CENTAUR CLASSICS

GENERAL EDITOR: J. M. COHEN

Sir John Harington's translation of

ORLANDO   FURIOSO

by Lodovico Ariosto

Edited and introduced by
GRAHAM HOUGH

Centaur Press

1962

© CENTAUR PRESS LTD. 1962

This edition is limited to 1500 copies
of which 750 are for sale in the
United States of America

Published by the Centaur Press Ltd.
11-14 Stanhope Mews West, London, S.W.7
and printed in Great Britain by
The West Yorkshire Printing Co., Ltd., Wakefield, England

CONTENTS

INTRODUCTION VII

EPISTLE DEDICATORY TO THE QUEEN'S MAJESTY XI

THE FORTY-SIX CANTOS OR BOOKS OF ORLANDO FURIOSO I

SYNOPSIS OF THE POEM 575

LIST OF PRINCIPAL CHARACTERS 579

INTRODUCTION

i. THE ROMANTIC EPIC

ORLANDO FURIOSO is one of the great narrative poems of Europe, and has perhaps given more sheer sparkling pleasure to its readers than any other poem on the same scale. It is the prime example of a celebrated literary kind, the Italian romantic epic; a kind that has furnished a long and brilliant chapter in the history of the European imagination. Until about a century ago the Italian epics played a considerable part in English poetical culture; they always had their following from Spenser and the courtiers of Queen Elizabeth to Scott and the nineteenth-century readers of romance. We have our own great poem in the same mode—Spenser's *Faerie Queene*—and it is not too much to say that the material and organisation of Spenser's poem (though not its moral temper) is the direct product of Ariosto's. But the taste for long narrative poems has declined with the rise of the novel. Spenser is less read than he used to be, and Italian literature is less known to the English-speaking world. So to many readers and students of poetry to-day the Italian epic is a quite unfamiliar field, and we should begin by saying something of its nature and its history.

The Orlando of Ariosto's poem is better known to us as Roland, the most famous of Charlemagne's peers; and the Italian romance-epics are late and utterly transformed descendants of the *chansons de geste* of France which celebrated the semi-legendary exploits of Charlemagne against the Saracens. The *chansons de geste*, with the *Chanson de Roland* at their head, date from the eleventh and twelfth century, and they are heroic poetry of the barest and austerest kind. They are simple in style, stern and restricted in their emotional range, without love-interest and romantic adventures. But their influence soon became very widely diffused. French literature spread to North Italy about the end of the twelfth century, and the influence was not confined to the courtly and the cultivated. The stories of Charlemagne and Roland were above all popular in their diffusion; they were sung in the market-places in a mixed dialect of Franco-Italian. Like most popular literature, they sprawled, spread, developed new heroes and many narrative offshoots. The austere outlines of the ancient epics became overlaid with innumerable fantastic adventures. A notable new motif is the Christian warrior who gets entangled with a pagan princess in remote Eastern lands. Magic and enchantment make their appearance, and the geographical range of the exploits stretches from Paris to Cathay. A note of irresponsible mockery finds its way into the tales, and we are left with what amounts to a wild perversion of the spirit of the French originals. About the beginning of the fifteenth century these stories were combined into a huge compilation called the *Reali de Francia* which performed somewhat the same service for the Charlemagne legend in Italy as Malory did for the Arthurian legend in England.

At the same time, however, this popular Carolingian material was losing favour in courtly circles. It dates from before the days of chivalry, and represents the manners of an earlier feudal age. The far more refined and sophisticated society that grew up in the later twelfth century began to find its satisfaction not in the old harsh stories, but in the subtler enchantments of Arthurian romance. The legends of King Arthur and his knights established themselves in France not in the least as what they originally were, the exploits of a Romano-British military leader, but as chivalric tales in which love, hunting, knight-errantry, tournaments—the sentiments and pageantry of courtly life—play the principal part. And in Italy, with its already tangled skein of popular tales, the two narrative traditions tend to become fused. It is the mixture of the Carolingian and the Arthurian cycles that produced the romantic epic of Italy.

It was above all the pervading love-theme that distinguished the Arthurian romances from the older epics. The *chansons de geste* had no heroines, or their role was of negligible importance; but love-adventures are the main substance of the Arthurian tales. The comparison of the old literature and the new was made by Boiardo, the predecessor of Ariosto and the first great poet of the Italian romantic epic:

> Britain the great was once glorious for arms and for love, whence its name is still spread abroad and brings great honour to King Arthur. . . . Charlemagne then held a great court in France, but it was not like that former one . . . because it shut the door against Love and gave itself only to the holy war. For it is Love that brings glory, and makes a man worthy and honoured; it is Love that brings victory and gives courage to the knight at arms.

Matteo Boiardo, count of Scandiano, wrote for the courtly society of Ferrara, and the idea behind his poem is the simple one of combining the legends of Charlemagne, Roland and the rest, engaged in the holy war against the Saracens, with the erotic interest and the refined and chivalrous manners of the Arthurian tales. The very title of his poem shows his intention: *Orlando Innamorato*, Roland in love. Who could think of Roland in love as long as he remained a hero of the *chansons de geste*? Now all is changed, and we are in a different world. And since Ariosto's poem is a continuation of Boiardo's we must look for a moment at Boiardo's world. The poem opens with Charlemagne sitting in his great hall for the feast of Pentecost, surrounded by his peers. Into the hall comes a beautiful maiden, attended by a single knight and guarded by four giants. She is Angelica; and it is her extravagant desirability that sets the story in motion and provides the mainspring of its action. Orlando and a number of the other knights instantly fall in love with her, and from then on the holy war against the infidel comes a bad second to the sorrows, jealousies and intrigues brought about by her beauty and her caprice. But any outline with which the story may have begun is quickly overlaid by a profusion of other characters and adventures. Other heroes besides Orlando are subject to the whims of Angelica—Rinaldo, Astolfo and Ferrau; there are other pairs of lovers, more tender and more faithful—Ruggiero and Bradamante, Brandimarte and Fiordiligi; there is the magician Atlante, the enchantresses Morgana and Alcina with their beguiling gardens; there is a magic lance, a magic ring, lions, dragons, hermits and savage men; there are intricate, proliferating adventures, feats of arms inspired by love, and a background, never quite forgotten, of Charlemagne's holy war.

ii. Ariosto and the *Orlando Furioso*

This is Boiardo's world, and it is Ariosto's world too. Not surprisingly, the *Orlando Innamorato* was left unfinished. Ariosto simply takes it up where Boiardo left off, takes over all the principal characters and their relationships, and assumes a knowledge of their previous history. Boiardo's work was begun about 1475 and first published in 1484. Ariosto's *Orlando Furioso* appeared between 1516 and 1532. Also a courtier of Ferrara, Ariosto wrote for the delectation of the same noble house. Without public ambition, which in any case had little scope in the Italy of his day, he cared for little but a gentle epicurean retirement and the delicacies of his art. He was always irked by his semi-official employment for the Cardinal Ippolito d'Este. He wrote comedies, satires, and love-poetry in both Latin and Italian; but it is only by the *Orlando Furioso* that he enters the great literature of the world. It is the more curious that he was content in this merely to prolong and expand an already well-established and well-loved romance. *Orlando Furioso* must be one of the very few examples of a great poem in its own right existing merely as a sequel to another. Later in the sixteenth century the critics sometimes said that the *Innamorato* and the *Furioso* should be regarded as one poem. But it is Ariosto's fame that has grown and survived; and having done credit to the delightful Boiardo as the inventor of the genre, we can see reasons for this. Boiardo's style is straightforward, easy and a little rustic. He tells his story carelessly, with an undertone of genial ironic humour. And he has an old-fashioned gentlemanly admiration for the virtues of chivalry. Ariosto's manner represents an infinite sophistication of this. His style is of the greatest variety and delicacy, capable of extremely varied shades of expression, from Virgilian pathos and grandeur to the cheerful wantonness of the *novella*. Any appearance of artlessness in the telling of his story is the result of a free but consummate art. His transitions from one episode to another and from one tone to another are made with the utmost lightness and grace. We seem to divine the figure of the narrator as a magician, serenely detached from his creations and handling them all with an exquisite ironical unconcern—or concern only for the life, beauty and variety of his vast panorama.

Ariosto inherited from Boiardo and the medieval romances a plan of multiple narration in which a number of stories are kept going at the same time. We begin with one, break it off in the middle and start another, break that off and start a third, or return to the original tale—until the various narrative threads are woven together into an extremely elaborate web. As the formalist critics of the later sixteenth century complained, no one could keep the plot of the *Orlando Furioso* in mind, or comprehend it in a single vision. There are a few leading narrative lines. The title, as it were, goes one better than Boiardo; Orlando is not only in love, he is now mad with love. His passion for Angelica, and her infidelities and caprices, form one of the main continuing motives of the plot. Contrasted with this are the faithful and honourable loves of Ruggiero and Bradamante. These two are made the mythical ancestors of the house of Este, the ducal family of Ferrara to whom the poem is addressed. There is one fixed central point, Paris, where Charlemagne is besieged by the Saracen hordes. And a faint recollection of the old epic theme of Christendom embattled against the infidel is pretty constantly in the background. But around these not very prominent structural lines there is a medley of supernumerary adventures, additional characters, and interpolated tales that often form separate *novelle* in themselves. No mere description can give any idea of the richness and diversity of the pattern.

The moral temper of the poem too is hard to describe. Ariosto can present the martyr's death of Brandimarte (XLI) or the touching fidelity of Cloridano and Medoro (XVIII); but side by side with them we shall find the Chaucerian bawdy of the Host's tale (XXVIII) and the ingenious naughtiness of Ricciardetto and Fiordispina (XXV). And though it would be wrong to regard *Orlando Furioso* as a simply comic poem, there is a sense in which we can say that one part of it is no more serious than another. All is enveloped in an atmosphere of serene irony. It is not easy to be precise about this quality. Croce speaks of "the Ariostan irony, so often observed and mentioned but never adequately defined." The Italian critics themselves have not been at one about it. During the Counter-Reformation serious persons who nevertheless continued to enjoy the pleasures of the *Orlando Furioso* insisted on seeing it as allegory and ascribed to it a set of moral significances that are only very faintly present to us. De Sanctis in the romantic age saw a poem absolutely deprived of all serious purpose. And Croce locates the seriousness on one plane only— the aesthetic: Ariosto's world is a world of pure art, in which the only value is the irridescent, continually changing play of varied patterns and textures. We need not presume to decide. There is at all events enough to satisfy the lover of poetry and romance for as long a time as he cares to spend with it.

Different readers will no doubt value it for different reasons. The sheer luxuriance and fertility of invention is perhaps its most evident quality. This is something that the modern reader of poetry is apt to forget. Generally orientated towards the lyric, he is unused to the enormous scale of Ariosto's canvas. The texture of the poem is indeed delicate enough to satisfy the most fastidious critic; but it is before all narrative, to be taken rapidly and in large draughts. Nor need it be taken as a whole, since so much of it can be enjoyed as separate episodes. The irony and the mockery are an immediate delight. But they should not be allowed to obscure other aspects of the work. The temptation that most besets the English reader is to undervalue the passages of heroism, pathos and heightened emotion, since they are in a rhetorical mode that has no exact parallel in our own poetry. In a work of such range and variety it would be vain to look for a single scene to typify the whole; but if I had to find a passage to represent the spirit of Ariosto it would perhaps be Astolfo's visit to the moon (XXXIV), where all the follies of the world are seen from another sphere, with a grave, benign, disillusioned humour. We may well regard this, and the whole poem of which it is a part, as the last brilliant flowering of the literature of the Italian Renaissance, before the formal pedantries of neo-classicism and the doctrinal pedantries of the Counter-Reformation diverted it into a new channel.*

iii. HARINGTON'S TRANSLATION

Harington's version of the poem, *Orlando Furioso in English Heroical Verse*, appeared in 1591. There were two more editions in the early seventeenth century, but it has not been reprinted since until the appearance of the present edition, and it has lately become a rare book. It is by far the liveliest and most readable translation of Ariosto in English. Sir John Harington was a godson of Queen Elizabeth and a noted court wit. The story goes (and it is reasonably well authenticated) that he first translated Canto XXVIII, notoriously bawdy and full of satirical reflections on women. This he circulated among the court ladies, greatly to their delight; and the Queen in indignation banished him from her presence until he had translated the remaining forty-five cantos. The dates are not clear, but this must have meant a fairly prolonged exile for Harington on his Somerset estate. He was not a poet by trade, his only previous works being a few slight epigrams; but he soon acquired a rapid and easy style and eventually succeeded in bringing his enormous task to an end. Perhaps we should note that Harington enjoys a second fame as the inventor of the water-closet. He described his ingenious device in a work called *The Metamorphoses of Ajax*, published in 1596.

Harington's translation is not a literal one. He uses the metre of the original, the *ottava rima* stanza, and he achieves a very close approximation to Ariosto's narrative energy and speed. But his tendency is to abbreviation and compression. He often runs two or three of Ariosto's stanzas into one. Sometimes he omits whole passages, and shortens battles and genealogies, which evidently bored him. Almost all his cantos are a little shorter than the originals. In return, he occasionally expands—oddly enough in moral and devotional passages. VII. 35-37, on vain pleasures, and XV. 73-77, on Astolfo's religious exercises in Jerusalem, are Harington's own. But in a poem of this informal structure and on this enormous scale the divergences are after all slight.

He becomes extremely skilful with the difficult octave stanza, indulging freely in antitheses, alliterations and elaborate polysyllabic rhymes. On the whole we must admit that the delicacy of Ariosto's verse tends to disappear, and the more subtle strokes of irony. His narrative is a more rough and ready affair and his humour a more simple burlesque. But *Orlando Furioso* is among other things a burlesque poem; its narrative is easy and irresponsible. Harington is not betraying his original, he is only accentuating some of its qualities at the necessary expense of others—other qualities that are intimately connected with the more sophisticated nature of the Italian language at that time. He is capable of dignity as well as comic bathos, and above all, he preserves a rapid flow and an entirely natural, racy choice of words. In this he stands alone. Hoole's version in the eighteenth century is in heroic couplets, and thus has an entirely different movement from the Italian. The nineteenth-century translation of Rose is close and literal and preserves the metre— but at the cost of hideous inversions and a stilted vocabulary. Above all, Harington is writing within half a century of Ariosto's death, in an England penetrated with Italian influence and deeply devoted to Italian letters. He gives us a rendering that is not only a source of vigorous enjoyment in itself, but is very close to the spirit of the original.

Graham Hough

---

* The best short account in English of Ariosto's life and work is to be found in volumes IV and V of John Addington Symonds' *Renaissance in Italy*.

TO THE MOST EXCELLENT,
VERTVOVS, AND NOBLE PRINCESSE,
ELIZABETH,
BY THE GRACE OF GOD, QUEENE OF
ENGLAND, FRANCE AND IRELAND,
DEFENDER OF THE FAITH, &c.

MOST renowned (and most worthy to be most renowned) Soveraigne Ladie; I presume to offer to your Highnesse this first part of the fruit of the little garden of my slender skill. It hath been the longer in growing, and is the lesse worthy the gathering, because my ground is barren and too cold for such dainty Italian fruits, being also perhaps over-shaded with trees of some older growth: but the beams of your blessed countenance, vouchsafing to shine on so poore a soile, shall soone disperse all hurtfull mists that would obscure it, and easily dissolve all (whether they be Mel-dews, or Fel-dews) that would sterve this shallow set plant. I desire to be briefe, because I love to be plaine. Whatsoever I am or can, is your Majesties. Your gracious favours have been extended in my poore family even to the third generation, your bounty to us and our heires. Wherefore this (though unperfect and unworthy worke) I humbly recommend to that gracious protection, under which I enjoy all in which I can take joy. If your Highnesse will read it, who dare reject it? if allow it, who can reproove it? if protect it, what Momvs barking, or Zoilvs biting can any way hurt or annoy it? And thus most humbly craving pardon for this boldnesse, I cease to write, though I will not cease to wish, that your high felicities may never cease.

Your most humble servant,

Iohn Harington.

THE FIRST BOOKE OF
ORLANDO FVRIOSO

THE ARGVMENT

Charles *hath the foyle,* Angelica *flies thence:*
Renaldos *horse holpe him his Love to find:*
Ferraw *with him doth fight in her defence:*
She flies againe, they stay not long behind.
Argalias *ghost reproves* Ferraws *offence,*
The Spaniard *to new vows himselfe doth bind:*
His mistris presence Sacrapant *enjoyeth,*
With Bradamant, Renaldo *him annoyeth.*

ORLANDO FVRIOSO

THE FIRST BOOKE

1

Of Dames, of Knights, of armes, of loves delight,
  Of courtesies, of high attempts I speake,
Then when the *Moores* transported all their might
  On *Africke* seas, the force of *France* to breake:
Incited by the youthfull heate and spight
  Of *Agramant* their King, that vow'd to wreake
The death of King *Trayano* (lately slaine)
Vpon the *Romane* Emperour *Charlemaine*.

2

I will no lesse *Orlandos* acts declare,
  (A tale in prose ne verse yet sung or said)
Who fell bestraught with love, a hap most rare,
  To one that erst was counted wise and stayd:
If my sweet Saint that causeth my like care,
  My slender muse affoord some gracious ayd,
I make no doubt but I shall have the skill.
As much as I have promist to fulfill.

3

Vouchsafe (O *Prince* of most renowmed race,
  The ornament and hope of this our time)
T'accept this gift presented to your grace,
  By me your servant rudely here in rime.
And though I paper pay and inke, in place
  Of deeper debt, yet take it for no crime:
It may suffice a poore and humble debter,
To say, and if he could it shoulde be better.

4

Here shall you find among the worthy peeres,
  Whose praises I prepare to tell in verse,
Rogero, him from whom of auncient yeeres
  Your princely stems derived, I reherse:
Whose noble mind by princely acts appeares,
  Whose worthy fame even to the skie doth perse:
So you vouchsafe my lowly stile and base,
Among your high conceits a little plase.

5

Orlando who long time had loved deare,
  Angelica the faire: and for her sake,
About the world, in nations far and neare,
  Did high attempts performe and undertake,
Return'd with her into the West that yeare,
  That *Charles* his power against the *Turks* did make:
And with the force of *Germanie* and *France*,
Neare *Pyren* Alpes his standard did advance.

6

To make the Kings of *Affrike* and of *Spaine*,
  Repent their rash attempts and foolish vaunts;
One having brought from *Affrike* in his traine,
  All able men to carry sword or launce,
The other mov'd the *Spaniards* now againe
  To overthrow the goodly Realme of *Fraunce*,
And hither (as I said) *Orlando* went,
But of his comming straight he did repent.

7

For here (behold how humane judgements are,
  And how the wiser sort art oft mistaken)
His Ladie whom he guarded had so farre,
  Nor had in fights nor dangers great forsaken,
Without the dint of sword or open warre,
  Amid his friends away from him was taken.
For *Charles* the great, a valiant Prince and wise,
Did this to quench a broile that did arise.

8

Betweene *Orlando* and *Renaldo* late,
  There fell about *Angelica* some brall,
And each of them began the tother hate,
  This Ladies love had made them both so thrall.
But *Charles* who much mislikes that such debate
  Betweene such friends should rise, on cause so small,
To *Namus* of *Bavier* in keeping gave her,
And suffred neither of them both to have her.

9

But promist he would presently bestow
  The damsell faire, on him that in that fight,
The plainest proofe should of his prowesse show,
  And danger most the *Pagans* with his might,
But (ay the while) the *Christians* take the blow,
  Their souldiers slaine, their Captaines put to flight,
The Duke himselfe a prisner there was taken,
His tent was quite abandon'd and forsaken.

10

Where when the damsell faire a while had stayd,
  That for the victor pointed was a pray,
She tooke her horse, ne farther time delayd,
  But secretly convay'd her selfe away,
For she foresaw, and was full sore afrayd,
  That this to *Charles* would prove a dismall day.
And riding through a wood, she hapt to meet
A Knight that came against her on his feet.

B

5

11

His curats on; his helmet not undone,
　And through the wood so swiftly he did runne,
　His sword and target ready to the same,
　As they that go halfe naked for a game.
　But never did a shepheards daughter shunne
　More speedily a snake that on her came,
　Then faire *Angelica* did take her flight,
　When as she once had knowledge of the Knight.

12

This valiant Knight was Lord of *Clarimount*,
　Duke *Ammons* sonne, as you shall understand,
　Who having lost his horse of good account,
　That by mishap was slipt out of his hand,
　He follow'd him, in hope againe to mount,
　Vntill this Ladies fight did make him stand,
　Whose face and shape proportion'd were so well,
　They seem'd the house where love it selfe did dwell.

13

But she that shuns *Renaldo* all she may,
　Vpon her horses necke doth lay the raine,
　Through thicke and thin she gallopeth away,
　Ne makes she choise of beaten way or plaine,
　But gives her palfrey leave to chuse the way,
　And being mov'd with feare and with disdaine,
　Now up, now downe, she never leaves to ride,
　Till she arrived by a river side.

14

Fast by the streame *Ferraw* she sees anone,
　(Who noyd, in part with dust, and part with sweat)
　Out of the battell hither came alone,
　With drinke his thirst, with aire to swage his heat;
　And minding backe againe to have bene gone,
　He was detain'd with an unlookt for let,
　Into the streame by hap his helmet fell,
　And how to get it out he cannot tell.

15

And hearing now the noise and mournfull crie
　Of one with piteous voice demaunding ayd,
　Seeing the damsell eke approching nie,
　That nought but helpe against *Renaldo* prayd,
　What wight it was, he guessed by and by,
　Though looking pale, like one that had bene frayd,
　And though she had not late bene in his sight,
　He thought it was *Angelica* the bright.

16

And being both a stout and courteous Knight,
　And love a little kindling in his brest,
　He promist straight to aide her all he might,
　And to performe what ever she request.
　And though he want an helmet, yet to fight
　With bold *Renaldo* he will do his best.
　And both the one, the other straight defied,
　Oft having either others value tried.

17

Betweene them two a combat fierce began,
　With strokes that might have pierst the hardest rocks.
　While they thus fight on foote, and man to man,
　And give and take so hard and heavy knocks,
　Away the damsell posteth all she can,
　Their paine and travell she requites with mocks.
　So hard she rode while they were at their fight,
　That she was cleane escaped out of sight.

18

When they long time contended had in vaine,
　Who should remaine the master in the field,
　And that with force, with cunning, nor with paine,
　The tone of them could make the other yeeld,
　Renaldo first did move the Knight of Spaine
　(Although he us'd such curtesie but seeld)
　To make a truce; ne was he to be blamed,
　For love his heart to other fight inflamed.

19

You thought (said he) to hinder me alone,
　But you have hurt your selfe as much or more,
　You see the faire *Angelica* is gone,
　So soone we leese that earst we fought so sore.
　Had you me tane or slaine, your gaine were none,
　Sith you were nere the nere your love therfore.
　For while we two have made this little stay,
　She lets us both alone and goes her way.

20

But if you love the Ladie, as you say,
　Then let us both agree to find her out,
　To have her first will be our wisest way,
　And when of holding her there is no doubt,
　Then by consent let her remaine his pray,
　That with his sword can prove himselfe most stout,
　I see not else after our long debate,
　How either of us can amend his state.

21

Ferraw (that felt small pleasure in the fight)
　Agreed a sound and friendly league to make:
　They lay aside all wrath and malice quight,
　And at the parting from the running lake,
　The Pagan would not let the Christen Knight
　To follow him on foote, for manners sake:
　But prayes him mount behind his horses backe,
　And so they seeke the damsell by the tracke.

22

O auncient Knights of true and noble hart,
　They rivals were, one faith they liv'd not under,
　Beside they felt their bodies shrewdly smart
　Of blowes late given, and yet (behold a wonder)
　Through thicke and thin, suspition set apart,
　Like friends they ride, and parted not asunder,
　Vntill the horse with double spurring drived,
　Vnto a way, which parts in two, arrived.

23

And being neither able to descrie
  Which way was gone *Angelica* the bright,
  Because the tracke of horses feet, whereby
  They seeke her out, appeare alike in sight:
  They part, and either will his fortune try,
  The left hand one, the other takes the right.
  The *Spaniard* when he wandred had a while,
  Came whence he went, the way did him beguile.

24

He was arriv'd but there, with all his paine,
  Where in the foord he let his helmet fall,
  And of his Ladie (whom he lov'd in vaine)
  He now had little hope, or none at all.
  His helmet now he thinkes to get againe,
  And seekes it out, but seeke it while he shall,
  It was so deeply sunken in the sand,
  He cannot get it out at any hand.

25

Hard by the banke a tall yong Popler grew,
  Which he cut downe, thereof a pole to make,
  With which each place in feeling and in vew,
  To find his scull he up and downe doth rake,
  But lo a hap unlookt for doth ensew,
  While he such needlesse frutelesse paine doth take,
  He saw a Knight arise out of the brooke,
  Breast-hie, with visage grim, and angry looke.

26

The Knight was arm'd at all points save the hed,
  And in his hand he held the helmet plaine,
  That very helmet that such care had bred
  In him that late had sought it with such paine.
  And looking grimly on *Ferraw*, he sed,
  Ah faithlesse wretch, in promise false and vaine,
  It greeves thee now this helmet so to misse,
  That should of right be rendred long ere this.

27

Remember (cruell Pagan) when you killed
  Me, brother to *Angelica* the bright:
  You said you would (as I then dying willed)
  Mine armour drowne, when finisht were the fight,
  Now if that fortune have the thing fulfilled,
  Which thou thy self sholdst have perform'd in right,
  Greeve not thy selfe, or if thou wilt be greeved,
  Greeve that thy promise cannot be beleeved.

28

But if to want an helmet thou repine,
  Get one wherewith thine honour thou maist save,
  Such hath *Orlando* Countie Paladine,
  Renaldo such, or one perchance more brave,
  That was from *Almont* tane, this from *Mambrine*:
  Win one of these; that, thou with praise maist have,
  And as for this, surecase to seeke it more,
  But leave it as thou promis'd me before.

29

Ferraw was much amaz'd to see the sprite,
  That made this strange appearance unexpected,
  His voice was gone, his haire did stand upright,
  His senses all were so to feare subjected.
  His heart did swell with anger and despight,
  To heare his breach of promise thus objected,
  And that *Argalia* (so the Knight was named)
  With just reproofe could make him thus ashamed.

30

And wanting time, the matter to excuse,
  And being guiltie of no litle blame,
  He rested mute, and in a senslesse muse,
  So sore his heart was tainted with the shame.
  And by *Lanfusas* life he vow'd to use
  No helmet, till such time he gat the same,
  Which from the stout *Almont Orlando* wan,
  When as they two encountted man to man.

31

But he this vow to keepe more firmely ment,
  And kept it better then the first he made,
  Away he parted hence a malcontent,
  And many daies ensuing rested sad.
  To seeke *Orlando* out is his intent,
  With whom to fight he would be very glad,
  But now what haps unto *Renaldo* fell,
  That tooke the other way, tis time to tell.

32

Not farre he walkt, but he his horse had spide,
  That praunsing went before him on the way,
  Holla my boy holla (*Renaldo* cride)
  The want of thee annoy'd me much to day.
  But Bayard will not let his master ride,
  But takes his heeles and faster goes away.
  His flight much anger in *Renaldo* bred:
  But follow we *Angelica* that fled.

33

That fled through woods and deserts all obscure,
  Through places uninhabited and wast,
  Ne could she yet repute her selfe secure,
  But farther still she gallopeth in hast.
  Each leafe that stirres in her doth feare procure,
  And maketh her affrighted and agast:
  Each noise she heares, each shadow she doth see,
  She doth mistrust it should *Renaldo* be.

34

Like to a fawne, or kid of bearded goate,
  That in the wood a tyger fierce espide,
  To kill her dam, and first to teare the throate,
  And then to feed upon the hanch or side,
  Both feare lest she might light on such a lot,
  And seeke it selfe in thickest brackes to hide,
  And thinkes each noise the wind or aire doth cause,
  It selfe in danger of the tygers clawes.

35

That day and night she wandred here and there,
 And halfe the other day that did ensue,
 Vntill at last she was arrived where
 A fine yong grove with pleasant shadow grew,
 Neare to the which two little rivers were,
 Whose moisture did the tender herbes renew,
 And make a sweete and very pleasing sound,
 By running on the sand and stonie ground.

36

Here she at last her selfe in safetie thought,
 As being from *Renaldo* many a mile,
 Tyr'd with annoy the heate and travell brought,
 She thinkes it best with sleepe the time beguile,
 And having first a place convenient sought,
 She lets her horse refresh his limbes the while,
 Who fed upon the bankes well cloth'd with grasse,
 And dranke the river water cleere as glasse.

37

Hard by the brooke an arbor she describe,
 Wherein grew faire and very fragrant floures,
 With roses sweet, and other trees beside,
 Wherewith the place adornes the native boures,
 So fenced in with shades on either side,
 Safe from the heate of late or early houres,
 The boughes and leaves so cunningly were mixt,
 No sunne, no light, could enter them betwixt.

38

Within, the tender herbes a bed do make,
 Inviting folke to take their rest and ease:
 Here meanes this Ladie faire a nap to take,
 And fals to sleepe, the place so well doth please.
 Not long she lay, but her a noise did wake,
 The trampling of a horse did her disease,
 And looking out as secret as she might,
 To come all arm'd she saw a comely Knight.

39

She knowes not yet if he be foe or friend,
 Twixt hope and feare she doubtfully doth stand,
 And what he meanes to do she doth attend,
 And who it was she faine would understand.
 The Knight did to the river side descend,
 And resting downe his head upon his hand,
 All in a muse he sitteth still alone,
 Like one transform'd into a marble stone.

40

He tarri'd in this muse an houre and more,
 With looke cast downe in sad and heavie guise,
 At last he did lament his hap so sore,
 Yet in so sweete and comely mournefull wise,
 So hard a heart no tyger ever bore,
 But would have heard such plaints with warrish eies.
 His heart did seeme a mountaine full of flame,
 His cheekes a streame of teares to quench the same.

41

Alas (said he) what meanes this divers passion?
 I burne as fire, and yet as frost I freese,
 I still lament, and yet I move compassion,
 I come too late, and all my labour leese.
 I had but words and lookes for shew and fashion,
 But others get the game, and gainefull fees:
 If neither fruite nor floure come to my part,
 Why should her love consume my carefull hart?

42

Like to the rose I count the virgine pure,
 That grow'th on native stem in garden faire,
 Which while it stands with wals environ'd sure,
 Where heardmen with their heards cannot repaire
 To favor it, it seemeth to allure
 The morning deaw, the heate, the earth, the aire.
 Yong gallant men, and lovely dames delight
 In their sweet sent, and in their pleasing sight.

43

But when at once tis gathered and gone,
 From proper stalke, where late before it grew,
 The love, the liking little is or none,
 Both favour, grace and beautie all adew.
 So when a virgin grants to one alone
 The precious floure for which so many sew,
 Well he that getteth it may love her best,
 But she forgoes the love of all the rest.

44

She may deserve his love, but others hate,
 To whom of love she shewd her selfe so scant,
 (Oh then my cruell fortune or my fate)
 Others have store, but I am starv'd with want:
 Then leave to love this ladie so ungrate:
 Nay live to love (behold I soone recant)
 Yea first let life from these my limbs be rent,
 Ere I to change my love shall give consent.

45

If some perhaps desirous are to know,
 What wight it was with sorrow so opprest,
 Twas *Sacrapant* that was afflicted so,
 And love had bred this torment in his brest:
 That trickling wound, that flattring cruell foe,
 Most happie they that know and have it least.
 The love of her I say procur'd his woe,
 And she had heard and knew it long ago.

46

Her love allur'd him from the Easterne land,
 Vnto the Westerne shores, where sets the Sunne,
 And here he heard how by *Orlandos* hand,
 A passage safe from th'Indies she had wonne.
 Her sequestration he did understand,
 That *Charles* had made, and how the same was done
 To make the Knights more venterous and bold,
 In fighting for the Floure de luce of gold.

47

And furthermore himselfe had present bene
 When *Charles* his men were overthrowne and slaine
 Since then, he travel'd farre to find this Queene,
 But hitherto it hath bene all in vaine.
 Now much despaire, and little hope betweene,
 So rufully thereof he doth complaine,
 And with such wailing words his woes rehearst,
 As might the hardest stonie heart have pearst.

48

And while in this most dolefull state he bides,
 And sighes full oft, and sheddeth many a teare,
 And speakes these same, and many words besides,
 (Which I to tell for want of time forbeare)
 His noble fortune so for him provides,
 That all this came unto his mistresse eare,
 And in one moment he prevailed more
 Then he had done in many yeares before.

49

Angelica with great attention hard,
 The mone, and plaint, that him tormented sore,
 Who long had loved her, with great regard,
 As she had triall, many yeares before,
 Yet as a marble pillar cold and hard,
 She not inclines to pittie him the more.
 Like one that all the world doth much disdaine,
 And deemeth none worthie her love againe.

50

But being now with danger compast round,
 She thought it best to take him for her guide,
 For one that were in water almost drown'd,
 Were very stout, if for no helpe he cride:
 If she let passe the fortune now she found,
 She thinkes to want the like another tyde.
 And furthermore for certaine this she knew,
 That *Sacrapant* had beene her lover true.

51

Ne meant she tho to quench the raging fires,
 That ay consum'd his faithfull loving heart,
 Ne yet with that a lover most desires,
 T'asswage the paine in all, or yet in part:
 She meanes he first shall pull her from the briers,
 And feed him then with words and womens art,
 To make him first of all to serve her turne,
 That done, to wonted coynesse to returne.

52

Vnto the river side she doth descend,
 And toward him most goddesse like she came,
 And said, all peace to thee my dearest friend,
 With modest looke, and cald him by his name,
 And further said, the Gods and you defend
 My chastity, mine honour and my fame,
 And never grant by their divine permission,
 That I give cause of any such suspition.

53

With how great joy a mothers minde is fil'd,
 To see a sonne, for whom she long had mourned,
 Whom she heard late in battell to be kild,
 And saw the troopes without him home returned,
 Such joy had *Sacrapant* when he behild,
 His Ladie deere: his teares to smiles are turned,
 To see her beautie rare, her comely favour,
 Her princely presence, and her stately havour.

54

Like one all ravisht with her heavenly face,
 Vnto his loved Ladie he doth runne,
 Who was content in armes him to embrace,
 Which she perhaps at home would not have done,
 But doubting now the dangerous time and place,
 She must go forward as she hath begun,
 In hope by his good service and assistance,
 To make her home returne without resistance.

55

And in most lov'ly manner she doth tell,
 The strange adventures, and the divers chance,
 That since they two did part to her befell,
 Both on the way, and since she came to France:
 And how *Orlando* used her right well,
 Defending her from danger and mischance,
 And that his noble force and magnanimitie,
 Had still preserv'd the floure of her virginity.

56

It might be true, but sure it was incredible,
 To tell to one that were discreet and wise,
 But unto *Sacrapant* it seemed possible,
 Because that love had dasled so his eyes:
 Love causeth what is seene, to seeme invisible,
 And makes of things not seene, a shape to rise.
 It is a proverbe used long ago,
 We soone beleeve the thing we would have so.

57

But to himselfe thus *Sacrapant* doth say,
 B'it that my Lord of *Anglant* were so mad,
 To take no pleasure of so faire a pray,
 When he both time and place, and power had,
 Yet am not I obliged any way,
 To imitate a president so bad,
 Ile rather take my pleasure while I may,
 Then waile my want of wit another day.

58

Ile gather now the fresh and fragrant rose,
 Whose beautie may with standing still be spent,
 One cannot do a thing (as I suppose)
 That better can a womans mind content:
 Well may they seeme much grieved for a glose,
 And weepe and waile, and dolefully lament,
 There shall no foolish plaints, nor fained ire,
 Hinder me to encarnat my desire.

59

This said, forthwith he did himselfe prepare,
　T'assault the fort that easly would be wonne,
　But loe a sodaine hap that bred new care,
　And made him cease his enterprise begonne,
　For of an enemy he was aware,
　He claspt his helmet late before undone,
　And armed all, he mounteth one his beast,
　And standeth ready with his speare in rest.

60

Behold a warrior whom he did not know,
　Came downe the wood in semblance like a Knight,
　The furniture was all as white as snow,
　And in the helme a plume of fethers white.
　King *Sacrapant* by proofe doth plainely show,
　That he doth take the thing in great despite,
　To be disturb'd and hindred from that pleasure,
　That he prefer'd before all other treasure.

61

Approching nie, the warrior he defide,
　And hopes to set him quite beside the seat:
　The other with such loftie words replide,
　As persons use, in choler and in heat.
　At last when glorious vaunts were laid aside,
　They come to strokes and each to do his feat,
　Doth couch his speare, and running thus they sped,
　Their coursers both encountred hed to hed.

62

As Lions meete, or Buls in pastures greene,
　With teeth & hornes, & staine with bloud the field,
　Such eger fight these warriers was betweene,
　And eithers speare had pearst the tothers sheild,
　The sound that of these strokes had raised beene,
　An eccho lowd along the vale did yeeld.
　T'was happie that their curats were so good,
　The Lances else had pierced to the blood.

63

For quite unable now about to wheele,
　They butt like rammes, the one the others head,
　Whereof the Pagans horse such paine did feele,
　That ere long space had past he fell down dead.
　The tothers horse a little gan to reele,
　But being spurd, full quickly up he sped.
　The Pagans horse thus overthrowne and slaine,
　Fell backward greatly to his masters paine.

64

That unknowne champion seeing thother downe,
　His horse upon him lying dead in vew,
　Expecting in this fight no more renowne,
　Determin'd not the battell to renew.
　But by the way that leadeth from the towne,
　The first appointed journey doth pursew,
　And was now ridden halfe a mile at least,
　Before the Pagan parted from his beast.

65

Like as the tiller of the fruitfull ground,
　With sodaine storme and tempest is astonish'd
　Who sees the flash, and heares the thunders sound,
　And for their masters sakes, the cattell punish'd,
　Or when by hap a faire old pine he found,
　By force of raging winds his leaves diminish'd,
　So stood amaz'd the Pagan in the place,
　His Ladie present at the wofull case.

66

He fetcht a sigh most deepely from his heart,
　Not that he had put out of joynt, or lamed
　His arme, his legge, or any other part,
　But chiefly he his evill fortune blamed,
　At such a time, to hap so overthwart,
　Before his love, to make him so ashamed:
　And had not she some cause of speech found out,
　He had remained speechlesse out of doubt.

67

My Lord (said she) what ailes you be so sad?
　The want was not in you, but in your steed,
　For whom a stable, or a pasture had
　Beene fitter then a course at tilt indeed.
　Nor is that adverse partie very glad,
　As well appeares, that paried with such speed,
　For in my judgement they be said to yeeld,
　That first leave off, and do depart the feeld.

68

Thus while she gives him comfort all she may,
　Behold there came a messenger in post,
　Blowing his horne, and riding downe the way,
　Where he before his horse, and honor lost,
　And comming nearer he of them doth pray,
　To tell if they had seene passe by that cost,
　A champion arm'd at all points like a Knight,
　The shield, the horse, and armour all of white.

69

I have both seene the Knight, and felt his force,
　(Said *Sacrapant*) for here before you came,
　He cast me downe and also kild my horse,
　Ne know I (that doth greeve me most) his name.
　Sir (quoth the post) the name I will not force,
　To tell, sith you desire to know the same,
　First, know that you were conquer'd in this fight,
　By valour of a damsell faire and bright.

70

Of passing strength, but of more passing hew,
　And *Bradamant*, this damsell faire is named,
　She was the wight, whose meeting you may rew,
　And all your life hereafter be ashamed.
　This said, he turn'd his horse and bad adew.
　But *Sacrapant* with high disdaine enflamed,
　Was first so wroth, and then so sham'd thereto,
　He knew not what to say, nor what to do.

71

And after he had staid a while and mus'd,
  That at a womans hands he had received
Such a disgrace as could not be excus'd,
  Nor how he might revenge it he perceived,
With thought hereof his mind was so confus'd,
  He stood like one of wit and sense bereaved.
At last he go'th, a better place to finde,
He takes her horse and makes her mount behind.

72

Now having rode a mile, or thereabout,
  They heard a noise, a trampling on the ground,
They thought it was some company or rout,
  That caused in the woods so great a sound:
At last they see a warlike horse, and stout,
  With guilded barb, that cost full many a pound,
No hedge, no ditch, no wood, no water was,
That stopped him where he was bent to passe.

73

Angelica casting her eye aside:
  Except (said she) mine eies all dazled be,
I have that famous horse *Bayardo* spide,
  Come trotting downe the wood, as seemes to me:
(How well for us our fortune doth provide)
  It is the very same, I know tis he:
On one poore nag to ride we two were loth,
And here he commeth fit to serve us both.

74

King *Sacrapant* alighted by and by,
  And thinkes to take him gently by the raine,
But with his heeles the horse doth streight reply,
  As who should say, his rule he did disdaine.
It happie was he stood the beast not nye,
  For if he had, it had beene to his paine,
For why, such force the horse had in his heele,
He would have burst a mountaine all of steele.

75

But to the damsell gently he doth go,
  In humble manner, and in lowly sort,
A spaniell after absence fauneth so,
  And seekes to make his master play, and sport,
For *Bayard* cald to mind the damsell tho,
  When she unto *Albracca* did resort,
And us'd to feed him for his masters sake,
Whom she then lov'd, and he did her forsake.

76

She takes the bridle boldly in her hand,
  And strok't his brest, and necke, with art and skill:
The horse that had great wit to understand,
  Like to a lambe, by her he standeth still,
And while *Bayardo* gently there did stand,
  The Pagan got him up, and had his will.
And she that erst to ride behind was faine,
Into her saddle mounted now againe.

77

And being newly setled in her seate,
  She saw a man on foote all armed runne,
Straight in her mind she gan to chafe and fret,
  Because she knew it was Duke *Ammons* sonne,
Most earnestly he sude her love to get,
  More earnestly she seekes his love to shunne.
Once she lov'd him, he hated her as much,
And now he loves, she hates, his hap was such.

78

The cause of this first from two fountaines grew,
  Like in the tast, but in effects unlike,
Plac'd in *Ardenna*, each in others vew,
  Who tasts the one, loves dart his heart doth strike,
Contrary of the other doth ensew,
  Who drinke thereof, their lovers shall mislike.
Renaldo dranke of one, and love him pained,
Shee drunke the other and his love disdained.

79

The liquor thus with secret venim mingled,
  Makes her to stand so stiffely in the nay,
On whom *Renaldos* heart was wholy kindled,
  Though scarce to looke on him she can away,
But from his sight desiring to be singled,
  With soft low voice the Pagan she doth pray,
That he approch no nearer to this Knight,
But flie away with all the speed he might.

80

Why then (quoth he) make you so small esteeme,
  Of me, as though that I to him should yeeld?
So weake and faint my forces do you deeme,
  That safe from him your selfe I cannot shield?
Then you forget *Albracca* it should seeme,
  And that same night, when I amid the field,
Alone unarmed did defend you then,
Against King *Agrican* and all his men.

81

No sir, said she (ne knowes she what to say)
  Because *Renaldo* now approcht so nie,
And threatned so the Pagan in the way,
  When under him his horse he did espie,
And saw the damsell taken as a pray,
  In whose defence he meanes to live and die.
But what fell out betweene these warriers fearce,
Within the second booke I do rehearse.

THE SECOND BOOKE OF
ORLANDO FVRIOSO

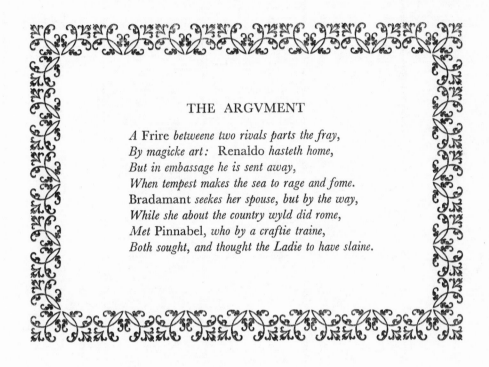

THE ARGVMENT

A Frire *betweene two rivals parts the fray,*
By magicke art: Renaldo *hasteth home,*
But in embassage he is sent away,
When tempest makes the sea to rage and fome.
Bradamant *seekes her spouse, but by the way,*
While she about the country wyld did rome,
Met Pinnabel, *who by a craftie traine,*
Both sought, and thought the Ladie to have slaine.

ORLANDO FVRIOSO
THE SECOND BOOKE

1

O Blind god Love, why takst thou such delight,
  With darts of divers force our hearts to wound?
  By thy too much abusing of thy might,
  This discord great in humane hearts is found.
  When I would wade the shallow foord aright,
  Thou draw'st me to the deepe to have me dround,
  From those love me, my love thou dost recall,
  And place it where I find no love at all.

2

Thou mak'st most faire unto *Renaldo* seeme
  Angelica, that takes him for a foe,
  And when that she of him did well esteeme,
  Then he dislikt, and did refuse her thoe.
  Which makes her now of him the lesse to deeme.
  Thus (as they say) she renders *quit pro quo*.
  She hateth him, and doth detest him so,
  She first will die, ere she will with him go.

3

Renaldo (full of stately courage) cride,
  Downe theefe from of my horse, downe by and by,
  So rob'd to be I never can abide,
  But they that do it dearely shall abye,
  Also this Ladie you must leave beside,—
  Else one of us in her defence will dye—
  A horse so good, and such a goodly dame,
  To leave unto a theefe it were a shame.

4

What? me a theefe? thou in thy throat dost lye,
  (Quoth *Sacrapant*, that was as hot as he)
  Theefe to thy selfe, thy malice I defie,
  For as I heare, the name is due to thee:
  But if thou dare thy might and manhood trie,
  Come take this Ladie, or this horse from me.
  Though I allow in this of thine opinion,
  That of the world she is the matchlesse minion.

5

Like as two mastive dogges with hungrie mawes,
  Mov'd first to hate, from hate to raging ire,
  Approch with grinning teeth, and griesly jaws,
  With staring eyes, as red as flaming fire,
  At last they bite, and scratch with teeth and claws,
  And teare themselves, and tumble in the mire.
  So after byting and reprochfull words,
  Did these two worthy warriers draw their swords.

6

One was on foote, the tother on a horse,
  You thinke perhaps, the horseman vantage had,
  No sure, no whit; he would have wisht to skorce,
  For why at last to light he must be glad,
  The beast did know thus much by natures force,
  To hurt his master were a service bad.
  The pagan could not nor with spur nor hand,
  Make him unto his mind to go or stand.

7

He stops, when he should make a full careire,
  He runnes or trots, when he would have him rest,
  At last to throw his rider in the mire,
  He plungeth with his head beneath his breast.
  But *Sacrapant* that now had small desire,
  At such a time, to tame so proud a beast,
  Did worke so well at last by sleight and force,
  On his left side, he lighted from his horse.

8

When from *Bayardos* over furious might,
  The Pagan had himselfe discharged so,
  With naked swords there was a noble fight,
  Sometimes they lye aloft, sometimes aloe,
  And from their blowes the fire flies out in fight:
  I thinke that *Vulcans* hammers beat more slow,
  Where he within the mountaine *Ætnas* chaps,
  Doth forge for *love*, the fearfull thunderclaps.

9

Sometimes they profer, then they pause a while,
  Sometime strike out, like masters of the play,
  Now stand upright, now stoup another while,
  Now open lye, then cover all they may.
  Now ward, then with a slip the blow beguile:
  Now forward step, now backe a little way:
  Now round about, and where the tone gives place,
  There still the other presseth in his place.

10

Renaldo did the Pagan Prince invade,
  And strike at once with all the might he cowd,
  The other doth oppose against the blade,
  A shield of bone and steele of temper good.
  But through the same a way *Fusberta* made,
  And of the blow resounded all the wood:
  The steele, the bone like yse in peeces broke,
  And left his arme benummed with the stroke.

11

Which when the faire and fearfull *damsell* saw,
  And how great damage did ensue thereby,
  She looked pale, for anguish and for aw,
  Like those by doome that are condemn'd to dye:
  She thinks it best her selfe from hence withdraw,
  Else will *Renaldo* take her by and by,
  The same *Renaldo* whom she hateth so,
  Though love of her procured all his wo.

12

Vnto the wood she turnes her horse in hast,
  And takes a little narrow path and blind;
  Her fearfull looks ofttimes she backe doth cast,
  Still doubting lest *Renaldo* came behind:
  And when that she a little way had past,
  Alow the vale a *Hermit* she did find:
  A weake old man, with beard along his brest,
  In shew devout, and holier then the rest.

13

He seem'd like one with fasts and age consumed,
  He rode upon a slouthfull going asse,
  And by his looke, a man would have presumed,
  That of his conscience scrupulous he was.
  Yet her young face, his old sight so illumed,
  When as he saw the damsell by to pass:
  (Though weake and faint, as such an age behoved)
  That charitie his courage somewhat moved.

14

The damsell of the *Hermit* askt the way,
  That might unto some hav'n town lead most neare,
  That she might part from France without delay,
  Where once *Renaldos* name she might not heare.
  The frier that could enchaunt, doth all he may,
  To comfort her, and make her of good cheare,
  And to her safetie promising to looke,
  Out of his bag forthwith he drew a booke.

15

A booke of skill and learning so profound,
  That of a lease he had not made an end,
  But that there rose a sprite from under ground,
  Whom like a page he doth of arrants lead.
  This sprite by words of secret vertue bound,
  Goes where these Knights their combat did intend:
  And while they two were fighting very hard,
  He enters them betweene without regard.

16

Good sirs (quoth he) for courtsie sake me show,
  When one of you the tother shall have slaine,
  And after all the travell you bestow,
  What guerdon you expect for all your paine,
  Behold, *Orlando* striking nere a blow,
  Nor breaking staffe, while you strive here in vaine,
  To *Paris* ward the Ladie faire doth carie,
  While you on fighting undiscreetly tarie.

17

I saw from hence a mile, or thereabout,
  Orlando with *Angelica* alone,
  And as for you, they jest and make a flout,
  That fight where praise and profit can be none.
  Twer best you quickly went to seeke them out,
  Before that any farther they be gone,
  Within the walls of *Paris* if they get,
  Your eye on her againe you shall not set.

18

When as the Knights this message had received,
  They both remain'd amazed, dumbe and sad,
  To heare *Orlando* had them so deceived,
  Of whom before great jealousie they had;
  But good *Renaldo* so great griefe conceived,
  That for the time, like one all raging made,
  He sware without regard of God or man,
  That he will kill *Orlando* if he can.

19

And seeing where his horse stood still untide,
  He thither goes: such hast he makes away,
  He offers not the Pagan leave to ride,
  Nor at the parting once adjeu doth say.
  Now *Bayard* felt his masters spurres in side,
  And gallops maine, ne maketh any stay.
  No rivers, rocks, no hedge, nor ditches wide,
  Could stay his course, or make him step aside.

20

Nor marvell if *Renaldo* made some hast,
  To mount againe upon his horses backe,
  You heard before how many dayes had past,
  That by his absence he had felt great lacke,
  The horse (that had of humane wit some tast,)
  Ran not away for any jadish knacke,
  His going only was to this intent,
  To guide his master where the Ladie went.

21

The horse had spide her when she tooke her flight,
  First from the tent, as he thereby did stand,
  And follow'd her, and kept her long in sight,
  As then by hap out of his masters hand.
  (His master did not long before alight,
  To combat with a Baron hand to hand)
  The horse pursude the damsell all about,
  And holpe his master still to find her out.

22

He followed her through valley, hill and plaine,
  Through woods and thickets for his masters sake,
  Whom he permitted not to touch the raine,
  For feare lest he some other way should take,
  By which *Renaldo* though with mickle paine
  Twise found her out, twise she did him forsake:
  For first *Ferraw*, then *Sacrapant* withstood,
  That by twise finding her he did no good.

23

Bayardo trusting to the lying sprite,
  Whose false (but likely) tale so late he hard,
  And doubting not it was both true and right,
  He doth his duty now with due regard.
  Renaldo prickt with love and raging spite,
  Doth pricke apace, and all to *Paris* ward,
  To *Paris* ward he maketh so great shift,
  The wind it selfe seemes not to go so swift.

24

Such hast he made *Orlando* out to find,
  That scant he ceast to travell all the night,
  So deeply stacke the storie in his mind,
  That was of late devised by the sprite:
  Betimes and late as first he had assign'd,
  He rode untill he saw the towne in sight:
  Where *Charles* whose chance all christned hearts did rew,
  With the small relikes of his powre withdrew.

25

And for he lookes to be assaulted then,
  Or else besieg'd, he useth all his care,
  To store himselfe with victuall and with men.
  The walls eke of the towne he doth repaire,
  And take advice, both how, and where, and when,
  For his defence each thing he may prepare.
  An armie new to make he doth intend,
  And for new souldiers into England send.

26

He minds to take the field againe ere long,
  And trie the hap of warre another day,
  And all in hast to make himselfe more strong,
  He sends *Renaldo* Englands ayd to pray.
  Renaldo thought the Emperour did him wrong,
  To send him in such hast, and grant no stay.
  Not that ill will to th'Iland he did carie,
  But for another cause he faine would tarie.

27

Yet now although full sore against his mind,
  As loth to leave the Ladie he so loved,
  Whom he in *Paris* hoped had to find,
  Because t'obey his Prince it him behoved,
  He taketh this embassage thus assign'd,
  And having straight all other lets removed,
  He posted first to *Callis* with great hast,
  And there embarkt ere halfe next day was past.

28

Against the mariners and masters minds,
  (Such hast he made to have returned backe)
  He takes the sea though swelling with great winds,
  And threatning ruine manifest and wracke.
  Fierce *Boreas* that himselfe despised finds,
  Doth beate on seas with tempest foule and blacke,
  By force whereof the waves were rais'd so hie,
  The very tops were sprinkled all thereby.

29

The mariners take in their greater saile,
  And by the wind they lie, but all in vaine,
  Then backe againe they bend without availe,
  Now they are out, they cannot in againe.
  No (said the wind) my force shall so prevaile,
  Your bold attempts shall put you to some paine.
  It was a folly any more to strive,
  Needs must they follow as the wind did drive.

30

In the foreship sometimes the blast doth blow,
  Straight in the poope, the seas breake to the skies.
  Needs must they beare a saile, though very low,
  To void the waves that higher still did rise:
  But sith my web so diverse now doth grow,
  To weave with many threds I must devise,
  I leave *Renaldo* in this dangerous place,
  And of his sister speake a little space.

31

I meane the noble damsell *Bradamant*,
  Of *Ammon* daughter, and dame *Beatrice*,
  In whose rare mind no noble part did want,
  So full of value, and so void of vice,
  King *Charles* and *France* of her might rightly vaunt,
  So chast, so faire, so faithfull and so wise,
  And in the feates of armes of so great fame,
  A man might guesse by that of whence she came.

32

There was a Knight enamourd on this dame,
  That out of *Affricke* came with *Agramant*,
  Rogero hight, so was his fathers name,
  (His mother was the child of *Agolant*)
  The damsell that of worthy linage came,
  And had a heart not made of adamant,
  Disdained not the love of such a Knight,
  Although he had but seeld bene in her sight.

33

Long travell and great paine she had endured,
  And rid alone her lover to have found,
  Ne would she thinke her saftie more assured,
  If with an armie she were garded round.
  You heard before how she by force procured
  King *Sacrapant* to fall and kisse the ground,
  The wood she past, and after that the mountaine,
  Vntill at last she saw a goodly fountaine.

34

A goodly fountaine running in a field,
  All full of trees, whose leaves do never fade,
  Which did to passengers great pleasure yeeld,
  The running streame so sweete a murmur made,
  Vpon the South, a hill the Sunne did shield,
  The ground gave floures, the grove a gratefull shade.
  Now here the dame casting her eye aside,
  A man at armes fast by the brooke describe.

35

A man at armes she spyed by the brooke,
  Whose banks with flowers of divers hew were clad,
  Of which sweet place he so small pleasure tooke,
  His face did shew his heart was nothing glad,
  His targe and helmet were not farre to looke,
  Vpon a tree where tide his horse he had:
  His eyes were swolne with tears, his mind oppressed
  With bitter thoughts that had his heart distressed.

36

The damsell faire entic'd by deepe desire,
  That all (but chiefly women) have to know,
  All strangers states, doth earnestly require
  The dolefull Knight his inward griefe to show.
  Who marking well her manner and attire,
  Her courteous speech with him prevailed so,
  He tels his state, esteeming by the sight,
  That needs she must have bene some noble Knight.

37

Good sir (said he) you first must understand,
  I served *Charles* against the King of *Spaine*,
  I horsemen had and footmen in my band,
  In ambush plac'd the Spanish King t'have slaine:
  I brought the fairest Ladie in this land,
  And my best loved with me in my traine,
  When sodainly ere I thereof was ware,
  There came a horseman that procur'd my care.

38

Perhap a man, or some infernall sprite,
  In humane shape, I cannot certaine say,
  But this I say, he tooke the damsell bright,
  Even as a faulcon seaseth on his pray,
  So he my loving Ladie did affright,
  And so affrighted bare her quite away.
  And when I thought to rescue her by force,
  Aloft in aire he mounted with his horse.

39

Even as a rav'nous kite that doth espie
  A little chicken wandring from the other,
  Doth catch him straight, and carries him on hie,
  That now repents he was not with his mother.
  What could I do? my horse wants wings to flie,
  Scant could he set one leg before the tother,
  He traveld had before so many dayes,
  Among the painfull hils and stonie wayes.

40

But like to one that were his wit beside,
  I leave my men to do my first intent,
  Not caring of my selfe what should betide,
  (So strongly to my fancie was I bent)
  And tooke the blind god *Cupid* for my guide,
  By wayes as blind to seeke my love I went.
  And though my sense, my guide, my way were blind,
  Yet on I go in hope my love to find.

41

A senight space abating but a day,
  About the woods and mountaines I did range,
  In savage deserts wilde and void of way,
  Where humane steps were rare and very strange.
  Fast by the desert place a plaine there lay,
  That shewed from the rest but little change,
  Save onely that a castle full of wonder
  Did stand in rockes that had bene clov'n asunder.

42

This castle shines like flaming fire a farre,
  Not made of lime and stone as ours are here:
  And still as I approcht a little narre,
  More wonderfull the building doth appeare.
  It is a fort impregnable by warre,
  Compacted all of mettall shining cleare.
  The fiends of hell this fort of steele did make,
  Of metall tempred in the *Stigian* lake.

43

The towres are all of steele, and polisht bright,
  There is on them no spot or any rust,
  It shines by day, by darke it giveth light,
  Here dwels this robber wicked and unjust,
  And what he gets against all lawes and right,
  The lawlesse wretch abuseth here by lust,
  And here he keepes my faire and faithfull lover,
  Without all hope that I may her recover.

44

Ah wo was me, in vaine I sought to helpe,
  I see the place that keepes that I love best,
  Even as a foxe that crying heares her whelpe,
  Now borne aloft into the Eagles nest,
  About the tree she goes, and faine would helpe,
  But is constrain'd for want of wings to rest.
  The rocke so steepe, the castle is so hie,
  None can get in except they learne to flie.

45

And as I tarri'd in the plaine, behold
  I saw two Knights come riding downe the plaine,
  Led by desire and hope to win this hold,
  But their desire and hope was all in vaine.
  Gradasso was the first of courage bold,
  A King of *Serican* that held the raine.
  Rogero next, a man of noble nation,
  Of yeares but yong, but of great estimation.

46

A little dwarfe they had to be their guide,
  Who told me that they came to trie their force
  Against the champion that doth use to ride
  Out of this castle on the winged horse.
  Which when I heard, to them for helpe I cride,
  And pray'd them of my case to take remorse,
  And that they would, if twere their chance to win,
  Set free my love that there was locked in.

47

And all my griefe to them I did unfold,
Affirming with my teares my tale too true:
No sooner I my heavy hap had told,
But they were come within the castles vew,
I stood aloofe the battell to behold,
And praid to God good fortune might ensue.
Beneath the castle lies a little plaine,
Exceeding not an arrow shoore or twaine.

48

And as they talkt who first should fight or last,
They were arrived to the castle hill,
At length *Gradasso* (whether lots were cast,
Or that *Rogero* yeelded to his will)
Doth take his horne, and blew therewith a blast,
The noise whereof the castle wals did fill.
And straight with greater speed then can be guest,
Came out the rider of the flying beast.

49

And as we see strange cranes are wont to do,
First stalke a while, ere they their wings can find,
Then soare from ground not past a yard or two,
Till in their wings they gather'd have the wind,
At last they mount the very clouds unto,
Triangle wise, according to their kind:
So by degrees this *Mage* begins to flie,
The bird of *Iove* can hardly mount so hie.

50

And when he sees his time, and thinkes it best,
He falleth downe like lead in fearfull guise,
Even as the faulcon doth the fowle arrest,
The ducke and mallard from the brooke that rise,
So he descending with his speare in rest,
Doth pierce the aire in strange and monstrous wise,
And ere *Gradasso* were thereof admonish'd,
He felt a stripe that made him halfe astonish'd.

51

The *Mage* upon *Gradasso* brake his speare,
Who strikes in vaine upon the aire and wind,
Away he flue without or hurt or feare,
And leaves *Gradasso* many a pace behind.
This fierce encounter was so hard to beare,
That good *Alfana* to the ground inclind,
This same *Alfana* was *Gradassos* mare,
The fair'st and best that ever saddle bare.

52

Aloft the starres the sorc'rer doth ascend,
And wheeles about, and downe he comes againe,
And on *Rogero* hee his force doth bend,
That had compassion on *Gradassos* paine:
So sore th'assault *Rogero* did offend,
His horse the force thereof could not sustaine,
And when to strike againe he made account,
He saw his foe up to the clouds to mount.

53

Sometimes the *Mage Rogero* doth assaile,
Straight way *Gradasso* he doth set upon,
And oft they strike againe without availe,
So quickly he at whom they strike is gone,
He winds about as ships do under saile,
His sailes are wings, and rest he gives them none,
But sets upon them in so sudden wise,
That he amaz'd and dazeld both their eyes.

54

Betweene this one aloft, and two alow,
This conflict did no little space endure,
Vntill at last the night began to grow,
With mistie clouds making the world obscure:
I saw this fight, the truth thereof I know,
I present was thereat, yet am I sure,
That very few (except the wiser sort)
Will credence give to such a strange report.

55

This heavenly hellish warriour bare a shield
On his left arme that had a silken case,
I cannot any cause or reason yeeld,
Why he would keepe it cover'd so long space:
It had such force, that who so it beheld,
Such shining light it striketh in their face,
That downe they fall with eyes and senses closed,
And leave their corps of him to be disposed.

56

The target like the carbuncle doth shine,
Such light was never seene with mortall eye,
It makes to ground the lookers on decline,
Be they farre off, or be they standing nie:
And as it clos'd their sight, it closed mine,
That in a trance no little space was I.
At last when I awakt and rose againe,
The aire was darke, and voided was the plaine.

57

The sorcerer hath tane them (I surmise)
Into his castle, as is likely most,
And by this light that dazeld all our eies,
My hope is gone, their liberty is lost:
This is the truth, ne do I ought devise,
You heare the same, I felt it to my cost.
Now judge if I have reason to complaine,
That have and do endure such endlesse paine.

58

When as this Knight his dolefull tale had done,
He sate him downe all chearlesse in the place,
This was Earle *Pinnabel Anselmus* sonne,
Borne in *Maganza* of that wicked race,
Who like the rest so lewd a course did runne,
He holpe the more his linage to deface:
For onely vertue noblenesse doth dignifie,
And vicious life a linage base doth signifie.

59

The Ladie faire attentive all this while,
  Doth hearken unto this *Maganzese* tale,
  Rogeros name sometime doth make her smile,
  Sometime againe for feare she looketh pale:
  But hearing how a sorcerer base and vile,
  Should in a castle so detaine him thrall,
  She pitied him, and in her mind she fretted,
  And oft desir'd to heare the tale repeated.

60

When at the last the whole she understood,
  She said, sir Knight mourne not, but take some pleasure,
  Perhaps our meeting may be to your good,
  And turne your enemie unto displeasure:
  Shew me this fort, for why it frets my blood,
  So foule a prison holds so faire a treasure
  And if good fortune favour mine intent,
  You will right well suppose your travell spent.

61

Ah (said the Knight) should I returne againe,
  To passe these mountaines hard and overthwart?
  Though for my selfe it is but little paine,
  To toile my bodie having lost my hart:
  For you to go where as you may be slaine,
  Or taken prisner were a foolish part:
  Which if it hap, yet me you cannot blame,
  Because I give you warning of the same.

62

This said, he riseth up his horse to take,
  The noble Ladie on the way to guide,
  Who meanes to venter for *Rogeros* sake,
  Or death or thraldome, or what ere betide,
  But loe a messenger great hast doth make,
  That comes behind, and (tarry ho) he cride,
  This was the post that told to *Sacrapant*,
  How she that foyld him was Dame *Bradamant*.

63

This messenger brought tidings in great post,
  Both from *Narbona* and from *Mompeleere*,
  How they were up in armes along the cost
  Of *Aquamort*, and all that dwelled neere,
  And how *Marfilias* men their hearts had lost,
  Because of her no tidings they could heare:
  And (for her absence made them ill apayd)
  They sent to have her presence and her ayd.

64

These townes and others many to the same,
  Betweene the streames of *Rodon* and of *Vare*,
  The Empror had assign'd this worthy dame,
  Committing them unto her trust and care.
  Her noble value gat her all this fame,
  Because in armes herselfe she bravely bare,
  And so the cities under her subjection,
  This message sent, requiring her direction.

65

Which when she heard, it made her somewhat pause,
  Twixt yea and no she stood a pretie space,
  Of one side honor and her office drawes,
  On th'other side love helpes to pleade the case,
  At last she meanes t'ensue the present cause,
  And fetch *Rogero* from th'inchanted place:
  And if her force cannot to this attaine,
  At least with him a prisner to remaine.

66

In curteous sort her answer she contrived,
  With gracious words, and sent away the post,
  She longs with her new guide to have arrived,
  To that same place where both their loves were lost.
  But he perceiving now she was derived,
  From *Clarimont* that he detested most,
  Doth hate her sore, and feareth to the same,
  Lest she should know he of *Maganza* came.

67

There was betweene these houses auncient hate;
  This of *Maganza*, that of *Clarimount*,
  And each of them had weakned others state,
  By killing men in both of great account.
  This *Pinnabel* (a vile and wicked mate,
  That all his kin in vices did surmount)
  Meanes with himselfe this damsell to betray,
  Or else to slip aside and go his way.

68

And this same fancie so his head did fill,
  With hate, with feare, with anger and with doubt,
  That he mistooke the way against his will,
  And knew not how againe to find it out,
  Till in the wood he saw a little hill,
  Bare on the top, where men might looke about,
  But *Bradamant* such amorous passions feeles,
  She followeth like a spannell at his heeles.

69

The craftie guide thus wandring in the wood,
  Intending now the Ladie to beguile,
  Said unto her forsooth he thought it good,
  Sith night grew on, themselves to rest a while:
  Here is, quoth he (and shewd which way it stood)
  A castle faire, and hence not many a mile:
  But tarry you a little here untill
  I may descrie the countrey from the hill.

70

This said, he mounted to the higher ground,
  And standing now the highest part upon,
  He cast about his eyes and looked round,
  To find some path whereby he might be gone.
  When unawares a monstrous cave he found,
  And strange cut out and hollow'd in the stone,
  Deepe thirtie cubits downe it doth descend,
  Having a faire large gate at lower end.

71

Such as great stately houses wont to have,
  Out of which gate proceeds a shining light,
  That all within most lightsome makes the cave,
  And all this while on this felonious Knight
  This noble Ladie due attendance gave,
  And never suffred him go out of sight.
  She follow'd *Pinnabel* hard at his backe,
  Because she was afeard to leefe the tracke.

72

When as this villaine traitor did espie,
  That his designements foolish were and vaine,
  Either to leave her, or to make her die,
  He thought it best to trie a further traine,
  Perswading her for to descend and trie,
  What Ladies faire within the cave remaine,
  For why (said he) within this little space
  I saw a goodly damsell in the place.

73

Both rich arayd and very faire of hew,
  Like one of noble linage and degree,
  And this her fortune made me more to rew,
  That here against her will she seem'd to be.
  And when I thought for to descend and vew,
  The cause of this her griefe to know and see,
  I was no sooner from my horse alighted,
  But with infernall hags I was afrighted.

74

The noble *Bradamant* that was more stout
  Then warie, who it was did her perswade,
  Hath such desire to helpe a damsell out,
  That straight the cave she meaneth to invade,
  She finds by hap a long bough thereabout,
  Thereof a pole of mightie length she made,
  First with her sword she hewes and pares it fit,
  That done she lets it downe into the pit.

75

She giveth *Pinnabel* the bigger end,
  And prayes him stand above and hold it fast,
  And by the same intending to descend,
  Vpon her armes her whole waight she doth cast.
  But he that to destroy her did intend,
  Doth aske if she would learne to leape a cast,
  And laughing, loos'd his hands that were together,
  And wisht that all the race of them were with her.

76

Yet great good hap the gentle damsell found,
  As well deserv'd a mind so innocent:
  For why the pole strake first upon the ground,
  And though by force it shiver'd all and rent,
  Yet were her limbes and life kept safe and sound,
  For all his vile and traiterous intent,
  Sore was the damsell mazed with the fall,
  As in another booke declare I shall.

THE THIRD BOOKE OF
ORLANDO FVRIOSO

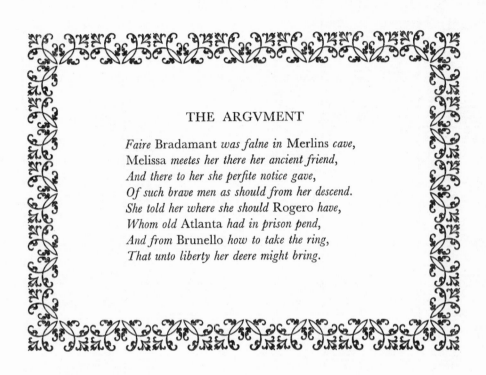

THE ARGVMENT

Faire Bradamant *was falne in* Merlins *cave,*
Melissa *meetes her there her ancient friend,*
And there to her she perfite notice gave,
Of such brave men as should from her descend.
She told her where she should Rogero *have,*
Whom old Atlanta *had in prison pend,*
And from Brunello *how to take the ring,*
That unto liberty her deere might bring.

ORLANDO FVRIOSO
THE THIRD BOOKE

1

Oh that my head were so well stor'd with skill,
  Of such a noble subject fit to treat,
  Oh that my wits were equall to my will,
  To frame a phrase fit for so high conceat:
  Ye Muses that do hold the sacred hill,
  Inspire my heart with flame of learned heat,
  While I presume in base and lowly verse,
  The names of glorious Princes to reherse.

2

Such Princes as excell all Princes far,
  In all the gifts of body and of mind,
  Temprat in peace, victorious eke in war,
  Themselves most noble, come of noble kind.
  And such (except my guesse do greatly er)
  As are by heav'ns eternall doome assign'd,
  In wealth, in fame, in rule and in prosperity,
  To live themselves, their children and posterity.

3

Nor can I now their severall actes most rare,
  Atcheev'd by ev'ry one of them recite,
  No though my verse with *Virgils* might compare,
  Or I as well as *Homer* could endite:
  With their great praise, great vollumes filled are,
  With large discourse, by them that stories write.
  I onely meane to shew what was foreshowne,
  Long ere their persons, or their deeds were knowne.

4

But first of *Pinnabel* a word to speake,
  Who as you heard with traiterous intent,
  The bonds of all humanity did break,
  For which ere long himselfe was after shent.
  Thus while base minds their wrongs do basly wreak,
  They do that once that often they repent,
  And curse that time, a thousand times, too late
  When they pursude their unrevenged hate.

5

With fainting heart, (for sin is full of feare)
  By stealing steps from hence he doth depart,
  And as he goes he prieth here and there,
  His fearefull looke bewraies his guilty hart,
  Nor yet his dread doth move him to forbeare,
  To heape more sin upon this ill desart.
  Appal'd with feare, but toucht with no remorse,
  Supposing she was slaine, he takes her horse.

6

But let him go untill another time,
  For I do meane hereafter you shall heare,
  How he was dealt with, when his double crime,
  In secret wrought, most open did appeare.
  Now unto *Bradamant* I bend my rime,
  Who with her fall, was yet of heavy cheare:
  And had beene taught a gamball for the nonce,
  To give her death and buriall at once.

7

Now when she came unto her selfe againe,
  And had recover'd memory and sence,
  She gets her on her feet, although with paine,
  In mind to seeke some way to get fro thence,
  When loe, before her face she seeth plaine,
  A stately portall built with great expence,
  And next behind the same she might descrie,
  A larger roome and fairer to the eie.

8

This was a Church most solemne and devout,
  That stands on marble pillars small and round,
  And rais'd by art on arches all about,
  That made each voyce to yeeld a double sound.
  A lightsome lampe that never goeth out,
  Did burne on altar standing in the ground:
  That though the roomes were large and wide in space,
  The lampe did serve to lighten all the place.

9

The noble damsell full of rev'rent feare,
  When as her selfe in sacred place she sees,
  (As one that still a godly minde did beare,)
  Begins to pray to him upon her knees,
  Whose holy side was perst with cruell speare,
  And who to save our lives his owne did leese:
  And while she stayes devoutly at her prayre,
  The sage *Melyssa* doth to her repaire.

10

Her gowne ungyrt, her haire about her head,
  Much like a priest or prophetesse arraid,
  And in her booke a little while she red,
  And after thus unto the damsell said:
  O thou by Gods appointment hither led,
  O *Bradamant*, most wise and worthy maid,
  I long have looked here for this thy comming,
  Foretold thereof by prophet *Merlins* cunning.

11

Here is the tombe that *Merline* erst did make,
  By force of secret skill and hidden art,
  In which sometimes the *Ladie* of the *lake*,
  That with her beautie had bewitcht his hart,
  Did make him enter fondly for her sake,
  From whence he never after could depart,
  And he was by a woman over reached,
  That unto others prophesied and preached.

12

His carkas dead within this stone is bound,
  But with dead corse the living soule doth dwell:
  And shall untill it heare the trumpet sound,
  That brings reward of doing ill or well.
  His voice doth live and answer and expound,
  And things both present past and future tell,
  Resolving men of ev'rie doubtfull case,
  That for his counsell come unto this place.

13

About a moneth or little more or lesse,
  It is since I repaird to *Merlins* grave,
  Of him about the studie I professe,
  Some precepts and instructions to have.
  And (for I willing was I must confesse)
  To meete you at your comming to this cave:
  For which he did prefixe this certaine day,
  This moved me of purpose here to stay.

14

Duke *Ammons* daughter silent stands and still,
  The while the wise *Melyssa* to her spake,
  Astonished at this unusuall skill,
  And doubting if she were asleepe or wake,
  A modest shame with grace her eyes doth fill,
  With which downe cast, this answer she doth make:
  Alas what good or merite is in me
  That prophets should my comming so foresee?

15

And glad of this adventure unexpected,
  She followeth her guide with great delight,
  And straight she saw the stately toombe erected,
  Of marble pure that held his bones and sprite,
  And (that which one would little have suspected)
  The very marble was so cleare and bright,
  That though the sunne no light unto it gave,
  The tombe it selfe did lighten all the cave.

16

For whether be the nature of some stone,
  A darkesome place with lightsomenes to fill,
  Or were it done by magike art alone,
  Or else by helpe of Mathematike skill,
  To make transparencies to meete in one,
  And so convey the sunne-beames where you will:
  But sure it was most curious to behold,
  Set forth with carved workes and guilt with gold.

17

Now when the damsell was approched nyre,
  To this strange toombe where *Merlins* bones were plast,
  Forth of the stones that shine like flaming fire,
  His lively voyce such speeches out doth cast:
  Let fortune ever favour thy desire,
  O *Bradamant* thou noble maid and chast,
  From out whose wombe an issue shall proceed,
  That all the world in glorie shall exceed.

18

The noble blood that came of ancient *Troy*,
  By two cleare springs in thee together mixt,
  Shall breed the flowre, the jewell and the joy,
  Of all on whom the sunne his beames hath fixt,
  Twixt those that heat, and those that cold annoy,
  From *Tage* to *Inde*, *Danub* and *Nile* betwixt,
  Emp'rors and Kings, and Dukes and Lords for ay,
  Of this thy linage carrie shall the sway.

19

And many a Captaine brave and worthy Knight,
  Shall issue from this stocke, that shall restore
  By warlike feates the glorie shining bright,
  That *Italy* possessed heretofore.
  And magistrates to maintaine peace and right,
  As *Numa* and *Augustus* did before,
  To cherish vertue, vice so to asswage,
  As shall to us bring backe the golden age.

20

Wherefore sith God hath by predestination,
  Appointed thee to be *Rogeros* wife,
  And means to blesse thine heirs and generation,
  With all the graces granted in this life,
  Persist thou firme in thy determination,
  And stoutly overcome each storme of strife,
  And worke his worthy punishment and paine,
  That doth thy lives delight from thee detaine.

21

This said: the prophet *Merline* holds his peace,
  And gives *Melissa* time to worke her will,
  Who when she did perceive the voice to cease,
  She purposeth by practise of her skill,
  To shew the damsell part of that increase,
  That should with fame the world hereafter fill.
  And for this purpose she did then assemble,
  A troupe of sprights their persons to resemble.

22

Who straight by words of secret vertue bound,
  In numbers great unto the cave repaire,
  Of whence I know not, whether under ground,
  Or else of those that wander in the aire:
  Then thrise she drawes about a circle round,
  And thrise she hallowes it with secret praire.
  Then opens she a triple clasped booke,
  And softly whispering in it she doth looke.

23

This done she takes the damsell by the hand
  Exhorting her she should not be afraid,
  And in a circle causeth her to stand,
  And for her more securitie and aid,
  And as it were for more assured band,
  Vpon her head some characters she laid.
  Then having done her due and solemne rites,
  She doth beginne to call upon the sprites.

24

Behold a crew of them come rushing in,
  In sundrie shapes with persons great and tall,
  And now they filled all the roome within,
  So readily they came unto her call,
  When *Bradamant* to feare did straight begin,
  Her heart was cold, her colour waxed pall.
  But yet the circle kept her like a wall,
  So that she needed not to feare at all.

25

Howbeit *Melyssa* caused them be gone,
  From thence unto the next adjoyning cave,
  And thence to come before them one by one,
  The better notice of their names to have,
  That at more leysure they may talke thereon,
  When as occasion so may seeme to crave
  Although (quoth she) this short time cannot serve
  To speake of ev'rie one as they deserve.

26

Lo here the first thy first begotten sonne,
  That beares thy favour and his fathers name,
  By whom the Lombards shall in fight be wonne,
  To *Defiderius* their Kings great shame,
  Who shall at *Pontyr* make the streames to runne,
  With blood in fields adjoyning to the same,
  And shall revenge the deeds and minds unpure,
  Of such as did his fathers fall procure.

27

And for this noble act among the rest,
  The Emperour shall give him in reward,
  The honours great of *Calaon* and *Est*,
  By which his family shall be prefard,
  The next *Vberto* is whose valiant brest,
  Shall be unto the church a gard,
  Defending it with valiant heart and hand,
  To th'honor of *Hesperyan* armes and land.

28

Alberto he is nam'd that third comes in,
  Whose triumphs are most famous ev'rie where,
  Then his sonne *Hugo* that did *Millain* winne,
  And for his crest two vipers us'd to beare,
  Next *Atso* is and next to him of kinne,
  That erst of *Lombardie* the crowne shall weare.
  Then *Albertasso* by whose meanes are wonne,
  The *Beringers* both father and the sonne.

29

To him shall *Othons* favour so encline,
  He shall in marriage give to him his daughter.
  Now *Hugo* comes againe, ô happie line,
  And happie man that sav'd so great a slaughter,
  When at *Christs* vicars rule *Rome* did repine,
  He daunteth them and so restor'd them after:
  The which by wit without the dint of sword,
  He shall effect in *Othons* time the third.

30

Now *Fulko* comes that to his brothers gave,
  His land in Italy which was not small,
  And dwelt in *Almany* his land to save
  Of *Samsony*, that unto him did fall.
  A Dukedome great that did with Castles brave,
  Accrew to him for want of issue male.
  By him that noble house is held and cherished,
  That but for him would be extinct and perished.

31

Then commeth *Atso* that misliketh warre,
  But yet his sonnes *Bertold* and *Albertasse*,
  With second *Henrie* shall be still at jarre,
  And bring the *Dutchmen* to a wofull passe.
  Next young *Renaldo* shining like a starre,
  Shall be unto the Church a wall of brasse,
  And worke the utter overthrow and losse,
  Of wicked *Fredrike* named *Barbarosse*.

32

Behold another *Atso* shall possesse,
  Verona with a stately territorie,
  Of *Oton* and *Honorius* no lesse,
  Shall be a marquesse made to his great glory,
  It would be long their names all to expresse,
  That shall protect the sacred consistorie,
  And in most valerous and marshall manner,
  Display and eke defend the Churches banner.

33

Obyso next and *Folko* you may view,
  With *Henries* two, the father and the sonne,
  Both *Guelfes* that fruitfull *Humbrya* shall subdew,
  And keepe the Dukedome there by conquest won.
  Behold him that the good state doth renew,
  Of *Italy* that late was quite undone.
  Cal'd *Atso* fift that bravely overthrew,
  The cruell *Esselino* and him slew.

34

That cruell *Esselyno* that was thought,
  To have beene gotten by some wicked divell,
  That never any goodnesse had beene taught,
  But sold his soule to sinne and doing evill,
  Comparing with the cruell acts he wrought,
  Fierce *Nero* were but myld and *Sylla* civill.
  Beside this *Atso* shall in time to come
  The powre of second *Fredrike* overcome.

35

And then he shall his brother *Albandrine*,
  Vnto the Florentines for monie gage,
  And *Othon* with the faction *Gebellyne*,
  He shall suppresse amid the furious rage,
  And raise the Church, nor letting it decline,
  But spending to defend it all his age.
  For which good service he shall justly merite,
  The Dukedome of *Ferrara* to inherite.

36

Next him *Renaldo* now ensu'th, whose lot,
  Shall be at *Naples* to be made away,
  A death his vertuous deeds deserued not,
  But wo to them that guiltlesse blood betray.
  Now followeth a worthy crue and knot,
  Whose acts alone to tell would spend a day:
  Obyso, Nicolas and *Aldbrandine*,
  Whose noble deeds shall honour much their line.

37

Then *Nicolas* is he that next ensu'th,
  That rul'd in tender yeares both neere and farre,
  That findes and eke revengeth their untruth,
  That sought his state by civill strife to marre.
  The sports and exercises of his youth,
  Are blowes and fights, and dangers great and warre,
  Which makes that ere to manly state he came,
  For martiall deeds he gets the onely name.

38

Lo *Lyonell* the glory of his age,
  Maintaining peace and quiet all his time,
  And keeping that with ease by wisedome sage,
  To which some others by much paine do clime,
  That fettred furie and rebuked rage,
  That locks up *Mars* in wals of stone and lime:
  That all his wit, his care and travell bent,
  To make his subjects live in state content.

39

Now *Hercles* comes, an *Hercules* indeed,
  Whose deeds shall merite ever during fame:
  That by his paines his countries ease shall breed,
  And put his enemies to flight and shame.
  Sharpe to devise, to execute with speed,
  Both stout t'attempt, and patient to the same,
  No Prince shall ever rule his countrie better,
  No Prince had ever countrie more his detter.

40

Not onely that he shall their moorish grounds,
  By great expence to pasture firme reduce,
  Not that the towne with wall environ round,
  And store with things behooffull to their use.
  Not that when warre in ech place shall abound,
  He shall mantaine them peaceable in truce,
  Not that he shall according to their asking
  Disburden them of payments and of tasking.

41

But that he shall more and above all these,
  Leave them behind him such a worthy race,
  As search within the circuit of the seas,
  You shall not find two to supplie their place.
  So shall the one the other strive to please,
  So shall the one the others love imbrace,
  As may for loving brotherly regard,
  With *Castor* and with *Pollux* be compard.

42

The elder of these two *Alfonso* hight,
  The next of them *Hyppolito* we call.
  Both passing stout and valiant in fight,
  Both passing wise and provident withall:
  And both in due defence of countries right,
  Shall seeme a bulwarke and a brazen wall:
  They both shall have of enemies good store,
  They both shall still subdue them evermore,

43

Their mother (if I may a mother name,)
  One more like *Progne* and *Medea* fell,
  Vnto her endlesse infamie and shame,
  Against her sonne *Alfonso* shall rebell,
  And joyne with *Venice* force (for this to blame)
  Though for the same ere long they paid full well,
  For those they thought to hurt, they did this good,
  To make the ground more fruitfull with their blood.

44

Not far fro thence the Spanish souldier hired,
  By pastors purse and in that pastors pay,
  That with a forcible assault aspired,
  To take a fort, and eke the captaine slay.
  But loe he comes and they perforce retyred,
  And have so short a pleasure of this pray,
  Scarse one of them in life is left abiding,
  To carrie notice of so heavie tiding.

45

His wit and valour shall him so advance,
  To have the honour of *Romania* field,
  Where by his meanes unto the force of *France*,
  The *Pope* and *Spaniards*, forced are to yeeld:
  And there in Christian blood, ô fatall chance,
  Shall horses swimme, such number shall be keeld,
  Nor shall not men enough alive remaine,
  To burie those that are in battell slaine.

46

The while his brother under Card'nals cap,
  Shall cover, nay shall shew a prudent head,
  Hyppolito (I meane) who shall have hap,
  With band of men but small (yet wisely led)
  To give to the *Venetians* such a clap,
  As few the like in stories have bene read.
  To take three times five *Gallies* at one tide,
  And barkes and boates a thousand more beside.

47

Behold two *Sygismonds* both wise and grave,
  Alfonso next, whose fame is talkt of rife,
  With his five sonnes, then *Hercles* that shall have
  The King of *France* his daughter to his wife,
  That towards him, her selfe shall so behave,
  Shall make him live most happie all his life.
  Hyppolito it is that now comes in,
  Not least for praise and glorie of his kin.

48

Next *Francis* named third, *Alfonsos* two,
  With many others worthy of renowne,
  The which to name might finde one worke to do,
  From Phœbus rising to his going downe.
  Now therefore if you will consent thereto,
  I here will end and send the spirits downe:
  To this the worthy damsell said not nay,
  And straight the spirits vanisht all away.

49

Then *Bradamant*, that all well marked had,
  Of whom her selfe should be the ancient mother,
  Did say, to learne she would be very glad,
  What two those were that differed from the other,
  That came with backward steps and lookt so sad,
  Vpon the good *Alfonso* and his brother.
  Melyssa sighs, misliking that suggestion,
  Which put it in her heart to ask this question.

50

And then as in a trance these words she spake,
  O thou more worthy sonne of worthy sire,
  They are thy bloud, on them compassion take,
  Let grace asswage, though justice kindle ire:
  Then unto *Bradamant* as new awake,
  I must (said she) denie you this desire,
  I say no more, content you with the sweet,
  For you, this sower morsell is not meet.

51

To morrow when the Sunne at breake of day,
  With light shall dim the light of ev'ry starre:
  I meane my selfe to guide you on your way,
  So as I will be sure you shall not arre.
  The place whereas your love is forc'd to stay,
  Is from the salt sea shore not very farre:
  That were you past a mile beyond this wood,
  The other way would easie be and good.

52

Of this nights stay the damsell was content,
  And in the cave with her she doth remaine,
  And most thereof in *Merlins* tombe she spent;
  Whose voice with talke did her still entertaine:
  Emboldning her to give her free consent,
  To love where she should sure be lov'd againe.
  Now gan the messenger of day to cro,
  When as her guide and she away did go.

53

The way they went was darke and unaccessible,
  By secret vaults and hollowes of the hill,
  To find it out had bene a thing impossible,
  But with a guide of knowledge great and skill:
  At last they came unto a path more passible,
  By which they cease not to ascend, untill
  They quite had left the darke and lothsome place,
  And saw the beames of *Phœbus* chearefull face.

54

And while that up this hill they slowly stalke,
  With pausing panting oft, and taking wind,
  To make lesse wearie seeme their wearie walke,
  Melyssa still doth store of matter find,
  And now of this, and then of that doth talke,
  But chiefly she the damsell puts in mind,
  Of her *Rogero*, how he had bene trained
  Into the prison where he now remained.

55

Atlanta that Magician strange is he
  That holdeth him (I trust) unto his cost,
  But had you *Pallas* strength or *Mars* (quoth she)
  And eke of armed men a mightie host,
  Yet to attempt by force to set him free,
  Your travell and your labour all were lost.
  Art must be wonne by art, and not by might,
  Force cannot free your welbeloved Knight.

56

For first the castle mounted is on hie,
  Impregnable with wals all over steeld,
  And next, the horse he rides hath wings to flie,
  And gallops in the aire as in the field:
  And last he dazleth ev'ry mortall eie,
  By hidden force of his enchanted shield,
  With light whereof mens senses are so dazed,
  With sight thereof they fall downe all amazed.

57

In all the world one onely meane hath beene,
  And is yet still to worke so rare a feat,
  A ring there is which from an *Indian* Queene,
  Was stole sometime, of price and vertue great:
  This ring can make a man to go unseene,
  This ring can all inchantments quite defeat:
  King *Agramant* hath sent his secretarie,
  Vnto *Rogero* this same ring to carie.

58

Brunello in his name that hath the ring,
  Most leud and false, but politike and wise,
  And put in trust especiall by his King,
  With it *Rogeros* safetie to devise:
  Which sith I wish not he, but you should bring,
  To bind him to you by this enterprise,
  And for I would not have the *Turke* protect him,
  Because I know he greatly doth affect him.

59

Do therefore this, when you do meete this man,
　Whose markes I wish in memory you beare,
His stature is two cubits and a span,
His head is long and gray, and thin of haire,
His nose is short and flat, his colour wan,
With beetle brow, eyes watrie not with teare,
His beard growes on his face without all stint,
And to conclude, his looke is all a squint.

60

Now when as you this comely man shall meet,
　As sure you shall within a day or two,
You may with curteous words him seeme to greet,
And tell him partly what you meane to do,
But speake not of the ring although you see't,
For so you may the matter all undo,
Then he great courtesie to you will offer,
And straight his companie to you will proffer.

61

But when unto the castle you come nie,
　Then see you set upon him on the way,
And take away the ring and make him die,
Nor give him any time, lest he convay
The ring into his mouth, and so thereby
Out of your sight he vanish quite away.
The worthy damsell markes her speeches well,
And so the one the other bids farewell.

62

Next day she hapt *Brunello* to espie,
　She knew him straight, she found him at her Inne,
She growes to question with him by and by,
And he to lie doth by and by beginne,
And she dissembles too, and doth denie
Her countrey, stocke and name, and sex and kinne.
Brunello pleasantly doth talke and tipple,
Not knowing he did halt before a cripple.

63

Now when they almost broken had their fast,
　She marking more his fingers then his eyes,
When much good talke between them two had past,
The most whereof were false and forged lies,
Behold mine host came unto them in hast,
And told them newes that made them sooner rise:
But here I meane to make a little pause,
Before I tell what was thereof the cause.

THE FOVRTH BOOKE OF
ORLANDO FVRIOSO

THE ARGVMENT

Bradamant *overcomes the false* Magician,
And sets Rogero *free, who by and by*
Leapt on a horse not knowing his condition,
Who bare him quite from sight of any eye.
Renaldo *sailed as he had commission,*
To England *ward, but borne by wind awrie,*
At Callidon *in* Scotland *he arrived,*
When faire Geneuras *foule death was contrived.*

D

ORLANDO FVRIOSO

THE FOVRTH BOOKE

1

Though he that useth craft and simulation,
  Doth seldome bend his acts to honest ends,
But rather of an evill inclination,
His wit and skill to others mischiefe bends:
Yet sith in this our worldly habitation,
We do not ever dwell among our friends,
Dissembling doubtlesse oftentimes may save
Mens lives, their fame and goods, and all they have.

2

If man by long acquaintance and great proofe,
  To trust some one man scant can be allured,
To whom he may in presence or aloofe,
Vnfold the secrets of his mind assured:
Then doth this damsell merit no reproofe,
That with *Brunello* (to all fraud inured)
Doth frame her selfe to counterfeit a while,
For to deceive deceivers is no guile.

3

Now while these two did to conferre begin,
  She to his fingers having still an eye,
The host and other servants of the Inne,
Came on the sodaine with a wofull crie,
And some did gaze without, and some within,
(As when men see a *Comet* in the skie)
The cause of this their wondring and their crying,
Was that they saw an armed horseman flying.

4

And straight by th'host and others they were told,
  How one that had in *Magicke* art great skill,
Not far from thence had made a stately hold,
Of shining steele, and plac'd it on a hill,
To which he bringeth Ladies yong and old,
And men and maids according to his will,
And when within that castle they have beene,
They never after have bene heard or seene.

5

No sooner can he spie a pretie maide,
  But straight he takes her up into the aire,
The which his custome makes them all afraid,
That either are or thinke that they be faire.
Those hardie knights that went to give them aide,
Of which sort many hither did repaire,
Went like the beasts to the sicke Lions den,
For all went in, but none return'd agen.

6

This tale in worthy *Bradamant* did breed
  A kind of pleasure and confused joy,
In hope (which after she perform'd indeed)
The sight of her beloved to enjoy,
She praid the host procure a guide with speed,
As though each little stay did breed annoy:
She sweares that in her heart she long'd to wrastle
With him that kept the captives in his castle.

7

Because that you sir knight should want no guide,
  (*Brunello* said) I will my selfe be he,
I know the way, and somewhat have beside,
By which may fortune you may pleasur'd be:
He meant the ring of force and vertue tride,
Although he meant not she the same should see.
Great thanks (quoth she) that you will take the pain,
In hope hereby the precious ring to gain.

8

Thus each from other hiding their intent,
  They forward set like friends by breake of day,
Brunello sometime foremost of them went,
Sometime behind, as chanced on the way.
Now had they certaine houres in travell spent,
When they arrived where the castle lay,
Whereas mount *Pyrene* stands above the plaine,
So high as may discover *France* and *Spaine*.

9

When as the castle did in sight appeare,
  So strange, so faire, so stately, and so hie,
In which that Knight whom she esteem'd so deare,
With many others, prisoner did lie.
She thought her fittest time drew very neare,
To take the ring, and make *Brunello* die.
Wherefore with open force she doth assaile him,
Whose strength with age and feare soon gan to faile him.

10

Her meaning was the Caitife to have kild,
  But unto that her noble heart said nay,
Small praise would come from bloud so basely spild,
She meanes to get the ring another way:
But first she bound him where he wild or nild,
And though with teares he did for pittie pray,
Yet left she him unto a tree fast tide,
And with the ring away she straight did ride.

11

And being in the greene fast by the towre,
   Straight (as the fashion was) her horne she blew,
   Out came that armed Knight that present houre,
   And seeing there a challenger in vew,
   He seemeth to assault her with great powre,
   But by the ring she all his falshood knew:
   She saw he carride neither sword nor speare,
   Nor any weapon that one need to feare.

12

He only carride at his saddle bow,
   A shield all wrapped in a crimson case,
   And read a booke by which he made to show
   Some strange and strong illusions in the place:
   And many that these cunnings did not know,
   He had deceiv'd and tane in little space.
   And caus'd both swords and lances to appeare,
   When neither sword nor lances them were neare.

13

But yet the beast he rode was not of art,
   But gotten of a *Griffeth* and a Mare,
   And like a *Griffeth* had the former part,
   As wings and head, and clawes that hideous are,
   And passing strength and force and ventrous hart,
   But all the rest may with a horse compare.
   Such beasts as these the hils of *Ryfee* yeeld,
   Though in these parts they have bin seene but seeld.

14

This monster rare from farthest regions brought
   This rare *Magician* ordred with such skill,
   That in one month or little more he tought
   The savage monster to obey his will:
   And though by conjurations strange he wrought,
   In other things his fancie to fulfill,
   (As cunning men still trie each strange conclusion)
   Yet in this *Griffeth* horse was one collusion.

15

The Ladie faire protected by the ring,
   Found all his sleights (although she seem'd not so)
   Her purpose to the better passe to bring,
   And first she seemes to ward a comming blow,
   And then to strike, and oft to curse the wing,
   That carride still away her flying fo,
   And sith to fight on horsebacke did not boote,
   She seemes as in a rage to light on foote.

16

The *Necromancer*, as his manner is,
   Disclosed at the last his shining shield,
   Supposing that the vertue would not misse,
   To make her (as it had done others) yeeld:
   So have I seene a craftie cat ere this,
   Play with a silly mouse of house or field,
   And let it go a while for sport and play,
   But kill at last and beare it quite away.

17

I say that he the cat, the other mise,
   Resembled had in every former fight,
   But now this ring had made this one so wise,
   That when she saw the strange enchanted light,
   She falleth not of force, but of devise,
   As though she were astonied at the sight,
   And lay like one of life and sense bereaved,
   By which the poore *Magician* was deceaved.

18

For straight he lighted from the flying horse,
   To take her as he had done many mo,
   The shield and booke in which was all his force,
   He left behind him at his saddle bow,
   But thinking to have found a senslesse corse,
   Amaz'd and dead, he finds it nothing so,
   For up she starts, so quite the case was altred,
   That with the cord he brought, himselfe was haltred.

19

And when with those selfe bonds she had him tide,
   By which he thought before her to have snared,
   She strong and yong, he wither'd, old and dride,
   Alas an unmeet match to be compared,
   Forthwith determining he should have dide,
   To strike his head from shoulders she prepared,
   Till she was mov'd to mercy with his teares,
   And with the sight of white and hoary haires.

20

For when he saw his force was overlaid,
   And that her strength was not to be withstood,
   O pardon life thou heavenly wight (he said)
   No honour comes by spilling aged blood.
   Which words to mercie mov'd the noble maid,
   Whose mind was always mercifull and good.
   Then why he built the castle she demanded,
   And what he was to tell her him commanded.

21

With wofull words the old man thus replide,
   I made this castle for no ill intention,
   For covetice or any fault beside,
   Or that I loved rapine or contention,
   But to prevent a danger shall betide
   A gentle Knight, I framed this invention:
   Who as the heavens hath shewd me in short season,
   Shall die in Christian state by filthy treason.

22

Rogero named is this worthy youth,
   Whose good and safetie faine I would advance,
   My name *Atlante* is to tell you truth,
   I bred him of a child, till his hard chance,
   And valiant mind (that breeds alas my ruth)
   With *Agramant* entist him into *France*.
   And I that (like mine owne child) alway lov'd him,
   From *France* and danger faine would have remov'd him.

23

By art and helpe of many a hellish elfe,
  This castle for *Rogero* I did build,
  And took him as I meant to take thy selfe,
  But that with greater art I was beguild,
  From dainty fare, and other worldly pelfe,
  Because he should not thinke himselfe exild,
  For company I brought him worthy wights,
  Both men and women, Ladies faire and Knights.

24

They have all plentie of desired pleasure,
  I bend to their contentment all my care,
  For them I spend my travell and my treasure,
  For musicke, clothes and games, and daintie fare,
  As hart can think, and mouth require with measure,
  Great store for them within this castle are.
  Well had I travel'd, well my time bestowed,
  But you have mard the fruits that I had sowed.

25

But if your mind be gracious as your looke,
  If stonie heart bide not in tender brest,
  Behold I offer thee my shield and booke,
  And flying horse, and grant my just request,
  Some two or three, or all the Knights I tooke,
  I give thee free, let but *Rogero* rest:
  Whose health, whose wealth, whose safty and welfare
  Have ever bene (and ever shall) my care.

26

Your care (quoth she) is very ill bestowne,
  In thraldome vile to keepe a worthy wight:
  As for your gifts you offer but mine owne,
  Sith by my conquest you are mine in right.
  Those dangers great you say to be foreshowne,
  And upon him in time to come must light,
  With figures cast and heavenly planets vewed,
  Cannot be knowne or cannot be eschewed.

27

How can you others harmes foresee so farre,
  And not prevent your owne that were so nie?
  I certaine shall suppose your art doth erre,
  And for the rest the end the truth shall trie:
  I now intend your matter all to marre,
  And that before these bonds I will untie,
  You shall set free and loose your prisners all,
  Whom in this castle you detained thrall.

28

When as the poore old man was so distrest,
  That needs he must for feare and dread obay,
  And that this same imperious dames behest,
  Could neither beare deniall nor delay,
  To do as she commands he deemes it best,
  And therefore takes th'inchanted place away.
  He breakes some hollow fuming pots of stone,
  And straight the wals and buildings all were gone.

29

This done, himselfe eke vanisht out of sight,
  As did the castle at that present hower,
  Then Ladies, Lords, and many a worthy Knight,
  Were straight releast from his enchanted power:
  And some there were had taken such delight
  In those so stately lodgings of that tower,
  That they esteemd that liberty a paine,
  And wisht that pleasant slavery againe.

30

Here were at freedome set among the rest,
  Gradasso, *Sacrapant*, two Kings of name,
  Prasyldo and *Iroldo* that from th'Est
  Into this country with *Renaldo* came.
  Here *Bradamant* found him she loved best,
  Her deare *Rogero* of renowned fame,
  Who after certaine notice of her had,
  Did shew to see her he was very glad.

31

As one of whom he great account did make,
  And thought himselfe to her most highly bound,
  Since she put off her helmet for his sake,
  And in her head receiv'd a grievous wound,
  Twere long to tell what toile they both did take,
  Both night and day each other to have found,
  But till this present time they had no meeting,
  Nor giv'n by word nor writing any greeting.

32

Now when before him present he beheld
  Her that from danger had him sole redeemed,
  His heart with so great joy and mirth was fild,
  The happiest wight on earth himselfe he deemed:
  And christall teares from her faire eyes distild,
  Embracing him whom she most deare esteemed.
  As oft we see a strong and sodaine passion,
  Bring forth effects quite of another fashion.

33

The Griffeth horse the while upon the plaine,
  Stood with the target at his saddle bow,
  The damsell thought to take him by the raine,
  But he then mounteth up, and like a crow
  Chast by a dog forthwith descends againe,
  And standeth still, or soareth very low,
  And when that some come nie in hope to take him,
  He flies away that none can overtake him.

34

But neare unto *Rogero* soone he staid,
  Which by *Atlantas* care was sole procured,
  Who for *Rogeros* danger was afraid,
  And thinkes his safetie never well assured.
  Wherefore he sent this monster for his aid,
  And by this meanes from *Europe* him allured,
  To his welfare his cares and thoughts he bendeth,
  To succor and preserve him he intendeth.

35

Rogero from his horse forthwith alighted,
  (The horse he rode on was Frontyno named)
And with this flying horse was so delighted,
  That though he saw him wanton and untamed,
Yet up he leapt, and soone was sore afrighted,
  He finds he would not to his mind be framed,
For in the aire the Griffeth sor'd so hie,
As doth the Faulcon that at fowle doth flie.

36

The damsell faire that now beheld her deare,
  Borne farre away by force of monsters wing,
Was sorrowfull and of so heavie cheare,
  That to their course her wits she scant could bring,
The tale of Ganymed she once did heare,
  Whom Poets faine to tend the heavenly King,
She doubts may true of her Rogero be,
That was as comely and as faire as he.

37

As long as eysight could at all prevaile,
  So long she viewd him still in all and part:
But when his distance made the sight to faile,
  At least she followed him in mind and hart,
To sob, to sigh, to weepe, lament and waile,
  She never leaves these chances overthwart.
And seeing plaine her love and she were parted,
She tooke Frontyno and away departed.

38

Now was Rogero mounted up so hie,
  He seem'd to be a mote or little pricke,
For no man could distinguish him by eie,
  Except his sight were passing fine and quicke:
All southerly this Griffeth horse doth flie,
  (Was never jade that serv'd man such a tricke)
But let him on his way, God speed him well,
For of Renaldo somewhat I must tell.

39

Who all the while with raging tempest strived,
  Borne where himselfe nor no man else did know,
By cruell stormie winds and weather drived,
  That dayes and nights surceased not to blow:
At last in Scotland weary he arrived,
  Where woods of Callidony first do show,
A famous wood wherein in times of old,
Brave deeds were done by ventrous Knights & bold.

40

Here have those famous Knights great honour won,
  At whose rare worth the world it selfe did wonder,
Here were most valiant acts atchiev'd and done,
  By Knights that dwelt there neare or far asunder,
And many a man hath here bene quite undone,
  Whose feeble force his enemie was under,
Here were, as proved is by ancient charter,
The famous Tristram, Lancellot and sir Arther.

41

At this same wood Renaldo from his fleet,
  Well mounted on his Bayards backe did part,
He points his men at Barwicke him to meet,
  The while himselfe alone with valiant heart,
Sometime on horsebacke, sometime on his feete,
  Doth march in mind to do some worthy part.
But seeing now the night came on so fast,
Vnto an Abbey he repaires at last.

42

The Abbot and his Monks with comely grace,
  As holy men of humane manners skilled,
Did welcome him, and in a little space,
  With costly fare his emptie stomacke filled.
Renaldo straight enquired of the place,
  What feates of armes had there bene late fulfilled,
And where a man by valiant acts may show,
If his exploits deserve dispraise or no.

43

They said that in that wood and forrest, find
  Adventures strange and feates of armes he might,
But as the place, so are the actions blind,
  That oft their doings never come to light.
But if (say they) we may perswade your mind,
  Attempt an action worthy of a Knight,
Where if you passe the perill and the paine,
Eternall fame shall unto you remaine.

44

For if you would performe an act indeed,
  Whereby great name and honour may be wonne,
Then this would be the best and noblest deed,
  That late or long time past was ever done:
Our Princes daughter standeth now in need,
  Of great defence, a danger great to shunne,
Against a Knight Lurcanio by name,
That seekes to take away her life and fame.

45

This Knight hath her unto the King accused,
  I thinke of malice rather then of right,
That he hath seene how she her selfe abused,
  And closely tooke her lover up by night.
Now by the lawes that in this land are used,
  Except she have a champion that by might
Within a month Lurcanio prove a lier,
She shall be straight condemned to the fier.

46

The Scottish law that breedeth all this strife,
  Appoints that all of base or better sort,
That take a man except she be his wife,
  And spends her time with him in Venus sport,
By cruell torment finish shall her life,
  Except she find some Knight that will support,
That she the hainous fact hath not committed,
But that in law she ought to be acquitted.

47

The King for faire *Geneura* takes great thought,
  Both for her safetie and her estimation,
  And seeks by all good meanes that may be wrought
  For her defence, and maketh proclamation,
  That by whose helpe from danger she is brought,
  (Provided he be one of noble nation)
  Shall have the goodly damsell for his wife,
  With livings large to keepe him all his life.

48

But if within this month that now ensu'th,
  (So little time for her defence is left her)
  No Knight will come that will defend her truth,
  Then friends and fame, and life will be bereft her,
  This enterprise would much commend your youth,
  The praise whereof would last a great while after:
  And from *Atlantas* pillars unto *Inde*,
  A fairer Ladie you shall never finde.

49

Now then beside the honour and the praise,
  To have a state, may make you live content,
  The Princes love (that helpeth many waies)
  Whose honour now is halfe consum'd and spent.
  Againe true Knights should helpe at all assaies,
  When any harme to Ladies faire is ment.
  The very law of knighthood hath commanded,
  To grant this aide that we have now demanded.

50

Renaldo paus'd, and after thus he spake,
  Why then (said he) must this faire damsell die,
  That for her true and secret lovers sake,
  Did condescend within his armes to lie?
  Accurst be they that such a law did make,
  Accurst be they that meane to live thereby,
  Nay rather point a punishment and paine
  For such as do their lovers true disdaine.

51

If faire *Geneura* had her friend or no,
  I stand not now the matter to decide,
  Yea I would praise her had she done it so,
  That by her foes it had not bene espide.
  Be as be may, my meaning is to go
  To fight for her, if I may have a guide
  That will but shew me where is her accuser,
  And I shall quickly prove he doth abuse her.

52

I know not of the fact she have committed,
  Nor can I say in this the certaine sure:
  But this I say, it ought to be remitted,
  Much rather then she should distresse endure.

I further say, they were but meanly witted,
  That did so straight a stature first procure.
  I also say, this law they ought recall,
  In place thereof a better to enstall.

53

Sith like desire the fancies doth possesse,
  Both of the male and of the female gender,
  To do that thing that fooles count great excesse,
  And quench the flame that *Cupid* doth engender,
  To grant the men more scope, the women lesse,
  Is law for which no reason we can render.
  Men using many never are ashamed,
  But women using one or two are blamed.

54

This law I say is partiall and naught,
  And doth to women plaine and open wrong,
  I trust in God they shall be better taught,
  And that this law shall be revokt ere long,
  The Abbot and his Monks in word and thought,
  Allowd *Renaldos* speech, both old and yong:
  They all condemne the law, and partly blame
  The king that may and mendeth not the same.

55

Next morning when *Renaldo* doth perceave
  The Sunne appeare, and starres their heads to hide,
  He thanks them for his cheare, and taketh leave,
  And takes a target bearer for his guide,
  For feare lest unknowne paths should him deceave,
  Himselfe all armed doth on *Bayard* ride,
  And to the *Scottish* court he goes a stranger,
  For to defend the damsell faire from danger.

56

And for they thought to take a way more nie,
  They leave the common way a mile or twaine,
  When suddenly they heard a piteous crie,
  Well like to one that feared to be slaine.
  In hast they spurre their horses by and by,
  Along the vale, and looking downe the plaine,
  A maide betweene two murderers they saw,
  That meant to take her life against all law.

57

The caitifes put the damsell in great feare,
  And shew'd that they were come to end her dayes,
  Which made her weepe, and shed full many a teare,
  To move their minds she trieth many wayes:
  And though the fact a while they did forbeare,
  Yet now they had removed all delayes,
  When as *Renaldo* came unto her aid,
  And made the malefactors sore afraid.

58

Away they fled and left the wench alone,
  For dread of death appald and sore affrighted,
Who all her cause of danger and of mone,
Vnto *Renaldo* straight would have recited,
But so great hast he maketh to be gone,
He gave no eare, nor from his horse alighted,
But to ensue the journey first assign'd him,
He caus'd the guide to take her up behind him.

59

And now on horsebacke marking well her face,
  And marking more her gesture and behaviour,
Her pleasing speech, and modest sober grace,
She now hath wonne a great deale more his favour,
And after he had rode a little space,
To tell her hard adventure he would have her:
And she began with humble voice and low,
As more at large hereafter I will show.

THE FIFT BOOKE OF

ORLANDO FVRIOSO

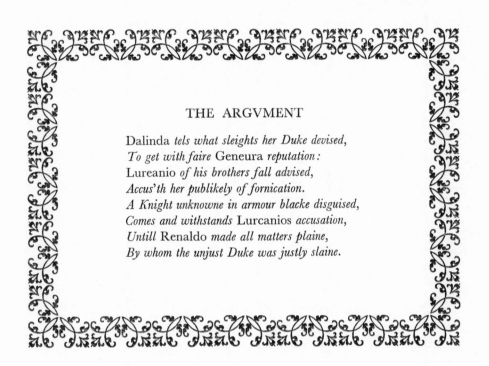

THE ARGVMENT

Dalinda *tels what sleights her Duke devised,*
To get with faire Geneura *reputation:*
Lureanio *of his brothers fall advised,*
Accus'th her publikely of fornication.
A Knight unknowne in armour blacke disguised,
Comes and withstands Lurcanios *accusation,*
Untill Renaldo *made all matters plaine,*
By whom the unjust Duke was justly slaine.

ORLANDO FVRIOSO

THE FIFT BOOKE

1

We see the rest of living creatures all,
  Both birds and beasts that on the earth do dwell,
  Live most in peace, or if they hap to brall,
  The male and female still agreeth well.
  The fierce, the faint, the greater nor the small,
  Against the law of nature will rebell.
  The savage Lions, Beares and Buls most wyld,
  Vnto their females shew themselves most myld.

2

What fiend of hell, what rage raignes here so rife,
  Disturbing still the state of humane harts?
  How comes it that we find twixt man and wife,
  Continuall jarres bred by injurious parts?
  The undefiled bed is filde by strife,
  And teares that grow of words unkind and thwarts:
  Nay oft all care and feare is so exiled,
  Their guilty hands with blood have bene defiled.

3

No doubt they are accurst and past all grace,
  And such as have of God nor man no feare,
  That dare to strike a damsell in the face,
  Or of her head to minish but a haire:
  But who with knife or poison would unlace
  Their line of life, or flesh in peeces teare,
  No man, nor made of flesh and blood I deeme him,
  But sure some hound of hell I do esteeme him.

4

Such were these theeves that would the damsell kill,
  That by *Renaldos* comming was recovered:
  They secretly had brought her downe the hill,
  In hope their fact could never be discovered,
  Yet such is God, so good his gracious will,
  That when she looked least she was delivered,
  And with a chearefull heart that late was sorie,
  She doth begin to tell the wofull storie.

5

Good sir (said she) my conscience to discharge,
  The greatest tyrannie I shall you tell,
  That erst in *Thebes*, in *Athens* or in *Arge*,
  Was ever wrought, or where worst tyrants dwell:
  My voice and skill would faile to tell at large
  The filthy fact, for I beleeve it well,
  Vpon this countrey *Phœbus* shines more cold,
  Because he doth such wicked acts behold.

6

Men seeke we see, and have in every age,
  To foile their foes, and tread them in the dust:
  But there to wreake their rancor and their rage,
  Where they are lov'd, is foule and too unjust.
  Love should prevaile, just anger to asswage,
  If love bring death, whereto can women trust:
  Yet love did breed my danger and my feare,
  As you shall heare if you will give me eare.

7

For entring first into my tender spring,
  Of youthfull yeares, unto the court I came,
  And served there the daughter of our King,
  And kept a place of honour with good fame,
  Till love (alas that love such care should bring)
  Envide my state, and sought to do me shame.
  Love made the Duke of *Alban* seeme to me,
  The fairest wight that erst mine eye did see.

8

And (for I thought he lov'd me all above)
  I bent my selfe to hold and love him best,
  But now I find that hard it is to prove,
  By sight or speech what bides in secret brest;
  While I (poore I) did thus beleeve and love,
  He gets my body, bed and all the rest.
  Nor thinking this might breed my mistres wrong
  Ev'n in her chamber this I practis'd long.

9

Where all the things of greatest value lay,
  And where *Geneura* sleepes her selfe sometime,
  There at a window we did finde a way,
  In secret sort to cover this our crime:
  Here when my love and I were bent to play,
  I taught him by a scale of cord to clime,
  And at the window I my selfe would stand,
  And let the ladder downe into his hand.

10

So oft we meete together at this sport,
  As faire *Geneuras* absence gives us leave,
  Who us'd to other chambers to resort
  In summer time, and this for heat to leave:
  And this we carried in so secret sort,
  As none there was our doings did perceave,
  For why, this window standeth out of sight,
  Where none do come by day nor yet by night.

11

Twixt us this use continu'd many dayes,
  Yea many months we us'd this privie traine,
Love set my heart on fire so many wayes,
That still my liking lasted to my paine.
I might have found by certaine strange delayes,
That he but little lov'd and much did faine,
For all his sleights were not so closely covered,
But that they might full easly be discovered.

12

At last my Duke did seeme enflamed sore,
  On faire *Geneura:* neither can I tell,
If now this love began or was before,
That I did come to court with her to dwell.
But looke if I were subject to his lore,
And looke if he my love requited well,
He askt my aid herein no whit ashamed,
To tell me how of her he was enflamed.

13

Not all of love, but partly of ambition,
  He beares in hand his minde is onely bent,
Because of her great state and hie condition,
To have her for his wife is his intent:
He nothing doubteth of the Kings permission,
Had he obtain'd *Geneuras* free assent.
Ne was it hard for him to take in hand,
That was the second person in the land.

14

He sware to me, if I would be so kind
  His hie attempt to further and assist,
That at his hands I should great favour finde,
And of the King procure me what me list:
How he would ever keepe it in his mind,
And in his former love to me persist,
And notwithstanding wife and all the rest,
I should be sure that he would love me best.

15

I straight consented to his fond request,
  As readie his commandment to obay,
And thinking still my time emploied best,
When I had pleas'd his fancy any way:
And when I found a time then was I prest,
To talke of him, and good of him to say.
I used all my art, my wit, and paine,
Geneuras love and liking to obtaine.

16

God knoweth how glad I was to worke his will,
  How diligent I follow'd his direction,
I spar'd no time, no travell nor no skill,
To this my Duke to kindle her affection:
But alwayes this attempt succeeded ill,
Love had her heart already in subjection,
A comely Knight did faire *Geneura* please,
Come to this countrie from beyond the seas.

17

From Italy for service (as I heare)
  Vnto the court he and his brother came,
In tourneys and in tilt he had no peere,
All Brittain soone was filled with his fame.
Our King did love him well and hold him deere,
And did by princely gifts confirme the same.
Faire castels, townes, and lordships, him he gave,
And made him great, such power great princes have.

18

Our Soveraigne much, his daughter likt him more,
  And *Ariodant* this worthy Knight is named,
So brave in deeds of armes himselfe he bore,
No Ladie of his love need be ashamed:
The hill of *Stoil* burneth not so sore,
Nor is the mount *Vesuvio* so inflamed,
As *Ariodantes* heart was set on fire,
Geneuras beautie kindling his desire.

19

His certaine love by signes most certaine found,
  Cause that my sute unwillingly was hard,
She well perceiv'd his love sincere and sound,
Enclining to his sute with great regard.
In vaine I seeke my Dukes love to expound,
The more I seeke to make the more I mard.
For while with words I seek to praise and grace him
No lesse with workes she striveth to deface him.

20

Thus being oft repulst (so ill sped I,)
  To my too much beloved Duke I went,
And told him how her heart was fixt alreadie,
How on the stranger all her mind was bent.
And praid him now sith there was no remedie,
That to surcease his sute he would consent,
For *Ariodant* so lov'd the princely maid,
That by no meanes his flames could be alaid.

21

When *Polynesso* (so the Duke we call)
  This tale unpleasant oftentime had hard,
And of himselfe had found his hopes were small,
When with my words her deeds he had compar'd,
Greev'd with repulse, and vexed therewithall,
To see this stranger thus to be prefar'd,
The love that late his heart so sore had burned,
Was cooled all, and into hatred turned.

22

Intending by some vile and subtill traine,
  To part *Geneura* from her faithfull lover,
And plant so great mislike betweene them twaine,
Yet with so cunning shew the same to cover,
That her good name he will so foule distaine,
Alive nor dead she never shall recover.
But lest he might in this attempt be thwarted,
To none at all his secret he imparted.

23

Now thus resolv'd (*Dalinda* faire) quoth he,
  (I so am cald) you know though trees be topt,
  And shrowded low, yet sprout yong shoots we see,
  And issue from that head so lately lopt:
  So in my love it fareth now with me.
  Though by repulse cut short and shrewdly cropt,
  The pared tops such buds of love do render,
  That still I prove new passions there engender.

24

Ne do I deeme so deare the great delight,
  As I disdaine I should be so reject,
  And left this griefe should overcome me quight,
  Because I faile to bring it to effect,
  To please my fond conceit this very night,
  I pray thee deare to do as I direct:
  When faire *Geneura* to her bed is gone,
  Take thou the clothes she ware and put them on.

25

As she is wont her golden haire to dresse,
  In stately sort to wind it on her wire,
  So you her poyson lively to expresse,
  May dresse your owne and weare her head attire,
  Her gorgets and her jewels rich no lesse,
  You may put on t'accomplish my desire.
  And when unto the window I ascend,
  I will my comming there you do attend.

26

Thus I may passe my fancies foolish fit,
  And thus (quoth he) my selfe I would deceive.
  And I that had no reason nor no wit,
  His shamefull drift (though open) to perceive:
  Did weare my mistresse robes that serv'd me fit,
  And stood at window, there him to receive.
  And of the fraud I was no whit aware,
  Till that fell out that caused all my care.

27

Of late twixt him and *Ariodant* had past,
  About *Geneura* faire these words or such,
  (For why there was good friendship in times past
  Betweene them two, till love their hearts did tuch)
  The Duke such kind of speeches out did cast,
  He said to *Ariodant*, he marvel'd much,
  That seeing he did alwaies well regard him,
  He should againe so thanklesly reward him.

28

I know you see (for needs it must be seene)
  The good consent and matrimoniall love,
  That long betweene *Geneur'* and me hath beene,
  For whom I meane ere long the King to move.
  Why should you fondly thrust your selfe betweene?
  Why should you rove your reach so farre above?
  For if my case were yours I would forbeare,
  Or if I knew that you so loved were.

29

And I much more (the other straight replies)
  Do marvell you sir Duke are so unkind,
  That know our love, and see it with your eyes,
  (Except that wilfulnesse have made you blind)
  That no man can more sured knots devise,
  Then her to me, and me to her do bind,
  Into this sute so rashly are intruded,
  Still finding from all hope you are excluded.

30

Why beare you not to me the like respect,
  As my good will requireth at your hand?
  Since that our love is growne to this effect,
  We meane to knit our selves in weddings band:
  Which to fulfill ere long I do expect,
  For know I am (though not in rents or land)
  Yet in my Princes grace no whit inferiour,
  And in his daughters, greatly your superiour.

31

Well (said the Duke) errors are hardly moved,
  That love doth breed in unadvised brest.
  Each thinkes himselfe to be the best beloved,
  And yet but one of us is loved best.
  Wherefore to have the matter plainly proved,
  Which should proceed in love, and which should rest,
  Let us agree that victor he remaine,
  That of her liking sheweth signes most plaine.

32

I will be bound to you by solemne oth,
  Your secrets all and counsell to conceale,
  So you likewise will plight to me your troth,
  The thing I shew you never to reveale.
  To trie the matter thus they greed both,
  And from this doome hereafter not repeale:
  But on the Bible first they were deposed,
  That this their speech should never be disclosed.

33

And first the stranger doth his state reveale,
  And tell the truth in hope to end the strife,
  How she had promist him in wo and weale,
  To live with him, and love him all her life:
  And how with writing with her hand and seale,
  She had confirmed she would be his wife,
  Except she were forbidden by her father,
  For then to live unmarride she had rather.

34

And furthermore he nothing doubts (he said)
  Of his good service so plaine proofe to show,
  As that the King shall nothing be afraid,
  On such a Knight his daughter to bestow:
  And how in this he needeth little aid,
  As finding still his favour greater grow,
  He doubts not he will grant his liking after
  That he shall know it pleaseth so his daughter.

35

And thus you see so sound stands mine estate,
  That I my selfe in thought can wish no more.
Who seekes her now is sure to come too late,
  For that he seekes is granted me before;
Now onely rests in marriage holy state,
  To knit the knot that must dure evermore.
And for her praise, I need not to declare it,
  As knowing none to whom I may compare it.

36

Thus *Ariodant* a tale most true declared,
  And what reward he hoped for his paine,
But my false Duke that him had fouly snared,
  And found by my great folly such a traine,
Doth sweare all this might no way be compared
  With his, no though himselfe did judge remaine,
For I (quoth he) can shew signes so expresse,
  As you your selfe inferiour shall confesse.

37

Alas (quoth he) I see you do not know
  How cunningly these women can dissemble,
They least do love where they make greatest show,
  And not to be the thing they most resemble.
But other favours I receive I trow,
  When as we two do secretly assemble,
As I will tell you (though I should conceale it)
  Because you promise never to reveale it.

38

The truth is this, that I full oft have seene
  Her ivory corpes, and bene with her all night,
And naked laine her naked armes betweene,
  And full enjoyde the fruites of loves delight:
Now judge who hath in greatest favour beene,
  To which of us she doth pertaine in right,
And then give place, and yeeld to me mine owne,
  Sith by just proofes I now have made it knowne.

39

Iust proofes? (quoth *Ariodant*) nay shamefull lies,
  Nor will I credit give to any word:
Is this the finest tale you can devise?
  What, hop'd you that with this I could be dord?
No, no, but sith a slander foule doth rise
  By thee to her, maintaine it with thy sword,
I call thee lying traitor to thy face,
  And meane to prove it in this present place.

40

Tush (quoth the Duke) it were a foolish part,
  For you to fight with me that am your friend,
Sith plaine to shew without deceit or art,
  As much as I have said I do intend.
These words did gripe poore *Ariodantes* hart,
  Downe all his limbes a shivering doth descend,
And still he stood with eyes cast downe on ground,
  Like one would fall into a deadly sound.

41

With wofull mind, with pale and chearlesse face,
  With trembling voice that came from bitter thought
He said he much desir'd to see this place,
  Where such strange feats and miracles were wrought.
Hath faire *Geneura* granted you this grace,
  That I (quoth he) so oft in vaine have sought?
Now sure except I see it in my view,
  I never will beleeve it can be trew.

42

The Duke did say he would with all his hart
  Both shew him where and how the thing was done,
And straight from him to me he doth depart,
  Whom to his purpose wholly he had wonne:
With both of us he playth so well his part,
  That both of us thereby were quite undone.
First he tels him that he would have him placed
  Among some houses falne and quite defaced.

43

Some ruin'd houses stood oppos'd direct
  Against the window where he doth ascend,
But *Ariodant* discreetly doth suspect
  That this false Duke some mischiefe did intend,
And thought that all did tend to this effect,
  By trechery to bring him to his end,
That sure he had devised this pretence,
  With mind to kill him ere he parted thence.

44

Thus though to see this sight he thought it long,
  Yet tooke he care all mischiefe to prevent,
And if perhap they offer force or wrong,
  By force the same for to resist he ment.
He had a brother valiant and strong,
  Lurcanio cal'd, and straight for him he sent,
Not doubting but alone by his assistance,
  Against twice twentie men to make resistance.

45

He bids his brother take his sword in hand,
  And go into a place that he would guide,
And in a corner closely there to stand,
  Aloofe from tother threescore paces wide,
The cause he would not let him understand,
  But prayes him there in secret sort to bide,
Vntill such time he hapt to heare him call,
  Else (if he lov'd him) not to stirre at all.

46

His brother would not his request denie,
  And so went *Ariodant* into his place,
And undiscover'd closely there did lie,
  Till having looked there a little space,
The craftie Duke to come he might descrie,
  That meant the chast *Geneura* to deface,
Who having made to me his wonted signes,
  I let him downe the ladder made of lines.

47

The gowne I ware was white, and richly set
  With aglets, pearle, and lace of gold well garnished,
My stately tresses cover'd with a net
  Of beaten gold most pure and brightly varnished.
Not thus content, the vaile aloft I set,
  Which only Princes weare: thus stately harnished,
And under *Cupids* banner bent to fight,
  All unawares I stood in all their sight.

48

For why *Lurcanio* either taking care,
  Lest *Ariodant* should in some danger go,
Or that he sought (as all desirous are)
  The counsels of his dearest friend to know,
Close out of sight by secret steps and ware,
  Hard at his heeles his brother follow'd so,
Till he was nearer come by fiftie paces,
  And there againe himselfe he newly places.

49

But I that thought no ill, securely came
  Vnto the open window as I said.
For once or twice before I did the same,
  And had no hurt, which made me lesse afraid:
I cannot boast (except I boast of shame)
  When in her robes I had my selfe arraid,
Me thought before I was not much unlike her,
  But certaine now I seemed very like her.

50

But *Ariodant* that stood so farre aloofe,
  Was more deceiv'd by distance of the place,
And straight beleev'd against his owne behoofe,
  Seeing her clothes that he had seene her face.
Now let those judge that partly know by proofe,
  The wofull plight of *Ariodantes* case,
When *Polynesso* came my faithlesse frend,
  In both their sights the ladder to ascend.

51

I that his comming willingly did wait,
  And he once come thought nothing went amisse,
Embrac'd him kindly at the first receit,
  His lips, his cheeks, and all his face did kisse,
And he the more to colour his deceit,
  Did use me kinder then he had ere this.
This sight much care to *Ariodante* brought,
  Thinking *Geneura* with the Duke was nought.

52

The griefe and sorrow sinketh so profound
  Into his heart, he straight resolves to die,
He puts the pummell of his sword on ground,
  And meanes himselfe upon the point to lie:
Which when *Lurcanio* saw and plainly found,
  That all this while was closely standing by,
And *Polynessos* comming did discerne,
  Though who it was he never yet could learne.

E

53

He held his brother for the present time,
  That else himselfe for griefe had surely slaine,
Who had he not stood nigh and come betime,
  His words and speeches had bene all in vaine.
What shall (quoth he) a faithlesse womans crime,
  Cause you to die or put your selfe to paine?
Nay let them go, and curst be all their kind,
  Ay borne like clouds with eu'ry blast of wind.

54

You rather should some just revenge devise,
  As she deserves, to bring her to confusion:
Sith we have plainly seene with both our eyes,
  Her filthy fact appeare without collusion.
Love those that love againe, if you be wise,
  For of my counsell this is the conclusion,
Put up your sword against your selfe prepared,
  And let her sinne be to the King declared.

55

His brothers words in *Ariodantes* mind
  Seeme for the time to make some small impression,
But still the curelesse wound remain'd behind,
  Despaire had of his heart the full possession.
And though he knew the thing he had assign'd,
  Contrary to a Christian knights profession:
Yet here on earth he torment felt so sore,
  In hell it selfe he thought there was no more.

56

And seeming now after a little pause,
  Vnto his brothers counsell to consent,
He from the court next day himselfe withdrawes,
  And makes none privie unto his intent.
His brother and the Duke both knew the cause,
  But neither knew the place whereto he went:
Divers thereof most diversly did judge,
  Some by good will perswaded, some by grudge.

57

Sev'n dayes entire about for him they sought,
  Sev'n dayes entire no newes of him was found,
The eight a peasant to *Geneura* brought
  These newes, that in the sea he saw him drown'd:
Not that the waters were with tempest wrought,
  Nor that his ship was stricken on the ground.
How then? Forsooth (quoth he) and therewith wept,
  Downe from a rocke into the sea he lept.

58

And further he unto *Geneura* told,
  How he met *Ariodant* upon the way,
Who made him go with him for to behold
  The wofull act that he would do that day.
And charged him the matter to unfold,
  And to his Princes daughter thus to say,
Had he been blind, he had full happie beene,
  His death should shew that he too much had seene.

59

There stands a rocke against the Irish ile,
  From thence into the sea himselfe he cast:
I stood and looked after him awhile,
  The height and steepnesse made me sore agast,
I thence have travel'd hither many a mile,
  To shew you plainly how the matter past.
When as the clowne his tale had verifide,
Geneuras heart was throughly terrifide.

60

O Lord what wofull words by her were spoken,
  Laid all alone upon her restlesse bed!
Oft did she strike her guiltlesse brest in token
  Of that great griefe that inwardly was bred:
Her golden tresses all were rent and broken,
  Recounting still those wofull words he sed,
How that the cause his cruell death was such,
Was onely this, that he had seene too much.

61

The rumor of his death spread farre and neare,
  And how for sorrow he himselfe had killed,
The King was sad, the court of heavy cheare,
  By Lords and Ladies many teares were spilled.
His brother most, as loving him most deare,
  Had so his mind with sorrow overfilled,
That he was scantly able to refraine,
With his owne hands himselfe for to have slaine.

62

And oftentimes repeating in his thought,
  The filthy fact he saw the other night,
Which (as you heard) the Duke and I had wrought,
  I little looking it would come to light,
And that the same his brothers death had brought,
  On faire *Geneura* he doth wreake his spight,
Not caring (so did wrath him overwhelme)
To leese the Kings good will and all his realme.

63

The King and Nobles sitting in the hall,
  Right pensive all for *Ariodants* destruction,
Lurcanio undertakes before them all,
  To give them perfect notice and instruction,
Who was the cause of *Ariodantes* fall:
  And having made some little introduction,
He said it was unchast *Geneuras* crime,
That made him kill himselfe before his time.

64

What should I seeke to hide his good intent?
  His love was such as greater none could be,
He hop'd to have your highnesse free assent,
  When you his value and his worth should see:
But while a plaine and honest way he went,
  Behold he saw another climb the tree,
And in the midst of all his hope and sute,
Another tooke the pleasure and the frute.

65

He further said, not that he had surmised,
  But that his eies had seene *Geneura* stand,
And at a window as they had devised,
  Let down a ladder to her lovers hand,
But in such sort he had himselfe disguised,
  That who it was he could not understand.
And for due proofe of this his accusation,
He bids the combat straight by proclamation.

66

How sore the King was griev'd to heare these newes,
  I leave it as a thing not hard to guesse,
Lurcanio plaine his daughter doth accuse,
  Of whom the King did looke for nothing lesse:
And this the more his feare and care renewes,
  That on this point the lawes are so expresse,
Except by combat it be prov'd a lie,
Needs must *Geneura* be condemn'd to die.

67

How hard the Scottish law is in this case,
  I do not doubt but you have heard it told,
How she that doth another man embrace,
  Beside her husband, be she yong or old,
Must die, except within two fortnights space,
  She find a champion stout that will uphold,
That unto her no punishment is due,
But he that doth accuse her is untrue.

68

The King (of crime that thinkes *Geneura* cleare)
  Makes offer her to wed to any Knight,
That will in armes defend his daughter deare,
  And prove her innocent in open fight.
Yet for all this no champion doth appeare,
  Such feare they have of this *Lurcanios* might.
One gazeth on another as they stand,
But none of them the combat takes in hand.

69

And further by ill fortune and mischance,
  Her brother *Zerbin* now is absent thence,
And gone to Spaine (I thinke) or else to France,
  Who were he here, she could not want defence,
Or if perhaps so lucky were her chance,
  To send him notice of her need from hence,
Had she the presence of her noble brother,
She should not need the aide of any other.

70

The King that meanes to make a certaine triall,
  If faire *Geneura* guilty be or no,
(For still she stiffly stood in the deniall,
  Of this that wrought her undeserved wo)
Examines all her maids, but they reply all,
  That of the matter nothing they did know.
Which made me seek for to prevent the danger,
The Duke and I might have about the stranger.

71

And thus for him more then my selfe afraid,
  (So faithfull love to this false Duke I bare)
I gave him notice of these things, and said,
  That he had need for both of us beware.
He prais'd my constant love, and farther praid,
  That I would credit him, and take no care.
He points two men (but both to me unknowne)
To bring me to a castle of his owne.

72

Now sir, I thinke you find by this effect,
  How soundly I did love him from my heart,
And how I prov'd by plaine course and direct,
  My meaning was not any wayes to start:
Now marke if he to me bare like respect,
  And marke if he requited my desart,
Alas how shall a silly wench attaine,
By loving truely to be lov'd againe.

73

This wicked Duke ungratefull and perjured,
  Beginneth now of me to have mistrust,
His guilty conscience could not be assured,
  How to conceale his wicked acts unjust,
Except my death (though causlesse) be procured,
  So hard his heart, so lawlesse was his lust.
He said he would me to his castle send,
But that same castle should have beene mine end.

74

He wild my guides when they were past that hill,
  And to the thicket a little way descended,
That there (to quite my love) they should me kill,
  Which as you saw, they to have done intended,
Had not your happy comming stopt their will,
  That (God and you be thankt) I was defended.
This tale Dalinda to Renaldo told,
And all the while their journey on they hold.

75

This strange adventure luckily befell
  To good Renaldo, for that now he found,
By this Dalinda that this tale did tell,
  Geneuras mind unspotted cleare and sound,
And now his courage was confirmed well,
  That wanted erst a true and certaine ground:
For though before for her he meant to fight,
Yet rather now for to defend the right.

76

To great S. Andrewes towne he maketh hast,
  Whereas the King was set with all his traine,
Most carefull waiting for the trumpets blast,
  That must pronounce his daughters joy or paine.
But now Renaldo spurred had so fast,
  He was arriv'd within a mile or twaine,
And through the Village as he then was riding,
He met a page that brought them fresher tiding.

77

How there was come a Warriour all disguised,
  That meant to prove Lurcanio said untreu,
His colours and his armour well devised,
  In maner and in making very new:
And though that sundry sundrily surmised,
  Yet who it was for certaine no man knew.
His page demaunded of his masters name,
Did sweare he never heard it since he came.

78

Now came Renaldo to the City wall,
  And at the gate but little time he staid,
The porter was so ready at his call:
  But poore Dalinda now grew sore afraid,
Renaldo bids her not to feare at all,
  For why he would her pardon beg he said:
So thrusting in among the thickest rout,
He saw them stand on scaffolds all about.

79

It straight was told him by the standers by,
  How there was thither come a stranger Knight,
That meant Geneuras innocence to try,
  And that already was begun the fight:
And how the greene that next the wall did ly,
  Was rail'd about of purpose for the fight.
This newes did make Renaldo hasten in,
And leave behind Dalinda at her Inne.

80

He told her he would come again ere long,
  And spurs his horse that made an open lane,
He pierced in the thickest preasse among,
  Whereas these valiant Knights had giv'n and tane,
Full many strokes, with sturdy hand and strong,
  Lurcanio thinks to bring Geneuras bane,
The other meanes the Lady to defend,
Whom (though unknown) they favor and commend.

81

There was Duke Polynesso bravely mounted,
  Vpon a courser of an exc'lent race,
Six Knights among the better sort accounted,
  On foot in armes do marshall well the place.
The Duke by office all the rest surmounted,
  High Constable (as alwaies in such case)
Who of Geneuras danger was as glad,
As all the rest were sorrowfull and sad.

82

Now had Renaldo made an open way,
  And was arived there in lucky howre,
To cause the combat to surcease and stay,
  Which these two knights applid with al their powre.
Renaldo in the Court appear'd that day,
  Of noble Chivalry the very flowre,
For first the Princes audience he praid,
Then with great expectation thus he said.

83

Send (noble Prince) quoth he, send by and by,
  And cause forthwith that they surcease the fight,
  For know, that which so ere of these doth dy,
  It certaine is he dies against all right.
  One thinks he tels the truth and tels a ly,
  And is deceiv'd by error in his fight,
  And looke what cause his brothers death procured,
  That very same hath him to fight allured.

84

The tother of a nature good and kind,
  Not knowing if he hold the right or no,
  To dy or to defend her hath assign'd,
  Lest so rare beauty should be spilled so.
  I harmelesse hope to save the faultlesse mind:
  And those that mischiefe mind to worke them wo,
  But first ô Prince to stay the fight give order,
  Before my speech proceedeth any farder.

85

Renaldos person with the tale he told,
  Mov'd so the King, that straight without delay,
  The Knights were bidden both their hands to hold,
  The combat for a time was caus'd to stay,
  Then he againe with voice and courage bold,
  The secret of the matter doth bewray,
  Declaring plaine how *Polynessos* lust
  Was first contriver of this deed unjust.

86

And proffreth of this speech to make a proofe,
  By combat hand to hand with sword and speare:
  The Duke was cal'd that stood not far aloofe,
  And scantly able to conceale his feare,
  He first denies, as was for his behoofe,
  And straight to battell both agreed were,
  They both were arm'd, the place before was ready,
  Now must they fight there could be no remedy.

87

How was the King, how were the people glad,
  That faire *Geneura* faultlesse there did stand,
  As Gods great goodnesse now revealed had,
  And should be proved by *Renaldos* hand.
  All thought the Duke of mind and maners bad,
  The proud'st and cruel'st man in all the land,
  It likely was as every one surmised,
  That this deceit by him should be devised.

88

Now *Polinesso* stands with doubtfull brest,
  With fainting heart, with pale dismaied face,
  Their trumpets blew, they set their speares in rest,
  Renaldo commeth on a mighty pace,
  For at this fight he finish will the feast,
  And where to strike him he designes a place:
  His very first encounter was so fierce,
  Renaldos speare the tothers sides did pierce.

89

And having overthrowne the Duke by force,
  As one unable so great strokes to bide,
  And cast him cleane six paces from his horse,
  Himselfe alights and th'others helme untide,
  Who making no resistance like a corse,
  With faint low voice for mercy now he cride,
  And plaine confest with this his later breath,
  The fault that brought him this deserved death.

90

No sooner had he made this last confession,
  But that his life did faile him with his voyce.
  Geneuras double scape of foule oppression,
  In life and fame did make the King rejoyce:
  In lieu of her to leese his crownes possession,
  He would have wisht, if such had beene his choyce:
  To leese his realme he could have beene no sadder:
  To get it lost he could have beene no gladder.

91

The combat done, *Renaldo* straight untide
  His beaver, when the King that knew his face,
  Gave thankes to God that did so well provide,
  So doubtlesse helpe in such a dangerous case.
  That unknowne Knight stood all this while aside,
  And saw the matters passed in the place,
  And ev'ry one did muse and marvell much,
  What wight it was whose curtesie was such.

92

The King did aske his name because he ment,
  With kingly gifts his service to reward,
  Affirming plainly that his good intent,
  Deserved thanks and very great regard.
  The Knight with much intreatie did assent,
  And to disarme himselfe he straight prepar'd,
  But who it was if you vouchsafe to looke,
  I will declare it in another booke.

THE SIXT BOOKE OF
ORLANDO FVRIOSO

THE ARGVMENT

Geneura *faire to Ariodant is given,*
And he a Duke is made that verie day.
Rogero *with the* Griffeth horse *is driven,*
Vnto Alcynas *Ile, and there doth stay.*
A mirtle in the middle strangly riven,
Alcinas *frands doth unto him bewray:*
Of which enform'd he thence would have departed,
But by the way he finds his purpose thwarted.

ORLANDO FVRIOSO

THE SIXT BOOKE

1

Most wretched he, that thinks by doing ill,
  His evill deedes long to conceale and hide,
  For though the voice and tongues of men be still,
  By foules or beasts his sin shall be descride:
  And God oft worketh by his secret will,
  That sinne it selfe the sinner so doth guide,
  That of his owne accord, without request,
  He makes his wicked doings manifest.

2

The gracelesse wight, Duke *Polinesso* thought,
  His former fault should sure have bin concealed,
  If that *Dalinda* unto death were brought,
  By whom alone the same could be revealed.
  Thus making worse the thing before was nought,
  He hurt the wound which time perhaps had healed.
  And weening with more sinne the lesse to mend,
  He hastned on his well deserved end.

3

And lost at once his life, his state, and frends,
  And honour too, a losse as great or more.
  Now (as I said) that unknowne Knight entends,
  Sith everie one to know him sought so sore,
  And sith the King did promise large amends,
  To shew his face which they saw oft before,
  And *Ariodant* most lovely did appeare,
  Whom they thought dead as you before did heare.

4

He whom *Geneura* wofully did waile,
  He whom *Lurcanio* deemed to be dead,
  He whom the King and court did so bewaile,
  He that to all the realme such care had bred,
  Doth live: the clownes report in this did faile,
  On which false ground the rumour false was spred.
  And yet in this the peasant did not mocke,
  He saw him leape downe headlong from the rock.

5

But as we see men oft with rash intent
  Are desperate and do resolve to die,
  And straight do change that fancie and repent,
  When unto death they do approch more nie:
  So *Ariodant* to drowne himselfe that ment,
  Now plung'd in sea repented by and by,
  And being of his limbes able and strong,
  Vnto the shore he swam againe ere long.

6

And much dispraising in his inward thought,
  This fond conceit that late his minde possest,
  At last a blind and narrow path him brought,
  All tyr'd and wet to be an hermits guest:
  With whom to stay in secret sort he sought,
  Both that he might his former griefe digest,
  And learne the truth, if this same clownes report,
  Were by *Geneura* tane in griefe or sport.

7

There first he heard how she conceiv'd such griefe,
  As almost brought her life to wofull end,
  He found of her they had so good beleefe,
  They thought she would not in such sort offend:
  He further heard except shee had releese,
  By one that would her innocence defend,
  It was great doubt *Lurcanios* accusation,
  Would bring her to a speedie condemnation,

8

And looke how love before his heart enraged,
  So now did wrath enflame, and though he knew wel
  To wreake his harme, his brothers life was gaged,
  He nathles thought his act so foule and cruell,
  That this his anger could not be asswaged,
  Vnto his flame love found such store of fewel:
  And this the more increast his wrath begun,
  To heare how every one the fight did shun.

9

For why *Lurcanio*, was so stout and wise,
  Except it were for to defend the truth,
  Men thought he would not so the King despise,
  And hazard life to bring *Geneuras* ruth,
  Which caused everie one his friend advise,
  To shunne the fight that must maintaine untruth.
  But *Ariodant* after long disputation,
  Meanes to withstand his brothers accusation.

10

Alas (quoth he) I never shall abide,
  Her, through my cause, to die in wo and paine,
  For danger or for death what may betide,
  Be she once dead my life cannot remaine,
  She is my saint, in her my blisse doth bide,
  Her golden rayes my eies light still maintaine,
  Fall backe, fall edge, and be it wrong or right,
  In her defence I am resolv'd to fight.

11

I take the wrong, but yet ile take the wrong,
  And die I shall, yet if I die I care not,
  But then alas, by law she dies ere long,
  O cruell lawes so sweete a wight that spare not:
  Yet this small joy I finde these griefes among,
  That *Polinesso* to defend her dare not,
  And she shall finde how little she was loved,
  Of him that to defend her never moved.

12

And she shall see me dead there for her sake,
  To whom so great a damage she hath done:
  And of my brother just revengement take
  I shall, by whom this strife was first begun,
  For there at least my death plaine proofe shall make
  That he this while a foolish thred hath spun,
  He thinketh to avenge his brothers ill,
  The while himselfe his brother there shall kill.

13

And thus resolv'd, he gets him armour new,
  New horse and all things new that needfull beene
  All clad in blacke, a sad and mournfull hew,
  And crost with wreath of yellow and of greene,
  A stranger bare his sheeld that neither knew
  His masters name nor him before had seene,
  And thus as I before rehearst, disguised
  He met his brother as he had devised.

14

I told you what successe the matter had,
  How *Ariodant* himselfe did then discover,
  For whom the King himselfe was even as glad,
  As late before his daughter to recover,
  And since he thought in joyfull times and sad,
  No man could shew himselfe a truer lover
  Then he that after so great wrong, intended
  Against his brother her to have defended.

15

Both loving him by his owne inclination,
  And prai'd thereto by many a Lord and Knight,
  And chiefly by *Renaldos* instigation,
  He gave to *Ariodant Geneura* bright.
  Now by the Dukes atteint and condemnation,
  Albania came to be the Kings in right.
  Which dutchie falling in so luckie houre,
  Was given unto the damsell for her dowre.

16

Renaldo for *Dalindas* pardon praide,
  Who for her error did so sore repent,
  That straight she vowd, with honest mind and staid,
  To live her life in prayer and penitence:
  Away she packt, nor further time delaid,
  In *Datia*, to a nunrie there she went.
  But to *Rogero* now I must repaire,
  That all this while did gallop in the aire.

17

Who though he were of mind and courage stout,
  And would not easily feare or be dismaid,
  Yet doubtlesse now his mind was full of doubt,
  His hart was now appal'd, and sore afraid.
  Farre from *Europa*, he had travail'd out,
  And yet his flying horse could not be staid,
  But past the pillars xij. score leagues and more,
  Pitcht there by *Hercles* many yeares before.

18

This *Griffeth horse* a bird most huge and rare,
  Doth pierce the skie with so great force of wing,
  That with that noble bird he may compare,
  Whom Poets faine, *Ioves* lightning downe to bring
  To whom all other birds inferior are,
  Because they take the Eagle for their king.
  Scarse seemeth from the clouds to go so swift,
  The thunderbolt sent by the lightnings drift.

19

When long this monster strange had kept his race,
  Straight as a line bending to neither side,
  He spide an Iland distant little space,
  To which he bends in purpose there to bide,
  Much like in semblance was it to the place,
  Where *Arethusa* us'd her selfe to hide,
  And seekes so long her love to have beguil'd,
  Till at the last she found her selfe with child.

20

A fairer place they saw not all the while,
  That they had travail'd in the aire aloft,
  In all the world was not a fairer ile,
  If all the world to finde the fame were sought:
  Here having travail'd many a hundred mile,
  Rogero by his bird to rest was brought,
  In pastures greene, and hils with coole fresh aire,
  Cleere rivers, shadie banks, and meddowes faire.

21

Heere divers groves there were, of dainty shade,
  Of Palme, or Orenge trees, of Cedars tall,
  Of sundrie fruites and flowers that never fade,
  The shew was faire, the plenty was not small.
  And arbours in the thickest places made,
  Where little light and heat came not at all:
  Where Nightingales did straine their little throtes,
  Recording still their sweete and pleasant notes.

22

Amid the lilly white and fragrant rose,
  Preserv'd still fresh by warme and temprate aire,
  The fearefull hare, and conny carelesse goes,
  The stag with stately head and body faire,
  Doth feed secure, not fearing any foes,
  That to his damage hither may repaire,
  The Bucke and Doe doth feed amid the fields,
  As in great store the pleasant forrest yeelds.

23

It needlesse was to bid *Rogero* light,
　When as his horse approched nigh the ground,
　He cast himselfe out of his saddle quite,
　And on his feet he falleth safe and sound,
　And holds the horses raines, lest else he might
　Fly quite away, and not againe be found,
　And to a mirtle by the water side,
　Betweene two other trees his beast he tide.

24

And finding thereabout a little brooke,
　That neere vnto a shady mountaine stands,
　His helmet from his head forthwith he tooke,
　His shield from arme, his gantlet from his hands,
　And from the higher places he doth looke,
　Full oft to sea, full oft to fruitfull lands,
　And seekes the coole and pleasant aire to take,
　That doth among the leaves a murmure make.

25

Oft with the water of that crystall well,
　He seekes to quench his thirst and swage his heate,
　With which his veines enflam'd did rise and swell,
　And caus'd his other parts to fry in sweate:
　Well may it seeme a marvell that I tell,
　Yet will I once againe the same repeate,
　He travel'd had above three thousand mile,
　And not put off his armour all the while.

26

Behold his horse he lately tyed there,
　Among the boughs in shady place to bide,
　Strave to go loose, and started backe for feare,
　And puls the tree to which the raines were tide,
　In which (as by the sequell shall appeare)
　A humane soule it selfe did strangely hide.
　With all his strength the steed strives to be loosed,
　By force whereof the mirtle sore was broosed.

27

And as an arme of tree from body rent,
　By peasant strength with many a sturdy stroke,
　When in the fire the moisture all is spent,
　The empty places fild with aire and smoke,
　Do boile and strive, and find at last a vent,
　When of the brand a shiver out is broke,
　So did the tree strive, bend, writh, wring and breake,
　Till at a little hole it thus did speake.

28

Right curteous Knight (for so I may you deeme,
　And must you call not knowing other name)
　If so you are as gracious as you seeme,
　Then let your friendly deed confirme the same,
　Vnloose this monster, sent as I esteeme,
　To adde some farther torment to my shame.
　Alas mine inward griefes were such before,
　By outward plagues they need be made no more.

29

Rogero mazed looked round about,
　If any man or woman he might see,
　At last he was resolved of his doubt,
　He found the voice was of the mirtle tree,
　With which abasht, though he were wise and stout,
　He said, I humbly pray thee pardon me,
　Whether thou be some humane ghost or spright,
　Or power divine that in this wood hast right.

30

Not wilfulnesse, but ignorance did breed
　Thine injury, mine error in this case:
　And made me do this unadvised deed,
　By which unwares thy leaves *I* did deface:
　But let thy speech so farre forth now proceed,
　To tell me how thou art that in this place,
　Dost dwell in tree amid the desert field,
　As God from haile and tempest thee may shield.

31

And if that I for this amends may make,
　Or now or after, or by paine or art,
　I sweare to thee by her, and for her sake,
　That holds of me, and shall the better part,
　That I shall not surcease all paines to take,
　To worke thy joy, or to asswage thy smart.
　This said, he saw again the mirtle shake,
　And then again he heard that thus it spake:

32

Sir Knight, your curtesie doth me constraine,
　To shew to you the thing that you desier,
　Although I sweat (as you may see) with paine,
　Like greenest boughes upon the flaming fier,
　I will discover unto you her traine,
　(Wo worth the time that ever I came nie her)
　That did for malice and by magicke strange,
　My lively shape to livelesse branches change.

33

I was an Earle, *Astolpho* was my name,
　Well knowne in *France* in time of warre and peace,
　Orlandos cosen and *Renalds*, whose fame
　While time shall last in earth shall never cease.
　Of *Oton* King of *English* Ile I came,
　And should succeed him after his decease,
　Both comely, young, carelesse of worldly pelfe,
　To none an enemy but to my selfe.

34

For as we turned from the *Estern* Iles,
　Whose banks are worne with surge of *Indian* wave,
　Where I and many more with witching wiles,
　Were straight inclosed in a hollow cave,
　Vntill *Orlando* did avenge the guiles,
　And found by force a meane his friends to save,
　We Westward went upon the shore and sand,
　That lieth on the North side of the land.

35

And as we travell'd homeward on our way,
  As chance did leade or destiny us drive,
  It was our fortune once on breake of day,
  Hard by *Alcynas* Castle to arrive,
  Where she alone, to sport her selfe and play,
  Such kind of gins for fishes did contrive,
  That though we saw no net, no bait, no hooke,
  Yet still we saw that store of fish she tooke.

36

The Dolphin strong, the Tunny good of tast,
  The Mullet, Sturgeon, Samon (princely fish)
  With Porpose, Seales, and Thornpooles came as fast,
  As she was pleased to commaund or wish.
  And still she tooke of each kind as they past,
  Some strange for shew, some dainty for the dish,
  The horsefish and the huge and monstrous whales,
  Whose mighty members harnest are with scales.

37

Among the rest that were too long to count,
  We saw the fish that men Balena call,
  Twelve yards above the water did amount
  His mighty backe, the monster is so tall:
  And (for it stood so still) we made account,
  It had beene land, but were deceived all,
  We were deceiv'd, well I may rew the while,
  It was so huge we thought it was an Ile.

38

I say this potent witch *Alcyna* tooke
  All sorts of fish without or net or aide,
  But only reading in a little booke,
  Or mumbling words, I know not what she said,
  But seeing me so well she lik't my looke,
  That at her sport but little time she staid,
  But sought forthwith to trap me by her skill,
  Which straight fell out according to her will.

39

For toward me with pleasant cheare she came,
  In modest maner and in comely sort,
  And did withall her speech demurely frame,
  And praid me to her lodging to resort,
  Or if I would be partner of her game,
  She offred me to shew me all the sport,
  And all the kinds of fish in seas that were,
  Some great, some small, some smooth, and some with
                                          (haire.

40

And if you lift a Mermaid faire to see,
  That can with song the raging stormes appease,
  At yond same little banke you may (quoth she)
  To which we two will safely passe with ease:
  (The banke which she pretends to shew to me,
  Was that same fish the monster of the seas)
  And I that too much loved to adventer,
  Vpon the fishes back with her did enter.

41

My cousins *Dudon* and *Renaldo* beckned
  To draw me thence, I heard not what they said,
  But of their speech and signes I little reckned,
  I had not wit enough to be afraid:
  But soone my courage was appal'd and weakned,
  I straight was faine in vaine to cry for aid,
  The monstrous fish that seem'd to me an Ile,
  Straight bare me from the shore full many a mile.

42

There was *Renaldo* like to have beene drownd,
  Who swam to save me if perhaps he might,
  But soddainly of him and of the ground,
  A misty cloud did take away the sight:
  Alcyna and I with seas environ'd round,
  Did travell on that monster all the night,
  And then with gracious speeches she began
  To give me all the comfort that she can.

43

And thus at last to this place we repaire,
  Of which by wrong *Alcyna* keepes possession,
  Deposing forcibly the rightfull heire,
  (Her elder lawfull sister) by oppression:
  The other two more vicious then faire,
  Are bastards, and begotten in transgression,
  I heard it told, and have it not forgotten,
  She and *Morgana* were in incest gotten.

44

And as their first beginning was of sinne,
  So is their life ungodly and defamed,
  Of law nor justice passing not a pinne,
  But like the heifer wanton and untamed,
  By warre they seeke their sisters right to winne,
  Their elder sister *Logistilla* named,
  And have so farre prevailed with their powers,
  They have of hers about an hundred towers.

45

And had ere this time taken all away,
  Save that the rest is strongly fenced round,
  For of one side the water stops the way,
  On th'other side the vantage of the ground,
  Which with a mighty banke doth make a stay,
  Much like the English and the Scottish bound:
  And yet the bastard sisters doe their best,
  And labour still to spoile her of the rest.

46

And why, because they see her good and holy,
  They hated her because themselves are vicious.
  But to returne, and tell you of my folly,
  That turn'd to me so hurtfull and pernicious,
  I now again grew somwhat bold and jolly,
  I see no cause to feare or be suspicious,
  And finding she lov'd me by signes most plaine,
  I wholly bent my selfe to love againe.

47

When I her dainty members did embrace,
  I deemed then there was none other blisse,
Me thought all other pleasures were but base,
  Of friends nor kin I had no want nor misse,
I onely wisht to stand in her good grace,
  And have accesse her corrall lips to kisse,
I thought my selfe the happiest of all creatures,
To have a Lady of so goodly features.

48

And this the more confirm'd my joy and pride,
  That toward me she shew'd such love and care,
By night and daily I was by her side,
  To do or speake against me no man dare,
I was her stay, I was her houses guide,
  I did commaund, the rest as subjects are:
She trusted me, alone with me she talked,
With me within she sat, without she walked.

49

Alas, why do I open lay my sore,
  Without all hope of medicine or releefe?
And call to mind the fickle joy before,
  Now being plung'd in gulfes of endlesse griefe?
For while I thought she lov'd me more and more,
  When as I deem'd my joy and blisse was chiefe,
Her wauing love away from me was taken,
A new guest came, the old was cleane forsaken.

50

Then did I find full soone, though too too late,
  Her wanton, wavering, wily womans wit,
Accustom'd in a trice to love and hate,
  I saw another in my seate to sit:
Her love was gone, forgone my happie state,
  The marke is mist that I was wont to hit:
And I had perfect knowledge then ere long,
That to a thousand she had done like wrong.

51

And least that they about the world might go,
  And make her wicked life and falshood knowne,
In divers places she doth them bestow,
  So as abrode they shall not make their mone,
Some into trees, amid the field that grow,
  Some into beasts, and some into a stone:
In rockes or rivers she doth hide the rest,
As to her cruell fancie seemeth best.

52

And you that are arriv'd by steps so strange,
  To this unfortunate and fatall Ile,
Although in youthfull sports a while you range,
  And though Alcina favour you a while,
(Although you little looke for any change,)
  Although she friendly seeme on you to smile,
Yet looke no lesse, but chang'd at last to be,
Into some brutish beast, some stone or tree.

53

Thus though perhap my labour is but lost,
  Yet have I giv'n you good and plaine advise,
Who can themselves beware by others cost,
  May be accounted well among the wise:
The waves that my poore ship so sore hath tost,
  You may avoid by heed and good devise,
Which if you do, then your successe is such,
As many others could not do so much.

54

Rogero did with much attention heare
  Astolfos speech, and by his name he knew
To Bradamant he was of kindred neare,
  Which made him more his wofull state to rew:
And for her sake that loved him most deare,
  To whom from him all love againe was dew,
He sought to bring him aid and some releefe,
At least with comfort to asswage his griefe.

55

Which having done, he asked him againe,
  The way that would to Logistilla guide,
For were it by the hils, by dale or plaine,
  He thither meant forthwith to runne or ride.
Astolfo answer'd it would aske much paine,
  And many a weary journey he should bide,
Because to stop this way Alcina sets
A thousand kinds of hindrances and lets.

56

For as the way it selfe is very steepe,
  Not passable without great toile and paine,
So she that in her mischiefe doth not sleepe,
  Doth make the matter harder to attaine,
By placing men of armes the way to keepe,
  Of which she hath full many in her traine.
Rogero gave Astolfo many thanks,
For giving him this warning of her pranks.

57

And leading then the flying horse in hand,
  Not daring yet to mount a beast so wilde,
Least (as before I made you understand)
  He might the second time have been beguil'd:
He meanes to go to Logistillas land,
  A vertuous Ladie, chast, discreet and mild,
And to withstand Alcina tooth and naile,
That upon him her force might not prevaile.

58

But well we may commend his good intent,
  Though missing that to which he did aspire,
Who judgeth of our actions by th'event,
  I wish they long may want their most desire.
For though Rogero to resist her ment,
  And feared her as children feare the fire,
Yet was he taken to his hurt and shame,
Even as the flie is taken in the flame.

59

For going on his way, behold he spies
  A house more stately then can well be told,
  Whose wals do seeme exalted to the skies,
  From top to bottome shining all of gold,
  A sight to ravish any mortall eyes,
  It seem'd some Alcumist did make this hold,
  The wals seem'd all of gold, but yet I trow
  All is not gold that makes a golden show.

60

Now though this stately sight did make him stay,
  Yet thinking on the danger him foretold,
  He left the easie and the beaten way,
  That leadeth to this rich and stately hold,
  And to her house where vertue beares the sway,
  He bends his steps with all the hast he could:
  But ere he could ascend the mountaines top,
  A crew of catives sought his way to stop.

61

A foule deform'd, a brutish cursed crew,
  In bodie like to antike worke devised,
  Of monstrous shape, and of an ugly hew,
  Like masking Mathachinas all disguised.
  Some looke like dogs, and some like apes in vew,
  Some dreadfull looke, and some to be despised,
  Yong shamelesse folke, and doting foolish aged,
  Some nak'd, some drunk, some bedlam-like enraged.

62

One rides in hast a horse without a bit,
  Another rides as slow, an asse or cow,
  The third upon a Centaurs rumpe doth sit,
  A fourth would flie with wings, but knows not how,
  The fift doth for a speare employ a spit,
  Sixt blowes a blast like one that gelds a sow.
  Some carrie ladders, others carrie chaines,
  Some sit and sleepe while others take the paines.

63

The Captaine of this honorable band,
  With belly swolne, and puffed blubber'd face,
  Because for drunkennesse he could not stand,
  Vpon a tortesse rode a heavy pace:
  His sergeants all were round about at hand,
  Each one to do his office in his place:
  Some wipe the sweat, with fans some make a wind,
  Some stay him up before, and some behind.

64

Then one of these that had his feet and brest
  Of manlike shape, but like unto a hound
  In eares, in necke, and mouth, and all the rest
  Doth utter barking words with currish sound,
  Part to command and partly to request
  The valiant knight to leave the higher ground,
  And to repaire unto *Alcynas* castle,
  Or els they two, for mastery must wrastle.

65

This monster seeing his request denide,
  Strake at *Rogeros* beaver with a launce,
  But he that could no such rude jests abide,
  With *Ballisarda* smote him in the paunch
  Out came the sword a foote on th'other side,
  With which he led his fellowes such a daunce,
  That some hopt headlesse, some cut by the knees,
  And some their arms, and some their eares did leese.

66

In vaine it was their targets to oppose
  Against the edge of his enchanted blade,
  No steele had force to beare those fatall blowes,
  Vnto the quicke the sword a passage made:
  But yet with numbers they do him inclose,
  Their multitude his force did overlade:
  He needs at least *Briarius* hundred armes
  To foile the foes that still about him swarmes.

67

Had he remembred to unfold the shield,
  Atlanta carrid at his saddle bow,
  He might have quickly overcome the field,
  And caus'd them all without receiving blow,
  Like men dismai'd and blind themselves to yeeld:
  But he perhaps that vertue did not know,
  Or if he did, perhaps he would disdaine,
  Where force did faile, by fraud his will to gaine.

68

But being full resolved not to yeeld
  Vnto such beasts, but ere he parted thence
  He would his carkasse leave amid the field,
  And manfully would die in his defence,
  Then lo good hap that failes the forward seeld,
  Provided him a meane to rid him hence.
  There came two Ladies, either like a Queene,
  And each of them most stately to be seene.

69

For each of them an Vnicorne did ride,
  As white as Lillies, or unmolten snow,
  And each of them was deck't with so great pride,
  As might most richly set them forth to show,
  But each of them was so divinely eide,
  Would move a man in love with them to grow,
  And each of them in all points was so choice,
  As in their sight a man would much rejoyce.

70

Then both of them unto the medow came,
  Whereas *Rogero* fought with all that rout,
  And both of them those brutish beasts did blame,
  That sought to harme a knight so strong and stout.
  Rogero blushing now with modest shame,
  Thank't them that had of danger holp't him out,
  And straight consented with those Ladies faire,
  Vnto *Alcynas* castle to repaire.

71

Those ornaments that do set forth the gate,
  Embost a little bigger then the rest,
  All are enrich't with stones of great estate,
  The best and richest growing in the East,
  In parted quadrons, with a seemely rate,
  The collons diamonds as may be guest:
  I say not whether counterfait or true,
  But shine they did like diamonds in view.

72

About these stately pillars and betweene
  Are wanton damsels gadding to and fro,
  And as their age, so are their garments greene,
  The blacke oxe hath not yet trod on their toe,
  Had vertue with that beautie tempred beene,
  It would have made the substance like the show:
  These maids with curteous speech and manners nice
  Welcome *Rogero* to this Paradise.

73

If so I may a Paradise it name,
  Where love and lust have built their habitation,
  Where time well spent is counted as a shame,
  No wise staid thought, no care of estimation,
  Nor nought but courting, dauncing, play and game,
  Disguised clothes, each day a sundry fashion,
  No vertuous labour doth this people please,
  But nice apparrell, belly-cheare and ease.

74

Their aire is alway temperate and cleare,
  And wants both winters storms, and summers heate,
  As though that Aprill lasted all the yeare,
  Some one by fountaines side doth take his seate,
  And there with fained voice and carelesse cheare,
  Some sonnet made of love he doth repeate:
  Some others, other where with other fashions,
  Describe unto their loves their loving passions.

75

And *Cupid* then, the captaine of the crew,
  Triumphs upon the captives he hath got,
  And more and more his forces to renew,
  Supplies with fresh the arrowes he hath shot,
  With which he hits (his levell is so true)
  And wounds full deepe, although it bleedeth not:
  This is the place to which *Rogero* went,
  And these the things to which our youth is bent.

76

Then straight a stately steed of colour bay,
  Well limb'd and strong was to *Rogero* brought,
  And deck't with faire capparison most gay,
  With gold and pearle and jewels richly wrought,
  The Griffeth horse (that whilome to obey
  The spurre and bit was by *Atlanta* taught)
  Because his journey long required rest,
  Was carrid to a stable to be drest.

77

The Ladies faire that had the knight defended,
  From that same wicked and ungratious band,
  Which as you heard at large before pretended,
  Rogeros passage stoutly to withstand,
  Told now *Rogero* how that they intended,
  Because his valew great they understand,
  Of him to crave his furtherance and aid,
  Against their fo that made them oft afraid.

78

There is (quoth they) a bridge amid our way,
  To which we are already verie nie,
  Where one *Erifila* doth all she may,
  To damage and annoy the passers by,
  A Giantesse she is, she lives by pray,
  Her fashions are to fight, deceive and lye:
  Her teeth be long, her visage rough with heare,
  Her nayles be sharpe, and scratching like a Beare.

79

The harme is great this monster vile doth doe,
  To stop the way that but for her were free,
  She spils and spoiles, she cares not what nor who,
  That griefe to heare, and pittie is to see:
  And for to adde more hatred hereunto,
  Know this, that all yon monsters you did see,
  Are to this monster either sonnes or daughters,
  And live like her by robberies and slaughters.

80

Rogero thus in curteous sort replide,
  Faire Ladies gladly I accept your motion,
  If other service I may do beside,
  You may command, I stand at your devotion:
  For this I weare this coat and blade well tride,
  Not to procure me riches or promotion,
  But to defend from injurie and wrong,
  All such as have their enemies too strong.

81

The Ladies did *Rogero* greatly thanke,
  As well deserv'd so stout and brave a Knight,
  That profer'd at the first request so franke,
  Against the gyantesse for them to fight.
  Now they drew nye unto the rivers banke,
  When as *Erifila* came out in sight:
  But they that in this story take some pleasure,
  May heare the rest of it at further leasure.

THE SEVENTH BOOK OF
ORLANDO FVRIOSO

THE ARGVMENT

When foule Erifila *was overcome,*
Rogero *guided by two stately dames,*
Vnto Alcynas *sumptuous court doth come,*
Where he his time in pleasure spends and games;
Melissa *him rebukes, he standeth dumme,*
And at her true reproofes he greatly shames.
In fine, by her good counsell and direction,
He frees himselfe from that most foule subjection.

ORLANDO FVRIOSO
THE SEVENTH BOOK

1

All they that to far countries do resort,
 Shall see strange sights, in earth, in seas, in skies,
Which when againe at home they shall report,
 Their solemne tales, esteemed are as lyes.
For why the fond and simple common sort,
 Beleeve but what they feele or see with eyes,
Therefore to them, my tale may seeme a fable,
Whose wits to understand it are not able.

2

But carelesse what the simple sots surmise,
 If they shall deeme it a device or deede,
Yet sure to those that are discreete and wise,
 It will no wonder nor no passion breed:
Wherefore my tale to such I do devise,
 And wish them to the same to take good heed,
For some there are, may fortune in this booke,
As in a glasse their acts and haps to looke.

3

For many men with hope and show of pleasure,
 Are carri'd far in foolish fond conceit,
And wast their pretious time, & spend their treasure,
 Before they can discover this deceit.
O happie they that keepe within their measure,
 To turne their course in time, and sound retreit,
Before that wit with late repentance taught,
Were better never had then so deare bought.

4

A little while before I did reherse,
 How that *Rogero* by two dames was brought,
To combat with *Erifila* the feerse,
 Who for to stop the bridge and passage sought.
In vaine it were for to declare in verse,
 How sumptuously her armor all was wrought,
All set with stones, and guilt with Indian gold,
Both fit for use, and pleasant to behold.

5

She mounted was, but not upon a steed,
 Insteed thereof she on a Wolfe doth sit,
A Wolfe whose match *Apulia* doth not breed,
 Well taught to hand, although she us'd no bit,
And all of sandie colour was her weed,
 Her armes were thus (for such a champion fit)
An ugly Tode was painted on her shield,
With poyson swolne, and in a sable field.

6

Now each the other forthwith had descride,
 And each with other then prepar'd to fight,
Then each the other scornefully defide,
 Each seekes to hurt the other all he might.
But she unable his fierce blowes to bide,
 Beneath the vizer smitten was so right:
That from her seat sixe paces she was heaved,
And lay like one of life and sense bereaved.

7

Rogero readie was to draw his sword,
 To head the monster lying on the sand,
Vntill those dames with many a gentle word,
 Asswag'd his heat and made him hold his hand:
He might in honour now her life affoord,
 Sith at his mercie wholly she doth stand:
Wherefore sir Knight put up your blade (say they)
Lets passe the bridge and follow on our way.

8

The way as yet unpleasant was and ill,
 Among the thornie bushes and betweene,
All stony, steep, ascending up the hill,
 A way lesse pleasant seldome hath been seene:
But this once past according to their will,
 And they now mounted up upon the greene,
They saw the fairest castle standing by,
That ere was seene with any mortall eye.

9

Alcyna met them at the outer gate,
 And came before the rest a little space,
And with a count'nance full of high estate,
 Salutes *Rogero* with a goodly grace,
And all the other courtiers in like rate,
 Do bid *Rogero* welcome to the place,
With so great showes of duty and of love,
As if some god descended from above.

10

Nor onely was this pallace for the sight,
 Most goodly, faire, and stately to behold,
But that the peoples courtsie bred delight,
 Which was as great as could with tongue be told.
All were of youth and beautie shining bright,
 Yet to confirme this thing I dare be bold,
That faire *Alcyna* past the rest as farre,
As doth the Sunne another little starre.

11

A shape whose like in waxe twere hard to frame,
    Or to expresse by skill of painters rare.
    Her haire was long, and yellow to the same,
    As might with wire of beaten gold compare:
    Her lovely cheekes with shew of modest shame,
    With roses and with lillies painted are,
    Her forehead faire and full of seemely cheare,
    As smooth as polisht Ivory doth appeare.

12

Within two arches of most curious fashion,
    Stand two gray eyes, that like to cleare suns shin'd,
    Of stedie looke, but apt to take compassion,
    Amid which lights, the naked boy and blind,
    Doth cast his darts that cause so many a passion,
    And leave a sweet and curelesse wound behind:
    From thence the nose in such good sort descended,
    As envie knowes not how it may be mended.

13

Conjoyn'd to which in due and comely space,
    Doth stand the mouth stain'd with Vermilion hew,
    Two rowes of precious perle serve in their place,
    To show and shut, a lip right faire to vew:
    Hence come the courteous words, and full of grace,
    That mollifie hard hearts and make them new:
    From hence proceed those smilings sweet and nice,
    That seeme to make an earthly paradice.

14

Her brest as milke, her necke as white as snow,
    Her necke was round, most plum and large her brest
    Two Ivory apples seemed there to grow,
    Full tender smooth, and fittest to be prest:
    They wave like seas, when winds most calme doth blow,
    But *Argos* selfe might not discerne the rest,
    Yet by presumption well it might be gest,
    That that which was concealed was the best.

15

Her armes due measure of proportion bare,
    Her faire white hand was to be viewed plaine,
    The fingers long, the joynts so curious are,
    As neither knot appear'd nor swelling vaine.
    And full to perfect all those features rare,
    The foote that to be seene doth so remaine,
    Both slender, short, little it was and round,
    A finer foote might no where well be found.

16

She had on every side prepar'd a net,
    If so she walke, or laugh, or sing, or stand:
    Rogero now the counsell doth forget,
    He had receiu'd late at *Astolfos* hand:
    He doth at nought those wholsome precepts set,
    That warned him to shun *Alcynas* land,
    He thought no fraud, no treason nor no guile,
    Could be accompani'd with so sweete a smile.

17

The dame of *France*, whom he so loved erst,
    He quite forgets, so farre awry he swarved:
    The tale *Astolfo* had to him reherst,
    He thinketh false, or else by him desarved:
    Alcynas goodly shape his heart so perst,
    She onely seem'd a mistresse to be sarved:
    Ne must you blame *Rogeros* inclination,
    But rather blame the force of incantation.

18

Now as abrode the stately courts did sound,
    Of trumpets, shagbot, cornets, and of flutes,
    Even so within there wants no pleasing sound,
    Of virginals, of vials and of lutes,
    Vpon the which persons not few were found,
    That did record their loves and loving sutes,
    And in some song of love and wanton verse,
    Their good or ill successes did reherse.

19

As for the sumptuous and luxurious fare,
    I thinke not they that *Nynus* did succeed,
    Nor *Cleopatra* faire, whose riot rare,
    To *Antonie* such love and losse did breed,
    Might with *Alcynas* any way compare,
    Whose love did all the others farre exceed,
    So deeply was she ravisht in the sight,
    Of this so valiant and so comely Knight.

20

The supper done, and tables tane away,
    To purposes and such like toyes they went,
    Each one to other secretly to say
    Some word, by which some pretie toy is ment,
    This helpt the lovers better to bewray
    Each unto other what was their intent,
    For when the word was hither tost and thither,
    Their last conclusion was to lie together.

21

These prettie kinds of amorous sports once ended,
    With torches to his chamber he was brought,
    On him a crew of gallant squires attended,
    That every way to do him honour sought.
    The chambers furniture could not be mended.
    It seem'd *Arachne* had the hangings wrought,
    A blanket new was made, the which once finish'd,
    The company by one and one diminish'd.

22

Now was *Rogero* couched in his bed,
    Betweene a paire of cambricke sheets perfumed,
    And oft he hearkens with his wakefull hed,
    For her whose love his heart and soule consumed:
    Each little noise hope of her comming bred,
    Which finding false, against himselfe he fumed,
    And curst the cause that did him so much wrong,
    To cause *Alcyna* tarry thence so long.

23

Sometime from bed he softly doth arise,
  And looke abroad if he might her espie,
  Sometime he with himselfe doth thus devise,
  Now she is comming, now she drawes thus nie:
  Sometime for very anger out he cries,
  What meaneth she, she doth no faster hie?
  Sometimes he casts least any let should be,
  Betweene his hand and this desired tree.

24

But faire *Alcyna*, when with odors sweet,
  She was perfum'd according to her skill,
  The time once come she deemed fit and meet,
  When all the house were now asleepe and still:
  With rich embroder'd slippers on her feet,
  She goes to give and take of joyes her fill,
  To him whom hope and feare so long assailed,
  Till sleepe drew on, and hope and feare both failed.

25

Now when *Astolfos* successor espide
  Those earthly starres, her faire and heav'nly eyes,
  As sulphur once in flamed cannot hide,
  Even so the mettall in his veines that lies,
  So flam'd that in the skin it scant could bide:
  But of a sodaine straight he doth arise,
  Leaps out of bed, and her in armes embraced,
  Ne would he stay till she her selfe unlaced.

26

So vtterly impatient of all stay,
  That though her mantle was but cyprous light,
  And next upon her smocke of lawne it lay.
  Yet so the champion hasted to the fight,
  The mantle with his fury fell away,
  And now the smocke remain'd alone in sight,
  Which smocke as plaine her beauties all discloses,
  As doth a glasse the lillies faire and roses.

27

And looke how close the Ivie doth embrace
  The tree or branch about the which it growes,
  So close the lovers couched in the place,
  Each drawing in the breath the other blowes:
  But how great joyes they found that little space,
  We well may guesse, but none for certaine knowes:
  Their sport was such, so well their leere they couth,
  That oft they had two tongues within one mouth.

28

Now though they keepe this close with great regard,
  Yet not so close but some did find the same,
  For though that vertue oft wants due reward,
  Yet seldome vice wants due deserved blame.
  Rogero still was more and more prefard
  Each one to him with cap and court'sie came,
  For faire *Alcyna* being now in love,
  Would have him plast the others all above.

29

In pleasure here they spend the night and day,
  They change their clothes so often as they lust,
  Within they feast, they dance, disport and play,
  Abroad they hunt, they hauke, they ride, they just,
  And so while sensuall life doth beare the sway,
  All discipline is troden in the dust.
  Thus while *Rogero* here his time mispends,
  He quite forgets his dutie and his frends.

30

For while *Rogero* bides in feast and joy,
  King *Agramant* doth take great care and paine,
  Dame *Bradamant* doth suffer great annoy,
  And travel'd farre to finde him all in vaine:
  She little knew *Alcyna* did enjoy
  Her due delights, yet doth she mone and plaine,
  To thinke how strangely this same flying horse,
  Bare him away against his will by force.

31

In townes, in fields, in hils, in dales she sought,
  In tents, in campes, in lodgings and in caves,
  Oft she enquir'd, but yet she learned nought,
  She past the rivers fresh and salt sea waves,
  Among the *Turkes* she leaves him not unsought,
  (Gramercy ring that her from danger saves:)
  A ring whose vertue workes a thing scant possible,
  Which holding in her mouth she goes invisible.

32

She will not, nor she cannot thinke him dead,
  For if a man of so great worth should die,
  It would some great report or fame have bred,
  From East unto the West, both farre and nie:
  It cannot sinke nor settle in her head,
  Whether he be in seas, in earth or skie,
  Yet still she seekes, and her companions are
  Sorrowes and sighes, and feares, and loving care.

33

At last she meanes to turne unto the cave,
  Where lie the great and learned *Merlins* bones,
  And at that tombe to crie so loud and rave,
  As shall with pitie move the marble stones:
  Nor till she may some certaine notice have
  Of her belov'd to stay her plaints and mones,
  In hope to bring her purpose to effect,
  By doing as that Prophet should direct.

34

Now as her course to *Poytiers* ward she bent,
  Melyssa using wonted skill and art,
  Encountred her, her journey to prevent,
  Who knew full well, and did to her impart,
  Both where he was, and how his time he spent,
  Which griev'd the vertuous damsell to the hart,
  That such a Knight, so valiant erst and wise,
  Should so be drown'd in pleasure and in vice.

35

O poyson'd hooke that lurkes in sugred bait,
　O pleasures vaine, that in this world are found,
Which like a subtile theefe do lie in waite,
　To swallow man in sinke of sinne profound:
O Kings and peers, beware of this deceit.
　And be not in this gulfe of pleasure dround:
The time will come, and must I tell you all,
When these your joyes shall bitter seeme as gall.

36

Then turne your cloth of gold to clothes of heares,
　Your feasts to fasts, to sorrowes turne your songs,
Your wanton toyes and smilings into teares,
　To restitution turne your doing wrongs,
Your fond securenesse turne to godly feares,
　And know that vengeance unto God belongs,
Who when he comes to judge the soules of men,
It will be late alas to mend it then.

37

Then shall the vertuous man shine like the sunne,
　Then shall the vicious man repent his pleasure,
Then one good deed of almes sincerely done,
　Shall be more worth then mines of Indian treasure,
Then sentence shall be giv'n which none shall shun,
　Then God shall wey and pay our deeds by measure,
Vnfortunate and thrice accursed thay,
Whom fond delights do make forget that day.

38

But to returne unto my tale againe,
　I say Melyssa tooke no little care,
To draw Rogero by some honest traine,
　From this same place of feasts and dainty fare,
And like a faithfull friend refus'd no paine,
　To set him free from her sweet senslesse snare,
To which his unkle brought him with intent
His destinie thereby for to prevent.

39

As oft we see men are so fond and blind,
　To carry to their sonnes too much affection,
That when they seeme to love, they are unkind,
　(For they do hate a child that spare correction)
So did Atlanta, not with evill mind,
　Give to Rogero this so bad direction,
But of a purpose, thereby to withdraw
His fatall end that he before foresaw.

40

For this he sent him past so many seas,
　Vnto the Ile that I before did name,
Esteeming lesse his honour then his ease,
　A few yeares life then everlasting fame.
For this he caused him so well to please
　Alcyna that same rich lascivious dame;
That though his time old Nestors life had finish'd,
Yet her affection should not be diminish'd.

41

But good Melyssa on a ground more sure,
　That lov'd his honor better then his weale,
By sound perswasions meanes him to procure,
　From pleasures court to vertues to appeale:
As leeches good that in a desperate cure,
　With steele, with flame, and oft with poison heale,
Of which although the patient do complaine,
Yet at the last he thankes him for his paine.

42

And thus Melyssa promised her aid,
　And helpe Rogero backe againe to bring,
Which much recomforted the noble maid,
　That lov'd this Knight above each earthly thing.
But for the better doing this (she said)
　It were behovefull that he had her ring,
Whose vertue was that who so did it weare,
Should never need the force of charmes to feare.

43

But Bradamant that would not onely spare
　Her ring (to do him good) but eke her hart,
Commends the ring and him unto her care,
　And so these Ladies take their leave and part.
Melissa for her journey doth prepare,
　By her well tried skill in Magicke art,
A beast that might supply her present lacke,
That had one red foot and another blacke.

44

Such hast she made, that by the breake of day
　She was arrived in Alcynas Ile,
But straight she chang'd her shape and her array,
　That she Rogero better might beguile:
Her stature tall she makes, her head all gray,
　A long white beard she takes to hide the wile,
In fine she doth so cunningly dissemble,
That she the old Atlanta doth resemble.

45

And in this sort she waiteth till she might
　By fortune find Rogero in fit place,
Which very seldome hapt, for day and night
　He stood so high in faire Alcynas grace,
That she could least abide of any wight,
　To have him absent but a minute space,
At last full early in a morning faire,
She spide him walke abroad to take the aire.

46

About his necke a carkneet rich he ware,
　Of precious stones, all set in gold well tride,
His armes that erst all warlike weapons bare,
　In golden bracelets wantonly were tide:
Into his eares two rings conveyed are,
　Of golden wire, at which on either side
Two Indian pearles in making like two peares,
Of passing price were pendent at his eares.

47

His locks bedew'd with waters of sweet savour,
  Stood curled round in order on his hed,
He had such wanton womanish behaviour,
  As though in *Valence* he had long bene bred:
So chang'd in speech, in manners and in favour,
  So from himselfe, beyond all reason led,
By these inchantments of this am'rous dame,
He was himselfe in nothing but in name.

48

Which when the wise and kind *Melyssa* saw,
  (Resembling still *Atlantas* person sage)
Of whom *Rogero* alwayes stood in aw,
  Even from his tender youth to elder age,
She toward him with looke austere did draw,
  And with a voice abrupt, as halfe in rage,
Is this (quoth she) the guerdon and the gaine,
I find for all my travell and my paine?

49

What was't for this that I in youth thee fed,
  With marrow of the Beares and Lions fell?
That I through caves and deserts have thee led,
  Where serpents of most ugly shape do dwell,
Where Tygers fierce and cruell Leopards bred,
  And taught thee how their forces all to quell:
An *Atis* or *Adonis* for to be,
Vnto *Alcyna* as I now thee see.

50

Was this foreshew'd by those observed starres,
  By figures and nativities oft cast,
By dreames, by oracles that never arres,
  By those vaine arts I studide in time past,
That thou should'st prove so rare a man in warres,
  Whose famous deeds to endlesse praise should last?
Whose acts should honord be both farre and neare,
And not be matcht with such another peare.

51

Is this a meane or ready way you trow?
  Which other worthy men have trod before,
A *Cæsar* or a *Scipio* to grow,
  And to increase in honor more and more?
But to the end a man may certaine know,
  How thrall thou art unto *Alcynas* lore,
Thou wearest here her chaines and slavish bands,
With which she binds thy warlike armes and hands.

52

If thou regard not thine owne estimation,
  To which the heav'ns ordaine thee if thou would,
Defraud not yet thine heires and generation,
  Of which I have thee oftentime foretold,
Appointed by eterne predestination,
  Except thou do their due from them withhold,
Out of thy loines and bowels to proceed
Such men whose match the world did never breed.

53

Let not so many a worthy soule and mind,
  Fram'd by the wisedome of the heav'nly King,
Be hindred of the bodies them assign'd,
  Whose of-spring chiefe must of thy issue spring:
Be not unto thine owne blood so unkind,
  Of whose great triumphs all the world shall ring,
Whose successors, whose children and posterity,
Shall helpe our country to her old prosperity.

54

What good hath this great Queene unto thee done,
  But many other queanes can do the same?
What certaine gaine is by her service wonne,
  That soone doth fancie, sooner doth defame?
Wherefore to make thee know what thou hast done,
  That of thy doings thou maist have some shame,
But weare this ring, and next time you repaire
To your *Alcyna*, marke if she be faire.

55

Rogero all abasht and mute did stand,
  With silent tongue, and looke for shame downe cast,
The good enchantresse tooke him by the hand,
  And on his finger straight the ring she plast,
But when this ring had made him understand
  His owne estate, he was so sore agast,
He wisht himselfe halfe buride under ground,
Much rather then in such place once be found.

56

But she that saw her speech tooke good effect,
  And that *Rogero* shamed of his sinne,
She doth her person and her name detect,
  And as her selfe (not *Atlant*) doth beginne,
By counsell and advice him to direct,
  To rid himselfe from this so dangerous ginne:
And gives him perfect notice and instruction,
How these deceits do bring men to destruction.

57

She shew'd him plainly she was thither sent,
  By *Bradamant* that lov'd him in sinceritie,
Who to deliver him from bondage ment,
  Of her that blinded him with false prosperity.
How she tooke *Atlants* person to th'intent
  Her countenance might carry more austeritie,
But finding now him home reduc'd againe,
She saith she will declare the matter plaine.

58

And unto him forthwith she doth impart,
  How that faire dame that best deserv'd his love,
Did send that ring, and would have sent her hart,
  If so her heart his good so farre might move,
The ring this vertue had, it could subvert
  All magick frauds, and make them vaine to prove:
Rogero as I said, no time did linger,
But put the ring upon his little finger.

59

When truth appear'd, *Rogero* hated more
  Alcynas trumpries, and did them detest,
  Then he was late enamored before,
  (O happie ring that makes the bearer blest)
  Now saw he that he could not see before,
  How with deceits *Alcyna* had bene drest,
  Her borrow'd beauties, all appeared stained,
  The painting gone, nothing but filth remained.

60

Ev'n as a child that taking from the tree
  An apple ripe, and hides it in some place,
  When he returnes the same againe to see,
  After a senight or a fortnights space,
  Doth scant beleeve it should the same fruite be,
  When rottennesse that ripenesse doth deface,
  And where before delight in it he tooke,
  Now scant he bides upon the same to looke.

61

Ev'n so *Rogero* plainly now describe,
  Alcynas foule disgraces and enormitie,
  Because of this his ring she could not hide,
  By all her paintings any one deformitie:
  He saw most plainly that in her did bide,
  Vnto her former beauties no conformity,
  But lookes so ugly, that from East to West,
  Was not a fouler old misshapen beast,

62

Her face was wan, a leane and writhled skin,
  Her stature scant three horseloaves did exceed:
  Her haire was gray of hue, and very thin,
  Her teeth were gone, her gums serv'd in their steed,
  No space was there between her nose and chin,
  Her noisome breath contagion would breed,
  In fine, of her it might have well bene said,
  In *Nestors* youth she was a pretie maid.

63

I feare her arts are learned now a dayes,
  To counterfait their haire and paint their skin,
  But reasons ring their crafts and guiles bewrayes,
  No wise men of their paintings passe a pin,
  Those vertues that in women merit praise,
  Are sober shewes without, chast thoughts within,
  True faith and due obedience to their make,
  And of their children honest care to take.

64

Now though *Rogero* (as before I sed)
  Detested sore the ugly witches sight,
  Yet by *Melyssas* counsell wisely led,
  He doth conceale the matter for a night,
  Till of provision he were better sped,
  With which he might more safely take his flight,
  And taking care his meaning close to hide,
  He doth forthwith his armour all provide.

65

And tels *Alcyna* he would go and trie,
  If that he were not waxen grosse or no,
  Because that idle he so long did lie,
  And never fought with any armed fo:
  His sword unto his girdle he doth tie,
  With armour on, a walking he doth go,
  And with a scarfe about his arme he lapt
  The shield that in the cypresse case was wrapt.

66

And thus arrai'd, he commeth to the stable,
  And tooke a horse (as wise *Melyssa* taught)
  A horse as blacke as any jeat or sable,
  So made as if in waxe he had bene wrought,
  Most swift for course, and strong of limbes and able,
  This horse hight Rabican was thither brought
  By Duke *Astolfo*, who by sorcerie
  Was turned late into a mirtle tree.

67

As for the Griffeth horse that there was by,
  Melyssa wisheth him to let him stand,
  And sayth, that she her selfe ere long would trie,
  To make him gentle to the spur and hand:
  And that she would hereafter time espie,
  To bring it him, and let him understand,
  How he should do with very little paine,
  To make him yeeld to spurre, to rod and raine.

68

She further said, his flight would be suspected,
  Except he let the flying horse to stay,
  Rogero none of all her words neglected,
  But did her counsell wise and sage obay:
  And so before his meaning was detected,
  From this misshapen hag he stole away,
  And meanes (if God will grant him so much grace)
  To be at *Logistillas* in short space.

69

Such men of armes as watched at the gate
  He slue, the rest he sodainly assailed,
  Good was his hap that scapt with broken pate,
  They tooke their heeles when as their hearts them failed.
  Alcyna now had notice all too late,
  Rogero was so farre it nought availed:
  But in another booke shall be contained,
  How him dame *Logestilla* entertained.

THE EIGHT BOOKE OF
ORLANDO FVRIOSO

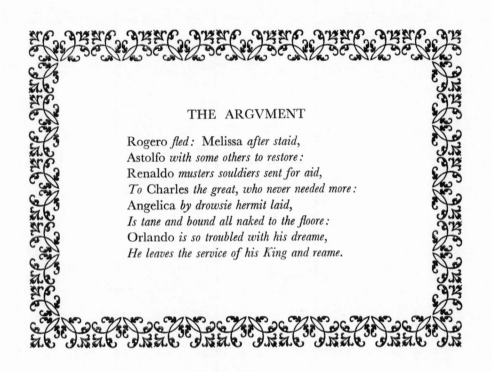

THE ARGVMENT

Rogero *fled:* Melissa *after staid,*
Astolfo *with some others to restore:*
Renaldo *musters souldiers sent for aid,*
To Charles *the great, who never needed more:*
Angelica *by drowsie hermit laid,*
Is tane and bound all naked to the floore:
Orlando *is so troubled with his dreame,*
He leaves the service of his King and reame.

ORLANDO FVRIOSO
THE EIGHT BOOKE

1

Oh strange enchantments used now adayes,
  Oh charmers strange among us dayly found,
  That find so many charms and subtle waies,
  Wherewith they hold fond lovers hearts fast bound,
  Not with conjured spirits that they raise,
  Nor knowledge of the stars and skill profound,
  But blinding mens conceits, and them fast tying,
  With simulation, fraud, deceit and lying.

2

But he that had the rule and ring of reason,   (cover,
  Should soone their frauds, their crafts and guiles dis-
  And finde a hoord of foule and lothsome treason,
  To lurke within the shew of such a lover:
  Well may they seeme most lovely for a season,
  When all their wrinkles they with painting cover,
  But unto men of wit and reason learned,
  Their subtleties shall quickly be discerned.

3

Rogero (as I said) in secret sort,
  With *Rabican* out of the castle went,
  And made the watch and guard unpleasant sport,
  That most of them his comming might repent:
  Some had their armes, and some their heads cut short,
  All put to flight, the gates in peeces rent.
  And then unto the wood he entred, when
  He met by chance one of *Alcynas* men.

4

This man did beare a faulcon on his fist,
  With which he went on hauking day by day,
  To flie in field, or river as he list,
  The countrie full of game still yeelded pray,
  He had a spaniell could not well be mist,
  And eke a hauking nagge not very gay,
  And meeting good *Rogero* halfe disguised,
  That he was fled away he straight surmised.

5

The servant rideth on, and at their meeting,
  He askt *Rogero* why he rode so fast,
  Rogero gave him very slender greeting,
  As though on such a squire he little past:
  Well (quoth the faulkner) though thou now art fleeting,
  I trust ere long to shew thee such a cast,
  That with my dogge, my faulcon and my horse,
  I do not doubt to fetch thee backe by force.

6

And first he lets the faulcon take her flight,
  But *Rabican* as fast as she did flie,
  Then from his horse the faulkner doth alight,
  His horse flue like an arrow by and by.
  Then went the dogge, who was of course so light,
  As is the wind that bloweth in the skie:
  And last of all himselfe ran with such shift,
  It seem'd the lightnings flame was not so swift.

7

Rogero thinketh it a foule disgrace,
  That any man should thinke he fled for feare,
  And more because he now was had in chase;
  Wherefore he doth a while the flight forbeare,
  And manfully to them he turnes his face,
  And seeing no man but the faulkner there,
  And that no weapon in his hand he saw,
  He much disdain'd on him his sword to draw.

8

But straight the dog doth bite his horses heeles,
  The hauke his head amazed with her wings.
  When *Rabycan* such strange foes forces feeles,
  He riseth up before, behinde he flings:
  Rogero thought the world had run on wheeles,
  And *Balisarda* out at once he brings,
  But they, it seem'd so well were seene in fence,
  That all his blowes to them brought no offence.

9

Both loth to stay, resolved not to yeeld,
  He takes his target from his saddle bow,
  And with the dazling light of that same sheeld,
  Whose force *Melyssa* lately made him know,
  He made them fall as if their eyes were seel'd,
  So that no farther let from them did grow,
  But having vanquisht them this wise with ease,
  He now may ride at leasure where he please.

10

These foes once foil'd their forces overcome,
  Alcyna straight had notice of his flight,
  For of the watchmen one to her was come,
  That while these things were done did stand in sight.
  This made her stand like one halfe dead or dumme,
  And after put her into such a fright,
  That forthwith for avoiding further harme,
  Through all the towne she made them crie alarme.

11

And calling oft her selfe a foolish beast,
   Because *Rogero* so from her was slipt,
   Sometime she beats her head, her face and breast,
   Sometime in rage her garments all she ript:
   She calleth all her men from most to least,
   A part of whom unto the sea she shipt,
   And of the rest she makes a mighty band,
   To fetch *Rogero* backe againe by land.

12

All were so busie to this service bent,
   That none remain'd the pallace faire to gard,
   Which greatly helpt *Melyssas* good intent,
   Which chiefly was as you before have hard,
   To set at large poore prisoners so long pent,
   Which now to do (she absent) was not hard,
   Dissolving all her circles and her knots,
   And stroying all her figures and her lots.

13

And thus in fields, in houses, and in woods,
   She set at large as many as she found,
   That had beene turn'd to trees, to stones and floods,
   And in that state by magicke art fast bound:
   Likewise to them she rendred all their goods,
   Who when they saw themselves so cleare unbound,
   Departing thence with all the hast they might,
   To *Logestilla* they arriv'd that night.

14

And first of all and chiefe of all the rest,
   The *English* Duke came to himselfe againe,
   Because *Rogero* lov'd and wisht him best,
   And lends the ring that makes inchantments vaine.
   But good *Melyssa* could by no meanes rest,
   Vntill she could his armour eke regaine,
   And that same famous worthie guilded launce,
   That had to him such honor done in *Fraunce*.

15

With which *Argalia* got no little fame,
   Who used oft the same in fight to beare.
   Now when *Melyssa* to the castle came,
   She found his other armour with the speare,
   And this atcheeu'd, the sage and friendly dame
   Mounts on the *Griffith horse* without all feare,
   And Duke *Astolfo* mounting on his crupper,
   To *Logestillas* came that night to supper.

16

Now was *Rogero* with no small ado,
   Tiring himselfe amid those craggie wayes,
   And striving all that he with paine may do,
   To cut off all those lothsome long delayes,
   That hindred him for sooner comming to
   That Ladie faire whose vertues merit praise,
   Till neare the Southerne sea with mickle paine,
   He came unto a sandy desert plaine.

17

Here was he plagu'd with thirst and parching heat,
   And with the sunne reflecting on the sand,
   Which from the South upon the banke did beat,
   Enflaming still the aire on either hand,
   But leaving now *Rogero* in this sweat,
   That still I may not in one matter stand.
   To *Scotland* now I will returne againe,
   And of *Renaldo* talke a word or twaine.

18

Great was his entertainment and his cheare,
   Made by the King and people of the land,
   Which feasts once done, the worthy valiant peare,
   As was his charge, doth let them understand,
   How *Charles* the great, whose state doth touch them neare
   In no small need of their good aid did stand,
   And how for this he sent him to their nation,
   And to this tale he ads an exhortation.

19

Then was it answer'd him without delay,
   That for King *Charls* and for the Empires sake,
   They all were ready to do all they may,
   And would for this behoofe short order take,
   And offred him to shew (if he would stay)
   What store of horse and footmen he could make:
   Namely the King himselfe would be right glad,
   To go in person, but his age forbad.

20

Nor yet should age with him so much have done,
   As make him from the battell to abide,
   Save that he had a wife and valiant sonne,
   Well able such a band of men to guide,
   Whose value had already praises wonne,
   And of his youth was now in floure and pride.
   This noble toward impe he doth intend,
   As captaine of his armed men to send.

21

Wherefore about his realme forthwith he sent,
   To get of horses and of men good store,
   With ships, and things to war most pertinent,
   As needfull meate, and mony needfull more:
   The while *Renaldo* into England went,
   The King to *Barwicke* companie him bore,
   And men report that when they should depart,
   The King was seene to weepe for tender hart.

22

Renaldo went with faire and prosprous wind,
   And past along upon the *English* coast,
   Vntill he hapt the noble *Tems* to find,
   Of which all *London* justly make their boast:
   Here he tooke land as first he had assign'd,
   And in twelve houres journey riding post,
   Vnto the Prince of *Wales* he was conducted,
   Whom of these matters fully he instructed.

23

The Prince that was Vicegerent to the King,
  (That *Oton* hight) who sojourn'd now in *France*,
From whom *Renaldo* did commission bring,
To take up horse, and men, and ordinance:
When he had once true knowledge of that thing,
Which of all other he would most advance:
He marshal'd men of armes without delay,
And points them meet at *Callice* by a day.

24

But here I must a while from hence digresse,
  Lest to one tale my pen should still be bound,
As good musitians do their skill expresse,
By playing on the strings of divers sound:
While *Renald* here is chear'd with great excesse,
(As ever in the *English* land is found)
I meane to tell how that faire Lady sped,
That twice before from this *Renaldo* fled.

25

I told you how *Angelica* the bright,
  Fled from *Renaldo* in a thicke dark wood,
How on a Hermit there she hapt to light,
And how her sight reviv'd his aged blood:
But she that tooke in him but small delight,
Whose hoary haires could do her little good,
With this good Hermit made but little stay,
But turn'd her horses rains and went away.

26

The Hermit seeing he contemned was,
  (Whom age long since, and love did newly blind)
Doth spurre a thousand times his silly asse,
Who still remained more and more behind,
And sith he saw he could not bring to passe,
To stop her course (afflicted much in mind)
In vaine he doth his poore asse beate and curse,
His trot was very bad, his gallop worse.

27

And being out of hope of comming nire,
  As having almost lost her horses tracke,
He studies now to compasse his desire,
With some rare stratageme to bring her back:
Vnto that art forthwith he doth retire,
(That damned art that is surnamed blacke)
And by his bookes of magicke he doth make,
A little sprite the Lady overtake.

28

And as the hound that men the Tumbler name,
  When he a hare or cony doth espie,
Doth seeme another way his course to frame,
As though he meant not to approch more nie,
But yet he meeteth at the last his game,
And shaketh it untill he make it die:
So doth the Hermit traverse all about,
At ev'ry turne to find the damsell out.

29

What he intends to do, full well I wot,
  And meane ere long the same to you to show,
The damsell travell'd still that knew it not,
The spright to do his office was not slow,
For straight within the horse himselfe he got,
As she on sands of *Gascoigne* seas did go,
The spright that fully had possest the horse,
Did drive her to the sea with all his force.

30

Which when the faire and fearefull damsell saw,
  Although she tride full oft with rod and raine,
Her palfrey from his dangerous course to draw,
Yet seeing plainly she did strive in vaine,
With colour chang'd for anguish and for aw,
And casting oft her looke to land againe,
At last she sitteth still, nor further striveth,
For needs they must go whom the divell driveth.

31

In vaine it was to strike the horse her bare,
  It was not done by that poore palfreis falt,
Wherefore she tucks her garments, taking care
Lest they should be bedew'd with waters salt,
Vpon her haire, which then all loose she ware,
The aire doth make an amorous assalt,
The greater winds were still, I thinke of duty,
That they acknowledge to so rare a beauty.

32

The waters more, the land still lesse she sees,
  At last she saw but one small peece of land,
And that small peece in small time she doth leese,
Now sees she neither shore nor any sand.
Then cold despaire all lively hope did freese,
When as her horse did turne to the right hand,
And at the twilight, or not long before,
Did bring her to a solitary shore.

33

Here she remaining helplesse and alone,
  Among the fruitlesse trees and senslesse rocks,
Standing her selfe all like the marble stone,
Save that sometime she tare her golden locks,
At last her eyes to teares, her tongue to mone,
She doth resolve, her faire soft breast she knocks,
And blames the God of heav'n and power divine
That did the fates unto her fall incline.

34

O fortune, fortune (thus the damsell cride)
  Fill now thy rage and execute thine ire,
And take this life that takest all beside,
And let my death accomplish thy desire:
I have and daily do thy force abide,
Feare still my mind, travell my limbs doth tire,
And makes me think in this great storme and strife,
That death were sweet to shorten such a life.

G

35

Can all thy malice do me further spite?
  Can any state be worse or more unstedy?
  That am from princely scepter banisht quite,
  A helplesse hap and hurt past all remedy,
  And worse then this, mine honor shining bright
  Is stained sore, and ev'n defast alredy,
  For though in act no ill I ever wrought,
  Yet wandring thus will make men think me nought.

36

What can a woman hold of any price,
  If once she leese her honor and good name?
  Alas I hate this beautie and despise,
  And wish it never had bene of such fame:
  Ne do I for this gift now thanke the skies,
  By which my spoile and utter ruine came,
  Which caus'd my brother *Argal* shed his blood,
  Ne could his armes enchanted do him good.

37

For this the King of Tartar *Agricane*,
  Sought of my father *Galafron* the spoile,
  Who whilome was in *India* cald great *Cane*,
  And after dide with sorrow of the foile.
  For this I dayly doubting to be tane,
  From place to place do passe with endlesse toile,
  And now to loose alas what hast thou left me,
  Since fame, and goods, and friends are all bereft me?

38

If drowning in the sea were not a death
  Severe enough to quench thy raging spite,
  Then send some beast out of this desert heath,
  To teare my limbs and to devoure me quite:
  I shall thee thanke for stopping of my breath,
  If to torment me thou have no delight,
  These wofull words vtterd the Ladie bright,
  When straight the hermit came within her sight.

39

Who all the while had in a corner stood,
  And heard her make this piteous plaint and mone,
  Proceeding from her sad and mourning mood,
  Enough to move a heart as hard as stone:
  It did the *senex fornicator* good,
  To thinke that he was there with her alone,
  Yet so devoutly commeth this old carrion,
  As though it had bene *Paul* or Saint *Hillarion*.

40

When as the damsell saw a man appeare,
  In such a desert solitary place,
  She straight began to be of better cheare,
  Though feare and dread appeare still in her face:
  And with a voice so loud as he might heare,
  She praid him pitie this her wofull case,
  Recounting all her dangers overblowne,
  To him to whom they were already knowne.

41

No sooner had the hermit heard her out,
  But straight to comfort her he doth begin,
  And shewes by many reasons and devout,
  How all these plagues were sent her for her sin:
  The while he puts his sawcie hands about,
  Sometime her breasts, sometime her neck and chin,
  And more and more still gathering heart of grace,
  He offers boldly her for to embrace.

42

But she that much disdain'd this homely fashion,
  Doth staine her cheekes with red for very shame,
  Thrust back his carren corpes without compassion,
  Reviling him with many a spitefull name,
  Who testy with old age and with new passion,
  That did him now with wrath and love inflame,
  Drawes out a bottle of a strange confection,
  That sleepe procureth by a strong infection.

43

With this he sprinkleth both the damsel's eies,
  (Those eyes whence *Cupid* oft his arrowes shet)
  Straight sound asleepe the goodly damsell lies,
  Subjected to the will of such a sot:
  Ne yet for ought he did or could devise,
  He could procure his curtall stir a jot,
  Yet oft he kist her lips, her cheekes, her brest,
  And felt and saw the beauties of the rest.

44

The dullerd jade still hangeth downe his head,
  Sturring or spurring could not make him praunce,
  The sundrier wayes he said, the worse he sped,
  His youthfull dayes were done, he could not daunce,
  His strength was gone, his courage all was dead,
  His weapon looked like a broken launce:
  And while himselfe in vaine he thus doth cumber,
  He falleth downe by her into a slumber.

45

But now another evill chance befell,
  (For one ill turne alone is seldome done)
  The which to th'end I may the better tell,
  Know this, about the setting of the sunne,
  There is an Ile, *Ebuda* as men tell,
  Whose habitants are welnigh all undone,
  By meanes that mightie *Proteus* thither sent
  An *Orke* that doth the people teare and rent.

46

Within this Ile, as auncient stories tell,
  (I not affirme how false they are or true)
  Sometime a King of mightie powre did dwell,
  That had a daughter passing faire of hue,
  The which faire Ladie *Proteus* lik't so well,
  When her on sands in walking he did vew,
  That though he dwelt in waters salt and cold,
  Yet fresh hot love on him had taken hold.

47

Which heate when all the sea could not asswage,
  He thought her milkwarm flesh could only quench,
And (for he saw she was of lawfull age)
  With her consent he forst the princely wench:
Which sinne did set her father in such rage,
  That straight condemning her in open bench:
Her of her life he publikely bereaved,
Nor spar'd the infant in her wombe conceaved.

48

This cruell act her lover so inflamed,
  On King and Iland he doth wreake his spite,
He sends that monster that before I named,
  With other beasts to stroy the Iland quite:
These monsters hurt their men, beat, kild and lamed,
  In fine put all the people in such fright,
That to escape the beast devoid of pitie,
They left their fields, and fled unto their citie.

49

And though men arm'd the gates and wals defend,
  Yet they within scant thought themselves secure,
And sith their harmes have neither ease nor end,
  And tir'd these tedious travels to endure,
Vnto *Apollos* oracle they send,
  To know how they their safetie might procure,
Who after humble sute and sacrifice,
Answer'd them of *Ebuda* in this wise.

50

Blood guiltlesse spilt did breed great *Proteus* ire,
  Inflam'd with love, and fed with beauty rare,
Blood guiltlesse must be spilt to quench this fire,
  Till one be found may with the first compare:
This you must do and if you peace desire,
  To take of damsels those that fairest are,
And offer one a day upon the shore,
Till he find one like unto that before.

51

This wofull answer breeding much despaire,
  And more dislike within their carefull hearts,
To thinke that ev'ry day a damsell faire,
  Must for a prey be giv'n without desarts:
This is the cause that maketh them repaire,
  (To find sufficient store) to sundry parts,
And get them Virgins faire and undefloured
Of this most ugly *Orke* to be devoured.

52

Now if this be of *Proteus* true or not,
  I meane not in defence of it to stand,
But this is certaine so, full well I wot,
  Men use this cruell custome in that land,
And day by day a maid is drawne by lot,
  And left for prey upon the rocke or sand,
Vnto the monster that doth them devoure,
Ev'n in their prime of youth and tender floure.

53

O wretched wights, whom subtle snares have brought
  To this unfortunate and fatall Ile,
Where damsels faire and handsome out are sought,
  To serve for food unto a monster vile:
Their pyrats bring them home, their vessels fraught
  With such they take by force, or trap with wile,
With which they fill their prisons and their towres,
To have them ready at appointed hours.

54

Thus sending out their vessels day by day,
  It chanc'd that one of them with tempest tost,
Hapt to arrive whereas the Hermit lay
  With that faire Lady hard upon the cost:
Oh cruell chance, oh precious peerlesse pray,
  Among the pirats either to be lost,
Or to be caried to the fatall Ile,
To be devoured of a monster vile.

55

That beauty rare that *Sacrapant* ay deemed
  More deare then living, liberty or life:
That beauty rare that to *Orlando* seemed
  Most fit of all the world to be his wife:
That beauty rare in India so esteemed,
  That bred so many a blow and bloody strife,
Is now so quite of aid and comfort reft,
Not one to speake a word for her is left.

56

The damsell faire drown'd in a deadly sleepe,
  Was tane and bound before she could awake,
Also the drowsie Fryer, to make him keepe
  Her company, away with them they take:
This done, they lanched out into the deepe,
  And with this precious prey they homeward make,
Where in a Castle they detain'd her thrall,
Vntill to dy her lucklesse lot should fall.

57

Yet such great force her passing beauty had,
  Among these barbarous and savage wights,
That they appeared sorrowfull and sad,
  To wey the danger of her dolefull plights,
It seemed all of them would have beene glad,
  To have preserv'd her many dayes and nights:
But such small store of others there remained,
At last to offer her they were constrained.

58

Who can the woes, the teares, the plaints rehearse,
  The lamentations & the mourning sound,   (pearce,
That seem'd the heavens themselves with noise to
  To rend the rocks, and stir the stedy ground?
Her iv'ry corps convay'd (as in a hearse)
  By wailing wights, where they must leave it bound:
The thought hereof in me such pang doth breed,
I can no further in this tale proceed.

59

Wherefore I must some other matter find,
  Vntill my Muse her sorrow may asswage,
For sure no cruell beast were so unkind,
  Nor Tyger in their greatest wrath and rage,
Nor any cruell tyrant can we find,
  (Although there are good store in ev'ry age)
That could behold or thinke without compassion,
A Lady bounden in so vile a fashion.

60

Oh had *Orlando* notice of her smart,
  Who was to *Paris* gone to seeke her out,
Or those two Knights whom late the fiend did part,
  The which for love of her together fought,
They would for her use all paine, care and art,
  Of death nor danger they would put no doubt:
But if they helpe not now, it is no wonder,
Sith they and she were plac'd so far asunder.

61

Now in this time to *Paris* siege was layd,
  By famous *Agramant Trajanos* sonne,
Of which at last they grew so sore afraid,
  The towne had almost of the *Turks* beene wonne,
Had not their vowes procur'd them heav'nly ayd,
  They had bin ruin'd all and quite undone,
The force of *France* had welnigh then bin foyled,
The holy Empire had almost bin spoyled.

62

For when that now the City was on fire,
  And when all hope of humane helpe was past,
Then mighty God forgetting wrath and ire,
  Vpon their teares, repentance true and fast,
At *Charles* his humble prayer and desire,
  With helpe from heav'n releev'd them at the last,
And sent such raine to aide the noble Prince,
As seld was seene before, and never since.

63

Now lay *Orlando* on his restlesse bed,
  And thinks with sleepe to rest his troubled sprite,
But still a thousand thoughts possest his head,
  Troubling his mind, and sleepe expelling quite:
As circles in a water cleare are spread,
  When sun doth shine by day, and moone by night
Succeeding one another in a ranke,
Till all by one and one do touch the banke.

64

So when his mistris entred in his thought,
  (As lightly she was never thence away)
The thought of her in him such circles wrought,
  As kept him waking ever night and day,
To thinke how he from *India* had her brought,
  And that she should thus on the sodaine stray,
Nor that he could of her true notice know,
Since *Charles* at *Burdels* had the overthrow.

65

The griefe hereof did him most neerely tuch,
  And caus'd him often to himselfe to say,
What beast would have been overrul'd so much?
  That when I might have made her with me stay,
(For why her love and zeale to me was such,
  That in her life she never said me nay)
Yet I must suffer *Namus* for to guard her,
As though my selfe but little did reguard her.

66

I should to *Charles* my selfe have rather scused,
  And as I did, have kept the damsell still,
Or if excuses all had bin refused,
  I might in stead of reason pleaded will:
And rather then have bin so much abused,
  All those that should resist me slay and kill,
At least I might have got her safer keeping,
And not have let her thus be lost with sleeping.

67

Where bidest thou, where wanderst thou my deare?
  So yong, so lovely, and so faire of hew?
Even like a lambe when starres do first appeare,
  (Her dame and shepheard being out of vew)
Bleateth aloud to make the shepheard heare,
  And in her kind her evill hap doth rew,
Vntill the wolfe doth find her to her paine,
The silly shepherd seeking her in vaine.

68

Where is my love, my joy, my lifes delight?
  Wanderst thou still? do not the wolves offend thee?
Or need'st not thou the service of thy Knight?
  And keepest thou the flowre did so commend thee?
That flowre that me may make a happy wight,
  That flowre for which I ever did defend thee,
That I forbare, to please thy mind (too chast)
Is not that flowre (alas) now gone and past?

69

O most unfortunate and wretched I,
  If they have tane that sweet and precious floure,
What can I do in such a case but dy?
  Yea I would kill my selfe this present houre,
I would this world and that to come defy,
  Earth first my coarse, and Hell my soule devoure,
And this unto himselfe *Orlando* said,
With care and sorrowes being overlaid.

70

Now was the time when man and bird and beast,
  Gives to his travel'd body due repose,
When some on beds, and some on boords do rest,
  Sleepe making them forget both friends and foes.
But cares do thee *Orlando* so molest,
  That scarce thou canst thine eyes a little close,
And yet that fugitive and little slumber,
With dreames unpleasant thee doth vex and cumber.

71

He dreamt that standing by a pleasant greene,
　Vpon a bank with fragrant flowers all painted,
He saw the fairest sight that erst was seene,
　I meane that face with which he was acquainted,
And those two stars that Cupid sits between　　(tainted,
　Whence came that shaft whose head his heart hath
The sight whereof did breed in him that pleasure,
　That he prefer'd before all worldly treasure.

72

He thought himselfe the fortunatest wight
　That ever was, and eke the blessedst lover:
But lo a storme destroy'd the flowers quite,
　And all the pleasant banke with haile did cover:
Then suddenly departed his delight,
　Which he remain'd all hopelesse to recover;
She being of this tempest so afraid,
　That in the wood to save herselfe she straid.

73

And there (unhappy wretch) against his will,
　He lost his Lady in unlucky howre:
But her to find againe he travel'd still,
　Employing to her safety all his powre,
The woods and deserts he with plaints doth fill,
　And cride, alas turn'd is my sweet to sowre:
And while these same and such like words he said,
　He thought he heard her voice demaunding aid.

74

At this same voice (well knowne) a while he staid,
　Then follow'd as the sound him guided most
With this mischance his mind was much dismaid,
　His body sore with toile and travell tost:
When straight he heard another voice, that said,
　Now hope no more, for all thy hope is lost.
And of the sodaine waking with the sound,
　His eies all full of watry teares he found.

75

So sore he was affrighted at this vision,
　That ev'n as though it had been so indeed,
And not a fancy vaine or apparition,
　Thinking his lady stood of him in need:
In secret sort he getteth all provision,
　To make repaire unto her aid with speed:
And (for he would not willingly be knowne)
　He tooke nor man nor armour of his owne.

76

His coate of armes, of colour white and red,
　He left behind for doubt of ill successe,
That if it fortun'd he but evill speed,
　At least the losse and foile should be the lesse:
Vpon his armour cypresse blacke he spred,
　With colour sad, his sorrow to expresse.
And thus disguis'd in sad and mourning hue,
　He parts, and biddeth not his friends adue.

77

Not of King *Charles*, whose kinsman he is neare,
　Nor taketh he his leave of *Brandimart*,
Nor yet to kinsman kind, or freind most deare,
　Doth he his meaning open or impart:
Nor untill day did all abrode appeare,
　Was *Charles* advised that he did depart,
But in great rage and choler when he knew it,
　He sware and vow'd *Orlando* sore should rue it.

78

At which good *Brandimart* was greatly greeved,
　As one that deem'd it was without desart,
And (that his frend by him might be releeved)
　To find him out from thence he straight doth part,
For by his words, he certainly beleeved,
　That he could ease his friend *Orlandos* smart,
But this to *Fiordeledge* he not imparted,
　For feare that she his purpose would have thwarted.

79

This *Fiordeledge* of him was dearely loved,
　A Lady of great beauty and cleare fame,
Of parents good, of manners unreproved,
　Both wealthy, wise and modest to the same,
Yet taketh he no leave of his beloved,
　But early in the morning from her came,
To turne that night was his determination,
　But was deceived of his expectation.

80

And when she waited had a month or more,
　Expecting his returne, and all in vaine,
For love of him she was inflam'd so sore,
　Alone she goes to find him out againe,
And many sorry haps she bid therefore,
　As in the story shall be shewed plaine,
For of *Orlando* now I have to say,
　That is of more importance then both thay.

81

Who having chang'd the armes he late did weare.
　Directly to the City gate he went,
And told the Sentnell, softly in his eare,
　What was his name, and what was his intent:
Who straight abast the bridge, without all feare,
　(Suposing sure his uncle had him sent:)
And straight upon the *Pagan* campe he lighted,
　As in the booke ensuing is recited.

THE NINTH BOOKE OF
ORLANDO FVRIOSO

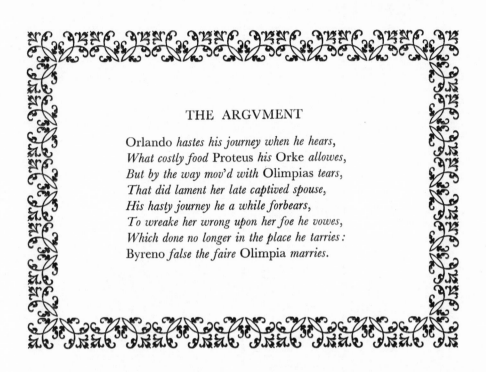

THE ARGVMENT

Orlando *hastes his journey when he hears,*
What costly food Proteus *his* Orke *allowes,*
But by the way mov'd with Olimpias *tears,*
That did lament her late captived spouse,
His hasty journey he a while forbears,
To wreake her wrong upon her foe he vowes,
Which done no longer in the place he tarries:
Byreno *false the faire* Olimpia *marries.*

ORLANDO FVRIOSO
THE NINTH BOOKE

I

Alas what dammage cannot *Cupid* bring,
  A noble heart once thralled to his lore?
That makes *Orlando* careles of his King,
  To whom of late most faithfull love he bore.
Who earst so grave and wise in every thing,
  And of the Church a Champion was before,
Now that in loves blind pathes he learns to plod,
Forgets himselfe, his country and his God.

2

Faine would I him disburden of this blame,
  Glad in my faults a fellow such to finde,
For to my good I feele me dull and lame,
  But prompt to ill, and swifter then the wind:
He not bethinking him how great a shame,
  It was to leave his helplesse friends behind,
Went where the Kings of *Affricke* and of *Spaine*,
Did ly in field encampt with all their traine.

3

Yet not encampt I can them call, for why
  They lay abroad dispersed with the raine,
Some twenty, ten, or eight together lie,
  Or sixe, or five, or foure, or three, or twaine:
Some farther off, and some are lodged nie,
  All weary with their former taken paine:
He might have kill'd of them a worthy crew,
Ne yet his *Durindana* once he drew.

4

The cause was this, so noble was his minde,
  To murther men asleepe he thought it base,
He lets them rest, and seekes his love to finde,
  By ev'ry person, and in ev'ry place,
And those he meets, with words and speeches kind,
  (Describing her apparell and her face)
He praies of all good fellowship to shoe,
Or where she is, or whither she did goe.

5

When light approcht and day began to breake,
  By day he seekes her in the host of *Turkes*,
His passions strong do make his reason weake,
  Yeeld to the fit that in his fancy workes.
Some helpe it was, he could their language speake,
  By which the safer he among them lurkes:
His words, his weeds, so like to theirs were seene,
As though he bred in *Tripoly* had beene.

6

But when he saw his staying was for nought,
  At three daies end away from thence he flang,
He left no towne of *France* and *Spaine* unsought,
  Ne yet this paine could ought asswage that pang:
Him Autumne first this wandring humor brought,
  When frutes do fade, his fruitlesse love first sprang,
And lasted still his force and rage renuing,
Both all the spring and summer next ensuing.

7

Now having travel'd as his custome was,
  From realme to realme, he came upon a day,
Where as the river cleare sometimes as glasse,
  That twixt the *Britans* and the *Normans* lay,
Was growne so high as now he could not passe,
  The snow and raine had borne so great a sway,
By force whereof the bridge was overthrowne,
The passage stopt, the foords were overflowne.

8

And looking round about the shore at large,
  Devising how to passe to th'other side,
He saw a little way from thence a barge,
  That seemed toward him the course to guide,
Of which a certaine damsell had the charge,
  To whom with voice aloud *Orlando* cride,
Intreating her because his hast was great,
Within the barge him to affoord a seat.

9

The maid affirm'd no price the barge could hire,
  And to command it he had no commission,
But promist she would grant him his desire,
  Vpon a certaine cov'nant and condition;
Which was to undertake by sword and fire,
  For to destroy an Ile, without remission,
A cruell Ile, *Ebuda* cald by name,
The wicked'st place where ever creature came.

10

For know (quoth she) beyond the *Irish* land,
  There lyes among the rest this gracelesse Ile,
That yeerely sends of wicked wights a band,
  To rob, to spoile, to fraud and to beguile:
All women kind that happen in their hand,
  They give for food unto a monster vile,
A monster vile that useth every day,
To have a maid or woman for his pray.

11

Of merchants and of pyrates that do come,
  They get them store, and of the fairest most:
  Now guesse by one a day how great a somme,
  Of women kind within this Ile are lost.
  If then of love you ever tasted cromme,
  Make one within the King of *Irelands* host,
  That make them ready shortly to proceed,
  To take a faire revenge of this foule deed.

12

No sooner had *Orlando* heard her out,
  But vow'd to be as forward as the first,
  To joyne himselfe with that same worthy rout,
  And now (for love doth ever cast the worst)
  Within himselfe begins to cast this doubt,
  Least that this wicked monster and accurst,
  Had got his Lady for a dainty bit,
  Because he heard no newes of her as yet.

13

And this conceit his minde so much possest,
  And in his heart made such a deepe impression,
  (For both in nature he did still detest
  All such as unto others do oppression)
  And much he fear'd his love among the rest,
  Might fall into the monsters vile possession,
  That straight he shipt, and by their due account,
  Within three daies he past S. *Michels* mount.

14

But having passed now the milke white sand,
  Of which the Ile of *Albion* takes his name,
  The wind that in the South before did stand,
  With so great fury to the Northwest came,
  In vaine it was against the same to stand,
  And therefore to retire it was no shame,
  Backe in one night the tempest draue them more
  Then they had sail'd three daies and nights before.

15

For when they saw it was no boote to strive,
  Against the fury of so feirce a winde,
  They went even as the weather did them drive
  Vntill the streame of *Antwerpe* they did finde,
  Where they to land with safety did arrive:
  There loe, an aged man with yeeres halfe blinde,
  Who deem'd *Orlando* of that crew the chiefe,
  To this effect utterd to him his griefe.

16

How that a certaine Dame of noble blood,
  Of vertue very great, of beauty rare,
  Of sober cheare and of behaviour good,
  (Though now opprest with misery and care)
  Requested him, except his hast withstood,
  That she to him a matter might declare,
  In which to aske his wise advise she ment,
  To which *Orlando* quickly did consent.

17

The Ladies pallace stood within the land,
  To which the Earle conducted was with speed,
  Where at the entry did the Lady stand,
  In mourning shew, and sorrowfull indeed,
  Who brought *Orlando* sadly by the hand,
  Into a chamber hang'd with mournfull weed,
  First him by her to sit she doth beseech,
  And then in ruefull sort she us'd this speech.

18

First (worthy Knight) I would you understood,
  I was the Earle of *Hollands* daughter deare,
  Who was to me so tender and so good,
  That though my brothers both were him as neare,
  Yet my desire in nothing he withstood,
  Nor spake the word that I was loth to heare:
  Thus whiles in state most steddy I did stand,
  A certaine Duke arrived in this land.

19

The Duke of *Zeland*, and his arrant was,
  To *Bisky* there against the *Moores* to fight,
  His age and beauty that did others passe,
  Moov'd me that had not tasted loves delight,
  Nor arm'd against his darts with steele or brasse,
  To yeeld my selfe his prisner without fight,
  Beleeving then as still I do and shall,
  That he to me doth carry love not small.

20

For while the windes contrary here him stay,
  Though naught for his, yet exc'lent for my drift,
  What time me seem'd each weeke was but a day,
  The pleasant houres did slide away so swift,
  We kept ourselves together day by day,
  Till at the last we made us so good shift,
  That ere we parted we had so procured,
  Each was to other man and wife assured.

21

Byreno was from hence but newly gone,
  (So is my deare beloved husbands name)
  But that a great Ambassador anon
  Directly from the King of Friseland came,
  To treat a certaine marriage upon
  With other of that nation of good fame,
  That to my Sire from *Holland* did repaire,
  That I might marry with his son and heire.

22

But I in whom faith tooke so deepe a roote,
  I could not change my new made choice, and tho
  I would, to strive with love it was no boote,
  That wounded me so lately with his bow,
  To stop the motions newly set on foote,
  Before they might to farther matter grow:
  I would not go, I flatly told my father,
  That I to dye a thousand deaths had rather.

23

My loving sire that chiefest care did take,
  That all he did might me his daughter please,
  Agreeing to my will, and for my sake,
  My griefe so new conceived to appease,
  Straightway the motion of this marriage brake,
  Which did so sore the *Friseland* King displease,
  He made sharpe warres on *Holland* in short space,
  By force whereof he ruin'd all my race.

24

For first he is of limbes and body strong,
  To meete his enemies in open field,
  And then so politicke in doing wrong,
  He makes their force unto his fraud to yeeld:
  He hath his other weapons strange among,
  A weapon strange, before this seene but seeld,
  A trunke of iron hollow made within,
  And there he puts powder and pellet in.

25

All closed save a little hole behind,
  Whereat no sooner taken is the flame,
  The bullet flies with such a furious wind,
  As though from clouds a bolt of thunder came.
  And whatsoever in the way it find,
  It burnes, it breakes, it teares and spoiles the same,
  No doubt some fiend of hell or divellish wight,
  Devised it to do mankind a spite.

26

And thus with this device and many other,
  In open field our battels twice he brake,
  And first in fight he slue mine elder brother,
  (The bullet through his curat way did make)
  And next inflight he tooke and kild the tother,
  Which caus'd my fathers aged heart to quake,
  Who notwithstanding stoutly did intend,
  His honor and my safety to defend.

27

But in a hold, that onely now was left him,
  They him besieg'd that all the rest had wonne,
  And by sharpe battell all the rest had reft him,
  Where to a loup one leveld so a gunne,
  The blow thereof of life and sense bereft him,
  So swift it came as none the same may shun.
  A weapon vile, wherewith a foolish boy
  May worthy Captaines mischiefe and annoy.

28

Thus was my father and my brothers slaine,
  Before this furious King his warre would cease,
  And I sole heire of *Holland* did remaine,
  Which made his former fancy more increase:
  He thinks by match with me my land to gaine,
  And offer'd to my people rest and peace,
  If I *Arbante* marry would his sonne,
  Which I before refused to have done.

29

And I (as well for hatred I did beare,
  Most just to him and all his generation,
  By whom my sire and brothers killed were
  By whom was spoil'd and robbed all our nation,
  As that to breake my promise I did feare,
  Which I *Byreno* made with protestation,
  That howsoever fortunes wheele should turne,
  Yet none should marry me till his returne)

30

Made answer this, that if for every ill
  I now abide I should have thousands more,
  Though they my corpes with cruell torments kill,
  I would not breake my promise given before.
  My countrymen perswade me change this will,
  First praying me, then threatning me full sore,
  Except I do, to yeeld me and my land
  (Desired prey) into mine enemies hand.

31

But finding still their threats and prayers vaine,
  And still that in my former mind I staid,
  Me and my country by a privy traine,
  Vnto the King of *Friseland* they berraid;
  Who thinking now with flattry me to gaine,
  First bid me not to feare or be dismaid,
  Then offred free to give me lands and life,
  If I would be his sonne *Arbantes* wife.

32

Then I that see my selfe inforced so,
  Although I meant that death should set me free,
  Yet loth as unrevenged hence to go,
  On those that had so greatly injur'd me:
  Did muse on many meanes to helpe my wo,
  At last I thought dissembling best to be,
  Wherefore I fained that I was relented,
  And that to have his son I was contented.

33

Among some servants that my father had,
  Two brethren strong and hardy I did chuse,
  Most apt to do what ever I them bad,
  And for my sake no danger to refuse,
  For each of them was brought up of a lad
  Within our house, I did their service use
  In warre and peace, and found their faiths as great
  As were their hearts to any hardy feat.

34

To these two men I open made my mind,
  They promist me their service and their aid,
  One into *Flanders* went a barke to find,
  The other with my selfe in *Holland* staid:
  Now was our day for marriage assign'd,
  When flying newes the strangers made afraid,
  With many sailes *Byreno* was reported,
  Into these parts newly to have resorted.

35

For when the first conflict and broile was fought,
  Wherein my brother cruelly was slaine,
  I straight by letters with *Byreno* wrought,
  To make all speed to succour us from *Spaine*.
  But while provision for each thing was sought,
  The *Friseland* King gate all that did remaine,
  Byreno hearing not what late was past,
  Conducts his navy hither in great hast.

36

The *Friseland* King that heard of his repaire,
  Doth leave the marriage for his eldest sonne,
  And to the sea he goes with navy faire,
  They meet, they fight the King of *Friseland* wonne,
  And to expell all comfort with despaire,
  Byreno prisner tane, I quite undone,
  Abrode *Byreno* captive like was carried,
  At whom unto his en'my I was married.

37

But when he thought in armes me to embrace,
  And have that due that wives their husbands ow,
  My servant standing in a secret place,
  Which I to him did for this purpose show,
  Affoords him to his sport but little space,
  And with a Pollax strake him such a blow,
  That staggring straight, and making little strife,
  He left his love, his living and his life.

38

And thus this youth borne in unhappy houre,
  Came to his death as he deserved well,
  In spite of all his sire *Cymoscos* powre,
  Whose tyranny all others did excell:
  Whose sword my sire and brothers did devoure,
  And from my native soile did me expell,
  And meant to enter upon all my lands,
  While I by marriage should be in their hands.

39

But when we once performed had this deed,
  And taken things of greatest price away,
  Before that any noyse or tumult breed,
  Out of the window we devis'd a way:
  And packing thence with all expedient speed,
  We came to sea before the breake of day,
  Whereas my servant waited with a barge,
  As he before receiv'd of me in charge.

40

I know not if *Cymosco* tooke more griefe,
  Or wrath or rancor kindled in his mind,
  To see his son that lay past all reliefe,
  To find nothing of value left behind,
  Then when his pride and glory should be chiefe,
  Then when to make a triumph be assign'd,
  And hoping all were at a wedding glad,
  He finds them all as at a buriall sad.

41

His hate of me and pitty of his sonne,
  Torment him night and day with endlesse griefe:
  But sith by teares no good the dead is done,
  And sharpe revenge asswageth malice cheefe,
  From dolefull teares to rage he straight doth runne,
  And seeks of all his sorrow this releese,
  To get me in his hands with subtile traines,
  Then me to kill with torments and with paines.

42

Those of my friends or servants he could find,
  Or that to me did any way retaine,
  He all destroyd, and left not one behind,
  Som hang'd, som burn'd, & som with torment slaine,
  To kill *Byreno* once he had assign'd,
  Of purpose onely to procure my paine,
  But that he thought his life would be a net,
  The sooner me into his hands to get.

43

Wherefore he set a hard, and cruell law,
  Except *Byrena* could in twelve months space,
  Find meanes by fraud or forces me to draw,
  To yeeld my selfe a prisner in his place,
  (Such Princes are that have of God no aw)
  Then dy he should without all hope of grace:
  So that to save his life, my death alone
  Must be the meanes, for other can be none.

44

All that by paine or cost procure I could,
  With diligence I have already done,
  Six Castles faire in *Flanders* I have sold,
  The mony spent, and yet no profit wonne,
  I sought to bribe those that him kept in hold,
  But they my craft with greater craft did shunne:
  I also mov'd our neighbours neere and farre,
  English and *Dutch* on him to make sharp warre.

45

But those I sent when they long time had staid,
  I thinke they would not, or they could not speed:
  They brought me many words, but little aid,
  My store decreast, but greater grew my need,
  And now (the thought whereof makes me afraid)
  That time drawes ny, when neither force nor meed,
  As soone as full expired is the yeere,
  From cruell death can safe preserve my deare.

46

For him my father and his sonnes were slaine,
  For him my state and living all is lost,
  For him those little goods that did remaine,
  I have consum'd to my great care and cost,
  For him with hearts disease and bodies paine,
  With troublous waves of fortune I am tost,
  Now last of all I must lay down my life,
  To save my spouse from blow of bloody knife.

47

And finding that my fortune is so bad,
  I must to save his life lay downe mine owne,
  To leese mine owne I shall be faine and glad,
  Where sorrow springs of seeds that love had sowne:
  This onely feare and doubt doth make me sad,
  Because I know not how it may be knowne,
  If I shall sure release *Byrenos* bands,
  By yeelding me into the tyrants hands.

48

I feare when he hath shut me in this cage,
  If all the torments I shall then endure,
  His fury to *Byreno* may asswage,
  Whose liberty I study to procure:
  I rather feare least following his rage,
  When he shall find he hath us both so sure,
  He will not care his oath and vow to breake,
  Vpon us both at once his wrath to wreake.

49

Behold the cause why I did long so sore
  To speake with you, demaunding your advice,
  As I have oft of others done before,
  Yet found I none so handy nor so wise,
  That would assure his freedome to restore,
  Whose love doth me to hate my selfe intice,
  The cause no doubt is this, they stand in feare
  Of those his guns, whose force no steele can beare.

50

But if your vertue do not disagree,
  With this your comely shape and manly show,
  Let me request you sir to go with me,
  Where I my selfe in prison shall bestow,
  And promise me to set *Byreno* free,
  If so the tyrant from his promise go.
  For I shall die with great content and joy,
  If by my death *Byreno* scape annoy.

51

Her dolefull tale the damsell here did end,
  Which oft was interrupted with her teares:
  Orlando loving not the time to spend
  In idle talke, all answers long forbeares,
  But in his mind he fully doth intend
  To foile her foes and rid her of her feares,
  He briefly said, that she should him commaund,
  To do much more then she did him demaund.

52

He meanes not tho that she her selfe should yeeld
  Vnto the cruell tyrant as a pledge,
  Except his sword (that failed him but seeld)
  Had on the sodaine lost his force and edge,
  He meanes (like common birders in the field)
  To catch the birds and never hurt the hedge,
  And thus resolv'd to do this worthy deed,
  From *Flanders* now by sea they go with speed.

53

The skilfull Pilot doth the vessell steare,
  Sometime on th'one, sometime on th'other side,
  The Iles of *Zeland* some before appeare,
  And some behind as fast themselves do hide,
  And straight to *Holland* they approched neare,
  Orlando went to land, but bids her bide:
  His meaning is that she shall understand,
  The tyrants death before she come on land.

54

Himselfe forthwith was mounted on a steed,
  A darke browne bay, with white starre in his face,
  Both large and strongly limb'd (like *Flemish* breed)
  But not so full of life nor swift of pace,
  Yet good enough to serve him at his need,
  When as his *Briliador* was not in place:
  And thus he came to *Dordreck*, where he found
  With men of armes the gates environ'd round.

55

The wayes, the wals, with arm'd men watched were,
  For tyrants still are most of such condition,
  (And chiefly new) that ay they stand in feare,
  And further now some newes had bred suspition,
  How that an armie great approched neare,
  Well stor'd with men, and stuffed with munition,
  The which they said *Byrenos* cosin brought,
  By force his kinsmans freedome to have wrought.

56

Orlando wils a watchman carry word
  Vnto their King, how that a wandring Knight
  Desires to prove his force with speare and sword,
  Whom if the King could overcome in fight,
  Then he should have the Ladie by accord,
  That slue *Arbante* on his wedding night:
  For he had taken her into protection,
  And could deliver her to his subjection.

57

But craved eke the King should bounden be,
  By promise firme (if he were overcome)
  To set his prisner (cald *Byreno*) free,
  And of his message this was all the summe:
  And this was told unto the King, but he
  That of true vertue never tasted crumme,
  Bent all his will and wit against all reason,
  To falshood foule, to false deceit and treason.

58

He makes account if he this Knight can stay,
  The which to do he meanes great meanes to make,
  That then the Ladie quickly get he may,
  And make him yeeld her for his safetie sake,
  He sendeth thirtie men a privie way,
  Him to inclose about and prisner take,
  Who fetching compasse to avoid suspicion,
  At last arrived where they had commission.

59

In this meane time with words he foded out,
  The worthy Earle, untill he saw his men,
  According as he bad them come about,
  Enclosing all the way behind, and then
  Out of the gates he rusheth with a rout,
  Of men on horse and foot of three times ten,
  As hunters do inclose the beasts in woods,
  Or fishers do inclose the fish in floods.

60

So doth the King *Cymosco* care and strive,
  To stop the wayes with all foresight and heed,
  And meaneth sure to have him tane alive,
  And thinks the same is such an easie deed,
  That of those guns with which he did deprive
  So many lives, he thinks there is no need,
  For such a weapon serveth very ill,
  Where he did meane to take and not to kill.

61

As cunning fowlers do the birds reserve,
  That first they take in hope of greater pray,
  And makes them for a bait and stale to serve,
  To take the rest by sport and pretie play,
  So meanes the King alive him to preserve,
  But unto this *Orlandos* force said nay:
  He meanes not to be handled in that sort,
  But breakes the nets and marreth all the sport.

62

The noble Earle with couched speare in hand,
  Doth ride where as he finds the thickest prease,
  Two, three and foure, that in this way did stand,
  The speare doth pierce, nor at the fift doth cease,
  It past the sixt the brodenesse of a hand,
  Nor that same handbredth maketh any peace,
  The seventh so great a blow therewith he strake,
  That downe he fell and never after spake.

63

Ev'n as a boy that shoots abroade for sport,
  And finds some frogs that in a ditch have bred,
  Doth pricke them with an arrow in such sort,
  One after one untill such store be dead,
  As that for more his shaft may seeme too short,
  From fethers fild already to the head,
  So with his speare *Orlando* him besturd,
  And that once left, he draweth out his sword.

64

That sword that never yet was drawne in vaine,
  Against whose edge doth armour little boote,
  At ev'ry thrust or blow he gave was slaine,
  A man on horse, or else a man on foote.
  The edge whereof with crimson still doth staine,
  And where it lights it pierceth to the roote.
  The *Friseland* King repents him now too late,
  That he for hast his guns behind forgate.

65

With voice aloud, and many a boistrous thret,
  He bids them bring his gun, but none doth heare,
  Who once within the gate his foot can get,
  Hee dare not once peepe out againe for feare:
  But when he saw none by his word did set,
  And that almost they all departed were,
  He thought it best to save himselfe by flight,
  From so great force of this same furious Knight.

66

He back retires, ne drawes the bridge for hast,
  Because *Orlando* now approcht so nie,
  And had not then his horse him speeded fast,
  As though he did not runne but rather flie,
  Orlando would have made him sore agast,
  Who caring not to make the poore sort die,
  Past by the rest and kept the King in chase,
  That sav'd himselfe by his good horses pace,

67

But yet ere long, againe he doth returne,
  And brings with him his iron cane and fire,
  Wherwith he doth beate down, and bruse and burne
  All those whom he to mischiefe doth desire:
  He hopes this weapon well shall serve his turne,
  Yet for all this he meanes to come no nire,
  But like a hunter privily doth watch,
  Where he the heedlesse beast may safest catch.

68

The King with this his engine ly'th in wait,
  A weapon tearing trees and rending rocks,
  Whose force no fence can ward with any sleight,
  It gives so sound and unexpected knocks:
  Thus having laine a little at receit,
  And watcht his vantage like a crafty foxe,
  When once the Earle within his reach he spide,
  He setteth fire unto his peeces side.

69

Straight like a lampe of lightning out it flies,
  And sendeth forth withall so great a sound,
  As seem'd to shake the everlasting skies,
  And to remove the unremoved ground,
  The shot gainst which no armour can suffice,
  But breaketh all that in the way is found,
  Doth whiz, and sing, and kindles as it went,
  Yet did not that effect the tyrant ment.

70

For whether twere his overhasty speed,
  And too great will to hurt did make him swerve,
  Or whether feare possest him in the deed,
  That not to guide his hand his heart could serve,
  Or whether God of mercy meere and meed,
  Was pleas'd his champion longer to preserve:
  It onely strake the horse with so great paine,
  That downe he fell and never rose againe.

71

The horse and horseman downe together fell,
  Downe lay the horse, up quickly rose the Knight,
And on his feet was straight recover'd well,
  More earnestly bent then before to fight,
And as the stories of *Antheus* tell,
  In whom each fall increased more his might:
So though *Orlando* with his fall was troubled,
His force and fury seemed to be doubled.

72

But when the King of *Friseland* plainly saw,
  How this bold Knight grew fiercer then before,
He thought it best by flight himselfe withdraw,
  His fainting heart with feare was pierst so sore:
Aside he turnes the horses foming jaw,
  Now full resolv'd to prove his force no more,
Orlando with such speed doth him pursue,
As doth an arrow from a bow of Yue.

73

And what he could not riding erst atchieve,
  He doth the same and more upon his feet,
And runs so swift as few men would believe,
  Except themselves had present bin to see it,
Vntill at last so hard he him did drive,
  He overtooke him in a narrow street,
And with his sword he cleft his head in twaine,
The senslesse corpes doth on the ground remaine.

74

Now as *Orlando* did this feate contrive,
  There grew new broiles from thence a little distance,
For then *Byrenos* cosin did arrive,
  With men on horse and foot for his assistance,
And finding none that durst against him strive,
  He entred had the gates without resistance,
So late a feare was in the people bred,
That none of them durst come to make a hed.

75

The silly Burgers knew not what to say,
  Nor who these were, nor what was their desire,
Vntill the *Zelanders* themselves bewray,
  Both by their speech and manner of attire:
Then made they peace, & promist them straightway,
  To do what ere the captaine should require,
Against the men of *Friseland* them to aid,
Who yet in prison still *Byreno* staid.

76

For why, that people alwaies had in hate,
  The King of *Friseland* and his men of warre,
Their Dukes late death, and altring their estate,
  Had mov'd their minds, but that that all did marre,
Was overtaxing them in such a rate,
  As alwaies breeds a great dislike and jarre.
Orlando twixt these men made such conclusion,
As turn'd unto the *Friseland* mens confusion.

H

77

For straight to ground they threw the prison gate,
  They fetch the prisners out without a kay,
Byreno to the Earle is not ungrate,
  With thanks a part of his due debt to pay:
And then they go to shew *Byrenos* state,
  To faire *Olympia* that at anchor lay,
For so they call the Lady chast and faire,
That of that Country was undoubted haire.

78

She that was thither by *Orlando* brought,
  Without all hope of any such successe,
Who lately (silly creature) onely sought,
  Her death might bring her lover from distresse:
Now was her safety and *Byrenos* wrought,
  When she suppos'd and lookt for nothing lesse:
The joy cannot with many words be told,
Wherewith the tone the tother did behold.

79

The people do the damsell faire restore,
  Vnto the state that unto her was due:
But she that vowd her selfe for evermore,
  To be unto *Byreno* lover true,
Persisting now as faithfull as before,
  Nor fearing any harme that might ensue,
Doth grant to him for love and meere affection
Of her and her estate the full protection.

80

Byreno leaves his cosin in his place,
  To guide that Country with sufficient gard,
His loving wife in *Zeland* he will place,
  That done, with forces march to *Friseland* ward:
And hopes to conquer it in little space,
  If that his fortune were not over hard,
And that which most assur'd him of this thing,
He had in hold the daughter of their King.

81

Whom he did meane to marry (as men say)
  Vnto a younger brother of his name:
Orlando shipt himselfe that present day,
  Byreno with him to his shipping came,
And offer'd him a large part of the pray,
  Because his valeour cheefly won the same,
Who nothing tooke but that same engin rare,
Which we before to lightning did compare.

82

Ne took he this away because he ment,
  To prove the force therof upon his foe,
Or use the same when he to battell went,
  His courage would not suffer him do so:
To hurle away the same was his intent,
  Where it mankind might never damage moe:
He lets nor powder nor the shot remaine,
Nor ought that did unto the same pertaine.

83

And when that now the shelves and shallow shore,
  Some twenty leagues or there about was left,
  No land discern'd behind nor yet before,
  Vpon the right hand or upon the left,
  Because (said he) hereafter never more,
  May any Knight of life and limb be reft
  By thee, or coward vaunt him with the stout,
  Lye there alow untill I fetch thee out.

84

O curst device found out by some foule fend,
  And fram'd below by *Belzebub* in hell,
  Who by thy meane did purpose and intend,
  To ruine all that on the earth do dwell,
  From whence thou camst, I thither thee do send:
  (This said) the peece unto the bottom fell:
  Orlando maketh all the speed he may,
  Himselfe unto *Ebuda* to convay.

85

I say the noble Earle in hast him hide,
  Vnto that cruell Ile to find that wight,
  Whom he more lov'd then all the world beside,
  On whom his thoughts were running day and night
  Nor would he by the way one whit abide,
  Lest of new stay might new occasion light,
  And cause him when he had his purpose mist,
  To cry with late repentance, had I wist.

86

His course he meanes of neither side to bend,
  Nor South nor North, such hast he meanes to make,
  But goes as that blind archer doth him send,
  That deepe with dart of golden head him strake.
  And here a while to leave him I intend,
  Returning to the match of which I spake:
  For you may thinke I lost it in the carriage,
  If you should heare no more newes of the marriage.

87

Great feasts were made in *Holland*, and great sport,
  Because of this new match and copulation;
  But greater shall in *Zeland* by report,
  For which there was great care and preparation:
  Yet would I not you thither should resort,
  Except you knew *Byrenos* inclination,
  For chaunces fell that spoiled all the cheare,
  As in the book ensuing you shall heare.

THE TENTH BOOKE OF
ORLANDO FVRIOSO

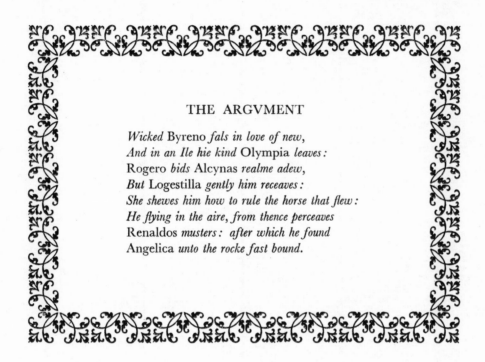

THE ARGVMENT

Wicked Byreno *fals in love of new,*
And in an Ile hie kind Olympia *leaves:*
Rogero *bids* Alcynas *realme adew,*
But Logestilla *gently him receaves:*
She shewes him how to rule the horse that flew:
He flying in the aire, from thence perceaves
Renaldos *musters: after which he found*
Angelica *unto the rocke fast bound.*

ORLANDO FVRIOSO
THE TENTH BOOKE

1

Among the mirrors rare of loyall love,
  That present are, or have bin in time past,
  Whose faith no force of fortune could remove
  With fauning cheare, nor yet with frowning blast:
  Olympia faire all others farre above,
  By just desert requireth to be plast:
  Whose stedfast love (to say I dare be bold)
  Doth passe the paterns of the new or old.

2

How could she signes more evident impart,
  Vnto *Byreno* of her loving mind?
  No, though she should have open laid her hart,
  Yet could she not have prov'd her selfe more kind:
  And if such love and duty, by desart
  May looke of due like love again to find,
  Her faith requires unto *Byreno* showne,
  That he should seeke her safety as his owne.

3

Nor onely not to leave her in annoy,
  Or her reject for any other dame,
  No not for her that bred the bane of Troy,
  Or any other of more worthy name,
  But her preferre before all worldly joy,
  Before his sences five, before his fame,
  Or any other thing of greater price,
  To be exprest by word or by device.

4

Now if *Byreno* did her well requite,
  If that he shew'd to her the like good will,
  If he regarded as he ought of right,
  To bend unto her liking all his skill,
  Nay if forgetting all her merits quite,
  Vngrate, unkind, he sought her life to spill:
  Behold I shall a tale to you recite,
  Would make a man his lip for anger bite.

5

And when that I shall have declared plaine,
  His cruelty, her loves unkind reward,
  I thinke you Ladies never will againe
  Beleeve mens words, your hearts will wax so hard;
  For lovers loved Ladies loves to gaine,
  Do promise, vow and sweare without regard,
  That God doth see and know their falshood still,
  And can and shall revenge it at his will.

6

Their othes but words, their words are all but wind,
  Vtter'd in hast, and with like hast forgotten,
  With which their faiths they do as firmely bind,
  As bundels are trust up with cords all rotten:
  Coynesse is naught, but worse to be too kind,
  Men care not for the good that soone is gotten:
  But women of their wits may justly bost,
  That are made wiser by an others cost.

7

Wherefore I wish you lovely dames beware,
  These beardlesse youths, whose faces shine so neate,
  Whose fancies soone like strawe fire kindled are,
  And sooner quencht amid their flaming heate:
  The hunter chaseth still the flying hare,
  By hill, by dale, with labour and with sweate,
  But when at last the wished prey is taken,
  They seeke new game, the old is quite forsaken.

8

Even so these youths, the while you say them nay,
  In humble sort they seeke, they sue, they serve,
  They like, they love, they honor, and obay,
  They wait, they watch your favours to deserve:
  A part they plaine, in presence of they pray,
  For love of you they mourne, they pine and starve:
  But having got that erst they sought so sore,
  They turne their sailes unto another shore.

9

Though this be true, I not perswade you tho,
  To leave to love, for that were open wrong,
  To cause you like a vine undrest to grow,
  Vncared for the briers and thornes among:
  But least on youths you should your selves bestow,
  That never in one fancy tarry long:
  The meane is best, young fruits the stomach gripe,
  The elder cloy when they be over ripe.

10

I shew'd you in the tale I told you last,
  How that *Byreno* had *Cymoscos* daughter,
  To marry whom a motion late was past,
  Because his brother lov'd and greatly sought her,
  But his owne mouth was of too lickrish tast,
  To leave so sweet a morsell, having caught her:
  He thought it were a point of foolish kindnesse,
  To part withall, a peece of so rare finenesse.

11

The damsell little passed fourteene yeare,
  Most tender, sweet and lovely, fresh and faire,
  As when the budding rose doth first appeare,
  When sunny beames in May make temperate aire,
  Byreno likes her face, her sober cheare,
  And us'd to her to make so oft repaire,
  That ev'n as Brimstone quickly taketh flame,
  So love tooke him to his perpetuall shame.

12

The streame of teares that for her sire she shed,
  A flaming fornace bred within his brest,
  The plaints she made, and dolefull words she sed,
  Doth breed his hope of getting his request,
  Thus foule desires with hopes as foule are fed,
  As water hote from boiling straight doth rest,
  When liquor cold is powred in the pot,
  So with new love his old was quite forgot.

13

From flow to ebbe thus turned was the tide,
  His late belov'd *Olympia* lothsome grew,
  To looke on her his heart could scant abide,
  His thoughts were all so setled on the new,
  Yet still the time might serve he thinks to hide,
  His filthy hate with faire and painted hew,
  And though in fancy he did her detest,
  Yet still great kindnesse he in shew profest.

14

And if he shew'd the other signes of love,
  (Although such love was worse then any hate)
  Yet none there was herein did him reprove,
  But tooke his meaning in another rate,
  They thought som good remorse his mind did move,
  In gracious sort to pity her estate,
  And that to her he charitably ment,
  Because she was so yong and innocent.

15

O mighty God, how much are men mistane?
  How oft with fained shewes they are deceaved?
  Byrenos wicked meaning and prophane,
  For good and godly was of men receaved:
  The marriners their oares in hand had tane,
  And from the shore the ship was quickly heaved,
  To *Zeland* ward the Duke with all his traine,
  With helpe of oares and sailes doth passe amaine.

16

Now had they lost the sight of *Holland* shore,
  And marcht with gentle gale in comely ranke,
  And (for the wind was westerly) they bore
  To come within the lue of *Scottish* banke,
  When as a sodain tempest rose so sore,
  The force thereof their ships had well nie sanke,
  Three dayes they bare it out, the fourth at night
  A barren Iland hapned in their sight.

17

Here faire *Olympia* from her ship to sand,
  From sands she passeth to the higher ground,
  Byreno kindly led her by the hand,
  (Although his heart another harbour found)
  They sup in their pavillion pitcht on land,
  Environ'd with a tent about them round:
  The supper done, to bed do go they twaine,
  The rest unto their ships returne againe.

18

The travell great she lately did endure,
  And had three dayes before her waking kept,
  And being now upon the shore secure,
  (Now glad of that for which ere long she wept)
  And taking her amid his armes secure,
  All this did cause that she the sounder slept,
  (Ah silly soule) when she was least afraid,
  Of her false husband thus to be betraid.

19

The trecherous *Byreno*, whom deceit
  And thought of leud intent doth waking keepe,
  Now having time for which he long did wait,
  Supposing faire *Olympia* sound asleepe,
  Vnto his ships he hies with short retrait,
  And makes them all lanch forth into the deepe:
  And thus with wicked practise and unjust,
  He her forsooke that chiefly him did trust.

20

Now were the sailes well charged with the wind,
  And beare him lighter then the wind away,
  The poore *Olympia* now was left behind,
  Who never waked till that breake of day,
  To lightsomnesse had chang'd the darknesse blind,
  And sunny beames had driv'n the mist away,
  She stretcht her armes betwixt asleep and wake,
  And thinks *Byreno* in her armes to take.

21

She findeth none, and drawing back againe,
  Again she reacht them out, but findeth none,
  Her leg likewise she reached out in vaine,
  In vaine, for he for whom she feeles is gone,
  Feare sleep expels, her eies she opens plaine,
  Nor yet she heares, she sees, nor feeles not one,
  With which amaz'd, the clothes away she cast,
  And to the shore she runneth in great hast.

22

With heart dismaid, and seeing her before
  Her fatall hap, unto the sea she hies,
  She smote her brest, her haire she rent and tore,
  Now looking (for all lightsome were the skies)
  If ought she could discerne, but even the shore,
  But even the shore, no other thing she spies:
  Then once or twise she cald *Byrenos* name,
  Then once or twise the caves resound the same.

23

And boldly then she mounted on the rocks.
  All rough and steepe, such courage sorrow brought,
  Her wofull words might move the stones and stocks,
  But when she saw, or at the least she thought,
  She saw the ships, her guiltlesse brest she knocks,
  By signes and cries to bring them backe she sought,
  But signes and cries but little now availes,
  That wind bare them away that fild their sailes.

24

What meanest thou (thus poore *Olympia* spake)
  So cruelly without me to depart?
  Bend back thy course, and cease such speed to make,
  Thy vessel of her lading lackes a part:
  It little is the carkas poore to take,
  Since that it doth already beare the hart:
  Thus having by the shore ende long in vaine,
  Vnto the tent she backe returnes againe.

25

And lying groveling on her restlesse bed,
  Moistning the same with water of her eies,
  Sith two on thee did couch last night (she sed)
  Why did not two from thee together rise?
  Accurst the wombe that false *Byreno* bred,
  Accurst the day that first I saw the skies.
  What shall I do? what can I here alone,
  Or who (wo me) can mitigate my mone?

26

I see no man, nor any signe I see,
  That any man within this Ile doth dwell:
  I see no ship that hence may carry me,
  With (at the least) some hope of being well:
  I here shall starve, it cannot other be,
  And buried how to be I cannot tell;
  Ah how if wolves that wander in this wood,
  Devoure my flesh, or drinke my guiltlesse blood?

27

Alas I doubt, and stand ev'n now in feare,
  Lest that some rav'nous wolfe that here abides,
  Some Lion, Tyger, or some vgly Beare,
  With teeth and clawes shall pierce my tender sides,
  Yet what beast could with greater torment teare,
  Then thou more fierce then any beast besides?
  For they contented are but once to kill,
  But thou my life a thousand times dost spill.

28

But presuppose some vessell here arrive,
  And take me from this place for pittie sake,
  And so perchance I may be left alive,
  The Beares nor Lions never shall me take,
  Yet will it be in vaine for me to strive,
  Againe to *Holland* my repaire to make:
  Thou keep'st by force the place where I was borne,
  Whence by deceit thou broughts me (false forsworn)

29

Thou took'st from me my living, by pretence
  And colour of thy friendship and alliance,
  Thy men of armes were paid by my expence,
  I gave thee all, such was my fond affiance:
  Or shall I turne to *Flanders?* sith from thence
  I sold my selfe, and am at flat defiance
  With all the nation, whom to set thee free
  I quite forsooke, that now ah wo is me?

30

Is there for me in *Friseland* any place?
  Where I refus'd for thee to be a Queene,
  The which refusall ruin'd all my race,
  As by the sequell was too plainly seene?
  O cruell hap, ô strange and monstrous case,
  The righteous God judge thee and me betweene.
  Was ever Tyger carried heart so hard,
  For so firme love to pay so foule reward?

31

But what and if some pyrat wanting feare
  Of God and man, shall take me as a slave?
  Thou God forbid, let Tyger, Wolfe and Beare,
  First carry me a prey into their cave,
  And there my flesh in peeces all to teare,
  That dying, I my chastitie may save.
  This said, her raging griefe her hands addresses,
  To offer force unto her golden tresses.

32

And even as *Hecuba* fell raging mad,
  With griefe of mind and sorrow sore oppressed,
  To see her *Polydorus* little lad,
  By kinsmans fraud and crueltie distressed:
  So rav'd *Olympia* faire, as though she had
  With twentie thousand divels bene possessed:
  At last she sitteth on the rocks alone,
  And seemes as senslesse as the senslesse stone.

33

And in this state I meane to let her stay,
  Till of *Rogero* I have talkt a while,
  Who travel'd in the hot and sandy way,
  Full many weary and unpleasant mile:
  And now it was the middle of the day,
  When as upon the South side of the Ile,
  He saw three Ladies neere a little towre,
  Did sport themselves within a pleasant bowre.

34

These Ladies faire were of *Alcynas* crew,
  And there refresht themselves a little space,
  They had great store of wines both old and new,
  And sundry kind of junkets in like case:
  A pretty barke there lay within their vew,
  That did attend their pleasures in the place,
  And wait when any little gale should blow,
  (For now was none) that they might homeward go.

35

Then one of these that had espide the Knight,
  At such a time, and in such way to ride,
  With courteous speech invites him to alight:
  The second brings him wine on th'other side,
  And makes him farre more thirstie with the sight,
  But these enticements could not cause him bide,
  He feares *Alcyna* prisner so might take him,
  If by this stay she hapt to overtake him.

36

Even as salt peeter mixt with brimstone pure,
  Inflameth straight when once it feeles the fire,
  Or as the sea with winds and aire obscure,
  Doth worke and swell, and ever riseth hier;
  So they that saw their words could not allure,
  His noble mind to follow their desier,
  Tooke high disdaine that they were so contemned,
  And him of great discourtesie condemned.

37

And straight the third as in a raging mood
  Said thus, O creature void of all gentilitie,
  And borne (no doubt) of base unworthy blood,
  And bred where never used was civilitie,
  Ay during life fro thee depart all good,
  Nor maist thou die in quiet and tranquillitie,
  But burned maist thou be, or cut in quarters,
  Or driven to hang thy selfe in thine owne garters.

38

With these and many bitter speeches mo,
  They raile on him, and then they take their barke,
  And coast along upon the Southerne shore,
  That they his passage and his course might marke.
  But he that now was gotten farre before,
  Did little to their threats or curses harke:
  And notwithstanding all that they contrived,
  Yet to his ship in safetie he arrived.

39

The Pilot doth *Rogero* much commend,
  That from *Alcyna* so himselfe did save,
  And as a wise and well experienc'd frend,
  Sound counsell and good precepts him he gave,
  And wisht that he his time would better spend,
  And leave fond toyes, embracing wisedome grave,
  And from the good the evill to discerne,
  As *Logestilla* used men to learne.

40

There is the food that fils and never cloyeth,
  There is the love, the beauty and the grace,
  That maketh him most blest that them enjoyeth,
  To which compar'd, all other joyes are base:
  There hope, nor feare, nor care the mind annoyeth,
  Respect of persons, nor regard of place:
  The mind still finding perfit contentation,
  That rests it selfe in vertuous contemplation.

41

There are (said he) some better lessons taught,
  Then dancings, dallyings, or daintie diet,
  There shal you learne to frame your mind & thought
  From will to wit, to temperance from riet:
  There is the path by which you may be brought
  Into the perfect paradise of quiet.
  This tale the Pilot to *Rogero* told,
  And all the while their course they forward hold.

42

But lo, they see a navie under saile,
  Of ships that toward them in hast did bend,
  Alcyna wrathfull striving tooth and naile,
  Doth thinke to fetch againe her fleeting frend:
  But all her diligence could not availe,
  Rogero to returne doth not intend,
  And of her forces he was not afraid,
  Because that *Logestilla* sent him aid.

43

For straight a watchman standing in a towre,
  So high that all the hils and shore was under,
  Did ring the larum bell that present houre,
  He saw her fleet, though distant farre asunder:
  And when that now approched was their powre,
  With cannon shot they made them such a thunder,
  That though *Alcyna* threatned much and braved,
  Yet was *Rogero* from her malice saved.

44

Then at his first arrivall to the shore,
  Foure damsels met him sent by *Logestilla*,
  Andronica that wisely sees before,
  And *Fronesis* the just, and chast *Drusilla*,
  And she that boldly fights for vertues lore,
  Descending from the Romane race *Camilla*:
  And straight rusht out of men a worthy band,
  Ay prest to meet their foes on sea and land.

45

Within a large and very quiet bay,
  A navie was of vessels big and tall,
  That readie at an howers warning lay,
  To go to fight at any little call.
  And now there was begun a great affray,
  By land and sea the conflict was not small,
  Which did the realme in hurly burly set,
  Alcyna late did from her sister get.

46

This strange to see of wars the strange successe,
  She that of late was counted of such might,
  Is now so driv'n in danger and distresse,
  That scant she could preserve her selfe by flight.
  Rogeros parting brought her griefe no lesse,
  Then did the foile, which both bred such despite,
  And such despaire, to die she had intended,
  (If so she might) to have her torments ended.

47

And as her selfe the dame of *Carthage* kild,
  When as the *Troyan* Duke did her forsake:
Or as her blood the Queene of *Ægypt* spild,
  For that so famous *Romane* captaines sake:
Even so *Alcyna* with like sorrowes fild,
  Wisht of her selfe with like death end to make,
But (either auncient folke beleev'd a lie,
Or this is true) a fairy cannot die.

48

But leave we now *Alcyna* in this paine,
  That from her elder sister fled apace,
And to *Rogero* let us turne againe,
  That was conducted to a better place,
Where finding now that he did safe remaine,
  He thanked God that gave him so much grace,
To see his foes of forces all deprived,
Himselfe within the castle safe arrived.

49

And such a castle that in stately show
  And costly substance others all surmounted,
The value of the wals can no man know,
  Except he first upon the same had mounted:
Men have not jewels of such price below,
  For Di'monds are to these but drosse accounted,
And Pearles but pelfe, and Rubies all are rotten,
Where stones of such rare vertue can be gotten.

50

These wals are built of stones of so great price,
  All other unto these come farre behind:
In these men see the vertue and the vice,
  That cleaveth to the inward foule and mind.
Who looks in such a glasse, may grow so wise,
  As neither flattering praises shall him blind
With tickling words nor undeserved blame,
With forged faults shall worke him any shame.

51

From hence doth come the everlasting light,
  That may with *Phœbus* beames so cleare compare,
That when the Sunne is downe there is no night,
  With those that of these jewels stored are:
These gems do teach us to discerne aright,
  These gems are wrought with workmanship so rare,
That hard it were to make true estimation,
Which is more worth the substance or the fashion.

52

On arches rais'd of prophiry passing hie,
  So hie that to ascend them seem'd a paine,
Were gardens faire and pleasant to the eie,
  Few found so faire below upon a plaine:
Sweet smelling trees in order standing by,
  With fountaines watring them in steed of raine,
Which do the same so naturally nourish,
As all the yeare both flowres and fruites do flourish.

53

No weeds or fruitlesse trees are in this place,
  But herbs whose vertues are of highest price,
As soveraigne sage, and thrift, and herbe of grace,
  And time, which well bestowed maketh wise,
And lowly patience, proud thoughts to abase,
  And hearts ease, that can never grow with vice.
These are the herbs that in this garden grew,
Whose vertues do their beauties still renew.

54

The Ladie of the castle greatly joyed,
  To see the safe arrivall of this Knight,
And all her care and travell she employed,
  That honor might be done him in her sight.
Astolfo (in his passage lesse annoyed)
  Doth take in his acquaintance great delight,
And all the other his good favour sought,
That by *Melyssa* to themselves were brought.

55

Now having all themselves some dayes reposed
  In *Logestillas* house, and taken rest,
And finding all themselves right well disposed,
  To make returne againe into the West,
The good *Melyssa* for them all proposed,
  Vnto the mighty Ladie this request,
That by her leave without incurring blame,
They might returne them all from whence they came.

56

To whom dame *Logestilla* thus replide,
  That after they a day or two had staid,
She would for them most carefully provide,
  For all their journey furniture and aid:
And first she taught *Rogero* how to ride
  The flying horse (of whom he was afraide)
To make him pace or passe a full careere,
As readily as other horses here.

57

When all was ready now for him to part,
  Rogero bids this worthy dame farewell,
Whom all his life time after from his hart
  He highly honored and loved well.
First I will shew how well he playd his part,
  Then of the *English* Duke I meane to tell,
How in more time, and with far greater paine,
He did returne to *Charles* his court againe.

58

Rogero mounted on the winged steed,
  Which he had learn'd obedient now to make,
Doth deeme it were a brave and noble deed,
  About the world his voyage home to take.
Forthwith beginneth Eastward to proceed,
  And though the thing were much to undertake,
Yet hope of praise makes men no travell shunne,
To say another day, we this have done.

59

And leaving first the *Indian* river *Tana*,
    He guides his journey to the great *Catay*,
    From thence he passeth unto *Mangiana*,
    And came within the sight of huge *Quinsay*:
    Vpon the right hand leaving *Sericana*,
    And turning from the *Scythians* away,
    Where *Asia* from *Europa* first doth draw,
    Pomeria, *Russia*, *Prutina* he saw.

60

His horse that hath the use of wings and feet,
    Did helpe with greater haste home to retire,
    And tho with speed to turne he thought it meet,
    Because his *Bradamant* did so desire,
    Yet having now of travell felt the sweet,
    (Most sweet to those to knowledge that aspire)
    When *Germany* and *Hungry* he had past,
    He meanes to visit *England* at the last.

61

Where in a medow on a morning faire,
    Fast by the *Tems* at *London* he did light,
    Delighted with the water and the aire,
    And that faire citie standing in his sight,
    When straight he saw that souldiers did repaire,
    To muster there, and asking of a Knight,
    That in the medow he had met by chance,
    He understood that they were bound for *France*.

62

These be the succors (thus the Knight him told)
    Renaldo sude for at his comming hither,
    With *Irish* men and *Scots* of courage bold,
    To joyne in hearts and hands and purse together.
    The muster's tane and each mans name enrold,
    Their onely stay is but for wind and wether,
    But as they passe I meane to you to shew them,
    Their names and armes, that you may better know
                                                    (them.

63

You see the standerd, that so great doth show,
    That joynes the *Leopard* and the *Flouredeluce*,
    That chiefest is, the rest do come below,
    And rev'rence this according to our use:
    Duke *Leonell* Lord generall doth it ow,
    A famous man in time of warre and truce,
    And nephew deare unto the King my master,
    Who gave to him the Dukedome of *Lancaster*.

64

This banner that stands next unto the Kings,
    With glittering shew that shakes the rest among,
    And beares in azure field three argent wings,
    To *Richard* Earle of *Warwicke* doth belong,
    This man the Duke of *Glosters* banner brings,
    Actæons head, except my guesse be wrong,
    The fierbrand the Duke of *Clarence* is,
    The tree the Duke of *Yorke* doth claime for his.

65

The launce into three sundry peeces rent,
    Belongs unto the worthy Duke of *Norfolke*:
    The lightning longs unto the Earle of *Kent*,
    The Griphin longs unto the Earle of *Pembroke*:
    The ballance ev'n by which just doome is ment,
    Belongs unto the noble Duke of *Suffolke*.
    The Dragon to the valiant Earle of *Cumberland*,
    The garland is the brave Earls of *Northumberland*.

66

The Earle of *Arundell* a ship halfe drown'd,
    The Marquesse *Barkly* gives an argent hill:
    The gallant Earle of *Essex* hath the hound,
    The bay tree *Darby* that doth flourish still:
    The wheele hath *Dorset* ever running round,
    The Earle of *March* his banner all doth fill
    With Cædar trees: the Duke of *Somerset*
    A broken chaire doth in his ensigne set.

67

The Faulcon hovering upon her nest,
    The Earle of *Dev'nshire* doth in banner beare,
    And brings a sturdy crew from out the West.
    The Earle of *Oxenford* doth give the Beare:
    The banner all with blacke and yellow drest,
    Belongs unto the Earle of *Winchester*.
    He that the cristall crosse in banner hath,
    Is sent from the rich Bishop of the *Bath*.

68

The archers on horse, with other armed men,
    Are two and fortie thousand more or lesse,
    The other footmens number doubles them,
    Or wants thereof but little as I guesse:
    The banners shew their captains noble stem,
    A crosse, a wreath, an azure bar, a fesse,
    Geffray and *Ermant*, *Edward* bold and *Harry*,
    Vnder their guide the footmen all do carry.

69

The Duke of *Buckingham* that first appeares,
    The next to him the Earle of *Salsbury*:
    Burgany next, a man well stricke in yeares,
    And *Edward* next the Earle of *Shrewsbury*.
    Now turne about, and lo the *Scottish* peares,
    Brave men, and well appointed you shall see,
    Where *Zerbin* sonne unto the *Scottish* King,
    Vnto the field doth thirtie thousand bring.

70

All chosen men from many a shire and towne,
    All ready to resist, assaile, invade,
    Their standerd is the beast of most renowne,
    That in his paw doth hold a glittering blade,
    This is the heire apparant to the crowne,
    This is the goodly impe whom nature made,
    To show her chiefest workmanship and skill,
    And after brake the mould against her will.

71

The Earle of *Otton* commeth after him,
  That in his banner beares the golden barre:
  The spotted Leopard that looks so grim,
  That is the ensigne of the Duke of *Marre*.
  Not far from him there commeth *Alcubrin*,
  A man of mighty strength and fierce in warre,
  No Duke, nor Earle, nor Marquesse as men say,
  But of the savages he beares the sway.

72

The Duke of *Trafford* beares in ensigne bright,
  The bird whose yong ones stare in *Phœbus* face:
  Lurcanio Lord of *Angus*, valiant Knight,
  Doth give a Bull, whom two dogs hold in chase;
  The Duke of *Albanie* gives blue and white,
  (Since he obtained faire *Geneuras* grace)
  Earle *Bohune* in his stately banner beares
  A Vulture that with clawes a Dragon teares.

73

Their horsemen are with jacks for most part clad,
  Their horses are both swift of course and strong,
  They run on horseback with a slender gad,
  And like a speare, but that it is more long:
  Their people are of warre then peace more glad,
  More apt to offer then to suffer wrong:
  These are the succors out of *Scotland* sent,
  That with the noble Prince *Zerbino* went.

74

Then come the *Irish* men of valiant harts,
  And active limbs, in personages tall,
  They naked use to go in many parts,
  But with a mantle yet they cover all:
  Short swords they use to carry and long darts,
  To fight both neare and farre aloofe withall,
  And of these bands the Lords and leaders are,
  The noble Earles of *Ormond* and *Kildare*.

75

Some sixteene thousand men or thereabout,
  Out of the Irish Ile at this time went,
  Beside the other Ilands thereabout,
  Sweveland and Island other succors sent;
  To good King *Charles*, for why they stood in doubt,
  If he were conquer'd they should all repent,
  And still their numbers daily did increase,
  Of those that better like of warre then peace.

76

Now while *Rogero* learnes the armes and name
  Of every *Brittish* Lord, behold a rout
  Of citizens and folke of all sorts came,
  Some with delight, and some with dread and doubt,
  To see a beast so strange, so strong, so tame,
  And wondring much, they compast him about:
  They thought it was a strange and monstrous thing,
  To see a horse that had a *Griffons* wing.

77

Wherefore to make the people marvell more,
  And as it were to sport himselfe and play,
  He spur'd his beast, who straight aloft did soare,
  And bare his master Westward quite away:
  And straight he was beyond our *English* shore,
  And meanes to passe the *Irish* seas that day,
  Saint *George* his channell in a little while,
  He past, and after saw the *Irish* Ile.

78

Where men do tell strange tales, that long ago
  Saint *Patrick* built a solitary cave,
  Into the which they that devoutly go,
  By purging of their sins their soules may save:
  Now whether this report be true or no,
  I not affirme, and yet I not deprave.
  But crossing from hence to Island ward he found
  Angelica unto the rock fast bound.

79

Both nak'd and bound at this same Ile of wo,
  For Ile of wo it may be justly called,
  Where peerlesse peeces are abused so,
  By monster vile to be devour'd and thralled,
  Where pyrats still by land and sea do go,
  Assaulting forts that are but weakly walled:
  And whom they take by flattry or by force,
  They give a monster quite without remorse.

80

I did declare not many books before,
  If you the same in memory do keepe,
  How certaine pyrats tooke her at a shore,
  Where that chast Hermit lay by her asleepe,
  And how at last for want of other store,
  Although their hearts did melt, and eies did weepe,
  Moov'd with a helplesse and a vaine compassion,
  Perforce they bound her on this wofull fashion.

81

And thus the caitives left her all forlorne,
  With nothing but the rocks and seas in sight,
  As naked as of nature she was borne,
  And void of succour, and all comfort quite.
  No vaile of lawne as then by her was worne,
  To shade the damask rose and lillies white,
  Whose colours were so mixt in every member,
  Like fragrant both in Iuly and December.

82

Rogero at the first had surely thought,
  She was some image made of alabaster,
  Or of white marble curiously wrought,
  To shew the skilfull hand of some great master.
  But vewing neerer he was quickly taught,
  She had some parts that were not made of plaster:
  Both that her eies did shed such wofull teares,
  And that the wind did wave her golden heares.

83

To see her bound to heare her mourne and plaine,
  Not onely made that he his journey staid,
  But caus'd that he from teares could scant abstaine,
  Both love and pity so his heart assail'd,
  At last with words to mitigate her paine,
  Thus much to her in louing sort he said,
  O Lady worthy onely of those bands,
  Wherewith love binds the hearts and not the hands.

84

And farre unfit for these or any such,
  what wight was found so cruell and unkind,
  To banish all humanity so much,
  Those polisht Ivory hands in chaines to bind,
  About that corps whom none can worthely tuch
  With hurtfull hands, unworthy bands to wind?
  This said, she blusht, seeing those parts were spide,
  The which (though faire) yet nature strives to hide.

85

Faine would she with her hand have hid her eyes,
  But that her hands were bound unto the stone,
  Which made her oft to breake to wofull cries,
  (Sole remedy where remedy is none)
  At last with sobbing voice she doth devise
  To tell the Knight the cause of all her mone:
  But from the sea a sodaine noise was heard,
  That this her speech and all the matter mard.

86

Behold there now appear'd the monster great,
  Halfe underneath and halfe above the wave,
  As when a ship with wind and weather beat,
  Doth hasten to the hav'n it selfe to save:
  So doth the monster hast, in hope to eate
  The dainty morsell he was wont to have:
  Which sight so sore the damsell did appall,
  Rogero could not comfort her at all.

87

Yet with his speare in hand, though not in rest,
  The ugly *Orke* upon the brow he strake,
  (I call him *Orke*, because I know no beast,
  Nor fish from whence comparison to take)
  His head and teeth were like a bore, the rest
  A masse, of which I know not what to make,
  He gave him on the brow a mighty knocke,
  But pierst no more then if it were a rocke.

88

And finding that his blow so small hurt brings,
  He turnes again on fresh him to assay,
  The *Orke* that saw the shadow of great wings,
  Vpon the water up and down to play,
  With fury great and rage away he flings,
  And on the shore doth leave the certaine pray,
  The shadow vaine he up and downe doth chase,
  The while *Rogero* layth him on apace.

89

Even as an Eagle that espies from hie,
  Among the herbs a party colour'd snake,
  Or on a bank sunning her selfe to lie,
  To cast the elder skin, a new to make,
  Lies hovering warily till she may spie
  A vantage sure the venom'd worme to take,
  Then takes him by the back, and beates her wings,
  Mauger the poison of his forked stings.

90

So doth *Rogero* both with sword and speare,
  The cruell monster warily assaile,
  Not where he fenced is with grizly heare,
  So hard as that no weapon could prevaile,
  But sometime pricks him neere unto his eare,
  Sometime his sides, sometimes his ugly taile:
  But nature had with such strong fences arm'd him,
  As all his blowes but small or nothing harm'd him.

91

So have I seene ere this a silly flie,
  With mastive dog in sommers heate to play,
  Sometime to sting him in his nose or eie,
  Sometime about his grizly jawes to stay,
  And buzzing round about his eares to flie,
  He snaps in vaine, for still she whips away,
  And oft so long she dallies in this sort,
  Till one snap comes and marreth all her sport.

92

But now *Rogero* doth this sleight devise,
  Sith that by force he cannot make him yeeld,
  He meanes to dazle both the monsters eyes,
  By hidden force of his enchanted sheeld.
  And being thus resolv'd to land he flies,
  And from all harme the Lady faire to sheeld,
  He puts the precious Ring upon her hand,
  Whose vertue was enchantments to withstand.

93

That ring that worthy *Bradamant* him sent,
  When she from false *Brunello* had it tane,
  With which *Melyssa* into *India* went,
  And wrought his freedome, and *Alcynas* bane,
  That ring he lends the damsell, with intent
  To save her eyes by vertue of the same,
  Then takes he forth the shield, whose light so dazed
  The lookers on, they fall down all amazed.

94

The monster now approaching to the shore,
  Amaz'd at this, resistance none did make,
  Rogero hewes upon him more and more,
  But his hard scales no harme thereby did take.
  Oh sir (saith she) unloosen me before
  Out of this maze the monster do awake,
  And let your sword slay me this present houre,
  So as this monster may not me devoure.

95

These wofull words mov'd so *Rogeros* mind,
  That straight he did unloose the Lady faire,
  And caus'd her by and by to get behind
  Vpon his horse, then mounting in the aire,
  He leaves his *Spanish* journey first assign'd,
  And unto little *Brittain* doth repaire,
  But by the way be sure he did not misse,
  To give her many a sweet and friendly kisse.

96

And having found a solitary place,
  A pleasant grove well water'd with a spring,
  Which never herd nor herdman did deface,
  Where *Philomela* used still to sing,
  Here he alights, minding to stay a space,
  And hither he the Lady faire did bring,
  But sure it seem'd he made his full account,
  Ere long upon a better beast to mount.

97

His armour made him yet a while to bide,
  Which forced stay a more desire did breed,
  But now in him it was most truly tride,
  Oft times the greater hast, the worse the speed,
  He knits with hast two knots, while one untide.
  But soft'tis best no furder to proceed,
  I now cut off abruptly here my rime,
  And keepe my tale unto another time.

THE ELEVENTH BOOKE OF
ORLANDO FVRIOSO

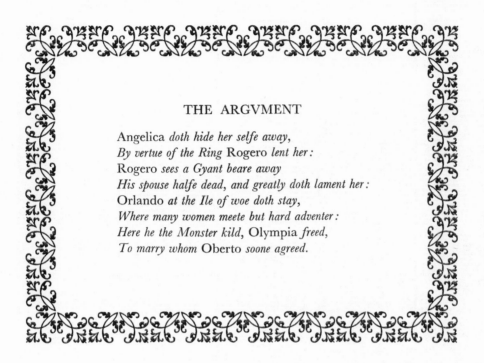

THE ARGVMENT

Angelica *doth hide her selfe away,*
By vertue of the Ring Rogero *lent her:*
Rogero *sees a Gyant beare away*
His spouse halfe dead, and greatly doth lament her:
Orlando *at the Ile of woe doth stay,*
Where many women meete but hard adventer:
Here he the Monster kild, Olympia *freed,*
To marry whom Oberto *soone agreed.*

ORLANDO FVRIOSO
THE ELEVENTH BOOKE

1

The gallant courser in his full carriere,
  Is made by man, to stop with slender raine:
But man himselfe his lust and fond desire,
Is seldome drawne by reason to refraine:
'Tis hard to stop, but harder to retire,
When youthfull course ensueth pleasure vaine,
As Bears do breake the hives and weake defences,
When smell of hony commeth to their sences.

2

No marvell if *Rogero* could not hold,
  But that he would now take a little sport,
That naked did *Angelica* behold,
Within a grove alone from all resort:
His love to *Bradamant* now waxeth cold,
Or at the least is temper'd in such sort,
He meanes therewith at this time to dispence,
And not to let this go a maiden hence.

3

Whose beauty was so rare as well it might
  Have made *Zenocrates* an Epicure,
No marvell then if this same gentle Knight,
Could not so great temptation well endure:
But while he hasten'd to his hop't delight,
Of which he thought him in possession sure,
There fell a strange and unexpected thing,
By meanes *Angelica* did know the ring.

4

This was the ring that she with her had brought
  To *France*, the very first time she was there,
What time by aid thereof so well she wrought,
She holp her brother to th'inchanted speare,
By vertue of this ring she set at nought
Those magike arts, that men so greatly feare:
With this *Orlando* County Palladine,
She did release from wicked *Dragontine*,

5

By helpe of this invisible she went,
  Out of the towre where *Atlant* had her set:
For this same Ring *Brunello* false was sent
By *Agramant*, who long'd the same to get.
To tell that story is not my intent,
For feare it might my other matter let,
But certaine tis, that when this Ring was lost,
In fortunes waves she had been ever tost.

6

Now when she saw this Ring was on her hand,
  She was so strooke with marvell and with joy,
That scarce she could discerne and understand,
If she were wake or if she dream'd some toy;
But to make tryall how the case doth stand,
And know if she this treasure doth enjoy,
Into her mouth the Ring she doth convay,
And straight invisible she goeth away.

7

Rogero that each minute thought an howre,
  (His armour off, and ready for the play)
Expecting now the damsell in a bowre,
Where he had pointed her for him to stay,
Found all too late, that by the Rings strange power,
She had unseene convai'd her selfe away.
He lent it her to save her eyes from blindnesse,
And for reward she quits him with unkindnesse.

8

With which her act displeas'd and ill apaid,
  He curst himselfe, and chafed in his mind:
O cruell and unthankfull wench (he said)
Is this the love that I deserv'd to find?
Dost thou reward him thus that brought thee aid?
To thy preserver art thou so unkind?
Take ring and shield, and flying horse and me,
This onely barre me not thy face to see.

9

This said, he go'th about where she had beene,
  Still groping as the weather had bin darke,
Embracing of the aire his armes betweene,
In steed of her, then heedfull he doth harke,
To find her by the sound that was not seene,
And whence the same doth come he wel doth mark.
But on went she untill it was her lote
To come into a silly shepheards cote.

10

And though this fame were far from any towne,
  Yet there she quickly did her selfe provide
Of meate and drinke, and of a simple gowne,
Sufficient for the time her bare to hide,
Not suting for a Ladie of renowne,
That had bin ever clad in pompe and pride,
Had gownes of crimson, purple and carnasion,
Of ev'ry colour, and of ev'ry fashion.

11

But yet no kind of weed so base or ill is,
  Her of her princely beauty to bereave,
They that so much extoll faire *Amarillis*,
  Or *Galate*, do but themselves deceave:
Cease *Tyteras* to praise thy golden *Phillis*,
  Peace *Melebe*, this passes by your leave;
Ye souldiers all that serve in *Cupids* garrison,
May not presume with this to make comparison.

12

Now here the damsell faire a palfrey hired,
  With other things most needfull for her way,
And meanes to her owne home to have retired,
  From whence she had bin absent many a day.
The while *Rogero* now with travell tired,
  Lamenting he had lost so faire a pray,
Doth seeke his horse who had not long bin idle,
But in his masters absence brake his bridle.

13

Which when he found, the raines in peeces torne,
  The horse soar'd far away with mighty wing,
How could such haps with patientnesse be borne,
  Of one great losse to find a greater spring?
He sitteth in a dumpe, like one forlorne,
  For losse of her, his horse, and of his ring,
Whose vertue great did make him much repent it,
But yet much more her vertue that had sent it.

14

And in this rage he puts his armor on,
  And on his shoulder carieth his shield,
Pursuing that first path he lights upon,
  He found it brought him to a goodly field,
One side whereof when he a while had gone,
  It seem'd the wood adjoyn'd some sound did yeeld,
And still the neare and nearer that he goes,
The plainer sound he heard of sturdy bloes.

15

A combat twixt a Giant and a Knight,
  He sees hard by most furiously begunne,
The Giant with a club doth think by might,
  The battell of the tother to have wonne;
The tother with his sword and nimble fight,
  His furious blowes with watchfull eye doth shunne,
Rogero seeing this great inequalitie,
Yet standeth still and shewes no partialitie.

16

But in his mind he wisht the Knight to win,
  When lo the Giant with new fury fed,
To lay on lode with both hands doth begin,
  And with one blow he layes him downe for dead,
And straight in cruell sort he steppeth in,
  For to disarme him, and cut off his head:
But when the Giant had the face disarmed,
Rogero knew the partie he had harmed.

17

He saw it was his *Bradamant* most deare,
  Whom this same Giant would have made to die,
Wherefore with courage stout he steppeth neare,
  The Giant to new combat to defie,
Who either heares him not, or would not heare,
  Or meaneth not a conflict new to trie,
But tooke her up, and on his shoulders layd her,
And so in hast away from thence convay'd her.

18

So have I seene a wolfe to beare away
  A lambe from shepheards fold, so have I seene
An Eagle on a silly Dove to pray,
  And soare aloft the skie and earth betweene:
Rogero hies him after as he may,
  Vntill he came unto a goodly greene,
But th'other ev'ry step so much out stept him,
That in his view *Rogero* scantly kept him.

19

But now a while of him I speake no more,
  And to *Orlando* I returne againe,
Who having lost the sight of Holland shore,
  Did hasten to *Ebuda* with much paine:
I did declare not many books before,
  How he *Cymoscos* engin strange did gaine,
And to the bottome of the sea did throw it,
That none might find it out againe or know it.

20

And though his meaning and intent was so,
  Yet vaine it was, as after was perceived,
For why, that serpent vile our auncient fo,
  That *Eva* first in Paradise deceived,
Not much above two hundred yeares ago,
  (As we from our forefathers have received)
From out the sea by necromancie brought it,
And then in *Almanie* afresh they wrought it.

21

They wrought it both in iron and in brasse,
  The cunning and the art increasing still,
As oft by proofe we find it comes to passe,
  The worse the worke, the greater growes the skill,
And to each kind a name assign'd there was,
  According to the first inventers will,
To tell the names of all were but a trouble,
Some demicanons, some are called double.

22

The Culverings to shoot a bullet farre,
  The Falcon, Saker, Minion and the Sling,
Not armed men, but walled townes to marre,
  Such diu'llish force is in this hellish thing.
Ye souldiers brave, and valiant men of warre,
  Now cease to field your manly darts to bring,
And get a hargubush upon your shoulder,
Or else in vaine you sue to be a souldier.

23

How didst thou find (oh filthy foule invention)
  A harbor safe in any humane hart?
  Thou mak'st a coward get the souldiers pension,
  And souldiers brave thou rob'st of due desart,
  Whole millions have bin slaine, as stories mention,
  Since first devised was this wicked art,
  France, Italy and *England* chiefe may rew it,
  Since first they us'd this art, and first they knew it.

24

The *English* bowmen may go burne their boes,
  And breake their shafts and cut in two the string,
  That weapon now may keepe the corne from croes,
  That did the *French* at *Agincourt* so sting:
  But to that wight I wish a world of woes,
  That did to light device so div'llish bring,
  Let him be giv'n into the hands of Sathan,
  To be tormented ay with *Core* and *Dathan*.

25

Now good *Orlando* though he greatly strived,
  With speed to get him to the Ile of wo,
  Yet first the *Irish* King was there arrived,
  By chance, or else that God would have it so,
  Because it might the better be contrived,
  On wrongfull wights his judgements just to show.
  But when *Ebuda* once in sight appeared,
  Orlando all the company straight cheared.

26

And putting off his armes of colour sable,
  He bids the master out to launch his boate,
  And in the same an anker strong and cable,
  With which he meanes unto this Ile to floate,
  Not doubting (if lucke serve) he will be able,
  To put the anker in the monsters throate,
  And thus alone the noble Knight doth venter,
  Into the Ile *Ebuda* then to enter.

27

Now was the time when as *Aurora* faire,
  Began to shew the world her golden head,
  And looke abroad to take the coole fresh aire,
  Tythono lying still in jealous bed,
  When as *Orlando* hither did repaire,
  By two blind guides, *Cupid* and *Fortune* led,
  When lo unto the shore his shipboate turning,
  He seem'd to heare a noise as one were mourning.

28

At which strange sound casting his eye aside,
  He might discerne a goodly damsell naked,
  With armes abrode unto the rocke fast tide,
  That what with cold and what with terror shaked,
  Eftsoones the hideous monster he espide,
  Whose sight might well have made stout harts have
  Orlandos mind therewith is not amated,   (quaked,
  Nor his high courage any whit abated.

29

He gets betweene the monster and his pray,
  That pray that he so hotly doth pursue,
  And (for before he was resolv'd what way
  He would attempt the monster to subdue)
  Vpon his shoulder doth the anker lay,
  And when he came within his ugly view,
  Even mauger all his malice, might and rancor,
  Into his open jawes he beares the ancor.

30

As they that dig in mine of cole or stone,
  The same in sundry places underprop,
  Lest it should fall when least they thinke thereon,
  And so their breath or else their passage stop:
  So is this anker fastend in the bone,
  Both in the bottome of his mouth and top,
  That though he would againe he could not close it,
  Nor wider open it for to unlose it.

31

Now having gagd his hideous chaps so sure,
  That out and in he can with safetie go,
  He enters with his sword the place obscure,
  And there bestoweth many a thrust and blow,
  And as that citie cannot be secure,
  That hath within her wals receiv'd her so,
  No safer could this *Orke* be now from danger,
  That in his entrals hath receiv'd a stranger.

32

But griped now with pangs of inward paine,
  Sometime he plungeth up unto the skie,
  Sometime he diveth to the deepe againe,
  And makes the troubled sands to mount on hie:
  Orlando feels the sea come in amaine,
  That forced him at last his swimming trie.
  He swims to shore with body strong and able,
  And beares upon his neck the ankers cable.

33

And as a savage Bull that unaware
  About his hornes hath now a cord fast bound,
  Doth strive in vaine to breake the hunters snare,
  And skips and leaps, and flings, and runneth round,
  So though *Orlando* with his strength so rare,
  Assaid to draw him nearer to the ground,
  Yet doth he fetch an hundred frisks and more,
  Ere he could draw him up upon the shore.

34

His wounded bowels shed such store of blood,
  They call that sea the red sea to this howre,
  Sometime he breathed such a sudden flood,
  As made the clearest weather seeme to lowre,
  The hideous noise fild ev'ry cave and wood,
  So that god *Proteus* doubting his owne powre,
  Fled straight fro thence, himselfe in corners hiding,
  Not daring longer here to make abiding.

35

And all the gods that dwell in surging waves,
  With this same tumult grew in such a feare,
  They hid themselves in rocks and hollow caves,
  Lest that *Orlando* should have found them there:
Neptune with triple mace by flight him saves,
  His charret drawne with dolphins doth him beare,
  Nor yet behind *Glaucus* or *Triton* taried,
  For feare in these new broiles to have miscaried.

36

Those Ilanders that all this while attended,
  And saw the monster drawne to land and tane,
  With superstition moved much, condemned
  This godly worke for wicked and profane;
  As though that *Proteus* would be new offended,
  That had before, and now might worke their bane.
  They doubt he wold (thus fools their good haps consters)
  Send to their land his flock of ugly monsters.

37

And therefore *Proteus* anger to appease,
  They meane to drowne *Orlando* if they can,
  Whose deed they deemd his godhead did displease:
  And ev'n as fire doth creepe from bran to bran,
  Vntill the pile of wood it wholy cease,
  So doth this fury grow from man to man,
  That they concluded all upon the matter,
  To throw *Orlando* bound into the water.

38

One takes a sling, another takes a bowe,
  This with a sword is arm'd, he with a speare,
  And some afore, and some behind him go,
  Some neare approch, some stand aloofe for feare:
  He museth much what his ungratefull fo
  Should meane, for benefits such mind to beare:
  And inwardly he was displeas'd and sory,
  To find such wrong where he deserved glory.

39

As little curres that barke at greatest Beare,
  Yet cannot cause him once his way to shunne,
  No more doth he these curlike creatures feare,
  That like a sort of mad men on him runne.
  And (for they saw he did no armor weare)
  They thought the feat would have bin easly done,
  They knew not that his skin from head to foote,
  Was such to strike on it, it was no boote.

40

But when that he his *Durindana* drew,
  He layd therewith about him in such sort,
  That straight their faintnes and his force they knew,
  They found to fight with him it was no sport.
  Thrise ten of them at blowes but ten he slew,
  Their fellowes fled that saw them cut so short,
  Which foes thus foild, *Orlando* now intended
  T'unloose the Ladie whom he had defended.

41

But now this while, behold the *Irish* band
  Arrived neare unto their chiefest citie,
  Who had no sooner set their foote on land,
  But that forthwith they put apart all pittie,
  And slue all sorts that came unto their hand,
  The fierce, the faint, the foolish and the wittie,
  Thus were't just doome, or were it cruell rage,
  They spar'd of neither sexe nor neither age.

42

Thus th'Ile of wo is made a wofull Ile,
  And for the peoples sake they plague the place,
  Orlando sets the Lady free the while,
  That there was bound in that unseemly case,
  To have bin given unto the monster vile:
  And viewing well, he cald to mind her face,
  And that it should *Olympia* be he guessed,
  But twas *Olympia* that had thus bin dressed.

43

Distrest *Olympia* thus unkindly served,
  Whom love and fortune made a double scorne:
  For first of him, of whom she best deserved,
  She was forsaken quite and left forlorne.
  And next by pyrats taken and reserved,
  Of monster vile to be in peeces torne.
  And in this case the good *Orlando* found her,
  And then with great compassion he unbound her.

44

And thus he said, now tell what strange annoy,
  Or evill hap hath hurt thy happy raigne?
  Whom late I left in solace and in joy,
  Why do I find in danger and in paine?
  How is the blisse that thou didst then enjoy,
  So chang'd and turn'd to misery againe?
  And she in wofull manner thus replied,
  When shame her cheeks with crimson first had died.

45

I know not if my chance or else my choice,
  If fortune or my folly be in blame.
  Shall I lament, or shall I now rejoyce,
  That live in wo, and should have dide in shame?
  And as she spake, the teares did stop her voice:
  But when againe unto her selfe she came,
  She told him all the wofull story weeping,
  How false *Byreno* had betraid her sleeping.

46

And how from that same Ile where he betray'd her,
  A crew of cursed pyrats did her take,
  And to this wicked Iland had convay'd her,
  For that same foule and ugly monsters sake,
  Where now it was *Orlandos* hap to ayd her:
  She walked naked when these words she spake.
  Looke how *Diana* painted is in tables,
  Among the rest of *Ovids* pleasant fables.

47

Of whose sharpe doome the Poet there doth tell,
  How she with hornes *Actæon* did invest,
  Because he saw her naked at the well:
  So stands *Olympia* faire, with face and brest,
  And sides, and thighes to be discerned well,
  And legs and feet, but yet she hides the rest.
  And as they two were talking thus together,
  Oberto King of *Irish* Ile came thither.

48

Who being moved at the strange report,
  That one alone the monster should assaile,
  And gag him with an anker in such sort,
  To make his strength, and life, and all to faile,
  Then draw him to the shore as ship to port
  Is tow'd with ropes, without or oares or saile.
  This made him go to find *Orlando* out,
  The while his souldiers spoiled all about.

49

Now when the King this worthy Knight did see,
  Though all with bloud and water foule distain'd,
  Yet straight he guest it should *Orlando* be,
  For in his youth in *France* he had remained,
  And knew the Lords and Knights of best degree,
  In *Charles* his court a page of honor trained:
  Their old acquaintance caus'd at this new meeting,
  They had a loving and a friendly greeting.

50

And then *Orlando* told the *Irish* King,
  How and by whom *Olympia* was abused,
  By one whom out of danger great to bring,
  She had no paine nor death it selfe refused,
  How he himselfe was witnesse of the thing.
  While they thus talke, *Oberto* her perused,
  Whose sorrowes past, renew'd with present feares,
  Did fill her lovely eyes with watry teares.

51

Such colour had her face, as when the Sunne
  Doth shine on watry cloud in pleasant spring,
  And ev'n as when the sommer is begunne,
  The Nightingales in boughes do sit and sing,
  So that blind god, whose force can no man shunne,
  Sits in her eyes, and thence his darts doth fling,
  And bathes his wings in her cleare cristall streames,
  And sunneth them in her rare beauties beames.

52

In these he heates his golden headed dart,
  In those he cooleth it, and temper'd so,
  He levels thence at good *Obertos* hart,
  And to the head he drawth it in his bow.
  Thus is he wounded deepe and feeles no smart,
  His armor cannot fend so fierce a blow:
  For while on her faire eyes and limbs he gaped,
  The arrow came that could not be escaped.

53

And sure *Olympias* beauties were so rare,
  As might well move a man the same to note,
  Her haire, her eyes, her cheeks most amorous are,
  Her nose, her mouth, her shoulders and her throte,
  As for her other parts that then were bare,
  Which she was wont to cover with her cote,
  Were made in such a mould as might have moved
  The chast *Hipolytus* her to have loved.

54

A man would thinke them fram'd by *Phydias* arts,
  Their colour and proportion good was such,
  And unto them her shamefastnesse imparts
  A greater grace to that before was much:
  I cease to praise those other secret parts,
  As not so fit to talke of as to tuch,
  In generall all was as white as milke,
  As smooth as ivory, and as soft as silke.

55

Had she in valley of Idea beene,
  When *Pastor Paris* hap did so befall,
  To be a judge three goddesses betweene,
  She should have got, and they forgone the ball.
  Had she but once of him bene naked seene,
  For *Helena* he had not car'd at all,
  Nor broke the bonds of sacred hospitalitie,
  That bred his country warres and great mortalitie.

56

Had she but then bene in *Crotana* towne,
  When *Zeuxes* for the goddesse *Iunos* sake,
  To paint a picture of most rare renowne,
  Did many of the fairest damsels make
  To stand before him bare from foote to crowne,
  A patterne of their perfect parts to take,
  No doubt he would have all the rest refused,
  And her alone in steed of all have chused.

57

I doubtlesse deeme *Byreno* never viewd,
  Her naked corps, for certaine if he had,
  He could not so all humane sence exclude,
  To leave her thus alone in state so bad:
  But briefly all this matter to conclude,
  It seem'd *Oberto* would have bin full glad,
  In this her wo, her misery and need,
  To comfort her by either word or deed.

58

And straight he promist that he would attend her,
  And set her in her country if he may,
  And mauger all her enemies defend her,
  And take revenge on him did her betray.
  And that he might both men and money lend her,
  He would to pawne his realme of *Ireland* lay,
  Nor till she were restor'd aske no repayment,
  And straight he sought about to get her raiment.

59

They need not travell farre to find a gowne,
  For why immediatly they found good store,
By sending to the next adjoyning towne,
  The which his men of warre had spoild before,
Where many a worthy Ladie of renowne,
  That had bene naked tide unto the shore,
And many a tender virgin and unsoiled,
Were of their raiment and their lives despoiled.

60

And yet for all they were so richly gownd,
  Oberto could not cloath her as he wold,
No not in Florence (though it doth abound
  With rich embroderies of pearle and gold)
Could any peece of precious stuffe be found,
  Of worth to serve to keepe her from the cold,
Whose shape was so exact in every part,
Even hard to match by nature or by art.

61

Orlando with this love was well content,
  As one that hither came with other end,
For sith he mist Angelica, he ment
  His journey backe to France againe to bend.
With them by ship to Ireland first he went,
  As in his way, and with the King his friend,
Not hearing, had his love bin here or no,
For all were dead that could have told him so.

62

At both their sutes he scant staid there one day,
  His passing love such passions in him bred,
But ere he went he doth Oberto pray
  To do for her as much as he had sed,
And parting so from thence he tooke his way,
  Ev'n as his fortune and his fancie led,
But good Oberto need not be desired,
To do as much or more then he required.

63

For few dayes past but that with her he went
  To Holland, where he raised such commotion,
That straight Byreno taken was and shent,
  Receiving on three trees a just promotion:
And all those countries did forthwith consent,
  To sweare them faith and be at their devotion.
Thus of a countesse she is made a Prince,
And lives in joy and solace ever since.

64

Orlando bends his course to Brittish shore,
  Whence he not long before to ship did mount,
Where he had left his famous Brilliadore,
  A goodly courser and of good account,
No doubt of valiant acts he did good store,
  Though what they were I cannot here recount,
For such a minde he carride still unto them,
He cared not to tell them, but to do them.

65

But in what fashion he did passe the rest
  Of that unfortunate and fatall yeare,
I say by me it cannot be exprest,
  Because thereof no record doth appeare,
But when the spring did ground with green invest,
  And sunne in Gemini made weather cleare,
Then did he acts both worthie of reciting,
And to be kept in everlasting writing.

66

From hils to dales, from woods to pastures wide,
  From waters fresh unto the salt sea shore,
To seeke his love he up and downe doth ride,
  The lesse he finds he seeketh still the more,
At last he heard a voice for helpe that cride,
  He drawes his sword and spurs his Brilliadore.
But to refresh the reader now tis reason,
And stay my storie to a better season.

THE TWELFTH BOOKE OF
ORLANDO FVRIOSO

THE ARGVMENT

Orlando *doth pursue with great disdaine,*
One that did seeme his love by force to carrie:
Rogero *led by such another traine,*
With him doth in the charmed pallace tarrie:
Orlando *parting from the place againe,*
He sees indeed her whom he faine would marrie,
Fights with Ferraw, *and foiles two* Turkish *bands,*
And findes faire Isabell *in outlawes hands.*

ORLANDO FVRIOSO
THE TWELFTH BOOKE

1

Faire *Ceres* when she hastned backe againe,
  From great Idea homeward to returne,
  There where *Enceladus* with endles paine,
  Doth beare mount Ætna that doth ever burne,
  When she had sought her daughter long in vaine,
  Whose losse so strange did make the mother mourne,
  She spoiles for spite her brest, cheeks, eyes and heare,
  At last two boughs from Pyne tree she doth teare.

2

In *Vulcans* forge she sets on fire the brands,
  And gives them powre for ever to be light,
  And taking one a peece in both her hands,
  And drawne in coach by yoaked serpents might,
  She searcheth woods and fields and seas and lands,
  And brooks and streames and dens devoyd of light,
  And hearing here on earth no newes to like her,
  At last she went to hell it selfe to seeke her.

3

Were good *Orlandos* powre to be compared,
  As well with *Ceres* as his loving minde,
  He would no paine, no place, nor time have spared,
  His deare belov'd *Angelyca* to finde,
  To go to rocks and caves he would have dared,
  And place to saints, and place to fends assign'd,
  He onely wanted one of *Ceres* waggons,
  In which she carried was with flying draggons.

4

How he did search all *France* before he told,
  Now *Italy* to search is his intent,
  And *Germany* and *Castill* new and old,
  And then to *Affrica* to passe he ment,
  And as he thus determined, behold
  He heard a voice that seemed to lament,
  And drawing nye, to understand what tyding,
  On a great horse he saw a horse man ryding.

5

Perforce he bare upon his saddle bow,
  A Lady sorrowfull and sore afrayd,
  That cryde aloud still making open show,
  Of inward griefe, and thus to him she said,
  O worthy wight (Lord of *Anglante*) know
  I dye, I dye without you bring me ayd,
  And then he thought comming more nie to vew her,
  It was *Angelyca*, and that he knew her.

6

I say not that it was, but that it seem'd,
  To be *Angelyca* that thus was cary'd,
  But he that justly great disgrace it deem'd,
  Thus in his sight, to have his mistresse hary'd,
  Whose love above all treasures he esteem'd,
  To take revenge hereof he nothing tary'd,
  But put his spurres to *Brilliadores* sides,
  And in great hast to that same horseman rydes.

7

With many bloodie words and cruell threats,
  He bids that horseman to come backe againe,
  But he at naught his words and speeches sets,
  Rejoycing in so rich a gotten gayne,
  The vilen still ground of *Orlando* gets,
  Vntill they came into a faire large plaine,
  Wherein a house of great estate was built,
  The gate hereof in gorgeous sort was gilt.

8

The building all of marble faire was wrought,
  Most costly carv'd and cunningly contrived,
  To this faire house, his pray the foule thiefe brought,
  Straight after him *Orlando* there arrived:
  Then he alights and all about he sought,
  For him that had him of his joy deprived,
  He maketh search in chambers all about,
  And galleries and halls to finde them out.

9

Each roome he finds set forth with rich aray,
  With beds of silke, and gold of curious art,
  But yet he finds not that desired pray,
  The want whereof did sore torment his heart.
  There might he finde with like affliction stray,
  Gradasso, *Sacrapant* and *Brandimart*,
  And feirce *Ferraw* possest with strange confusion,
  Procured in that place by strong illusion.

10

They all complaine in anger and in rage,
  How of this house the master them hath used,
  One lost his horse, another lost his page,
  Another doubts his mistresse is abused:
  Thus are they kept like birds within a cage,
  And stand with sense and wits and words confused
  And manie with this strange deception carried,
  Within this place both weeks & months had tarrid.

11

Orlando when he saw he could not learne,
  Where this same theefe his mistresse had convaid,
  Though she was carride out at some posterne,
  Wherefore within no longer time he staid,
  But walkes about the castle to discerne,
  If that were true of which he was afraid:
  But as he walked up and downe the plaine,
  He thought he heard her call him backe againe.

12

And to a window casting up his eye,
  He thought he saw her face full of divinity,
  And that he heard her plainly thus to crie,
  O noble wight of proved magnanimitie,
  Helpe now, or never helpe, alas shall I
  In mine *Orlandos* sight leese my virginitie?
  Kill me, or let a thousand deaths befall me,
  Rather then let a villaine so to thrall me.

13

These wofull speeches once or twise repeted,
  Caus'd him returne into the house againe,
  And searching once againe he chafte and freted,
  (Hope still asswaging somewhat of his paine)
  And oft he heard the voice that counterfeted
  The speech of his *Angelica* most plaine.
  From side to side he follow'd still the sound,
  But of *Angelica* no signe he found.

14

Now while *Orlando* tarrid in this trance,
  In hope for to avenge his mistresse harmes,
  Rogero (who I told you had this chaunce)
  To see his *Bradamant* in gyants armes,
  (Drawne to this place with such another daunce)
  Namely by force of some unusuall charmes,
  Saw first the gyant in this castle enter,
  And after him he boldly doth adventer.

15

But when he came within the castle walls,
  And made much narrow search, as in such case,
  In garrets, towrs, in parlers and in halls,
  And under staires and many a homely place,
  Oft casting doubts what hurt his love befalls,
  Or lest the theefe were gone in this meane space,
  Forthwith he walketh out into the plaine,
  And heares a voice recall him backe againe.

16

That voice that lately did *Orlando* make
  Returne in hope *Angelica* to finde,
  Rogero now for *Bradamant* doth take,
  Whose love no lesse possest his carefull minde:
  And when the voice unto *Gradasso* spake,
  Or *Sacrapant*, or *Brandimart* most kinde,
  To every one of these it plainely seemed,
  To be her voice whom each one best esteemed.

17

Atlanta had procur'd this strange invention,
  Thereby to keepe *Rogero* from mischance,
  Because he saw it was the heavens intention,
  That he by treason should be kil'd in *France*,
  Ferraw and those of whom I last made mention,
  With all whom vallew highest did advance,
  To keepe him companie he here detained,
  With good provision while they here remained.

18

And while these knights with strange enchantments bound
  Do here abide, behold the *Indian* queene
  Angelica that late her ring had found,
  (Whose vertue can her cause to go unseene,
  And also frustrate magick still profound)
  Now longing home, where long she had not been,
  And being now of needfull things provided,
  Yet wants she one that her might home have guided.

19

Orlandos company she would have had,
  Or *Sacrapant*, she car'd not which of twaine,
  Not that of eithers love she would be glad,
  For them and all the world she did disdaine,
  But (for the way was dangerous and bad,
  In time of warre to travell *France* and *Spaine*)
  She wisht for her owne safetie and her ease,
  To have the company of one of these.

20

Wherefore a while she travels up and downe,
  To seeke for them that long in vaine had sought her,
  And passing many woods and many a towne,
  Vnto this place at last good fortune brought her,
  Where whē she saw these knights of great renowne,
  Thus seek for her, she scant abstaines from laughter,
  To see *Atlantas* cunning and dissembling,
  Her person and her voice so right resembling.

21

Her selfe unseene sees them and all the rest,
  Now meanes she sure to take one of them two,
  But yet she knowes not which (her doubtfull brest
  Did stay as unresolved what to do)
  Orlandos valour could defend her best,
  But then this doubt is added thereunto,
  That when she once so highly had prefard him,
  She shall not know againe how to discard him.

22

But *Sacrapant* although she should him lift
  High up to heaven yet maketh she no doubt,
  But she will find some sleight and pretie shift,
  With her accustom'd coynesse him to lout:
  To him she goes, resolved of this drift,
  And straight the precious ring she taketh out
  From of her mouth, which made her go concealed,
  With mind to him alone to be revealed.

23

But straight came in *Orlando* and *Ferraw*,
  That both desired, her to have enjoy'd,
Thus all of them at once their goddesse saw,
  Not being now by magick art annoyd,
For when the ring on finger she did draw,
  She made unwares all their enchantments voyd,
These three were all in complete armor, save
Ferraw no headpeece had, nor none would have.

24

The cause was this, he solemnely had sworne,
  Vpon his head no helmet should be set,
But that that was by stout *Orlando* worne,
  Which he did erst from *Trajans* brother get,
Ferraw to weare a helmet had forborne,
  Since with the ghost of *Argall* he had met:
Thus in this sort they came together armed,
By vertue of her ring now all uncharmed.

25

All three at once do now the damsell view,
  All three at once on her would straight have seased,
All three her faithfull lovers were she knew,
  Yet with all three at once she is displeased,
And from all three she straight her selfe withdrew,
  Who (haply) one at once would her have pleased,
From henceforth none of them she thinks to need,
But that the ring shall serve in all their steed.

26

She hastens hence and will no longer stay,
  Disdaine and feare together make her swift,
Into a wood she leades them all the way,
  But when she saw there was none other shift,
Into her mouth the ring she doth convay,
  That ever holpe her at the deadest lift,
And out of all their sights forthwith she vanish'd,
And leaves them all with wonder halfe astonish'd.

27

Onely one path there was, and that not wide,
  In this they follow'd her with no small hast,
But she first caus'd her horse to step aside,
  And standeth still a while till they were past,
And then at better leisure she doth ride,
  A farre more easie pace, and not so fast,
Vntill they three continuing still their riding,
Came to a way in sundry parts dividing.

28

And comming where they found no further tracke,
  Ferraw, that was before the tother two,
In choler and in fury great turn'd backe,
  And askt the other what they meant to do,
And (as his manner was to brag and cracke)
  Demaunded how they durst presume to wo,
Or follow her, whose propertie he claimed,
Except they would of him be slaine or maimed.

29

Orlando straight replide, thou foolish beast,
  Save that I see thou doest an helmet want,
I would ere this have taught thee at the least,
  Hereafter with thy betters not to vant:
Ferraw doth thanke him for his care (in jeast)
  And said it shew'd his wits were very scant,
For as he was he would not be afraid,
To prove against them both that he had said.

30

Sir, said *Orlando* to the Pagan King,
  Lend him your headpeece, and ere we go hence,
I will this beast in better order bring,
  Or sharply punish him for his offence.
Nay soft (said *Sacrapant*) that were a thing,
  The which to grant might shew I had no sence,
Lend you him yours, for Ile not go to schoole,
To know as well as you to bob a foole.

31

Tush (quoth *Ferraw*) fooles to your faces both,
  As though if I had bin dispos'd to weare one,
I would have suffer'd (were you leive or loth)
  The best and proudest of you both to beare one,
The truth is this, that I by solemne oth
  Vpon a certaine chance did once forsweare one,
That on my head no helmet should be donne,
Vntill I had *Orlandos* helmet wonne.

32

What (quoth the Earle) then seems it unto thee,
  Thy force so much *Orlandos* doth surmount,
That thou couldst do the same to him, that he
  Vnto *Almonta* did in *Aspramount*?
Rather I thinke, if thou his face should see,
  Thou wouldst so farre be wide of thine account,
That thou wouldst tremble over all thy body,
And yeeld thy selfe and armour like a nody.

33

The *Spanish* vaunter (like to all the nation)
  Said he had often with *Orlando* met,
And had him at advantage in such fashion,
  That had he list he might his helmet get,
But thus (quoth he) the time brings alteration,
  That now I seeke, I then at naught did set,
To take his helmet from him then I spared,
Because as then for it I little cared.

34

Then straight *Orlando* mov'd in rightfull anger,
  Made answer thus, thou foole and murren lier,
I cannot now forbeare thee any longer,
  I am whom thou to find do'st so desire,
When met we two that thou didst part the stronger?
  Thou thought'st me farder, thou shalt feele me nier,
Try now if thou beest able me to foyle,
Or I can thee of all thy armour spoyle.

K

35

Nor do I seeke to take this ods of thee,
  This said, forthwith his helmet he untide,
And hung the same fast by upon a tree,
  Then drew his *Durindana* from his side;
And in like sort you might the *Spaniard* see,
  That was no whit abated of his pride,
How he his sword and target straight prepar'd,
And lay most manfully unto his ward.

36

And thus these champions do the fight begin
  Vpon their coursers fierce, themselves more fierce,
And where the armour joynes, and is most thin,
  There still they strive with sturdy strokes to pierce:
Search all the world, and two such men therein
  Could not be found, for as old books rehearse,
Their skins were such, as they had bin unarmed,
Yet could they not with weapons have bin harmed.

37

Ferraw had in his youth inchantment such,
  That but his navell, hard was all the rest,
Vnto *Orlando* there was done as much,
  By prayer of some saint (as may be guest)
Save in his feet, which he let no man tuch,
  Take it for truth, or take it for a jest,
Thus I have found it wrote, that they indeed
Ware armor more for shew then any need.

38

Thus twixt them two the fight continues still,
  Yet not so sharpe in substance as in show;
Ferraw imploying all his art and skill,
  Sharpe thrusts upon the tother to bestow:
Orlando that hath ever strength at will,
  Layth on the Spaniard many a lustie blow:
Angelica doth stand fast by unseene,
And sees alone the battell them betweene.

39

For why the Pagan Prince was gone the while,
  To find her out, when they together fought,
And by their strife, that he might both beguile,
  He hopes, and had conceived in his thought:
He rides away, and travels many a mile,
  And still his deare beloved mistris sought.
And thus it came to passe that she that day,
Was onely present at so great a fray.

40

Which when she saw continue in such sort,
  Nor yet could guesse by ought that she did see,
Which was most like to cut the others short,
  She takes away the helmet from the tree,
And thinks by this to make her selfe some sport,
  Or they by this might sooner sundred be,
Not meaning in such sort away to set it,
But that the worthy Earle againe may get it.

41

And with the same away from hence she goes,
  The while they two with paine and travell tired,
In giving and in taking deadly bloes,
  Ferraw (that mist the headpeece first) retired,
And for he did most certainly suppose,
  That *Sacrapant* had tane it undesired,
Good Lord (said he) what meane we here to do?
This other Knight hath cousened us two.

42

And unawares the helmet tane away,
  Orlando hearing this, doth looke aside,
And missing it, he doth beleeve straight way,
  As did *Ferraw*, and after him they ride:
They came at last into a parted way,
  That in two parts it selfe doth there divide,
Fresh tracke in both of them was to be seene,
This of the Knight, that of the *Indian* Queene.

43

Orlandos hap was to pursue the Knight,
  Ferraw, that was more luckie of the twaine,
Happen'd upon *Angelica* to light,
  Who to refresh her former taken paine,
Fast by a fountaine did before alight,
  And seeing sodainly the knight of *Spaine*,
Straight like a shadow from his sight she past,
And on the ground the helmet left with hast.

44

But as the sight of her did make him glad,
  In hope by this good fortune her to get,
So thus againe to loose her made him sad,
  And shew'd that she did him at nothing set:
Then curst he as he had bin raging mad,
  Blaspheming *Trivigant* and *Mahomet*,
And all the Gods ador'd in *Turks* profession,
The griefe in him did make so deepe impression.

45

Yet when he had *Orlandos* helmet spide,
  And knew it was by letters writ thereon,
The same for which *Trajanos* brother dide,
  He takes it quickly up and puts it on,
And then in hast he after her doth ride,
  That was out of his sight so strangely gone,
He takes the helmet, thinking little shame,
Although he came not truly by the same.

46

But seeing she away from him was fled,
  Nor where she was he knew nor could not guesse,
Himselfe from hence to *Paris* ward he sped,
  His hope to find her waxing lesse and lesse:
And yet the sorrow that her losse had bred,
  Was part asswag'd, the helmet to possesse,
Though afterward when as *Orlando* knew it,
He sware great othes that he would make him **rew** it.

47

But how *Orlando* did againe it get,
　And how *Ferraw* was plagued for that crime,
　And how they two betweene two bridges met,
　Whereas *Ferraw* was killed at that time,
　My purpose is not to declare as yet,
　But to another story turne my rime:
　Now I must tell you of that *Indian* Queene,
　By vertue of her ring that goeth unseene.

48

Who parted thence all sad and discontented,
　That by her meanes *Ferraw* his will had got,
　That she (with this unlookt for hap prevented)
　Left him the helmet, though she meant it not,
　And in her heart her act she sore repented,
　And with her selfe she said, alas God wot,
　I silly foole tooke it with good intention,
　Thereby to breake their strife and sharpe contention.

49

Not that thereby this filthy *Spaniard* might
　By helpe of my deceit and doing wrong,
　Keepe that by fraud he could not win by might,
　Alas to thy true love and service long,
　A better recompence then this of right,
　From me (my good *Orlando*) should belong:
　And thus in this most kind and dolefull fashion,
　She doth continue long her lamentation.

50

Now meaneth she to travell to the East,
　Vnto her native soile and country ground,
　Her journey doth her other griefes digest,
　Her ring doth in her journey keepe her sound;
　Yet chanced she, ere she forsooke the West,
　To travell neare a wood, whereas she found
　A fine yong man betweene two dead men lying,
　With wound in bleeding brest even then a dying.

51

But here a while I cease of her to treate,
　Or *Sacrapant*, or of the Knight of *Spaine*,
　First I must tell of many a hardy feate,
　Before I can returne to them againe:
　Orlandos actions I will now repeate,
　That still endur'd such travell and such paine,
　Nor time it selfe, that sorrowes doth appease,
　Could grant to this his griefe an end or ease.

52

And first the noble Earle an headpeece bought,
　By late ill fortune having lost his owne,
　For temper or the strength he never sought,
　So it did keepe him but from being knowne.
　Now *Phœbus* charret had the daylight brought,
　And hid the starres that late before were showne,
　And faire *Aurora* was new risen when
　Orlando met two bands of armed men.

53

One band was led by worthy *Manilard*,
　A man though stout, yet hoary haird for age,
　Who with his men did make to *Paris* ward,
　He not for warre, but fit for counsell sage:
　Alsyrdo of the other had the guard,
　Then in the prime and chiefe floure of his age,
　And one that passed all the *Turkish* warriers,
　To fight at tilt, at turney or at barriers.

54

These men with other of the *Pagan* host,
　Had layne the winter past not far fro thence,
　When *Agramant* did see his men were lost,
　By vaine assaults unto his great expence,
　And therefore now he sweares and maketh bost,
　That he will never raise his siege fro thence,
　Till they within that now had left the field,
　Were forst by famine all their goods to yeeld.

55

And for that cause, now sommer comes againe,
　He gets together all the men he may,
　With new supplies of *Affrike* and of *Spaine*,
　And some of *France* that did accept his pay,
　But that in order due they may remaine,
　He points them all to meet him in one day,
　Who by commandement hither came in clusters,
　To make appearance at the pointed musters.

56

Now when *Alsyrdo* saw *Orlando* there,
　Inflam'd with pride and glory of his mind,
　He longed straight with him to breake a speare,
　And spurs his horse, but quickly he doth find
　Himselfe too weake so sturdy blowes to beare,
　And wisheth now that he had staid behind,
　He falleth from the horses back downe dead,
　The fearfull horse without his master fled.

57

Straight there was rais'd a mighty cry and shout,
　By all the souldiers of *Alsyrdos* band,
　When as they see their captaine (late so stout)
　Throwne downe and killed by *Orlandos* hand:
　Then out of ray they compast him about
　On ev'ry side in number as the sand,
　They that are nie, with blowes do him assaile,
　And those aloofe throw darts as thicke as haile.

58

Looke what a noise an herd of savage swine
　Do make when as the wolfe a pig hath caught,
　That doth in all their hearings cry and whine,
　They flocke about as nature hath them taught:
　So do these souldiers murmure and repine,
　To see their captaine thus to mischiefe brought,
　And with great fury they do set upon him,
　All with one voice, still crying, on him, on him.

59

I say the nearer fight with sword and speare,
  And those aloofe send shafts and many a dart,
  But he that never yet admitted feare
  To lodge in any harbour of his hart,
  Vpon his shield a thousand darts doth beare,
  And thousands more on every other part,
  Yet of them all makes no more care nor keepe,
  Then doth a Lion of a flocke of sheepe.

60

For when at once his fatall blade he drew,
  That blade so often bath'd in *Pagans* blood,
  No steele there was of temper old or new,
  Nor folded cloths the edge thereof withstood,
  About the field, heads, legs, armes, shoulders flew,
  The furrowes all did flow with crimson flood,
  Death goeth about the field rejoycing mickle,
  To see a sword that so surpast his sickle.

61

This made the *Pagan* rout so sore agast,
  He that could swiftest runne was best apaid,
  And as they came, so fled they now as fast,
  One brother for another never staid:
  No memory of love or friendship past,
  Could make one stay to give another aid,
  He that could gallop fastest was most glad,
  Not asking if the wayes were good or bad.

62

Onely one man there was in all the field,
  That had so long in vertues schoole bin bred,
  That rather then to turne his backe or yeeld,
  He meaneth there to leave his cark as dead:
  Old *Manylard*, who taking up his sheeld,
  Even as his valiant heart and courage led,
  Sets spurs to horse, and in his rest a lance,
  And runs against the *Palladine* of France.

63

Vpon *Orlandos* shield his speare he brake,
  Who never stird for all the manly blow,
  But with his naked sword againe he strake,
  And made him tumble ore the saddle bow:
  Fortune on vertue did some pitie take,
  For why, *Orlandos* sword fell flatling tho,
  That though it quite amaz'd and overthrew him,
  Yet by good hap it maim'd him not nor slew him.

64

With great confusion all the other fled,
  And now of armed men the field was voyd,
  Save such as were or seemed to be dead,
  So as *Orlando* now no more annoy'd,
  Went on his journey as his fancie led,
  To seeke her, in whose sight he onely joy'd,
  Through plains and woods, through sandy ways and
  He travels making still of her enquiry.   (miry,

65

Vntill it was his fortune toward night
  To come fast by a mountaine, in whose side
  Forth of a cave he saw a glims of light,
  And towards it he presently doth ride:
  Then at the mouth thereof he doth alight,
  And to a bush fast by his horse he tide,
  He douts, as ever love is full of feare,
  That his belov'd *Angelica* was there.

66

Ev'n as the hunters that desirous are,
  Some present pastime for their hounds to see,
  In stubble fields do seeke the fearfull hare,
  By ev'ry bush, and under ev'ry tree:
  So he with like desire and greater care,
  Seeks her that sole of sorrow can him free,
  He enters boldly in the hollow cave,
  And thinks of her some tidings there to have.

67

The entrance straight and narrow was to passe,
  Descending steps into a place profound,
  Whereas a certain faire yong Ladie was,
  Kept by some outlawes prisner under ground,
  Her beautie did the common sort surpasse,
  So farre as scant her match was to be found,
  So as that darke and solitary den,
  Might seeme to be a Paradise as then.

68

On her an aged woman there did wait,
  The which (as oft with women doth befall)
  About some matter of but little waight,
  Did happen at that time to chide and brall,
  But when they saw a stranger comming, straight
  They held their peaces, and were quiet all,
  Orlando doth salute them with good grace,
  And they do bid him welcome to the place.

69

Then after common words of salutation,
  Although at first of him they were afraid,
  Yet straight he enter'd in examination,
  By whom in that same cave they had bin staid
  And who they were in so unseemly fashion,
  That kept a comely and a noble maid?
  And said, he saw it written in her face,
  Her nurture and her linage were not base.

70

She told him straight how long she there had beene,
  And by what hap she had bin thither brought,
  Amid her words the sighs do passe betweene,
  The corall and the pearle by nature wrought,
  Sweet teares upon her tender cheeks were seene,
  That came from fountaine of her bitter thought:
  But soft, lest I should do the Reader wrong,
  I end this booke, that else would be too long.

THE THIRTEENTH BOOKE OF
ORLANDO FVRIOSO

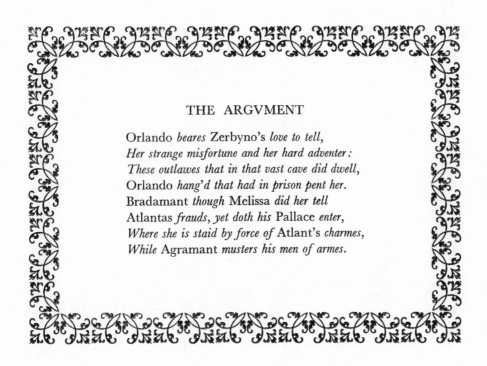

THE ARGVMENT

Orlando *beares* Zerbyno's *love to tell,*
Her strange misfortune and her hard adventer:
These outlawes that in that vast cave did dwell,
Orlando *hang'd that had in prison pent her.*
Bradamant *though* Melissa *did her tell*
Atlantas *frauds, yet doth his* Pallace *enter,*
Where she is staid by force of Atlant's *charmes,*
While Agramant *musters his men of armes.*

ORLANDO FVRIOSO

THE THIRTEENTH BOOKE

1

Fvll ventrous were the noble knights of old,
　And worthy that their fame should aye endure,
That durst with valiant heart and courage bold
　Find out in dens and places all obscure,
Such as in courts we now but seeld behold,
　Faire dames, of beauty, mind, and manners pure:
As erst I told you how *Orlando* found
A brave young Lady hidden under ground.

2

Now in my former matter to proceed,
　I say when he had view'd her person well,
And mark'd her face and haviour with great heed,
　He doth request the damsell faire to tell,
Who was the author of so foul a deed,
　To force her in so unfit place to dwell:
And she as plaine and briefly as she can,
In this sweet sort her woful speech began.

3

Most worthy knight (she said) although I know,
　That I shall buy my speech to you full deare,
(For sure I am, this woman here will show
　My words to him that first did place me here)
Truth I will tell, though truth increase my woe,
　And make him look on me with angry cheare:
Despaire hath ever danger all contemn'd,
What should she feare that is ev'n now condemn'd?

4

I am that *Isabel* that somtime was
　A daughter deare unto the king of *Spaine*,
Well did I say I was, for now alas,
　I am the child of anguish and of paine:
Love, onely love this great change brought to passe,
　Love, only love of thee I may complaine,
That flattring alwaies in thy first beginnings,
Yeeld'st certaine losse in stead of hoped winnings:

5

Then in good state I spent my happy daies,
　Noble and young, honest and rich, and faire,
Now base, despised, poore, and wanting praise:
　Drown'd in a dungeon of most deep despaire,
Thus love throwes down whom fortune high doth raise,
　And marrs the sport in which he is a plaier:
He that in art of love did shew his skill,
Saith, love and majestie agrees but ill.

6

But that I plainly may declare my mind,
　Thus it fell out, my father twelve moneths since,
To make a famous triumph had assign'd,
　Vnto the which came many a Lord and Prince:
Now whether liking did my eys so blind,
　Or that his vertue did it selfe convince:
Zerbin (me thought) the king of *Scotlands* son
In this same triumph honour chief had won.

7

The passing feats of armes I saw him do,
　In which he was compared with the best,
His person and his beauty joyn'd thereto,
　In which he far surpassed all the rest,
Did cause that he no sooner did me wo,
　But I as quickly granted his request:
Interpreters nor other means none wanted,
To make the seeds to grow that love had planted.

8

When as these feasts and solemne shewes were ended,
　My *Zerbin* back againe to *Scotland* hasted,
Wherewith how grievously I was offended,
　Well may you guesse, if ever love you tasted:
But he that cannot be too much commended,
　Whose love to me no lesse in absence lasted,
With purpose and with promise firm to marry me,
Studi'd all means away from hence to carry me.

9

'Twere vaine he thought to ask me of my sire,
　(*Zerbin* a *Christen*, I a *Sarazine*)
Our country law contrari'd that desire,
　To which our loves so wholly did incline:
This feat doth some new stratagem require,
　More heedfull, secret, circumspect and fine:
When love hath knit two hearts in perfit unity,
They seldome faile to finde their opportunity.

10

An house of great estate in *Bayon* towne,
　My father had with gardens sweet and faire,
In which with large descents still going down
　Vnto a river comes the garden staire,
Here (if ill fortune on us do not frown)
　He means when I shall walk to take the aire,
Soon to surprise me walking in an ally,
And so convey me to his armed gally.

11

But sith with him the case did then so stand,
  Not to be present at this enterprise,
He sent me letters written with his hand,
  By *Oderike* of *Byskie* stout and wise,
Expert in service both of sea and land,
  And wils me do as he should me advise,
Whose faith he nothing doubteth to be found,
As one to him by benefits much bound.

12

This firm and fast, and sure obliged friend,
  Of proved courage, value and of skill,
Against the time appointed he doth send:
  And I that for their comming looked still,
Against the time appointed did descend,
  To give him scope to work his masters will,
And he accordingly came unespi'd,
With armed men under the garden side.

13

I seeing them, my selfe most fearfull faine,
  They seeing me soon of their purpose sped,
Those that resistance made, forthwith were slaine,
  And some afraid and faint, like cowards fled,
The rest with me as prisners do remaine;
  Then straight we were unto the gally led,
And gone so farre, we could not be recovered,
Before my father had the fact discovered.

14

Of this departure I my selfe was glad,
  In hope ere long my *Zerbin* to have found,
But lo a sudden tempest made us sad,
  And neare to *Rochell* almost had us drownd,
The master of the ship no cunning had,
  To keep the keel from striking on the ground:
It booted not against the waves to strive,
Vpon sharp rocks the tempest doth us drive.

15

In vaine it was to pull down all our sailes,
  And on the foreboord close to couch the mast,
No paine against the raging sea prevailes,
  On land we look each minute to be cast:
Divine help oft doth come, when humane failes,
  And when in reason all reliefe is past:
For doubtlesse I do deem by power divine,
We were preserved in this dang'rous time.

16

The *Byskin* that the danger well doth note,
  Doth meane a desprate remedy to trie,
He straightway launcheth out the little bote,
  He and two more go down therein, and I,
This done, he cuts the rope and lets her flote,
  Threatning with naked sword that he should die,
That durst presume to give so bold adventer,
Against our wils into the boat to enter.

17

The rope now cut, away the boat was carried
  By force of waves unto the shallow shore,
And by great fortune none of us miscarried,
  So great a plunge I never scap'd before,
But they (poore soules) that in the gally tarried,
  Were drown'd, the vessell quite in peeces tore,
Where though my losse of stuffe and jewels griev'd me,
My hope to see my *Zerbin* still reliev'd me.

18

Now being come to land (in lucklesse houre)
  And trusting onely *Oderikes* direction,
Love (that doth ever love to shew his power,
  In tempring or distempring our affection)
My good to ill, my sweet doth turn to sower,
  My hope to hurt, my health into infection:
He in whose trust *Zerbin* so much relieth,
Freezeth in faith, and in new fancie frieth.

19

Now whether first at sea this humour grew,
  Or els he moved was with new occasion,
To have me here alone with so small crew,
  As from his will I could not make evasion,
He bids all faith and honesty adieu,
  And yeelds himselfe unto this foul perswasion;
And that he may his pleasure surely warrant,
He sends the servants of a sleevelesse arrant.

20

Two men there were that had so lucky lot,
  With us into the ship-boat to descend,
One hight *Almonio*, by birth a *Scot*,
  A valiant man, and *Zerbins* trusty friend,
Odrike tels him, that it beseemed not,
  So few upon a Princesse to attend,
And that the daughter of the King of *Spaine*
Should go on foot, and with so small a traine.

21

Wherefore he wisheth him to go before
  To *Rochell*, there a palfrey to provide,
And hire some men, a dozen or a score,
  Me to my lodging mannerly to guide:
Almonio went, then was there left no more,
  But *Coreb*, one of wit and courage tri'd,
In whom the *Byskin* put the more affiance,
Because that he was one of his alliance.

22

Yet long he seem'd in doubtfull minde to hover,
  Faine (if he could) he would have rid him thence,
At last he thinks so fast a friend and lover
  Will with his friends iniquity dispence:
Wherefore he doth to him his minde discover,
  In hope that he would further his offence,
And do as friends in our dayes have a fashion,
Advance their pleasure more then reputation.

23

But he whose honest minde could not suppose,
  That *Oderike* had had so little grace,
  The fact not only threatens to disclose,
  But cals him false and traitor to his face:
  From bitter words unto more bitter blowes,
  They came and fought together in the place;
  And I in this prospect no whit delighting,
  Fled to the wood while they two were a fighting.

24

Between them two the combat was not long,
  But lo the worser cause the better sped,
  Whether he were more skilfull or more strong,
  Odrike doth lay *Corebo* there for dead:
  That done, he runs the woods and fern among,
  And followes fast the way that I had fled,
  I think that he god *Cupids* wings did borrow,
  He made such hast to hasten on my sorrow.

25

Feare made me swift, for I was sore afraid,
  Love made him swifter run to overtake me,
  Then sore against my will my course he staid,
  Then sundrily both foul and faire he spake me,
  Somtime he promised, somtime he praid,
  Somtime he threatned he by force would make me:
  With suit, with gifts with threats he oft did prove me,
  With suit, with gifts, with threats he nought did move
                                                      (me.

26

But when he could not with his words prevaile,
  He doth resolve no further time to stay,
  With open force he then did me assaile,
  As doth a hungry Beare cease on his pray,
  And I defended me with tooth and naile,
  And cries, and skreeks, and all the wayes I may,
  Nor was I in mine own defence afeard,
  To scratch his eyes, and pull away his beard.

27

I know not if it were my skreetch and crie,
  That might have well bin heard a league and more,
  Or if it were their use that dwell thereby,
  To come to seek some shipwracks on the shore,
  But straight upon the hill we might descry,
  Come toward us of company good store,
  Which makes my *Byskie* man away to run,
  And to surcease his enterprise begun.

28

Thus this unlook'd for crew preserv'd me then,
  And hindred him of his unjust desire:
  But I was sav'd, as is the flounder, when
  He leapeth from the dish into the fire.
  For though these barbarous and savage men
  To touch my person did not once aspire;
  No vertuous thought did breed this moderation,
  But hope of gaine and greedy inclination.

29

The Leader of this miserable band
  Did think his market will be raised much,
  In selling me, when men shall understand,
  He sels a maid whom none did ever touch,
  And now I heare a merchant is in hand,
  Of him to buy me, if his luck be such;
  From whom into the East I shall be sent,
  Where to the *Souldan* they will me present.

30

And in this sort her wofull tale she told,
  And mingled sighs with tears in rufull fashion,
  Expressed with such dolefull words as would
  Have mov'd a stony heart to take compassion:
  It eas'd in part her mind, thus to unfold
  The bitter cause of her unpleasant passion.
  Now while *Orlando* to this tale attended,
  The crew of caitives to the cave descended.

31

A barbarous and foul misshapen crew,
  Armed, one with a spit, one with a prong,
  Mouthes, eyes and face most ugly were to view,
  One had no nose, anothers was too long:
  But when their leader somwhat nearer drew,
  And saw *Orlando* standing there among,
  Turning to his companion he said,
  Lo here a bird for whom no net we laid.

32

Then to the Earle he said, I am right glad
  To find one so well armed in my cave,
  For long for such an armour long'd I had,
  And surely now this I suppose to have:
  How think you, when my person shall be clad
  With this your coat, shall not I then be brave?
  Wherefore good sir, think not your welcome scant,
  That come so fitly to supply my want.

33

Orlando turning with a sower smile,
  Answer'd, his armour was of price too high,
  And that he greatly did himselfe beguile,
  That thought of him his armour there to buy:
  And as they nearer came, he stoopt the while,
  And took a brand that in the fire did lie,
  And straight he threw it at the caitives head,
  And laid him there along the floor for dead.

34

A short thick plank stood on a scrubby post,
  That serv'd them for a boord to drink and eat,
  This like a coight at them *Orlando* tost,
  And (for the same full heavy was and great)
  It fell down there among them to their cost,
  They never saw before so strange a feat:
  By which scarce one of them escaped harm,
  In head, in leg, in brest, in side or arm.

35

So shall you see a country man that takes
    In time of spring a brickbat or a stone,
    And throwes the same upon a knot of snakes,
    That lie together cluster'd all in one,
    How great a spoile the stone among them makes,
    And those that scape, how quickly they be gone:
    So did *Orlando* with these peasants play,
    That glad were they that scap'd to run away.

36

Those that could scape the heavy tables fall,
    Vnto their feet commended their defence,
    Which were (as *Turpin* writes) but seven in all,
    Which seven were glad to run away from thence:
    But yet their flying brought them help but small,
    Orlando means to punish their offence,
    Their feet, nor yet their fence could them so guard,
    But that he brought them to the hanging ward.

37

Now when the foresaid aged woman saw,
    In how bad sort these friends of hers were serv'd,
    She was affeard, for well she knew by law,
    That no lesse punishment she had deserv'd.
    Forthwith from thence she stale away for aw,
    And up and down the desart wood she swerv'd,
    Vntill at last a warriour stout her met,
    But who it was I may not tell as yet.

38

The tender damsell doth *Orlando* pray,
    Her chastity and honour to protect,
    Who made her go with him, and from that day
    Had unto her a fatherly respect:
    Now as they went, a prisner by the way
    They saw, whose name I may not now detect.
    Now should I speak of *Bradamant* by right,
    Whom erst I left in such a dolefull plight.

39

The valourous Lady looking long in vaine,
    When her *Rogero* would to her return,
    Lay in *Marsilia* to the Pagans paine,
    Where ev'ry day she did them some shrewd turn;
    For some of them in *Provence* did remaine,
    And *Languedock* where they did spoile and burn,
    Till with her value she did them rebuke,
    Supplying place of captaine and of duke.

40

Now on a day as she sate still and mused,
    The time of his appointment long expir'd,
    Doubting lest she by him might be abus'd,
    Or that her company he not desir'd;
    And often when she blam'd, she straight excus'd:
    Thus while with carefull thought her self she tir'd,
    Melissa whom she thought not to be neare her,
    Came suddenly of purpose for to cheare her.

41

With pleasant countenance *Melissa* sage,
    Much like to those that carie welcome newes,
    Wils her, her causlesse sorrow to asswage,
    And good *Rogero's* absence doth excuse,
    Swearing that she durst lay her life to gage,
    He would not absent be, if he might chuse,
    And that he did now in his promise hault,
    Was not by his but by anothers fault.

42

Wherefore (quoth she) get you to horseback straight
    If you would set your faithfull lover free,
    And I my selfe intend on you to wait,
    Till you his prison with your eye shall see,
    Whereas *Atlanta* with a strange deceit
    Detaineth men, of base and high degree,
    And showes by strange illusion distrest,
    Each one the party whom he loveth best.

43

Each one doth deeme he sees in great distresse,
    His love, his friend, his fellow or his page,
    According as mens reasons more or lesse,
    Are weak or strong such passion to asswage:
    Thus do they follow this their foolish guesse,
    Vntill they come like birds into a cage,
    Searching the pallace with a pensive heart,
    The great desire not suffring them to part.

44

Now then (said she) when you shall once draw nigh,
    Where this same *Necromancer* strange doth dwell,
    He will your comming and the cause descry,
    And to delude you (mark me what I tell)
    He straight will offer there unto your eye
    (By help of some inhabitants of hell)
    Rogero's person, all in wofull plight,
    As though he had been conquered in fight.

45

And if you follow, thinking him to aid,
    Then will he stay you as he doth the rest,
    But kill him therefore, and be not afraid,
    For so you shall your friend deliver best:
    So shall your foe *Atlanto* be betraid
    In his own trap when as he looketh left,
    And feare not when he commeth by to strike him,
    Though he your deare resemble, and look like him.

46

I know full well how hard 'twill be to try,
    And how your heart will faile, and hand will tremble
    When you shall go about to make one dy,
    That shall *Rogero's* shape so right resemble:
    But in this case you may not trust your ey,
    But all your sprites and forces all assemble:
    For this assure you, if you let him go,
    You work your own and your *Rogero's* wo.

47

The Proverb saith, one that is warn'd is arm'd,
  The which old saw, doth prove by due construction,
That they that after warning had are harm'd,
  Did ill regard or follow good instruction.
Now *Bradamant* rides to the place so charm'd,
  And vow'd that old *Magicians* destruction,
  And that they may the tedious way beguile,
  They spend the time in pleasant talk the while.

48

And oft *Melissa* doth to her repeat
  The names of those that should be her posterity,
That should in force and deeds of armes be great,
  But greater in Religion and sincerity,
Atchieving many a strange and worthy feat,
  And use both head and hand with great dexterity,
  In ruling just, and bountifull in giving,
  Cæsars in fight, and Saints in godly living.

49

Now when *Melissa* sage such things did show,
  The noble Lady modestly repli'd,
Sith God (quoth she) doth give you skill to know,
  The things that shall in future times betide,
And means on me (unworthy) to bestow
  An issue such as few shall have beside,
  Tell me, among so many men of name,
  Shall there no woman be of worthy fame?

50

Yes many a one (said she) both chast and wise,
  Mothers to such as beare imperiall crownes,
Pillars and stayes of royall families,
  Owners of realmes, of countries and of townes,
Out of thy blessed off-spring must arise,
  Such as shall be ev'n in their sober gownes,
  For chastity and modesty as glorious,
  As shall their husbands be in warre victorious.

51

Nor can I well, or do I now intend,
  To take upon me all their names to tell,
For then my speech would never have an end,
  I find so many that deserve so well,
Onely I mean a word or two to spend,
  Of one or two that do the rest excell:
  Had you but talk'd hereof in *Merlins* cave,
  You should have seen the shapes that they shall have.

52

Shall I begin with her whose vertue rare
  Shall with her husband live in happy strife,
Whether his valiant actions may compare,
  Or be prefer'd before her honest life?
He fights abroad against king *Charles* at Tare,
  She staid at home a chast and sober wife:
  Penelope in spending chast her dayes,
  As worthy as *Ulisses* was of praise.

53

Then next dame *Beatrice* the wife somtime
  Of *Lodwicke Sforze*, surnamed eke the *More*:
Wise and discreet, and known without all crime,
  Of fortunes gifts, and vertues having store:
Her husband liv'd most happy all her time,
  And in such state as few have liv'd before:
  But after fell from being Duke of *Millen*,
  To be a captive fetter'd like a villen.

54

To passe the famous house I should be sorie,
  Of *Aragon*, and that most worthy queen,
Whose match in neither greek nor latine storie,
  Or any writer els hath ever been:
And full to perfect her most worthy glory,
  Three worthy children shall of her be seen:
  Of whom the heavens have pointed her the mother,
  Isbell by name, *Alfonso* and his brother.

55

As silver is to tin, as gold to brasse,
  As roses are to flowers and herbs more base,
As diamonds and rubyes are to glasse,
  As cedars are to fallowes: in like case
Shall famous *Leonora* others passe,
  In vertue, beauty, modesty and grace:
  But above all, in this she shall excell,
  In bringing up her children passing well.

56

For as the vessell ever beares a tast
  Of that same juyce wherewith it first was fil'd,
And as in fruitfull ground the seed growes fast,
  That first is sowne when as the same is til'd:
So look what lore in youthfull yeares is plac'd,
  By that they grow the worse or better wil'd,
  When as they come to manly age and stature,
  Sith education is another nature.

57

Then next her neece, a faire and famous dame,
  That hight *Renata* I may not forget,
Daughter to *Lews* the xij king of that name,
  Whom of the *Britten* Dutches he did get:
Whose vertue great shall merit lasting fame,
  While fier shall be warm or water wet,
  While wind shall blow, and earth stand firm & sound,
  And heav'nly sphears shall run their courses round.

58

I passe all those that passe all these some deale,
  Whose soules aspiring to an higher praise,
Despising pomp and ease, and worldly weale,
  In sacred rites shall spend their blessed dayes:
Whose hearts and holy love and godly zeale,
  To heav'nly joyes from earthly thoughts shall raise,
  That to good works, to prayer and pure divinitie,
  Shall consecrate their lives and their virginitie.

59

Thus doth *Melyssa* unto her discourse,
    Of those should come hereafter of her seed,
    And while they talked oft by entercourse,
    They in their journey onward do proceed,
    And oftentimes *Melyssa* hath recourse,
    To will her of *Atlanta* take great heed,
    And least she should with faint and foolish kindnes
    Be led unwares in errour and in blindnes.

60

Now when they neare approched to the place,
    Then *Bradamant* departed from her guide,
    And after she had rode a little space,
    She saw one brought with hands together ti'd,
    Exceeding like *Rogero* in the face,
    In voice, in stature, haire and all beside:
    Bound fast with chaines betweene two gyants led,
    That threatned him ere long he should be dead.

61

But when the damsell saw within her view,
    The lamentable state and hard condition,
    Of him whose face she certaine thought she knew,
    She changeth straight her trust into suspicion,
    Doubting *Melyssa* of some malice new,
    Or hidden hate had giv'n her such commission,
    To make *Rogero* for a greater spite,
    Be slaine by her in whom he doth delight.

62

Is not this he (thus to her self she spake)
    Whom still mine heart and now mine eyes do see?
    If my *Rogero* I can so mistake,
    I never shall have knowledge which is he:
    I either dream and am not now awake,
    Or els no doubt it can none other be,
    Melyssa? what, may not *Melyssa* lye?
    Shall I believe her tale, and not mine eye?

63

Now while that thus she thought and thus she said,
    And in this unwise thought did thus persever,
    She thought she heard him speak and ask for aid,
    Saying (my love) assist me now or never,
    What shall I in thy sight be so betraid?
    Dost thou forsake me? then farewell for ever:
    These unkind words her heart so greatly daunted,
    She followes him into the house inchanted.

64

No sooner was she enter'd in the gate,
    But that the common error her possest,
    Wandring about the house betimes and late,
    Nor night nor day she taketh any rest;
    The strange inchantment brought her in that state,
    That though she saw the man that lov'd her best,
    And spake with him, and met him every houre,
    To know the tone the tother had no power.

65

But let not now the reader be displeas'd,
    Although I leave her in this charmed place,
    I mean ere long her travell shall be eas'd,
    And she shall see and know *Rogero's* face,
    Ev'n as the tast with diverse meats is pleas'd,
    So think I by this story in like case;
    The friendly reader shall be lesse annoy'd,
    If with one matter long he be not cloy'd.

66

With sundry threds a man had need to weave,
    To make so large a web as I intend,
    Wherefore all other matters I must leave,
    Of *Agramant* a little time to spend:
    Who sorely at the *flower de luce* did heave,
    And all his might to mar the same did bend,
    Sending for men to *Affricke* and to *Spaine*,
    Those to supply that in the field were slaine.

67

Thus all on war his heart was wholly fixt,
    His new supplies with sundry captains led
    Were come, with men of sundry nations mixt,
    With whom that no disorder may be bred,
    A day for viewes and musters was prefixt,
    That ev'ry one might know his guide and head:
    Then fell they to their mustring and their viewing,
    As shall be shew'd you in the book ensuing.

THE FOVRTEENTH BOOKE OF
ORLANDO FVRIOSO

THE ARGVMENT

Agramant *mustring of his men, doth misse*
Two bands that by Orlando *late were slaine:*
Mandricard *vowes to be reveng'd of this,*
But by the way he haps to entertaine
Dame Doralice, *whose beauty was his blisse.*
An Angell brings Renaldo *and his traine*
Unseene, there where the Pagan *did encampe,*
And sendeth discord to the Turkish *campe.*

ORLANDO FVRIOSO
THE FOVRTEENTH BOOKE

1

Among the fierce assaults, and cruell blowes,
  That *France* hath felt from *Affrick* and from *Spaine*,
  In which so many men fed Wolves and Crowes,
  That were on both sides in the battell slaine:
  Although the *French* were foiled by their foes,
  That long they came not to the field againe,
  Yet was this foile sore to the *Pagans* cost,
  For diverse Lords and Princes that they lost.

2

So bloudy was the victory they gate,
  That scant this joy did countervaile that wo,
  And if we may compare things done of late,
  (Renown'd *Alfons*) to things done long ago,
  Ravenna's fall by fortune or by fate,
  In which your vertue great did flourish so,
  To win the field so bloudy and so hard,
  With this of theirs may justly be compar'd.

3

For when the souldiers of the *Spanish* band
  Whom then the *Pope* retained in his pay,
  Had almost got the victory in hand,
  The *Frenchmen* ready now to run away,
  Thou cam'st to succour with that noble band
  Of valiant youths, that merited that day
  The honour of the gilded spurre and hilt,
  In recompence of bloud so bravely spilt.

4

So didst thou bruise the Akornes rich of gold,
  So didst thou break the yellow staffe and red,
  So didst thou then the *Flower de luce* uphold,
  When as the captaine was in battell dead,
  For which the Lawrell crown they ware of old,
  By just desert belongeth to thy head;
  And Civill crown, no lesse in honour precious,
  For saving unto *Rome* her own *Fabricius*.

5

Colonna nam'd a collum true indeed,
  Vnto the state of *Rome* and Romane name,
  Whom you by value took, and sav'd by meed,
  By which more honour true and worthy fame,
  Vnto your self you did procure and breed:
  Then in the overcomming all that came,
  From *Aragon*, from *Castill* and *Navar*,
  For all their speares and new devised car.

6

Now though we all our lives and safeties ow,
  To you that this great conquest did atchieve,
  Yet our side did receive so great a blow,
  As scarce that joy this sorrow did relieve:
  And that the dames of *France* most plainly show,
  Whom this so bloudy triumph still doth grieve,
  Witnesse their widowes in their mourning gownes,
  And watry eyes in villages and townes.

7

King *Lews* of *France* had need in time prepare,
  For captains new to these unruly bands,
  That wickedly without all feare or care,
  Of lawes of God, of nature, or of lands,
  No sort, nor sex, nor age, nor order spare,
  From force of their unchast and bloudy hands.
  Christs body in the Sacrament they tare it,
  To beare away the silver plate that bare it.

8

Wretched *Ravenna* better had it been,
  That thou the *French* shouldst not at all resist,
  Thou mightst by *Brescy* have been warn'd I ween,
  Now thou a warning art for such as list
  To shun like losse, by thy mishaps fore-seen,
  Not stubbornly in folly to persist;
  So *Riminy* and *Fæns* were preserv'd,
  By marking in what sort thou hadst been serv'd.

9

As now king *Lews* (I say) had need to send
  New captains to supply their rooms were dead,
  So then the *Pagan* Princes did intend
  To see their men from sundry countries led,
  And all disorders and defects to mend,
  To point them captains that do lack a head;
  First then *Marsilio* all his souldiers view'th,
  And *Agramant* next after him insew'th.

10

The chief of those are of *Marsilio's* traine,
  Are first the *Catalins*, men of great land,
  And of the best and noblest blood of *Spaine*:
  The next that do to them in order stand,
  Are of *Navar*, whose King was lately slaine
  At *Burdels* by *Renaldos* valiant hand,
  Marsilio sore laments the sorie case,
  And pointeth *Isolir* supply his place.

11

Bulligant governeth those of Lion,
    Grandonius for th'Algarbys doth provide,
Marsilio's brother called Falsiron,
    Doth those of lesser Castile rule and guide:
Those of Mallaga do attend upon
    Madrasso, so doth Civill all beside,
There where as Betis water so abounds,
As all about it makes them fruitfull grounds.

12

Tessyra, Baricond and Stordilan,
    Vnto the field do bring their forces in,
Granado this, Majorick he hath tane,
    The first to rule in Lisbon doth begin,
Where Larbin late was brought unto his bane,
    Tessyra unto Larbyn next of kin,
Those of Gallicia Serpentine doth guide,
Since valiant Maricold in battell di'd.

13

Those of Toledo and of Galatrave,
    Whom Synagon did lead not long ago,
Now Matalist their government must have,
    Because that he was slaine by Christen so:
Then Pisardin a man in battell brave,
    With all the band of Salamance doth go.
With many other souldiers of Pagenza,
Of Avila, Zamorra and Palenza.

14

Those of the court and of Marsilio's traine,
    With those of Saragose, Ferraw doth guide,
The chiefest flour, and the chief host of Spaine,
    Well arm'd, well hors'd, well furnished beside,
With whom two kings that late had lost their raigne,
    Morgant and Malsatise did there abide,
And in the state of private men remain'd,
And were by him most friendly entertain'd.

15

The name of many a Duke, and Lord, and Knight,
    For brevity I purpose to omit,
Such as were stout and hardy men in fight,
    Such as were wise and politike in wit,
With th'Earle of Sagunt Archidant that hight,
    Langiran, Ammirant, and Malagit:
There was great Fulliron, Marsilio's bastard,
That in that fight did shew himself no dastard.

16

After the Spanish hoast was view'd and past,
    Before king Agramant, the next that came,
Was one that all the rest in stature past,
    The governour and king of great Orane,
Then came a band whose leader small time past,
    At Burdels field was brought unto his bane,
Lamenting that the king of Garamant
Was conquer'd by the Lady Bradamant.

17

Then came the third, and that a headlesse crew,
    Whose captaine Argust was in battell slaine,
To this the second and the fourth, anew
    King Agramant doth leaders fresh ordaine.
But few there were that for these roomes did sew,
    So few sufficient men there did remaine:
Buraldo and Argonio for the best,
And Ormida he chose among the rest.

18

Then came Brunello with a chearlesse face,
    And look for shame still fixed on the ground,
For late he fell in Agramants disgrace,
    Who doubted that his faith had not been sound,
Ere since he went unto th'inchanted place,
    Where to a tree dame Bradamant him bound,
Because he lost his ring, whose losse so griev'd him,
That though he told him true, he not believ'd him.

19

But Isolir the brother of Ferraw,
    That was the first that found him and unti'd him,
Avouch'd to Agramant the thing he saw,
    How that by force some enemy had ti'd him,
So as the King his anger did with-draw,
    Although he never after well could bide him,
But swore the next offence that he committed,
An halter should unto his neck be fitted.

20

With those of Esperie came Soridano,
    And Doribon did come with those of Set,
With those of Nasomanie Prusiano,
    King Agricalt Amonios charge did get,
Malabusers came with them of Fisano,
    The rest doth Finadure in order set,
Ballastro those that follow'd erst Tardocco,
Those of Canaria and of Morocco.

21

From Mulga and Arsilla others came,
    The first their former captaine still doth hold,
Vnto the next the King a new doth name,
    One Corineus a trusty man and bold,
Then Balivesse a man of evill fame,
    Clarindo next of whom great deeds are told,
Sobrino next a man of elder age,
In all the camp was none more wise and sage.

22

Those of Getulia came with Rimedont,
    With Maribaldo those of Bolga went,
And those of Cosca came with Balnifront,
    Their former Lord his life in battell spent:
Then came the king of Algier Rodomont,
    That lately into Turkie had been sent,
To bring some new supplies of horse and men,
And back againe was new return'd as then.

23

In all the camp was not a man more stout,
  In all the camp was not a man more strong,
  Nor one of whom the *French* stood more in doubt,
  Was there the *Turkish* army all among,
  In *Agramants* nor in *Marsilio's* rout,
  Nor all the followers did to them belong.
  Beside he was (which made them dread him chief)
  The greatest enemy to our belief.

24

Then *Puliano* came, a gallant king,
  And *Agramantes* cousen *Dardanell*,
  Whether some Owle did at their window sing,
  Or other lucklesse bird, I cannot tell,
  As oft we see it is an usuall thing,
  That some presage ones mischief shall foretell;
  But sure it was prefixt in heav'n on high,
  What time and hour next day they both should die.

25

Now all their bands were muster'd saving two,
  Those of *Noritia* and of *Tremisen*,
  King *Agramant* doth marvell what they do,
  He knowes not where to heare of them nor when:
  Now as he was dispatching hereunto
  Some messenger, behold one of the men
  That serv'd the king of *Tremisen*, in hast
  Came and discover'd all that had been past.

26

Sir king (quoth he) by fortune and ill chance,
  The noble kings *Alsird* and *Manilard*,
  Happen'd to meet a cruell knight of *France*,
  While with their bands they travel'd hitherward,
  He overthrew them both, (oh hard mischance)
  And kild and spoil'd, and drave away their guard,
  And sure (quoth he) I think his force is such,
  To all your camp he would have done as much.

27

Among the rest that to this tale gave eare,
  There was a Prince that late from *Affricke* came,
  To whom king *Agramant* great love did beare,
  And *Mandricardo* was the Princes name,
  His heart was stout, and far from any feare,
  His body strong and able to the same:
  And that which greatest glory did him yeeld,
  He had in *Sorie* conquer'd *Hectors* field.

28

Now that the messenger his tale had done,
  Which made the hearers hearts for sorrow cold,
  This valiant Prince king *Agricanes* son,
  Straight was resolv'd with heart and courage bold,
  That to win praise no paine did ever shun:
  Although his purpose secret he did hold,
  To be revenged on this bloudy knight,
  That had so many slaine and put to flight.

29

He ask'd the messenger what clothes he ware,
  And in what colour'd garments he was clad?
  Black (quoth the messenger) his raiments are,
  No plume nor bravery his helmet had:
  And true it was, *Orlando's* inward care
  That made his heart so sorrowfull and sad,
  Caus'd that his armour and his open shoes
  Had like resemblance of his inward woes.

30

Marsilio had before a day or twaine,
  Giv'n unto *Mandricard* a gallant steed;
  His colour bay, but black his taile and maine,
  Of *Frizland* was the dam that did him breed,
  The Sier was a villan brave of *Spaine*:
  On this brave beast this brave man mounts with speed.
  Swearing he will not to the camp turn back,
  Till he had found the champion all in black.

31

He meets the silly people in the way,
  Halting, or maim'd, or weeping for their friends,
  Their wofull looks their fearfull hearts bewray,
  (Weeping in such a losse but small amends)
  But when he came where the dead bodies lay,
  In viewing of their wounds some time he spends,
  As witnesses of his strong hand that gave them,
  Him he envies, and pities them that have them.

32

Ev'n as a Wolfe by pinching famine led,
  That in the field a carren beast doth find,
  On which before the dogs and rav'ns have fed,
  And nothing left but hornes and bones behind,
  Stands still, and gazeth on the carkasse dead:
  So at this sight the *Pagan* Prince repin'd,
  And curseth oft, and cals himself a beast,
  For comming tardy to so rich a feast.

33

But when the mourning knight not here he found,
  From thence he travel'd many a weary mile,
  Vntill he found a meadow compast round,
  With running streames that almost made an Ile,
  Save one small entrance left of solid ground,
  Which guarded was with armed men that while,
  Of whom the *Pagan* asketh why they stand
  To guard the place with weapons in their hand.

34

Their captaine viewing well his brave attire,
  Doth think he was a man of great regard,
  And said king *Stordilano* did then hire,
  Into these parts his daughter deare to guard,
  Espous'd to king of *Sarza* by her Sire,
  Who shortly for the mariage prepar'd:
  And here (quoth he) we do this passage keep,
  That none may trouble her while she doth sleep.

35

To morrow to the camp we mind to go,
  Where she unto her father shall be brought,
Who means on *Rodomont* her to bestow,
  By whom this noble match is greatly sought.
Now when the captaine had him answer'd so,
  This Prince that setteth all the world at nought,
Why then (quoth he) this maid belike is faire,
I pray thee cause her hither to repaire.

36

My hast is great, but were it greater far,
  Yet would I stay to see a prettie maid:
Alas you misse your mark your aime doth arr,
  (Gentle sir foole) to him the captaine said:
Thus first they gan with bitter words to jar,
  And then from blowes but little time they staid,
For straight the Prince did set his speare in rest,
And smote therewith the captaine through the brest.

37

And straightwayes he recovered his speare,
  And at the next that came therewith doth run,
For why none other weapon he did weare,
  Since he the *Trojan Hectors* armor won,
At what time he most solemnly did sweare,
  To win the sword worn by *Trajano's* son,
Cal'd *Durindan*, a blade of temper rare,
That *Hector* erst, and now *Orlando* bare.

38

Great was the force of this *Tartarian* knight,
  That with his speare and weapon none beside,
Durst with so many joyn'd together fight:
  Yet sets he spurs to horse, and stoutly cri'd,
Where is a man that dare withstand my might,
  Who dares forbid me where I list to ride?
And with that speare himselfe he so bestir'd,
That small prevail'd against him bill or sword.

39

But when his speare in peeces burst he saw,
  The trunchen huge he takes in both his hands,
His blowes were such, not bloud but life to draw,
  All dead or fled, not one his force withstands:
As Ebrew *Samson* with the Asses jaw,
  Did heap on heaps the proud *Philisten* bands,
So *Mandricard* smote oft with so great force,
As one stroke kil'd both horsman and his horse.

40

Now though they took this thing in high disdaine,
  To be thus conquer'd with a broken stick,
Yet when they learned had unto their paine,
  It was in vaine against the wall to kick,
Though unrevenged lie their fellowes slaine,
  They leave the dead, rather then loose the quick:
But he so eager was to kill and slay,
That scant he suffer'd one to scape away.

41

And as the reeds in marishes and lakes,
  Dri'd with the Sun, or stubble in the field,
When as by hap the fire among it takes,
  May not it selfe against that fury shield:
Ev'n so this crew but small resistance makes,
  And ev'n of force is driv'n at last to yeeld,
And leave her undefended to their shame,
For whose defence they from *Granata* came.

42

Now when the passage open did appeare,
  He hastens in the Lady faire to see,
Whom he doth finde in sad and mourning cheare,
  And leaning of her head against a tree,
All down her cheeks ran streames of cristall cleare,
  She makes such mone, as greater could not be,
And in her countenance was plainly shown
Great grief for others harms, feare of her own.

43

Her feare increast when as he nearer drew,
  With visage stern and all with bloud distain'd,
The cries were great of her and of her crew,
  That to their gods of their ill haps complain'd:
For why, beside the guard whom late he slew,
  She had (that privately with her remain'd)
Laund'rers and nurses, playfellowes and teachers,
With learn'd Physitions, and heathnish Preachers.

44

Now when the *Pagan* Prince saw that faire face
  Whose fairer was not to be found in *Spaine*,
He thinks if weeping give her such a grace,
  What will she prove when she shall smile againe?
He deemeth *Paradise* not like this place,
  And of his victory he seeks this gaine,
To have his prisner suffer him to wo her,
And yeeld himself a prisner unto her.

45

Howbe't he maketh her against her minde,
  Vpon her ambling nag with him to ride,
Her masters, maids, and servants left behinde,
  And promis'd them he will for her provide,
He will be servitor, and nurse, and hinde,
  And playfellow, and governour, and guide,
Adieu my friends (quoth he) I you enlarge,
For of your Mistris I will take the charge.

46

The wofull folk all mourning part away,
  With scalding sighs, cold hearts, and watry eyes,
And one unto another thus they say,
  How deep revenge will her stout spouse devise,
How will he rage to leese so faire a pray?
  Oh that he had been at this enterprise,
No doubt but he would quickly wreak this slaughter,
And bring againe king *Stordilano's* daughter.

47

Of this faire prey the Prince was well apaid,
Which fortune gate him joyned to his might,
And now it seem'd his hast was well alaid,
That late he made to meet the mourning knight,
Before he rode in post, but now he staid,
Bethinking where to rest himself that night,
To finde a place was now his whole desire,
Where he might quench his lately kindled fire.

48

And first to comfort and asswage the paine,
Of Lady *Doralice* (so was her name)
He frames a tale, and most thereof doth faine,
And sweares that he allured by her fame,
Had purposely forsook his home and raigne,
And for her love into these quarters came,
Not that he ought to *France* and *Spaine* that duty,
But only to the beames of her rare beauty.

49

If love deserveth love (quoth he) then I
Deserve your liking, that have lov'd you long;
If stock you do esteem, my stock is high,
Sith I am sonne to *Agrican* the strong:
If state may stand in stead, who can denie,
To God alone our homage doth belong?
If value in your choise be of behoof,
I think this day thereof I have show'd proof.

50

These words and such as love had then him taught,
Who lent him eloquence to serve his turne,
So sweetly in her tender fancie wrought,
That in a little while she ceast to mourne,
And first her feare asswag'd, and then her thought,
A pleasing looke doth to her eye returne,
By which the Prince (in love no novice) guest,
That she ere long would grant him his request.

51

Now doth the night approch, and *Phœbus* face
In *Ocean* sea begins it selfe to hide,
The which did cause them somwhat mend their pace
And on their way with greater speed to ride:
And now they travel'd had but little space,
When first a smoke and then a light they spide,
Then came they where they heard the bandogs bark
When as the aire was now obscure and dark.

52

A few poore cotages where heardmen dwell,
They find, and there together they alight,
The houses poore, but such as very well
Might serve them to repose them for a night,
Their fare was meane, fit hunger to expell,
To which the heardmen friendly them invite,
As curtesie oft times in simple bowres
Is found as great as in the stately towres.

53

But after supper what did passe betweene
Dame *Doralyce* and *Agricanes* haire,
May not be told, because it was not seene,
But they may guesse, that have with Ladies faire
By night alone in place convenient beene,
Where to disturbe them no man did repaire,
I doubt he did not so his passion bridle,
To let so faire a dame lie by him idle.

54

But sure I am when day light did appeare,
They both arose well pleas'd and well content,
And thankt the heardmen for their friendly cheare,
And so from thence they both together went,
Vntill they came unto a river cleare,
Before the forenoone of the day was spent,
And riding downe along the river side,
Two horsemen with a damsell they espide.

55

But let them go, for why my high conceat
Forbiddeth me long in one path to tread,
And cals me back of *Agramant* to treat,
Who being newly troubled in his head,
To heare there were from *England* succors great,
Vnder the conduct of Renaldo led,
To counsell cald the Princes sage and wise,
Some remedie for mischiefs to devise.

56

They all conclude the next ensuing day,
With scaling ladders on the wals to mount,
Lest dangers new be bred by long delay,
And succors fresh hinder their first account:
Thus *Agramant*, thus doth *Marsilio* say,
Sobrina sage, and cruell *Rodomont*,
Who to destroy *Paris* alone doth threate,
And to pull downe the sacred *Romane* seate.

57

And to this end they straight provide in hast,
Innumerable ladders apt to scale,
With timber towres upon great wheeles so plast,
As that they may approch the citie wall,
From whence they may broade bridges safely cast,
And passe without all jeopardie to fall,
And throw their balls compact of firy matter,
Then have they rams, the walls to bruse and batter.

58

But *Charles*, the day that went before that day,
The *Painims* meant to do their worst and best,
Did cause the Priests and Friers masse to say,
Did cause the people all to be confest,
And humbly prostrate unto God to pray,
To save and pittie them that were opprest,
And then they all receiv'd in Christen union,
The blessed Sacrament, that high communion.

59

Himselfe with Lords and Barons of great fame,
  (An humble feare of God in him so wrought)
In person publikly performes the same,
And by example others duties tought,
And calling on our Saviours blessed name,
O Lord (said he) though I my selfe be nought,
Let not my sinne, my wickednesse and ill,
Move thee thy faithfull peoples blood to spill.

60

And if it be thy sacred will (O God)
  To punish us for our so great transgression,
And make us feele thy hand and heavy rod,
At least defer this plague and just oppression,
That by thy foes we be not overtrod,
We that of thy true faith do make profession,
Lest they blaspheme thy name (we overthrowne)
And say thou couldest not defend thine owne.

61

So shall our fall make them thy law despise,
  So shall their wicked number still increase,
So shall the power of *Babylon* arise,
So shall thy Sacraments and Gospell cease,
Looke on this people Lord with gracious eyes,
Turne foiles and warres to victories and peace,
That when these dogs and runnegates be daunted,
Thy tombe and temple may be daily haunted.

62

Alas our merits are of none effect,
  To pay a portion of our grievous debt,
Except thy grace our weaknesse so protect,
That our misdeeds out of thy sight be set,
Lord heale our soules with grievous vice infect,
Forgive our faults, our errors all forget,
And though our sinnes the sands in number passe,
Yet let thy mercies greatnesse them surpasse.

63

Thus praid the Prince most sorrowfull and sad,
  With humblenesse of heart and great contrition,
And to this prayre he then a vow doth ad,
Well suting to his state and high condition.
Nor small effect these vowes and prayers had,
For presently without all intermission,
His Angell good up to our Saviour mounted,
And there his vowes and prayers all recounted.

64

And thousand pray'rs alike at that same time,
  By messengers alike to God were brought,
When lo the goodnesse, and the powre divine,
That never shall, nor never vaine was sought,
His gracious eare doth to their prayre incline,
Those whom he made, & whō he deare had bought:
Then to the Angell *Michael* straight he beckned,
Who not a little of his calling reckned.

65

And thus he said, go thither straight in post,
  Where now in *Picardie* the Christens land,
And so to *Paris* guide that *English* host,
Let not their foes their comming understand,
In this attempt shall Silence helpe you most,
Will him this enterprise to take in hand,
This done, then see you find dame *Discord* out,
And will her hast unto the *Pagan* rout.

66

And charge her there according to her skill,
  Among the best to sow such foule dissention,
That they may one the other wound and kill,
And fill their camp with brauls and with contention:
Let some men like their entertainment ill,
And grudge because they have no bigger pension,
And let them all so vary out of measure,
That they may do their Prince but little pleasure.

67

The blessed Angell not a word replies,
  But doth his makers holy will obay,
Forthwith ev'n in a moment downe he flies,
And where he goes the clouds do fleet away:
But by the way he thinks and doth devise,
Of ev'ry place where *Silence* find he may,
Though he an Angell were he could not tell,
Where this same enemy of speech doth dwell.

68

At last he fully doth himselfe perswade,
  To find him in some houses of devotion,
That first for life monasticall were made,
Where godly men, despisers of promotion,
Dwell farre from all this worldly wicked trade,
With minds abhorring flesh and fleshly motion,
Where idle words should counted be a shame,
And where on ev'ry wall they write his name.

69

Wherefore into an Abbey he doth go,
  And makes no question *Silence* there to find,
And Peace and Charitie, and Love also,
And lowly thoughts, and well contented mind:
But soone he was aware it was not so,
All contrary their humors were inclind,
For *Silence* in that Abbey doth not host,
His name was onely writ upon a post.

70

Nor *Quietnesse*, nor *Humblenesse*, nor *Peace*,
  Nor *Charitie*, nor godly love was here,
They were somtimes, but now those times do cease,
Now *Covetise*, and *Ease*, and *Belly cheare*,
Pride, Envie, Sloth, and *Anger*, so increase,
That *Silence* banisht is and comes not neare.
With wonder great the Angell them doth vew,
And findeth *Discord* in this cursed crew.

71

Her whom the heav'nly King did will him find,
　Next after *Silence*, her he findeth furst,
　To seeke her out in hell he had assign'd,
　Among the spirits damned and accurst,
　It sore did grieve his pure unspotted mind,
　Where he expected best, to find them worst,
　It seem'd to him a thing uncouth and strange,
　In sacred place to find so great a change.

72

He knew her by her weed of sundry hew,
　All parcht with infinite unequall lists,
　Her skin in sundry places naked vew
　At divers rents and cuts, he may that lists:
　Her haire was gray, and red, and blacke and blew,
　And hard, and soft, in laces some she twists,
　Some hangeth downe, upright some standeth staring,
　As if each haire with other had bene squaring.

73

Her lap was full of writs and of citations,
　Of processes, of actions and arrests,
　Of bils, of answers, and of replications,
　In courts of Delegates and of Requests,
　To grieve the simple sort with great vexations:
　She had resorting to her as her guests,
　Attending on her circuits and her journeys,
　Scriv'ners and Clarks, and Lawyers and Atturneys.

74

The Angell calleth her, and bids her go,
　Vnto the *Turks* as fast as she can hie,
　Among their Kings such seeds of strife to sow,
　As one of them may cause the tother die.
　Then he demaundeth her if she do know,
　Within what place *Silence* doth use to lie,
　He thought that she that travel'd much about,
　In stirring strife might hap to find him out.

75

I cannot call to mind (quoth she) as yet,
　That I have talkt with *Silence* any time,
　I heare them talke of him, and praise his wit,
　And secretnesse to cover any crime;
　But my companion *Fraud* can serve you fit,
　For she hath kept him companie sometime,
　And which was *Fraud* she pointeth with her finger,
　Then hence she hies and doth no longer linger.

76

Fraud shew'd in comely clothes a lovely looke,
　An humble cast of eye, a sober pace,
　And so sweet speech, a man might her have tooke,
　For him that said, haile *Marie* full of grace,
　But all the rest deformedly did looke,
　Full of all filthinesse, and foule disgrace,
　Hid under those large garments that she ware,
　Close under which a poison'd knife she bare.

77

The Angell asketh her if she do know
　The place where *Silence* makes his habitation.
　Forsooth (quoth *Fraud*) he dwelled long ago
　With the wise sages of the Greekish nation.
　Archytas and *Pythagoras* (I trow)
　That chiefe to vertue had their inclination,
　And afterward he spent these latter yeers
　With *Carmelit* and with Saint *Bennet* friers.

78

But since these old Philosophers did faile,
　And these new saints their saintlike life did change,
　He sought new places for his most availe,
　And secret and uncertaine he doth range:
　Sometime with theeves that true men do assaile,
　Sometime with lovers that delight in change,
　Sometime with traitors he doth bide, and furder,
　I saw him late with one that did a murder.

79

With clippers and with coyners he doth stay,
　Sometime in secret dens and caves obscure,
　And oft he changeth places day by day,
　For long he cannot in a place endure.
　But I can tell you one most ready way,
　Where you to find him out shall be most sure,
　Go where as *Sleepe* doth dwell, and out of doubt,
　At midnight you shall find him thereabout.

80

Though *Fraud* by custome use to lie and faine,
　Yet was this tale so evidently trew,
　The Angell now no longer doth remaine,
　But with his golden wings away he flew
　To *Arabie*, where in a country plaine,
　Far from all villages and cities vew,
　There lieth a vale with woods so overgrowne,
　As scarce at noone the day light there is showne.

81

Amid this darke thicke wood, there is a cave,
　Whose entrance is with Ivie overspread,
　They have no light within, nor none they crave,
　Here *Sleepe* doth couch his ever drowsie head,
　And *Sloth* lies by, that seems the gout to have,
　And *Idlenesse*, not so well taught as fed,
　They point *Forgetfulnesse* the gate to keepe,
　That none come in nor out to hinder *Sleepe*.

82

She knowes no names of men, nor none will learne,
　Their messages she list not understand,
　She knowes no businesse doth her concerne,
　Silence is sentinell unto this band,
　And unto those he comming doth discerne,
　To come no neare he beckens with his hand,
　He treadeth soft, his shoes are made of felt,
　His garment short, and girded with a belt.

83

To him the Angell go'th, and in his eare
  He tels him thus, *Iehovah* bids you guide
  Renaldo, with the succors he doth beare,
  To *Paris* walls, so as they be not spide,
  Nor let the *Pagans* once suspect or feare
  Their comming, nor for it at all provide,
  And let them heare no incling of these foes.
  Vntill they find their force and feele their bloes.

84

No answer *Silence* made, but with his head
  He made a signe, as who should say he would,
  And with the Angell straight himselfe he sped,
  In greater hast then can be thought or told,
  To *Picardie*, from whence the *Angell* led,
  That present day the bands of souldiers bold,
  To *Paris* walls, an hundred miles asunder,
  Yet no man was aware it was a wonder.

85

And *Silence* still surveyeth all the rout,
  Before, beside, behind, with great regard,
  And with a cloud doth compasse them about,
  No man of them was seene, no noise was heard,
  Then walketh he among the *Pagans* scout,
  And unto them that kept their watch and ward,
  And brought them somewhat (what I do not find)
  That made them for the time both deafe and blind.

86

Now while *Renaldo* came with so great hast,
  As well it seem'd an Angell did him guide,
  And as he went, with so great silence past,
  As by his foes his comming was not spide:
  King *Agramant* had now his footmen plast
  By *Paris* walls, fast by the ditches side,
  He meanes the citie to assaile that day,
  On ev'ry side by all the meanes he may.

87

He that would take upon him to declare,
  Of *Agramantas* host the certaine number,
  That to destroy this Citie did prepare,
  Shall seeme himselfe as frutelesly to cumber,
  As if he told what flowres in *Hyble* are,
  What fish in sea, what water drops in *Humber*,
  What starres in skie at midnight when it covers
  The unchast acts of close and secret lovers.

88

The larum bell in ev'ry place doth ring,
  About the towne with strange disorderd sound,
  In Churches Mattens they do say and sing,
  Some kneeling down, some groveling in the ground,
  If gold were unto God so gratefull thing,
  As fond men think, no doubt there would be found,
  Enough in this extremity, that would
  Make all the saints new images of gold.

89

There might you see godly old men and just,
  Lamenting that their lives so long did last,
  And call them happie that were laid in dust,
  And buried many yeares and ages past;
  But gallant youths, devoid of all mistrust,
  Not with these perils any whit agast,
  Whom enemies nor engines none appals,
  Go to defend right manfully the walls.

90

Bold Barons, Earles and Dukes of great degree,
  With souldiers, forreiners, and of the towne,
  Did come to *Charles*, and praid him to agree,
  To let them out, and let the drawbridge downe:
  Glad was King *Charles* their forward minds to see,
  To fight for *Christs* religion and his crowne,
  But yet as then he doth not thinke it best,
  In this one point to grant them their request.

91

He rather thinks it better them to place,
  The forces of the fierce assault to breake,
  With distant bands a great or little space,
  According as the wall was strong or weake:
  Himselfe with chearfull vigor in his face,
  Vnto them all most curteously doth speake,
  These he doth comfort, them he doth encourage,
  And fill the stout with hope, the faint with courage.

92

Faire *Paris* lieth in a pleasant plaine,
  Ev'n in the navell, rather in the hart
  Of *France*, the river cuts the same in twaine,
  And makes an Iland of the better part,
  The rest that doth in greatnesse more containe,
  A ditch and wall doth from the plaine depart,
  King *Agramant* assaults the Westerne side,
  As having Westward gotten all beside.

93

Marsilio with the warlike bands of *Spaine*,
  He points to keepe the field in armed ranks,
  Sobrino sage and those with him remaine,
  Are placed upon *Sequans* fruitfull banks.
  Himselfe with an innumerable traine,
  With ladders, bridges, fagots, barres and planks,
  Doth thinke to fill the ditch and make it levell,
  And at the walles do keepe unruly revell.

94

What should I speake of *Rodomont* most fell,
  Blaspheming God, not onely scorning men,
  That knew to use a glittering blade so well,
  As I so well know not to use my pen:
  His deeds alone would aske a day to tell,
  That in few houres he did performe as then:
  As for the rest they came like swarmes of flies,
  And fild the aire with shouts and hideous cries.

95

And they no lesse provided are within,
  With rampers, bulwarks, and with double dikes,
  And where their foes to climbe do once begin,
  They push them down with bils, with staves & pikes;
  If one be kild, another steppeth in,
  Ho man his place for feare of hurt mislikes,   (water,
  Some throw down bricks, some stones, some scalding
  And grieve them much with all, most with the later.

96

Some throw among them newly flaked lime,
  That burneth most when most it seems to quench,
  With pots of brimstone, pitch and turpentine,
  Annoying them with heate, and smoke, and stench,
  The rest are still employ'd, and leese no time,
  With wreathed stakes to fortifie, the trench:
  Thus all within were busie, all without,
  On both sides fortune standing still in doubt.

97

The while the king of *Sarza* brought about
  His owne and men of divers other lands,
  Himselfe to shew his might and courage stout,
  That made him counted valiant of his hands,
  From *Cupids* campe was not excluded out,
  But rather soly subject to such bands,
  A Lion geuls he gives in loftie banner,
  A Ladie bridling him in lowly manner.

98

So by the beast he meant his owne fierce mind,
  And by the dame his mistris faire was ment,
  The bridle was to shew how love could bind
  His loftie heart, and bow it to her bent.
  He little knew, that shew'd himselfe so kind,
  How of his purchase others tooke the rent:
  He knew not *Mandricard* did pleade possession,
  Of her to whom he makes this kind profession.

99

Straight to the wals are thousand ladders plast,
  With double ranks that two may climbe at once,
  And up the souldiers get on them in hast,
  One shoulders up another for the nonce:
  He that goes slow, and he that climbes too fast,
  Are each in perill of a broken sconce.
  Their enemies assailing still the hier,
  Their captains those that linger or retier.

100

Thus ev'ry one do clammer up the wall,
  For value some, and other some for feare,
  And some are slaine, and some are made to fall,
  Repenting late that ever they came there:
  Fierce *Rodomont* alone (contemning all)
  No paine, no place for perill doth forbeare,
  But rusheth on, more despratly then stoutly,
  Blaspheming God while others pray devoutly.

101

A paire of curats passing hard he ware,
  Made of an ugly Dragons scaly skin,
  This armour his great auncestor first bare,
  He that to build *Babel* did first begin:
  (A towre whose height shold with the clouds cōpare)
  And thought from God the rule of heav'n to win:
  And to the same effect likewise he made,
  Of passing proofe an helmet, shield and blade.

102

Thus *Rodomont* that came of *Nimrods* kind,
  As proud and irreligious as was he,
  Regardeth not a passage safe to find,
  Or where the wall might weakest guarded be,
  But with a heart to mischiefe all inclind,
  Where he the same defended best doth see,
  (Protected with his shield) he makes no bones,
  To go through fire and water, darts and stones.

103

When once upon the battlement he was,
  Where all the wall was broade and largely paved,
  How did he slay the *Christens* then alas,
  How fierce he unto them himselfe behaved?
  His blade doth pierce their plates of steele and bras,
  All were not priests whose crownes that day were
  He kild alone so many as their blood   (shaved,
  Did cause the ditch to fill with crimson flood.

104

Beside the baser sort, these men of name,
  At this same first conflict by him were slaine,
  Orgetto Duke, that late from *Flanders* came,
  Arnold and *Hugo*, two of *Charles* his traine,
  And *Lews* that governd *Provence* with great fame,
  Walter and *Denis*, *Hawnce* of *Satalline*,
  Some were thrust through, some had (past all releefe)
  Their helmets and their heads clov'n to the teeth.

105

And some by force from off the wall he cast,
  Among the which was one *Moschino* hight,
  That by his will would never water tast,
  But still in wine did put his whole delight:
  But lo his lucke was to be drown'd at last,
  Within this dirtie ditch for further spite,
  And he that never water could abide
  In all his life, now here in water dide.

106

Thus while that *Rodomont* did kill and slay,
  All that he found upon the utmost wall,
  His band of men the while had found the way,
  To passe the ditch and so the wall to scale.
  But now within another dike there lay,
  The sight whereof their courage did appall,
  For why the *Christens* sent such store of shot,
  As this same place did seeme to them too hot.

107

The dike was drie, the bottome ev'n and plaine,
  Both sides were steep, but steepest next the towne,
  At this the souldiers curtesie do straine,
  Which of them first shall venter to go downe,
  Within the citizens had made a traine,
  With labour great and cost of many a crowne,
  That when the ditch with armed men was filled,
  With heat and smother they should all be killed.

108

It cubits had in bredth thrise ten and more,
  And in the bottome there were closely plast,
  Barrels of pitch, brimstone, and oyle good store,
  All matter quick to kindle, long to last.
  The captaine led them all the way before,
  And thousand souldiers follow'd them as fast,
  But *Rodomont* as though he had had wings,
  Quite ore the dike like to a grehound springs.

109

And being placed on the inner side,
  Arm'd and unarmed men to him are like,
  No steele there was his forces could abide,
  Death follow'th ev'rie blow that he doth strike:
  Which when a while to their great cost they tride,
  They do of force abandon quite the dike,
  He follows slaying without all remorse,
  So sharpe his sword, so furious is his force.

110

But when the souldiers thought the banke to mount,
  With scaling ladders, as they did the wall,
  They found themselves deceiv'd of their account,
  For straight the fier works were kindled all,
  Whose sudden flames the clouds themselves surmount
  Which sight the Pagans greatly did appall;
  And so increase their terror and their wonder,
  It made a noise like to continuall thunder.

111

The *Christens* do rejoyce at this reliefe,
  To see their practise had succeeded well:
  The *Pagans* plagu'd, with heat, and smother chiefe,
  In great dispaire do rore alowd and yell:
  Thus twixt the noise of fier and cries of griefe,
  They make an harmony most meete for hell.
  And here I meane to leave them in the fire,
  For to repose my selfe I now desire.

THE FIFTEENTH BOOKE OF
ORLANDO FVRIOSO

THE ARGVMENT

Faire Paris *is assail'd on ev'rie part,*
By those of Affricke, *and by those of* Spaine:
From Logestill' Astolfo *doth depart,*
And takes Calligorant *in his owne traine,*
Then slew Orillo, *that by Magicke art*
Reviv'd, when by the brothers he was slaine:
Stout Sansonet Astolfo *kind doth use,*
But Gryphin *of his mistres beares ill newes.*

ORLANDO FVRIOSO
THE FIFTEENTH BOOKE

1

To winne the field against our armed foes,
  Is counted honourable any waies,
  Although it be with policie or blowes,
  Yet bloody conquests staine the Captaines praise,
  But chiefest honour doth belong to those,
  Whom Fortune to such height of hap doth raise,
  To have their foe supprest and overthrowne,
  With little losse and damage of their owne.

2

Such was the victorie that you then gain'd,
  O stout *Hyppolito* you conquer'd so,
  When the *Venetian* Navie had obtain'd,
  With armed vessels all the streame of *Poe*,
  Your policie and vallue them constrain'd,
  With losse inestimable thence to go:
  Their marriners and souldiers all destroying,
  Our marriners and souldiers not annoying.

3

The Pagan *Rodomont* did want this skill,
  That forst ten thousand men the trench to enter,
  By his commandment sore against their will,
  Vpon so perillous a place to venter,
  Where straight the smother doth their bodies kill,
  And send their sinfull soules beneath the center,
  Himselfe in safetie sees them there a dying,
  Still swearing, cursing, heav'n it selfe defying.

4

Now *Agramant* an hot assault and fearce,
  Gave where he thought the same was lest expected
  He strives the wals to batter, break and pearce
  With engines strong, and rams thereto erected:
  Those Kings whose names I did before rehearse,
  Brought men some stout, & some with fear infected,
  And such as rather wish to stand aloofe,
  Then weare a corslet of the surest proofe.

5

But *Agramant* herein was much deceaved,
  For where he thought them weake and unprepar'd,
  He found that manfully he was receaved,
  And that the King himselfe the place did guard,
  With thousands more readie to be bereaved
  Of life and limbe, and such as nought regard,
  Before that they would take so great disgrace,
  As in their masters sight to leese their place.

6

But here I cease untill another time,
  To tell of these assaults the hard successe,
  Of damage like to both sides: now my rime
  Vnto the *English* Duke I must addresse,
  Astolfo sonne of *Oton* whom sometime
  Alcynas witchcraft held in great distresse,
  Who like another *Cyrce* men transformed,
  To trees, to beasts, and foules of shapes deformed.

7

You heard before how all her strange deceits,
  Melyssa sage did with the ring discover,
  And how she gave them also good receits,
  As made them all their former shapes recover,
  How after having scaped all their sleights,
  They did no longer in such fancies hover,
  But to be surely able to resist her,
  They fled unto her vertuous elder sister.

8

Where when they had with comfort great remained,
  Desirous to their countries to retire,
  They asked leave of her, and leave obtained,
  Of her that never hinders just desire:
  But ere they went she frendly them constrained,
  With precious gifts to be endowed by her,
  Such gifts as were of precious price indeed,
  And all their lives should stand them all in steed.

9

But chiefly to this *English* Duke she gave,
  Of secret skill a little written booke,
  Containing many a precept wise and grave,
  The which of her most thankfully he tooke;
  These teach a man from charmes himselfe to save,
  That in the same advisedly doth looke,
  And that to find them out he may be able,
  The booke had in the end a perfit table.

10

Beside this booke on him she doth bestow,
  Another gift of as great price and more,
  A horne in which if he do once but blow,
  The noise thereof shall trouble men so sore,
  That all both stout and faint shall flie therefro,
  So strange a noise was never heard before;
  When to the Duke these rare gifts were imparted,
  He humblie tooke his leave and thence departed.

M

11

And least *Alcyna* should by force attempt,
    To bring him backe or worke him some disease,
Andronica was with a navie sent,
    To wafte him safe till he were past those seas,
And vertuous *Sophrosina* with him went,
    To see him passe with safety and with ease,
So good a conduct and so sure a guide,
As was not found in all the world beside.

12

And thus she sail'd along that *Indian* shore,
    And sees and leeseth sight of sundry Iles,
Those called *fortunate* and others more,
    That distant are, some few, some many miles,
And (for he never heard of them before)
    He askt his guide some questions other whiles,
As whether from those *Indian* seas perchance,
A ship may saile to *England, Spaine*, and *France*.

13

She answer'd thus; to put you out of doubt,
    First know the earth it selfe is like an Iland,
Invironed with waters round about,
    That compasse in on ev'ry side their drie land,
And though to this day no man hath found out,
    Nor thinks there can be any way but by land,
Because they judge the lands length there is such,
That it the other *Hemispher* doth tuch.

14

Yet I foresee, ere many ages passe,
    New marriners and masters new shall rise,
That shall find out that erst so hidden was,
    And shall discover where the passage lies,
And all the men that went before surpasse,
    To find new lands, new starres, new seas, new skies,
And passe about the earth as doth the Sunne,
To search what with *Antipodes* is done.

15

Behold I see the signe of holy crosse,
    A signe within these quarters seene but seeld,
I see where ten a thousand put to losse,
    And to th'imperiall banner all do yeeld,
I see in spite of ev'ry thwart and crosse,
    The house of *Aragon* still wins the feeld,
I see that fortune is dispos'd to lift
Vp unto heav'n the name of *Charles* the fift.

16

It pleaseth God to keepe the waies unknowne,
    Vnto these parts as they have bene and are,
Vntill seven hundred yeares be overblowne,
    What time he meanes to raise an Emp'ror rare,
That shall both find and make them all his owne,
    And one that shall most worthily compare,
In warre for courage, and in peace for justice,
With *Trajan*, with *Aurelius* or *Augustus*.

17

I see the will of heav'n doth so incline,
    The house of *Austria* and of *Arragon*,
Shall linke together in a happie line,
    And be by match united both in one:
I see a braunch grow by the banke of *Ryne*
    Out of this house, as like there hath bene none,
Whose match (thus much to say I dare be bold)
May not be found in writers new or old.

18

By him againe *Astrea* shall be brought,
    And be restored from her long exile,
And vertues that have long bene set at nought,
    Shall raigne and banish fraud deceit and guile:
For which great works by him so nobly wrought,
    God meanes to grant him all this earthly Ile,
And under this wise Prince his deare annointed,
One shepheard and one flocke he hath appointed.

19

Which that it may the better be effected,
    He gives them Captaines both by sea and land,
That shall win places never yet detected
    And none shall dare their forces to withstand;
Cortese first, by whom shall be erected,
    The Emp'rors banner in the *Indian* sand,
Who by his valiant hand and wise direction,
Shall win and keepe those *Indies* in subjection.

20

Loe, with the noble Marques of *Pescare*,
    Prosper Colonna prosperous in fight,
Loe him that may with both of them compare,
    Or be preferred if you do him right,
I meane the Marques *Vast*, whose vallew rare,
    In tender youthfull yeares shall shine most bright,
Like to a horse that running swiftest pace,
Doth last set out, and first doth win the race.

21

In him shall faith and courage be so mixt,
    That when his years shall seeme but young & tender
As passing not the twenty yeare and sixt,
    Yet shall his fame and forces not be slender;
On him shall eyes and hearts of men be fixt,
    To him shall townes and forts, and castles render,
As to a Captaine with such worth endewed,
As he alone the world might have subdewed.

22

What should I speake of famous *Andrew D'Orie*,
    That to the pyrats so much terror breeds,
As *Pompey* so much prais'd in *Latin* storie?
    This *Andrew* either matches or exceeds:
What nobler name can be, what greater glorie,
    Then to roote out such hurtfull cursed weeds?
So as men may with saftie and with ease,
From *Italy* to *Nylus* passe the seas.

23

By his assistance, furtherance and his aide,
  In *Italy Cæsar* a crowne obtaines,
For which good service though he be well paid,
Yet for himselfe thereby he nothing gaines:
The paine is his (ô noble mind well staid)
The profit to his country sole remaines:
And whereas some to rule their country sought,
By him his countries freedome shall be wrought.

24

This love by him unto his country showne,
  In honor true shall more his name advance,
Then both the *Cæsars* victories well knowne,
  In *England, Spaine,* in *Italy* and *France:*
For though their enemies were overthrowne,
  By valour oft, and oftentimes by chance,
Yet this did blot their praise and make it lesse,
That both their countries freedome did oppresse.

25

Wherefore let them and others all beside,
  That tyrannize their countries be ashamed,
And hanging downe their heads, their faces hide,
  When they shall heare this noble *Andrew* named,
By whose rare temperate and happie guide,
  His countries peace and freedome shall be framed:
And thus *Andronica* the Duke foretold,
What men in future ages come there shold.

26

The while with prosperous winds the vessels drived,
  Came first within the view of *Persian* shore,
And then from thence their way they so contrived,
  They past the gulfe (so called long before)
And there to land so happily arrived,
  Misdoubting of *Alcynas* might no more,
He thanks these guides that all the way defend him,
And humbly to their Ladie recommend him.

27

More woods then one, more fields then one he past,
  More then one valley, more then one high hill:
He meeteth theeves by night, by dayes as fast,
  That lie in wait poore travellers to kill:
Of beasts, of serpents huge he was agast,
  That with their terror those wild deserts fill,
But when he blew his horne they fled away,
No man nor beast durst in the hearing stay.

28

He travels through the happie *Arabie,*
  So called for the store of spices sweet,
There where the bird that burnes and doth not die,
  To dwell of all the world hath thought most meet:
Thence went he to the sea, that once was drie,
  Which *Iacobs* sons went through upon their feet,
Proud *Pharao* following them unto his cost,
Himselfe and all his charets drown'd and lost.

29

Fast by the banks of *Trajans* streame he rides;
  There where as *Nylus* doth receive the same,
An horse of passing swiftnesse he bestrides,
  That was ingendred twixt the wind and flame,
Not such a beast in all the world besides,
  And *Rabycano* is this horses name:
Now as along the rivers banke he past,
He saw a boate make toward him in hast.

30

A simple hermit did the vessell steare,
  Whose beard with age was overgrowne and gray,
And when he came so nie that he might heare,
  These words to him he fatherly doth say,
My sonne if you do hold your safetie deare,
  Except you meane to die this present day,
Proceed no farther in the way you ride,
But ferrie over to the other side.

31

For if you do that fatall way proceed,
  You shall within a mile a giant meet,
Whose stature other men doth farre exceed,
  For why his height is counted fourteene feet,
He makes a sport of ev'ry cruell deed,
  The flesh of man unto his tast is sweet,
He eateth some alive, and some he slayeth,
He quarters some, and other some he flayeth.

32

Amid this crueltie he hath great sport,
  To use the service of a certaine net,
Which in the common way in secret sort,
  With dust and gravell cover'd he doth set,
And then when strangers do that way resort,
  First if he may, behind them he doth get:
And then with hideous outcries he them scares,
Vntill they fall into his net unwares.

33

But having caught them once in such a cage,
  Of birth or merit he hath no respect,
Of wealth nor sex, of country nor of age,
  No priviledge from him can them protect,
Their carkases his hunger must asswage,
  Their sculs like monuments he doth erect,
In posts and windowes hanging them on pins,
His chambers all are hanged with their skins.

34

Take then (my sonne) take then this other way,
  Where with more ease and safetie you may go.
Thanks (gentle Frier) the *English* Duke doth say,
  Yet can I not your counsell follow tho,
Though danger bids go safest way one may,
  Yet what saith honor? honor saith not so,
Let none retire with shame, thus honor seath,
The worst that can befall one is but death.

35

But contrary, if I may him intrap,
  As he to do to other doth devise,
  And take himselfe in his prepared trap,
  The good is great that hereof may arise.
  Well, quoth the hermit, God grant blessed hap,
  And send his Angell *Michael* from the skies,
  That may deliver him into thy hand,
  Or give thee strength his forces to withstand.

36

On goes the Duke blest by the simple Frier,
  Much trusting in his sword, more in his sound:
  And being now approcht a little nier,
  The cruell giants gracelesse house he found,
  Environ'd all with marish ground and mier,
  His chambers all within were furnisht round
  With skins and skuls of many a wofull hed,
  Of such as evill chance had thither led.

37

As hunters that by forrest wild do dwell,
  Naile by on post the heads and pawes of Beares,
  And of their dangers do delight to tell,
  And call to mind their hardly scaped feares:
  So looke who did in strength the rest excell,
  The giant kept some speciall limbs of theirs,
  The rest in ditches carelesly he throwes,
  To rot and be devour'd by dogs or crowes.

38

Calygorant (so is this giants name)
  Stands looking at his gate with watchfull eie,
  Rejoycing much when any stranger came,
  And namely now the Duke he doth espie,
  Not doubting but by him to do the same,
  He had to others done, and make him die;
  But first he seekes behind the Duke to get,
  And thinks hereby to drive him to the net.

39

When as the Duke the Giant fierce espide,
  He staid his horse and would not forward go,
  For feare lest in the net he might be tide,
  Of which the hermit had forwarn'd him tho:
  Then bloweth he his horne of vertue tride,
  That in the hearers terror breeds and wo,
  Which so possest his senses altogether,
  As straight he fled, and saw not where nor whether.

40

It seemed with his heart he lost his eies,
  And still he fled, and cares not how nor where,
  Right to the place where that most strange net lies,
  Which he to take the Duke had placed there,
  The net his armes and all his members ties,
  Which then *Astolfo* saw (now out of feare)
  He lights and drawes his sword, intending then
  To venge the death of thousand guiltlesse men.

41

But finding him so sure and strongly bound,
  He thought it were a base ungentle part,
  To slay a prisner whom in bands he found,
  So as he could not stir, nor no way start:
  God *Vulcan* wrought this net in caves profound,
  Of flaming *Ætna*, with such skill and art,
  That though the wires did seem but smal and weak,
  Yet could no force the same consume nor breake.

42

I say this curious net then *Vulcane* wrought,
  When certaine jealous thoughts his heart inflamed,
  His spouse therwith in *Mars* his armes he caught,
  And openly then made them both ashamed,
  At which prospect though many gods then laught,
  Yet many wisht in like sort to be shamed:
  Slie *Mercury* did after steale this net,
  His lovely *Cloris* therewithall to get.

43

Faire *Cloris* who flies out before the morne,
  And sprinkleth aire with smell of fragrant flowres,
  That in her lovely lap about are borne,
  From whence do fall the pleasant Aprill showres:
  But *Mercury*, sith she his love did scorne,
  Lay with his net in waite not many houres,
  Till at the last by *Nylus* banks he caught her,
  And there to daunce *la volta* then he taught her.

44

The net in *Anubs* temple he did leave,
  Where many yeares in safetie it did bide,
  Vntill *Calygorant* not asking leave,
  And caring not what should thereof betide,
  Of this great relique did the Church bereave,
  With all the plate and ornaments beside:
  And to this wicked use the net employed,
  By which the passengers were sore annoyed.

45

Now of this net *Astolfo* tooke a wire,
  And (like a theefe) behind him tide his hands,
  Who now was meeke as any could desire,
  And like a lambe by him most gently stands:
  At least the waight thereof himselfe might tire,
  First having bound his prisner sure in bands,
  He makes him carry that upon his backe.
  And usde him like a mule to beare a packe.

46

And thus he parteth thence triumphing so,
  And led the giant prisner in a string,
  And all about the country him doth show,
  (A sight that to them all great joy did bring)
  To *Memphis* Pyramids he then doth go,
  Most famous for the tombe of many a King,
  More hie in height then fiftie times *Pauls* steeple,
  Then saw he *Cayr* so huge and full of peeple.

47

But not so peopled as they now report,
  That thousands in the streets by night do lie
For want of roome, yet builded in such sort,
  That ev'ry house is made three stories hie,
Where runnegates do dwell, that make a sport,
  Their faith and their salvation to denie:
Of which the *Sowdan* for his owne behoofe,
Keepes fifteene thousand lodging in one roofe.

48

Thence went *Astolfo* to the banks of Nyle,
  To *Damyat* a citie thereabout,
And here he heard within a dozen myle
  Orillo dwelt, a hardy theefe and stout,
That rob'd poore men, and kild them other while,
  As travellers of him stood sore in doubt,
And (that which him with greater wonder filled)
The common voice was he could not be killed.

49

Full many a thrust, full many a cruell blow,
  Of many men in fight he had endured,
And unto many men great care and wo,
  And death it selfe he often had procured:
But his owne body was enchanted so,
  As ev'ry wound he had forthwith was cured,
I thinke some *Fayry* was his dame, or rather
I thinke some *Incubus* had bene his father.

50

The worthy Knight this wicked creature sought,
  Vntill at last he came unto the place,
Where then *Orillo* with two champions fought,
  The combat having held no little space,
Yet at his hands they both had gained nought,
  Though both of them gave sundry blowes apace,
Their names were these that held this mongrell tack,
Griffin the white and *Aquilant* the black.

51

The Necromancer fought with vantage great,
  He rode upon a cruell hideous beast,
A *Crocodile* that flesh of men doth eat,
  And birds and beasts, and doth them all digest,
Yet had the brethren throwne him from his seat,
  And further had the *Crocodile* distrest:
But him to wound and kill in vaine they strived,
For still his wounds did heale, and he revived.

52

Sometime they cleft his head by force in twaine,
  As butchers cleave a bullocks with an axe,
But straight he joyneth both the parts againe,
  As if they had bene made of melting waxe.
Who so hath seene the *Alcumists* most vaine,
  That work with *Mercurie* their cunning knacks,
Which quite disperst, rejoyneth ev'ry member,
Would soone by this be made that to remember.

53

Fierce *Aquilant* among so many bloes,
  With one, his head from off his shoulders strake,
About he seekes and gropeth as he goes,
  And in the dust to find his head doth rake,
And finding it, he takes it by the nose,
  Or by the locks, nor more ado doth make,
But sets it on as if it were but glewed,
And fights as if his forces were renewed.

54

Stout *Griffin* at a blow cuts off his arme,
  And takes it up and flings it in the brooke,
But he like one that had receiv'd no harme,
  Doth dive the same within the streame to looke,
Which found, he joynes (I know not with what charme)
  Vnto the place it late before forsooke:
Two dames stood by in white and blacke attire,
The combat being fought at their desire.

55

These were the courteous dames that with great care
  Had brought them up ev'n from their swathing bāds,
For these two brothers did by fortune rare
  In their first childhood chance into their hands:
These two to *Oliver*, *Gysmonda* bare,
  Though straight they were convaid to forren lands,
Where these two Ladies kept them as their owne,
I need not tell at large a tale so knowne.

56

Now was the time that neare approcht the night,
  That makes each thing with shadow shew obscure,
So that not want of force, but want of light,
  Did cause the combat could no longer dure:
The Ladies clad in garments blacke and bright,
  That (as I said) this conflict did procure,
On this condition did them all dismisse,
That to returne next day they do not misse.

57

But when that *English* Duke both saw and knew,
  The valiant youths *Griffin* and *Aquilant*,
Not onely by their armes he saw in vew,
  But by their blowes, of which they were not scant,
He doth acquaintance old with them renew,
  And they no point of courtesie do want,
For straightway by the Ladies he was led,
To take with them a supper and a bed.

58

Then in a garden sweet they did provide
  Great store of daintie meats and costly wine,
Fast by a coole and pleasant fountaines side,
  As best agreeth with the sommer time,
The while the giant with strong chaines they tide
  Vnto the body of an auncient Pine,
Lest he might hap to trouble and molest them,
While they determin'd to refresh and rest them.

59

The boord with rich and costly fare was filled,
  And yet their smallest pleasure was their meat,
  The Knights in languages and learning skilled,
  Talke of *Orillo* and the wonder great,
  To see one wounded so, and yet not killed,
  It seem'd to them a dreame and strange conceat,
  And ev'n the wisest and most learn'd did wonder,
  How he rejoyn'd his members cut in sunder.

60

Astolfo onely in his booke had read,
  (That booke that taught all charmes to overthrow)
  How this *Orillo* never could be dead,
  While in his head one fatall haire did grow,
  But having puld this haire from off his head,
  He should be subject unto ev'ry blow,
  Thus said the booke, but precept there was none,
  Among so many haires to find that one.

61

Astolfo joyfull of this good instruction,
  Not doubting but by this to make him die,
  First makes some circumstance of introduction,
  And prayes the brothers give him leave to trie,
  If he could bring *Orillo* to destruction,
  And they this friendly sute do not denie,
  Not doubting he alone would strive in vaine,
  With him that late resisted had them twaine.

62

Now had the Sunne remov'd the nights darke vaile,
  When as *Orillo* turned to the field,
  And then the *English* Duke did him assaile,
  Both fought on horseback, both with spear & shield.
  Ev'n then *Orillo* felt his heart to faile,
  (A hap to him that hapned had but feeld)
  Eu'n then some strange presage did him offend,
  That shew'd his dayes drew shortly to their end.

63

Their speares now broke their naked swords they drew,
  Astolfo layes on blowes on him a maine,
  About the field *Orillos* members flew,
  But he together gathers them againe,
  And straight his fight and forces doth renew,
  The English Duke dismembring him in vaine,
  Vntill at length one blow so luckie sped,
  That by his shoulders he cut off his hed.

64

And having headed him so ev'n and just,
  Straight with his head on horsebacke he doth mount
  And rides away, *Orillo* in the dust
  Doth grope to find the same as he was wont,
  But missing it and full of new mistrust,
  To overtake him yet he makes account,
  He rides, and would have cride ho tarrie tarrie,
  But in his hand the Duke his tongue doth carrie.

65

But though his head were lost, he finds his heeles,
  To spurre and pricke he never doth forbeare,
  The headlesse body never stirs nor reeles,
  But sits as sure as if the head were there:
  The while the skull *Astolfo* puls and peeles,
  Among such store to find th'inchanted haire,
  For in the haires no difference was in sight,
  To know if he did take the wrong or right.

66

But sith to make sure worke he thought it best,
  He makes his sword serve for a barbers knife,
  To shave the skull therewith he doth not rest,
  Vntill he finisht had the bloudy strife:
  He cuts that haire by chance among the rest,
  That haire that held *Orillo* in his life,
  The face looks pale, devoid of lively heate,
  The body backward fals out of the seate.

67

This done, the Duke brought in his hand the head,
  Returning to the company againe,
  And shew'd them where he left the carkas dead,
  Which when they saw with certain signes and plaine
  A kind of envious joy in them it bred,
  For glad they were their enemie was slaine,
  But inwardly they were displeas'd and sorie,
  That this same Duke had got from them the glorie.

68

The women also were not well content,
  That he had slaine *Orillo* in the fight,
  Because it hindred had their first intent,
  Which was to stay these youths al means they might,
  In hope thereby some mischiefes to prevent,
  Which they foresaw should unto them alight:
  Straight all that country was with rumor filled,
  How th'*English* Duke *Orillo* fierce had killed.

69

For as in all those cities they do use,
  The keeper of the next adjoyning fort,
  Sent by a Dove a letter of the newes,
  From *Damiat* unto the nearest port,
  By which device most rare they cannot chuse
  But heare and send with speed each true report:
  And thus in ev'ry country and in towne,
  They do extoll this *English* Dukes renowne.

70

The worthy Duke the brothers doth perswade,
  From thence their courses into *France* to bend,
  To do the dutie for which man was made,
  Gods honour and their countries to defend,
  Which now the *Turks* and *Painims* did invade,
  And neare had brought the same to wofull end:
  Which counsell from so great a Prince proceeding,
  They follow straight with forwardnesse exceeding.

71

The women now with teares in watry eies,
  Bid them farewell, and so they parted thence:
  And for they heard the holy citie lies
  Not passing sixe or sev'n dayes journey thence,
  To take it in their way they do devise,
  To see the place, where for humane offence,
  True God, true man descending from above,
  Did die for us unworthy of such love.

72

And sith the way betweene was large and wide,
  And void of fruits for sustenance of man,
  They do good store of bread and wine provide,
  With needfull things, as for the time they can,
  And on the giants shoulders them they tide,
  Who like a sumpter horse them after ran,
  And on this sort with most devout intent,
  Like pilgrims to *Ierusalem* they went.

73

Six dayes they traveld in their weary way,
  Nor seeing man, nor beast, nor bird alive,
  The seventh immediat after breake of day,
  In that most blessed city they arrive:
  Then visit they the tombe where *Iesus* lay,
  When with his death he did us dead revive,
  And brought hell, sinne and death into subjection,
  With suffring, dying, and his resurrection.

74

Now while the tombe with great heed they behold,
  Bare head and feet in shew of meek submission,
  And with more inward joy then can be told,
  Yet joyned with a deepe and sad contrition,
  That strake their hearts in awe and made them cold,
  With true remorse devoid of superstition,
  And with themselves they still continued musing,
  Each one himselfe in such like words accusing.

75

Why then, where thou deare Lord didst for our sake,
  With water and with blood the ground distaine,
  Shall not mine eyes some small amends to make,
  Shed teares in memory of so great paine?
  Oh drowsie heart that dost not now awake,
  Oh frozen heart that meltest not in raine,
  Oh stony heart that dost not now relent,
  Lament thee now, or else for ay lament.

76

Thus with an humble and repentant sprite,
  They tarride at the tombe no little space,
  When lo the priest appeared in their sight,
  Whose office was to keepe the holy place,
Who seeing them so lowly and contrite,
  He doth impart to them this speciall grace,
  (Sith to amendment they were now resolved)
  Them of their sinnes forepassed he absolved.

77

This done, they went about and view'd the towne,
  Held in those happy dayes by Christen hands,
  Who striving now to keepe each other downe,
  With causlesse warres do trouble sea and lands,
  Or leesing or neglecting that renowne,
  In which Gods honour and their safetie stands:
  But letting this great enemy increase,
  By their seeld making, never keeping peace.

78

A gallant knight whom *Sansonet* they call,
  This city govern'd under *Charles* the great,
  Who then intended to repaire the wall,
  And make the town a strong and stately seat:
  Astolfo gave to him the *Giant* tall,
  For strength and stature fit for such a feat,
  To serve his present purpose for the nonce,
  Vnto the wals to carie heavy stones.

79

And *Sansonet* doth eke on him bestow
  A curious belt and hangers for a blade,
  And spurs of gold, in substance rich and show,
  That for that knight were thought to have bin made
  That slue the *Dragon* with a deadly blow,
  Which did the Lady chast and faire invade:
  Thus gifts both giv'n and tane on either part,
  Each from the other friendly doth depart.

80

Now going from *Ierusalem*, behold
  They met a Greekish pilgrim by the way,
  That such ill newes to good *Griffino* told,
  As made him out of temper all the day:
  It was his evill fortune, deare to hold,
  And give his heart unto her for a prey,
  That had a pleasing hue, and faire smooth skin,
  But false, unchast, and trecherous within.

81

Her name was *Origilla*, whom of late
  He left at *Constans* of an ague sick;
  And hoping now to find her in good state,
  He heares she hath him serv'd a sluttish trick,
  As namely she had got a new-found mate,
  Not caring if that he were dead or quick:
  She thought that for her yong yeares 'twas no reason
  To lie alone in that sweet pleasant season.

82

This newes his mind doth gripe, his heart doth bite,
  He mournes by day, by night he takes no rest,
  That breeds him paine, that others breeds delight,
  And this torments him more than all the rest,
  He shames, and shuns to have it come to light,
  What was his griefe that did him so molest.
  And this to keep it close the rather made him,
  Because from her his brother did disswade him.

83

But all in vaine, for he was wholly bent
  To follow her, although he knew her nought,
  Yet to himselfe he keepeth his intent,
  That secretly his going may be wrought:
  He vowes to make th'adulterer repent,
  Who now to *Antiochia* her had brought:
  But in another book I will expresse,
  Of his departure what was the successe.

THE SIXTEENTH BOOKE OF
ORLANDO FVRIOSO

THE ARGVMENT

Stout Griffin *finds his subtill mistresse straying,*
With vile Martano, *but is pacifi'd:*
The Turks *and* Christians *all their force displaying,*
Do fight, on both sides many thousands di'd:
Both man and house by sword and fire decaying,
Do make a wofull sight on either side:
Without the towne the Christians *plague the* Turks,
Within fierce Rodomont *much mischiefe works.*

ORLANDO FVRIOSO
THE SIXTEENTH BOOKE

1

Great paines in love full many men have found,
  Of which my self have prov'd so great a part,
  As by my skill some good may hap redound,
  To such as are lesse skilfull in this art:
  Wherefore what I affirme with judgement sound,
  To breed just cause of lesse or greater smart,
  Believe what I set downe for your behoofe,
  Probatum est, I know 'tis true by proofe.

2

I do affirm, and have, and ever shall,
  That he that binds himselfe in worthy bands,
  Although his mistresse shew him grace but small,
  Although he find no favour at her hands,
  Sharp words, coy looks, smal thanks, hope none at all,
  Though more and more aloofe from him she stands,
  Yet so his heart and thoughts be highly plac'd,
  He must not mourn, no though he die disgrac'd.

3

Let him lament, let him mourn, pine, and die,
  Whom wanton wandring eyes, whom flaring haire
  Have made a slave, when under them doth lie
  A heart corrupt, a tongue that false will sweare,
  Like wounded Deere in vaine he seekes to flie,
  And in his thigh the shaft about doth beare;
  And this above the rest torments him chiefe,
  He is asham'd and dares not shew his griefe.

4

Such was the hap, such was the wofull state
  Of *Griffin* now possest with foolish love,
  He knew her mind and manners worthy hate,
  Yet could not he this fancy fond remove:
  His reason faine his passion would abate,
  But appetite is placed her above:
  That be she ne'r so false, ingrate or nought,
  Yet needs of him she must be lov'd and sought.

5

Away he steales from hence in secret sort,
  Nor to his brother once adieu doth say,
  For feare lest that his brother would dehort
  Him from her love, as oft he did assay:
  And that his journey may be cut more short,
  He coasts the country for the nearest way,
  He travels all the day and half the night,
  Vntill *Damasco* came within his sight.

6

Fast by this town this trull he overtooke,
  That lovingly with her new love did ride,
  And all old friends and lovers all forsooke,
  He was her Champion, he her onely guide:
  A man might boldly sweare it on a book,
  He were a husband fit for such a bride,
  He false, unconstant, trecherous, so was she:
  She had a modest look, and so had he.

7

He rode all arm'd upon a stamping steed,
  With gilded barb that cost full many a crown;
  She ware no lesse magnificent a weed,
  A rich embroidered purple velvet gown;
  Thus to *Damasco* ward they do proceed,
  Where late there was proclaimed in the towne,
  A solemne feast that should endure some dayes,
  For justs, for tilt, for turneyes, and for playes.

8

Now when the queen good *Griffin* had espi'd,
  (For whom she knew her squire would be too weak)
  Though sore appal'd, as scant she could it hide,
  Lest he his wrath on both at once should wreak,
  Yet as the time permits she doth provide,
  Consulting with her guide before she speak:
  And when they had agreed how to deceive him,
  With open armes she runneth to receive him.

9

And framing then her speech with great regard,
  To answer fit unto her gestures kind,
  Deare sir (quoth she) is this the due reward,
  My loyall love to you deserves to find?
  That from your sight I should a yeare be bard,
  Your sight that wholly can content my mind?
  You left me grieved with a burning fever,
  But burning more in love of you for ever.

10

Where I your comming look'd for long in vaine,
  Each houre a day, each moneth did seem a yeare,
  And of your absence long I did complaine,
  Enquiring oft, if I of you could heare:
  Alas how full is carefull love of paine?
  So sad mine heart, so heavy was my cheare,
  As being in despaire which way to mend it,
  I loath'd my life, and did desire to end it.

11

But lo how fortune when I looked least,
  Hath now provided me of double aid,
  And sent my brother, this most welcome guest,
  With whom I have without dishonour staid,
  And now your selfe whose presence makes me blest,
  For had your comming longer been delaid,
  So was my heart and soule to you inclin'd,
  That sure for grief I should have di'd and pin'd.

12

Thus flattring words wherewith her tongue abounds,
  Holp her in so good sort her tale to frame,
  That now on him the greater fault redounds,
  As glad he was to scuse himselfe from blame,
  And her strong reasons sounded on weak grounds,
  Do cleare both her, and him that with her came,
  And makes him deem'd a kinsman and a brother,
  That did his best to make this maid a mother.

13

So that he did not onely not reprove
  Her that so trech'rously had him betraid,
  So that he did not wreak as did behove,
  Th'adulterer that false with her had plaid;
  But thinks it well if he the blame remove,
  Which to his charge so probably she laid:
  And as for him (love makes him see so blindly)
  He calls him kinsman, and salutes him kindly.

14

Thus *Griffin* of his love no whit abates,
  But keeps her company as with his own,
  Vntill they came within *Damasco* gates,
  Where none of them were seen before or known.
  The town was full of Lords and great estates,
  The rumor of the feast so far was blown,
  Which that they might have more securely haunted,
  The king to all that came safe conduct graunted.

15

But here I cease to talk of *Origill*,
  And of her mate with her as fitly met,
  As knavish jack could be for whorish gill,
  Vnchast and false, as ever water wet:
  To flatter and dissemble passing skill,
  And all was fish that came into her net:
  Now here I leave good *Griffin* in her armes,
  And turne me to the *Turkish* men of armes.

16

I left where *Agramant* assaulted hard,
  A gate which he had hoped to have found,
  But weak and feeble, naked, unprepar'd,
  And easie to be beaten to the ground:
  I told you how king *Charles* the place did guard,
  Inviron'd with selected souldiers round:
  As namely *Guydons* strong, and *Angilero*,
  With *Oton* stout *Ovolyo Berlingero*.

17

Thus either band in sight of either king,
  Doth fight in hope of great reward and praise,
  And thinks such honour back that day to bring,
  As should themselves and all their of-spring raise.
  But such great store of darts the Christens sling,
  As still the *Turks* are foiled many wayes,
  They die, and by their deaths do others reach,
  How hurtfull 'tis to rove beyond their reach.

18

But *Rodomont* whose men consum'd with fire,
  Do fill their masters mind with double rage,
  Yet to avenge their deaths doth so desire,
  As nought but blood his thirst of blood can swage:
  He spares not in the passion of his ire,
  Nor men nor women, order, sex nor age,
  Away do run the silly people crying,
  And leave their children, friends, and wives a dying.

19

They happy were whose feet did serve them best,
  The fury of this cruell *Turke* to shun,
  For some were killed in the flight, the rest
  Vnto the Churches or strong houses run,
  And lock the gates against so fierce a guest,
  That in the streets had so great mischiefe done:
  And of them all that had been slaine in chase,
  Not one of them was wounded in the face.

20

But as the Tyger kils the fearfull Doe,
  That but by flight cannot it self defend,
  Or as the Wolves do spoile the sheep: ev'n so
  This cruell *Turke* their guiltlesse blood doth spend:
  They neither know to strike nor ward a blow,
  To hurt their foe nor yet to help their friend:
  Thus past the Pagan to S. *Michels* bridge,
  And none there was his passage to abridge.

21

He kils alike the sinner and the good,
  The reverend father and the harmlesse child,
  He spils alike the yong and aged blood,
  With widowes, wives, and virgins undefil'd;
  And though that all did yeeld, and none withstood,
  Yet mercy from his mind was so exil'd,
  He shew'd to such as things can truly value,
  Great signes of cruelty, but none of value.

22

Nor doth the cruell rage and fury cease,
  With seeing of so many people slaine,
  But rather still it growes and doth increase,
  Against those other that alive remaine:
  Nor grants he to the Churches any peace,
  But ev'n as though the walls could suffer paine,
  He maketh furious warres against the walls,
  And flings against them store of fiery balls.

23

Their houses all were built in *Paris* then,
　Of timber (and I judge this present houre
　Of brick and stone there are not six of ten)
　Which made the *Pagan* then to bend his power,
　To burn the houses, having kil'd the men:
　And though that fire do of it self devoure,
　Yet he doth help the fire and overthrew them,
　And those that lurk'd within he spoil'd and slue them.

24

Had *Agramant* had like successe without,
　As had within this wicked *Rodomount*,
　The wals of *Paris* had not kept him out,
　On which so oft he did assay to mount:
　But now this while the Angell brought about
　Renaldo stout the flower of *Clarimount*,
　Both with the *English* and the *Scots* supplies,
　As secretly as *Silence* could devise.

25

And that they might them more unwares assaile,
　They cast a bridge a league above the towne,
　And passe the river to their best availe,
　And so in battell order comming downe,
　Not doubting if their footing do not faile,
　To get that day great glory and renowne:
　And still among the ranks *Renaldo* rides,
　And for things needfull evermore provides.

26

Two thousand horse in good Duke *Edmonds* guide,
　And thrice two thousand archers he doth send,
　To get to *Paris* on the tother side,
　To help within the city to defend:
　(The cariages and other lets beside,
　To leave behind a while he doth intend)
　These succours greatly help the town within,
　And at Saint *Dennis* gate they let them in.

27

Renaldo takes the conduct of the rest,
　Appointing each his office and his place,
　As in his skill and judgement seemeth best,
　Sev'ring each band from others with a space:
　And seeing ev'ry one was prone and prest,
　As was to be required in such case,
　He calleth all the Lords and Leaders chiefe,
　And us'd to them this pithy speech and briefe.

28

My Lords (quoth he) I need not to repeat
　Your weighty businesse unto you at large,
　I onely say, you have just cause and great,
　To give God thanks your duties to discharge,
　That here hath sent you, where with little sweat,
　But giving on your foes one valiant charge,
　You may obtaine true fame and glory more,
　Than all your ancestors obtain'd before.

29

God, onely God that gives and guides good chance,
　Hath offer'd unto you this good occasion,
　Your names and glories highly to advance,
　Which is in noble minds a strong perswasion:
　Behold the kings of *England* and of *France*,
　Endanger'd greatly by the *Turks* invasion,
　Shut up in trenches and in wals with shame,
　You may set free to your immortall fame.

30

The very law of nature and humanity
　Wils noble hearts to help the weak distres'd;
　But more the lawes of state and Christianity,
　Without your help now like to be oppres'd,
　And right Religion turn'd to Turkish vanity,
　Of which what harms will grow, may soon be guest,
　Our temples faire with their foule idols fil'd,
　Our virgins (chast by vow) deflour'd and kil'd.

31

No mean, no stay, no end will be of slaughter,
　Of rapes and rapines wicked and unjust;
　No man shall keep his sister, wife, or daughter,
　From out the reach of their unruly lust:
　But now if you these sorrowes turn to laughter,
　And raise your honour troden in the dust,
　They must owe you the freedomes and the lives
　Of them, their friends, their children, and their wives.

32

In ancient times a lawrell Civick crown
　To him that sav'd one citizen they gave,
　If then they had such honour and renown,
　How many crownes shall you deserve to have,
　If (not a townsman, but) a noble town,
　And thousand innocents therein you save?
　In you it lies them to preserve and cherish,
　That (but for you) in wo should pine and perish.

33

Which if they should (as God forbid they should)
　By these vile *Saracens* be over-run,
　Then were the *Romane* Empire bought and sold,
　The holy Church were spoil'd and quite undone:
　In you it is these huge harms to with-hold,
　By you alone must this exploit be done,
　Tread then this path of praise so large and ample,
　Ile lead the way, follow but mine example.

34

This speech by him pronounc'd with so good spright,
　With voice so audible, with comely grace,
　Incensed them with such desire to fight,
　That tedious seem'd to them each little space.
　And as we see in riding men delight
　To spurre a horse, although he run apace:
　So stir'd *Renaldo* with this exhortation
　Those of the *English* and the *Scottish* nation.

35

And having thus confirm'd their forward hearts,
  And promis'd largely in his masters name,
  Great recompence to ev'ry mans deserts,
  Vnto the river walls he closely came,
  His army he divides in sundry parts,
  Lest breach of order bring them out of frame,
  And with the *Irish* band he first indents,
  To spoile their lodgings, and to rob their tents.

36

The rest he thus in prudent sort divides,
  The wayard *Zerbin* hath in government,
  The Duke of *Lancaster* the battell guides,
  The Duke of *Clarence* with the rereward went,
  Renaldo with some chosen men besides,
  Gives first the charge by generall consent:
  Then on a sodaine they do raise a shout,
  And fil'd our side with courage, theirs with doubt.

37

Renaldo riding out afore the rest,
  (With mind to do as much as he had said)
  Puts spurs to horse and sets his speare in rest,
  His onely sight the *Pagans* greatly fraid,
  With fainting hearts, pale looks, and panting brest,
  They shew most certaine signes of minds dismaid,
  Yet stout king *Puliano* shewes no token
  Of heart astonished or courage broken.

38

But trusting to his strength, and void of feare,
  And ranging out in sight of all his band,
  He met him man to man and speare to speare,
  He met him horse to horse, and hand to hand:
  But straight it plainly was discerned there,
  Sleight without force in little steed doth stand:
  This kind of fight was of a rougher sort,
  Then running of a course at tilt in sport.

39

Thus was king *Pulian* overthrown and tane,
  To no small terrour of the *Pagan* host,
  Next came the king (that giant) of *Oran*,
  That of his goodly stature much doth bost,
  But soon *Renaldo* brought him to his bane,
  His horse, his weapon, and his life he lost:
  The horse was glad to find himselfe inlarg'd,
  And of his heavy burden so discharg'd.

40

Nor was *Renaldo* of his sword more spare,
  Then of his speare before himselfe he show'd,
  His blade *Fusberta* pierced to the bare,
  When he his thrusts or deadly blowes bestow'd:
  No shields, no coats of so good temper are,
  Nor cloth in hundred folds together sow'd,
  That this same fatall blade of his withstood,
  But that at ev'ry blow it fetcht the blood.

41

Nor did *Zerbino* merit common praise,
  That of his value shewd that day good proof,
  He met the stoutest *Turks* at all assaies,
  On horse, on foot, at hand, and farre aloof,
  Attempting and performing sundry waies,
  That might be for their harm and his behoof:
  And all his band in fight was fierce and hot,
  As is the nature of the valiant *Scot*.

42

And thus their fiery heat and courage bold,
  Well shew'd by blowes they to the *Pagans* gave,
  Did make their stomacks faint, their courage cold,
  And glad in th'end by flight themselves to save:
  For *Sobrin* one in yeares and judgement old,
  (Though no lesse stout thē those lesse age that have)
  Doth now a little with his band retire,
  To shun the fury of the *Scottish* fire.

43

The worthy Dukes of *Albanie* and *Mar*,
  Ensu'd in valiant sort the good successe,
  And with the same prevailed had so far,
  As they had brought the *Turks* to great distresse,
  Till *Isolir* the new king of *Navar*,
  Came with his band their fury to represse;
  And on that side the battell did restore,
  Almost now lost, at least declin'd before.

44

Then grew the fight on both sides firm and stable,
  Both sides defend, both sides alike invade,
  They cast on both sides darts innumerable,
  And make therewith a dark unpleasing shade:
  An endlesse work it were to write the rable,
  The *Christens* kil'd with bow, with bill, with blade,
  Somtime the sway goeth hither, somtime thither,
  Like waters driv'n with doubtfull tides and weather.

45

When one is slaine, his room another fils,
  When one is hurt, another takes his place,
  And he that now another smites and kils,
  Fals dead himself within a little space;
  Great heaps of bodies dead make little hils,
  The earth it selfe doth look with bloudy face,
  The green wherewith it erst was overspread,
  Is turn'd to sanguine and vermilion red.

46

My pen would faile, and skill would be too scant,
  To tell the famous acts that *Zerbin* wrought,
  How his new brother noble *Ariodant*,
  A fresh supply against the *Pagans* brought,
  And how still one supplying tothers want,
  Against the *Turks* with mutuall forces fought;
  Then namely when the Prince was almost slaine,
  By bastards two of *Aragen* in *Spaine*.

47

Chelindo one, the other *Mosco* hight,
  These two at once on *Zerbin* bent their force,
  In hope that if their hands could hit aright,
  To wound him sore, or at the least unhorse,
  They wound him not, yet forc'd him to alight,
  For under him so sore they hurt his horse,
  To serve his Lord he was no longer able,
  But made the field his everlasting stable.

48

This foile and fall his courage more do whet,
  To lose the service of his trusty steed,
  But from the saddle quickly he doth get,
  His losse his wrath, his wrath revenge doth breed:
  He means not long to tarry in their debt,
  That to his horse did this unworthy deed:
  And first he gave to *Mosco* such a thrust,
  As made him tumble senslesse in the dust.

49

But when *Chelindo* saw his brother dead,
  Revenge and feare in him together strave,
  His inward eare provok'd him to have fled,
  Himselfe from danger imminent to save,
  But straight revenge another humour bred,
  Expelling feare, and makes him bold and brave,
  He spurs his horse in hope to over-run him,
  But *Zerbin* slightly steps aside to shun him.

50

And such a blow he lent him as he past,
  Vpon his shoulders from the reredemaine,
  That horse and man unto the ground were cast,
  Whence neither of them rose alive againe:
  And now the *Spanish* band came in so fast,
  As noble *Zerbin* had almost been slaine;
  But *Ariodante* then himselfe bestir'd,
  And makes an open lane by dint of sword.

51

The while the Duke of *Clarence* doth assaile
  Their rere that was by *Baricondo* led,
  The *English* archers shoot as thick as haile,
  Which to their horsemen great annoyance bred:
  On ev'ry side the *Christens* do prevaile,
  On ev'ry side the fearfull *Pagans* fled,
  Great store were slaine, and many prisners taken,
  Their battell now declined sore and shaken.

52

And had been lost, had not *Ferraw* by chance
  Come to their aid as yong *Olimpio* fell,
  Slaine by a knight of *Scotland* or of *France*;
  A cruell knight, whose name I cannot tell:
  Ferraw was sore aggriev'd at this mischance,
  He knew this youth and lov'd him passing well,
  Because his skill in musick was so choice,
  Both for sweet stroke, and for his pleasing voice.

53

Had not the humour of ambition vaine
  With crotchets new his foolish fancy fil'd,
  He might have better staid at home in *Spaine*,
  Than come abroad to be in battell kil'd:
  But thus we see they get but losse and paine,
  That deale in that in which they be not skil'd;
  I wish musitions meddle with their songs,
  And pray the souldiers to revenge their wrongs.

54

Ferraw that saw ten thousand slaine before,
  Without or fetching sigh or shedding teare:
  With this his minions death was griev'd so sore,
  As scarce he could ev'n then to weep forbeare,
  But he that kil'd him shall abuy therefore,
  By *Macon* and *Lanfusa* he doth sweare,
  And straight perform'd it to the knights great paine,
  For with his polax out he dasht his braine.

55

Nor so content, he runs among the presse,
  And in his rage so many *Scots* he slew,
  That their late forwardnesse he did represse,
  And caus'd that they in hast themselves withdrew:
  Then to the tents was sent the king of *Fesse*,
  To make resistance to the *Irish* crew,
  That spoil'd their lodgings having rob'd the best,
  And went about to set on fire the rest.

56

Then when the stout king *Agramant* espi'd,
  The danger great he and his men were in,
  And how these new supplies on ev'ry side,
  Made his retire, and ground of them did win:
  To save his own in time he doth provide,
  And lets alone the wals, and them within,
  Himselfe with Lords and other Princes store
  Came where *Ferraw* was entred late before.

57

And in such strength they do their forces link,
  And with such fury they restore the fight,
  That now the *Scots* began to faile and shrink,
  Save that *Renaldo* came ev'n then in sight,
  And cri'd, O worthy *Scots*, and do you think
  To save your selves by so unworthy flight?
  Will you so leese the honour late you wonne?
  Care you no more to save your masters sonne?

58

Do you no more regard your reputation,
  By you in sundry bloudy battels got,
  To leave the flower and jewell of your nation,
  Amid his foes as if you lov'd him not?
  Ye shame your selves and all your generation,
  If you distaine you with so foule a blot,
  Turn, turn I say, and take some heart of grace,
  And meet and smite these *Panims* in the face.

N

59

They that before were sore with feare possest,
  Were now so heartned, that with honest shame,
  Each one doth seem his safety to detest,
  Each one his mind with anger doth inflame,
  And where they left their captaine halfe distrest,
  With this so forward guide as fast they came:
  So *Zerbin* rescu'd was from *Turkish* forces,
  And mounted straight one of the empty horses.

60

Renaldo that did ever take delight
  To set on those that were most strong and stout,
  When once king *Agramant* was come in sight,
  Him from the rest forthwith he singles out:
  But when between them was begun the fight,
  They sundred were by those that stood about,
  I meane the *Turks*, who their chief Prince defended,
  Who els perhap his raigne ev'n then had ended.

61

Now while without the wals the battell so,
  On either side with fury was renew'd,
  Fierce *Rodomont* within did work such wo,
  More rufull sight with eye was never view'd;
  To wrack profane the holy temples go,
  He setteth fire on all, and to conclude,
  He did alone so spoile the goodly citie,
  As might have mov'd a stony heart to pitie.

62

And (while king *Charles* that was farre off from thence,
  Did entertaine the new-come *English* host,
  The which *Renaldo* sent for their defence)
  Behold there came a messenger in post,
  That look'd like one bestraught of wit and sence,
  His voice with hast and feare was welnigh lost,
  And when his broken words were plainly heard,
  Ah well away (he cries) we all are mar'd.

63

Some fiend of hell (for sure a fiend of hell
  It is that doth our city so destroy)
  Is sent from Belzebub with us to dwell,
  To work our utter ruine and annoy:
  This day we must bid all good dayes farewell,
  This day must be the last day of our joy,
  Lo yonder how our sacred temples smoke,
  Nor one in their defence dares strike a stroke.

64

Look how a man would be amaz'd to heare
  A noise confus'd of backward ringing bels,
  And after find, when he approcheth neare,
  New set on on fire his house wherein he dwels;
  In such amazement and in such a feare
  Was *Charles* to heare the tale this poore man tels,
  And as he thither nearer came and nearer,
  He sees the buildings clearer burn and clearer.

65

Of hardy Squires he culs a gallant crew,
  And means to drive away this wicked wight,
  If man it be, or sprite with humane hue,
  That doth unto the town this fowle despight:
  Now came he where he plaine might see in view
  Men murdred, houses burn'd, a wofull sight.
  But now although perhap my story please you,
  To pawse a little may refresh and ease you.

THE SEVENTEENTH BOOKE OF
ORLANDO FVRIOSO

THE ARGVMENT

Fierce Rodomont *leave* Paris *is constrain'd,*
Martano *at* Damasco *tilts most vily,*
Stout Griffin *thinks his running thereby stain'd,*
And goes from thence, the while Martano *slily*
Doth steale his coat and horse, and so obtain'd
Great gifts, and of the king is graced highly:
But Griffin *taken in* Martano's *clothing,*
Receives disgrace, each one his presence lothing.

ORLANDO FVRIOSO
THE SEVENTEENTH BOOKE

1

The most just God, when once mans sins do grow
  Beyond the bounds of pardon and of grace,
  Because that men his judgements just may know,
  No lesse then love, to rule on earth doth place,
  Vile monsters, such as tyrannize us so,
  With wrong the right, with lust they lawes deface:
  For this same cause were *Sylla* sent and *Marius*,
  The *Nerons* both, and filthy minded *Varius*.

2

For this *Domician* held in *Rome* the raigne,
  And *Antoninus* of that name the last,
  And *Massimin* a base unworthy swaine,
  To plague mankind in Princely throne was plac'd:
  For this in *Thebes* did cruell *Creon* raigne,
  With other tyrants more in ages past,
  For this of late hath *Italie* been wonne,
  By men of *Lumbardie*, of *Goth*, and *Hunne*.

3

What should I of unjust *Attyla* speak?
  Of *Esselin*, and of an hundred more?
  Whom God doth send his anger just to wreak,
  On us that still neglect his sacred lore.
  The times forepast long since, the present eke,
  Of such examples yeelds us wofull store,
  How we unthankfull and unfruitfull sheep
  Are giv'n to hungry rav'ning Wolves to keep.

4

Such Wolves as would not onely by their wils,
  Seaze all our goods and substance as their pray,
  But also send beyond the *Alps* high hils,
  For other wolves more hunger-sterv'd than they:
  The bones of men that *Thrasimeno* fils,
  The fights of *Treb* and *Cannas* are but play,
  If with our bloudy slaughters they compare,
  Of *Adda, Mela, Ronco*, and of *Tare*.

5

No doubt but God in heav'nly throne that sits,
  And thence our deeds and thoughts doth plainly see,
  Vs to be spoild and conquer'd thus permits,
  By those that are perhaps as ill as we:
  But if to please him we would bend our wits,
  Then from these foes he soone would set us free,
  And we shall see their punishment ere long,
  That us oppresse by villany and wrong.

6

But now to turn from whence I did digresse,
  I told you how when *Charles* the newes had heard,
  Of houses burn'd, and men in great distresse,
  By him that doth nor God nor man regard:
  Vnto their aid he doth himself addresse,
  And chuse some speciall men to be his guard,
  And meeting such as fled their course he staid,
  And these or such like words to them he said.

7

O simple fooles, what mean you hence to run?
  Turn back for shame, turn back, and do not flie,
  You chuse the greater ill the lesse to shun,
  To live with shame, and may with honour die;
  What city have you left when this is won?
  What hope is left a fortune new to trie?
  Shall one vile *Pagan* boast another day,
  That he alone hath driv'n you all away?

8

This said, he came unto the pallace gate,
  Where now the *Pagan* Prince triumphant stood,
  Most like a Serpent fierce that hath of late,
  His old skin cast and left it in the wood,
  Rejoycing now of his renewed state,
  Of his fresh strength, of young and lusty bloud,
  He shewes his forked tongue and comes apace,
  And ev'ry beast that sees him gives him place.

9

Thus scornfull and thus proud the Pagan stands,
  With threats to spoile the Pallace and deface,
  And not a man that once his force withstands,
  Vntill king *Charles* appeared in the place;
  Who looking on his old victorious hands,
  Said thus; and is now alter'd so the case,
  That these my hands that wonted were to win,
  To yeeld and to be faint should now begin?

10

Why should the strength, the vigour and the might,
  That I was wont in you to feel now faile?
  Shall this same *Panim* dog ev'n in my sight,
  My people slay, my dwelling house assaile?
  No, first on me a thousand deaths alight,
  No death can make a princely heart to quaile;
  And with that word with couched speare in rest,
  He runs and smites the *Pagan* on the breast.

11

And straight the other of the chosen crew,
  On ev'ry side the *Pagan* do beset,
But how he scap'd, and what did then ensew,
Another time ile tell, but not as yet:
For first some matters past I must renew,
And namely *Griffin* I may not forget,
And crafty *Origilla* with the tother,
That was her bedfellow and not her brother.

12

These three unto *Damasco* came together,
  The fair'st and richest town of all the East,
What time great lords and knights repaired thither,
Allured by the fame of such a feast.
I told you from the holy city hither,
Was five or six dayes journey at the least:
But all the townes about both small and great,
Are not like this for state and fruitfull seat.

13

For first, beside the cleare and temp'rate aire,
  Not noid with sommers heat nor winters cold,
There are great store of buildings large and faire,
Of carved stone most stately to behold,
The streets all pav'd where is their most repaire,
And all the ground is of so fruitfull mold,
That all the yeare their spring doth seem to last,
And brings them store of fruits of dainty tast.

14

Above the City lies a little hill,
  That shades the morning sun in early houres,
Of waters sweet (which here we use to still)
They make such store with spice and juyce of flowrs,
As for the quantity might drive a mill,
Their gardens have faire walks and shady bowrs:
But (that which chief maintaineth all the sweets)
Two christall streams do run amid the streets.

15

Such was the native beauty of the town:
  But now because they look for great resort,
Of Princes and of Lords of great renown,
They deck their city in another sort:
Each Lady putteth on her richest gown,
Each house with Arras hang'd in stately port:
The noble youths do stand upon comparison,
Whose horse doth best, who wears the best caparison.

16

Thus *Griffin* and his mates come to this place,
  And first they view these showes with great delight,
And after they had rode a little space,
A courteous squire perswades them to alight,
And prayeth them to do his house that grace,
To eat and take their lodgings there that night:
They thank him for his kind and friendly offer,
And straight accept the courtsie he doth profer.

17

They had set down before them costly meat,
  Of sundry wines there was no little store,
Of precious fruits the plenty was so great,
As they had seldome seen the like before:
The while their host doth unto them repeat,
The cause of all this feasting, and wherefore
The king appointed all these solemne sports,
To draw together knights of sundry sorts.

18

But *Griffin* (though he came not for this end,
  For praise and bravery at tilt to run,
But came to find his fleeting female friend)
Yet was his courage such he would not shun,
In these brave sports some little time to spend,
Where of well doing honour might be won.
He promis'd straight (though little were his leisure)
Before he go, to see and shew some pleasure.

19

And first he asketh farther of the feast,
  If it were new ordain'd, or els of old?
His host replieth thus (my worthy guest)
I shall in briefe to you this thing unfold:
Our Prince the greatest Prince in all the East,
Hath newly pointed this great feast to hold;
This is the first, but all of his retinue
Mind each fourth month this custome to continue.

20

In token of great gladnesse and great joy,
  By all the city is the feast begun,
In token of the danger and annoy
That *Norandin* (our king) did lately shun,
Lock'd up foure months, where he could not enjoy
The use of earth, of water, aire, nor sun:
Yet at the foure months end by hap he scap'd
The death with yawning mouth that on him gap'd

21

(But plaine to shew you whence did come the seed,
  Of which this danger seemed first to grow)
Love did to *Norandin* this danger breed,
The king of *Cypres* daughter pleas'd him so,
Because her beauty did the rest exceed,
To see her, needs (in person) he would go:
He saw he lik'd, he woo'd, he won, he married her,
And homward then by ship he would have caried her

22

But lo a wind and tempest rose so sore,
  As three dayes space they looked to be drown'd,
And made them land upon an unknown shore,
Where straight we pitcht our tents upon the ground,
And (for of trees and grasse there was good store)
The King in hope some venson to have found,
Into the next adjoyning wood doth go,
Two pages beare his quiver and his bow.

23

His meaning was some stag or buck to kill,
  We wait his comming in the tent at ease,
When suddenly such noise our eares doth fill,
  As wind in woods, and waves do make in seas,
And aye more nigh us it approched, till
  We plaine might see unto our sore disease,
A monster huge that ran along the sand,
Destroying all that in the way did stand.

24

This *Orke* (for so men do the monster call)
  Directed straight his course upon our tent,
His eyes were out, how ere it did befall,
  But yet he was so quick and sharp of sent,
As all his blindnesse holp not us at all,
  He hunteth like a spaniell by the vent,
His sent is such as none can hope to shun him,
His pace is such as no man can outrun him.

25

Thus whether they prepar'd to fight or fly,
  Or whether feare both fight and flight did let,
He takes them as his prisners by and by,
  Of forty, ten scarce to the ship could get,
Among the other prisners tane was I,
  Whilst I our Queene in safety would have set,
But all in vaine to flie, it did not boot,
He was so quick of sent, and swift of foot.

26

As shepheards hang a wallet at their wast,
  So at his girdle hangs a mighty sack,
In which the better sort of us he plac'd,
  The rest he bound together in a pack,
And to his cave that was most huge and vast,
  He beares us (hopelesse ever to come back)
A comely matron in this den he had,
Maids faire and foule, some poore, some richly clad.

27

Beside this female family of his,
  He hath a cave wherein he keeps his flock,
That cave in length and largenesse passeth this,
  Made all by hand out of the stony rock:
And (for mans flesh his chiefest dainty is)
  Into the cave he safely doth us lock,
The while he leads abroad his goats and sheep,
Which in the fields adjoyning he doth keep.

28

The king not knowing this, returned back,
  The silence that he found some feare did breed:
But when he found his wife and men were lack,
  He then to sea did hast him with great speed:
He sees plaine signes of hast, of spoile, of wrack,
  Yet knowes he not the author of this deed,
Vntill he had his ship by hap recover'd,
Then by his men the fact was plaine discover'd.

29

When he had heard at last the wofull newes,
  How greatly was his heart surpris'd with griefe?
What gods, what fortune did he not accuse
  For all his losses, but *Lucyna* chiefe?
But dangers all and death he first will chuse,
  Ere he then leave his love without reliefe,
He either will her libertie procure,
Or els he will like chance with her endure.

30

He leaves his ship, and goes by land apace,
  There where the monster had his love convaid,
And often wailes her hard and wofull case,
  Desiring and despairing of her aid.
Now came he in the kenning of the place,
  And stands twixt halfe amaz'd and halfe afraid:
At last he enters (love expelling feare)
When by good hap the monster was not there.

31

His wife was there, who with compassion mov'd,
  Admonish'd him to make but little stay,
But hasten thence, if so his life he lov'd,
  Lest that her husband find him in the way:
Yet from his purpose this him not remov'd,
  But to the sober matron he doth say,
In vaine you seek to drive me hence by terror,
Desire hath hither brought me, and not error.

32

By my ill hap while I abroad was riding,
  The *Orko* bare away my dearest wife,
I hither come of her to heare some tiding,
  Or having lost my love to leese my life,
I care not I, if she in life be biding,
  If she be dead, my death shall end this strife,
Love in this point so resolute hath made me,
You should but leese your labour to disswade me.

33

The gentle matron in this sort replies,
  Know this, thy wife in safety doth remaine,
But hard it is to compasse or devise,
  Which way to get her from his hand againe,
His want of sight, his passing sent supplies,
  To strive with him by force it were but vaine,
He spoileth men, but women do not die,
Save onely such as strive away to flie.

34

But those he finds his company to shun,
  With hatred great he doth for aye pursue,
Some he doth hang all naked in the sun,
  And day by day their torments doth renue;
And some immediately to death are done,
  Both yong and old, both foule or faire of hew,
So that to seek to set *Lucyna* free,
May harm her much, and little profit thee.

35

Wherefore my sonne depart the while thou may,
  (The matron saith) *Lucyna* shall not die,
For hither shortly he will her convay,
Where she shall fare no worse than these and I,
Depart? (quoth he) nay here I mind to stay,
And fall what shall, I will my fortune trie,
And if my hap be such I cannot free her,
At least I meane before I die to see her.

36

The matrons mind with much compassion moved,
  To see his loving and most constant mind,
That from his purpose would not be removed,
To bring him aid and comfort was inclin'd:
And then she told him how it him behoved,
If so to see his wife he had assign'd,
To use some such device as she would tell him,
That when the *Ork* should come he might not smell him.

37

She had that hanged in the houses roofe,
  The hairie skins of many a bearded goate,
And knowing best what was for his behoofe,
Of one of them she makes him make a coate,
And with goates suet for a further proofe,
To noint his body from the foote to throate:
And in this sort his shape and favour hiding,
He commeth to the place where we were biding.

38

Now night drew neare, his horne the *Orke* doth blow,
  And all his heards came backe unto his fold,
And *Norandin* among the goates doth go,
And enters in, love maketh him so bold,
The *Orko* shuts the doore, and leaves us so,
Shut up as safe as in a towre or hold,
Then doth the King at large unto his lover,
His comming and the meanes thereof discover.

39

Lucina doth not onely not rejoyce,
  To see her husband come thus strangely clad,
But with most lamentable mournfull voyce,
She blam'd him that such perill ventred had,
And sweares that if she might have had her choyce,
She would alone have felt this fortune bad,
And that before it somewhat eas'd her paine,
To thinke that he in safetie did remaine.

40

Thus said *Lucina* faire with watred eies,
  As seeming now more dolefull then before;
But *Norandino* in this sort replies,
Think'st thou my deare I loved thee no more?
Yes sure, and will ev'n now a meane devise
Both thee and these to freedome to restore,
And to deliver from this servile slavery,
By helpe of this same skin and grease unsavery.

41

And straight he taught us as himselfe had tride,
  Each one to kill a goate and take the skin,
And outwardly to weare the hairy hide,
And to be nointed with the grease within.
Thus ev'ry one doth for himselfe provide,
Before the sunne did yet to shine begin,
Then came the *Orke* and mov'd away the stone,
And out the bearded goates came one and one.

42

The smelling *Orko* at the doore doth stand,
  We past like goates and make no noise nor speech,
Yet oft he groped with his hideous hand,
But poore *Lucina* could not chuse but skreech;
Or that he hapt to touch her with his wand,
Or else too roughly paw'd her by the breech,
So back he puts her straight, and locks her up,
And sweares that she should drinke a sory cup.

43

Himselfe drives out his flocke (as wont he was)
  And we like goates among the goates do keepe,
And when as they were feeding on the grasse,
The monstrous heardman laid him downe to sleepe.
Thus we escapt, but our good King alas,
(That mist his love) doth nought but waile and weep
And save that still he hop't of her reliefe,
He would no doubt have dide of very griefe.

44

At night he turneth back with like desire,
  As he before had come to set her free,
And he conceales himselfe with like attire,
From him that wants his instrument to see.
The *Orke* inflam'd with cruell rage and ire,
And finds himselfe deceived thus to be,
This recompence he points her for her paines,
Vpon that hill to hang each day in chaines.

45

A cruell doome, but who could it resist?
  Away went we, each for himselfe afraid,
But *Norandino* ever doth persist
In his first purpose of procuring aid,
Lamenting that so narrowly he mist
To bring her out, among the goates he staid,
And like a goate (forgetting his estate)
He go'th out early, and returneth late.

46

She sees him go and come, but all in vaine,
  She maketh signes to him to have him part,
He constantly resolveth to remaine,
The love of her possesseth so his hart,
Despising danger and enduring paine,
He hopeth hopelesse still to ease her smart,
At foure months end (good fortune so prepard)
Gradasso thither came and *Mandricard*.

47

And (for her father was their loving frend)
  They gave this bold attempt to set her free,
  And to her father straight they do her send,
  Who was full glad and joyfull her to see,
  And that her dangers had this happie end:
  But *Norandino* was more glad then he;
  Who with the goats no longer now did stay,
  But while the *Orko* slept he stale away.

48

And now for joy of this great perill past,
  In which he stay'd so wofull and forlorne,
  And that the memorie thereof may last,
  To those that shall be, and are yet unborne,
  (For never Prince before such wo did tast,
  Nor stay'd so long in misery and scorne,
  And it shall be just sixteene weeks to morow,
  That he remained in this wo and sorow.)

49

Therfore I say the King prepares this sport,
  With very great magnificence and bost,
  Inviting hither men of ev'ry sort,
  Such as in chivalrie excell the most,
  That far and neare may carie the report,
  Of these great triumphs unto ev'ry cost.
  This tale the courteous host did tell his guest,
  Of him that first ordaind the sumptuous feast.

50

In this and such like talke they spend the night,
  And then they sleepe upon their beds of downe,
  But when that once it shined cleare and light,
  The trumpets sounded over all the towne,
  And *Griffin* straight puts on his armor bright,
  Aspiring after fame and high renowne;
  His leud companion likewise doth the same,
  To shew a hope as well as he of fame.

51

All armed thus they came unto the field,
  And view the warlike troupes as they did passe,
  Where some had painted on their crest and shield,
  Or some device that there described was,
  What hope or doubt his love to him did yeeld,
  They all were *Christens* then, but now alas,
  They all are *Turks* unto the endlesse shame,
  Of those that may and do not mend the same.

52

For where they should employ their sword and lance,
  Against the Infidels our publike foes,
  Gods Word and true Religion to advance,
  They to poore *Christens* worke perpetuall woes:
  To you I write, ye Kings of *Spaine* and *France*,
  Let these alone, and turne your force on those:
  And unto you also I write as much,
  Ye nations fierce, *Zwizzers* I meane and *Dutch*.

53

Lo, tone of *Christen* Kings usurps a name,
  Another *Catholike* will needs be called:
  Why do not both your deeds declare the same?
  Why are Christs people slaine by you and thralled?
  Get backe againe *Ierusalem* for shame,
  That now the *Turke* hath tane from you and walled
  Constantinople get that famous towne,
  That erst belonged to th'Imperiall crowne.

54

Dost not thou *Spaine* confront with *Affrike* shore,
  That more then *Italy* hath thee offended?
  Yet to her hurt thou leavest that before,
  Against the Infidels thou hadst intended:
  O *Italy* a slave for evermore,
  In such sort mard, as never can be mended,
  A slave to slaves, and made of sinne a sinke,
  And sotted sleepe like men orecome with drinke.

55

Ye *Swizzers* fierce, if feare of famine drive you,
  To come to *Lombardie* to seeke some food,
  Are not the *Turks* as neare? why should it grieve you
  To spill your foes, and spare your brothers blood?
  They have the gold and riches to relieve you,
  Enrich your selves with lawfull gotten good,
  So shall all *Europe* be to you beholding,
  For driving them from these parts, and withholding.

56

Thou Lion stout that holdst of heav'n the kayes,
  (A waightie charge) see that from drowsie sleepe
  Thou wake our realme, and bring her joyfull dayes,
  And from these forren wolves it safely keepe,
  God doth thee to this height of honor raise,
  That thou mayst feed and well defend thy sheepe,
  That with a roring voice and mighty arme,
  Thou mayst withold thy flock from ev'ry harme.

57

But whither roves my rudely rolling pen,
  That waxe so sawcie to reprove such peeres?
  I said before that in *Damasco* then
  They *Christend* were (as in records appeares)
  So that the armor of their horse and men
  Was like to ours (though chang'd of later yeares)
  And Ladies fild their galleries and towrs,
  To see the justs as they did here in ours.

58

Each strives in shew his fellow to exceed,
  And to be gallant in his mistris sight,
  To see each one manage his stately steed,
  Was to the standers by a great delight:
  Some praise unto themselves, some shame do breed,
  By shewing horses doings wrong or right,
  The chiefest prize that should be of this tilt,
  An armor was rich, set with stone and gilt.

59

By hap a merchant of *Armenia* found
  This armour, and to *Norandin* it sold,
  Who, had he knowne how good it was and sound,
  Would not have left it sure for any gold,
  (The circumstance I cannot now expound,
  I meane ere long it shall to you be told)
  Now must I tell of *Griffin* that came in,
  Iust when the sport and tilting did begin.

60

Eight valiant Knights the chalenge did sustaine,
  Against all commers that would runne that day,
  These eight were of the Princes private traine,
  Of noble blood, and noble ev'ry way,
  They fight in sport, but some in sport were slaine,
  For why as hotly they did fight in play,
  As deadly foes do fight in battell ray,
  Save that the King may when he list them stay.

61

Now *Griffins* fellow was *Martano* named,
  Who (though he were a coward and a beast)
  Like bold blind Bayard he was not ashamed,
  To enter like a Knight among the rest,
  His countenance likewise in shew he framed,
  As though he were as forward as the best,
  And thus he stood and view'd a bitter fight,
  Between a Baron and another Knight.

62

Lord of *Seleucia* the tone they call,
  And one of eight that did maintaine the just,
  The Knight *Ombruno* hight of person tall,
  Who in his vizer tooke so great a thrust,
  That from his horse astonied he did fall,
  And with his lively blood distain'd the dust:
  This sight amaz'd *Martano* in such sort,
  He was afraid to leese his life in sport.

63

Soone after this so fierce conflict was done,
  Another challenger straight steppeth out,
  With whom *Martano* was requir'd to runne,
  But he (whose heart was ever full of doubt)
  With fond excuses sought the same to shunne,
  And shew'd himselfe a faint and dastard lout,
  Till *Griffin* egd him on, and blam'd his feare,
  As men do set a mastive on a Beare.

64

Then tooke he heart of grace, and on did ride,
  And makes a little florish with his speare,
  But in the middle way he stept aside,
  For feare the blow would be too big to beare:
  Yet one that would seeke this disgrace to hide,
  Might in this point impute it not to feare,
  But rather that his horse not good and redie,
  Did shun the tilt, and raune not ev'n nor stedie.

65

But after with his sword he dealt so ill,
  Demosthenes him could not have defended,
  He shew'd both want of courage and of skill,
  So as the lookers on were all offended,
  And straight with hissing and with voices shrill,
  The conflict cowardly begun was ended:
  In his behalfe was *Griffin* sore ashamed,
  His heart thereto with double heate inflamed.

66

For now he sees how much on him it stands,
  With double value to wipe out the blot,
  And shew himselfe the more stout of his hands,
  Sith his companion shew'd himselfe a sot,
  His fame or shame must flie to forren lands,
  And if he now should faile one little jot,
  The same wold seem a foule and huge transgression,
  His mate had fild their minds with such impression.

67

The first he met Lord of *Sidona* hight,
  And towards him he runs with massie speare,
  And gave a blow that did so heavie light,
  As to the ground it did him backward beare:
  Then came of *Laodice* another Knight,
  On him the staffe in peeces three did teare,
  Yet was the counterbuffe thereof so great,
  The Knight had much ado to keepe his seate.

68

But when they came with naked swords to trie,
  Which should the honor and the prise obtaine,
  So *Griffin* did with deadly strokes him plie,
  At last he left him stoni'd on the plaine.
  Straightway two valiant brothers standing by,
  That at *Griffino* tooke no small disdaine,
  The tone *Corimbo*, tother *Tirse* hight,
  These two forthwith do challenge him to fight.

69

Successively them both he overthrew,
  And now men thought that he the prise would win,
  But *Salintern* that saw them downe in vew,
  To envie good *Griffino* doth begin,
  This man the stoutst of all the courtly crew,
  Doth take a speare in hand, and enters in,
  And to the combat *Griffin* straight defies,
  And scornes to have a stranger win the prize.

70

But *Griffin* chose one staffe among the rest,
  The biggest and the strongest of a score,
  And with the same he pierceth backe and brest,
  That downe he fell and never stirred more;
  The King that loved and esteem'd him best,
  Laments his death, and maketh mone therefore,
  But yet the common sort were faine and glad,
  That knew his mind and manners were but bad.

71

Next after him two others he doth meet,
  Ermofilo the captaine of his guard,
And *Carmond* Admirall of all his fleet,
  With these a while he had a conflict hard,
The first unhorst was left upon his feet,
  The other with a blow was almost mard.
Thus of eight challengers remain'd but one,
The rest were quite subdude by him alone.

72

This one was he of whom at first I spake,
  Lord of *Seleucia* a valiant man,
This one to *Griffin* did resistance make,
  And long it was ere ought of him he wan,
But one blow on his head so fierce he strake,
  As he likewise to stagger now began,
Had not the King made them to have bene parted,
Sure *Griffin* had him kild ere he had parted.

73

Thus all those eight, that all the world defide,
  By one alone were vanquished and slaine,
So as the King was forced to provide,
  An order new for those that do remaine;
(By parting runners some on either side)
  For yet was spent not past an houre or twaine,
Lest this his triumph should have end too soone,
He makes them spend therein the afternoone.

74

But *Griffin* full of wrath and discontent,
  Backe to his host with his companion came,
The praise he wan did him not so content,
  As he was griev'd at his companions shame:
Wherefore to leave the towne they do consent,
  While men were busie looking on the game,
And to a little towne fast by he goes,
And meanes himselfe a while for to repose.

75

The travell sore he had before endured,
  So great a wearinesse in him had bred,
And such desire of sleepe withall procured,
  As straight he gat him to his naked bed.
The while *Martano* to all fraud inured,
  And using aid of her mischievous head,
(As he did soundly sleepe) devis'd the while
A stratageme most strange, him to beguile.

76

They do conclude to take *Griffinos* steed,
  And cote, and ev'ry warlike implement,
And that *Martano* in *Griffinos* steed,
  Himselfe to *Norandino* shall present.
This they devis'd, this they perform'd in deed,
  And boldly backe againe *Martano* went,
In *Griffins* armor stoutly stepping in,
As did the Asse that ware the Lions skin.

77

He rusheth in among the thickest presse,
  An houre before the setting of the sunne,
The King and all the rest straightway do guesse,
  That this was he that had such honor wonne:
And straight great honour they to him addresse,
  And cause the like by others to be done,
And his base name, not worthy to be named,
About the towne with honor was proclaimed.

78

Fast by the King he rideth cheeke by cheeke,
  And in his praise they songs and verses make,
In *Hebrew* tongue, in *Latin* and in *Greeke*.
  And now this while did *Griffin* hap to wake,
And seeing that his armour was to seeke,
  He first begins some small mistrust to take,
Yet hardly could it sinke into his reason,
That she had giv'n consent to such a treason.

79

In feare and doubt no little time he hovered,
  But when his host the truth had plaine declar'd,
And that he saw the falshood plaine discovered,
  By which she had in follies bands him snar'd,
Then truth shewd plain, that love before had covered,
  And to revenge this wrong he straight prepar'd,
But wanting other furniture (perforce)
He tooke *Martanos* armor and his horse.

80

And backe unto *Damasco* he doth ride,
  Arriving there within an houre of night,
And entring at the gate upon the side,
  The pallace of the King stood plaine in sight,
Where then the King a banket did provide,
  For many a Duke and Lord, and valiant Knight,
And *Griffin* boldly sate among the rest,
Forgetting that he ware the scorned crest.

81

And taken for the man whose coate he ware,
  His presence did the better sort offend,
Of which when vile *Martano* was aware,
  That of the table sate at th'upper end,
And sees that to disgrace him they forbare,
  And thinke him his companion and his frend:
His friendship and acquaintance he renounced,
And this hard doom of him he straight pronounced.

82

O King (quoth he) it seems that for my sake,
  You graciously forbeare to do him shame,
That of his basenesse shamefull proofe did make
  This day, and now againe confirmes the same:
But you the matter and the man mistake,
  I know not him, his nation, nor his name,
By chance I met him onely on the way,
I never saw him I, till yesterday.

83

Wherefore might I herein your grace advise,
  You should a sample make him for the rest,
That here presents unto your princely eies,
Himselfe unworthy, and unwelcome guest,
Let him tormented be in cruell wise,
(This is my doome) let him be hang'd at least,
And unrevenged let him not be borne,
That Knighthood should receive so great a scorne.

84

Thus much the vile and base *Martano* seth,
  And *Origilla* sooth'd it with as much,
And wisht an halter stop the villains breth.
Nay (quoth the King) the sinne is nothing such,
As is in law or reason worthy death,
His life or yet his liberty to tuch:
This, for examples sake I thinke it meet,
To do him some disgrace in open street.

85

And straight he rounds a Sergeant in his eare,
  And secretly appoints him what to do,
Who came forthwith unto the table where
Griffino sate, and made no more ado,
But leadeth him, that no such thing did feare,
A secret prison and a sure unto,
And for that night he clapt him up in fetters,
Where theeves do use to lie and evill debters.

86

Next day *Martano* that did greatly dread,
  Lest this his foule device would come to light,
If *Griffin* should be heard his cause to pleade,
Therefore as soone as *Phœbus* shined bright,
(Pretending businesse) away he sped,
And leaves *Griffino* in this wofull plight:
But ere he goes, the King to him imparts
No small rewards for his, not his desarts.

87

But let him go his wayes, and do not doubt,
  That this unknowne and unreveng'd shall be:
Straight was *Griffino* from the jayle put out,
And carted so as all men might him see,
Tide hand and foot, and people all about,
Of which the most were but of meane degree,
Also the armor whence this error came,
Was hald about unto his farder shame.

88

With many filthy words they him revile,
  From filthy tongues, that hard it is to stop,
And shew'd him round about the towne the while,
At ev'ry crosse, and house, and stall and shop:
Then thinking him for ever to exile,
They led him of that hill unto the top,
And there his bonds they loose with great disgrace,
And then they will him packe him thence apace.

89

With scornfull sound of bason, pot and pan,
  They thought to drive him thence like Bees in swarmes,
But when he was untide, then he began
To make them know their error to their harmes,
Then he did lay about, and play the man,
Now having use of both his warlike armes,
But in what sort he them dismayd and scared,
Within another booke shall be declared.

THE EIGHTEENTH BOOKE OF
ORLANDO FVRIOSO

THE ARGVMENT

Now Griffin's *knowne and felt :* Algyre *doth threaten*
The Tartar *Prince :* Charles *fighteth and prevailes :*
Martano *like a coward is well beaten,*
Marfisas *force* Damasco *warriers quailes :*
From thence with tempest tost, and weather beaten,
Both she and Griffin *and* Astolfo *sailes :*
Medor *and* Cloridan *with care and paine,*
Seeke for the carkas of their master slaine.

ORLANDO FVRIOSO
THE EIGHTEENTH BOOKE

1

Most worthie Prince your vertues high and rare,
  With tongue and penne I praise, and ever shall,
  Although my words and verse inferiour are,
  In number and in worth to match them all:
  But all above this one I do compare,
  And far prefer, and pure divinest call,
  That giving gracious care to those are greeved,
  Yet ev'ry tale is not by you beleeved.

2

Oft have I heard your highnesse hath refused,
  Although the same most earnestly were sought
  To heare the guiltlesse absent man accused,
  (And when a great complaint to you was brought)
  You have the matter and the man excused:
  Suspending still your judgement and your thought,
  And keeping till the truth were truly tride,
  Ever one eare for the contrarie side.

3

Had *Norandino* had so great a grace,
  As not to credite tales so lightly told,
  He had not offerd *Griffin* this disgrace,
  No though thereby he might have gained gold:
  But so doth rashnes vertue oft deface,
  As here was proved that was said of old;
  The silly people beare the scourge and blame,
  Oft when their Princes do deserve the same.

4

For *Griffin* (as in part I told before)
  When as his hands and feete were once untide,
  Did deale about of blowes and thrusts such store,
  As well was he could for himselfe provide,
  His wrath was such as none he then forbore,
  The old, the young, the strong, the feeble dide:
  And they that laught before to see him carted,
  Now for their labor whinde as much and smarted.

5

The people faint and mazed fled away,
  From him whom late they did deride and scorne,
  He follow'd them and kild them by the way,
  Dastards more meet to die, then to be borne.
  But in this chase a while I let him stay,
  Triumphing now that lately was forlorne:
  Of *Rodomont* now somewhat must be spoken,
  On whom at once I said eight speares were broken.

6

Eight speares at once upon the scaly skin,
  Did light, and divers darts were throwne aloofe,
  For speares and darts he passeth not a pin,
  Such was his strength, so sure his armors proofe:
  But when he saw that more and more came in,
  To part from thence he thinks his best behoofe,
  For why on ev'ry side they do assaile him,
  That needs at length his breath and strength must faile
                           (him.

7

Ev'n as the Lions whelps that see a Bull,
  Are at the first of his great strength affraid,
  But when they see their sire to teare or pull
  His throte and sides, they runne their sire to aid,
  And flie upon his face and horned scull,
  Till prostrate on the ground they have him laid:
  So now when *Charles* himselfe was in the place,
  Each one tooke armes, each one took hart of grace.

8

Who so hath seene a huge well baited Beare,
  With many dogs, men standing close about,
  When he by hap the stake or cord doth teare,
  And rusheth in among the thickest rout,
  How suddenly they runne away with feare,
  And make a lane to let the Beare go out:
  He might (I say) compare by such a sight,
  The manner of this *Pagans* fight and flight.

9

He rusheth out, and with his two hand blade,
  He florisheth about in so fierce sort,
  That soone a way for him to passe was made,
  To hinder him his way it was no sport,
  And those that by the way did him invade,
  Except they shifted better, were cut short:
  Thus in despite of *Charles* and all his realme,
  He came unto the banks of *Sequans* streame.

10

And standing from the banke a little distance,
  That few or none behind could him enclose,
  An howers space and more he made resistance,
  Against King *Charles*, whose powre stil greater groes
  Till in the end in hope of no assistance,
  Displeas'd, but not disgrast away he goes:
  He takes the river fretting in his minde,
  That he had left a man alive behinde.

11

And so he swell'd in anger and in pride,
  That he had thought to turne him backe againe,
  And to have mounted on the other side,
  And all that should withstand him to have slaine:
But lo a messenger he then espide,
  That made him from that rash attempt refraine,
  But who did send him, and what word he bare,
  I meane to you another time declare.

12

But first what Discord did I meane to show,
  Who as you heard was by the Angell sent
  Among the *Pagans*, seeds of strife to sow,
  And as she was commanded thither went:
Yet leaving *Fraud* behind the coales to blow,
  Least all the fire of strife should quite be spent,
  And to augment his strength, as much as may be,
  He carrid *Pride* with him out of the Abby.

13

Pride leaves *Hypocrisie* to keepe his place,
  And thus these jarring friends togither go,
  And when they traveld had a little space,
  They found by hap dame *Ielousie* also,
That met a dwarfe that run a trudging pace,
  Ev'n as she wanderd idlely to and fro:
  And learning unto whom this page was sent,
  To go with him she quickly did consent.

14

You call to mind (for sure you cannot chuse,
  But call to mind so late a written storie)
  How *Mandricardo Doralice* did use,
  And kept with joy whom he did win with glorie:
She secretly sent notice of this newes,
  (Though afterward her selfe perhap was sorie)
  To *Rodomont*, and sharply him incited,
  To venge her rape as I before recited.

15

The messenger arrived then by hap,
  When from the streame the *Pagan* did ascend,
  And told him all the tale of her mishap,
  And how another did possesse his frend:
Cold *jelousie* straight enterd in his lap,
  And *Pride* with *Discord* do the matter mend,
  Alledging if he put up this disgrace,
  Then let him nere looke Ladie in the face.

16

Like as a Tyger that her young hath lost,
  Suppris'd by hunters hand and borne away,
  Doth follow on the foote through ev'ry cost,
  No dikes nor waters wide can make her stay:
So *Rodomont* with love (and anger most)
  Enflamed, could endure no more delay,
  And though he want his horse, that did not boote,
  To cause him stay, he rather goes on foote.

17

He meanes what ever horseman next he spide,
  To take his horse of frend or else of foe,
  At this is *Discord* pleas'd, and said to *Pride*,
  That she was glad their bus'nes cotned so:
I will (quoth she) a horse for him provide,
  An horse shall cost him deare enough I trow;
  But what of him and of that horse befel,
  Another time not now I meane to tell.

18

This while the most renowned *Christen* King,
  That had expulst the *Pagan* from the towne,
  His valiant men of armes about doth bring,
  And on the sodaine lets the draw bridge downe,
And with a fresh assault their foes so sting,
  While fortune smild on him, on them did frowne,
  That they had runne away like men dismaid,
  Had not *Ferraw* couragiously them staid.

19

My mates in armes (quoth he) brethren and frends,
  Prov'd valiant heretofore, now hold your place:
  More happie far is he his life that spends,
  In honour, then that keeps it in disgrace;
Loe me your generall that here entends,
  No way to staine the blood of *Spanish* race;
  The patterne follow that I shew you furst,
  And then I care not, let them do their worst.

20

Thus in that part *Ferraw* the fight renewd,
  And draws with him the chosen *Spanish* band,
  That oft in *Christen* blood their hands imbrewd,
  And none almost but they did now withstand:
But destinie can never be eschewd,
  As may by their successe be rightly scand;
  Behold *Renaldo* comes, and as he came,
  It seem'd he carrid lightning fierce or flame.

21

Not long before *Almontes* valiant sonne,
  Hight *Dardanell*, had slaine a Christian Knight,
  And proud of that his glorie lately wonne,
  And of this good successe he had in fight,
About the field he carelessely did runne,
  Vntill he hapt to see a wofull sight,
  He saw *Alfeo* yeelding up the ghost,
  A youth whom he esteem'd and loved most.

22

Lurcanio was the man that did the deed,
  And *Dardanell* to venge it doth intend,
  Lurcanio follow'd on and tooke no heed,
  The other all on him his force doth bend,
And with a waightie speare, him and his steed,
  Vnto the earth together he doth send,
  And pierst his thigh, and put him in such paine,
  As scant he able was to rise againe.

23

But *Ariodant* (that deare his brother loved)
  And sees him in such paine and danger lie,
  Was therewithall in wrath so greatly moved,
  He meaneth to avenge his hurt, or die:
  But though that he attempted oft and proved,
  Yet could he not to *Dardanell* come nie,
  For still of other men, the throng and number,
  Did him in this attempt molest and cumber.

24

No doubt the heav'ns had *Dardanell* ordained,
  To perish by a more victorious hand;
  Renaldos blade must with his blood be stained,
  And was, as after you shall understand:
  By him this praise and glory must be gained,
  The fame whereof must fill both sea and land:
  But let these westerne warres a while remaine,
  And of *Griffino* talke we now againe.

25

Who taught those of *Damasco* to their harmes,
  What wrong they did to cart him in such sort,
  They fill the towne with uprores and alarmes,
  Mens mouthes and eares were full of this report:
  The King brings forth five hundred men in armes,
  And sends five more to fortifie the fort:
  For why this tumult brought him in perswasion,
  That sure some host of men did make invasion.

26

But when he saw no men, no host, no band,
  No troupes of horse the citie to invade,
  Onely one man (well knowne) that there did stand,
  And of his people such a slaughter made,
  (Mov'd with remorce) he stretcheth out his hand
  Naked, in shew of peace, as is the trade,
  And openly his rashnesse he lamented,
  That such a Knight to harme he had consented.

27

And *Griffin* when to find he now begunne,
  The King was of so good an inclination,
  And that the wrong to him before was done,
  Not of his owne, but others instigation:
  To make a friendly concord doth not shunne,
  Because hereby he lost no reputation:
  And there he tarid at the Kings request,
  To cure his wounds and take a little rest.

28

This while his brother *Aquilant* the blacke,
  That with *Astolfo* still in *Iewrie* staid,
  And sees his brother now so long did lacke,
  Was in his mind all sad and ill apaid:
  They heard no newes of him, they found no tracke,
  Though wait about in ev'ry place was laid,
  Vntill the Greekish pilgrim they had met,
  By whom of him some inkling they did get.

29

He told them how a certaine wanton dame,
  Hight *Origilla*, with a ruffian knave,
  That kept her openly without all shame,
  Yet going in apparell fine and brave,
  These two (the pilgrim said) together came,
  From *Antioch* (as forth in speech they gave)
  And to *Damasco* then they meant to go,
  But what became of them he did not know.

30

And further unto *Aquilant* he told,
  How he *Griffino* met this other day,
  And did to him the matter all unfold,
  And how forthwith *Griffino* went his way,
  With chase enough, and swearing that he would
  Kill this same vile adultrer if he may:
  No sooner had his speech the pilgrim ended,
  In post to follow, *Aquilant* intended.

31

In post he follow'd to *Damasco* ward,
  And when he travel'd had a day or twaine,
  (Behold that God that ever doth reward
  The good with blessings and the bad with paine)
  That gracelesse couple that before you heard,
  Betraid *Griffino* with that divellish traine,
  Into the hands of *Aquilant* did give,
  While they in pleasure most securely live.

32

I say that *Aquilant* by Gods permission,
  Doth meet the vile *Martano* on the way,
  His horse, his coate, and outward apparition,
  So like unto *Griffino* ev'ry way,
  That *Aquilant* at first without suspition,
  Went to embrace him, and began to say,
  Brother well met, I joy of your welfare,
  Your absence bred in me much feare and care.

33

But when he saw the tother not replide,
  But shrunke away like one that were afraid,
  Ah traitor villain; yeeld thy selfe, he cride,
  Thou hast my brother spoiled and betraid,
  Tell me (thou wretch) doth he in life abide?
  To whom in humble sort *Martano* said,
  (With fainting hart, with quaking voice & trembling
  Yet in the midst of all his feare dissembling.)

34

Oh pardon sir, your brother is alive,
  And like to live, and hath no hurt, nor shall,
  The truth is this, I being loth to strive
  With him, because I found him stout and tall,
  Did with no ill intent this drift contrive,
  To save my selfe and do him hurt but small,
  For this same womans sake that is my sister,
  With open force not daring to assist her.

35

It grieved me to see how he by lust
  Did her abuse whom nature made me love,
  And for I thought it was both meet and just,
  Her from this wicked custome to remove,
  And sith I did his valew great mistrust,
  I thought it best by pollicie to prove:
  I stale his horse and coate while he was sleeping,
  And so convaid her quite out of his keeping.

36

Well might *Martano* beare away the bell,
  Or else a whetstone challenge for his dew,
  That on the sodaine such a tale could tell,
  And not a word of all his tale was trew,
  But yet in shew it all agreed well,
  Save one which *Aquilant* most certaine knew,
  Was false, and he in vaine did seeke to smother,
  He was her bedfellow, and not her brother.

37

With hand and tongue at once he doth replie,
  And in one instant he both strake and spake,
  I know (quoth he) vile villaine thou dost lie,
  And on the face so fiercely him he strake,
  He makes two teeth into his throate to flie;
  Then with great violence he doth him take,
  And him and her he binds in bitter bands,
  Like captives carrid into forren lands.

38

And thus in hast unto *Damasco* riding,
  He swears that he these bands would not unbind,
  Till of his brother he do heare some tiding,
  Whom in *Damasco* after he did find;
  Who now with cunning Phisicke and good guiding,
  Was almost heald in body and in mind,
  And when he saw his unexpected brother,
  They both saluted and embrac'd each other.

39

And after they had made in speech some sport,
  About full many a foolish accident,
  (For *Aquilant* had heard a large report
  Of *Griffins* carting, and his punishment)
  At last he asketh *Griffin* in what sort
  They should this couple worthily torment;
  To hang and draw, and burne their privie parts,
  Was not too much for their too foule desarts.

40

The King and all his Councell thought it good,
  Because their fault was such so open knowne,
  That they should publikely dispill their blood,
  And their desarts might publikely be showne:
  But yet that motion *Griffin* straight withstood,
  Pretending private causes of his owne,
  Onely he wisht *Martano* should be stript,
  And at a cart drawne through the street and whipt.

41

And as for her, although she had deserved
  A punishment as great as he, or more,
  Yet was the sentence of her doome reserved
  Vntill *Lucina* came, and not before:
  So that by *Griffins* meane she was preserved,
  So great a sway love in his fancie bore:
  Here *Aquilant* by *Griffin* was procured,
  To bide with him untill his wounds were cured.

42

Now *Norandin* that all his powre still bends,
  To honor *Griffin* all the meanes he may,
  And with great courtesie to make amends,
  For that disgrace he did him th'other day;
  To make another triumph he intends,
  Set forth with pompe and state, and rich array:
  And that the same may flie to forraine nations,
  He notifies it straight by proclamations.

43

At foure weekes end the triumph should begin,
  The same whereof about so farre was blowne,
  Without the land of *Iewrie* and within,
  At last unto *Astolfo* it was knowne,
  Who asking *Sansonets* advice herein,
  Whose wisedome he preferd before his owne,
  At last for company they both agree,
  To go together these same justs to see.

44

Now as they went upon their way, behold
  They met a gallant and a stately dame,
  With whom this Duke acquainted was of old,
  Marfisa was this noble Ladies name:
  She traveld like a Knight, her heart was bold,
  Her body passing strong unto the same,
  And when she knew both why and where they went,
  To go with them she quickly did consent.

45

And thus these three their journey so contrive,
  As just against the day and solemne feast,
  Together at *Damasco* they arrive,
  Each one well mounted on a stately beast,
  The King that specially did care and strive,
  To honor *Griffin* more then all the rest,
  By all the meanes and wayes he could devise,
  Augmented much the valew of the prise.

46

And where it was, as I before declar'd,
  A single armor rich and finely wrought,
  Now *Norandino* at this time prepard,
  To set it out with things not lightly bought,
  To this he adds a horse most richly barb'd,
  By riders skill to great perfection brought,
  Wel shapt, wel markt, strong limb'd, & passing swift,
  The beast alone, fit for a Princes gift.

47

All this he did, because great hope he saw,
That *Griffin* once againe the prise would win,
But then was verifide the old said saw,
Much falls betweene the Challice and the chin:
For when *Marfisa* (void of feare or aw)
Without had view'd this armor and within,
And finds it had bene hers by marks well knowne,
She seizeth straight upon it as her owne.

48

The King that ill so great disgrace could brooke,
Did shew himselfe therewith much discontent,
And with a princely frowne and angry looke,
His silence threatned that she should repent,
And in so great despite the thing he tooke,
That straight some sergeants unto her he sent,
With souldiers, some on foote and some on horse,
Deceiv'd much in her sex, more in her force.

49

For never did a child take more delight,
With gawdie flowres in time of spring to play,
Nor never did yong Ladie brave and bright,
Like dauncing better on a solemne day,
Then did *Marfisa* in the sound and sight
Of glittring blades and speares delight to stay:
And this did cause her take therein more pleasure,
Because her strength was great beyond all measure.

50

Those few that were to apprehend her sent,
And punish her for this unlawfull deed,
Were caus'd their comming quickly to repent,
And others by their harmes tooke better heed:
The armed Knights most diversly were bent,
Some standing still to mark what this would breed,
Some to the sergeants thought to bring reliefe,
Of whom were *Griffin* and his brother chiefe.

51

The *English* Duke doth deeme it were a shame,
To leave *Marfisa* in this dangerous case,
Sith chiefly for his company she came,
And *Sansonet* doth deeme it like disgrace,
Wherefore they meane how ere the matter frame,
Not leave her unassisted in the place,
Astolfo had a charmed speare all gilt,
With which he used oft to runne at tilt.

52

The vertue of this charmed speare was such,
Besides the gilding bright and faire of hew,
That whom so ere the head thereof did tuch,
Straight him from off his horse it overthrew,
Griffino first although disdaining much,
He quite unhorst, nor who it was he knew:
Then *Aquilant* that to revenge it ment,
Vnto the ground in manner like was sent.

53

Thus did these warriers three themselves behave,
But chiefe *Marfisa*, who would never rest,
But would in spite of all, the armor have,
Nor once vouchsafe to aske it or request;
She doth the King and all his nobles brave,
And when the best of them had done his best,
On ev'ry side she beat the people downe,
And from them all made way out of the towne.

54

Sansonet and *Astolfo* did the like,
King *Norandinos* men of armes pursew,
The foolish people crie stop, kill and strike,
But none comes neare, but stand aloofe to vew:
A narrow bridge there was, this place they pike,
And to defend it against all the crew,
Till *Griffin* came, having his horse recovered,
And by some markes the *English* Duke discovered.

55

And straight his brother *Aquilante* came,
And of *Astolfo* both acquaintance take,
And then in civill termes they somewhat blame
Her litle count she of the King did make,
Astolfo friendly told to them her name,
And in defence of her some words he spake,
The rest that came marvell to what it tends,
To heare them talke together now like friends.

56

But when that *Norandinos* souldiers hard
Her name, so dreaded over all the East,
They surely thought that they should all be mard,
And that the citie would be tane at least,
Therefore they pray the King to have regard.
But now *Marfisa* (moved by request
Of those two brothers) friendly doth consent,
Herselfe before the Prince for to present.

57

And thus without much reverence she spake,
Sir King, I marvell what your highnesse ment,
A prise and gift of such a thing to make,
As is not yours without I give consent:
The Armes this armor hath plaine proofe do make,
Namely a crowne into three peeces rent:
Once I put off this armor in a way,
To chase a theefe that stale from me a pray.

58

Then said the King, faire dame the truth is so,
Of one *Armenian* merchant I them bought,
I make no question be they yours or no,
Nor needs for proofe more witnesse to be brought,
For though they were not, I would them bestow
On you, if so the same by you were sought:
As for *Griffino* unto whom I gave them,
He shall be pleas'd I hope, and not to have them.

59

I will him recompence some other way,
  And give him gifts of as great worth or more;
  Thanks to your highnesse *Griffin* straight doth say,
  Preserve me in your grace, I aske no more:
  But when *Marfisa* saw that ev'ry way
  They honor'd her, she chang'd her mind before,
  To shew magnificence she us'd this drift,
  That he must take this armor as her gift.

60

And thus good friends all turned back againe,
  And then with double joy the feast they hold,
  In which chiefe praise did *Sansonet* obtaine,
  The other foure did then themselves withhold,
  Wishing the praise should unto him remaine,
  And then with greater cheare then can be told,
  By *Norandino* they were nobly feasted,
  And there themselves they well repos'd and rested.

61

Sev'n dayes or eight the King them entertained,
  And those once past, of him their leave they take,
  The which with gifts and honor great obtained,
  Vnto the towne of Tripoly they make,
  And in one company these five remained,
  And mind not one the other to forsake,
  As long as one of them was left alive,
  Vntill in *France* they safely should arrive.

62

And straight they get a vessell for their hire,
  A merchants ship new laden from the West,
  The master of the ship an auncient sire,
  Consented to their wils with small request,
  The wind as then serv'd fit for their desire,
  And blowes a gentle gale all from the East,
  So that with filled sailes in little while,
  They came as farre as *Cypres*, *Venus* Ile.

63

Here ev'ry place was full of odours sweet,
  Of gardens faire or spice of pleasant tast,
  The people lustfull (for dame *Venus* meet)
  From tender yeares to doting age do last,
  With wanton damsels walking in each street,
  Inviting men to pleasure and repast,
  From hence againe they loosed, at what time,
  Don Phœbus charret unto th'East did clime.

64

The weather still was temperat and cleare,
  A pleasant gale their swelling sailes did fill;
  No signe of storme or tempest did appeare,
  To such as in the weather had best skill:
  But loe the weather oft doth change her cheare,
  Ev'n as a woman oft doth change her will,
  For sodainly they had such stormes of wether,
  As if that heav'n and earth would come together.

65

The aire doth on the sodaine grow obscure,
  But lightned oft with lightnings dreadfull light,
  And save their houreglasse kept them reckning sure
  Twas hard for to discerne the day from night:
  The desprat marriners do all endure,
  As men inured to the waters spight,
  The heav'ns above, the waves beneath do rore,
  Yet are not they dismaid one whit therefore.

66

One with a whistle hang'd about his necke,
  Showes by the sound which cord must be undone,
  And straight the shipboy ready at a becke,
  Vnto the tops with nimble sleight doth runne,
  The other marriners upon the decke,
  Or at the steere the comming waves do shunne,
  And then by turnes they pump the water out,
  By paine and care preventing ev'ry doubt.

67

Now while this noble crew with tempest tost,
  Went in the sea as wind and weather drave,
  And looke each minute to be drown'd and lost,
  The *Christians* with a fresh assault and brave,
  Set on the *Pagans* sorely to their cost:
  Who now began the worser side to have,
  But chiefly then their courage gan to quaile,
  When noble *Dardanellos* life did faile.

68

Renaldo him had noted from the rest,
  Full proud of slaughter of so many foes,
  And to himselfe he said tis surely best,
  To crop this weed before it higher growes,
  Therewith he sets his fatall speare in rest,
  And cries to *Dardanello* as he goes,
  Alas poore boy, much wo to thee they bred,
  That left to thee that sheild of white and red.

69

Ile trie if you defend those colours well,
  (He saith) which if with me you cannot do,
  Against *Orlando* fierce, I can you tell,
  For to defend them will be great adoe.
  Thus said *Renaldo*, and noble *Dardanell*,
  In valiant wise thus answer'd thereunto,
  Know this (quoth he) that these my colours I
  Will bravely here defend, or bravely die.

70

With that he spurr'd his horse (as this he spake)
  And with great force *Renaldo* did assaile,
  But loe the staffe upon his armor brake,
  So as his blow but little did availe,
  But straight *Renaldos* speare a way did make,
  And pierce the double folds of plate and maile,
  And went so deepe into the tender skin,
  The life went out there where the staffe went in.

71

Looke how a purple flowre doth fade and drie,
  That painefull plowman cutteth up with sheare,
Or as the Poppeys heads aside do lie,
When it the bodie cannot longer beare;
So did the noble *Dardanello* die,
And with his death fild all his men with feare,
As waters runne abrode that breake their bay,
So fled his souldiers breaking their array.

72

They flie unto their tents with full perswasion,
  That of the field the masterie was lost,
Wherefore to fortifie against invasion,
They spare no time, no travell, nor no cost;
Now *Charles* by forhead meanes to take Occasion,
And follows them full close with all his host,
And comming to their tents so bravely venterd,
That he with them themselves almost had enterd.

73

Had not his valiant attempt bene staid,
  By over hastie comming of the night,
So that of force as then it was delaid,
And either side was driv'n to leave the fight,
But with this difference, all the *Turks* dismaid,
And newly gather'd from their fearfull flight,
The *Christians* on the tother side pursewing,
And day by day their hope and powre renewing.

74

The number of the *Turks* that day were slaine,
  Was more then fourscore thousand (as they say)
Their bloud did fat the ground of all that plaine,
And makes the ground more fertile to this day:
Among the dead some men halfe dead remaine,
Left there for theeves and robbers as a pray,
Within the *Pagan* campe great mone they make,
Some for their friends, some for their kinsfolks sake.

75

Two youths there were among so many more,
  Whose friendship fast and firme, whose faithfull harts
Deserved to be plast the rest before,
And to be praised for their good desarts,
Their names were *Cloridano* and *Medore*,
Both borne farre hence, about the Estern parts,
Their parents poore, and not of our beleefe,
Yet for true love they may be praised chiefe.

76

The elder of the two hight *Cloridan*,
  An hunter wilde in all his life had beene,
Of active limbs, and eke an hardie man,
As in a thousand men might well be seene:
Medoro was but yong, and now began
To enter too, of youth the pleasant greene,
Faire skind, black eyd, and yellow curled heare,
That hang'd in lovely locks by either eare.

77

These two among the rest kept watch that night,
  And while the time in sundry speech they spent,
Medoro oftentime most sadly sight,
His masters death did cause him to lament,
Oh (said *Medoro*) what a wofull spight:
What cruell scourge to me hath fortune sent?
That *Dardanel Almontes* worthy sonne,
So sodainly should unto death be done?

78

Behold his noble corse is left a prey,
  To be devoured by the wolfe and crow,
A food too fine to be so borne away,
But I shall remedy that hap I trow,
Ile find the meane his corse thence to convay,
I am resolv'd my selfe will thither go,
That for the good he did me when he liv'd,
At least his corse by me may be reliev'd.

79

When *Cloridano* heard this saying out,
  He stood amaz'd, and musing in his mind,
In tender yeares to find a heart so stout,
Vnto so dangerous attempt inclin'd,
And straight disswades him, casting many a doubt,
To make him change the thing he had assign'd:
But still *Medoro* doth resolve to trie,
To bury *Dardanell*, or els to die.

80

When *Cloridan* so resolute him found,
  Of his own frank accord he vow doth make
To follow him in broken state and sound,
And never him to leave or to forsake;
And straight they two do leave this fenced ground,
And pointing new supplies their roomes to take,
They find the *Christen* camp lie all neglected,
As those that feare no harm, nor none suspected.

81

I say those *Christens* that the watch should keep,
  Lay as they cared not for foe nor friend,
Their senses so possest with wine and sleep,
That none of them their office did attend:
But *Cloridan* that saw them drown'd so deep,
(Said thus) *Medoro*, now I do intend
To get for our great losse this small amends,
To kill some foes, that killed all our friends.

82

Stand thou and watch, and harken ev'ry way,
  And for the rest let me alone to trie,
This said, he goes where one *Alseo* lay,
That took upon him knowledge in the skie,
By which he dream'd he should live many a day,
And in his wives beloved bosome die:
But all was false, his cunning him deceiv'd,
For now this *Pagan* him of life bereav'd.

83

And many more whom here I do not name,
  That sleep on boards, or making straw their bed:
At last where wretched *Grillo* lay he came,
  That on an empty barrell couch'd his head,
Himselfe had emptied late before the same,
  A deadly sleep the wine in him had bred,
The *Turke* his sword within his bowels fix'd,
Out came the blood and wine together mix'd.

84

Neare *Grillo* slept a *Dutchman* and a *Greeke*,
  That all the night had pli'd the dice and drink,
To both of them at once he did the like,
  That dream'd perhaps of sev'n and of sysesink:
They had been better watched all the week,
  Then at so bad a time as this to wink:
Death certaine is to all, the Proverb saith,
Vncertaine is to all the houre of death.

85

Look how a Lion fierce with famine pin'd,
  That comes unto a flock of silly sheep,
Where neither fence, nor people he doth find,
  Doth spoile the flock the while the shepheards sleep;
So *Cloridano* with as bloudy mind,   (keep,
  That found those husht that watch and ward should
Could not his cruell rage and malice bridle:
Nor was this while *Medoro's* weapon idle.

86

For he that did disdaine to make to die,
  Those of the common and the baser sort,
Came there where Duke *Labretto* then did lie,
  Embracing of his Lady in such sort,
As yvie doth the wall, they lay so nie,
  Now soundly sleeping after *Venus* sport,
So close, the aire could not have come betweene;
Medore their heads at one blow cuts off cleane.

87

Oh happy state, ô life, ô death most sweet,
  For sure I think their soules embracing so,
In heav'nly seat do oft together meet,
  And in good peace and love did thither go.
Then next a captaine of the *Flemish* fleet,
  And th'Earle of *Flaunders* sonnes with other mo,
Medoro kil'd, and so far forward went,
He came but little from the Emp'rors tent.

88

But loe they both with shedding bloud now tir'd,
  And fearing lest at length some few might wake,
Ere long time past, both by accord retir'd,
  And mind their first attempt in hand to take,
(as both, but as *Medoro* chiefe desir'd)
  Most secretly unto the field they make,
They mean although they both were faint & weary,
The noble *Dardanellos* corse to burie.

89

The heaps of men that in the field remaine,
  Some dead, and some between alive and dead,
Had made their labour to have been in vaine,
  Had not the moone shew'd out her horned head,
So bright, as cleare discover'd all the plaine,
  That then was cover'd with Vermillion red,
Were it a chance or els his earnest prayer,
That made the moon at that time shine so faire.

90

Now after search by *Phœbe's* friendly light,
  The good *Medore* espi'd him on the ground,
Who when he saw that grievous wofull sight,
  He was for sorrow ready there to sound;
And out he cries, alas ô wo thy wight,
  Not worthy, in this sort to have been found;
Now my last duty do I mean to pay,
And then to say, farewell to you for ay.

91

Thus spake *Medoro* shedding many a teare,
  And minding now no longer time to tarrie,
The loved corse doth on his shoulders beare,
  And *Cloridano* holp the same to carrie,
And they that erst were stout and void of feare,
  Were waxen now so timerous and warie,
Not for their own, but this deare burdens sake,
That ev'ry little noise did cause them quake.

92

This while the noble *Zerbin*, having chast
  His fearfull foes while others were asleep,
That had his heart on vertues lore so plac'd,
  As did to noble deeds him waking keep,
Came with his troope where these two made great hast
  By hils, by dales, by stony waies and steep,
The carkas of their Lord to beare away,
When much it wanted not of break of day.

93

The *Scots* that were of noble *Zerbins* band,
  And saw two men go loden down the plaine,
Make after them a gallop out of hand,
  In hope to light upon some prey or gaine:
When *Cloridano* spying ore the land,
  Did say 'twas best to let the corse remaine,
Alledging that it was a foolish trick,
In saving one dead man to lose two quick.

94

And herewithall his hold he letteth slide
   And thinks *Medoro* would the same have done,
   He meanes himselfe in the next wood to hide,
   And toward it in great hast he doth run;
   But good *Medoro* that could not abide,
   To leave the office he so late begun,
   Although with double paine and duller pace,
   With all the burthen fled away in chase.

95

And to the wood the nearest way he went,
   In hope to get it ere the horsemen came,
   But now his breath and strength were so farre spent,
   As they had very neare him overtane,
   Yet in his deed he doth no whit relent,
   To leave his Lord he counts it such a shame.
   But they that think this story worth the reading,
   Must take a little respite in proceeding.

THE NINETEENTH BOOKE OF
ORLANDO FVRIOSO

THE ARGVMENT

Angelica *doth heale, and wed* Medore:
Marfisa, *with that other worthy crew,*
Lands (after travell long) upon the shore
Of Amazons: *where when the law they knew,*
Stout Guydon, *that came thither late before,*
Fought with Marfisa, *who his nine men slue;*
But when the combat ceast for want of light,
Then Guydon *prayth them lodge with him that night.*

ORLANDO FVRIOSO
THE NINETEENTH BOOKE

1

e can deeme right who faithfull friends do rest,
'hile they beare sway and rule in great degree,
›r then both fast and fained friends are prest,
'hose faiths seeme both of one effect to be:
it then revolts the faint and fained guest,
'hen wealth unwindes, and fortune seems to flee,
it he that loves indeed remaineth fast,
nd loves and serves when life and all is past.

2

l mens thoughts were written in their face,
›me one that now the rest doth overcrow,
›me other eke that wants his soverains grace,   (know:
'hen as their Prince their inward thoughts should
he meaner man should take the betters place,
he greater man might stoop and sit below.
it tell me now how poore *Medoro* sped,
hat lov'd his master both alive and dead.

3

aine he sought to get him to the wood,
y blind and narrow paths to him unknown,
heir swift and his slow pace the same withstood,
›rc'd by the burden that he bare alone.
it now, when *Cloridano* understood
'edoro's case, he made for him great mone,
nd curs'd himselfe, and was full ill apaid,
hat he had left his friend devoid of aid.

4

'oro all about so straight beset,
o leave his loved load was then constrain'd,
it all in vaine he sought from thence to get
is masters carkas that behind remain'd,
'as unto him so fierce and strong a let;
 staid his weary steps, and him retain'd,
v'n as a Beare that would defend her whelp,
bout doth hover though she cannot help.

5

:ood *Medore* about the corse did hover,
he while that *Cloridano* commeth back,
nd (for the day was dawn'd) he might discover,
ow greatly his *Medore*, his help did lack;
'herefore to do his best him to recover,
e takes his bow and quiver from his back,
nd at a *Scot* he took his aime so well,
e strake him in the braine that down he fell.

6

The fall and death so sodaine of the *Scot*
    Abated much the courage of the rest,
    And much they marvel'd whence should come this shot,
    And sore this accident did them molest:
    But *Cloridan* for this forbare them not,
    But shot another in about the brest,
    The which inflam'd *Zerbinos* mind so sore,
    That for revenge he would have slaine *Medore*.

7

And fastning in his golden curled haire,
    His warlike hand, thou shalt (said he) abuy,
    Thou shalt the penance and the burthen beare
    Of him, that here hath made my men to die:
    Yet for all this, *Zerbino* did forbeare
    To kill him, when he saw with gracious eye,
    His sweet sad look, and harkned to his speech,
    That in this sort for pardon did beseech.

8

Sir knight (he said) for thy *Messias* sake,
    I thee do pray and earnestly conjure,
    So much compassion now on me to take,
    To let me give my Lord his sepulture.
    I little care what spoile of me ye make,
    What paines or tortures I my selfe endure,
    I onely sue, so long my life to save,
    As I may lay my master in his grave.

9

Now while *Medoro* spake these words and such,
    Whereby *Zerbino* was to mercy mov'd,
    And to his favour was inclined much,
    As one that gratefulnesse had ever lov'd,
    A vile base swaine so rudely did him touch,
    As him not onely from his place remov'd,
    But with his staffe most rudely overthrew him,
    That ev'ry one do deem him dead that view him.

10

This fact did so *Zerbino's* mind offend,
    That presently the villain he did chase,
    And to have killed him he did intend,
    And had, but that the other fled apace:
    But when that *Cloridano* saw his friend,
    With bleeding wound lie prostrate in the place,
    He means himselfe no longer now to hide,
    But ev'n to die by deare *Medoro's* side.

11

And as he purpos'd, so he did indeed,
 For fighting manfully he there was slaine,
 The *Scots* do onward on their way proceed,
 Medoro halfe alive doth now remaine:
 And still his brest in wofull sort doth bleed,
 The staffe had cut therein so large a veine,
 And sure he had bled out his life and all,
 But for one rare good hap did him befall.

12

For lo, a damsell came, though meanly clad,
 In shepheards weeds, yet fresh and faire of favour,
 And such a one as in those base clothes had
 A shew of princely birth and high behaviour,
 She finding him lie there in case so bad,
 Did think it charity to be his saviour:
 This was (if you forget) the Lady faire,
 That of *Cataya* was undoubted heire.

13

I shewd you by what hap she gat the ring,
 And how the same had fil'd her with such pride,
 And her into so high conceit did bring,
 That all her suters now she flat deni'd,
 She careth not for Earle, nor Duke, nor King,
 Orlando she and *Sacrapant* defi'd,
 But chiefly she would blush and be asham'd,
 If she but hapt to heare *Renaldo* nam'd.

14

So great her folly grew, so vaine her pride,
 As she esteemed all the world at nought,
 The which when once the blind boy had espi'd,
 (Not blind when any mischiefe may be wrought)
 He will no longer this presumption bide,
 And for a fit occasion long he sought,
 And finding this, he thought himselfe now sped,
 And up he drawes his arrow to the head.

15

Now when this *Indian* Queene did there behold
 A lovely youth lie dying in the place,
 His body feeble in a mortall cold,
 A deadly pale amid his lively face,
 A kind of passion straight on her took hold,
 That mov'd her mind to pitie this his case,
 And much the rather when he did declare
 The wofull cause that bred him all this care.

16

She having learn'd of Surgerie the art,
 An art which still the *Indians* greatly prize,
 Which fathers to their children to impart,
 Whose knowledge in tradition chiefly lies,
 Which without books the children learn by hart,
 I say *Angelica* doth then devise,
 By skill she had in juyce of herbs and flowers,
 For to renew *Medoro's* lively powers.

17

And calling to her mind she late had seen,
 An herb whose vertue was to stanch the blood,
 As *Dittamie*, or some such herb I ween,
 That for such purpose wholsome was and good;
 Straightway she seeks this herb upon the green,
 With all the hast and diligence she could;
 And finding it, she takes thereof a branch,
 Whose vertue was the course of blood to stanch.

18

Then comming back againe, she met by hap,
 A silly shepheard seeking of his cow,
 That brake out of his ground at some small gap,
 And now was straid he knew not where nor how,
 She prayes him take the herbs were in her lap,
 (A servitor more fit to serve a sow)
 And beare her company unto the place,
 Where poore *Medoro* lay in dang'rous case.

19

Then from their horse she and the shepheard light,
 And straight between two tiles those herbs she brus'd
 And took the juyce between her fingers bright,
 And so into the wound the same infus'd,
 Whose vertue great reviv'd *Medoro's* spright,
 To find himselfe so well and kindly us'd,
 That doubt it was which most his wound did salve,
 The precious surgeon or the precious salve.

20

And now he had recover'd so much force,
 As what with hers, and with the shepheards aid,
 He clamer'd up upon the shepheards horse,
 Howbeit in the place so long he staid,
 Vntill he saw his loved masters corse,
 Into a grave with *Cloridanos* laid;
 And then, and not before he did agree,
 To do as they by her should pointed be.

21

From thence unto the shepheards house she went,
 And made her patient eke with her to go,
 And there to bide with him she was content,
 Till he were clearely rid of all his wo:
 But in this while she felt her heart relent,
 With sundry qualms that wonted not be so,
 And when his comely personage she saw,
 A secret heat she felt her heart to gnaw.

22

For while she heal'd his wound, another dart
 Did wound her thoughts, and high conceits so deep,
 As now therewith was ravisht her proud heart,
 Possessing it although she wake or sleep:
 Her wound to heale, there was no herb nor art,
 For more and more like flame the same doth creep,
 Yet her chiefe care is him to help and cure,
 That all this torment doth to her procure.

23

Thus while *Medoro* better growes and better,
　She feels her self tormented more and more,
　And he that for his love to her was debter,
　Is he alone that plagueth her so sore:
　Wherefore though modesty a while did let her,
　Yet now perforce no further she forbore,
　But plainly to *Medoro* told her grief,
　And at his hands as plainly ask'd relief.

24

O stout *Orlando*, valiant *Sacrapant*,
　O fierce *Ferraw*, ô hundreds more beside,
　Where are those valiant acts of which you vaunt?
　Where is your pomp, your glory, and your pride?
　One poore *Medore* all your desires doth daunt,
　One poore *Medore* doth all your power deride,
　And she whom all of you have woo'd in vaine,
　To woo *Medoro* doth not now disdaine.

25

She suffers poore *Medoro* take the flowre,
　Which many sought, but none had yet obtain'd
　That fragrant rose, that to that present houre
　Vngather'd was, behold *Medoro* gain'd,
　And over her to give him perfect power,
　With sacred rites a marriage was ordain'd,
　And with the veile of this so sacred order,
　She covers this her folly and disorder.

26

Now when the solemne marriage was done,
　Of which god *Cupid* ask'd the banes (I trow)
　She going forward as she hath begun,
　Continu'd there with him a month or mo,
　From rising to the setting of the Sun,
　With him she doth sit, talk, lie, stand and go,
　Forgetting so all maidenly sobrietie,
　That she of him could never have satietie.

27

If in the house she staid, then would she crave
　Medoro in the house with her to stay,
　If in the field she walk, then must she have
　Medoro lead or guide her in the way:
　And by a river in the shady cave,
　They oft did use to spend the heat of day:
　Like to that cave where (shunning stormy weather)
　The Trojan Duke and *Dido* met together.

28

Amid these joyes (as great as joyes might be)
　Their manner was on ev'ry wall within,
　Without on ev'ry stone or shady tree,
　To grave their names with bodkin, knife, or pin,
　Angelica and *Medore*, you plaine might see,
　(So great a glory had they both therein)
　Angelica and *Medore* in ev'ry place,
　With sundry knots and wreathes they enterlace.

29

Now when she thought in this well pleasing place,
　She had already made sufficient stay,
　And, for she long'd to do *Medore* that grace,
　To give to him her kingdome of *Catay*,
　From whence she had been absent so long space,
　From this poore house she means to go away,
　Yet minds she ere she go, her host to please,
　With whom she found such pleasure and such ease.

30

Angelica had since she was a gerle,
　Worn on her arm (as for *Orlando's* sake)
　A bracelet rich, of precious stone and pearle,
　Which as a token she of him did take,
　And though she had it of this worthy Earle,
　Yet did she thereof chiefest reckning make,
　Not that the giver she did much esteem,
　But for the gift was rich, and so did seem.

31

By her this bracelet many yeares was worn,
　Not onely in her time of peace and joy,
　But ev'n when she remained most forlorn,
　And subject to each danger and annoy,
　Ev'n then when nak'd as ever she was born,
　The *Orko* came in hope her to enjoy.
　This bracelet (wanting store of coine and pence)
　She gives her host as for a recompence.

32

Next day betime she getteth on her way,
　And makes *Medoro* sole her Lord and guide,
　He kept her company both night and day,
　And none but he with her did go and ride;
　Their meaning is at *Berselon* to stay,
　A port in *Spaine*, untill they may provide
　A vessell that with help of oare and wind
　May them transport from *Spanish* seas to *Inde*.

33

But ere they were arrived at this port,
　They met a mad man of his wit bestraught,
　Besmear'd with dirt and mire in filthy sort,
　His outward sense expel'd with inward thought:
　This mad man made them but ilfavour'd sport,
　And had made worse, had he them rightly caught,
　But as it was, he put them in great danger,
　And flies at them as dogs do at a stranger.

34

But how she scaped and away did get
　With her new love, hereafter I declare:
　For why *Marfisa* I may not forget,
　And those with her that in the tempest are,
　With *Griffin*, *Aquilant*, and *Sansonet*,
　And th'*English* Duke that hath the horn so rare,
　Which five I left in danger and disease,
　Tost terribly in the tempestuous seas.

35

Now while the wind continu'd blowing hard,
    And of his rage did small or nothing bate,
    The master sets his compasse and his card,
    And cals to counsell first the masters mate,
    And then the mariners of best regard
    Consulting of the weather and their state,
    And ev'ry one doth tell his guesse and thought,
    Neare to what coast the tempest had them brought.

36

Some say *Lymisso*, *Tripoly* some say,
    Some say *Satila*, full of rocks and sands,
    And sweare that all of them were cast away,
    Except they keep aloofe from off those lands;
    This causeth some to curse and some to pray,
    And lift to heav'n their wofull hearts and hands,
    Their stuffe nor merchandize none care to save,
    But hurle the same into the greedy wave.

37

Well might they bost of iron heart and breast,
    That could at such a time be void of feare:
    The stout *Marfisa* at that time confest,
    She wisht with all her heart not to be there,
    So sore the swelling seas did them molest,
    As though it would the ship in peeces teare,
    Nor was there any signe the wind would cease,
    And that the sea would grant them any peace.

38

One vowes a journey to the holy tombe,
    Another to *Galicia* vowes to go,
    Vnto Saint *Iames*, some others unto *Rome*,
    Or other hallowed places that they know:
    The mariners feare nought but want of roome,
    Sea roome they wish, then care they for no mo,
    At foure daies end it clear'd and waxed faire,
    Or were't the season, or their earnest praier.

39

And as the weather grew more cleare and cleare,
    They did discover plaine a goodly coast,
    And to the port as they drew neare and neare,
    Born in by tide, their sailes and tackle lost,
    Behold a goodly city did appeare,
    With towres and stately buildings of great cost,
    Of which when once the master was aware,
    It bred in him no little feare and care.

40

To cast his anker straight he doth provide,
    For vaine it was to labour to go back,
    The vessels wanted sailes to stem the tide,
    The tempest had put all things so to wrack,
    And yet he feared on the other side,
    They of the town would sure be on his jack;
    In fine so full his mind was of confusion,
    He knew not whereupon to make conclusion.

41

Now while he stood confused in this sort,
    The *English* Duke demaunds what cause of doubt
    Made him refuse so faire and safe a port,
    And strive against the streame to keep still out?
    Sir (quoth the master) briefly to report
    To you the cause, know this, that hereabout
    And namely in that city dwels a nation,
    That use a barbarous and cruell fashion.

42

They call them *Amazons* that here do dwell,
    Here women guide, and rule, and govern all,
    The men from government they do expell,
    Some they do kill, the rest keep bond and thrall,
    He sole shall scape that runs at tilt so well,
    As first to make ten men of theirs to fall,
    And next in Venery and flesh delight,
    Can satisfie ten women in one night.

43

And if a man performe the first of these,
    And have such hap to overthrow the men,
    And yet at night his force do faile to please
    In act of generation damsels ten,
    He must be kild or drowned in the seas,
    Or kept a prisner in some cave or den;
    But they that both perform, shall have their lives,
    And those ten damsels ever for their wives.

44

When as the pilot out his tale had told,
    Of women that delight in spoile and murder,
    The *English* Duke could hard his laughter hold,
    To heare of so fantasticall an order,
    And all the five affirmed straight they would
    Land at this place, and go by sea no further;
    Each place to them was safe and out of feare,
    Where they might have the use of sword and speare.

45

But all the shipmen carried other minds,
    As men that better were to stormes inur'd,
    And would have thought their lives in waves & winds
    More then in conflicts and in fights assur'd:
    But whether reason leads or causes binds,
    Or that the better part the same procur'd,
    The ship with broken mast and tackle torn,
    By force of tide into the hav'n was born.

46

No sooner was the vessell in the port,
    But straight a gally ready for such need,
    Stor'd with artillery of ev'ry sort,
    And one that could both row and saile with speed,
    Did board them, and (to make the matter short)
    A woman clad in grave and ancient weed,
    As old as *Sibill*, or as *Hectors* mother,
    Spake in effect these words, with many other.

47

My friends (quoth she) or yeeld or look to die,
  For hope is none to scape away by flight,
But thus if any of you mean to trie,
  If he alone can vanquish ten in fight,
And afterward with twice five maidens lie,
  And of them maids make women in one night;
Then such a one shall rule among us chiefe,
And save his friends from punishment and griefe.

48

But if that any shall the fact attempt,
  And faile but in the first or in the last,
Then he shall die because of his contempt,
  And into prison ye shall all be cast.
They made her answer all, they were content,
  Not one man there was therewithall agast
For in both kinds the knights had so been prov'd,
As with the danger they were nothing mov'd.

49

The *English* Duke with these three youths of *France*,
  Straight for this enterprise themselves prepare,
But chiefe the Duke that doubted no mischance,
  By vertue of his book and horn most rare:
Marfisa eke (though for the second daunce
  She was not fit) so manly mind she bare,
As she would needs her force and fortune trie,
And sware her sword all weapons should supplie.

50

And straight they all agreed some lots to draw,
  And to conclude, on her the hazard fell,
But she that quite was void of feare and aw,
  Did promise to perform her office well:
This sword (quoth she) shall abrogate this law,
  And plague them all that in this city dwell,
And to undo these doubts I will provide,
As *Alexander Gordius* knots unti'd.

51

No forreiner hereafter shall bewaile,
  The wicked law of this ungodly land:
This said, she putteth on her coat of maile,
  In hope alone against ten men to stand.
Then came the ten were pointed to assaile,
  But he that was the foremost of the band,
As farre as by apparance might be guest,
Was one that farre surpassed all the rest.

52

His horse was black as pitch, or polisht jet,
  Save in one foot, and in his brow a starre,
A shining spot of white, not very great,
  A lofty reine, an eye that threatned warre;
Such as the horse, such was his own conceit,
  His sorrowes did exceed his joyes so farre,
And deadly care so drown'd his small delight,
As did the black the little spot of white.

53

This knight (that ever vantage did eschew)
  Would not accompany those other nine,
But standeth still on horseback taking view,
  Which way the victory did most incline:
Marfisa rode a horse of dainty hew,
  Giv'n unto her of late by *Norandine*,
His colour pide, powder'd with many a spot,
Small head, fierce look, clean limb'd, and lofty trot.

54

Now when that giv'n of battell was the signe,
  On her alone all nine at once did flie,
And she alone sustain'd the force of nine:
  The tenth (I said) was quiet standing by,
As one that did against that use repine,
  When more then one should seek to make one die:
And with the first encounter thus she sped,
She laid down foure of them on ground for dead.

55

The fift she justles, and by force unhorses,
  And with a trunch the sixt she gave a blow,
That to the ground both man and horse inforces,
  With mazed head, and foltring feet to go.
The standers by admire her passing forces,
  And chiefe their wives that saw them killed so,
For as a chainshot sweeps all in the way,
So with those nine *Marfisa* then did play.

56

She bath'd her blade in blood up to the hilt,
  And with the same their bodies all she mangled,
All that abode her blowes, their bloud was spilt,
  They scaped best that here and thither ranged,
Or those whose horses overthrown at tilt,
  Lay with their masters on the earth intangled.
Thus of nine enemies remained none,
For all were kil'd, or maim'd, or overthrown.

57

The knight that was arraid in black attire,
  And stood aside, and saw this hardy fight,
To shew that he for feare did not retire,
  But to make known his curtsie shining bright,
Straight steppeth out, and first he doth desire
  To speak with her whom he esteem'd a knight,
For he could not imagine nor suppose,
A woman could have giv'n such manly blowes.

58

And thus he saith, me seems the odds too great,
  That I of you should take, to fight straightway,
Sith both your horse and you are in a sweat,
  Mine offer is to respite you a day,
Till you may be refresht with rest and meat,
  That with mine honour fight with you I may:
For I should think my selfe disgraced sore,
To vanquish one wean'd and spent before.

59

Weari'd and spent (quoth she) alas the while,
    Think you I am so weari'd and so spent?
    Your courteous offer causeth me to smile,
    To think how quickly you will it repent;
    You do deceive your selfe, and much beguile,
    To think that I to pawse would be content,
    I doubt not you shall find but little cause,
    (When you have tri'd) to offer me to pause.

60

Well, said the knight, if you will trie it straight,
    That you accept, I cannot well refuse:
    Forthwith two speares of mighty strength & waight
    Were brought, and he doth bid *Marfisa* chuse:
    Now was the Sun foure houres past his haight,
    When as these two began their speares to use;
    The trumpets sound, they set their speares in rest,
    And each determining to do their best.

61

The speares in spels and sundry peeces flew,
    As if they had been little sticks or cane,
    Yet of the blowes to both did hurt ensew,
    Their steeds were welnigh brought unto their bane,
    Quite overthrown in all the peoples view,
    As though their legs had quite from them been tane,
    So both their horses tumbled on the ground,
    Yet both themselves from hurt were safe and sound.

62

An hundred and an hundred knights and more,
    Marfisa had subdu'd (it was well known)
    Yet such a chance she never had before,
    To have her horse so strangely overthrown:
    Also the knight that black apparell wore,
    Doth marvell whence this great mishap was grown,
    And not a little wondred at her force,
    That had so stoutly overthrown his horse.

63

Forthwith on foot the combat they apply,
    In which the tone the tother doth not spare,
    And either thinks to make the other die,
    And either of the tother doth beware.
    But all the while among the standers by,
    Appeared great attentivenesse and care,
    For never could they guesse from the beginning,
    Which of the two was in best hope of winning.

64

Now gan *Marfisa* to her selfe to say,
    It happy was that he before stood still,
    For had he holp the tother nine to day,
    No doubt with me it could have been but ill,

That now alone so hard doth hold me play,
    As scant I save my selfe with all my skill,
    Thus to her selfe the stout *Marfisa* thought,
    And all the while couragiously she fought.

65

Contrary, to himselfe the knight thus saith,
    'Twas well for me, that he before was spent,
    For had he been but fresh in perfect breath,
    I doubt me that ere this I had been shent,
    Surely (thought he) I scant had scaped death,
    If he to rest himselfe had giv'n consent,
    No question I did great advantage take,
    That he refus'd that offer I did make.

66

Thus did the combat long 'twixt them endure,
    And neither party boasted of their gaine,
    Vntill the nights dark shadow and obscure
    Did cover city, wood, and vale, and plaine,
    And that that rest to all things doth procure,
    Did force them two to respit this their paine;
    And first the knight thus said, what can we do?
    Behold how night is come to part us two.

67

You may (said he) one night prolong your life,
    And longer not, such is the cursed law,
    Against my will (God knowes) I hold this strife,
    And now I feare and have no little aw,
    Lest ev'ry one that was to them a wife,
    Whom late you kil'd, will from your beds you draw,
    For ev'ry one of those unhappy men
    Whom erst you slue, was husband unto ten.

68

So that for those same nine that you have slaine,
    Nine times ten women seek revenge to take:
    Wherefore I wish that you and all your traine
    Within my roofe this night abode do make,
    For so perhap from wrong they will abstaine,
    If not for right, at least for rev'rence sake,
    Ile take your offer sir, *Marfisa* saith,
    So that hereof to me you give your faith.

69

That as in fight you shew your value great,
    As I have proved in this present place,
    So I may find your words without deceit,
    Lest falshood should your noble deeds deface:
    I will accept your lodging and your meat,
    And will perswade my fellowes in like case;
    But rather then for feare you should it think,
    Let's fight it out by light of torch and link.

70

And thus in fine they all of them agreed,
   That unto him that night they would be guest:
Straight to a sumptuous pallace they proceed,
   By torch-light brought to chambers richly drest:
But when that each put off their warlike weed,
   Then each of them with wonder was possest:
She, that the knight did by his face appeare,
To be a boy, of age but eighteene yeare.

71

And he, when by her haire her sex he knew,
   Wonder'd to see a woman of such might,
As namely that in sight nine tall men slue,
   And after had with him prolong'd the fight:
And either pleased in the others view,
   Behold the one the other with delight,
Then each desir'd the others name to learn,
As in th'ensuing book you shall discern.

THE TWENTIETH BOOKE OF
ORLANDO FVRIOSO

THE ARGVMENT

With Guidon *all his worthy guests agree,*
*To breake from th'*Amazons *the morrow morne :*
Astolfo *doubting lest it would not be,*
Doth drive them thence and scares them with his horne :
Zerbino *laughs* Gabrina *gay to see ;*
Marfisa *seemes to take it in great scorne,*
And 'gainst his will commits her to his guiding,
By whom he heares of Isabella *tiding.*

ORLANDO FVRIOSO
THE TWENTIETH BOOKE

1

ght wondrous deeds by diverse dames were done,
In times of old, as well by sword as pen,
Whereby their glory shined like the sun,
And famous was both farre and neare as then,
The same *Harpalice* in battell wonne,
Camillas worth is eke well known to men,
Corinnas praise, and *Saphos* are discern'd,
Above the rest, because they both were learn'd.

2

hat art so deep? what science is so high,
But worthy women have thereto attain'd?
Who list in stories old to look, may trie,
And find my speech herein not false nor fain'd,
And though of late they seem not to come nigh,
The praise their sexe in former times have gain'd,
No doubt the fault is either in backbiters,
Or want of skill and judgement in the writers.

3

r sure I see in this our present age,
Such vertuous parts in their sweet sex to grow,
The young so sober, and the rest so sage,
And all so chast, as writers shall (I know)
Have work enough to fill full many a page,
With their great praise that from their worth will flow,
To win the fame their ancestors did leese,
And passe *Marfisa* not in few degrees.

4

t now to turn my speech to her againe,
I say that when the knight did ask her name,
She made him answer, and did not disdaine,
To tell both what she was, and whence she came,
Yet (as her fashion was) both brief and plaine;
She saith thus to the knight, I called am
Marfisa: and she need to say no more,
For all the world had heard the rest before.

5

e tother, when his turn to speak came in,
First making long and farther circumstance,
In such like manner doth his tale begin,
(And sighing deep) you all have heard perchance,
Both of my fathers house, and of my kin,
Of fame in *Italie*, in *Spaine*, and *France:*
For sure I am the house of *Clarimount*,
In all the world is known and of account.

6

He that *Charello* and *Mambrino* slew,
And did their kingdomes ruine and deface,
Out of one stock with me together grew,
Although we were not all born in one place,
For why at *Ister* stood (to tell you true)
My father me begat, and in that case
My mother great with child he left behind,
And went to *France* by help of saile and wind.

7

Thus sev'nteen yeares I liv'd like one exil'd,
Vntill I able was to break a lance,
And for that place me seem'd too base and vild,
I mean to seek my friends and kin in *France:*
They name me *Guidon* savage of a child,
As yet I could not much my name advance,
For hither by a tempest I was born,
As you were now, with ship and tackle torn.

8

Here first *Argillon* with nine men I kil'd,
Elev'n months since, and that same day at night,
The office of an husband I fulfil'd,
Vnto ten *Amazons* in flesh delight:
This done, to take my choice then was I wil'd,
Of any ten that pleased best my sight,
And these remaine my wives, and must untill
One come that me with other nine can kill.

9

Vnto the knights this seem'd a marv'lous storie,
And much they wondred at this government,
They marvell that so great a territorie
For want of men was not consum'd and spent:
They thought no lesse the women would be sorie,
For want of men to live so continent:
'Twas strange one man sufficed ten of these,
Sith one with us can scant one woman please.

10

And straight they were inquisitive to know,
When first this foolish order there began,
And upon what occasion it did grow,
That women in that country ruled man?
Then *Guidon* answer'd thus, I shall you show
The whole discourse as briefly as I can,
According as my selfe have heard the same,
Since (by mishap) into this realme I came.

11

When as the *Greekes* had quite defaced *Troy*,
  And after twice ten yeares returned home,
  (For ten whole yeares in danger and annoy,
  Of surging seas they up and down did rome)
  They found their wives that had but little joy,
  So long a time, to live and lie alone,
  Each one a lusty lover to have chosen,
  Lest with the cold they might be serv'd and frozen.

12

Their houses full of bastard brats they see:
  In fine, they purpose after consultation,
  To pardon all their wives, and set them free,
  But for these boyes that bred some alteration,
  To drive them out a doore they do agree,
  And make them seek a forraine habitation;
  It was contrary much to their desires,
  That others brats should warm them at their fires.

13

Thus some thrown out, some close their mothers keep
  In corners, from their angry husbands sight,
  And when as elder yeares on them do creep,
  Each one betakes him to his most delight;
  Some plow, some get them herds of goats and sheep,
  Some sciences, and some do learn to fight,
  Thus ev'ry one betook him to some trade,
  As he assignes that all the world hath made.

14

Among the rest that art of war ensue,
  Phalanto sonne of *Clytemnestra* Queene,
  But eighteen yeares of age, and fresh of hue,
  And in the flower of youths well pleasing greene,
  This one to him an hundred gallants drue,
  And getting ships and things that needfull been,
  With writs of Mart (a thing that breeds much sorrow)
  He gets him to the sea, in mind to borrow.

15

Now while *Phalanto* with his cursed fleet
  Abode at sea with that more cursed traine:
  It fortun'd at that time that they of *Creet*,
  Had *Idumeo* driv'n out of his raigne:
  Wherefore for better strength they thought it meet
  Phalanto and his men to entertaine:
  They give to him great hire, and great reward,
  The city of *Ditea* for to guard.

16

Ditea was a town of great estate,
  Rich, and frequented with no small resort,
  And yeelds in plenty large, betimes and late,
  Of sundry kinds of pleasures, and of sport;
  And as they all men us'd, so in like rate,
  They us'd their soldiers in so friendly sort,
  As though they had agreed by sound accords,
  To make them all their masters and their Lords.

17

But chief they found with women so great grace,
  As they wan most of them unto their lure;
  But when the warres were ended in short space,
  And that their pay no longer did endure,
  They all prepar'd to leave this pleasant place,
  Which to the damsels did great griefe procure;
  To leese their husbands brother, or their father,
  Then these new lovers ev'ry one had rather.

18

And when they saw they could not make them stay,
  By no device of theirs, nor no request,
  They do agree with them to steale away,
  And take such things as were of value best;
  Thus came these damsels loden with their prey,
  And thence to sea, and were now gone at least
  An hundred leagues, with these new lawlesse lovers,
  Before *Ditea* this their flight discovers.

19

The wind so good then for their purpose blew,
  Phalanto quickly landed in this coast,
  And here the amorous and wanton crew
  Vnto their loves of this their lewdnesse boast;
  But now that saying was confirmed true,
  That pleasant things, do often cloy the most:
  And there can be a greater clog to no man,
  Then to be weary of a wanton woman.

20

Wherefore like men that were, and had been ever
  Of gaine most greedy, sparing of expence:
  They secretly consulting, do endever
  To take the goods, and then to steale from thence.
  Thus while the women still in love persever,
  They that regard not pleasure more then pence,
  Load with their wealth, of which there was good store,
  Stale to the sea, and left them on the shore.

21

Sore were the damsels daunted and dismaid,
  When once they saw their loves had them forsaken,
  For what more spite can be, then be betraid
  Of him to whom one hath her selfe betaken?
  And sith they find that weeping doth not aid,
  They meane betime some order shall be taken,
  What they shall do, and how hereafter live,
  An ev'ry one doth straight her verdit give.

22

One, home to turne againe doth thinke it best,
  And to their kin and friends them to submit,
  And with repentance pardon to request,
  And vow the like fault never to commit;
  Another that good motion doth detest,
  And sweares it shew'd the mover had no wit,
  And that with greater honestie or ease,
  They might go drowne them headlong in the seas.

23

Among the rest one *Orontea* hight,
  That lineally of *Mynos* was descended,
  And past the rest in beautie and good sprite,
  And had lesse grievously then they offended,
  For to *Phalanto* she her troth did plight,
  And to have bene his honest spouse intended:
  This one declareth thus her resolution,
  And makes the rest put it in execution.

24

She wishes them to tary in this land,
  That had both fruitfull earth and pleasant aire,
  And fountaines sweet, and woods on ev'ry hand,
  And medowes greene, and pastures fresh and faire,
  Beside large hav'ns, where ships at ease might stand,
  To which the merchants often made repaire,
  By tempest driven, well loden with good trafficke,
  Of things that came from *Ægypt* and from *Affrick*.

25

Wherefore this place she minds not to forsake,
  But that they may as chiefly they desire,
  A sharpe revenge on men for ever take,
  They vow to put to sacke, to sword and fire,
  Such ships as to their hav'n repaire do make,
  And kill the men, and this they all conspire:
  And still when any come, this trade they use,
  Nor left a man alive to carry newes.

26

But when this cruell law some yeares had lasted,
  Which they had meant to have confirm'd for ay,
  They find that they so fast consum'd and wasted,
  That this their barren kingdome would decay,
  Except to find some remedy they hasted,
  And having long consulted on the way,
  They meane of this their law to bate some rigor,
  Yet leave the substance still in strength and vigor.

27

And thus they do, they chuse among such men,
  As tempests drive to this their wicked nation,
  Some few as were so lustie, as with ten
  They could performe the act of generation,
  All in one night, the rest into a den
  They cast, and kill them in most cruell fashion,
  And build unto revenge a solemne alter,
  And over this they make them stretch a halter.

28

Such men as live are to this order sworne,
  To kill all such as hither shall repaire,
  And all men children that to them are borne,
  They sell or change as in an open faire,
  So when some die with age and weaknesse worne,
  Then other women do the want repaire,
  Their powre and number thus doth still increase,
  Their wealth and pomp augmented, with long peace.

29

But after many yeares it thus befell,
  Elbanio, one of *Hercles* noble race,
  A comely tall strong man, and favord well,
  And in his speech and manners passing grace,
  Arrived where these homicids do dwell,
  And ere he knew the fashion of the place,
  The cruell sergeants tooke him as they found him,
  And like a fellon hand and foote they bound him.

30

It fortund as they carrid him to slaughter,
  Among the rest that did the same behold,
  Was *Alessandra, Oronteas* daughter,
  A fine yong girle, about twise eight yeare old,
  Elbanio humbly as he went besought her,
  To be a meane this foule death to withhold,
  That like a man he might be kild at least,
  And not be drawne to slaughter like a beast.

31

To beg my life (quoth he) it were a vanitie,
  (Which in your service I would gladly spend)
  Where humane hearts be void of all humanitie,
  But all the sute that I to make intend,
  (Which to denie were too too much immanitie)
  Is this, that thus my life I may not end,
  But with my sword in hand to fight with men,
  With sev'n at once, or eight, or nine or ten.

32

This he to her, thus she to him replies,
  Though to mankind we all professe hostilitie,
  Yet thinke not (this she spake with watrie eyes)
  That all our hearts are void of all gentilitie,
  What *Progne* or *Medea* could despise
  Your passing beautie, courage and nobilitie?
  And were my fellowes all so ill inclind,
  Yet I my selfe would beare a better mind.

33

And though the rigor of our law be such,
  That no man can obtaine a pardon free,
  And ev'n this small you aske, to graunt is much,
  If our law strictly should observed be,
  Yet such remorse I feele my heart doth tuch,
  To grant thy sute if others will agree
  Although I feare thou wilt in such a strife,
  Prolong thy paine, and not preserve thy life.

34

Oh (said *Elbanio*) blest were such a day,
  That in the field my manhood I might trie,
  Could but your credit carry such a sway,
  Not ten, but ten times ten I would defie.
  This said, she caus'd the execution stay,
  And to her mother goes she by and by,
  With thousand strings of *Cupid* in her brest,
  And unto her expoundeth his request.

35

Straight *Orontea* doth her counsell call,
  And in such sort thereof to them she spake,
  In guarding of our hav'n and citie wall,
  Tis good that of the strongest men we take:
  Therefore to know who be most stout and tall,
  I thinke it very good some proofe to make,
  For else we shall unto our selves do wrong,
  To save the weaker men, and kill the strong.

36

And who can wish to make a better triall,
  Then for one man to fight with five and five,
  And if he vanquisht them and make them die all,
  Twere certes meet he should be kept alive:
  Thus *Orontea* said, and they replie all,
  That in this point with her they cannot strive,
  Save old *Artemia* (carren witherd jade)
  Mislikt the motion, and this answer made.

37

The cause that first we did some men admit,
  Was not to keepe our hav'ns or citie wall,
  For we our selves have strength enough and wit,
  To keepe our towne (I trust) and ever shall.
  Were we as well for procreation fit,
  Without mans helpe, not one should live at all;
  Now for necessitie some few we spare,
  Such as most able for that service are.

38

This motion quite gainsaith our auncient law,
  To keepe one man as strong as halfe a score:
  How many women would he keepe in aw?
  Had we ten such we should beare rule no more.
  And further, tis an old and certaine saw,
  Both us'd and proved many yeares before,
  That they that give a weapon to their stronger,
  Are like themselves to carry rule no longer.

39

But put the case this one by our consent,
  And his good hap ten of the others kill,
  How shall an hundred widowes then lament,
  That long must lie alone against their will?
  If he an hundred women would content,
  Then him to save I should not thinke it all,
  Then were he to be lov'd, admir'd and wonderd,
  If he alone could satisfie an hunderd.

40

This cruell speech did all the rest displease,
  And loth they were *Elbanio* should be slaine,
  His comely shape their sharpnesse did appease,
  And chiefly she that over all did raigne,
  Doth seeke herein her daughters mind to please,
  With many reasons answring her againe,
  And point by point did all her speech confute,
  And in the end obtaind her daughters sute.

41

Thus to *Elbanio* pardon they impart,
  Provided if he overcome the men,
  And after bravely play the husbands part,
  Not with an hundred women, but with ten.
  Elbanio thanketh them with chearfull hart,
  Then was he freely loosed from the den:
  In fine, when all things ready were ordained,
  In both exploits the conquest he obtained.

42

Then *Alessandra*, in whose tender mind
  Love had already made so deepe impression,
  With other nine, were unto him assignd,
  And princely mace was put in his possession.
  But first by solemne vow they do him bind,
  To hold this law for ever by succession,
  To sacrifice all men, save such as trie,
  To kill ten men, and with ten women lie.

43

And though that many have in ages past
  Attempted both, yet few have had successe,
  To scape the first exploit, and trie the last,
  In which to faile, the danger were no lesse,
  But he that both performes, forthwith is plast
  In princely seate, and free from all distresse:
  And this their law (as by records appeares)
  Alreadie lasted hath two thousand yeares.

44

The last but I, that held this cursed place,
  Argillon hight, whom I in combat killed,
  And him and his thereby I did displace,
  And then their roomes with me and mine I filled,
  Where we have tarrid now a twelvemonths space,
  Among these wights of goodnesse all unskilled,
  And leade a life full of disdaine and scorne,
  As better had bene never to be borne.

45

For why these dallyings and wanton toyes,
  That wonted are to please our foolish youth,
  With costly fare, gay clothes, and *Venus* joyes,
  Of which repentance is the frute ensewth,
  Doth breed to me but anguish and annoyes,
  And pensive cares, and ever during ruth;
  And chiefly when unto my mind I call,
  My liberty is lost, and I a thrall.

46

To loose my lustie time in this vile place,
  Remov'd from kin and friends, and countrey farre,
  A wofull and remedilesse disgrace,
  Mov'd by some ill aspect of angry starre,
  Ev'n as a stallion kept for breed and race,
  Whom some mishap hath made unfit for warre,
  By losse of sight and foundring of his feete,
  For service quite unable and unmeete.

47

The while this tale the savage *Guidon* told,
  The *English* Duke that all this while stood by,
  And heard his speech, and did his face behold,
  And noted all his grace with watchfull eye,
  And made by all these observations bold,
  He runneth to embrace him by and by,
  And said, deare cosin, I were much too blame,
  Except I lov'd the house from whence you came.

48

Your mother could not tie a better lace
  About your necke, to make your linage knowne,
  Then this your value in this present place,
  Against *Marfisa* in the battell showne:
  I am *Astolfo* one of *Ammons* race,
  Friend to your house, and kinsman of your owne,
  I much rejoyce to find by this mischance;
  So neare a kinsman so far off from *France*.

49

But he that otherwise would have bene glad,
  To meet a friend, a Prince of kin so neare,
  Now on the other side he was full sad,
  And shewd the same in countenance and cheare,
  For ev'ry way the sequell must be bad,
  For if he win they die, the case is cleare,
  And if he do not win, he is but ded,
  Thus by ones good the tothers harme is bred.

50

On th'other side his yeares and tender age,
  Did all of them so farre with pittie move,
  And did *Marfisas* heate so much asswage,
  Her enmitie was welnigh turn'd to love:
  At last she makes a motion wise and sage,
  Which was, that all to scape by force should prove,
  She sweares if he would take part with his cosen,
  Not all the towne could vanquish that halfe dosen.

51

Most glad (said *Guidon*) I would take your part,
  Though vaine it is against so great a number,
  To enterprise by force hence to depart,
  Their very multitude will us so cumber:
  For often (to the terror of mine hart)
  Ten thousand armed women I do number
  Here in the streets, and with as many more,
  They do defend the port, the hav'n and shore.

52

Tush (quoth *Marfisa*) this I not regard,
  Were they in number as the sands of seas,
  To valiant hearts no enterprise is hard,
  Take you but part, and joyne with me and these.
  Yes, answer'd *Guidon*, be I made or mard,
  Or bee't with paine, with danger or disease,
  I will take part with you, but if I may,
  I would advise you to a safer way.

53

If we this matter wisely take in hand,
  This is the safest way that I do know,
  They let no men to touch the salt sea sand,
  Lest any should attempt from hence to go:
  And sith tis hard their forces to withstand,
  Ile trie a better way then that, I trow,
  Among my ten I have one speciall wife,
  Vpon whose trust I venter dare my life.

54

She shall a barke provide in secret sort,
  And other needfull things for us prepare,
  And when as to the tilt-yard they resort,
  And of our fight in expectation are,
  We suddenly will make unto the port,
  And ship our selves ere any be aware:
  To leade the way my selfe I am content,
  So you and yours to follow will consent.

55

Marfisa straight, and all the rest agreed,
  That *Guidon* for that time should be their guide,
  And that accordingly they would proceed,
  As he for them had promist to provide:
  Though (said *Marfisa*) saving this my weed,
  My shape and sexe from all of them doth hide,
  I know my selfe from harme could be excused,
  And of them all both welcome and well used.

56

But now (said she) such part I mind to take,
  As you shall tast (how good or bad it prove)
  That night with his *Aleria Guidon* spake,
  (So was her name that bare him chiefest love)
  And points that she provision good should make,
  For things that needfull were for their remove.
  And she no time, nor paine, nor travell spar'd,
  But out of hand a galley straight prepar'd.

57

And that her fellowes might no fraud suspect,
  To go to seeke a prize she doth pretend,
  And with great diligence she doth direct,
  All meanes to serve their passage to defend:
  And they within no time nor meane neglect,
  To bring their stout designement to an end.
  Thus ev'ry one their charge so well attended,
  That ere the morning all was done and ended.

58

No sooner came the dawning of the day,
  But that those *Amazons* like bees in swarmes,
  That seeke new dwellings in the month of May,
  So came they well appointed all in armes,
  To see an end of that unended fray,
  Not looking for such new and strange alarmes,
  For straight those six I nam'd and all their traine,
  Came with intent to scape or else be slaine.

59

First *Guidon* breakes the way to all the rest,
  Soone after him *Marfisa* did ensew,
  Then *Sansonet* and th'*English* Duke were prest,
  And next two brothers came, then all the crew;
  But yet with numbers they were so opprest,
  Both with the shafts they shot, and darts they threw,
  That notwithstanding all they had devised,
  They were in danger great to be surprised.

60

But when the *English* Duke the danger saw,
  Vnto himselfe these words or such he said,
  I see our foes in troupes together draw,
  I see our friends are weakned and dismaid,
  Now will I strike our enemies in aw,
  Now will I bring our friends unlookt for aid,
  With this he tooke his horne and blew a blast,
  That made the hearers ev'ry one agast.

61

So great a terror in their minds was bred,
  That straight as if with sprites they had bene scard,
  This way and that, confusedly they fled,
  And left the gates without defence or guard,
  As tumults often are at stage-playes bred,
  When false reports of sudden fires are heard,
  Or when the overloden seates do cracke,
  One tumbling downe upon anothers backe.

62

One breakes a leg, another breakes an arme,
  And some are choakt and stifled in the presse,
  Some kill themselves for feare of further harme.
  And whence the danger comes they cannot guesse,
  But all of them in hast themselves unarme,
  And unto fearefull flight themselves addresse:
  Nor women onely with this feare are punish'd,
  But even the men themselves were all astonish'd.

63

Yea even *Marfisas* courage, late so fierce,
  (So great a vertue this inchantment had)
  That strange and sudden feare the same did pearce,
  And she by flight to save her selfe was glad:
  The Knights likewise whom late I did rehearse,
  And all the men, as if they had bene mad,
  To seaward fled, as doth a fearfull Dove,
  When any noise doth scare her from above.

64

Thus doth the blast annoy both friends and foes,
  Yet so as all the men to shipboord went:
  Astolfo stil about the citie goes,
  For them to terrifie is his intent,
  And more and more in all the streets he bloes,
  And chiefly those where they do most frequent,
  The while his frends were now to shipboord gotten,
  And launched out, and him had quite forgotten.

65

The ship *Aleria* did before provide,
  And *Guidon* taking ship with all the rest,
  Would not consent neare to the shore to bide,
  But stale away with dreadfull feare possest.
  Now came the Duke unto the water side,
  And seeing all were gone, he thought it best
  Some other meane and way to take in hand,
  By which he might convey him home by land.

66

But how he gate him home, and there did speed,
  When from those countries he was come to *France*,
  And how his horne did stand him in great steed,
  Defending him from danger and mischance,
  Hereafter I will shew, now I proceed
  To her whose deeds do still her name advance,
  I meane *Marfisa* stout, that made great hast,
  To shun the hearing of the fearfull blast.

67

But when they were removed from the shore,
  By helpe of sailes and oares, so great a space,
  As now the fearfull sound was heard no more,
  Each thought them guilty of a great disgrace,
  And of their feare they were asham'd so sore,
  One shund to looke another in the face,
  The while their bark had so good wind and wether,
  As all arriv'd in *Tyrrhen* seas together.

68

And to *Marsilia* thence by sea they went,
  Where *Bradamant* bare all the rule and sway,
  Who late as governesse was thither sent,
  Though thence she had bene absent many a day:
  For had she present bene, by her assent,
  Vnentertaind they should not go away.
  Here when they were refresht with meate and rest,
  Marfisa tooke her leave of all the rest.

69

And said she thought it great disgrace and shame,
  So many in one company to see,
  For crowes (quoth she) and pigeons do the same,
  And Deere, and sheepe, and beasts that fearfull be,
  But Falcons that do flie at stately game,
  With other birds and beasts in their degree,
  That feare not others force, and trust their owne,
  Shun company, and love to go alone.

70

But yet the rest that were of other mind,
  Together kept, and bad the Dame farewell,
  Vntill by hap a castle they did find,
  Wherein a Lord of great estate did dwell,
  That in appearance courteous seem'd and kind,
  But not in acts, as after I shall tell,
  For he surpris'd them all that night asleepe,
  And made them sweare a cruell law to keepe.

71

The while *Marfisa* on her way doth ride,
　Appareld like a Knight of some renowne,
　And as she passed by the river side,
　She met a woman in a tawnie gowne,
　Ilfavourd, crooked, old and hollow eyd,
　Her forehead furrow'd with continuall frowne,
　Her body tyr'd with travell and ill fare,
　Her guilty mind afflicted more with care.

72

This filthy hag, this carren wither'd jade,
　Was she whom in the cave *Orlando* found,
　When of the theeves such massacre he made,
　That kept faire *Isabella* under ground:
　This wretch that holpe them in that wicked trade,
　And fear'd the plague that might on her redound,
　Fled from all company for feare of danger,
　Vntill she hapt to light upon this stranger.

73

And for she saw her clad in strange array,
　Though gracelesse, yet she gathers heart of grace,
　And at the foord her comming she doth stay,
　And when *Marfisa* came unto the place,
　Sir Knight (for so she seem'd) I shall you pray,
　(Said this old hag) to do me so much grace,
　That on your horse behind you I may ride,
　Till I be past the streame on th'other side.

74

Marfisa that was ever from her cradle,
　Of courteous kind, doth grant her her desire,
　And made her clamber up behind her sadle,
　To passe the river and a filthy mire,
　That to her horse had almost bene a stable:
　And when they were ascended somewhat higher,
　They met a faire yong Ladie with a Knight,
　Both richly clad, both comely to the sight.

75

But both their minds were false, their manners bad,
　And therefore matcht together very fit,
　For he was *Pinnabell*, that lately had
　Faire *Bradamant* deceiv'd at *Merlins* pit,
　She was his love, for whom he was so sad,
　When *Bradamant* on him did hap to hit,
　Till after by this noble Damsels meane,
　That strange inchantment was dissolved cleane.

76

This Ladie that was *Pinnabellos* love,
　And was both proud and scornfull of behaviour,
　And sees this hag, did straight her laughter move,
　To scorne her writheld skin and evill favour:
　For which *Marfisa* stout doth her reprove,
　And with a sharpe reply she straight doth brave her,
　Because (quoth she) I find thou dost disdaine her,
　Against thy Knight and thee I will maintaine her.

77

I say this woman fairer is then thou,
　Now let thy Knight come fight in thy defence,
　For I by force my saying will avow,
　And if that I prevaile, ere thou go hence,
　Thou shalt thy horse and garments all allow
　To this old woman for a recompence.
　Then *Pinnabell* to fight doth him addresse,
　Because in manhood he could do no lesse.

78

But when they met (*Marfisas* passing force,
　Was such) she quickly vanquished the Knight,
　And overthrew him quite beside his horse.
　This done, she makes the stately dame to light,
　And with the aged woman cloths to scorse,
　At which the tone tooke sport, the tother spite,
　She tooke likewise the Ladies ambling nagge,
　And thereupon she sets the trotting hagge.

79

Who in this youthfull tyre and rich array,
　Doth looke in shew more ugly then before,
　Thus three dayes with *Marfisa* she did stay,
　Before they hapt to meet with any more;
　The fourth they met *Zerbino* on the way,
　The Scottish Prince that would have sav'd *Medore*,
　And now in anger great the *Scot* pursude,
　That in his presence prov'd himselfe so rude.

80

Now though *Zerbino* were but ill apaid,
　Yet was he straight with laughter great surprisde,
　To see an aged woman so arraid,
　In youthfull cloths as though she were disguisde:
　And to *Marfisa* merily he said,
　Sir Knight it seemeth you are well advis'd,
　To get so faire a peece to carrie by you,
　As you are sure that no man will envie you.

81

The woman seem'd some hundred yeares of age,
　Her wither'd skin such store of wrincles had,
　And like an ape or monkie in a cage,
　So looked she in this apparrell clad:
　But now she looked worse, when with new rage,
　Her eyes enflamed were, and she halfe mad:
　For what more spite can be a woman told,
　Then if one say she looketh foule and old?

82

Marfisa seemeth wroth (to make some sport)
　And thus she saith, surcease your slandrous toung,
　Your vertue of her beautie commeth short,
　She is (in spite of you) both faire and young:
　And if you dare contrarie my report,
　Or that hereby you feele your courage stoung,
　I will maintaine against you ev'ry word,
　On horse, or foote, by speare or else by sword.

83

Zerbino at this challenge did but laffe,
  And said he would not leese their friendship so:
Tis fit (quoth he) that swine should feed on draffe,
I am not I, so mad and fond I trow,
For her to draw a sword or breake a staffe,
But as you came you may together go:
No doubt you are a fitly matched paire,
If you as lustie be as she is faire.

84

Wherefore I list not paine and travell take,
  To get a conquest better lost then wonne:
Then (answer'd stout *Marfisa*) I will make
Another offer which you may not shunne,
On this condition let us for her sake,
A course at field one with the other runne:
That if you win then I will keepe her still,
If I, then you shall serve her while she will.

85

Content (quoth *Zerbin*) and with that they ran,
  With couched spears, and met amid the plaine;
But *Zerbin* had the worse, *Marfisa* wan,
As better horst, and stronger of the twaine:
Who seeing *Zerbin* downe, she then began,
To talke with him and jest with him againe,
Behold (quoth she) I here to you present,
This lovely damsell for your more content.

86

Now see you keepe your promise and your troth,
  To this faire dame to be a champion trew,
And do not breake the bands of sacred oth,
And so (quoth she) for now I bid adew.
Zerbin was mov'd with shame and anger both,
Shame for his foile, a thing most strange and new:
And wrath for her whom he thereby did gaine,
Which he might deeme the greater losse of twaine.

87

Then of his mistresse new he doth enquire,
  What Knight it was that did him overthrow,
She willingly did grant him his desire,
Supposing so his griefe might greater grow,
It was a Ladie in a Knights attire,
Marfisa hight (quoth she) that layd you low,
The which strange news I thinke not much did lacke
To make his armor blush upon his backe.

88

Vpon his horse in anger great he gets,
  And curst himselfe he had not sit more sure,
He bites his lips, and inwardly he frets,
And she in him more anger to procure,
With byting words his discontentment whets;
Yet he doth for his oth sake all endure,
Like tired horse he quiet all abides,
That hath the bit in mouth, and spurs in sides.

89

At last into this bitter plaint he burst,
  On thee ô fortune well I may complaine,
And call my selfe unhappie and accurst,
That dost at once two plagues for me ordaine,
Two plagues that of all plagues I count the worst,
As first this foile, my former fame to staine;
And having lost a Ladie of rare features,
To have this mistresse, fowlest of all creatures.

90

She, whose surpassing beautie well deserved,
  All worldly blisse, whose match was never found,
She from misfortune could not be preserved,
But that by cruell stormes she must be dround,
And this, who if she had bene rightly served
Ought long ere this, have fed worms under ground,
Thou hast these many yeares and still dost save,
That I by her at last this plague might have.

91

By these and such like words as *Zerbin* spake,
  That aged woman gives assured guesse,
That this was he, to whom, and for whose sake,
Faire *Isabell* (kept erst in great distresse,
There where *Orlando* did from theeves her take)
Was wont so great affection to professe,
And to describe his parts and shape so trew,
As ev'rie one might know him at a vew.

92

And now that by his words she plainely found,
  That this was *Zerbin*, and that he beleeved
Faire *Isabella* was in tempest dround,
With which conceit she saw he sore was greeved,
She that did know her to be safe and sound,
Yet meaning not his griefe should be releeved,
She telleth onely that that would disease him,
And doth conceale that which she thought would please
                                                    (him.

93

You sir (quoth she) that me so greatly scorne,
  If you but knew what tydings I could tell,
Of her whom you lament as dead and lorne,
You would both speake me faire and use me well:
But first I will with horses wild be torne,
And suffer all the paines of earth and hell,
Before that I will condescend to show it,
Or then by me you ever come to know it.

94

Looke how a gentle grewnd, that doth assaile
  And flies upon a stranger at the furst,
Will on the sodaine faune and wag his taile,
If so of bread one profer him a crust:
So *Zerbin* that before on her did raile,
And bitterly unto her face her curst,
Now he intreates her, and doth pray and flatter,
To give him farther notice of the matter.

95

At last with long intreatie she replies,
  And saith, faire *Isabella* is not ded,
  But so she lives, that sure she death envies:
  And never hope to have her maidenhed,
  For I have seene (quoth she) with these mine eyes,
  How twentie lawlesse men her captive led,
  And ev'ry one might have her at their pleasure,
  As having liberty, and lust, and leasure.

96

Ah wicked hagge, thou know'st it is a lie,
  And yet behold how thou canst paint it out,
  Thou know'st that none of them with her did lie,
  Thou know'st *Orlando* thence did fetch her out:
  And made the malefactors all to die,
  That of her danger now there was no doubt.
  But now alas this lying storie bred,
  A thousand jealousies in *Zerbines* hed.

97

He askt her where and when his love she saw,
  He speakes her oftentimes both foule and faire,
  But not a word more could he from her draw,
  Neither by threatning words, nor yet by prayre:
  He feeles a corzie cold his heart to gnaw,
  His little hope was turn'd to great dispaire:
  And thus this old ilfavour'd spitefull Callet,
  Gave good *Zerbino* such a choking sallet.

98

What patience thus provoked could have borne,
  At such a womans hands so vile a spite?
  And save he was unto her service sworne,
  No doubt he would have done her then her right.
  Thus she of malice full, and he of scorne,
  Went on their way, untill they met a Knight:
  But what became hereof if you will know,
  The booke ensuing shall the sequell show.

THE TWENTY-FIRST BOOKE OF
ORLANDO FVRIOSO

THE ARGVMENT

Most worthie Zerbin *by his promise bound,*
Defends Gabrina *most unworthie wight,*
And for her sake he overthrowes to ground
Hermonida, *unluckie* Flemish *Knight:*
Who doth to him her most lewd life expound,
Increasing by his speech, her cruell spite:
Yet still the good Zerbino *travels with her,*
And many a wearie mile they rode togither.

ORLANDO FVRIOSO

THE TWENTY-FIRST BOOKE

1

Nor Iron nailes make fast a planke or boord
  More firme, nor cords a burden surer binde,
Then faith once giv'n by promise or by word,
  Tyes most assuredly the vertuous minde,
Old times to us good store of samples foord,
  How praise devine was unto faith assinde,
And how in garments white she still was painted,
That ech smal spot or staine might shew her tainted.

2

Faith ever should be kept in secret sort,
  Although to one, or whether given to more,
Although in deserts farre from all resort,
  Or else a judge or multitude before:
What though the witnesse wants to make report?
  Yet must we keepe our cov'nant evermore,
As well by word and private protestation,
As by record and publike obligation.

3

And so did *Zerbin* as before I told,
  His promise firme unviolate preserve,
And though *Gabrina* was both foule and old,
  Though her misdeeds all rigor did deserve:
Yet he his faith and promise firme doth hold,
  And left his former busines her to serve,
Till as they traveld on the way by chance,
They met a *Flemish* Knight late come to *France*.

4

The Knight of stature comly was and tall,
  And in his shield he bare an azure bend,
His name *Ermonida* they use to call,
  It seem'd he was not this old womans frend,
For straight his sight her heart did so appall,
  Vnto her guide her life she doth commend:
And praid him (as he promist) to vouchsafe,
From this her enemie to keepe her safe,

5

This man (quoth she) my guiltlesse father killed,
  For malice onely that to me he bare:
This man my onely brothers blood hath spilled,
  Because he wisht my safetie and welfare:
Yet with revenge his rage cannot be filled,
  But still he seekes to worke my farther care.
Well (quoth *Zerbino*) be of better cheare,
For none shall do thee harme whilst I am heare.

6

Now when the Knight of *Flaunders* saw that face,
  That of all faces he did most detest:
With me to combat in this present place,
  You must prepare (quoth he) and trie your best,
Or yeeld to me this woman void of grace,
  That as she hath deserv'd she may be drest:
If you resistance make you will be slaine,
For so it fals to such as wrong maintaine.

7

Zerbino curteously doth thus replie,
  Bethinke your selfe with more consideration,
To make a woman of your hand to die,
  What staine it is to Knightly reputation;
As for the combat if you needs will trie,
  Her to defend is my determination:
For I am sworne to fight in her defence,
And therefore cannot with mine oth dispence.

8

This, and to this effect much more in vaine
  He spake, him from his purpose to perswade,
At last they were so kindled with disdaine,
  That one the other fiercely did invade:
Zerbino was the stronger of the twaine,
  And strake the tother through the shoulder blade,
So as he fell halfe dead and halfe alive,
Not able any more with him to strive.

9

But *Zerbin* doubting lest he had bene dead,
  With much compassion from his horse did light,
And first he loos'd his helmet from his head,
  And seeketh to revive him if he might;
Who looking firmely on *Zerbino* sed,
  I cannot much lament that such a Knight,
Hath hurt me in this fight and overthrowne,
In whom such valew and such worth is showne.

10

In this alone my hap I do lament,
  That it should be for such a womans sake,
And much I marvell that you would consent,
  To your protection such a one to take,
Which I am sure you would full sore repent,
  If I to you her deeds should open make,
And that you should so greatly damage me,
For such a wicked caitive as is she.

11

And save my voice and strength will faile I doubt,
  Before my tale will come to perfect end,
I will declare if you will heare it out,
The wicked life of this ungracious fend;
I had a brother valorous and stout,
In *Holland* borne, who (for he did intend
To win by service honour and renowne)
Heraclio serv'd that bare of *Greece* the crowne.

12

A noble Gentleman *Argeo* hight,
  Neare the confines of *Servia* did dwell,
Who in my brother tooke so great delight,
That in short space they were acquainted well.
Argeo marride had this cursed wight,
Of whom the present storie I do tell,
And tooke in her (unworthy) so great pleasure,
As past the bands of reason and of measure.

13

But she more light then leaves in Autumne season,
  That ev'ry blast doth blow about and change,
Against all wively care, all cause and reason,
Because she doth delight her selfe in change,
With wicked hart and head full fraught with treason,
So farre she lets her raging love to range,
She sues to have my brother to her lover,
And doth to him the foule desire uncover.

14

But neither doth a rocke more firmely stand
  Vpon the shore against the surging wave,
Nor doth the Cedar more upon the land
Resist the tempest that doth rage and rave,
Then doth my brother her desire withstand,
Though she at sundrie times the same doth crave,
And though she seeketh many a meane and triall,
Yet still she turneth with a flat deniall.

15

At last it fell (as oft it doth befall
  To valiant men that love to fight and quarell)
My brother was sore wounded in a brall,
So that it seem'd his life was in some parell:
Wherefore he gets within the castle wall,
Both that his frend might know & venge his quarell,
And other needfull things may be procured,
By which his hurt might be the sooner cured.

16

Now while my brother staid in this ill state,
  His friend *Argeo* sometime absent thence,
This woman early visits him and late,
And offers him good store of pounds and pence:
But he that alwaies villany did hate,
And would not do his friend so great offence,
Thought (as in evill cases is the best)
Of two great mischiefes to chuse out the lest.

17

He meanes to leave *Argeos* friendship quite,
  And get him home againe from whence he came,
Or hide himselfe where this most wicked wight
Shall never see his face nor heare his name:
This, though it griev'd him, as it ought of right,
He chuseth as a way lesse worthy blame,
Then yeelding to her lust for to abuse her,
Or to her loving husband to accuse her.

18

Wherefore (though of his wound both faint and weak)
  He doth resolve to part with constant mind,
He gets him thence, and not a word doth speake,
And leaves this filthy minded beast behind:
But fortune ill his purpose good doth breake,
And alter'd quite the course he had designd,
Home came her husband finding her alone,
Complaining grievously and making mone.

19

Her cheekes with teares all blubberd were and red,
  Her lookes did shew her mind was ill apaid,
Her lockes all torne did hang about her hed,
With which her loving husband sore afraid,
Did aske her oft what chance such change had bred,
Till at the length the wicked wretch thus said,
With spiteful heart, with wicked voice & trembling,
And faind a cause, the cause it selfe dissembling.

20

Alas (quoth she) what should I seeke to hide
  My wicked act and hainous deadly sinne,
Which though from you, and all the world beside,
I could conceale, yet doth the soule within,
And conscience grudge, a burden such to bide,
So as the inward torment I am in,
Doth passe the plague or penance far away,
That mortall man upon my sinne can lay.

21

If so a sinne of right you may it name,
  That one is forst unto against her will,
But thus it is, your friend that hither came,
(I thinking he had thought nor meant none ill)
Inforced me to my perpetuall shame,
Against all lawes, all honestie and skill:
And doubting that I would the fact bewray,
Forthwith he gate him hence and fled away.

22

But though my body he have so defil'd,
  Yet is my mind from sinne devoid and cleare,
Although from sight of men I am exil'd,
Nor dare I once in publike place appeare:
This said, with thousand names she him revil'd,
So that *Argeo* that the tale did heare,
Beleeved it, and straight withall intended
To punish him that never had offended.

23

He taketh horse forthwith and follow'th post,
    All on revenge his mind was wholly bent,
    And, for he perfitly did know the cost,
    And for my brother faire and softly went,
    He met him in an hower at the most,
    Bidding him stand or else he should be shent:
    My brother would disswade him if he might,
    But all in vaine, *Argeo* needs would fight.

24

The tone was strong and full of fresh disdaine,
    The tother weake and loth to hurt his frend,
    So that himselfe defending long in vaine,
    My brother was constrain'd to yeeld in th'end:
    And thus at last he prisner doth remaine,
    And yeelds, himselfe unable to defend:
    Which seene, *Argeo* doth surcease to strike,
    But speaketh unto him these words or like.

25

God never let my heart so farre be moved,
    With rightfull wrath that I thy blood should spill,
    Since once I thee esteemed well and loved,
    Whom once I loved, I will never kill:
    And though thy act may justly be reproved,
    The world shall see my goodnesse by thine ill,
    For be it love, or be it in disdaine,
    I will be found the better of the twaine.

26

Another meane then death to use I mind,
    In punishing this sinne and foule misdeed,
    This said (with willow bands he there did find)
    He makes a hurdle fit to serve such need,
    On which my brothers body he doth bind,
    That with old hurts and new did freshly bleed;
    And to his castle he doth him convay,
    In mind to keepe him there a prisner ay.

27

Yet though with him a prisner he remaind,
    In other things he felt no lacke nor want,
    Save that his liberty was him restraind:
    But lo, this wretch that late did him supplant,
    And to her husband so of him complaind,
    Thought she would trie if he would yet recant,
    And (for at her command she had the kayes)
    She goes to him, and thus to him she sayes.

28

Now sir (quoth she) I trust you feele the frute,
    That this your foolish constancie hath wrought,
    Had you not better bene to graunt the sute,
    That I in friendly sort so often sought?
    You see tis vaine to argue or dispute,
    Say what you can, you are a traitor thought:
    And he to whom you shew'd so great fidelity,
    Imputes to you treason and infidelity.

29

I thinke both for your ease and reputation,
    You had bene better graunted my request,
    You see you have a sorie habitation,
    And in the same for ever looke to rest,
    Except you change your first determination,
    And mollifie your stonie hearted brest,
    Which if you yet will do, I do assure you,
    Both libertie and credite to procure you.

30

No, never hope, no said *Filandro*, never,
    (So my unhappie brothers name they call)
    In vaine to change my mind youd do endever,
    And though *Argeo* causlesse keepe me thrall,
    Yet I in faith and troth will still persever,
    Sufficeth me, that he that seeth all,
    Doth know mine innocencie and doth see me,
    And when he list can both reward and free me.

31

I care not though the world of me thinke ill,
    I hope another world will make amends,
    Yet let *Argeo* slay me if he will,
    Or let him (as it seemeth he intends)
    Though wrongfully, in prison hold me still,
    Yet one day he will find he hurts his frends,
    And know by proofe how he hath bene beguil'd,
    When truth appears, and time brings forth her child.

32

Yet for all this, this woman void of shame,
    Did cease no whit *Filandro* still to tempt,
    And oftentimes in vaine to him she came,
    And ever turnes repulst and with contempt,
    And in this frantike fancie she doth frame
    A thousand sleights to further her attempt,
    And many things in mind she doth revolve,
    Before on any one she doth resolve.

33

Six months entire she doth her selfe absent,
    Nor ever came *Filandro* to entice,
    Which made him hope that she was now content
    To cease her sute, and follow his advice;
    But lo, how fortune (that is ever bent
    To further wicked persons in their vice)
    Doth unto her a fit occasion lend,
    To bring her wicked lust to wofull end.

34

There had bene hate and enmity of old,
    Betweene her husband and another Knight,
    Morando cald, who often would be bold,
    If so *Argeo* absent were a night,
    To come with force and to assault his hold,
    Or thereabout to do him some despight:
    But if he were at home, then all that whiles
    He came not neare him by a dozen miles.

35

Wherefore to be reveng'd on this his fo,
　That often did him wrong and great outrage,
　Argeo gives it out that he will go
　Vnto *Ierusalem* on pilgrimage,
　And from his house disguysd he parted so,
　In secret sort, without or man or page,
　And ev'ry night comes in at the posterne,
　That none but she his comming might discerne.

36

Thus all the day he wanders all about,
　In woods, in groves, in pastures here and thither,
　To see if he could find *Morando* out,
　That in his absence used to come hither:
　And farre he keepes himselfe from any rout,
　Vntill that darknesse doth obscure the wether,
　Then would he get him home a secret way,
　Of which his wife did keepe a privie kay.

37

Thus all but she, *Argeo* absent thought,
　By which his wicked wife with wonted skill,
　Another meanes and new occasion sought,
　To bring to passe her foule unbridled will:
　With weeping eyes (her eyes to weepe she tought)
　And all with teares her bosome she doth fill,
　Then came she to my brother and complained,
　That (but he helpe) her honour would be stained.

38

Nor mine alone, but mine *Argeos* too,
　Who were he here (quoth she) I would not care,
　You know what harme *Morando* wonts to doo,
　When as mine husbands absence makes him dare,
　And now behold the caitive me doth woo,
　And to intrap me sets full many a snare,
　And offred servants great reward and hire,
　So they would helpe to further his desire.

39

And hearing that *Argeo* was away,
　And would continue so no little space,
　He came within the castle wall to day,
　(His absence gave him so much heart of grace)
　Where, had my husband bene but in the way,
　He durst not onely not have shew'd his face,
　But sure he would not have presum'd at all,
　To come within a kenning of the wall.

40

And what by message he before had done,
　Now face to face by mouth he doth the same,
　So as I hardly know which way to shunne,
　That which to do, would breed my endlesse blame.
　Had not my sugred speech his favour wonne,
　By faining I my will to his would frame,
　He would perforce have had his foule intent,
　Which now he hopes to get by my assent.

41

I promist him (but promise made for feare
　Is voyd) and I performance never ment,
　But so that act I made him to forbeare,
　Which he to do by force was fully bent.
　Now if you be a friend, or ever were,
　Vnto *Argeo*, you may this prevent,
　Nor onely save mine honour thus distressed,
　But his to whom such love you have professed.

42

Which if you me denie, then I may say,
　Not honestie, of which your bost you make,
　But crueltie did cause you say me nay,
　And of my sute so small regard to take:
　And that you were not moved any way
　With friendships rule, or for *Argeos* sake:
　Although twixt us it might have secret beene,
　But now my shame must needs be knowne & seene.

43

Tush (quoth *Filandro*) this is more then need,
　To use much circumstance in such a case,
　As I began, so meane I to proceed,
　And though *Argeo* hold me in disgrace,
　Yet unto him I not impute this deed,
　But ready will be still in time and place,
　To do him service any way I may,
　So you but shew to me the meane and way.

44

Sir then (said she) the way were this, to kill
　Him that doth seeke my husbands shame and mine,
　Which you may easly do, if so you will
　A while unto my words your eare incline:
　I have put off his comming hither, till
　It be betwixt the houres of ten and nine,
　What time I promist him so to provide,
　To let him in, so as he were not spide.

45

Now then my counsell is, that you do stay
　Here in my chamber, untill I procure
　Him to disarme himselfe, so as you may
　Slay him with small ado, and make him sure.
　This is (quoth she) the onely ready way,
　And safest for your selfe, I you assure:
　To this device *Filandro* doth assent,
　Thinking hereby his friends hurt to prevent.

46

Now more and more approcht the cursed night,
　When as his wife (if I a wife may call)
　This hellish hag and foule infernall sprite,
　Did place my brother arm'd behind a wall,
　And as she wisht, ev'n so it fell aright,
　For ill device amisse doth seldome fall;
　Her husband in the ev'ning somewhat late,
　Enterd his castle at the posterne gate.

47

Filandro at one blow cuts of his hed,
　Taking him for *Morando* in exchange,
　She stands fast by that him had thither led,
　Nor shewes in word or gesture any change:
　Argeo there remaineth slaine and ded,
　And kild by him (ô chance most hard and strange)
　That while he friendly thought to do him good,
　Most cruell and unfriendly shed his blood.

48

Now when this feate had thus bene brought to passe,
　Gabrina (so is this good womans name)
　That doth in craft the fiends of hell surpasse,
　Vnto my brother for his weapon came,
　Which he deliverd as his promise was,
　And that once done, then she without all shame,
　Prayes him to take in hand a lighted candle,
　And view him well whom he so ill did handle.

49

There first he saw how he had kild his frend,
　A sight that made him at the heart repent,
　And she afresh the matter to amend,
　Doth threate, except he would to her assent,
　That she should bring his life to shamefull end,
　For to accuse him of this fact she ment,
　Wishing him though his life he did despise,
　To shunne a shamefull death if he be wise.

50

Filandro maz'd, and full of feare did stand,
　When of his error he was first aware,
　He thought at first to kill her out of hand,
　By whom he was intrapt in such a snare,
　But she had got his weapons in her hand,
　And to defend her selfe did straight prepare:
　But sure he could have found it in his hart,
　By peicemeale to have torne her ev'ry part.

51

Like as a ship in midst of seas opprest,
　Betweene two winds that do together strive,
　Can have no time of respite or of rest,
　But goes what way the stronger wind doth drive:
　So now *Filandro* doubting which was best,
　To die, or in such sort to bide alive,
　Stood long in doubt; and neither way did bend,
　Yet chose the worser bargain in the end.

52

His reason open layes before his face,
　The danger great if once the fact were knowne,
　Beside the infamie and great disgrace,
　That would about the world of him be blowne:
　Beside to chuse he had but little space,
　So as his wit and sence was scant his owne:
　At last he doth conclude what ever come,
　To swallow this unsav'ry choking plum.

53

Wherefore against his will, inforst by feare,
　He promiseth to take her for his wife,
　And unto her he solemnely doth sweare,
　To marry her if now she save his life:
　And (for it was not safe to tarry theare)
　When once the murder should be publisht rife,
　He turnes unto the place where he was borne,
　And leaves behind him infamie and scorne.

54

And still he carrid in his pensive heart,
　His friends mishap, lamenting it in vaine,
　How for a just reward of such desart,
　A *Progne* and *Medea* he did gaine;
　And save his oth restrained him in part,
　No doubt he would the wicked hag have slaine:
　But yet he hated her like toade or snake,
　And in her company small joy did take.

55

From that to this, to laugh or once to smile,
　He was not seene, his words and looks were sad,
　With often sighs, and in a little while,
　He grew much like *Orestes*, when he had
　First slaine his father by his mothers guile,
　Then her, and last of all fell raging mad,
　With spirits vext so was my brothers hed,
　Still vext till sicknes made him keepe his bed.

56

But when this cursed strumpet plainly saw,
　How small delight in her my brother tooke,
　She doth her fervent love from him withdraw,
　And in short space that fancie she forsooke:
　And lastly she resolves against all law,
　So soone as she can fit occasion looke,
　To bring *Filandros* life to wofull end,
　And after her first husband him to send.

57

An old Physition full of false deceit,
　She findeth out most fit for such a feat,
　That better knew to give a poisond bait,
　Then for to cure with herbs or wholesom meate:
　Him, that for gaine most greedily doth wait,
　By profers large she quickly doth intreate,
　To take upon him this ungracious cure,
　With poysond cup to make her husband sure.

58

Now while my selfe was by, and others more,
　This old Physition came to him ere long,
　And brought a cup, in which was poyson store,
　And said, it cordiall was, to make him strong:
　But lo, *Gabrina* that devis'd before,
　Ev'n in the prise of wrong, to do some wrong,
　Before *Filandro* of the cup did tast,
　Stept twixt the leach and him in no small hast.

59

And taking in her hand against his will,
  The cup in which the poysond drinke was plast,
She said, good Doctor do not take it ill,
That I require you first the drink to tast,
I will not have my husband drinke, untill
You have your selfe before him tane the tast:
  I will (said she) be certaine by the rood,
  That this you give him, wholsome is and good.

60

Now in what pickle thinke you was the leach?
  The time was short to take a sound advice,
He might not use perswasion now nor speach,
He durst not tell how she did him intice,
Nor could he guesse what was herein her reach,
To make him tast first of the poysond spice,
  Wherefore to take a tast he thought it best,
  And then he gives my brother all the rest.

61

Even as a hawke that hath a partidge trust
  In griping talents, sits and plumes the same,
Oft by a dog whom she doth not mistrust,
Is kild her selfe and reaved of her game:
So this Physition gracelesse and vnjust,
While he to greedie gaine his mind doth frame,
  Was us'd by her even as he well deserved,
  And so I wish all such Physitions served.

62

The poore old man that felt his stomacke ake,
  Began to take his leave, and homeward hasted,
He thinks some strong *Antidoton* to take,
Against the poysond cup he lately tasted:
She sweares his home returne he may not make,
While th'operation of the potion lasted,
  And that she will see plainly ere he go,
  If so it do her husband good or no.

63

By humble sute and offers he doth trie,
  That with her licence he may thence depart,
But all in vaine, his sute she doth denie:
Now had the liquor welnigh toucht his hart,
Wherefore perceiving plainly he must die,
He doth the secret to us all impart:
  Thus to himselfe he did the same at last,
  Which oft he did to others in time past.

64

And straight in little space my brother dyde,
  And after him dide this same false Phisition,
We that had heard and seene the matter tride,
Of which my selfe before had some suspition;
Both hand and foote we then this monster tyde,
And bring her unto such as had commission,
  Where her confession, and our accusation,
  Made them pronounce her doome of condemnation.

65

Thus in the gaile in fetters she was laid,
  Adjudged to be burned at a stake,
Thus (said the Knight) and more he would have said
How she escapt, and how she prison brake,
But so he fainted, as they were affraid,
He would have sounded at those words he spake:
  Wherefore his page him to his horse doth lift,
  And then to binde his wounds they make a shift.

66

Then *Zerbin* tooke his leave and made a skuse,
  That he had hurt the knight in her defence,
Affirming he had done, as is the use,
To save his charge from damage and offence:
And that thenceforth with him he would have truce,
This said, he tooke his leave and parted thence,
  And promist him with words of great civillity,
  To further him unto his best ability.

67

Sir (said the Knight) for this I do you thanke,
  And wish you of that woman to beware,
Lest that she serve you some such slipperie pranke,
As may procure your farther woe and care:
For hard shall any scape from danger franke,
That in her company long season are:
  Gabrina silent all the while stands by,
  For hard it is to prove the truth a lye.

68

Thus hence they part, and for his promise sake,
  At her commandment *Zerbin* doth attend,
And wisht in heart, the divell might her take,
Though with his hand he must her still defend:
And those last words the Knight of *Holland* spake,
To give him warning of the cursed fend,
  Do fill his mind with so great griefe and spight,
  That now he scant could well abide her sight.

69

And this same old and weather-beaten trot,
  Perceiving how *Zerbino* was inclin'd,
Would not once yeeld or be behind a jot,
In spitefull wishing, nor in evill mind:
Her eye and tongue and looke conceale it not,
Nor yet her deeds as after he did finde,
  Thus in this harmony and concord good,
  It was their hap to travell through the wood.

70

Now when the time approched neare the night,
  They heard a noise of bustling and of blowes,
Caus'd as they guessed by some brall or fight,
But where it was yet neither of them knowes,
Zerbino longed much to see the fight,
And thitherwards in no small hast he goes,
  And in no lesse, *Gabrina* maketh after,
  As shall be shewd you more at large hereafter.

THE TWENTY-SECOND BOOKE OF
ORLANDO FVRIOSO

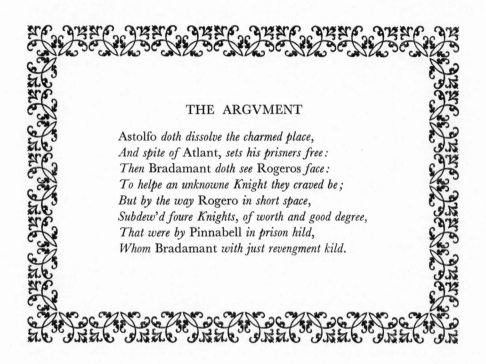

THE ARGVMENT

Astolfo *doth dissolve the charmed place,*
And spite of Atlant, *sets his prisners free:*
Then Bradamant *doth see* Rogeros *face:*
To helpe an unknowne Knight they craved be;
But by the way Rogero *in short space,*
Subdew'd foure Knights, of worth and good degree,
That were by Pinnabell *in prison hild,*
Whom Bradamant *with just revengment kild.*

ORLANDO FVRIOSO
THE TWENTY-SECOND BOOKE

1

Ye courtly dames, that are both kind and true,
  Vnto your loves, if kinde and true be any,
  As sure I am in all your lovely crue,
  Of so chast minde, there are not over many,
  Be not displeas'd with this that doth ensue,
  For neither must I leave it, neither can I,
  And beare with me for that I said before,
  When on *Gabrina* I did raile so sore.

2

Mine ernest words, nor yet her great offence,
  Cannot obscure in honour and cleare fame,
  Those few, whose spotlesse lives want no defence,
  Whom hate nor envie no way can defame:
  He that his master sold for thirtie pence,
  To *Iohn* nor *Peter* breeds no blot nor blame:
  Nor men of *Hipermestra* worse have thought,
  Although her sisters were unchast and nought.

3

For one that in this verse I shall dispraise,
  As driv'n by course of this my present storie,
  Whole hunderds are whom I intend to praise,
  And magnifie their well deserved glory,
  If this then be offensive any waies,
  To all or any, I can be but sorie:
  Now of the *Scottish* Prince a word or two,
  That heard a noise, and went forthwith thereto.

4

Betweene two mountaines in a shadie dale,
  He doth descend that way the noise him led,
  But when he came he saw upon the vale,
  A Baron lately slaine and newly ded.
  But ere I enter further in this tale,
  I first must tell you how *Astolfo* sped:
  Whom late I left in that most cursed citie,
  Where women murther men without all pittie.

5

I told you how his horne with mightie blast,
  Not onely all his foes had driven away,
  But also made his friends so sore agast,
  As not the stowtest of them there durst stay:
  Wherefore (I said) he was constraind at last,
  Alone to get him homward on his way,
  Forthwith on *Rabicano* he doth mount,
  An horse of which he makes no small account.

6

His horne that serves him still at all assayes,
  He carries with him and his learned booke,
  First by *Armenia* he goes his wayes,
  Then *Brusia* and the way of Thrase he tooke,
  So that within the space of twentie daies,
  The streame *Danubio* he quite forsooke:
  Then from *Boemia* ward he doth decline,
  Vnto *Franconia* and the streame of *Rhyne*.

7

Then through *Ardennas* wood to *Aquis grave*,
  And thence to *Flanders* where he shipping found,
  What time a Northeast winde, did blow so brave,
  As set him soone in sight of *English* ground:
  So that no whit annoyd with winde nor wave,
  His native soile receiv'd him safe and sound:
  He taketh horse, and ere the Sunne was downe,
  At *London* he arriv'd the chiefest towne.

8

Here at his first arrivall straight he heares,
  How that the *Turkes* faire *Paris* did beseege,
  And how his sire (a man well stroke in yeares)
  Was there, and sent for ayd to raise the seege:
  And how of late the Lords and chiefest peares,
  Were gone with new supplies to helpe their leege,
  But little stay he makes these words once hard,
  But taketh ship againe to *Callice* ward.

9

And for the winde serv'd then not very well,
  They were by force thereof borne quite aside,
  So that the master scant himselfe could tell,
  What course he held, they were borne downe so wide,
  Yet at the last so luckie it befell,
  Within a kenning they some land had spide,
  And drawing neare they found the towne of *Roan*,
  Where presently the Duke tooke land alone.

10

And crossing through a wood when time drew neare,
  That neither day could well be cald nor night,
  He hapt to finde a christall spring and cleare,
  And by the side thereof he did alight,
  With mind to quench his thirst and rest him heare,
  As in a place of pleasure and delight,
  He ties his horse unto a tree, and thinketh
  To have him tarrie safe there while he drinketh.

11

Strange things may fall betweene the lip and cup,
  For scant *Astolfo* yet had wet his lip,
  But from a bush a villaine started up,
  Vntide the horse, and on his backe doth skip:
  The Duke that scant had tasted yet a sup;
  And finds himselfe thus tane in such a trip,
  Forgets to drinke, and followes in a rage,
  For wrath not water doth his thirst asswage.

12

The little villaine that the horse had got,
  (Like one that did in knavish pranks delight)
  Although he might have run, yet did it not,
  Because *Astolfo* should not leese his sight:
  But with false gallop, or a gentle trot,
  He leads the Duke unto that place aright,
  Where many Knights and Lords of high degree,
  Without a prison, more then prisners be.

13

Astolfo, though his armour doth him cumber,
  Yet fearing least he might arrive too late,
  In following the villaine doth not slumber,
  Vntill he came within the pallace gate,
  Where (as I said) of Lords no little number,
  Were wandring up and downe in strange estate:
  Astolfo of their presence doth not force,
  But runneth up and downe to finde his horse.

14

The craftie villaine was in no place found,
  Though many a homely place for him was sought,
  Yet still the Duke doth search the pallace round,
  And for his beast he takes no little thought:
  At last he guest it was enchaunted ground,
  And as by *Logestilla* he was tought,
  He tooke his booke and searcheth in the table,
  How to dissolve the place he might be able.

15

And straight in th'index for it he doth looke,
  Of pallaces fram'd by such strange illusion,
  Among the rest, of this (so saith the booke)
  That it should never come unto confusion,
  Vntill a certaine stone away were tooke,
  In which a sprite was kept by strange inclusion,
  And if he did but lift the threshold stone,
  The goodly house would vanish and be gone.

16

The Duke not doubting now of good successe,
  Go'th to the threshold where the stone was laid,
  And which it was he presently doth guesse,
  And then by force to move it he assaid:
  But *Atlant*, that expected nothing lesse,
  And sees his bold attempt, was sore affraid,
  And straight an hundred meanes he doth devise,
  To hinder him from this bold enterprise.

17

He makes the Duke, by this his divellish skill,
  To seeme of divers shapes unto the rest,
  To one a dwarfe, of face and favour ill,
  To one a gyant, to a third a beast,
  And all their hearts with hatred he doth fill,
  He thinkes by them the Duke should be distrest:
  By seeming unto ev'rie one the same,
  For which each one into the pallace came.

18

Behold *Rogero* stout, and *Brandimart*,
  Prasildo, *Bradamant*, and others moe,
  Vpon *Astolfo* set with cruell hart,
  As to revenge themselves upon their foe:
  But with his horne the Duke then plaid his part,
  And brought their loftie stomackes somwhat low:
  But had not th'horne procur'd him this exemption,
  No doubt the Duke had dyde without redemption.

19

For when they heard the strange and fearfull blast,
  They forced were for feare away to runne,
  As fearfull Pigeons flie away agast.
  When men do ring a bell or shoot a gunne;
  The Sorcerer himselfe was not the last,
  That sought by flight the fearfull noise to shunne:
  Yea such it was, that neither rat nor mouse,
  Durst tarrie in the circuit of the house.

20

Among the horses that did breake their bands,
  Was *Rabican* of whom before I told,
  Who by good hap came to *Astolfos* hands,
  Who was full glad when of him he had hold,
  Also *Rogeros* Griffith horse there stands,
  Fast tyed in a chaine of beaten gold,
  The Duke, as by his booke he had bene tought,
  Destroyed quite the house by magicke wrought.

21

I do not doubt but you can call to minde,
  How good *Rogero* lost this stately beast,
  What time *Angelica* his eyes did blinde,
  Denying most unkindly his request:
  The horse that sored swifter then the winde,
  Went backe to *Atlant* whom he loved best,
  By whom he had bene of a young one bred,
  And diligently taught, and costly fed.

22

This *English* Duke was glad of such a pray,
  As one that was to travell greatly bent,
  And in the world was not a better way
  For him to serve his purpose and intent;
  Wherefore he meaneth not to let him stray,
  But takes him as a thing from heav'n him sent,
  For long ere this he had of him such proofe,
  As well he knew what was for his behoofe.

23

Now being full resolv'd to take in hand,
  To travell round about the world so wide,
  And visite many a sea and many a land,
  As none had done, nor ever should beside,
  One onely care his purpose did withstand,
  Which caus'd him yet a little time to bide,
  He doth bethink him oft, yet doth not know
  On whom his *Rabicano* to bestow.

24

He would be loth that such a stately steed
  Should by a peasant be possest or found,
  And though of him he stood then in no need,
  Yet had he care to have him safe and sound,
  In hands of such as would him keepe and feed;
  While thus he thought and lookt about him round,
  Next day a while before the Sunne was set,
  A champion all in armes unwares he met.

25

But first I meane to tell you what became
  Of good *Rogero* and his *Bradamant*,
  Who when againe unto themselves they came,
  The pallace quite destroyd of old *Atlant*:
  Each knew and cald the other by their name,
  And of all courtesies they were not scant,
  Lamenting much that this inchanted pallace,
  Had hinderd them so long such joy and sollace.

26

The noble maid to shew her selfe as kind,
  As might become a virgin wise and sage,
  Doth in plaine termes as plaine declare her mind,
  As thus, that she his loves heate will asswage,
  And unto him her selfe in wedlocke bind,
  And spend with him all her ensuing age,
  If to be christned first he were content,
  And afterwards to aske her friends consent.

27

But he that would not onely not refuse
  To change his life for his beloveds sake,
  But also if the choise were his to chuse,
  To leese his life and all the world forsake,
  Did answer thus, my deare, what ere ensues
  I will performe what ere I undertake.
  To be baptiz'd in water or in fire,
  I will consent if it be your desire.

28

This said, he goes from thence with full intent,
  To take upon him christend state of life,
  Which done he most sincerely after ment,
  To aske her of her father for a wife;
  Vnto an Abby straight their course they bent,
  As in those days were in those places rife,
  Where men devout did live with great frugalitie,
  And yet for strangers kept good hospitalitie.

29

But ere they came to that religious place,
  They met a damsell full of heavy cheare,
  That had with teares bedewed all her face,
  Yet in those teares great beautie did appeare,
  Rogero, that had ever speciall grace
  In courteous acts and speech when she came neare,
  Doth aske of her what dangers or what feares,
  Did move her so to make her shed such teares.

30

She thus replies, the cause of this my griefe,
  Is not for feare or danger of mine owne,
  But for good will, and for compassion chiefe,
  Of one yong Knight, whose name is yet unknowne,
  Who if he have not great and quick reliefe,
  Is judgd into the fier to be throwne,
  So great a fault they say he hath committed,
  That doubt it is it will not be remitted.

31

The fault was this, there was good will betweene
  Him and the daughter of the King of *Spaine*,
  And lest his love should be descride and seene,
  He finely doth himselfe a woman faine,
  And went and spake as if he had so beene,
  And thus he plaid (to tell the matter plaine)
  The maid in shew, the man in deed so well,
  That in a while he made her belly swell.

32

But out alas, what can so secret be,
  But out it will when we do least suspect?
  For posts have eares, and walls have eyes to see,
  Dumbe beasts and birds have tongues ill to detect,
  First one had found it out, then two or three:
  And looke how fire doth creepe that men neglect,
  So this report from mouth to mouth did spring,
  Till at the last it came unto the King.

33

The King straight sends a trustie servant thether,
  Who making search when they two were in bed,
  Found out the troth, and tooke them both together,
  Found him a man, and found her belly sped,
  Away they carrid her I know not whether,
  Away unto the prison he was led,
  And must be burnd this day or else to morow,
  The thought wherof doth move my mind to sorow.

34

This made me purposely to come from thence,
  And not to see one of so comely shape,
  So sharply punisht for this small offence,
  As if it were for murder or for rape,
  Nor any hope could sinke into my sence,
  How possible it were for him to scape,
  And who could see or thinke without compassion,
  A fine yong youth tormented in such fashion?

35

Twas strange to thinke how nie this tale did touch
  The noble *Bradamants* most tender hart,
  It seem'd she pittide this mans state as much,
  As if her brother had playd such a part:
  Some cause there was to make her fancie such,
  As afterward at large I shall impart:
  And straight she makes this motion that they twaine
  Might save this wofull youth from being slaine.

36

Rogero much commends her noble mind,
  And to the mourning damsell thus they said,
  We both are to this enterprise inclind,
  If fortune serve we will the yong man aid,
  But when they saw that still she mournd and whind,
  Tush (quoth *Rogero*) cease to be afraid,
  Tis more then time that we were going hence,
  Not teares but force must serve for his defence.

37

These comfortable words *Rogero* spake,
  With that his warlike looke and manly show,
  Did cause her heart of grace forthwith to take,
  Yet still she doubts which way were best to go,
  Not that she feard the right way to mistake,
  For all the wayes she perfitly did know,
  To turne the way she came she was afraid,
  Lest in the way they haply might be staid.

38

There are (quoth she) two wayes unto the place,
  Of which the tone is easie, faire and plaine,
  The tother foule, and farre the greater space,
  Yet at this time the safer of the twaine,
  But yet I feare, except God send more grace,
  That ere we thither come, he may be slaine:
  Thus stood this damsell still, not little musing,
  Betweene the nearer way and safer chusing.

39

Rogero that was resolute and stout,
  Did aske what reason moov'd her to perswade
  Them two to take the farther way about;
  And straightway she to them this answer made,
  Forsooth (said she) the cause that moves my doubt
  Is this, I feare that some will you invade,
  By meanes that *Pinnabell* (*Anselmus* sonne)
  Hath here of late a custome leud begunne.

40

As namely that who ever that way ride,
  Of what estate soever or degree,
  Must leese their horses first and then beside
  Must of their clothes and raiment spoiled be.
  Foure valiant youths of strength, and courage tride,
  Are sworne to this, so that no he nor she
  Can passe that way without this evill paiment,
  That he must weapons leese, and she her raiment.

41

The custome is, as yet but three dayes old,
  By *Pinabello* and his wife devised,
  Who meeting haply (as I heard it told)
  A Knight, or one in Knightly clothes disguised,
  With whom a woman ugly to behold,
  And by this couple scorned and despised,
  This *Pinnabell* the worse had of the quarrell,
  His wife was spoild of horse and of apparrell.

42

This spite enraged so the womans mind,
  That wishing to revenge, not knowing how,
  Yet wrath and folly so her sence doth blind,
  That straight she makes a foolish solemne vow,
  And he that was to evill deeds inclind
  No lesse then she, doth of the same allow:
  The vow was this, for anger of this foile,
  A thousand others in like sort to spoile.

43

That very night came to that house by chance,
  Foure valiant Knights as ever armor bare,
  To fight on horse or foot with sword or lance,
  But few may with the worst of them compare,
  These foure I say were first that led this dance,
  By night surprised ere they were aware,
  Both *Griffin*, *Aquilant* and *Sansonet*,
  And *Guidon Savage*, scant a man as yet.

44

These foure in shew he gently entertained,
  And makes them friendly countenance and cheare,
  With courteous speech and friendly manner fained,
  As if he lov'd them well and held them deare:
  But while secure they in their beds remained,
  And when Sunne rising now approched neare,
  He did beset the lodging where they lay,
  And tooke their armor and their clothes away.

45

And further bound them in that present place,
  Both hand and foote as if they prisners were,
  And ere he did those causlesse bonds unlace,
  He makes them solemnly to vow and sweare,
  To keepe this order for a twelvemonths space,
  That whosoever hapned to come there,
  They foure endevour should with all their forces,
  To take away their raiment and their horses.

46

To this by solemne oth are sworne they foure,
  Constrain'd thereto by this their cruell host,
  And though herewith they were offended sore,
  Yet must they sweare for feare of farther cost,
  Already not so few as twise a score,
  Their horses and their furniture have lost,
  And none as yet so able have bene found,
  But one of these have laid him on the ground.

47

But if some one do hap so strong to be,
　　To make his partie good with one of those,
　　Then straight the order is, the other three
　　Must him assist, thus none unconquerd goes.
　　Wherefore if you will be advis'd by me,
　　Tis best to shun this way as I suppose,
　　Sith each of these is such as I recited,
　　How great thinke you will be their force united?

48

But presuppose that you their force withstand,
　　As your great courage makes me thinke you might,
　　Yet needs it hinder must the cause in hand,
　　And make you tarry hereabout all night:
　　Sith then this case so dangerously doth stand,
　　I would perswade you now to shun this fight,
　　Lest while you in this enterprise remaine,
　　The poore yong man may fortune to be slaine.

49

Tush quoth *Rogero*, have no doubt at all,
　　Let us endevor still to do our best,
　　And then hap good or ill, fall what may fall,
　　Let God and fortune governe all the rest:
　　I hope this enterprise I finish shall
　　So well, as I shall eke do your request,
　　And there arrive to save him in good time,
　　That should be burned for so small a crime.

50

This said, he gets him on the nearest way,
　　Fast by the place where *Pinnabell* doth dwell,
　　And at the bridge they forced were to stay,
　　And straight a man (whose name I know not well)
　　Came out in hast, and stand to them doth say,
　　And then begins their order them to tell,
　　Perswading them, if they will shunne the perill,
　　To yeeld in peace their horses and apparell.

51

Peace (quoth *Rogero*) leave thy foolish prating,
　　A tale already knowne thou dost repeate,
　　Children with bugs, and dogs are scard with rating,
　　With me it small availes to brag or threate,
　　I leese but time with thee to stand debating,
　　Shew me the men that mind to do this feate,
　　My hast is such that long I may not stay,
　　Wherefore I pray you bid them come away.

52

Lo here comes one of them, this old man sed,
　　And as he spake the word, out came a Knight,
　　A tall strong man, all arm'd from foot to hed,
　　His armor like a fornace shined bright,
　　His colours that he ware were white and red,
　　This was the first, and *Sansonet* he hight,
　　And, for he was a man of mighty strength,
　　Two massie speares he brought of mighty length.

53

The one of these he to *Rogero* gave,
　　The other to himselfe he doth reserve,
　　Then each in hope the victory to have,
　　To spurre their stedie steeds that will not swerve,
　　Rogeros shield from wounding doth him save,
　　The others did him not so well preserve,
　　The speare both pierst his shield and prickt his arme,
　　And overthrew him to his further harme.

54

You do not sure, nor cannot yet forget,
　　What of *Rogeros* shield before I told,
　　That made the fiends of hell with toyle to swer,
　　And shin'd so bright as none could it behold,
　　No marvell then though valiant *Sansonet*,
　　Although his hands were strong and hart were bold,
　　Could not prevaile so strong a shield to pierce,
　　Of so great force as late I did rehearse.

55

This while was *Pinnabell* approched nie
　　To *Bradamant*, and askt of her his name,
　　That in their sight his force so great did trie,
　　To overthrow a Knight of so great fame.
　　(Lo how the mighty God that sits on hie,
　　Can punish sinne when least men looke the same)
　　Now *Pinnabell* fell in his enemies hands,
　　When in his owne conceit most safe he stands.

56

It was his hap that selfe same horse to ride,
　　Which eight months past from *Bradamant* he stale,
　　Then when he falsly let the pole to slide,
　　At *Merlins* cave (if you did marke the tale)
　　But now when she that traitor vile had spide,
　　That thought by trechery to worke her bale,
　　She stept forthwith betweene him and his castle,
　　And sweares that she with him a pull would wrastle.

57

Looke how a fox, with dogs and hunters chast,
　　That to come backe unto her hole did weene,
　　Is utterly discourag'd and agast,
　　When in her way she nets and dogs hath seene:
　　So he that no such perill did forecast,
　　And sees his fo stept him and home betweene,
　　With word him threatning and with sword assailing,
　　Doth take the wood his heart and courage failing.

58

Thus now on flight his onely hope relying,
　　He spurd that horse that chiefe his trouble bred,
　　No hope of helpe, and yet for helpe still crying,
　　For doubt of death almost already ded,
　　Sometime the fact excusing or denying,
　　But she beleeving not a word he sed,
　　None in the castle were of this aware,
　　About *Rogero* all so busied are.

59

This while forth of the gate came th'other three,
  That to this law so solemnly had sworne,
Among the rest that came was also she
  That caus'd this law, full of disdaine and scorne,
And none of these but sooner would agree
  With horses wilde to be in peeces torne,
Then to distaine their honor and good name,
With any act that might be worthy shame.

60

Wherefore it griev'd them to the very gall,
  That more then one at once should one assaile,
Save they were sworne to runne together all,
  If so the first of victorie did faile:
And she uncessantly on them did call,
  What meane you sirs (quoth she) what do you aile?
Do you forget the cause I brought you hither?
Are you not sworne to take part altogether?

61

Fie, answered *Guidon*, what a shame is this?
  Let rather me alone my fortune trie,
And if of victory I hap to misse,
  At my returning backe then let me die.
Not so quoth she, my meaning other is,
  And you I trust will not your word denie:
I brought you hither for another cause,
Not now to make new orders and new lawes.

62

Thus were they urged by this scornfull dame,
  To that which all their hearts abhorred sore,
And which they thought to them so great a shame,
  As never like had chanced them before;
Also *Rogeros* words increast the same,
  Vpbraiding them, and egging more and more,
And asking why they made so long delay,
To take his armor and his horse away.

63

And thus in maner forst and by constraint,
  They came all three *Rogero* to invade,
Which act they thought wold sore their honors taint,
  Though full account of victory they made,
Rogero at their comming doth not faint,
  As one well us'd through dangers great to wade,
And first the worthy *Oliveros* sonnes,
With all their force against *Rogero* runnes.

64

Rogero turn'd his horse to take the field,
  With that same staffe that lately overthrew
Stout *Sansonet*, and with that passing shield,
  That *Atlant* made by helpe of hellish crew,
That shield, whose ayd he used very seeld,
  Some unexpected danger to eschew:
Twise when *Alcynas* kingdome he forsooke,
Once when the Indian Queene from th'*Ork* he took.

65

Save these three times he never us'd the aid
  Of this his shield, but left it coverd still,
If he abroade, or if within he staid,
  He never left it open by his will.
As for these three, he was no more afraid
  Of all their strength, their number nor their skill,
Nor made no more account with them to fight,
Then if they had seemd children in his sight.

66

And first he met the yonger of the twaine,
  That *Griffin* hight, who had so great a blo,
As in the saddle he could scant remain,
  But quite amazed reeled to and fro;
He strake *Rogero*, but it was in vaine,
  For why, the stroke fell overthwartly so,
That quite beside *Rogeros* shield it slipt,
But yet the case it all to tare and ript.

67

Now when the renting of the silken case,
  In which *Rogero* usd the shield to hide,
Had cast out such a light in each mans face,
  That none of them the force thereof could bide,
They fell downe all amazed in the place,
  Admit they sit, or stand, or go, or ride,
Rogero with the cause not yet acquainted,
Did marvell how his foes so soone had fainted.

68

But when he once was of the cause aware,
  And how the cover of his shield was rent,
By meane whereof it open lay and bare,
  And thence such light unto the lookers sent:
He lookes about where his companions are,
  Because forthwith to get him thence he ment,
I meane his *Bradamant*, and that same maid,
That for that youth did erst demaund his aid.

69

But his belov'd as then he found not, where
  He erst had left her when he went to just,
And when he plainly saw she was not there,
  And that that happend he could not mistrust,
He parted thence, and with him he doth beare
  The maid that made to him the sute so just,
Who lay that time amazed with the rest,
With sudden blasing of the light distrest.

70

He takes her kirtle, and with it doth hide,
  The light that did so dazle all their eyes,
That light on which to looke none could abide,
  As if two Sunnes had shone at once in skies:
Forthwith himselfe all malcontent doth ride,
  To have this combat ended in such wise,
As might imputed be to Magicke art,
And not his prowesse or his valiant hart.

71

Now while this thought such passions did him yeeld,
　That though he had indeed most bravely donne,
　Yet men would thinke the glory of the field,
　Not by his valiantnesse to have bene wonne,
　But by the force of that inchanted shield,
　That cast a light more piercing then the Sunne,
　I say as thus he thought, he passed by
　A large deepe well, that by the way did lie.

72

A well at which the beasts in summers heate
　Did use their thirstie drought to quench and coole,
　And chew againe their undigested meate,
　And walke about the shallowes of the poole.
　Here did *Rogero* oft these words repeate,
　Thou shield, that late didst make me such a foole,
　To cause me get a conquest with such shame,
　Lie there (quoth he) with thee go all my blame.

73

With that he threw the shield into the well,
　The well was deepe, the shield of mighty weight,
　That to the bottome suddenly it fell,
　The water over it a monstrous height:
　But lo dame Fame the thing abroad doth tell,
　How he because he would not win by sleight,
　But by meere value, had his target drownd,
　Where it should never afterward be found.

74

Yet many (that had heard the strange report)
　Of those that dwelled thence, some farre, some nire,
　To seeke the target thither did resort,
　And to have found it out had great desire,
　But it was cast away in such a sort,
　As none unto their purpose did aspire,
　For why the maid that onely did behold it,
　And knew which well it was, yet never told it.

75

But when the Knights came to themselves againe,
　And were awake, and one the other saw,
　That late were vanquisht with so little paine,
　As if to him they had bene men of straw,
　They wondred much what troubled had their braine,
　And all of them did thence themselves withdraw,
　And all that day they argue and devise,
　How that same light should dazle so their eyes.

76

This while came notice of the wofull fall
　Of *Pinnabell*, whom *Bradamant* had killed,
　With which they greatly were displeased all,
　Not knowing why or who his blood had spilled;
　His wife and sire that heard what was befall,
　His sonne, her spouse, the place with outcries filled,
　And curst and chased with too late repentance,
　That none on *Pinnabell* had giv'n attendance.

77

Now when the damsell justly had him slaine,
　And tane away his horse, sometime her owne,
　She would have turnd the way she came againe,
　But that the same was unto her unknowne;
　To purpose small, she travels with great paine,
　To seeke it out, as after shall be showne:
　For here to stay is my determination,
　And pawse a little for my recreation.

THE TWENTY-THIRD BOOKE OF

ORLANDO FVRIOSO

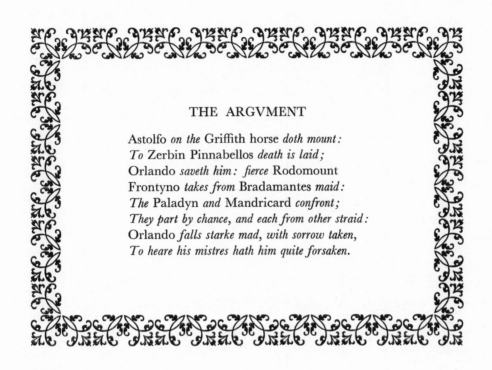

THE ARGVMENT

Astolfo *on the* Griffith horse *doth mount:*
To Zerbin Pinnabellos *death is laid;*
Orlando *saveth him: fierce* Rodomount
Frontyno *takes from* Bradamantes *maid:*
The Paladyn *and* Mandricard *confront;*
They part by chance, and each from other straid:
Orlando *falls starke mad, with sorrow taken,*
To heare his mistres hath him quite forsaken.

ORLANDO FVRIOSO
THE TWENTY-THIRD BOOKE

1

Let ev'rie one do all the good they can,
  For seldom commeth harme of doing well,
  Though just reward it wanteth now and than,
  Yet shame, and evill death it doth expell,
  But he that mischieveth another man,
  Doth seldome carrie it to heav'n or hell:
  Men say it, and we see it come to passe,
  Good turns in sand, shrewd turns are writ in brasse.

2

Seeld mountaines meet, but men may often meet,
  (The Proverbe saith) and who so sets a trap,
  May catch himselfe, as here you plainly see't
  In him, that thought his dame in woes to wrap,
  But hurts himselfe, a punishment most meet;
  God still defending her from all mishap:
  God her preserv'd, and will all those preserve,
  As shunne all vice, and him sincerely serve.

3

It little did availe to *Pinnabell*,
  To be amid his kinsfolke and his frends;
  And neare the castle, where his sire did dwell,
  Where ev'ry one, him honours and attends,
  Loe here the end of him doth plainly tell,
  How wicked lives have often wretched ends;
  But to proceed, I said when he was slaine,
  The noble damsell sought her way againe.

4

Which when she saw she could by no meanes know,
  But more and more uncertainly did rove;
  And sees the sunne was now declining low,
  She meanes that night to rest her in the grove:
  And sleepe sometime, or else sometime (I trow)
  To looke on *Mars*, on *Saturne*, or on *Iove*,
  But chiefly, whether she awakes or sleepes,
  Rogeros image in her heart she keepes.

5

Oft times she fretting to her selfe would say,
  Loe; hate with me farre more prevailed hath,
  Then love could do, that now have lost my way,
  And left my comfort to avenge my wrath,
  Nor had my wit so much forecast or stay,
  To take some marke of my foretrodden path:
  I did (quoth she) as fooles are wont to do,
  Take one shrewd turne to do another two.

6

These words and many like to these she spake,
  To passe the rest of that her restlesse night,
  Till starres gan vanish and the dawning brake,
  And all the Eastern parts were full of light,
  Then at adventure she her way doth take,
  Not knowing yet if it were wrong or right;
  And having traveld in that way some miles,
  By hap *Astolfo* came that way the whiles.

7

He rides the winged horse, but in his hand,
  He leades the famous *Rabican* behinde,
  And ev'n as then, in great doubt he did stand,
  Where to bestow a beast of so good kind:
  She knowing him, went to him out of hand,
  With words, with showes, and with embracements kind,
  And joyd to find this kinsman of her owne,
  And unto him her selfe she maketh knowne.

8

Astolfo much rejoyst at this their meeting,
  Then one the other askt of their well fare,
  And after their long talke, and friendly greeting,
  In which each shewd of other loving care:
  Sith I (quoth he) intend hence to be fleeting,
  To see what sights in forren countries are,
  This horse of me, I shall request you take,
  Till I returne, and keepe him for my sake.

9

Also he said, this corslet and this speare,
  With you I leave till I returne againe,
  (This speare the sonne of *Galafron* did beare,
  Whom as you heard before *Ferraw* had slaine,)
  With head whereof, if any touched were,
  Straight wayes to fall to ground they must be faine,
  All these he left behind to make him light,
  Before that he begins to take his flight.

10

Thus leave once tane, away the Duke doth sore,
  First low, and after still more hye and hye,
  Till at the length she could him see no more;
  So doth the Pylot first, with watchfull eye,
  Guide out his vessell softly by the shore,
  While he doth thinke the rocks and shallowes nye:
  But after when he dreads no more such doubts,
  He fayles apace, and claps on all his clouts.

S

11

Now when the Duke was from the damsell gone,
  What she might do she mused in her minde,
  And carefully she meditates thereon:
  How she may take the journey first assign'd,
  And not neglect her kinsmans charge; anon
  A wandring peasant twas her hap to finde,
  To him she doth betake the horses spare,
  Though of the wayes they both unskilfull are.

12

Her meaning was to go to *Vallumbrose*,
  As first her love and she concluded had,
  Whom there to finde, she certaine doth suppose;
  Whom there to find, she would have bene full glad,
  But loe a quite contrary course she goes,
  And sees a sight that made her then full sad,
  Her fathers house *Montalbanie* she spide,
  In which as then her mother did abide.

13

If she shall forward go, approching nire,
  She shall be stayed there, she stands in doubt,
  If she stand still, or backward do retire,
  She feares to meet acquaintance thereabout;
  If she be staid, she feeles such burning fire,
  Of longing love as cannot be put out:
  She chaunst amid these thoughts, and many other,
  To meet *Alardo* there her younger brother.

14

This meeting in her minde bred much vexation,
  When as she found her brother her had spide,
  And made her alter her determination,
  Which that she might from him the better hide,
  She us'd some common words of salutation,
  And to *Montalban* with him she doth ride,
  Where as her mother, full of care and feare,
  Had wisht, and wayted for her comming there.

15

But all those kind embracings and those kisses,
  She had of parent, kinsmen kinde, and frends,
  She deems of little vallue to those blisses,
  That she had lost, and thought them small amends:
  But sith to meet *Rogero* now she misses,
  To send a messenger she now intends,
  Some such to whom she may commit the charge,
  To tell her mind unto her love at large.

16

And if neede were to pray him in her name,
  As he had promist her, to be baptised,
  And to excuse, that thither she not came,
  As they together had before devised:
  Besides his horse *Frontino*, by the same,
  She sent a horse of goodnes not despised,
  No horse in *France* or *Spaine* esteemed more,
  Bayardo sole except, and *Brigliadore*.

17

Rogero (if you call it well to minde)
  What time the *Griffith* horse he first did take,
  That soard away as swift as western winde,
  And forst him quickly *Europe* to forsake,
  That gallant beast *Frontino* left behind,
  Whom *Bradamant* then, for his masters sake,
  Tooke home, and with much care and costly feeding,
  Made him by this time, faire and fat exceeding.

18

And straight her mayds and women servants all,
  That skilfull were to sow, to weave, and knit,
  She doth to worke in hast together call,
  And she her selfe among them all doth sit,
  To worke a net, of art and cost not small,
  For his caparison to make it fit:
  When this was done, and finisht, straight way after,
  She calls her nurse *Callitriscas* daughter.

19

This mayd knew best her minde of all the rest,
  And oft had heard her praising to the skyes,
  Rogeros comly shape, and valiant brest,
  His sugred speech, sweet face, and lov'ly eyes;
  This mayd with secrets all shee trusted best,
  On this mayds secrecie, she much relyes:
  Hyppalca named was this trustie mayd,
  Her then she cald, and thus to her she said.

20

Hyppalca mine, you know of all my crew,
  Of women servants, I esteeme you most,
  As one that hath bene secret, wise, and trew,
  A praise of which we women seld can bost)
  My meaning is to make a choise of you,
  To have you to *Rogero* ride in post;
  And unto him mine absence to excuse,
  And shew, that I could neither will nor chuse.

21

Your selfe (quoth she) may ride a little nagge,
  And in your hand lead by *Frontino* spare,
  And if perhap some foole will be so bragge,
  As that to take the horse from you he dare,
  To make him that he shall no farther wagge,
  But tell who owes the horse, and do not care:
  She thought *Rogero* was of so great fame,
  That ev'ry one would quake to heare his name.

22

Thus when *Hyppalca* was instructed well,
  Of all that to her arrant did belong,
  And that no more remain'd behind to tell,
  She tooke her horse, and there she stayd not long,
  In ten miles space (so luckie it befell)
  None offer made to do her any wrong,
  No traveller, no Knight, nor peasant staid her,
  Nor once with word or deed so much as frayd her.

23

About the time the Sun to South did mount,
  She met (poore soule) a Knight, unto her cost,
  That *Turke* most terrible cald *Rodomount*,
  That follow'd arm'd on foote, a page in post;
  Who when he saw an horse of such account,
  He God blasphem'd and all the heav'nly host,
  That such a gallant serviceable beast,
  In some mans hand, he had not found at least.

24

He had before profest by solemne vow,
  When wanting horse, he traveld on his feet,
  That wer't from knight, or knave that drives a plow,
  To take perforce the next horse he should meet:
  Yet though he lik't the horse, to take this now,
  And rob a mayd thereof, he thought unmeet,
  He sees her leade a horse, and he doth lacke,
  And oft he wisht his master on his backe.

25

I would he were (quoth she) he soone would make,
  You change your mind, and glad to get you hence,
  And you should find how much you do mistake,
  Your strength and force to offer him offence.
  And who (quoth he) is this, of whom you cracke?
  Rogero she replies: forsooth, and sence
  So great a champion is the horses owner,
  I may (said he) then take him with mine honor.

26

To take his horse (quoth he) I now intend,
  For of a horse you see I stand in need:
  And if I find it true as you pretend,
  That he so stout a champion is in deed,
  I *Rodomont* this action will defend,
  Now on my present journey I proceed,
  And where I go my vertues shine so bright,
  He soone may find me if he list to fight.

27

This said, with cruell threats, and part with force,
  He gat his will, full sore against her will,
  And straight he mounteth up upon that horse,
  She cursing follow'd him, and banning still,
  But of those curses he doth little force;
  Then winners bost, when leesers speake their fill,
  Best pleas'd was he, when as she wisht him worst,
  As still the foxe fares best when he is curst.

28

But what she saith he little doth regard,
  Suppose she curst, or prayd, or rayld, or cride,
  He seekes out *Doralice* and *Mandricard*,
  And had the little dwarfe to be his guide,
  No little hast he maketh thither ward:
  But here a while mine author steps aside,
  And to that place of purpose makes digression,
  Where *Pinnabell* was shriv'n without confession.

29

The noble Dame no sooner left the place,
  Where late this caitive by her hand was slaine,
  But *Zerbin* there arriv'd in little space,
  With old *Gabrina*, who perceiving plaine,
  One murtherd, straight he followed the trace,
  (Lest murther unrevenged should remaine)
  He minds if fortune be so much his furderer:
  To be revenged sharply on the murderer.

30

Gabrina to the quarrie straight approcheth,
  Looks all about, searching the corse and prying,
  (As one that still on ev'rie gaine encrocheth)
  To win both by the living and the dying,
  In purses and in pockets all she pocheth,
  Of him that murther'd on the ground was lying,
  As having this, conjoyn'd to other evills,
  In covetise to passe the very devills.

31

She would have had his cote and armor faine,
  Save that she knew not how them to have hidden,
  But from great part of that desired gaine,
  By want of leysure she was then forbidden;
  Howb'it she did convay away his chaine,
  And ere *Zerbino* backe againe was ridden,
  She put it safely where it was not seene,
  Her upper gowne and peticote betweene.

32

And sore it grieved her to leave the rest,
  But now *Zerbino* was returned backe,
  And for the time drew nigh of taking rest,
  And night came now to spred his mantell blacke,
  To seeke some lodging out they thought it best,
  Of which, in that wild countrie was great lacke.
  They leave the valley, and they came that night,
  Vnto a castle *Altariva* hight.

33

They thither went, and long they had not stayd,
  But in came people with great exclamation,
  With wofull news, that many hearts dismayd,
  And fill'd their mouths and eyes with lamentation,
  How *Pinnabell* was murderd and betrayd,
  And lost his life, and worldly habitation,
  And straight they brought the corse with light of torches
  And led the same through all the courts and porches.

34

Great were the plaints, the sorow and the griefe,
  By kindred made, by tenants and his frends;
  But by his father, old *Anselmus* chiefe,
  Who, though revenge be but a small amends,
  And his sonnes life was now past all reliefe,
  By search to find the murdrer he intends.
  Zerbino hereof makes himselfe a stranger,
  As well to shunne suspition as danger.

35

Now when the funerals in stately sort,
  Ordained were with pompe and superstition
  To which great store of people did resort,
  And all that would, had franke and free permission,
  Straight with oyes, a cryer doth report,
  Thereto assigned by that Earles commission,
  That who so could the murderer bewray,
  Should have a thousand duckats for his pay.

36

This newes from mouth to mouth, from eare to eare,
  (As newes are wont to do) did flie so fast,
  That old *Gabrina*, being present there,
  Among the rest, heard of it at the last:
  Who either for the hatred she did beare,
  To good *Zerbino*, for some matters past,
  Or else for gaine of that so great reward,
  Straight to destroy *Zerbino* she prepard.

37

And that she might more surely him entrap,
  With th'Erle himselfe to speake she doth request,
  And probably, she tels how this mishap,
  Was by *Zerbino* wrought his new come guest:
  And straight she puld the chaine out of her lap,
  Which sole might serve to verifie the rest:
  That aged sire, that all the tale beleeved,
  Was sore inrag'd herewith, not onely grieved.

38

And lifting up his hands unto the skies,
  With age now feeble, feeble now with woe,
  With fainting voice he spake, and watrie eies,
  (My sonne) thou shalt not unrevenged go:
  And while in bed secure *Zerbino* lyes,
  Not thinking he had bene betrayed so,
  With armed men his lodging was beset,
  He naked tane, as is a byrd in net.

39

With as great cruelty as could be showne,
  His princely armes were piniond fast behind him,
  And to a dungeon deepe he straight was throwne,
  And that vile place, to bide in was assignd him,
  Vntill the sentence of his death were knowne:
  In fine *Anselmus* (so did passion blind him)
  (Her likely tale, his wrath so rashly leading)
  Condemned him, and never heard him pleading.

40

Thus was this worthy Prince without all cause,
  Condemnd to die (such is the wofull being,
  Where hests of lawlesse lords, must stand for laws,
  Though from all lawes and reason disagreeing)
  Now neare and neare his execution drawes,
  And gazing people, greedie still of seeing,
  In clusters march and follow all confused,
  On horse, on foot, as at such time is used.

41

But loe how God that ever doth defend,
  Those innocents that put in him their trust,
  A helpe unlooked for did thither send,
  And freed him from this doome of death unjust:
  Orlando did ev'n then the hill ascend,
  Orlando is the man that save him must,
  And at that time there did with him remaine,
  The daughter of *Galego*, King of *Spaine*.

42

This was that *Isabell*, whom he of late,
  Recover'd from the outlawes in the cave,
  And having brought her out of that ill state,
  Yet still he promist care of her to have,
  And whatsoever danger or debate,
  To him befell, yet her he still did save:
  Orlando all that great assemblie saw,
  That did the Knight to execution draw.

43

He thither went and askt of him the cause,
  Why he was drawne unto a death so cruell,
  Forsooth (*Zerbino* said) against all lawes,
  I am condemn'd if you the matter knew well,
  Anselmus rage, that will admit no pause,
  Vnto this flame, doth kindle all the fewell:
  Beleeving falsely that I slue his sonne,
  Whereas by me (God knowes) it was not done.

44

Thus *Zerbin* said, and said it in such sort,
  As made *Orlando* vow him to releeve,
  For very apt he was, each ill report,
  Of any of *Maganza* to beleeve;
  Each house still thought to cut the other short,
  Each house still sought the other how to greeve:
  Each house long time, had tane a pride and pleasure,
  To worke the tother danger and displeasure.

45

Vnloose the Knight ye catives (straight he cride)
  Else looke for death to be your due reward:
  What man is this (quoth one) that gapes so wide?
  And speakes so foolishly without regard?
  Were he of steele, of strength and temper tride,
  And we of straw, his sute might hap be hard.
  This said, he taketh up a mighty launce,
  And runnes against the *Palladine* of *Fraunce*.

46

Orlando ran at him with couched speare,
  And though his armour were both good and sure,
  As namely that *Zerbino* erst did weare,
  Yet was the stroke too grievous to endure,
  For though the beaver did it stifly beare,
  Yet did the blow a greater hurt procure:
  For on the cheeke, it gave him such a checke,
  That though it pierced not, it brake his necke.

47

Nor at that course did all his furie cease,
  Six other of that speare the force then felt,
  Then with his sword among the thickest prease,
  Such store of thrusts, and deadly blowes he delt,
  That many in the place did straight decease;
  And ev'n as snow against the Sunne doth melt,
  So melted they and fainted in his sight,
  That in an houre he put them all to flight.

48

When they were fled, he set *Zerbino* free,
  Who would have kist the ground whereon he trod,
  And done him reverence humbly on his knee,
  But that the Earle such courtsie him forbod:
  But yet he thankt him in the high'st degree,
  As one he honourd most, excepting God:
  Then did he put his armor on againe,
  Which late was worne by him that there was slaine.

49

Now while *Zerbino* there a little staid,
  Preparing with *Orlando* to go hence,
  Behold faire *Isabell*, that princely maid,
  That all the while had staid a little thence,
  And sees no farther cause to be affraid,
  Came neare, & brought great joy and great offence,
  By divers passions bred of one desire,
  Some cold as ice, and some as hot as fire.

50

For where before *Zerbino* thought her drownd,
  Now certaine he rejoyced very much,
  To see her in his presence safe and sound,
  And that her misadventure was not such;
  But weying in whose hand he had her found,
  A jealous feare forthwith his heart doth tuch,
  And inwardly a greater anguish bred,
  Then late it had, to heare that she was ded.

51

To see her in the hands of such a Knight,
  It greatly did him anger and displease,
  From whom to offer, her to take by might,
  It were no honestie nor haply ease,
  But for *Orlandos* sake he ought of right,
  All passions both of love and wrath appease;
  To whom in thankfulnesse it were but meete,
  To lay his hands under *Orlandos* feete.

52

Wherefore he makes no words, but on he goth
  In silent sort, till comming to a well
  To drinke they lighted, being thirstie both,
  And each his drought with water doth expell,
  But when the damsell saw and knew for troth,
  That was *Zerbino* whom she lou'd so well,
  (For when to drinke his bever he untide)
  Straight she her love had through his bever spide.

53

With open armes she runs him to embrace,
  And hangs about his necke a pleasant yoke,
  And speechlesse she remaind a pretie space,
  And with her cristall teares (before she spoke)
  Surpris'd with joy, she all bedewd his face,
  And long it was ere into speech she broke,
  By which the noble Earle did plainly see,
  That this could no man but *Zerbino* be.

54

Now when she had againe her vitall sprites,
  And that she able was her mind to show,
  First she *Orlandos* great desarts recites,
  That rescude her from place of shame and wo,
  Commending him above all other Knights,
  That undefiled had preserv'd her so,
  And pray'd her deare, when she had made recitall
  Of his good deeds, to make him some requitall.

55

Great thanks were giv'n, and profers great there were
  Of recompence and service on each side,
  But lo a hap that made them speech forbeare,
  For why an armed Knight they had espide:
  Twas *Mandricardo* that arrived there,
  Who as you heard, these many dayes did ride
  To seeke this Earle, till meeting by the way
  Faire *Doralice*, a while it made him stay.

56

You heard how *Mandricard* sought out the tracke,
  (Mov'd thereunto by envie and disdaine)
  Of this fierce Knight, appareld all in blacke,
  By whom the King of *Tremysen* was slaine,
  And those *Noritians* all, so put to wracke,
  As few of them unwounded did remaine,
  And now he found him as it came to passe,
  Yet knew he not that this *Orlando* was.

57

But marking well, the signes and tokens eke,
  To those he heard, of such as thence were fled,
  You are (quoth he) the selfe same man I seeke,
  By whom so many of my friends are ded:
  I have (he said) traveld above a weeke
  To find you out, and now at last am sped,
  You are the man that I have sought (I guesse)
  And sure your manly looke doth shew no lesse.

58

Sir (quoth *Orlando*) though I want your name,
  A noble Knight you are it may be guest,
  For sure a heart so thirsting after fame,
  Is seldome bred in base unnoble brest:
  But if to see me onely now you came,
  I straight herein will graunt you your request:
  And that you may behold me to your fill,
  I will put off mine armour if you will.

59

But when you well have view'd me all about,
　If yet you have a farther mind to trie,
　Which of us two can prove himselfe most stout,
　And first in field can make the tother flie:
　Attempt it when you list, and make no doubt,
　But hereunto right soone agree shall I:
　That (quoth the *Pagan*) is my mind indeed,
　And thus to fight together they agreed.

60

But when *Orlando* view'd the *Pagan* King,
　And saw no pollax at his saddle bow,
　No sword by side, no bow, nor dart, nor sling,
　But ev'n a speare, he needs of him would know,
　When that were burst, unto what other thing
　He then would trust, to give or beare a blow:
　Tush (quoth the *Pagan* Prince) you need not feare,
　But I will match you onely with the speare.

61

I have (quoth he) an oath most solemne sworne,
　Since first the noble *Hectors* armes I wan,
　That by my side should never sword be worne,
　Nor other iron weapon, till I can
　Get *Durindana* by *Orlando* borne,
　Though how he gate it, well I cannot scan,
　But since he gate it, great reports do flie,
　That noble deeds of armes he doth thereby.

62

No lesse (quoth he) I faine on him would wreake
　My fathers death, whom falsly he betraid,
　For well I wot my sire was not so weake,
　With any *Christen* to be overlaid:
　At this *Orlando* could not chuse but speake,
　It is a lie (quoth he) that thou hast said,
　I am *Orlando*, and I will not beare it,
　This sword is *Durindan*, win it and weare it.

63

And though this sword is justly wholly mine,
　Yet for this time I frankly do agree,
　A while it shall be neither mine nor thine,
　And if in combat you can vanquish me,
　Then tak't, and thereat I shall not repine:
　This said, he hang'd the sword upon a tree,
　Indifferently betweene them both to stand,
　Vntill the strife by combat might be scand.

64

Now one at th'other ran with couched speare,
　And on the head-peece each the other strake,
　The staves in sundry peeces rend and teare,
　But by the blowes the men small hurt do take:
　And now the trunchens onely left them were,
　And at foure blowes the trunchens likewise brake,
　Thus when they saw all other weapons mist,
　At last they were inforst to fight with fist.

65

So have I seene two clownes fall at debate,
　About some watercourse or marke of land,
　And either clap the tother on the pate,
　With crabtree staffe, or with as crabbed hand;
　Such of this conflict was the present state,
　And each of them doth to his tackle stand,
　And being tyr'd with giving frutelesse stripes,
　At last they flatly fell to handie gripes.

66

The *Pagan*, part by sleight and part by force,
　Thought to have done as *Hercles* in time past,
　To fierce *Antheus* did, and th'Earle inforce,
　To yeeld himselfe, or leave his horse at last.
　Orlando that could surely sit his horse,
　With all his strength bestrides the saddle fast,
　Yet did the *Pagan* heave him with such strength,
　That all his gyrses broken were at length.

67

Downe came the Earle, yet kept his saddle still,
　Nor what had happend was he well aware,
　But as he fell, intending by his will,
　Vnto the *Pagan* King to worke some care,
　He meant (but his attempt succeeded ill)
　To overthrow the horse the *Pagan* bare,
　But missing hold, the horse unhurt remaines,
　Yet off he puld his headstall and his raines.

68

The horse that had at liberty his hed,
　Runs over ditch and valley, hedge and wood,
　As partly feare, and partly courage led,
　For nothing was that his mad course withstood:
　But *Mandricard* still beates him on his head,
　And ev'n as if he speech had understood,
　He threatens him (except he stay) to beate him,
　And with faire speech somtime he doth intreat him.

69

But all was one, three mile outright he rode,
　Ere he could make the harebraine horse to stay,
　Or cause him once to make a small abode,
　But more and more he gallops still away:
　At last with hast the horse and eke the lode
　Fell downe into a ditch, and there they lay,
　Both horse and man all soyld and rayd with durt,
　Yet neither horse nor man had any hurt.

70

This while Dame *Doralice* that saw her guide
　Thus post away against his will amaine,
　She thought it were not safe behind to bide,
　And therefore follow'd him though with great paine,
　And seeing that he could no farther ride,
　Because his wilfull horse did want a raine,
　She prayes him take her horses raine and bit,
　For mine (quoth she) will go though wanting it.

71

Much did the *Pagan* praise her gentle offer,
    Yet did refuse it as a part too base,
    To let her want and take her bridle of her,
    He thought it were to him a great disgrace.
    But lo good chance a better meane did profer,
    Gabrina came unwares unto the place,
    She that betraid of late the *Scottish* Prince,
    And heard (of like) of his delivery since.

72

And therefore fearing punishment and blame,
    And clog'd with guilty conscience, fled the light,
    Vntill by hap unwares she thither came,
    And on this couple fortuned to light:
    They could not chuse but make great sport & game,
    To see so strange and unagreeing sight,
    As such a witherd old ilfavord hag,
    To ride in purple on an ambling nag.

73

He that of right or wrong did little passe,
    Meanes with her store his lacke there to supply,
    Nor once demaunded who or what she was,
    But takes away her bridle by and by:
    She skreecheth out, and weepes, and cries alas,
    Ev'n ready fearing hurt, unhurt to die:
    Hereafter I shall tell what became on her,
    Now for a farewell shame I wish upon her.

74

This while *Orlando* had his girses mended,
    And new provided what before did lacke,
    And mounting on his horse, a while attended
    To see if so the *Pagan* would come backe;
    But seeing that he came not, he intended
    To follow him, and find him by the tracke:
    But first (as one that well good manners knew)
    He bad *Zerbino* and his spouse adew.

75

Faine would *Zerbino* with this Earle have gone,
    And take such part of ev'ry hap as he,
    But that the noble Earle hereof would none,
    And said there could not more dishonor be,
    Then for a Knight to shun to fight alone;
    Wherefore he would not thereunto agree:
    Thus *Zerbin* loth doth from this Earle depart,
    Poore *Isbell* shedding teares for tender hart.

76

But ere they went this Earle *Zerbino* praid,
    If first he hapt on *Mandricard* to light,
    To tell him how long time for him he staid,
    And meant to seeke him out againe to fight,
    Now that his comming was so long delaid,
    He meant to *Paris* ward to go that night,
    To *Charles* his camp, and if he sought him there,
    He should assured be of him to heare.

77

Thus much he praid, and thence away he went,
    To seeke out *Mandricard*, but found him not,
    And (for the day now more then halfe was spent,
    The Sunne and season waxing somewhat hot)
    A shadie grove he found, and there he ment
    To take some ease, but found small ease God wot:
    He thinks his thirst and heate a while to swage,
    But found that set him in worse heate and rage.

78

For looking all about the grove, behold
    In sundry places faire ingrav'n he sees,
    Her name whose loue he more esteemes then gold,
    By her owne hand in barkes of divers trees,
    This was the place wherein before I told,
    Medoro us'd to pay his surgeons fees,
    Where she, to bost of that that was her shame,
    Vs'd oft to write hers and *Medoros* name.

79

And then with true love knots and pretie poses,
    (To shew how she to him by love was knit)
    Her inward thoughts by outward words discloses,
    In her much love to shew her little wit.
    Orlando knew the hand, and yet supposes
    It was not she that had such posies writ;
    And to beguile himselfe, tush, tush (quoth he)
    There may be more *Angelicas* then she.

80

Yea, but I know too well that pretie hand,
    Oft hath she sent me letters of her writing:
    Then he bethinks how she might understand
    His name and love by that same new inditing,
    And how it might be done long time he scand,
    With this fond thought so fondly him delighting.
    Thus with small hope, much feare, all malcontent,
    In these and such conceits the time he spent.

81

And ay the more he seekes out of his thought
    To drive this fancie, still it doth increase,
    Ev'n as a bird that is with birdlime caught,
    Doth beate her wings, and strives, and doth not cease
    Vntill she hath her selfe all overwrought,
    And quite intangled in the slimie grease:
    Thus on went he, till him the way did bring
    Vnto a shadie cave and pleasant spring.

82

This was a place, wherein above the rest,
    This loving paire, leaving their homely host,
    Spent time in sports that may not be exprest,
    Here in the parching heate they tarrid most,
    And here *Medore* (that thought himselfe most blest)
    Wrote certaine verses as in way of bost:
    Which in his language doubtlesse sounded prittie,
    And thus I turne them to an *English* dittie.

83

Ye pleasant plants, greene herbs, and waters faire,
  And cave with smell, and gratefull shadow mixt,
  Where sweet *Angelica*, daughter and heire
  Of *Galafronne*, on whom in vaine were fixt
Full many hearts, with me did oft repaire
  Alone, and naked lay mine armes betwixt;
  I poore *Medore*, can yeeld but praise and thanks,
  For these great pleasures found amid your banks.

84

And pray each Lord whom *Cupid* holds in pay,
  Each Knight, each dame, and ev'ry one beside,
  Or gentle or meane sort that passe this way,
  As fancie or his fortune shall him guide,
That to the plants, herbs, spring, and cave he say,
  Long may the Sun and Moon maintaine your pride,
  And the faire crew of Nymphs make such purveyance
  As hither come no heards to your annoyance.

85

It written was there in th'Arabian tong,
  Which tong *Orlando* perfect understood,
  As having learnt it when he was but yong,
  And oft the skill thereof had done him good,
But at this time it him so deeply stoong,
  It had bin well that he it never coud,
  And yet we see, to know men still are glad,
  And yet we see much knowledge makes men mad.

86

Twise, thrise, yea five times he doth reade the rime,
  And though he saw and knew the meaning plaine,
  Yet, that his love was guilty of such crime,
  He will not let it sinke into his braine,
Oft he perused it, and ev'ry time
  It doth increase his sharpe tormenting paine,
  And ay the more he on the matter mused,
  The more his wits and senses were confused.

87

Ev'n then was he of wit welnigh bestraught,
  So quite he was giv'n over unto griefe,
  (And sure if we beleeve as proofe hath taught,
  This torture is of all the rest the chiefe)
His sprite was dead, his courage quaild with thought,
  He doth despaire and looke for no reliefe,
  And sorrow did his senses so surprise,
  That words his toong, and teares forsooke his eyes.

88

The raging pang remained still within,
  That would have burst out all at once too fast:
  Ev'n so we see the water tarry in
  A bottle little mouth'd, and bit in wast,
That though you topsie turvy turne the brim,
  The liquor bides behind with too much hast,
  And with the striving oft is in such taking,
  As scant a man can get it out with shaking.

89

At last he comes unto himselfe anew,
  And in his mind another way doth frame,
  That that which there was written was not trew,
  But writ of spite his Ladie to defame,
Or to that end, that he the same might vew,
  And so his heart with jealousie inflame:
  Well be't who list (quoth he) I see this clearly,
  He hath her hand resembled passing nearly.

90

With this small hope, with this poore little sparke,
  He doth some deale revive his troubled sprite,
  And for it was now late, and waxed darke,
  He seekes some place where he may lie that night,
At last he heares a noise of dogs that barke,
  He smels some smoke, and sees some candle light,
  He takes his Inne, with will to sleepe, not eate,
  As fild with griefe, and with none other meate.

91

But lo his hap was at that house to host,
  Where faire *Angelica* had layne before,
  And where her name on ev'ry doore and post,
  With true love knots was joyned to *Medore*,
That knot his name whom he detested most,
  Was in his eye and thought still evermore:
  He dares not aske, nor once the matter tuch,
  For knowing more of that he knowes too much.

92

But vaine it was himselfe so to beguile,
  For why his host unasked by and by,
  That saw his guest sit there so sad the while,
  And thinks to put him from his dumps thereby,
Beginneth plaine without all fraud or guile,
  Without concealing truth or adding lie,
  To tell that tale to him without regard,
  Which divers had before with pleasure heard.

93

As thus, how at *Angelicas* request
  He holpe unto his house to bring *Medore*,
  Who then was sorely wounded in his brest,
  And she with surgery did heale his sore:
But while with her owne hands the wound she drest,
  Blind *Cupid* wounded her as much or more,
  That when her skill and herbs had cur'd her patient,
  Her curelesse wound in love made her unpatient.

94

So that, admit she were the greatest Queene
  Of fame, and living in those Eastern parts,
  Yet so with fancie she was overseene,
  To marry with a page of meane desarts;
Thus love (quoth he) will have his godhead seene,
  In famous Queens, and highest Princes harts:
  This said (to end the tale) he shew'd the jewell
  That she had giv'n him, which *Orlando* knew well.

95

This tale, and chiefly this same last conclusion,
  Was ev'n a hatchet to cut off all hope,
  When love had after many a vaine collusion,
  Now for his farewell lent him such a rope
  To hang himselfe, and drowne him in confusion,
  Yet faine he would denie his sorrow scope,
  And though a while to shew it he forbeares,
  It breaketh out at last in sighs and teares.

96

And as it were inforst he gives the raine
  To raging griefe, upon his bed alone,
  His eyes do shed a very showre of raine,
  With many a scalding sigh and bitter grone,
  He slept as much as if he had then laine
  Vpon a bed of thornes, and stuft with stone.
  And as he lay thereon and could not rest him,
  The bed it selfe gave matter to molest him.

97

Ah wretch I am (thus to himselfe he sed)
  Shall I once hope to take repose and rest me
  In that same house? yea ev'n in that same bed
  Where my ungratefull love so leudly drest me?
  Nay, let me first an hundred times be ded,
  First wolves devoure and vultures shall digest me.
  Strait up he starts, and on he put his clothes,
  And leaves the house, so much the bed he lothes.

98

He leaves his host, nor once doth take his leave,
  He far'd so ill, he bids them not farewell,
  He leaves the towne, his servants he doth leave,
  He rides, but where he rides he cannot tell.
  And when alone himselfe he doth perceave
  To weepe and waile, nay ev'n to houle and yell,
  He doth not cease to give his griefe a vent,
  That inwardly so sore did him torment.

99

The day the night to him were both aleeke,
  Abroade upon the cold bare earth he lies,
  No sleepe, no food he takes, nor none would seek,
  All sustenance he to himselfe denies.
  Thus he began, and ended halfe the weeke,
  And he himselfe doth marvell, whence his eyes
  Are fed so long with such a spring of water,
  And to himselfe thus reasons on the matter.

100

No, no, these be no teares that now I shed,
  These be no teares, nor can teares run so rife,
  But fire of frenzie drawth up to my head,
  My vitall humor that should keepe my life;
  This streame will never cease till I be dead,
  Then welcome death and end my fatall strife:
  No comfort in this life my wo can minish,
  But thou who canst both life and sorrow finish.

101

These are not sighs, for sighs some respite have,
  My gripes, my pangs, no respite do permit,
  The blindfold boy made me a seeing slave,
  When from my eyes my heart he first did hit.
  Now all inflam'd, I burne, I rage and rave,
  And in the midst of flame consume no whit:
  Love sitting in my heart a master crewell,
  Blowes with his wings feeds with his will the fewell.

102

I am not I, the man that earst I was,
  Orlando, he is buried and dead,
  His most ungratefull love (ah foolish lasse)
  Hath kild *Orlando*, and cut off his head:
  I am his ghost, that up and downe must passe,
  In this tormenting hell for ever led,
  To be a fearfull sample and a just,
  To all such fooles as put in love their trust.

103

Thus wandring still in wayes that have no way,
  He hapt againe to light upon the cave,
  Where (in remembrance of their pleasant play)
  Medoro did that epigram ingrave.
  To see the stones againe, his woes display,
  And her ill name, and his ill hap deprave,
  Did on the sudden all his sence inrage,
  With hate, with fury, with revenge and rage.

104

Straightwayes he draweth forth his fatall blade,
  And hewes the stones, to heav'n the shivers flee,
  Accursed was that fountaine, cave and shade,
  The arbor and the flowres and ev'ry tree:
  Orlando of all places havocke made,
  Where he those names together joyn'd may see,
  Yea to the spring he did perpetuall hurt,
  By filling it with leaves, boughs, stones and durt.

105

And having done this foolish franticke feate,
  He layes him downe all weary on the ground,
  Distemper'd in his bodie with much heate,
  In mind with paines that no tongue can expound,
  Three dayes he doth not sleepe, nor drinke, nor eate,
  But lay with open eyes as in a sound.
  The fourth with rage, and not with reason waked,
  He rents his clothes, and runs about starke naked.

106

His helmet here he flings, his poulderns there;
  He casts away his curats and his shield:
  His sword he throws away, he cares not where,
  He scatters all his armor in the field:
  No ragge about his bodie he doth beare,
  As might from cold or might from shame him shield,
  And save he left behind this fatall blade,
  No doubt he had therewith great havocke made.

107

But his surpassing force did so exceed,
  All common men, that neither sword nor bill,
  Nor any other weapon he did need,
  Meere strength suffic'd him to do what he will,
  He rootes up trees as one would root a weed:
  And ev'n as birders laying nets with skill,
  Pare slender thornes away with easie strokes,
  So he did play with ashes, elmes and okes.

108

The heardmen and the shepheards that did heare,
  The hideous noise and unacquainted sound,
  With feare and wonder great approched neare,
  To see, and know, what was hereof the ground.
  But now I must cut off this treatise heare,
  Lest this my booke do grow beyond his bound;
  And if you take some pleasure in this text,
  I will go forward with it in the next.

THE TWENTY-FOVRTH BOOKE OF

ORLANDO FVRIOSO

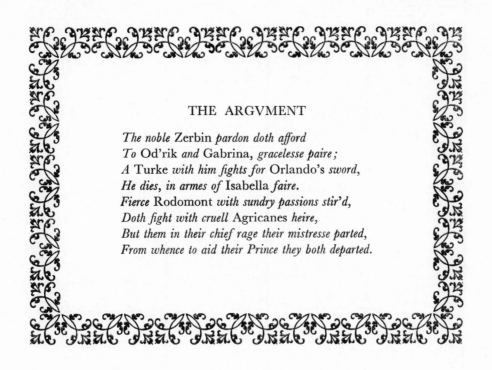

THE ARGVMENT

The noble Zerbin *pardon doth afford*
To Od'rik *and* Gabrina, *gracelesse paire;*
A Turke *with him fights for* Orlando's *sword,*
He dies, in armes of Isabella *faire.*
Fierce Rodomont *with sundry passions stir'd,*
Doth fight with cruell Agricanes *heire,*
But them in their chief rage their mistresse parted,
From whence to aid their Prince they both departed.

ORLANDO FVRIOSO
THE TWENTY-FOVRTH BOOKE

1

Who so shall set on Cupids snares his foot,
  Must seeke to draw it backe, least it be caught,
And madnes meer, in love to overshoot,
  The fool hath felt, the wise hath ever taught,
And though in all alike it take not root,
  Yet all shall find that love's a thing of naught,
For sure it is an open signe of madnesse,
To have anothers pleasure breed thy sadnesse.

2

Now though effects prove not in all alike,
  Yet all are mad in sort, all go astray,
As in a wildernesse where men do seek,
  And more and more in seeking lose their way,
Wherefore let no man this my wish mislike,
  In whom fond love shall carie long the sway,
I wish for due reward such doting dolts,
Like wilfull prisners, store of iron bolts.

3

Some man perhap will say, what soft, my friend,
  You spie our faults, in your own errors blind;
And true it is, yet speak I to this end,
  To bring us both into a better mind.
As for my selfe, I hope ere long to mend,
  And from these bonds in time my selfe unwind:
Though it had tane in me such root, I proove it,
As hard 'tis on the sudden to remoove it.

4

I shew'd you in the book that went before,
  By what mishap *Orlando* waxed mad,
And lost not onely care of vertues lore,
  But reason, wit, and all the sense he had:
His armor he disperst, his clothes he tore,
  The very clothes wherewith his corps was clad:
And though he wander'd all unarm'd and naked,
Yet at his presence all the country quaked.

5

The countrimen that heard the noise aloof,
  Of trees, that with their fall made no small crack:
Came neare, and saw by plaine and open proof,
  His monstrous strength, by their so monstrous wrack;
And straight they found it best for their behoof,
  With all the hast they could to get them back;
For those he caught he did this lesson teach,
To keep aloof from out a mad mans reach.

6

Away they fled, but he pursu'd so fast,
  That some he caught, and some surpris'd with feare,
Stood still (as oft it happens) all agast,
  Not knowing how to hide themselves, nor where:
Some other ploughmen seeing what had past,
  Thought it but little wit to tarie there,
But clim'd (for feare) their houses and their churches,
Not trusting strength of elmes, of beech, and burches.

7

Among the rest he takes one by his heel,
  And with his head knocks out anothers braine,
Which caused both of them such paine to feel,
  As till doomes day they never shall complaine,
Another with his fist he made to reel,
  Till paine it selfe made him past sense of paine,
And when the men fled all away affeard,
Then with like rage he set upon their heard.

8

The voice of men, the bellowings of beast,
  About the country rais'd so great a sound,
As might have well been heard five leagues at least,
  And all the people straight were raised round;
Each man providing (as he could) the best,
  And for the present time might then be found,
With bows, with bils, with staves, & pikes, & prongs
To be reveng'd on these outragious wrongs.

9

Look how the waves are driv'n by western blast,
  And one and one, do rise still more and more,
Vntill their force so great be at the last,
  They sprinkle all the banks, and beat the shore;
So now these country folk came in so fast,
  By two, and three, a dozen, and a score;
Till at the last they grew so great a number,
Their very multitude themselves did cumber.

10

But when they saw their force could do no good,
  And that his skin so strange protection had,
That though they smote thereon, they drew no blood,
  They thought that they might worse be thought then
To fight with one that all them so withstood,   (mad,
  Wherefore they parted home dismaid and sad,
The mad man went unto the nearest village,
Although he cared not for spoile or pillage.

11

And finding no man there, nor small, nor great,
  For all were fled away from thence for aw;
  As famine forc'd him, he sought out some meat,
  And were it fine or course, the first he saw,
  In greedy sort he doth devoure and eat,
  Not caring if it rosted were or raw;
  And when thus homely he had tane repast,
  About the country bedlam-like he past.

12

He scares both man and beast without regard,
  He takes swift goats and fallow deere in chase,
  Somtimes a Lion fierce, a Bore, a Pard,
  He kils by strength and swiftnesse of his pace.
  At last he came whereas a knight did guard
  The passage of a bridge, and by the place
  Had built a towre of no small work and charge,
  As shall be show'd hereafter more at large.

13

Now must I tell what hap *Zerbino* had,
  Who with faire *Isabell* together rode.
  Along that place where this good Earle fell mad;
  But by the way, these two made some abode,
  Where they beheld two men in armour clad,
  That drive a horse that bare a wofull lode,
  A knight a prisner, to *Zerbino* known,
  That had been once a servant of his own.

14

This prisner *Oderike* of *Biskie* hight,
  In whom the Prince had put so great a trust,
  He made chiefe choice of him as of a knight,
  That of his promise would be firm and just:
  But he (fond beast) esteeming small delight,
  And fruitlesse hope of his unbridled lust,
  Above his sacred oath and promis'd fealtie,
  Would have defloured her against all lealtie.

15

Faire *Isabell* by hap ev'n then was telling,
  How in the boat she desperately was sav'd;
  And having scap'd the stormy seas and swelling,
  How trecherously this wretch himselfe behav'd,
  That (had not outlawes thereabout been dwelling)
  He would have forc'd her unto that he crav'd,
  And ev'n as these, or some such words she said,
  She saw the man she spake of captive led.

16

Those two that led the wicked *Od'ricke* ti'd,
  Knew well their Lord when as they came in view,
  Both by the Lady that was by his side,
  And by the rampant Lion red of hew,
  Born by the Prince, not for a shew of pride,
  But his as from his predecessors dew,
  They light, and with a courtsie to the ground,
  And cap in hand, salute their Lord thus found.

17

Zerbino knew and cal'd them both by name,
  Corebo tone, *Almonio* tother hight,
  Which two with *Isabell* from *Bayon* came,
  In conduct of that most unworthy wight.
  And straight *Almonio* thus his speech doth frame,
  My Lord (said he) I shall to you recite
  Some little part of that unpleasant story,
  That till this houre had made my heart full sory.

18

Sith (thank'd be God) this Lady here doth live,
  Who felt these stormes, and therein chiefly smarted,
  I know that she thereof could notice give,
  And hath ere this to you the same imparted;
  I onely shall declare what did me grieve,
  And what had hapned since from her I parted,
  What time by this vile wretches lewd intent,
  For horse and men to *Rochell* I was sent.

19

And as I went, so back I turn'd in hast,
  With men and horse as good as I could get,
  To seek them out mine eyes about I cast,
  But yet mine eyes on them I could not set,
  Their track I found, and following that full fast,
  It brought me to a wood whereas I met
  My fellow *Coreb*, panting then and groning,
  This caitife cursing and himselfe bemoning.

20

He told me how he (fighting in defence
  Of *Isabella*) was so sorely wounded,
  That from that place he had not stirred since,
  And how with bleeding much he oft had sounded,
  At which report I took so great offence,
  That in my wits I was wellnigh confounded:
  And to revenge my heart so sharp was whet,
  That *Corebs* danger quite I did forget.

21

But when in vaine this wretch I long had sought,
  To *Coreb* I returned back againe,
  Who was so weak and low by bleeding brought,
  That scant the life did in his limbs remaine:
  For which his wofull state I took great thought,
  As one that deem'd it fitter to ordaine
  Some Priests and Friers, buriall to procure him,
  Then Surgeons or Physitions that might cure him.

22

Yet him unto the town at last I caried,
  Where by such help our friendly host procur'd,
  It pleased God, *Corebo* not miscaried,
  But of his grievous hurts was soundly cur'd;
  Which done, no longer in those parts we taried,
  But being there by sundry men assur'd,
  That *Odricke* in *Alfonsos* court was biding,
  We thither went to heare of him some tiding.

23

And there I challeng'd *Odricke* face to face,
  And by the noble justice of the King,
  And chiefly (as I deem) by Gods great grace,
  That onely rules and governes ev'ry thing,
  I took him prisner in the present place,
  From whence alive I did him hither bring.
  For why that king that heard his great offence,
  Did grant us liberty to bring him thence.

24

I might have slaine him, as he well deserv'd,
  But yet I chused rather of the twaine,
  Vnto your doom to have his life reserv'd,
  That you might point him death with worthy paine,
  And much I joy that luck so well hath serv'd,
  That we so safe have found your grace againe:
  And much more I rejoyce, if much more may be,
  At health and welfare of this noble Lady.

25

Thus much *Almonio* said, and then did cease,
  Expecting what *Zerbino* would reply,
  Who all the while stood still and held his peace,
  And view'd the prisner with an heedfull eye,
  And much it did his griefe of mind increase,
  To think a friend could stray so farre awry.
  Then sighing deep; what *Odricke* is this true,
  Wherewith (quoth he) *Almonio* chargeth you?

26

The caitive humbly prostrate on the ground,
  Forgive my Lord (said he) your servants crime,
  What wight on earth can void of fault be found?
  What Saint is such as doth not sin sometime?
  'Tween good and bad this diffrence sole is found,
  That good men sin but seeld, and mend betime,
  The bad man (making scruple none or question)
  Yeelds wilfully to ev'ry lewd suggestion.

27

If you to me some fortresse had committed,
  And I the same had wittingly betraid,
  I graunt such fault were not to be remitted,
  But if I had with force been overlaid,
  Then sure I am my case would have been pitied,
  At least no sin should to my charge be laid:
  For when the enemy is once the stronger,
  'Tis vaine to make resistance any longer.

28

Ev'n so my Lord, my faith I ought to guard,
  No other then a fortresse or a hold,
  Put in my charge with carefull watch and ward,
  As long as strength will serve me it to hold:
  And so I kept my faith with due regard,
  Nor was I any way to be controld
  Vntill at last I was so strong assail'd,
  That faith gave place, and fancy then prevail'd.

29

Thus *Odricke* said, and what he said beside,
  I doubt it somwhat tedious were to tell,
  As namely, none so great assault could bide,
  That love all other passions doth excell,
  But sure if it were ever plainly tride,
  That humble speech doth often wrath expell;
  Now *Odricke* found of lowly words the fruit,
  That holp him to obtaine so hard a suit.

30

Zerbino stood a while in mind confus'd,
  To punish or to pardon his offence,
  Somtime his thoughts all clemency refus'd,
  Somtime the love and service done long since,
  Asswag'd his wrath, and tothers fault excus'd,
  And mov'd him with his folly to dispence:
  And still as rage did kindle fire of wrath,
  To quench it mercy store of water hath.

31

Now while in this same doubt *Zerbino* staid,
  Behold by hap *Gabrina* there was brought,
  She that of late had this good Prince betraid,
  And had to him so great a danger wrought;
  Her horse that heard where other horses naid,
  Came to the noise, as nature had them taught,
  Against her will she wanting force to sway him,
  And having lost the reines wherewith to stay him.

32

The beastly wretch cri'd help, and out alas,
  While thus her horse ran over fields and lands,
  But when the *Scottish* Prince saw who she was,
  And how she thither came he understands,
  He gave God thanks that so had brought to passe,
  To give those two at once into his hands,
  Which two for their misdeeds above the rest,
  He had great cause to malice and detest.

33

And after he had made a little pause,
  Vnto his servants turning thus he said,
  Sirs, *Odricke* shall not die, although by lawes
  His fact deserves no lesse uprightly waid,
  For sith he saith affection was the cause,
  Content I am, on love the fault be laid,
  The sin to which a man by love is driven,
  So much the rather ought to be forgiven.

34

The force of strong affection hath ere this
  Distemper'd, yea and somtime overthrown
  A wiser and a staider head then his,
  As is to me by mine experience known,
  And that herein he did his duty misse,
  I must confesse, the fault was part mine own,
  That gave to him such charge and did not know
  How quickly flaming heat can kindle tow.

T

35

Then to the caitive *Odricke* thus he spake,
  Here I forgive thee, and do thee enlarge,
  But yet the penance I will have thee take,
  Is this, to take this woman in thy charge,
  And sweare to me thou shalt her not forsake
  For one whole yeare, but this thine oath discharge
  And that thou shalt if any would offend her,
  Do thy dever, and unto death defend her.

36

This was the punishment on him he laid,
  And certainly this same had been enow,
  If so the circumstance were duly waigh'd,
  And *Odericke* had right perform'd his vow.
  For why? so many men she had betraid,
  And done such sinnes ev'n from her youth till now,
  That wheresoere they had together travel'd,
  In her defence he must at last be gravel'd.

37

Thus *Zerbin* let this wicked couple go,
  And thinks sufficiently to plague them both,
  But sweares if ever he did hap to know,
  That he therein should violate his troth,
  His flesh should serve as feeding for the crow,
  A fit reward for such as break their oath;
  Thus went this honest couple thence together,
  Lurking in corners, wandring here and thither.

38

But what in th'end of these same two became,
  I know not, and mine author doth not write,
  I onely heard a speech, or flying fame,
  That when they once were quite from *Zerbins* sight
  Odricke (to shun the quarrels and the shame,
  That by her company on him might light)
  Did hang her up, and after in short space,
  Almonio made him run the selfe same race.

39

The Prince that faine some tidings would have heard,
  Of that Earle *Palladine*, who tother day,
  Fought hand to hand with lofty *Mandricard*,
  Vntill his rainlesse horse bare him away,
  Doth travell on his way to *Paris* ward,
  Though faire and soft, and lingring by the way,
  And his two servants he doth send before,
  And kept with him his Lady, and no more.

40

They rode not farre but that they found the cave,
  And that same pleasant arbor and the spring,
  At which *Medoro* us'd such sport to have,
  With that faire daughter of the *Indian* king;
  Where she their names together did ingrave,
  All ti'd with truelove knots (a wondrous thing)
  They look, and see the stones, the words and letters
  All cut and mangled in a thousand fitters.

41

And as they mus'd hereon, they might espie
  Orlandos armour, and his famous blade,
  High *Durindana* on the ground to lie,
  That sword that first for *Hector* had been made,
  They saw where *Brigliador* was feeding by
  Vpon the grasse amid the pleasant shade:
  This sight did make them both exceeding sad,
  Yet little did they deem that th'Earle was mad.

42

Had they but seen one little drop of blood,
  They would have surely thought he had been slaine,
  But while in this most carefull doubt they stood,
  Behold there came a country silly swaine,
  That with no little speed ran through the wood,
  And scap'd the mad mans fury with great paine;
  He told them how a man bestraught of senses,
  Had done these outrages and great offences.

43

And further gave them perfect information,
  And told each circumstance at their request:
  Zerbino standeth still in admiration,
  And (as the manner is) himselfe he blest,
  And with great griefe of mind and lamentation,
  He takes the sword and armour, and the rest,
  And *Isabella* helpeth them to gather,
  And so they lay them on a heap together.

44

This while by hap came by faire *Fiordeliege*,
  Who (as I told before) with pensive heart
  Went to seek out her loved Lord and Liege,
  I mean *Orlandos* friend, King *Brandimart*,
  Who leaving *Paris* in the wofull siege,
  To seek *Orlando* did from thence depart,
  Till *Atlant* to that cage him did intice,
  Which he had fram'd by magicall device.

45

The which inchantment being now defeated,
  By good *Astolfos* value and his skill,
  And all the knights as I before repeated,
  At liberty to go which way they will,
  King *Brandimart*, though much in mind he fretted,
  To think how long in vaine he had stood still,
  Back unto *Paris* ward his course he turn'd,
  Yet missing her the way that he return'd.

46

Thus (as I said) faire *Fiordeliege* by chance,
  Saw much of that which hap'd, and heard the rest,
  How that same worthy *Palladine* of *France*,
  With inward griefe of mind, and thought opprest,
  Or by some other great and strange mischance,
  Went like a man with some ill sprite possest,
  And she likewise enquiring of the peasant,
  Heard all the circumstance, a tale unpleasant.

47

Zerbino being farre from any town,
   Hangs all *Orlandos* armour on a Pine,
   Like to a Penon, and lest any clown
   Or peasant vile should take a thing so fine,
   He writes upon the tree, let none take down
   This armour of *Orlando Palladine;*
   As who should say, if any man attempt it,
   Orlando would ere long cause him repent it.

48

And having brought this worthy work to end,
   And ready now to take his journey hence,
   Fierce *Mandricard* hapt thither to descend,
   And when he saw the tree, he ask'd of whence
   Those weapons were? which known, he doth intend
   To take away good *Durindana* thence,
   He steps unto the tree, and takes the sword,
   Nor so content, he adds this spitefull word.

49

Ah sir (quoth he) this hap doth make me glad,
   My claime unto this sword is not unknown,
   And though before I no possession had,
   Yet now I lawfully seize on mine own:
   Alas poor fool, and doth he faine him mad?
   And hath away his sword and armour thrown,
   Because he was not able to maintaine it,
   And was afeard that I by force would gaine it?

50

Zerbino crieth out, what? peace for shame,
   Take not his sword, or think not I will beare it,
   If by the coat of *Hector* so you came,
   You stale it, and unworthy are to weare it:
   Tush (quoth the *Pagan*) I will beare that blame,
   As for your threatning, do not think I feare it:
   Thus tones sharp answers, tothers sharp replying
   Made them to fall to termes of flat defying.

51

And either shewing signes of plaine hostilitie,
   Prepares the tother fiercely to invade,
   Zerbino with his skill and great agilitie,
   His party good against the *Pagan* made,
   And voided all the blowes with much facilitie,
   Though having great disvantage in the blade,
   And in that armour massie so and strong,
   That in times past to *Hector* did belong.

52

Look how a Grewnd that finds a sturdy Bore,
   Amid the field far straying from the heard,
   Doth run about, behind him and before,
   Because of his sharp tusks he is afeard.
   So *Zerbin* that had seen oft heretofore
   That blade, and of the force thereof had heard,
   With heedfull eye to shun the blowes he watched,
   Because he was in weapons overmatched.

53

Thus warily this worthy Prince did fight,
   And though by heedfull skill he scaped oft
   The furious blowes of this *Tartarian* knight,
   Yet lo at last one blow came from aloft,
   And *Durindan* so heavy did alight,
   As pierced through the hard unto the soft,
   A finger deep, and went in length a span,
   Down from the place where first the wound began.

54

The Prince so earnest was, he felt no smart,
   Yet ran the blood out of the brest amaine,
   And of his curats all the former part
   With crimson streame of blood it did distaine:
   So have I seen her hand that to mine heart,
   Hath been a cause of anguish and much paine,
   When she a purple seam or flower hath drawn,
   In silver kirtle, or in sleeve of lawn.

55

The wound was great, but yet did greater show,
   Which sight faire *Isabella* much amated,
   The Prince that seemed not the same to know,
   With force increased rather then abated,
   Vpon the *Pagans* brow gave such a blow,
   As would (no doubt) have made him checkt & mated,
   Save that (as I to you before rehearst)
   His armour was not easie to be pierst.

56

The blow was such as caused him to reel,
   And on his styrups staggringly he stood,
   Had not his armour been of passing steel,
   The blow would sure have entred to the blood,
   The grievous paine that he thereof did feel
   Did put him in so fierce a raging mood,
   So that for all *Zerbinos* skill and sleight,
   He wounded him in places sev'n or eight.

57

Which when his loving *Isabella* saw,
   She went to *Doralice*, and her doth pray,
   The fury of her husband to withdraw,
   And joyne with her to part the bloudy fray,
   Who both because she was in feare and aw,
   Lest yet the Prince her spouse indanger may,
   And for of nature kind she was and meek,
   Or that good motion she doth not mislike.

58

Thus those two Ladies this fierce battell parted,
   In which the Prince received many a wound,
   Though being (as he was) most valiant hearted,
   He never gave the *Pagan* inch of ground:
   From thence each couple presently departed,
   Fierce *Mandricard* to *Pagan* camp was bound,
   To *Paris* ward the Prince, but driv'n to stay,
   By reason of his bleeding by the way.

59

Dame *Fiordeliege* that stood this while aloof,
  And saw how *Mandricard* prevailed had,
  And how the Prince had fought with evill proof,
  Departed thence all sorrowfull and sad,
  Reviling *Mandricard* with just reproof,
  That of this evill gotten sword was glad,
  And wished that her husband *Brandimart*,
  Had present been to take *Zerbinos* part.

60

But as she travel'd homward to the camp,
  She saw the noble *Palladine* of *France*,
  Not like himselfe, but of another stamp,
  Besmear'd and nak'd as anticks wont to dance:
  Quite was extinguished the shining lamp,
  Of vertue bright that did his name advance:
  This fight in *Fiordeliege* much sorrow bred,
  But tell me now how good *Zerbino* sped.

61

Who on his way with painfull steps proceeding,
  With *Isabella* onely and no more,
  His former taken hurts still freshly bleeding,
  Which now with cold were stiffe and waxed sore,
  And yet this griefe in him the rest exceeding,
  To think that sword of which I spake before,
  Should mauger him, be by a *Turke* possest,
  I say this griev'd him more then all the rest.

62

Now gan the dreadfull pangs of death assaile him,
  So great a streame of blood his wound had drain'd,
  His eyes were dim, his speech began to faile him,
  Strong hart to yeeld to weak limbs was constrain'd:
  What can poore *Isabella* do but waile him?
  She blam'd the heav'ns and fates that had ordain'd,
  Her to escape such dangers and such harmes,
  And now to have her deare die in her armes.

63

Zerbino though he scant could draw his breath,
  Yet hearing her lamenting in such fashion,
  Doth ope his closed lips, and thus he saith,
  Both shewing then, and moving much compassion:
  So might I (my deare love) ev'n after death,
  Be deare to thee as I do feel great passion,
  To think when as my death frō hence shall reave me,
  Alone in wo and danger I shall leave thee.

64

Might I have left thee in some safer place,
  I should esteem my death a blessed hap,
  And that the heav'ns had giv'n me speciall grace,
  To end my life in thy beloved lap,
  Now grieves it me to think of thine hard case,
  In what a world of woes I thee shall wrap,
  When I must die, and leave thee here alone,
  And none to help thy harm, or heare thy mone.

65

To this the wofull *Isabell* replies,
  With watred eyes, and heart surpriz'd with anguish,
  Her face to his, and joyning her faire eyes
  To his that like a wither'd rose did languish,
  No thought (said she) my deare in thee arise
  For me, for know I neither do nor can wish
  Thee to surviue, I will be thine for ever,
  Life could not, and death shall not us dissever.

66

No sooner shall thy breath thy brest forsake,
  But I will follow thee I care not whither,
  Griefe or this sword of me an end shall make,
  And if some stranger after shall come hither,
  I hope of us such pitie he will take,
  To lay our bodies in one grave together:
  This said, about his neck her arms she clasp'd,
  And drawes the fainting breath that oft he gasp'd.

67

The Prince inforcing his sorefeebled voice,
  Saith thus, I thee conjure my sole delight,
  By that deare love that made me first thy choice,
  And thee from native soile to take thy flight,
  If ever in my love thou didst rejoyce,
  If to command thee I have any right,
  That thou still live (as long as God shall graunt thee)
  And not despaire how ever fortune daunt thee.

68

Th'almighty God from danger and from ill
  Hath hitherto, and will (I trust) thee save;
  Ev'n as he sent that noble Earle to kill
  Those caitives that did keep thee in their cave,
  And sav'd thee from the *Biskins* wicked will,
  First having thee preserv'd from salt sea wave,
  Live then my deare, and trust in him above,
  And while you live be mindfull of my love.

69

These latter words his lips had scantly past,
  When death unto his heart was softly crept;
  And as the lamp goeth out when oyle doth wast,
  So quietly the noble *Zerbin* slept:
  What tongue can tell how sore she was agast,
  How she lamented, wailed, mourn'd and wept,
  To her own eyes and faire haire doing force,
  When as she saw her deare a senslesse corse?

70

And griefe had set her in so great a rage,
  With *Zerbins* sword she thinks an end to make
  Of her own life, her sorrow to asswage,
  Neglecting those last words *Zerbino* spake:
  But lo, a certaine saintlike personage,
  That sword from hand, that thought from heart doth
  A certaine godly hermit and devout,   (take,
  That was by hap abiding thereabout.

71

Who came and said, oh damsell leave despaire,
  Mans nature weak, and womens sex is fraile,
  Feare him that rules both heav'n, and earth, and aire,
  Who saith the word, and his word cannot faile,
  That those that unto him for help repaire,
  And put their trust in him, shall never quaile:
  Then shew'd he her, to prove his saying true,
  Examples out of Scriptures old and new.

72

Of saintlike women that in time of old,
  Their lives in prayer and chastity had spent;
  And further to the damsell faire he told,
  And prov'd and shew'd by reasons evident,
  That worldly things are vaine and have no hold,
  Alone in God is joy and true content:
  In fine, he makes to her this godly motion,
  Her future life to spend in true devotion.

73

His godly speech by help of heav'nly grace,
  Powr'd in her heart by high divine infusion,
  Wrought such effect, and found so great a place,
  She ceast to seek or work her own confusion:
  But leaving the profession of her race,
  Profest her selfe a *Christen* in conclusion;
  She gave her selfe to praier and pure divinity,
  And vow'd to God her life and her virginity.

74

Yet did she not remove out of her thought,
  The fervent love *Zerbino* had her born,
  But by the hermits help the corse she brought,
  And thinks it sin to leave it so forlorn,
  And in some village thereabout she bought
  Sweet balmes to fill the flesh all cut and torn,
  Then in a Cypres coffin she doth close it,
  Not being yet resolv'd where to dispose it.

75

That aged sire, though being wise and staid,
  Yet would not trust in his own stay so well,
  To carry such a faire and goodly maid
  To sojourn with him in his little cell,
  'Twere perill great (thus to himselfe he said)
  That fire and straw should nigh together dwell,
  Wherefore he means to *Province* her to carie,
  And there to place her in a monestarie.

76

But as he thitherward with *Isbell* went,
  And by the way devoutly did her teach,
  All things unto religion pertinent,
  And of the same most learnedly did preach:
  Behold a *Pagan* fierce with foule intent,
  This purpose and their journey doth impeach,
  As I shall shew more largely afterward,
  Now back I must return to *Mandricard*.

77

Who having ended that same cruell fight,
  In which the worthiest Prince alive was slaine,
  Soon after by a shady bank did light,
  And turn'd his horse a grazing on the plaine,
  Dame *Doralice* in whom he took delight,
  Alone with him in that place did remaine,
  When looking sodainly by chance aside,
  An armed knight come toward them she spide.

78

She guest, but yet she knew not by the view,
  Who it might be, untill she spi'd her page
  That came with him, then certainly she knew
  'Twas *Rodomont*, full of revenge and rage,
  Wherefore unto her knight she nearer drew,
  And said (my Lord) mine honour I dare gage,
  That yon is *Rodomont* mine ancient lover,
  Who thinks by fight from you me to recover.

79

Look how the Falcon in the aire doth mount,
  When she espies a Bittor or a Hern,
  So when this Prince espied *Rodomount*,
  And by his hast his fury did discern,
  Like one that made of conquest full account,
  He starteth up with visage grim and stern:
  Straight arm'd and hors'd he is, his foe to meet,
  In hand the reines, in styrups are his feet.

80

When as the tone the tother came so neare,
  As each might hearken what the tother said,
  Fierce *Rodomont* spake lowd as he might heare,
  With threatning gesture both of hand and head:
  And said, be sure Ile make thee buy it deare,
  That with a short vaine pleasure hast been led,
  To do to one so foule and open wrong,
  That can and will it wreak on thee ere long.

81

The *Tartar* Prince that for him little car'd,
  Made answer thus, in vaine you me do threat:
  Poore boyes with words, or women may be scar'd,
  Not I that fight as willingly as eat:
  Prove when you please, I am not unprepar'd,
  At any time for any warlike feat,
  On horse, on foot, in field, or in the list,
  I shall be ready; try me when you list.

82

Thus words bred wrath, and wrath engendred blowes,
  And blowes increas'd their sharp avenging will,
  Ev'n as the wind that first but calmly blowes,
  But after more and more increasing still,
  At last it trees and houses overthrowes,
  And seas and lands with tempest it doth fill:
  So cruell grew the fight them two between,
  Whose match might hardly in the world be seen.

83

Their hearts were stout, so were their bodies strong,
  Desire to win in both alike was great,
  One doth maintaine, tother would venge his wrong,
  And love their fury equally doth whet,
  In equall peise the fight endured long,
  Nor each of tother any gaine could get,
  But each of them so firmly kept his ground,
  As if each inch thereof had cost a pound.

84

Among an hundred blowes the *Tartar* smit,
  Of which small hurt to *Rodomont* did rise,
  Yet one at last so heavily did hit
  Vpon his helmet, over both his eyes;
  His senses all were so amaz'd with it,
  He thought he saw more starres then are in skies,
  And almost down he was ev'n in her sight,
  For whom he first began this cruell fight.

85

But as a strong and justly temper'd bow
  Of *Pymount* steel, the more you do it bend,
  Vpon recoile doth give the bigger blow,
  And doth with greater force the quarrell send,
  Ev'n so the *Sarzan* king that stoop'd so low,
  As highly to revenge it doth intend,
  And to acquit himselfe of this disgrace,
  He striketh at the *Tartar* Princes face.

86

So fierce he strake in this so furious mood,
  An inch or little more above his sight,
  That save those armes of *Hector* was so good,
  No doubt that blow had finish'd all the fight,
  But so aston'd therewith the *Tartar* stood,
  He could not tell if it were noon or night:
  And while in this amazement he abode,
  The tother ceaseth not to lay on load.

87

The *Tartars* horse that saw the glittering blade,
  That *Rodomont* about his head so tost,
  Did start aside, and with a turn he made,
  Rescu'd his master, sore to his own cost:
  Down with the blow fals this unluckie jade,
  And with his starting he his life hath lost:
  To ward his head he wanted *Hectors* shield,
  And therefore dead he tumbleth on the field.

88

Now came his master to himselfe againe,
  Inflam'd with greater anger then before,
  To see his horse so pitifully slaine,
  But *Rodomont* forbeares him ne'er the more.
  But spurrs on him, and thinks with fury maine,
  To beare him down, but he so strongly bore
  The push, and thrust withall *Frontino* back,
  He made his master glad to leave his back.

89

Thus now with minds more alien'd from all peace,
  In eager sort the combat is renew'd,
  To strike, to thrust each other doth not cease,
  In hope with bloud their swords to have embrew'd,
  Fell rancor, wrath and pride do still increase,
  And death of one or both must have ensew'd,
  Ere either of them would from thence have started,
  Had not a certaine messenger them parted.

90

One that had travel'd all about the cost,
  To seek them out, to ask their help and aid,
  To raise the siege, that by the *Christen* host,
  Vnto the camp of *Agramant* was laid:
  Yet though he came in peace, and eke in post,
  To speak to them at first he was affraid,
  And though his office were sufficient warrant,
  Yet to themselves he dares not do his arrant.

91

But seeing *Doralice*, to her he told,
  How *Agramant*, *Marsilie*, *Stordylan*,
  And others more, like men pent up in hold,
  Were in great danger to be kild or tane,
  Wherefore he wisheth her for to unfold
  Thus much to them, that sought each others bane:
  And to perswade them to so good accord,
  As they might go to help their soveraigne Lord.

92

She that a woman was of passing sprite,
  And knew that neither of them would offend her,
  Stept them between, and charg'd them stay the fight,
  As they their honour and her love did tender,
  And help their king that is in wofull plight,
  And end this fray begun of cause so slender,
  At least defer so long to trie this quarrell,
  Till *Agramant* their king were out of perill.

93

When she thus much to them declared had,
  Then doth the messenger declare the rest,
  And other strong perswasions he doth add,
  And doth expound to them their kings request,
  Alledging that their absence made him sad,
  That but they help, the camp would be distrest,
  And that if they to rescue him neglected,
  A present ruine were to be expected.

94

With his report and with her strong perswasion,
  The hardy knights the combat do defer,
  Till *Agramant* be freed from this invasion,
  And all the *Christen* forces moved are,
  Thus of this friendly truce she is occasion,
  That first was causer of their deadly war,
  To her they bind themselves by solemne oth,
  That untill then they will be quiet both.

95

There *Discord* was and *Pride*, and what they may,
  They do this league to interrupt and break,
But at that time *Love* bare so great a sway,
That to withstand him, they were both too weak:
In vaine it was to argue and gainsay,
When once dame *Doralice* the word did speak,
By her perswasion firmly they agreed,
Like friends upon their journey to proceed.

96

One onely want there was, that let them sore,
  Which was that *Mandricardos* horse was dead,
But lo ev'n then came thither *Brygliadore*,
That since his masters madnesse there had fed,
Full glad the Prince of *Tartar* was therefore,
Of such a horse so quickly to be sped:
But least my tale with tediousnesse molest you,
I wish you lay aside the book, and rest you.

THE TWENTY-FIFT BOOKE OF
ORLANDO FVRIOSO

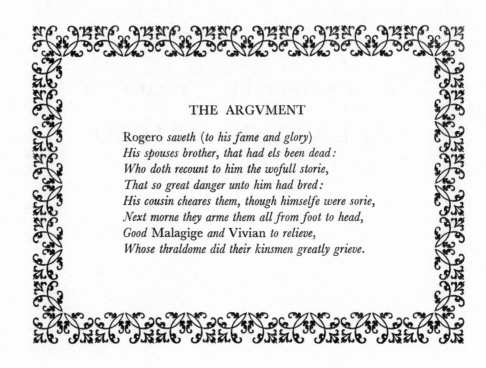

THE ARGVMENT

Rogero *saveth (to his fame and glory)*
His spouses brother, that had els been dead:
Who doth recount to him the wofull storie,
That so great danger unto him had bred:
His cousin cheares them, though himselfe were sorie,
Next morne they arme them all from foot to head,
Good Malagige *and* Vivian *to relieve,*
Whose thraldome did their kinsmen greatly grieve.

ORLANDO FVRIOSO
THE TWENTY-FIFT BOOK

1

The strife is great that growes in youthfull mind,
  When honour falls at variance with affection,
  Nor could it yet be known or well defin'd,
  Which passion keepes the tother in subjection,
  For both allure, both do our judgements blind,
  And both corrupt the heart with strong infection:
  Yet lo sometimes these hurts procure our weal,
  Ev'n as one poyson doth another heale.

2

For here you see these princes that of late,
  Strave fiercely tone the tother to subdue,
  Agreed to respit this their sharp debate,
  And to repaire unto the *Turkish* crew,
  To succour *Agramants* distressed state,
  To whom they ought in duty to be true,
  And yet herein love claimeth halfe the praise,
  For she commanded them to go their waies.

3

And on they went without more disagreeing,
  Faire *Doralice* with these her servants twaine,
  The tone in suit, one in possession being,
  And yet as then in concord they remaine:
  At last they came unto a place, where seeing
  Foure knights themselves did solace on a plaine,
  (Of which two were unarm'd, two armour bare)
  With them a Lady was of beauty rare.

4

With these a while they staid, but who these were,
  And what they did, and whither then they went,
  A little while to tell I do forbeare,
  For to *Rogero* now my tale is meant,
  Who would no more the shield enchanted beare,
  But in the well did drown it, with intent
  That men might know his valiant deeds of armes,
  Were done by force of vertue, not of charmes.

5

He scant had gone a mile or little more,
  From this same well, but that he met a post
  From *Agramant*, of which there went good store,
  The Captaines to recall unto the host,
  He told him how the king (besieged sore,
  And like (if succour come not) to be lost)
  Commanded him as his true Lord and Liege,
  To come without delay to raise the siege.

6

Much was *Rogero* with the message mov'd,
  And diverse passions strave within his mind,
  He faine would have his Princes siege remov'd,
  Yet loth he was to leave his love behind;
  But be his doing praised or reprov'd,
  He was so to the present cause inclin'd,
  First with his guide he goes to stay the slaughter,
  Of him that had deflowr'd *Marsilios* daughter.

7

They came unto the place an houre ere night,
  Where this same execution should be done,
  A castle that belong'd to *Charles* of right,
  But late the *Spanish* king the same had wonne,
  And kept it in the midst of *France* by might,
  By count'nance of the great *Trajanos* sonne:
  Rogero commeth in, and none deni'd him,
  Because they knew the damsell that did guide him.

8

There first he saw prepar'd a flaming fire,
  In which they meant to burne the wofull youth,
  He thought so small a sinne did not require
  Such punishment, no more it doth in truth:
  But when he markt his face and his attire,
  And heard and saw the manner of his ruth,
  Now sure I know (quoth he) I am not I,
  Or this is *Bradamant* that here should die.

9

Tis certaine she, I see which way it went,
  Belike while I at yonder castle staid,
  She hither came afore me, with intent
  To bring vnto the prisner here some aid,
  For which (poore soule) her self should now be **shent**,
  Yet I am glad and very well apaid,
  That I am hither come in so good season,
  To save her that should die against all reason.

10

And even with that, most furiously he flies
  Wiht naked sword upon the gazing rout,
  Who ever standeth in his way he dies,
  With so great force he hurles his blade about:
  Then straight the prisners fetters he unties,
  Nor was there one so hardie or so stout,
  That once durst make resistance or forbid it,
  No not so much as aske him why he did it.

11

As fearfull fowle that in the sunshine bright,
  Sit pruning of themselves upon a banke,
  When as a Faulcon doth among them light,
  Flie without care of order or of ranke:
  So when these caitives saw this noble Knight,
  Forthwith they from his manly presence shranke,
  So did their fearfull hearts and courage faile them,
  When as they felt *Rogero* once assaile them.

12

No marvell tho, for why *Rogeros* force
  Was not as mens that now borne later are,
  The strength of Lion, Beare, or Bull, or Horse,
  Were nothing, if with his they do compare,
  And chiefe sith now he doth himselfe inforce,
  To do as much as he or can or dare,
  Hereby from danger thinking to recover,
  Her unto whom he was professed lover.

13

Now when the youth from danger quite was freed,
  And all that sought his death away were fled,
  He thanks the author of this worthy deed,
  And thanketh her that had him thither led
  Then, when of helpe he stood in greatest need,
  When otherwise he doubtlesse had bin dead,
  And executed like a malefactor,
  Agnizing him his Lord and benefactor.

14

And furthermore he doth *Rogero* pray,
  To let him understand his name and nation;
  Rogero musing to himselfe doth say,
  What meaneth this so strange congratulation?
  In face, in shape, in gesture, in array,
  This is my love, I see no alteration,
  Yet strange it is her voice should be so changed,
  More strange that she from me is so estranged.

15

It doubtlesse is not she, for if it were,
  Could she within three houres my name forget?
  Wherefore to tell his name he doth forbeare,
  Vntill he may more perfect notice get:
  And thus he said, I have, I know not where,
  Seene you ere this, and I bethinke me yet
  Where it might be, for sure I know your face,
  Though now I have fogot the time and place.

16

Most noble sir (said tother) I agree,
  You may have seene me, though I know not when,
  I rather judge it should my sister be,
  That fights and carries armes as well as men:
  My mother at one birth bare her and me,
  And we be both so like, that now and then
  Our servants, yea our father and our mother
  Have tane us in exchange the tone for tother.

17

Chiefly since in her head she had a wound,
  For which she was constrain'd to cut her haire,
  Twere long the circumstances to expound,
  How she was hurt and heald, by whom and where,
  Since that betweene us difference none is found,
  Save sex and names that from our birth we beare,
  She *Bradamant*, I *Richardet* am cald,
  She sister, and I brother to *Renald*.

18

And further if you please, I shall you tell,
  As we do onward on our journey go,
  A strange mishap that unto me befell,
  By being tane for her not long ago;
  A hap that at the first I liked well,
  But after wrought my danger great and wo:
  Yes with good will, *Rogero* said, and than
  Yong *Richardetto* thus his tale began.

19

It happend (as in part I toucht before)
  My valiant sister passing through a wood,
  Was hurt with certaine *Sarazins* so sore,
  As had her cost almost her vitall blood,
  Which wound to cure, her tresses short she wore,
  For so as then her surgeon thought it good;
  The wound once cur'd, for which her head was pold
  Abroade to go againe she waxed bold.

20

And having traveld till the heate of day,
  All clad in armor, as her manner was,
  At noone she tooke occasion to make stay,
  Fast by a watrie streame as cleare as glasse,
  And putting off her helmet, downe she lay,
  Vpon a pleasant banke well cloth'd with grasse,
  And sleepe at last her heavie eyes did close,
  The place inviting her to take repose.

21

Now while she did there fast asleepe remaine,
  There happend to arrive unto that place,
  The daughter of *Marsilio* King of *Spaine*,
  That there by chance was hunting in the chase,
  And seeing signes of manhood very plaine,
  With that her sweet and amiable face,
  As horse, and sword, and target all of steele,
  A little amorous passion she doth feele.

22

And taking then my sister for a man,
  As by all circumstances well she might,
  She offers her all courtsie that she can,
  And askt her if in hunting she delight;
  And then to chuse a standing they began,
  And finding one far off from others sight,
  She opened more plainly that affection,
  That had her heart already in subjection.

23

And save her maiden modestie forbad,
　She would the same in words have plainly told,
　Howb'it with sighs, with rufull looks and sad,
　And silent signes she doth her griefe unfold:
　And when she thus long time discoursed had,
　Surpris'd with hope, she could no longer hold,
　But steps unto her, and gives her such a kisse,
　As that alone shewes what her meaning is.

24

My sister at the first doth thinke it strange,
　That such a sute should unto her be made,
　And finding she had tane her in exchange,
　She thinks it best (before she further wade,
　Or let the tothers humor further range)
　Tell troth, for thus she doth her selfe perswade,
　Tis better to be knowne a Ladie gentle,
　Then to be deem'd a base man and ungentle.

25

For what could be more cullen-like or base?
　Or fitter for a man were made of straw,
　Then standing in a faire yong Ladies grace,
　To shew himselfe a cuckow or a daw,
　And leese occasion both of time and place?
　My sister therefore that this ill foresaw,
　And knew she wanted that, that her should aid,
　Told her by circumstance she was a maid.

26

And thus she told her how the worthy fame,
　Hippolita and stout *Camilla* wonne,
　In deeds of armes, mov'd her her mind to frame,
　To do the like while others sow'd and sponne:
　And that she thought it to her sex no shame,
　To do as women of such worth had done;
　She told her this, in hope this would appease her,
　But this alas did so much more disease her.

27

For why the fancie was so firmly fixt,
　That in her mind she had before conceived,
　By meanes of speech had passed them betwixt,
　That sore it griev'd her to be thus deceived,
　Before, her feare with some good hope was mixt,
　But now ev'n hope it selfe was her bereaved:
　And this is one extremest point of griefe,
　Still to despaire and hope for no reliefe.

28

He that had heard her wofull plaint and mone,
　Must needs have greatly at the same bin grieved,
　Ah wo is me (she said) that I alone
　Should live in such despaire to be relieved:
　In passed times I thinke there hath bene none,
　In time to come it will not be beleeved,
　That love should make by such a strong infection,
　One woman beare another such affection.

29

O *Cupid*, if thou didst my state envie,
　And that thou hadst a mind me to torment,
　To send such paines as others more do trie,
　At least me thinke thou shouldst have bin content:
　Shall in so many ages none but I,
　Yeeld of so uncouth love such president?
　The female with the female doth not wish
　To couple, nor in beast, nor foule, nor fish.

30

I sole am found in earth, aire, sea, or fire,
　In whom so strange a wonder thou hast done,
　On me thou shewst the power of thine ire,
　And what a mighty conquest thou hast wonne.
　The wife of *Nynus* had a strange desire,
　To joyne in copulation with her sonne;
　Faire *Myrrba* by her sire was made a mother,
　And made *Adonis* both her sonne and brother.

31

Pasyphae, except it be a tale,
　Was buld, inclosed in a woodden cow;
　Yet in all these the female sought the male,
　But nature doth my fancie disallow;
　No *Dedalus* could remedy my bale,
　Nor art can frame, nor sense imagine how,
　This knot dame nature hath so firmely knit,
　It cannot be dissolv'd by any wit.

32

This *Fiordispina* faire (so was her name)
　In piteous sort her wofull state doth waile,
　My sister unto her, her speech doth frame,
　As chiefly to her comfort might availe:
　And wisht her this unbridled will to tame,
　Sith nature could not suffer it prevaile,
　And that she would let that desire be daunted,
　Which possibly by no meanes could be graunted.

33

All this but all in vaine my sister said,
　To seeke that fancie from her mind to wrest,
　She that for comfort car'd not, but for aid,
　Doth more and more her selfe vexe and molest:
　Now night grew on as they together staid,
　What time all creatures seeke repose and rest,
　The Ladie prayes my sister for her sake,
　A lodging at her castle then to take.

34

To this request doth *Bradamant* assent,
　And so together to that place they came,
　Where I (but that you did my harme prevent)
　Should have bene cast into the burning flame:
　She that all kindnesse to my sister ment,
　By many outward courtsies shewd the same:
　And caused her to weare a womans weed,
　That men might know that she was one indeed.

35

For why the semblance false she saw before,
  Of manly shape to her was so pernicious,
  She would now see her in those weeds no more,
  The rather eke lest folke should be suspicious,
  (If she had bene as shewd the weed she wore)
  Lest that they two did live together vicious:
  She further was by physick rules assured,
  That contraries by contraries are cured.

36

But nought could salve that sore, nor swage her woes,
  That night they lay together in one bed,
  But sundry and unlike was their repose,
  One quiet slept, the tothers troubled hed
  Still waking, or if she her eyes but close,
  That little sleepe strange dreames and fancies bred:
  She thought the gods and heav'n would so assist her,
  Into a better sex to change my sister.

37

As men tormented with a burning fever,
  Do dreame with drinke they swage their grievous thirst,
  But when they wake, they feele their thirst persever,
  And to be greater then it was at first;
  So she whose thoughts from love, sleepe could not sever,
  Did dreame of that, for which she wake did thirst,
  But waking felt and found it as before,
  Her hope still lesse, and her desire still more.

38

How fervently did she to *Macon* pray?
  What vowes did she unto her prayre annex?
  If so by mighty miracle he may,
  Her bedfellow turne to a better sex?
  Now neare approcht the dawning of the day,
  When she in vaine her selfe doth grieve and vex:
  And so much more her passion grew the stronger,
  Because my sister now would stay no longer.

39

When *Fiordispina* saw she would be gone,
  She caus'd a gallant gennet to be brought,
  All richly barbd, and furniture thereon,
  Which with her owne hand partly she had wrought,
  This frankly she bestoweth her upon,
  My sister takes it kindly, as she ought,
  And takes her leave, and on her way doth get,
  And home she came that night ere Sunne was set.

40

We that long time of her had heard no tiding,
  I meane her mother, brothers, and her kin,
  Do welcome her, and aske of her abiding,
  Why she so long from us had absent bin?
  Who straight from us the troth of nothing hiding,
  Doth tell us how great danger she was in;
  And opned from the ending to beginning,
  The course of all her leesing and her winning.

41

As namely first how hardly she had sped,
  And in a conflict had receiv'd a wound,
  For which she was constrain'd to pole her head,
  Before her health she could recover sound;
  She told how fortune afterwards her led,
  Where that faire huntresse had her sleeping found;
  She told us how the Ladie did her woo,
  And all the circumstance that long'd thereto.

42

To heare this story I was passing glad,
  For why at *Saragoza* I had seene
  This *Fiordispina*, and some knowledge had
  Of her likewise when she in *France* had beene;
  And lik't her well, yet was I not so mad,
  In vaine to set my love on such a Queene:
  But now againe I gave that fancie scope,
  When by this tale I had conceav'd some hope.

43

Love was my counsellor that me advised,
  My meaning secret I to none impart,
  This was the stratageme that we devised,
  This was the plot, the cunning, and the art,
  To go in *Bradamantas* clothes disguised,
  And for a while to play the womans part:
  I knew my face my sisters so resembling,
  Would be the better helpe for my dissembling.

44

The day ensuing ere it yet was light,
  I tooke my way, my love and fancie guiding,
  I there arriv'd an houre before twas night,
  Such hap I had, such hast I made in riding:
  No sooner came I in the servants sight,
  But well was he of me could carry tiding:
  They looke (as Princes oft to give do use)
  Some recompence for bringing so good newes.

45

Straight out she came, and met me halfe the way,
  And tooke me fast about the necke and kist me,
  And told me how in this my little stay,
  In anguish great and sorrow she had mist me,
  Then she did cause me alter mine array,
  In which with her owne hands she doth assist me;
  A cawl of gold she set upon my crowne,
  And put on me a rich and stately gowne.

46

And for my part to helpe the matter, I
  Did take great heed to all I did or said,
  With sober cast I carrid still mine eye,
  And bare my hands before me like a maid;
  My voice did serve me worst, but yet thereby
  Such heed I us'd, my sex was not bewraid:
  And thus arrayd, my Princesse led me with her,
  Where many Knights and Ladies were togither.

47

My looke and clothes did all them so beguile,
  They all had thought I had a woman beene,
  And honour such was done to me that while,
  As if I were a Dutchesse or a Queene:
  And (that which made me oftentime to smile)
  Some youths there were of yeers & judgement green
  That cast upon me many a wanton looke,
  My sex and quality they so mistooke.

48

At last came meate, both store of flesh and fish,
  What kinds of both, to tell I overslip,
  I maidenly tast here and there a dish,
  And in the wine I scant do wet my lip,
  The time seem'd long that staid my wanton wish,
  And still I doubted taking in some trip:
  When bed time came, she told me I must be
  Her bedfellow, the which well pleased me.

49

Now when the maids and pages all were gone,
  One onely lampe upon the cubbard burning,
  And all coasts cleare, thus I began anon:
  Faire dame I thinke you muse of my returning,
  And cause you have indeed to muse thereon,
  For yesterday when I did leave you mourning,
  I thinke both you and I did thinke as then,
  We should not meet againe till God knowes when.

50

First let me tell you why from you I went,
  Then why I come, hereafter I shall show:
  Deare Ladie (thus it was) I did lament
  Your fruitlesse love on me was placed so,
  And though I could have ay bene well content,
  To waite on you, and never part you fro,
  Yet since my presence did but make you languish,
  I thought mine absence minish would your anguish.

51

But riding on my way, I somewhat straid,
  As fortune and adventure did me guide,
  And lo I heard a voice that cride for aid,
  Within a thicket by the river side:
  A *Satyr* taken had a naked maid,
  And with a twisted cord her hands had tide,
  And in his usage seemed so to threate her,
  As if that he would kill her straight, and eate her.

52

I rusht to them with naked sword in hand,
  And death to him, and freedome I did give her,
  She diving under water out of hand,
  Vnrecompenst thou shalt not me deliver,
  Quoth she, for I will have you understand,
  I am a Nymph that dwell here in this river;
  And for this courtsie I do much regard you,
  And am well able richly to reward you.

V

53

Aske of me what you list, and I will give it,
  For I upon the elements have powre;
  I can with charms bring down the *Moon*, beleeve it,
  I can swage stormes, and make faire weather lowre,
  What is so hard but my skill can atchieve it?
  To drayne the sea, or build in aire a towre?
  Yea ev'n with simple words (and if I will)
  I can inforce and make the Sunne stand still.

54

When as the *Nymph* had made me this great offer,
  (Lo Ladie what great love to you I bare)
  I neither askt with gold to fill my coffer,
  Nor victory, of which some greedy are,
  This favour onely I demaunded of her,
  To make me able to asswage your care:
  Nor nam'd I any meanes for feare of erring,
  The onely way and meanes to her referring.

55

No sooner this request to her I told,
  But in the christall streame againe she dived,
  And sprinkled me with drops of water cold,
  Which to my skinne no sooner were arrived,
  But I was chang'd from that I was of old,
  And of my former state I was deprived;
  I felt, I saw, yet scant beleeve I can,
  That of a woman I was made a man.

56

And saving that ev'n now I am so nie you,
  As you may quickly prove my tale not fained,
  Else you might thinke I said it but to trie you;
  Now lo, since I for you this wish obtained,
  Aske what you please, I nothing shall denie you,
  Enjoy that which my love for you hath gained:
  When I had pleaded thus, and she had heard it,
  On sight of evidence she gave her vardit.

57

As one whose state is overwhelm'd with debt,
  By lending or by spending out of measure,
  That looks ech houre when prouling shreevs will fret
  Himselfe to ward, and of his goods make seasure,
  If some unlookt for gaine he hap to get,
  By some mans death, or by some trovie treasure,
  Is so surpris'd with joy, he scant doth know,
  If true it be, or if he dreamed so.

58

So she that now did see, and feele, and touch,
  That which she long had longed for in vaine,
  It overfild her mind with joy so much,
  It seemed in a trance she did remaine;
  Therein her incredulity was such,
  As to resolve her I did take much paine:
  If these be dreames (quoth she) for these dreams sake
  I ever wish to dreame and never wake.

59

Not sound of drum, of trumpet, or of phife,
  Nor warlike instrument of any sort,
Did sound alarum to our friendly strife,
  But dovelike billing follow'd lovely sport,
This battell hazards neither limbe nor life,
  Without a ladder I did scale the fort;
And stoutly plant my standard on the wall,
And under me I made my fo to fall.

60

If that same bed were full the night before,
  Of teares, of plaints, of anguish and annoyes,
No doubt but now it had in as great store,
  Both smilings, sports, and solaces and joyes:
No Iuy doth embrace the pillar more,
  Then she did me, nor Apes can find more toyes,
Then we yong fooles did find to make us merie,
Till joy it selfe of joy did make us wearie.

61

The thing twixt us did secret long remaine,
  And certaine months this pleasure did endure,
Till some had found, and told it to my paine,
  As you well know that did my life assure:
Yet I confesse great griefe I still sustaine,
  Not knowing how her safetie to procure.
This Richardetto to Rogero told,
And all the while their journey on they hold.

62

By that time Richardettos tale was done,
  They gan up to a little hill to mount,
And when an houre and more was set the Sunne,
  They came unto the castle Agrismount,
Kept then by Aldiger the bastard sonne
  Of Bovo, of the house of Clarimount,
A wise and sober man and of good qualitie,
And bountifull in keeping hospitalitie.

63

And after he had bid them welcome both,
  One as his kinsman, tother as his friend,
I heare ill newes (quoth he) that I am loth
  To tell to you, lest it should you offend:
But thus it is, to let you know the troth,
  I heare that Bertolage doth sure intend
To buy the prisners that Ferraw hath tane,
As namely Malagige and Viviane.

64

Lanfusa taketh upon her to sell them,
  And as I heare to morrow is the day,
Vnto your brothers I sent one to tell them,
  But they be absent hence so farre away,
As ere they come, from hence they may expell them,
  I am too weake to force, too poore to pay,
My love is great, to wish all good unto them,
But powre so small, as good I can none do them.

65

Young Richardetto much mislikt the newes,
  So did Rogero for the tothers sake,
And when he saw they both were in a muse,
  Nor knew what counsell, or what course to take,
No feare (quoth he) let me this matter use,
  On me this enterprise Ile undertake,
So I shall handle this affaire so handsome,
This sword alone shall pay your kinsmens ransome.

66

This spake Rogero his companions chearing,
  But notwithstanding Aldiger, his host,
Gave to those loftie promises such hearing,
  As if there were great boast and little rost:
Which unto Richardetto plaine appearing,
  Who knew his vallew, greater then his bost:
Good cosen if you knew him well that sed it,
You would said he unto his word give credit.

67

Then Aldiger on better information,
  Gave eare and credit to his noble guest,
And made him cheare to sute his reputation,
  And plast him at the boord above the rest:
And supper done, he was in seemely fashion,
  In chamber lodgd, of all the house the best,
The master of the house in nothing scant,
His worthy guest will suffer nothing want.

68

Now was the time when all men soundest sleepe,
  Rogero onely cannot sleepe a winke,
For cares and thoughts that him do waking keepe,
  And in his troubled braine profoundly sinke;
The siege of Agramant doth pierce him deepe,
  And what dishonor men of him may thinke,
And deeme his heart but faint, his faith but fickle,
To leave his Soveraigne in so wofull pickle.

69

Had he revolted at some other time,
  Men might have thought that true religion mov'd him,
None could have it imputed as a crime,
  Nor no man probably could haue reprov'd him:
Now, when his masters fortune did decline,
  And when to aid him chiefest it behoov'd him,
Feare, men will thinke, his change procured chiefe,
Nor just remorse, nor zeale of true beliefe.

70

This troubled him, and little lesse then this,
  It troubled him, to thinke of his deare hart,
Whom now by evill fortune he doth misse,
  Nor cannot once salute ere he depart;
Wherefore to write to her his purpose is,
  And so to her at large his mind impart,
Both that of him she may have certaine newes,
As that he may his sodaine going scuse.

71

The chamberlaines both prudent and discreet,
  Vpon *Rogero* quicke attendance gave,
  Providing him of needfull things and meet,
  Inke, paper, light, and what he else would crave:
  Then (as the manner is) he doth her greet,
  Vpon the front, as letters use to have;
  Thus after very harty commendations,
  Or some such phrase of friendly salutations.

72

Then tels he her how that the *Turkish* Prince,
  Had for his ayd, by speciall message sent,
  Who is besieg'd, and hath bene long time since;
  And how to rescue him is his intent:
  Least men of cowardise might him convince,
  That he away in time of danger went:
  And now would leave his lawfull Lord and liege,
  Then when his enemies did him besiege.

73

He prayeth her to weigh, how foule a deed,
  How full it were of infamy and shame,
  To yeeld his Prince no aid in such a need,
  That sent to him of purpose for the same:
  He wisht her for her owne sake to take heed,
  That no such staine might spot her spouses name,
  That being she, so true and so sincere,
  She should no blemish in her husband beare.

74

He further doth his zeale to her protest,
  As erst he had in word so now in writing,
  And sweares that when his Prince were undistrest,
  The siege quite rais'd, by concord or by fighting,
  That foolish people might not make a jest,
  To his reproch, that common speech reciting,
  Rogero loves to take the surer side,
  And turnes his sailes, as fortune turnes her tide.

75

I shall (he writes) when that time doth expire,
  Which in a month I hope will be effected,
  Finde some occasion from them to retire,
  And of no breach of honour be suspected.
  Then shall I full accomplish your desire,
  And do, as I by you shall be directed:
  This onely for my honour I demand thee,
  And after this thou ever shalt command mee.

76

These things, and like to these *Rogero* wrate,
  As then by hap came in his troubled hed,
  To certifie his love of his estate,
  And of the cause that his departure bred:
  By that time he had done, it was full late,
  And then againe he got him to his bed,
  And clos'd his eyes, when he had clos'd the letter,
  And after tooke his ease a great deale better.

77

Next day they all arose at breake of day,
  With minde to go to set their kinsmen free,
  And though *Rogero* earnestly did pray,
  That none might take that enterprise but he,
  Yet both the other stifly said him nay,
  And thereunto by no meanes would agree,
  Vnto the place assign'd they ride togither,
  And by the time appointed they came thither.

78

The place they came to was a goodly plaine,
  In which no tree nor bush was to be seene,
  Here *Bertolage* did point to take them twaine,
  As were agreed *Lanfuse* and him betweene,
  But first they met, while here they did remaine,
  One that a *Phenix* bare in field all greene,
  With armor faire embost, and guilt with gold,
  As in the booke that follows shall be told.

THE TWENTY-SIXT BOOKE OF
ORLANDO FVRIOSO

THE ARGVMENT

The learned Malagige *strange riddles showes,*
To his companions out of Merlins *well:*
With Mandricard *the* Sarzan *thither goes,*
And each tooke quarrels new, as there befell:
For Discord *seed of strife among them sowes,*
But Doralices *horse, by fiend of hell*
Affrighted, doth his mistres beare away,
Which caus'd the Pagans *both breake off the fray.*

ORLANDO FVRIOSO
THE TWENTY-SIXT BOOKE

1

Right worthy dames there were in times of old,
   That more esteem'd of vertue then of wealth,
But now our iron age is all for gold,
   For bad, and worse, in sicknes and in health,
But she that will that elder custome hold,
   And leave this new, deserves where ere she dwelth,
Here in this life to have a happie choice,
And in the next for ever to rejoyce,

2

Such was the noble *Bradamantas* mind,
   Who sought not after wealth and rich ability,
Nor state, nor pompe, that many women blind,
   But after vertue pure, the true nobility:
And well deserved he to find her kind,
   That shew'd in him such proofs of high gentility,
And tooke upon him actions for her sake,
Which time to come for miracles may take.

3

Rogero (as before I did recite)
   With *Aldiger* and *Richardetto* came,
To rescue those two prisners (if they might)
   That should be sold with great reproch and shame.
I told you how they met a gallant Knight,
   Whose shield had painted that same bird of fame,
That still renewes it selfe, and never dies,
And onely one, in all the world there flies.

4

Now when this Knight was of these three aware,
   That stood like men new plast in battell ray,
He comes to them, and seeing what they are,
   Will there (quoth he) some one of you assay,
If so his value can with mine compare,
   With staffe, with sword, or any other way?
If any will, come then, and let us trie it,
If none, then say so quickly, and denie it.

5

Sir answer'd *Aldiger*, I were content,
   To trie my selfe with you, a bout or two,
But we three came not here for this intent;
   We come, a greater feate then this to do,
And at this time, a little time mispent,
   May hinder us, and little pleasure you,
We three intend (if God do say Amen)
To take two prisners from six hundred men.

6

Sure (said that other) if you mind indeed,
   So great an enterprise to take in hand,
No doubt it doth of valiant mind proceed,
   And pittie t'were, your purpose to withstand:
I rather shall assist you in this deed,
   If you vouchsafe to make me of your band,
And by my service I will quickly shoe,
Good proofe if I deserve such grace or no.

7

Perhap that some would know, and if they may,
   What valiant Knight this was that did intreat,
To take *Rogeros* part in such a fray,
   Whereas the danger could not be but great.
Now she, not he, hereafter I must say,
   Marfisa was, of whom I did repeat,
How she both fought, and foyld a little since,
And with *Gabrina*, charg'd the *Scottish* Prince.

8

Rogero stout, and they of *Clarimount*,
   Of her and of her offer well esteemed,
She joyn'd with them, they making full account
   That she had bene of that same sex she seemed.
Straight ready on their horses backes they mount,
   They see a loose a cornet (as they deemed)
Of horse, and mingled some on foote together,
And all of them directly tending thether.

9

Their march, their ensignes, penons, and their flags,
   Did cause for *Moores* they knowne were & descride,
Amid this crew, upon two little nags
   The prisners rode with hands behind them tide,
That must be chang'd for certaine golden bags,
   That *Bertolage* had promist to provide;
Come (saith *Marfisa*) to the other three,
Now let the feast begin, and follow me.

10

Soft (quoth *Rogero*) there be wanting some
   Of those that to the banquet must be bidden,
And to begin afore the guest be come,
   In reason and good manners is forbidden;
By this, the tother crew had overcome
   The hill, that late before from them were hidden,
These were the traitrous wretches of *Magaunse*,
And now was ready to begin the daunce.

11

Maganza men of one side, merchant like,
　Brought laden moyles with gold and costly ware,
　The *Moors* their prisners brought with sword & pike,
　Environd round about with heed and care;
　The Captains meet with mind a match to strike,
　The prisners present at the bargaine are,
　And now are bought and sold (for ought they know)
　To *Bertolage* their old and mortall foe.

12

Good *Aldiger* and noble *Ammons* sonne,
　Could hold no longer seeing *Bertolage*,
　But both together at him they do runne;
　With hearts all set on fierce revenge and rage,
　His force nor fate their fury could not shunne,
　Their speares his armor and his brest did gage,
　Downe falls the wretch, his wealth him cannot save,
　Such end I wish all wicked wretches have.

13

Marfisa and *Rogero* at this signe,
　Set out without expecting trumpets blast,
　And with two staves of straight well seasond Pine,
　Twise twenty men unto the ground they cast;
　The Captaine of the *Moores* doth much repine,
　They of *Maganza* murmured as fast:
　For each side deemed, as they might in reason,
　That this had happend by the tothers treason.

14

Wherefore each side with wrath and fury kindled,
　Vpbraiding tone the tother with untruth,
　With swords and bils, pel mel together mingled,
　Do fight, and then a bloudy fray ensu'th,
　The *Moorish* Duke was by *Rogero* singled,
　A man ev'n then in prime and strength of youth,
　But youth, nor strength, nor armour could not save him,
　From such a blow as good *Rogero* gave him.

15

Marfisa doth as much on tother side,
　And in such sort besturd her with her blade,
　That looke which way soever she did ride,
　An open lane for her the people made;
　If any were so stout the brunt to bide,
　Yet soone they found their forces overlaid;　(enter,
　Through coats of proof they prov'd her sword would
　She sent their soules below the middle center.

16

If you have seen the hony making Bees
　To leave their hives, and going out in swarmes,
　When as their kings and masters disagrees,
　And they make camps in th'aire like men at armes,
　Straight in among them all the Swallow flees,
　And eates and beates them all unto their harmes:
　So thinke *Rogero* and *Marfisa* then,
　Did deale among these bands of armed men.

17

Now *Aldiger* and *Richardet* no lesse,
　Vpon *Maganza* merchants lay on lode,
　Both free to set their kinsmen from distresse,
　And for they hated them like snake or tode,
　They that the cause nor quarrell could not guesse,
　And saw their Captaine dead, made short abode:
　Their plate, their coine and treasure all they yeeld,
　And were the first that faintly left the field.

18

So flie from Lions silly heards of Goates,
　That have devourd and spoild them at their list,
　And torne their sides, their hanches and their throtes,
　Yet none of them their fellowes dare assist:
　So fled these men, and cast away their coates,
　And weapons all, and durst no more resist:
　Nor marvell if these two had Lions harts,
　That ready find such two to take their parts.

19

Whose acts at large to tell I do refraine,
　At which that age did not a little wonder,
　And now to tell them, men would thinke I faine,
　Yea though my words their actions far were under;
　For at one blow oft horse and man was slaine,
　From head to foote whole bodies clov'n in sunder,
　And either standing on their reputation,
　Bred for their foes a costly emulation.

20

Still tone of them markt tothers valiant deed,
　And each of tother fell in admiration,
　She deemes him *Mars*, or one of *Mars* his seed,
　And farre above all humane generation:
　And save he was deceived in her weed,
　He would have giv'n her equall commendation,
　And likned her, as well he liken might,
　Vnto *Bellona* for her valiant fight.

21

Thus of two bands these foure the battell wonne,
　And all their stuffe and carriages they got,
　The prisners loos'd, their bands were all undone,
　Their foes all foild, such is their happie lot:
　The man was well whose horse could swiftest runne,
　Small count they make of amble or of trot:
　The tone side leave their gold on asses loden,
　The tother of their captives are forboden.

22

The noble vanquishers do seize the pray,
　Which was both rich and sumptuous to behold,
　Of *Flanders* worke an hanging rich and gay,
　(To hang a stately roome) of silke and gold;
　They also found rich clothing and array,
　That should have bene unto *Lanfusa* sold,
　And namely mong the rest a gallant gowne,
　Embroderd round with cost of many a crowne.

23

They further found good vittels and good store,
Wine bottels coole and fresh, and good of tast,
With which (not having eate that day before)
They do agree to baite and breake their fast,
And ev'ry one prepares himselfe therefore,
And to that end their curats they unlast:
Now when *Marfisa* had put off her beaver,
To be a woman each one doth perceave her.

24

Her golden haire trust up with carelesse art,
Her forehead faire, and full of stately grace,
Her eye, her lip, and ev'ry other part,
So suting to her comely shape and face,
As bred ev'n then in each beholders hart,
A rev'rend love and wonder in like case;   (them,
And straight they askt her name, the which she told
And with as great delight she doth behold them.

25

But she her selfe farre more then all the rest,
Rogeros shape and person doth regard,
His vallew great, his unappalled brest,
Before the others all she much prefard,
To him alone her speeches she addrest,
Of him alone she would her speech were hard:
Thus she in him, and he delighted in her,
The while the other had prepard their dinner.

26

The place they din'd in was a pleasant cave,
And one of foure that famous *Merlin* wrought,
Where he in milke white marble did ingrave
Strange stories, which things future strangely taught,
The very images seem'd life to have;
And saving they were dumb, you wold have thought
Both by their lookes and by their lively features,
That they had mov'd, and had bene living creatures.

27

From out a desert wood an ugly beast
There seem'd to come, whose shape was thus defined
An asses eares, a wolfe in head and brest,
A carkas all with pinching famine pined,
A Lions grizly jaw, but all the rest
To foxlike shape did seeme to be inclined:
In *England*, *France*, in *Italy* and *Spaine*,
Yea all the world this monster seemd to raigne.

28

Where ere this cruell monster set his foote,
He kild and spoild of ev'ry sort and state,
No height of birth or state with him did boote,
He conquerd Kings and clownes, all in a rate,
Yea this beasts powre had tane so deepe a roote,
It enter'd in *Christ* his vicars sacred gate,
And vexed *Cardinals* and *Bishops* chiefe,
And bred a scandall ev'n in our beliefe.

29

Vnto this beast men seem'd to bow and bend,
This beast brake through each wall and ev'ry fence,
No citie could it selfe therefrom defend,
Strong castles made from it but weake defence,
In fine, her powre did seeme so farre extend,
That many were so fond and void of sence,
To thinke and to beleeve this monster fell,
Had powre of all things both in heav'n and hell.

30

But when this beast had rang'd a while, behold
One wearing on his head a lawrell crowne,
With three that wore the *flowre de luce* of gold,
Embroder'd richly on their purple gowne,
And with these three a stately Lion bold,
Did joyne his force to put the monster downe;
The titles and the names that them concerned,
Might in their garments plainly be discerned.

31

One that with sword the beast thrusts in the paunch,
Was he whose praise no time shall ever smother,
Francis the first of that name King of *France*,
Of Austria *Maximillen* is another,
Then *Charles* the fift that with a mighty launce
Smites through the beast, from tone side to the tother:
The fourth that in the brest with arrow wounds him
Was *Henrie* th'eight, the writing so expounds him.

32

Leo the tenth, the Lion fierce is called,
Who chast him, and fast caught him by the eare,
And in the chase the beast so tyrd and galled,
As others tooke him while he held him there:
By this the world seem'd freed that erst was thralled,
By this men seem'd secure and void of feare,
Seeing that beast whose look late made them tremble
Stroyd by the powre of this so brave assemble.

33

This story so set forth (as I have told)
With costly workmanship, great pleasure bred,
In all their minds that did the same behold,
And on this sight more then their meat they fed,
And chiefe *Marfisa* wisht to heare it told,
What men these were, if men already dead,
Or else a *prophecie* of things ensuing,
By hidden skill, laid ope to each mans vewing.

34

Then *Malagigi* was by them requested,
As one in Mathematikes seene right well,
And had the method thereof so digested,
As he all hidden mysteries could tell,
To shew what monster thus the world molested,
And who be these that him from earth expell: (them,
For though they saw their names, they did not know
But he they knew by his great skil could show them.

35

Know then (quoth he) that these whose names appeare
  In marble pure, did never live as yet,
  But long time hence, after six hundred yeare,
  To their great praise in princely throne shall sit,
  Merlin the *English* prophet plast them here
  In *Arthurs* time, and by his passing wit,
  Set here (as yet) their unperformed deeds,
  And noted all their names upon their weeds.

36

This beast you saw, had first her habitation
  Beneath amongst the wicked fiends of hell,
  And staid there till that wicked generation,
  (I meane the iron age) on earth did dwell,
  When none durst trust without an obligation,
  When fraud first came tween them that buy and sel,
  And when the mighty (to their great reproch)
  First on the poore mens livings did incroch.

37

Then first this monster cruell got abrode,
  And ever since her powre doth still increase,
  And wheresoere she maketh her abode,
  There is no friendship firme, nor godly peace;
  Conscience and justice under foote are trod,
  Good government and wholsome lawes do cease,
  That *Python Phœbus* kild with thousand darts,
  Was monster lesse then this by thousand parts.

38

Thus *Malagigi* said, and then he told
  Who those should be that should the monster kill,
  That should come then when as the world were old,
  That should renew each good, and mend each ill,
  Whose names in sacred stile to be inrold
  Deserve and to be prais'd and honourd still,
  That should in time to come, as he did conster;
  With bountie kill that miserable monster.

39

Those five I nam'd, and more by five times five,
  Mine author names, that holpe to slay the beast,
  Rogero and the rest, the time did drive,
  In such like talke during the present feast,
  And ere they rose, behold there did arrive
  Vnto this cave unwares another guest,
  By name that maid from whom of late by force,
  Fierce *Rodomont* had tane *Rogeros* horse.

40

She having heard by hap upon the way,
  Her mistris brother was at *Merlins* cave,
  Where she had bin her selfe another day,
  Not thinking now *Rogero* there to have;
  Him when she saw, she not one word doth say
  To him, nor any show or inckling gave,
  Like one that knew so well to do her arrant,
  As she durst go, sometime beside her warrant.

41

But unto *Richardet* she frames her tale,
  Yet so as tother might her speeches heare,
  How one from her a gallant courser stale,
  Which *Bradamant* her mistris held full deare,
  The horse (quoth she) *Frontyno* she did call,
  As I had led him thirty mile well neare,
  Marfilia toward, where she bad me stay,
  And pointed me to meet me at a day.

42

So fond was I, I feared no mans force,
  Nor doubted no mans will to do me wrong,
  When once I should but shew them how the horse
  Vnto *Renaldos* sister did belong:
  Yet one fierce *Pagan* voide of all remorse,
  Met me, and tooke him from me, and ere long
  Did meet a fo, with whom I fighting left him,
  That hath (I hope) by this of life bereft him.

43

Rogero with this tale was so much moved,
  That scant hereof *Hippalca* made an end,
  But *Richardetto* straight by him was moved,
  Yea and conjurd, as he would be his frend,
  That this attempt might sole by him be proved,
  And (but this damsell) none might him attend:
  That she may bring him to the *Pagans* sight,
  That tooke away her horse against all right.

44

Stout *Richardet* (though thinking too much wrong,
  So oft to let another undertake
  Those enterprises that to him belong)
  Yet sith so earnestly *Rogero* spake,
  He gives consent, and tother staid not long,
  But of the company his leave doth take,
  And leaves them all, in wonder great to see,
  That such hie worth could in a yong man be.

45

Now when *Hippalca* was quite out of sight,
  She opned to *Rogero* all the troth,
  How she that counts him her beloved Knight,
  And voweth to be his by solemne oth,
  Sent her of purpose to him this last night,
  Which she before conceald (as being loth
  Her mistris brother should her counsell know,
  How she that horse upon him did bestow.)

46

She told him how that he that tooke the steed,
  Did adde these proud and scornfull words beside,
  Because it is *Rogeros* horse indeed,
  So much the rather on the horse I ride,
  And if he will be griev'd at this my deed,
  Tell him I do not mind my selfe to hide,
  For I am *Rodomont* (he said) whose name
  Where ere I passe filleth the world with **fame.**

47

One might have seene it in *Rogeros* face,
  In how great dudgen this great wrong he tooke,
Both for the gift and giver in like case,
  And grosse abuse, for which he did not looke:
He thinks what infamy and foule disgrace
  It were to him, so great despite to brooke;
Which if he would, then justly ev'ry body,
Might take him for a dastard and a nody.

48

Wherefore with heart upon revenge full set,
  He followeth forthwith his female guide,
She that did thinke the fray unparted yet,
  That *Rodomont* and *Mandricardo* tride,
By darke blind wayes, the nearest she could get,
  Vnto the place directly she did ride,
But as you heard, they had deferd the quarell,
And hasted thence to help their Liege from perell.

49

And as I toucht before, their hap them brought
  Vnto the foresaid *Merlins* famous cave,
There where before good *Malagigi* taught,
  What secret meaning all the pictures have:
Now had *Marfisa* (by the rest besought)
  Put on a womans garment passing brave,
Which lately for *Lanfusa* had bin made,
And so attyrd, refresht her in the shade.

50

When that *Tartarian* Prince had spide this dame,
  Straight in his mind he plots this new found drift,
I will (thought he) by conquest win the same,
  And give her *Rodomontee* as my gift,
(As though that love were but a sport and game,
  That might be sold and changed for a shift)
For why (he thought) what needs a man complaine,
If leesing one, he do another gaine?

51

Wherefore the tothers damage to repaire,
  And that he might his owne in quiet have,
And for *Marfisa* seemly was and faire,
  As no man need a dame more comely crave:
He doth forthwith unto them make repaire,
  Denouncing straight the challenge stout and brave,
That he with those foure knights at tilt wold runne,
Till they slue him, or he their Ladie wonne.

52

Straight stept out *Malagige* and *Vivian*,
  Both prest in her defence to breake a speare,
Nor fearing to encounter man to man,
  With those two *Pagans* they saw present there;
But when the fray betweene them now began,
  Fierce *Rodomont* stood still and doth forbeare,
As comming thither with another mind,
And not to change his purpose first assignd.

53

Now of the brothers *Vivian* was the first,
  That with great might the *Pagan* did invade,
Vpon whose crest in vaine his speare he burst,
  His blow no hurt it did, no signe it made,
His force was least, so was his fortune worst,
  For *Mandricard* (more perfect in his trade)
With so great strength and skill his speare inforced,
That he was overthrowne and quite unhorsed.

54

To venge his brother, *Malagige* thought,
  But of his thought he quickly was deceived,
His force thus overmatcht prevailed nought,
  From off his saddle he was quickly heaved.
Next *Aldiger* his comming dearly bought,
  For in his side a great wound he received,
So downe upon the grasse he fell halfe dead,
His visage waxing pale, his armor red.

55

Then *Richardetto* came with mighty lance,
  And prov'd himselfe by his great force to be
Worthy the name of *Palladine* of *France*,
  As oft his foes did feele, his friends did see;
But at this time one overthwart mischance
  Did hap, that downe among the rest lay he,
His horse wherein he put so great a trust,
Fell downe with him, and tumbled in the dust.

56

When as no other champion did appeare,
  But all were overthrowne in this late fight,
Thinking this conquest now obtained cleare,
  Without more stay he from his horse doth light,
And comming unto her with smiling cheare,
  Faire dame (quoth he) you now are mine by right,
You cannot it denie, or once excuse it,
For by the lawes of battell so we use it.

57

Indeed (*Marfisa* said) it were no wrong,
  And I were yours I grant by law of warre,
If I were theirs, or did to them belong,
  That you have foiled in this present jarre,
But I shall make you know I hope ere long,
  You misse your marke, your aime did greatly arre,
I am mine owne, mine owner is within me,
He that will have me, from my selfe must win me.

58

I handle can (quoth she) both sword and speare,
  And have ere this made more then one man bleed,
Then cald she for her armor which was there,
  Which by a page was brought to her with speed
Off go'th her gowne, and for she still did weare
  A slender trusse beneath her womans weed,
Her well shap't limbs therein were plainly seene,
In shape like *Mars*, in face like *Ægypts* Queene.

59

When at all peeces she was armed round,
  She vauteth nimbly up into her seate,
  And twise or thrise she makes her horse to bound,
  To bate a little of his furious heate,
  And makes a turne or two above the ground,
  Then turnes she to her fo to do her feate;
  Such was (I judge) *Pentheseleas* fight,
  Against *Achilles* famous *Greekish* Knight.

60

Thus each themselves upon their horse advances,
  And with their couched speares forthwith they run,
  Vp in a thousand splinters flies the lances,
  But unto them no hurt at all is done:
  The *Pagan* greatly marvels how it chances,
  That she should scape, and curses *Moone* and *Sun;*
  And she with her successe as ill content,
  Blasphemeth eke the heav'ns and firmament.

61

Then they assayd with swords most dreadfull dint,
  To wound the tone the tother, and to kill,
  Their strokes were such as might have pierst the flint,
  And to their force was joyned passing skill:
  They lay on lode amaine, and do not stint,
  The sound doth all the place with eccho fill,
  But never was it more for their behoofe,
  To have their armour of so passing proofe.

62

But while they now did most apply the fray,
  Fierce *Rodomont* doth step them both betwixt,
  And blames him much for making such delay,
  Of that which late by him was firmely fixt;
  And then with courteous speech he her doth pray,
  With lowly words and loftie, quaintly mixt,
  That she would helpe to aid *Trajanos* sonne,
  Whose tents were in much danger to be wonne.

63

To this request *Marfisa* doth assent,
  As well to helpe King *Agramant* thereby,
  As for she came to *France* with that intent,
  The forces of the *Palladines* to try;
  This while *Rogero*, wroth and malcontent,
  After the stealer of his horse doth hie;
  And having found of him the perfect tracke,
  He sends againe his guide *Hippalca* backe.

64

And for he thought that none could do it better,
  The messenger he makes her of his mind,
  And sends by her his lately written letter,
  Protesting he will still continue kind,
  And that he doth himselfe acknowledge debter,
  And would himselfe to her for ever bind,
  He onely prayes her for a time excuse
  His absence, which he would not, might he chuse.

65

With this dispatch *Hippalca* went her way,
  And came to mount *Albano* that same night,
  Rogero made but very little stay,
  Vntill he had *Frontino* in his sight;
  Which seen & known, forthwith there was no way,
  But he will have his horse againe, or fight
  With him, that had with so unnoble force,
  The damsell robbed of the gallant horse.

66

And straight in shew of warre he coucht his speare,
  And to his face the *Pagan* he defide,
  But *Rodomont* doth patiently forbeare,
  Ev'n as a *Iob*, and all his words abide;
  Not that of him he had one sparke of feare,
  For his great value often had bin tride,
  But that the danger of his Lord and King,
  Weyd more with him then any other thing.

67

Wherefore he gently tels him for what cause
  He may not fight, and him exhorted to
  What all divine, and what all humane lawes,
  Vnto his Prince commands a man to do.
  I (said *Rogero*) am content to pawse,
  In this respect, and make a truce with you,
  So that this horse againe to me you render,
  Which so to take, your reason was but slender.

68

Now while these two herein do square and brave,
  The *Tartar* King doth unto them approch,
  And when he saw what armes *Rogero* gave,
  He set another brabble straight abroch.
  Mine are (quoth he) these armes that now you have,
  How dare you on my titles thus incroch?
  The cause why *Mandricardo* spake these words,
  Was that *Rogero* gave the King of burds.

69

An *Eagle* argent in a field of blew,
  Rogero gave, whilom the crest of *Troy*,
  As one that thence deriv'd his pedegrew,
  And did by due descent the same enjoy;
  But hereof *Mandricardo* nothing knew,
  Or nought beleev'd, and calld it but a toy,
  And tooke it as an injury and scorne,
  To see the same by any other worne.

70

For he himselfe did give, as for his cote,
  That bird that bare up *Ganimed* on hie,
  Ere since he wan (as I before did note)
  Don *Hectors* armes, and wan such praise thereby,
  The good successe hereof makes him aflote,
  So that he did *Rogero* straight defie,
  I shall (quoth he) some better manners teach thee,
  Then in such sawcie sort to overreach thee.

71

As wood well dride will quickly fall on fire,
　If so a man a little do it blow;
　So was *Rogero* kindled now in ire,
　To heare the *Pagan* reprehend him so;
　Thou thinkst (quoth he) to have thy fond desire,
　By charging me now with a double fo,
　But know that I my partie good will make,
　From him mine horse, from thee mine arms to take.

72

Did not we two about this matter boord?
　And then to take thy life I did abstaine,
　Because that by your side I saw no sword;
　But now sith you begin this brawle againe,
　This shall be fight in deed, that was but word,
　And that your crest shall turne you to much paine,
　Which unto me descent and propagation
　Hath left, but you do hold by usurpation.

73

Nay thou usurp'st, the tother straight doth say,
　And with that word he *Durindana* drew,
　That sword that erst *Orlando* flang away,
　And then a cruell fray was like ensew:
　But straight the tother two did cause them stay,
　And chiefly *Rodomont* did seeme to rew,
　That *Mandricard* of lightnesse shewd such token,
　That twise by him his promise had bin broken.

74

First when to get *Marfisa* he had thought,
　He had conflicted more then twise or thrise,
　And now with tother quarrelled for nought,
　About a bird or some such fond devise:
　Nay then (quoth he) if needs you would have fought,
　We two should trie the title of our prise,
　Which by consent should stand still undecided,
　Vntill our Princes safetie were provided.

75

Wherefore for shame do as you have agreed,
　And let us cease and lay all quarrels by,
　And when our Prince from danger shall be freed,
　Then first betweene us two the matter trie,
　And after if you live, you may proceed
　To fight it out with him, and so will I:
　Though well I wot, when I have done with you,
　But little will remaine for him to do.

76

Tush (saith the *Tartar* Prince) for him nor thee,
　Nor all the world beside, I passe one straw,
　For though you fight, or though you do agree,
　Of neither of you both I stand in aw,
　As water in a spring, so strength in me
　Shall still supply much more then you can draw;
　I hope by that time I have done my feate,
　From head to foot with blood Ile make you sweate.

77

Thus one ill word another doth draw on,
　And wrathfull *Mandricard* them both defies:
　Rodomont would have peace, but they would none,
　If this speake sharpe, then that more sharpe replies;
　If one strife be compounded, yet anon
　Another strife as bad or worse doth rise;
　In vaine *Marfisa* labours to compound them,
　For more and more untoward still she found them.

78

Ev'n as the painfull husbandman doth thinke,
　By care to keepe the river in his bounds,
　That swels with raine, readie to passe the brinke,
　And overflow his mow'd or sowed grounds,
　He strengthens ev'ry place that seems to shrinke,
　Yet more and more the water still abounds,
　And while he stops one vent, another groweth,
　Till over all perforce at last it floweth.

79

So when the dame, of whom I last made mention,
　Saw how *Rogero* stout and *Mandricard*,
　With *Rodomont* continude in contention,
　And each would seeme for tother two too hard,
　She willing to compound this sharpe dissention,
　Perswades them, but they little it regard,
　For still as one at her request forbeares,
　The other two are at it by the eares.

80

When as she saw their furie still increase,
　Let either us (quoth she) our Prince assist,
　And in the meane time let all quarrels cease;
　Or if you in this fury still persist,
　Then I with *Mandricard* will have no peace,
　Do herein (quoth *Rogero*) as you list,
　For I resolved am to have my horse,
　Although it be by faire meanes or by force.

81

Then do (said *Rodomont*) your worst and best,
　For with that horse to part I not agree,
　But here before you all I do protest,
　That if our King by this stay damag'd be,
　And that for want of ayd he be distrest,
　The cause thereof did not proceed of me;
　Rogero little weyes his protestation,
　But firmly holds his first determination.

82

And at the *Sarzan* furiously he flies,
　And with his shoulder gave him such a thrust,
　He lost his stirrops, and so loos'd his thies,
　That hard he scaped lying in the dust.
　What? hold *Rogero*, *Mandricardo* cries,
　Either not fight, or fight with me you must,
　And in great rage, as that same word he spake,
　Rogeros beaver with great might he strake.

83

The blow was such, as made him forward leane,
  And ere that he himselfe againe could reare,
  Vpon him smote the sonne of *Ulyen*,
  With so great strength as no strength might it beare
That had his armor bene of temper meane,
  No doubt they had an end made of him there:
  Rogeros hands flie ope with senslesse paine,
  The tone his sword, the tother leaues his raine.

84

His horse away beares him about the greene,
  And *Balisard* his blade is left behind:
  Marfisa that had to *Rogero* beene
Fellow in armes that day, was griev'd in mind,
  To see him us'd so hardly them betweene,
  And being strong of limbes, and stout by kind,
  She smiteth *Mandricardo* on the crowne
  So hard, as wants not much to fell him downe.

85

After *Rogero Rodomont* doth get him,
  And now *Frontino* had welnigh bin wonne,
  But by the way stout *Richardetto* met him,
And with him joyn'd his cousin *Bovos* sonne;
  Tone justles him, and furder off doth set him,
  The tother, namely *Vivian*, doth runne,
  Vnto *Rogero* that by this was waked,
  And lends his sword vnto his right hand naked.

86

Now backe he doth returne, enrag'd with scorne,
  Minding to pay his damage home againe,
  Ev'n as a Lion, whom the Bull hath borne
Vpon his head, is full of fierce disdaine,
  Flies at him still, nor feares his cruell horne,
  His anger making him forget his paine,
  And on his beauer with such force he thundered,
  As though he wold his head in twain haue sundered.

87

And sure he had perform'd it very neare,
  If *Balisarda* had bene in his hand,
  Which he let fall, as you before did heare,
Now when as *Discord* saw how things did stand,
  She thinks no peace can possibly be here,
  And taking *Pride* her sister by the hand,
  Now sister let vs turne vs to our Priers,
  For here (quoth she) are rais'd sufficient fiers.

88

And so away they went, and let them go:
  And let me tell you how *Rogero* sped,
  Who gaue to *Rodomont* so fierce a blow,
That such a great amazement in him bred,
  That twise or thrise he reeled to and fro;
  Frontino with his senslesse master fled,
  Also his sword had falne out of his fist,
  But that a chaine did tie it to his wrist.

89

This while *Marfisa* held the tother tacke,
  And yet on either side the conquest swayd,
  Each had so good an armor on their backe,
Of piercing it they need not be afrayd,
  Yet by a chance *Marfisa* hapt to lacke,
  And likewise hapt to haue *Rogeros* ayd,
  For in a turne she made, her horse did trip,
  And in the durt vpon one side did slip.

90

And as againe he labourd up to rise,
  The cruell *Tartar* justled him so crosse,
  That on his side the horse constrained lies,
Foundring againe vpon the slimie mosse;
  Which when *Rogero* from aloofe espies,
  How neare she was to danger great and losse,
  He steps to *Mandricard*, fiercely assailing him,
  While *Rodomont* stands mazd, his senses failing him.

91

The *Tartar* doth as fiercely him resist,
  But yet *Rogero* strake so great a blow,
  Both to auenge himselfe, and her assist,
Whom *Mandricardo* hapt to overthrow,
  That sure I thinke that blow had little mist,
  Quite to haue clov'n him to the saddle bow,
  Saue that the *Tartars* armor was so hard,
  And that *Rogero* wanted *Balisard*.

92

By this the *Sarzan* King againe did wake
  And seeing none but *Richardetto* neare,
  He cals to minde how for *Rogeros* sake,
That youth to him was troublesome while eare.
  Straight with great rage he toward him doth make,
  Minding to make him buy that curtsie deare:
  And sure good *Richardetto* had repented it,
  But that his cosin with great art preuented it.

93

His cosin *Malagige*, whose skill was great,
  In all that doth to magicke art pertaine,
  With words that he without booke could repeat,
Did conjure vp a spryte of hellish traine,
  And by this meanes he works a passing feat:
  For (though he nam'd no place) he doth ordaine,
  This sprite in *Doralices* horse to enter,
  And beare her thence away at all adventer.

94

The sprite thus conjurd, quickly doth his part,
  Into the damsels gentle nag he crept,
  And so his quiet nature did peruart,
That on the sudden thirtie foot he lept,
  And ten foot high, yet with so easie start,
  That *Doralice* still the sadle kept,
  Yet cride she out, in doubt to haue miscarried,
  For in the diuels name she thence was carried.

95

Forthwith to helpe her *Rodomonte* go'th,
　Because she fled, and cride to him for aid,
　To stay behind the *Tartar* is as loth,
　For feare betweene them he may be betraid,
　He leaves *Rogero* and *Marfisa* both,
　Nor in the place so little time he staid,
　As to accord with them upon some truce,
　Or make at least some mannerly excuse.

96

This while *Marfisa* was got up againe,
　And now she means to venge her on her fo,
　But he was gone, at which in great disdaine,
　She frets and chafes, that he had serv'd her so,
　Rogero chafes as much, for all in vaine,
　He knew it would be, after them to go:
　They know their steeds (and this doth grieve them more)
　Cannot outrun *Frontin* and *Brigliadore.*

97

Wherefore supposing (as it was indeed)
　That they were gone unto the *Turkish* host,
　To follow them forthwith these two agreed,
　Though not to follow as they went in post,
　Not doubting but when *Agramant* were freed,
　At leasure them to meet, and to their cost:
　They onward go, but yet *Rogero* ment,
　To bid his friends farewell afore he went.

98

Downe from his horse he gently doth descend,
　And *Richardetto* he aside doth take,
　And promist him for ay to be his frend,
　And to his noble sister for his sake:
　To whom (said he) I pray you me commend,
　Yet in such pretie sort the same he spake,
　His inward love was not thereby detected,
　Nor her great love to him, one whit suspected.

99

Thus solemne leave once tane on either side,
　And profers of great love and curtsie made,
　To him was hurt, and all the rest beside,
　As still among great nobles is the trade,
　Rogero with *Marfisa* on doth ride,
　But how they did the *Christen* campe invade,
　And what great losse did *Charles* thereby receive,
　In next ensuing booke you may perceive.

THE TWENTY-SEVENTH BOOKE OF
ORLANDO FVRIOSO

THE ARGVMENT

Rogero *and those other* Pagan *Kings,*
Make Charles *againe to* Paris *wals retire :*
Among the Turks *new seed of quarrell springs,*
And kindles in their hearts a quenchlesse fire :
Which all their campe in great disorder brings.
Agramant *to appease them doth desire ;*
Fierce Rodomont *doth leave the campe in wrath,*
Because his mistres him forsaken hath.

ORLANDO FVRIOSO
THE TWENTY-SEVENTH BOOKE

1

Among the many rare and speciall gifts,
 That in the female sex are found to sit,
 This one is chiefe, that they at sodaine shifts,
 Give best advice, and show most readie wit:
 But man, except he thinks and chews, and sifts,
 How ev'ry part may answer tother fit,
 By rash advice doth often overshoot him,
 And doth attempt the things that do not boot him.

2

Good *Malagigi* thought he had done wisely,
 In making *Doralice* to *Paris* fly,
 But if he had the matter wayd precisely,
 (Though *Richardetto* was preserv'd thereby)
 He would have sure confest it done unwisely,
 His safetie with so great a losse to buy:
 For by this act (which he then not forethought)
 A losse unspeakable to *Charles* was wrought.

3

Alas how much might he have better done,
 If he had made the fiend the wench convay,
 Vnto the fall or rising of the Sunne?
 To West, or East, or any other way,
 Where *Rodomont* and *Agricanes* sonne,
 From *Paris* wals might have gone far astray?
 But he that ever wisheth *Christens* evill,
 So at this time did prove himselfe a Devill.

4

The fiend her silly horse most slily enterd,
 And, not before prescribed any place,
 He quickly all the company distemperd;
 Nor bare he her away a common pace,
 But over brooks, and streams, and ditches venterd:
 She crying still for ayd as in such case,
 Nor leaves her beast to fling, run, snore and stampe,
 Vntill she quite was past the *Christen* campe.

5

There did she come ev'n as she could desire,
 Among the midst of *Agramantes* traine,
 And there at last she found the King her sire,
 That of *Granata* did possesse the raigne:
 The while her lovers both themselves do tire,
 And in pursuing her do take great paine,
 By tracing her with as great toile and care,
 As huntsmen do with pleasure trace the Hare.

6

Now *Charles* tis time for thee to looke about,
 Vnto thy wals and strengths in time betake thee,
 Thou never canst escape this plunge, I doubt,
 Except thou stir up quickly, and awake thee,
 Thy strength, the lamps of *France* are quenched out
 I meane thy frends & champions chiefe forsake thee,
 Orlando thee, his wits have him relinquished,
 And all his vertues drownd and quite extinguished.

7

Likewise *Renaldo*, though not fully mad,
 Yet little lesse then mad seekes there and heare,
 For faire *Angelica*, and is full sad,
 To see that he of her no news can heare;
 For why a certaine old inchaunter had
 Told him a forged tale, that toucht him neare,
 How she, to whom of love he made profession,
 Was in *Orlandos* keeping and possession.

8

This made him at the first so loth to go
 To *England*, whither he was sent for ayd;
 This made him backe againe to hasten so,
 Then when the *Turks* his presence so dismaid,
 And thinking after that, some news to know,
 By privie search the *Nunries* all he laid,
 And Castels all, in *Paris* and about,
 To see if he by search could finde her out.

9

But when he heard of her no news nor tiding,
 And that *Orlando* there likewise did want,
 He could in *Paris* make no longer biding,
 Doubting his rivall sought him to supplant,
 But up and downe about the countrie riding
 Sometime to *Brava*, sometime to *Anglant*,
 Supposing still *Orlando* her had hidden,
 Lest of his pleasure he might be forbidden.

10

And thus the wicked fiend his time espide,
 To give the *Christens* such a fatall blo,
 When as these two, in whom they most asside,
 Were absent now their Prince and countrie fro;
 Furder for souldiers of the *Turkish* side,
 All that were valiant men, or counted so,
 Were all against this time entised hither,
 Wholly uniting all their force togither.

11

Gradasso stout, and *Sacrapantee* fearce,
　　That in that charmed castell long had dwelt,
　　Which th'*English* Duke, as I did late rehearse,
　　Dissolved quite, and caus'd like snow to melt.
　　These two likewise the *Christen* campe do pearce,
　　The forces of these two the *Christens* felt.
　　Rogero and *Marfisa* made lesse hast,
　　And so it happend, they arrived last.

12

The first two couple neare the *Christens* tents,
　　Did meet, and then after long consultation,
　　Each unto other shewing their intents,
　　They all conclude with one determination,
　　And all of them to this give their consents,
　　In spite of all the *Christen* generation,
　　To succour *Agramant* their Lord and Liege,
　　And mauger *Charls* his might, to raise the siege.

13

Straight in one crew they foure togither knit,
　　Breake through the *Christen* watch by force amaine,
　　Neither in hugger mugger did they it,
　　But crying lowdly, *Affrica* and *Spaine*,
　　They lay on lode, and ev'rie one they hit,
　　Dead or astonished doth there remaine:
　　Alarum then all ore the campe was rung,
　　Though few could tel the cause frō whence it sprung.

14

Some thought the *Gascoigns* or the *Switzers* bold,
　　By mutiny had made some insurrection,
　　And their surmise unto the *Emp'ror* told,
　　Who came with minde to give them due correction
　　But when he did the bodies dead behold,
　　Incurable untill the resurrection,
　　He standeth still like one with wonder mazed,
　　And on their wofull wounds long time he gazed.

15

Ev'n as a man that with a bolt of thunder,
　　Hath seene his dwelling house smit unaware,
　　Straight searcheth with no little feare nor wonder,
　　Which way the bolt did passe that caus'd his care:
　　So *Charles* that saw mens bodies cut in sunder,
　　Inquires, of so great wounds who authours are,
　　And when he knew how few they were that did it,
　　Did wish himselfe there present to forbid it.

16

This while *Marfisa* on another side,
　　With good *Rogero* do them sore impeach,
　　And through the campe in spite of them they ride,
　　Killing or wounding all within their reach:
　　As in a mine that lies close unespide,
　　With trayns of gunpowder men make a breach:
　　Or as a tempest goes along by coast,
　　So suddenly these two brake through the host.

17

Many that scapt the tother foure by flight,
　　In flying, fell unwares upon these twaine;
　　And felt by proofe that neither flight nor fight,
　　Can save a man ordained to be slaine.
　　Ev'n as a Foxe, whom smoke and fire doth fright,
　　So as he dare not in the ground remaine,
　　Bolts out, and through both smoke & fire she flieth,
　　Into the Tartars mouth, and there he dieth.

18

Thus last of all, by this most noble paire,
　　The *Christen* armie once againe was sundred,
　　And then to *Agramant* they all repaire,
　　Who welcoms them, and at their value wondred.
　　Now hope and courage, drive away dispaire,
　　One *Turke*, of *Christens* straight defide an hundred,
　　So great a boldnesse in their mind doth rise,
　　By helpe and succour of these new supplies.

19

Straightway on both sides out their men were brought
　　Their standerds and their banners all displaid,
　　And there that day a bloodie field was fought,
　　And neither side made shew to be dismaid,
　　For hopes alike in either armie wrought,
　　Tones passed conquests, tothers present aid.
　　But fortune on the *Christens* so did frowne,
　　That they againe were driv'n unto the towne.

20

The passing force of cruell *Rodomount*,
　　The strength and value great of *Mandricard*,
　　Rogeros vertue, that doth all surmount,
　　Gradassos courage of no small regard,
　　Marfisas heart, of principall account,
　　The skill of *Sacrapant*, with best compard,
　　These were the causers of good *Charles* his losse,
　　And sent the *Christens* home by weeping crosse.

21

Great store were drown'd in *Sequana* with hast,
　　The bridge so narrow was for to receive them,
　　Wishing (as *Dedals* sonne had in time past)
　　Some wings wherewith aloft in ayre to heave them,
　　Some thrusting, strave to get them in so fast,
　　That strength & breath, & life at last did leave them
　　But that, whereby King *Charles* was chiefly shaken,
　　Was this, that many *Palladyns* were taken.

22

Thus fortune once againe did turne the wheele,
　　The good King *Charles* had her, but could not hold her,
　　And of this foile this hurt he then did feele,
　　It fainter made his friends, his foes the bolder:
　　The Marquis of *Vienna* true as steele,
　　Was at that service wounded in his shoulder,
　　And many hurt, but none did play his part,
　　So well that day, as valiant *Brandimart*.

23

He stoutly bare it out, no little space,
 And when he saw there was no other way,
 Then to the furie prudently gave place,
 And spar'd himselfe, against another day:
 Now once againe is *Charles* in wofull case,
 Now once againe to *Paris* siege they lay.
 Yong Orphans, and old widdows prayre and cries,
 Againe unto Gods heav'nly throne arise.

24

The Angell *Michel*, was but ill appaid,
 Finding the cause of those good *Christens* teares,
 He thought his maker was but ill obaid,
 And that he may be blamd therefore he feares;
 He cals himselfe deceived and berraid;
 By her should set the *Pagans* by the eares,
 From which (it seemed) now she did so vary,
 As she had rather done the quite contrary.

25

Ev'n as the Servitor whose love and zeale,
 More then his memory may be commended,
 Forgetting in some waighty cause to deale,
 That by his Lord to him was recommended,
 Would with new care his former fault conceale,
 That ere his master know, it may be mended:
 So this good *Angel*, went not up to God,
 Till he had done as much as he was bod.

26

To seeke dame *Discord* he doth leave the skie,
 And to the Abby he returnes againe,
 Where her amid the monks he might espie,
 That change old officers, and new ordaine:
 She laughs to see their portises to flie,
 Readie to knocke out one anothers braine:
 The *Angel* takes her by her painted locks,
 And with great furie gives her many knocks.

27

He brake a crosses handle on her crowne,
 And grievously doth beat her, backe and side,
 The wretch upon her mary bones fals downe,
 At th'*Angels* feet, and mercy, mercy cride:
 Packe to the *Pagans* then, that siege yon towne,
 (Quoth he) and see that you among them bide,
 For if this place againe thou ever trouble,
 Assure thy selfe, thy payment shall be double.

28

Though *Discords* back & arms were sore with beating
 Yet thence with all the hast she could she went;
 Sore terrifi'd with that great *Angels* threating,
 Doubting againe in like sort to be shent:
 Yet in this hast, behind her not forgetting,
 Bellows and coles, in steed of those were spent,
 By which in many minds, and hearts invincible,
 She quickly kindle might a fire inquenchible.

29

Rogero, Mandricard, and *Rodomont*,
 Gan now their quarrels to renew,
 As making of the *Christians* small account,
 That unto *Paris* walls themselves withdrew:
 Wherefore to *Agramant* they do recount
 Their quarrels & the grounds of whence they grew,
 Each one by challenge his just cause averring,
 The combats order to the King referring.

30

Also *Marfisa* doth the King intreat,
 That she may end her combat first begunne,
 With as great hast thereof, and as great heat,
 Against the *Tartar, Agricanes* sonne:
 This she desires with hast and instance great,
 As one that thinks, great wrong to her was done,
 If in regard of any state or powre,
 She should attend one day, or yet one howre.

31

But *Rodomont* alledgeth that of right,
 He first should end the matter with his rivall,
 Sith by accord they first deferd the fight,
 Till time might serve, after their here arrivall:
 No lesse *Rogero* for his horse takes spight,
 And sweares, that whether they agree or strive all,
 To take *Frontino*, no man should restraine him,
 Or else to fight with him that doth detaine him.

32

Further, the matter farther to entangle,
 The argent *Eagle* in the azure field,
 Gave to the *Tartar* matter more to jangle,
 And quarrell with *Rogero* for his shield:
 And so confusedly he then did wrangle,
 As though with all at once he would the field,
 And in his furie sure he had attempted it,
 But that the Kings commandment flat prevented it.

33

Who first with grave and frendly admonition,
 To peace and good attonement did exhort them,
 But when beyond all meanes of composition,
 He saw that wrath and furie did transport them,
 To certaine *Marshals* he doth give commission,
 According to the law of armes to sort them:
 And of all wayes, this was not thought the worst,
 To trie by lots, which two should combat furst.

34

Foure little scrowles were put into a pot,
 The first had *Rodomont* and *Mandricard;*
 Rodomont and *Rogero* next they wrot;
 The third *Rogero* was and *Mandricard;*
 The fourth paire that must trie the present lot,
 Was stout *Marfisa* joynd to *Mandricard:*
 When lots were cast, these two first out were tane,
 Fierce *Rodomont* and sonne of *Agrican*.

35

Mandricard and *Rogero* next they finde,
  Rodomont and *Rogero* next was said:
Mandricard and *Marfisa* staid behinde,
  With which the stately dame was ill apaid:
Nor was *Rogero* well content in minde,
  Doubting that when they first their parts had plaid,
The combat will be such betweene them two,
He and *Marfisa* should have nought to do.

36

Not farre from *Paris*, lay a levell ground,
  That was in compasse scant a thousand paces,
This plain with rayles, and bars was compast round,
  And tents therein were set with equall spaces,
With scaffolds rays'd upon the outward bound,
  To give to lookers on convenient places:
Now came the time these strifes should be decided,
Among those Knights, those tents were thus devided.

37

In the pavillion bordring on the East,
  Stands *Rodomont* with visage sterne and grim,
Ferraw and *Sacrapant* were readie prest,
  To put his scaly serpents hide on him:
In tother tent that was upon the West,
  Gradasso and stout *Falsyron* do trim,
With *Hectors* armes so stately and so faire,
The valiant Prince, King *Agricanes* haire.

38

On one side in a high tribunall seat,
  Do sit the Kings of *Affrica* and *Spaine*,
With *Stordilan* and other Princes great,
  Both feard and followd of the *Turkish* traine:
Happie was he that day, that could but get,
  A place to sit or stand although with paine,
On ridge of house, or wall, or top of tree,
In so great presse, the goodly shew to see.

39

On tother side sat Ladies of great name,
  In stately sort, to see and to be seene,
That out of divers realmes and countries came,
  To visit or attend the *Spanish* queene:
There *Doralyce* was plast, that lovely dame,
  Who wears a robe of crimson cut on greene,
Yet was the crimson staind in such a fashion,
It rather seemd inclining to carnation.

40

Among the rest *Marfisa* sat that day,
  In short light clothes most sumptuously arraid,
The fashion of such kind, as well it may
  Become a warrior, and yet a maid,
Hippolita (I thinke) us'd such array,
  When in the field her banner she displaid,
Thus each thing was prepared for the fight,
And each man was prepared for the sight.

41

An *Herald* in his coate of armes steppes out,
  And of the law of armes expounds the guise,
Professing to resolve each little doubt,
  That in such case accustoms to arise:
The people gasing standeth all about,
  Attent with listning ears, and longing eyes,
When from the tent of valiant *Mandricard*
Behold a sodaine noyse and sturre was hard.

42

The cause was this, the King of *Sericane*,
  Who (as before I did rehearse) was one,
That holpe to arme the sonne of *Agricane*,
  Taking his sword in hand to put it on,
Saw written in the handle, *Durindane*,
  And looking more advisedly thereon,
He saw *Almontes* armes grav'n on the blade,
The which strange sight him greatly wonder made.

43

And glad he was when once he did espy it,
  (The chiefest cause that first to *France* he came)
Although before he never could come by it,
  Wherefore he questions straight upon the same,
If *Mandricardo* wan it, or did buy it?
  Who in this sort his answer then did frame:
I with *Orlando* for this sword did quarrell,
And ear I had it, put my life in perrell.

44

Further unto this answer he doth ad,
  A farther lie, his glorie to increase,
How that *Orlando* for the feare he had,
  That for this sword he never should have peace,
Had throwne away the sword, and faind him mad,
  That thereby he might cause his quarrell cease:
Doing herein, as is the *Castor* wonted,
Bite of his stones, when he is nearly hunted.

45

Well (quoth *Gradasso*) what *Orlando* ment,
  I cannot now discusse, nor do I know,
But sure I am it is not mine intent,
  Now I have found it here to let it go,
The money, men, munition I have spent,
  Deserve as good a thing as this I trow:
You did but finde it, you your selfe confesse it,
And now I challenge it and do possesse it.

46

If you denie my claime, here I will prove it,
  This field the court, this list my pleading bar,
My plea is such, as no writ can remove it,
  My judge must be the sequell of the war.
War said the other, who, can better love it
  Then I? these words to me as musicke are,
If so the King of *Sarza* will agree,
To stay his combat, till I fight with thee.

47

Be sure Ile answer thee, and all beside,
  That dare presume to offer me offence:
With that *Rogero* stept betweene and cride,
  Ho sirs, with this I minde not to dispence,
Or let the fight proceed, as lots have tride,
  Or I my selfe will put you to your fence:
Shall he denie the sword and shall I yeeld,
That you shall weare mine *Eagle* on your shield?

48

Wherefore preserve that order first agreed on,
  From which in honour, you may no way start,
Or if to breake it further you proceed on,
  I breake will all, if you do breake a part.
Tush (quoth the *Tartar*) threats we have no need on,
  If *Mars* were in you both, and tooke your part,
Yet both should finde it folly to attempt,
Me of my shield, or sword once to prevent.

49

And with that word forthwith he bent his fist,
  And on *Gradassos* hand so fierce he strake,
That sodainly, or ear *Gradasso* wist,
  He made him unawares the sword forsake:
Who much repind he thus his purpose mist,
  And that so unprepard he could him take,
And much more griev'd it him, that this disgrace,
Was offerd him in such an open place.

50

Wherefore to be aveng'd of so great wrong,
  He steppeth backe and out his sword he drawes,
The tother doth no farther time prolong,
  Though in respect of order there was cause,
Nay which was more, he thought himselfe so strong
  To fight with all at once, he askt no pause,
But to them both at once he makes defiance,
In his owne strength he had so great affiance.

51

This man is mad, but let me with him trie it,
  Gradasso said, Ile make him wise againe:
Nay softly (quoth *Rogero*) I deny it,
  For this same combat doth to me pertaine:
Stand backe saith tone, saith tother nay not I yet,
  Backe you; yet both still in their place remaine.
Thus do these three with malice great and spite,
Strangely begin a combat tripartite.

52

And sure to much confusion it had growne,
  Had not some men, more stout perhap then wise,
Themselves among them undiscreetly throwne,
  With courage great, but yet with small advise,
To succour others danger with their owne:
  Yet could no force them part, nor no devise,
Till *Agramant* himselfe, their dreaded Lord,
In person came their quarrell to accord.

53

The rev'rence great that unto him they beare,
  Made them forthwith their forces to restraine,
Who straight the causes of these broiles did heare,
  And to compound them sought, but all in vaine,
For scant *Gradasso* could be made forbeare,
  The sword so long with tother to remaine,
Vntill the fight were ended now in hand,
Of which the sequell could not yet be scand.

54

Scarse had the King with words of great perswasion,
  This quarrell new begun, a while appeas'd,
But that another strife, by new occasion,
  In *Rodomontes* tent them all diseas'd:
An hurlyburly and a fierce invasion,
  There grows betweene two Princes sore displeas'd,
Betweene stout *Sacrapant* and *Rodomount*,
As I to you will presently recount.

55

King *Sacrapant*, as late before I told,
  Helping to arme the cruell *Sarzan* King,
With those selfe armes that *Nimrod* ware of old,
  From whom this Prince, his pedigree did bring,
Whiles he (I say) did curiously behold
  His furniture, and ev'rie other thing,
That to his horse, or unto him belong,
To see they might be sure and firme, and strong.

56

While he, that stately steed *Frontino* vew'd,
  That proudly champing stood upon his bit,
And all his raines with snowlike fome bedew'd,
  Without regard, whose hands embroder'd it,
A thought unpleasant in his mind renew'd,
  And to his heart did seeme full neare to sit,
He thinks this horse was very like in sight,
To one of his, that *Frontlat* whilom hight.

57

And more and more with heedfull looke still eying,
  The markes and shape, and colour of the steed,
After his long and very curious prying,
  He saw and knew it was his horse indeed:
Which horse from him (then at *Albracca* lying)
  Brunello stale, for want of better heed;
And shew'd him an unusuall cunning knacke,
To steale his horse while he sate on his backe.

58

Brunello stale that time more things beside,
  By name *Orlandos* sword hight *Balisard*,
Angelicas faire ring, of vertue tride,
  Which she recoverd as before you heard:
Likewise a sword ev'n from *Marfisas* side:
  This done, he gave *Rogero* afterward,
Orlandos sword, and this horse to the same,
But to *Frontino* first he chang'd his name.

59

Now then I say, when *Sacrapant* was sure,
  This horse was *Frontlat* that sometime was his,
  And that the markes he saw did him assure,
  That he therein tooke not his marke amis,
  To hold his peace he could not long endure,
  But said, good sir, know mine *Frontino* is,
  Stolne late from me, as I can make good proofe,
  Although (I trow) mine owne word is inough.

60

One at *Albracca* stale from me this steed,
  Yet for our late acquaintance I consent,
  Because I see that now you stand in need,
  That you shall use him now I am content:
  Conditionally, that first it be agreed,
  You shall acknowledge him not yours, but lent,
  Else here I claime him as my goods and chattell,
  And will defend my right in open battell.

61

The *Sarzan* King, that past (I thinke) in pride,
  All Kings and Knights that ever carrid sword,
  And past (I thinke) in strength and courage tride,
  All samples that old stories us afford,
  Made answer thus; if any man beside,
  Durst unto me have spoken such a word,
  He should have found, I took it in such scorne,
  He had bin better have bin speechles borne.

62

But for our late begunne acquaintance sake,
  I am content this at your hands to beare,
  So as you this, do as a warning take,
  The like attempt hereafter to forbeare,
  And if you will but harke what end I make,
  With *Mandricardo*, then I do not feare,
  But you shall see such sample of my force,
  Shall make you glad, to pray me take your horse.

63

Then villany is courtesie with thee,
  (Saith *Sacrapant* inflam'd with high disdaine)
  When you be offerd faire you cannot see,
  Wherefore my purpose is, I tell you plaine,
  My horse shall service do to none but mee,
  And with these hands I will my right maintaine:
  And that is more, if these same hands should faile,
  I will defend my right with tooth and naile.

64

Thus galling speech, betweene them multiplying,
  Till each last word, the former worser made,
  At last they fell to acts of flat defying,
  And tone the tother fiercely doth invade:
  Rodomont on his strength and armes relying;
  Yet tother so defends him with his blade,
  And makes it so about his head to hover,
  That seemes alone his body all to cover.

65

Ev'n as a charret wheele that runnes apace,
  Seemes to the eye all solid, firme and sound,
  Although twixt ev'rie spoke there is a space,
  Concealed from our sights by running round:
  So *Sacrapant* seem'd armed in that place,
  Though armour then about him none was found,
  So dextrously himselfe he then besturd,
  As well it stood upon him with his sword.

66

But quickly *Serpentino* and *Ferraw*,
  With naked sword in hand, stept them betwixt,
  With others more that present were and saw,
  As friends of either part togither mixt,
  Yet them no force, nor prayre could once withdraw,
  Their loftie hearts were on revenge so fixt,
  And wrath had quite so put them out of frame,
  Till *Agramant* to them in person came.

67

Vpon the sight of him, their soveraigne Lord,
  They both agreed their furie to withhold,
  Who straight perswaded them to good accord,
  And much good counsell to them both he told:
  But peace and good perswasions they abhord,
  And either on his manhood made him bold;
  Their King doth but among them leese his winde,
  For more and more he froward them doth finde.

68

By no meanes *Sacrapant* will be intreated,
  Vnto the *Sarzan* King his horse to lend,
  Except that he (as I before repeated)
  To borrow it of him, would condiscend:
  The tother at this very motion freated,
  And sweares nor heaven, nor he should make him bend,
  To seek to have by prayer or request,
  A thing of which by force he was possest.

69

King *Agramant* doth aske by what mischance,
  He lost his horse, or who it from him stale?
  The tother opend all the circumstance,
  And blusht for shame, when as he told the tale;
  Namely, how late before he came to *France*,
  One tooke him napping, as it did befall,
  And underpropt his saddell with foure stakes,
  And so from under him his courser takes.

70

Marfisa, that was come to part this fray,
  Hearing of this stolne horse among the rest,
  Was griev'd in minde, for why that very day,
  Her sword was stolne as she most truly guest;
  And then King *Sacrapant* she knew straight way,
  Whom erst she knew not, and that gallant beast,
  For which of late those two began to fight,
  She knew, and said belong'd to him in right.

71

While these things passed thus, the standers by,
　　That oft hereof had heard *Brunello* bost,
　　Straight in such sort to him did cast their eye,
　　As turned greatly to *Brunellos* cost:
　　By which *Marfisa* plainly did descrie
　　Him, by whose theft her sword she late had lost,
　　To be *Brunello*, whom she saw there sitting,
　　Among great Lords, a place for him unfitting.

72

She heard, and much it grieved her to heare,
　　How for these thefts and many mo beside,
　　The King rewarded him, and held him deare,
　　Whereas in law for them he should have dide:
　　These news so greatly chang'd *Marfisas* cheare,
　　That hardly she her wrath could longer hide,
　　Let *Agramant* accept it as he will,
　　She minds *Brunello* presently to kill.

73

Straight way she armed is from head to heele,
　　And makes her page her helmet close to claspe,
　　To him she goes, and with her glove of steele,
　　She gives him such a blow as made him gaspe,
　　And while the paine hereof doth make him reele
　　With her strong hand, his weak corse she doth graspe
　　As doth the Faulcon fierce the Mallard gripe,
　　To which a while before she gave a stripe.

74

With furie great from thence away she flings,
　　While he for helpe, and oft for mercy cride,
　　But will he, nill he, him away she brings,
　　Like to a thiefe with hands together tide,
　　Where *Agramant* among the meaner Kings,
　　Sate like a judge their causes to decide,
　　Then making some obeysance for good manner,
　　She speaketh thus in short but stately manner.

75

Sir King, I minde to hang this thiefe your man,
　　That by desart should long ere this have dide,
　　For when he stale that horse from him, ev'n than
　　He stale my sword that hanged by my side:
　　But if there any be, that dare or can
　　Deny my words, or say that I have lide;
　　Here in your presences I do desire,
　　To trie by combat whether is the lier.

76

But least some should, as some by fortune may,
　　Affirme, I chuse this time to make new strife,
　　Alone at such a time, on such a day,
　　When other quarrels in the campe are rife,
　　I am content a day or two to stay,
　　And to prolong this wretched caitives life,
　　To see if any man will him defend,
　　And after sure to hang him I intend.

77

I meane (quoth she) to bring him three mile hence,
　　And keepe him as a prisner in yon towre,
　　And with his life I promise to dispence,
　　For two dayes space, and longer not an howre,
　　If any list to fight in his defence,
　　There let him come and trie my force and powre:
　　Away she gallopt when she this had said,
　　And on her saddle bow the wretch she laid.

78

The King was sore displeas'd at this attempt,
　　And much it did his princely mind enrage,
　　And minds himselfe to wreake so great contempt,
　　Vntill *Sobrino*, one both grave and sage,
　　Told him in wisdome he must be content,
　　His choler in this matter to asswage;
　　And said it were a base part for his highnesse,
　　To fight for one sprung up by theft and slinesse.

79

Yea though before hand he were sure to win,
　　Yet would such victorie dishonor have,
　　Because a woman vanquisht were therein:
　　Wherefore (quoth he) if you his life might save,
　　With one words speech, to speake that word were sin;
　　For sure she doth but law and justice crave:
　　And Princes never do themselves more wrong,
　　Then when they hinder justice, or prolong.

80

You may (said he) to satisfie your mind,
　　Send after her, in manner of request,
　　And promise her, that if just cause you find,
　　He shall be hang'd, and so all strife may rest;
　　But if to this you find her not inclind,
　　Give her her will, for so I thinke tis best;
　　So that she firmely in your friendship bide,
　　Hang up *Brunello*, and all theeves beside.

81

This good direction *Agramant* obaying,
　　Went not himselfe, nor sent none to molest her,
　　But yet according to *Sobrinos* saying,
　　He sent a messenger that might request her:
　　Himselfe the while doth travell in allaying
　　The tumults fierce that all his campe do pester:
　　Pride laughs at this, and *Discord* so rejoyces,
　　As up to heav'n flie their eternall voyces.

82

Five men most resolute have set their rest,
　　To be the first that will begin the fight,
　　The strife so intricate, as would molest
　　Apollo to decide or set it right,
　　Yet *Agramant* still strives to do his best,
　　And to compound the matter if he might:
　　And thus to end the matter he begonne,
　　Twixt *Rodomont* and *Agricanes* sonne.

83

He makes to them this good and friendly motion,
  That sith for *Doralice* they onely strave,
  They would agree to stand at her devotion,
  And let her take her choise which she will have,
  And that once made, to raise no more commotion.
  This pleas'd them both, to this consent they gave;
  A certaine hope and trust them both alluring,
  Each on himselfe of her firme love assuring.

84

The *Sarzan* King doth thinke, that needs she must
  Give sentence on his side, and be his owne,
  Sith oft he had in turneys and in just,
  Her favours worne, and his affection showne:
  How can she love (thinkes he) or put her trust
  In one, whō she scant three daies space hath knowne?
  Nor was alone his owne opinion such,
  But all the campe beside did thinke as much.

85

They all thinke *Mandricardo* overseene,
  And made no question but she would reject him:
  But he that knew what past had them betweene,
  And found that she did inwardly affect him,
  Was sure, although his service were unseene,
  And done by night, that she would not neglect him;
  Wherefore of her good will he nothing doubting,
  Did scorne their scorns, and flouted at their flouting.

86

Thus having put the matter in her choyce,
  And put the choice in her owne declaration,
  She with a sober looke and lowly voice,
  Chose *Mandricard*, against all expectation:
  The *Tartar* Prince hereat did much rejoyce,
  But all the rest were filld with admiration,
  And *Rodomont* himselfe was so astound,
  As hardly he could lift his eyes from ground.

87

But when his wonted wrath had driv'n away
  That bashfull shame that dyde his face with red,
  Vnjust he cals that doome, and curst that day,
  And clapping hand upon his sword, he sed,
  This better arbitrate our matters may,
  Then womens foolish doome by fancie led,
  Who oftentimes are so perverse in chusing,
  They take the worst, the offerd best refusing.

88

Go then (quoth *Mandricard*) I little care,
  I hope that fight shall yeeld you like successe:
  And thus againe to fight they ready are,
  But *Agramant* doth soone that rage represse,
  And said, upon this point againe to square,
  Quite were against all lawes of armes expresse:
  And *Rodomont* he sharply then controld,
  That in his sight was against law so bold.

89

The *Sarzan* King that saw himselfe that day,
  So noted by those Peeres with double scorne,
  Both from his Prince, whom he must needs obay,
  And her to whom so great love he had borne,
  With fury great he flings from thence away,
  And counts himselfe disgrast and quite forlorne:
  Of all his traine two men he onely taketh,
  The King, the campe, the place he quite forsaketh.

90

And as a Bull his loved heard that leaves,
  By his strong rivall forced to be gone;
  Among the trees all clad with thickest leaves,
  Doth hide himselfe, and seekes to be alone:
  So he, whom shame of comfort all bereaves,
  Flies sight of men, yet still he thinks thereon;
  And chiefe when he remembers what disgrace
  His mistris did him in so open place.

91

Rogero gladly would have him pursude,
  To get his horse, but yet he doth refraine,
  Lest men should thinke he had the fight eschude,
  That did twixt *Mandricard* and him remaine.
  But *Sacrapant* whom no cause doth include,
  Pursues the *Sarzan* King, the horse to gaine:
  And doubtlesse had outgone him that same day,
  But for mishap that chanced by the way.

92

A damsell fell by hap into a river,
  And was in perill great to have bin drownd;
  He lighting from his horse backe to relieve her,
  Lept in, and brought her out all safe and sound:
  But doing this good act, her to deliver,
  Scarce all that day his horse againe he found,
  His horse got loose, and he with all his cunning,
  Could scantly catch him in six howers running.

93

At last with much ado he doth him get,
  And after *Rodomont* he then doth make;
  But where, and how long after him he met,
  And how the *Sarzan* did him prisner take,
  I may not now proceed to tell as yet:
  First tell I what vild words the *Sarzan* spake,
  That cald his Prince and mistris both unkind,
  And for her fault doth raile at all her kind.

94

With scalding sighes, that inward pangs bewrayd,
  He breathes out flames in places where he goes,
  From rocks and caves his plaints doth eccho ayd,
  And takes compassion on his rufull woes;
  O womens wits, how weake you are (he said)
  How soone to change you do your selves dispose?
  Observers of no faith, nor good direction,
  Most wretched all that trust in your protection.

95

Could neither service long, nor sured love,
 By me above a thousand wayes declared,
 Thy fickle mind to fastnesse so farre move,
 But wilfully to let thy selfe be snared?
 If reason could have led thy mind to prove,
 Was *Mandricard* with me to be compared?
 Hereof can reason be alledgd by no man,
 But this alone, my mistris is a woman.

96

I thinke that nature, or some angry God,
 Brought forth this wicked sex on earth to dwell,
 For some great plague, or just deserved rod
 To us, that wanting them had lived well:
 As in the wormes, an Adder, Snake and Tode:
 Among the Beasts, Beares, Wolves and Tygers fell:
 And makes the aire the Flie and Waspe to breed,
 And Tares to grow among the better seed.

97

Why did not Nature rather so provide,
 Without your helpe that man of man might come,
 And one be grafted on anothers side,
 As are the Apples with the Peare and Plom?
 But Nature can no meane nor rule abide,
 But still she must exceed in all or some;
 Full easie tis the cause thereof to render,
 For Nature selfe is of the womans gender.

98

Yet be not therefore proud and full of scorne,
 O womankind, that men come of your seed;
 The fragrant Rose growth on the pricking thorne,
 The Lilly faire comes of a filthy weed;
 In lothsome soyle men sow the wholsome corne;
 The basest mould, the fairest flowre doth breed:
 Vngratefull, false and craftie y'are and cruell,
 Borne of our burning hell to be the fuell.

99

These words, and like to these the *Pagan* fearce,
 Doth spend amid his rage and frantike fumes;
 And like a mad man did the same rehearse,
 Sometime in hie, oft times in baser tunes:
 I tremble to set downe in my poore verse,
 The blasphemie that he to speake presumes;
 And writing this I do, know this that I
 Full oft in heart do give my pen the lie.

100

But Passion did this *Pagans* sense so blind,
 And left within the same so sharpe a sting,
 That he not onely blam'd his love unkind,
 But also rag'd against his soveraigne King,
 And cursed him, and wished in his mind,
 That fortune so great woes on him might bring,
 That he might loose his state and princely crowne,
 And see his country turn'd quite upsidowne.

101

And being to such miseries once brought,
 And with adversitie assaild so sore,
 That then by him his freedome might be wrought,
 And that he might his former state restore,
 That *Agramant* might by such proofe be taught,
 Of faithfull friends indeed to set more store,
 And learne to know, that such a friend as he,
 Deserv'd in right and wrong preferd to be.

102

Thus blaming oft his Lord, more oft his love,
 To his owne native soyle his course he bent,
 But changing place, could not his sorrow move,
 Nor travels paine, his paine of mind relent;
 It seem'd his horse *Frontino* well to prove,
 Before his bridle should be drawne, he ment,
 To *Sonna* he doth ride without a bait,
 And minds fro thence to passe to *Provence* strait.

103

And there to cast away all care and carke,
 And all his anguish quickly to appease,
 For *Affrica* he will himselfe imbarke,
 And passe the large *Mediterranian* seas;
 But, for the weather, now waxt dim and darke,
 First in his Inne he minds to take his ease,
 For all the country, ev'n as farre as *Spaine*,
 In *Agramantes* powre did then remaine.

104

Now he resolves to lodge about the cost,
 And long he is not of a place to seeke,
 For straight he was invited by an host,
 To take his house, if so it might him like:
 It pleas'd the *Pagan* well, to heare him bost,
 That he had *Corsike* wine, and *French* and *Greeke*,
 For though he were a *Turke* in all the rest,
 Yet did he like *French* fashion drinking best.

105

The pleasant host, that was indeed of those,
 That can with double diligence attend,
 As having sav'd, amid both friends and foes,
 His goods, and gain'd by that which both do spend;
 When by that princes view he did suppose
 Him some great man, he straight abroade did send,
 And thither doth his kin and friends request,
 To helpe to waite, and welcome such a guest.

106

But loe, his guest sits musing all apart,
 And of his Mistres runneth all his thought,
 Which (though he would forget) spite of his heart,
 He thinks on still, so strong the fancy wrought:
 The standers by are not so malipart,
 To talk to him, till he occasion sought:
 Which having found, up from his chaire he started,
 And salutations to them all imparted.

107

Then askt he many questions of them all,
  And as occasion serv'd, discourses vari'd;
  But still we find, and ever find we shall,
  By thought of heart the speech of tongue is cari'd:
  For last to treat of marriage he doth fall,
  And asketh of the men if they be mari'd:
  And if they be, he prayth them to declare,
  Of their wives truths, what their opinions are.

108

Straight all of them made answer they had wives,
  And but mine host, all prais'd the happy state;
  And said they were the comforts of their lives,
  That draw a happy yoke without debate:
  A playfellow that farre off all griefe drives,
  A steward, early that provides and late;
  Both faithfull, chast, and sober, mild, and trusty,
  Nurse to weak age, and pleasure to the lusty.

109

Tush (quoth mine host) under your good correction,
  (Most noble guest) these fellowes say not right,
  But either with fond love, or foule subjection,
  So blinded are, they take the black for white:
  I once my selfe was toucht with this infection,
  But now I see that then I wanted sight:
  And now I know, as being better taught,
  That theirs and mine be all unchast and naught.

110

For as the *Phœnix* is a bird alone,
  And of that kind the whole world hath no more;
  So (think I) of all wives there is but one,
  That liveth chast in love and vertues lore:
  He blest may be that lighteth her upon,
  Small hope (think I) there is in so scant store,
  That many should have one of such a kind,
  Of which in all the world but one I find.

111

I once so blinded was as now be these,
  Till by good hap unto my house there came
  A gentleman of *Venice* from the seas,
  Francis Valerio was he cal'd by name:
  He knew, and could declare them all with ease,
  All womens wiles, and stories to the same
  He had of old; and of the later times,
  To shew both wives, and single womens crimes.

112

He said, and bad me hold it as my creed,
  That all of them are false, if they be tri'd:
  If some seem'd chast, it did of this proceed,
  They had the wit to do, and not be spi'd,
  And knew by deep dissembling and good heed,
  With sober looks their wanton lusts to hide:
  And this to prove, he told me such a tale,
  As while I live I still remember shall.

113

And if it like you sir to lend me eare,
  In my rude fashion I shall it recite;
  Right glad (quoth *Rodomont*) by heav'ns I sweare,
  For thou hast hit my present humour right:
  Wherefore (said he) sit down I pray thee there,
  For in thy speech already I delight:
  But here I end this book, for doubt I have,
  That in his tale mine host will play the knave.

THE TWENTY-EIGHT BOOKE OF

ORLANDO FVRIOSO

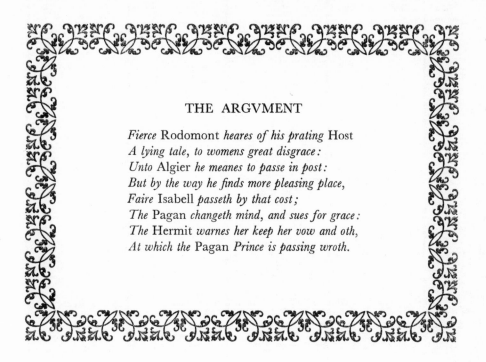

THE ARGVMENT

Fierce Rodomont *heares of his prating* Host
A lying tale, to womens great disgrace:
Unto Algier *he meanes to passe in post:*
But by the way he finds more pleasing place,
Faire Isabell *passeth by that cost;*
The Pagan *changeth mind, and sues for grace:*
The Hermit *warnes her keep her vow and oth,*
At which the Pagan *Prince is passing wroth.*

ORLANDO FVRIOSO
THE TWENTY-EIGHT BOOKE

1

You Ladies, ye that Ladies hold in prize,
  Give not (perdie) your eare to this same tale,
  The which to tell, mine Host doth here devise,
  To make men thinke your vertues are but small:
  Though from so base a tongue there can arise,
  To your sweet sexe, no just disgrace at all;
  Fooles will find fault without the cause discerning,
  And argue most of that they have no learning.

2

Turn ov'r the leaf, and let this tale alone,
  If any think the sex by this disgrac'd,
  I write it for no spite, nor malice none,
  But in my Authors book I find it plac'd;
  My loyall love to Ladies all is known,
  In whom I see such worth to be imbrac'd,
  That theirs I am, and glad would be therefore,
  To shew thereof a thousand proofes and more.

3

Peruse it not; or if you do it read,
  Esteeme it not, but as an idle bable;
  Regard it not; or if you take some heed,
  Believe it not, but as a foolish fable:
  But to the matter, thus it was indeed,
  When all the guests were cheared at the table;
  Neare *Rodomont* (so was the *Pagan* nam'd)
  Down sate mine *Host*, and thus his tale he fram'd.

4

Astolfo, whilom king of Lumbardy,
  To whom his elder brother left his raigne,
  Was in his youth so fresh and faire to see,
  As few to such perfection could attaine:
  Apelles match, or *Zeuces* he might be,
  That such a shape could paint without much paine,
  Great was his grace, and all the world so deem'd it,
  But yet himselfe of all men most esteem'd it.

5

He did not of his scepter take such pride,
  Nor that degree that common men are under,
  Nor wealth, nor friends, nor meaner kings beside,
  That thereabout dwelt neare or far asunder:
  But of his beauty, which he would not hide,
  At whose rare worth he thought the world did wonder,
  This was his joy, and all that he intended,
  To heare his comely face and shape commended.

6

Among his courtiers, one above the rest,
  Fausto by name, by birth a *Romane* knight:
  Who hearing oft so prais'd, as they know best,
  His face, and hands, and all that praise he might,
  The king did bid him tell at his request,
  Neare or farre off if he had seen that wight,
  That in all parts so perfectly was wrought:
  But he was answer'd as he little thought.

7

My Liege (quoth *Fausto*) plainly to declare,
  Both what my selfe doth see, and others say,
  But few with your rare beauty can compare,
  And that same few were none, were one away:
  Iocundo hight, a man of beauty rare,
  And brother mine, excepting whom, I may
  Prefer your grace before all other creatures,
  But he doth match or passe you for his features.

8

The king to heare such tidings strange it thought,
  As having still till that day kept the prize,
  And with a deep desire straightwayes he sought,
  To know this man, and see him with his eyes:
  In fine, with *Fausto* so far forth he wrought,
  To bring him to his court he must devise:
  Although (quoth he) to bring my brother to it,
  I shall be sure of work enough to do it.

9

The cause is this, my brother never went
  Forth of the gates of *Rome* scant all his life,
  And such small goods as Fortune hath him lent,
  He hath enjoy'd in quiet, free from strife,
  Left by our sire, and them he hath not spent,
  Nor yet increast, his gaines are not so rife:
  And he will think it more to go to *Pavy*,
  Then some would think to th'*Indies* in a Navy.

10

But I shall find it hardest when I prove,
  To draw him from his loving wife away;
  To whom he is so link'd in chaines of love,
  That all is vaine, if once his wife say nay:
  But yet your grace is so far all above,
  You shall command me, certes all I may.
  Thanks (quoth the king) and addeth such reward,
  As might have moved any to regard.

11

Away he posts, arriving in few dayes
At *Rome*, and to his brothers house he went,
And with such earnest words his brother prayes,
That to return with him he doth consent:
Also his sisters love he so allayes,
That she doth hold her peace as halfe content,
Beside great thanks, laying before her eyes
Preferments large, that hereof might arise.

12

Iocundo now resolv'd to go his way,
Gets men and horse against he should depart,
Sets forth himselfe with new and rich array,
As still we see nature adorn'd by art,
His wife at night in bed, at board by day;
With watry eyes to shew a sorie heart,
Complaines his absence will so sore her grieve,
Till his return she doubts she shall not live.

13

Ay me, the thought (quoth she) makes me so fraid,
That scant the breath abideth in my brest;
Peace my sweet love and life (*Iocundo* said)
And weeps as fast, and comforts her his best:
So may good fortune ay my journey aid,
As I return in threescore dayes at least:
Nor will I change the day I set thee down,
No though the king would grant me half his crown.

14

All this might not asswage this womans paine,
Two moneths were long, yea too too long she cries,
Needs must I die before you come againe,
Nor how to keep my life can I devise:
The dolefull dayes and nights I shall sustaine,
From meat my mouth, from sleep will keep mine eyes;
Now was *Iocundo* ready to repent,
That to his brother he had giv'n consent.

15

About her neck a jewell rich she ware,
A crosse all set with stone in gold well tride,
This relick late a *Boem* Pilgrim bare,
And gave her father other things beside:
Which costly things he kept with no small care,
Till comming from *Ierusalem* he di'd:
And her of all his goods his heire he makes,
This precious crosse to her goodman she takes.

16

And prayes him for her sake to weare that token,
And think on her: the man that was most kind,
Receiv'd it with more joy then can be spoken,
Although he needed not be put in mind,
For why no time, nor no state sound nor broken,
Nor absence long, a mean should ever find,
To quaile his love, not onely while his breath
Maintaines his life, but neither after death.

17

That very night that went before the morrow,
That they had pointed surely to depart;
Iocundos wife was sick, and sounds for sorrow,
Amid his armes, so heavy was her heart;
All night they wake, and now they bid Godmorrow,
And give their last farewell, and so they part;
Iocundo on his way with all his traine,
His loving wife doth go to bed againe.

18

Scant had *Iocundo* rode two mile forthright,
But that his crosse now came into his mind,
Which on his pillow he had laid last night,
And now for hast had left the same behind:
He would devise to scuse it if he might,
But no excuse sufficient could he find:
But that his love must needs be much suspected,
To find the precious jewell so neglected.

19

When no excuse within his mind could frame,
But that all seemed frivolous and vaine;
To send his man he counted it a shame,
To go himselfe it was but little paine:
He staid, and when his brother did the same,
Ride soft (quoth he) till I return againe:
For home againe I must, there is no nay,
But I will overtake you on the way.

20

Th'affaire is such as none can do but I,
But doubt you not, I will return as fast;
Away he spurres as hard as he could hie,
Alone without or man or page, for hast:
Now had the suns new rising clear'd the skie,
With brightest beames, ere he the streame had past,
He hies him home, and finds his wife in bed,
Full sound asleep, such cares were in her head.

21

He drawes the curtaine softly without sound,
And saw that he would little have suspected;
His chast and faithfull yokefellow he found
Yok'd with a knave, all honesty neglected:
Th'Adulterer, though sleeping very sound,
Yet by his face was easily detected:
A beggars brat, bred by him from his cradle,
And now was riding on his masters saddle.

22

Now if he stood amaz'd and discontent,
Believe it ye, to trie that would be loth;
For he that tries it, doubtlesse will repent,
As poore *Iocundo* did, who was so wroth,
That out he drew his sword, with just intent,
For their ungratefull act to kill them both:
But lo, the love he bare her, did withstand,
Against his heart, to make him hold his hand.

23

O ribald love, that such a slave couldst make,
  Of one that now was subject to thy force;
  He could not break her sleep for pities sake,
  That brake all bonds of faith without remorse;
  But back he goes before they did awake,
  And from his house he gets him to his horse:
  Love so pricks him, and he so pricks his steed,
  He overtakes his company with speed.

24

His look is sad, all changed is his cheare,
  Full heavy was his heart they well perceiv'd,
  They see no cause of griefe, nor guesse they neare,
  And they that guesse most likely, are deceiv'd;
  They thought he went to *Rome*, but you do heare
  How at *Cornetto* he his hurt receiv'd:
  Each man espi'd that love procur'd that passion,
  But none descri'd the manner nor the fashion.

25

His brother deems that all his griefe doth grow,
  Because his loving wife is left alone;
  But he a cleane contrary cause doth know,
  Her too much company did cause his mone:
  He bends his browes, his looks he casts alow,
  With powting lips, and many a grievous grone;
  In vaine doth *Faustus* comfort seek to bring him,
  For why he knowes not where the shoe doth wring him.

26

He gives a salve afore the sore is found,
  His plaisters are as poison to the smart;
  He seeks to heale, and wider makes the wound,
  He names his wife, but her name kils his heart:
  Gone was his tast, his sleeps do grow unsound,
  Nature decayth, and little helpeth art;
  And that faire face that erst was of such fame,
  Is now so chang'd, it seemeth not the same.

27

His eyes are sunk so deep into his head,
  It made his nose seem bigger then it should,
  His flesh doth shrink, his bones do seem to spread,
  He was so chang'd, as more cannot be told;
  At last an ague makes him keep his bed,
  And bait at innes more often then he would:
  His faire complexion now is pale and withered,
  Much like the Rose that yesterday was gathered.

28

With this mishap was *Faustus* sore agriev'd,
  Not onely for his brothers wofull state,
  But fearing of his Prince to be reprov'd,
  Vnto whose grace he undertook so late,
  To shew the goodliest man, as he believ'd,
  Now growne uncouth, by force of inward bate:
  Yet as they could their way they so contriv'd,
  That at the last in *Pavie* they arriv'd.

29

He would not straightway shew him to the King,
  Lest ev'ry one might deem his judgement small,
  But sent by letters notice of the thing,
  And what mishap his brother did befall;
  How scant alive he could him thither bring,
  A secret griefe so greatly did him gall,
  And with an ague pul'd him down so sore,
  He seem'd not now the man he was before.

30

And yet behold this noble King is glad
  That he is come, and meanes to make him cheare,
  As if he were the dearest friend he had,
  So sore he had desir'd to see him here:
  Nor would the worthy natur'd Prince be sad,
  In praise of beauty to have found a Peere;
  He knew *Iocundos* beauty had excel'd,
  But that by this disease it was expel'd.

31

He placeth him to his own lodging nigh,
  He visits him each day and ev'ry houre,
  Great plenty of provision he doth buy,
  To welcome him he bendeth all his power:
  But still *Iocundo* languishing doth lie,
  His wives misdeeds makes all his sweet seem sowre,
  No songs, no sighs, which oft he heard or saw,
  One dram of this his dolour could withdraw.

32

Fast by his lodging was (amongst the rest)
  A faire large room, which very few did use,
  Here would he walk, as one that did detest
  All pleasing sights, and comforts all refuse:
  Here the wide wound he bare within his brest,
  With thousand thoughts unpleasant he renewes;
  Yet here he found (which few would have believ'd)
  A remedy for that which had him griev'd.

33

For at the upper end of this old hall,
  There was a place of windowes void, and light,
  Save that the lime new molten from the wall,
  Let in a little beame that shined bright;
  Here did he see (which some may think a tale)
  A very strange and unexpected sight,
  He heard it not, but saw it in his view,
  Yet could he scant believe it should be true.

34

For at the chink was plainly to be seen
  A chamber hang'd with faire and rich array,
  Where none might come, but such as trusty been:
  The Princesse here in part doth spend the day,
  And here he saw a Dwarfe embrace the Queen,
  And strive a while; and after homely play
  His skill was such, that ere they went asunder,
  The Dwarfe was got aloft, and she lay under.

35

Iocundo standeth still as one amaz'd,
  Supposing sure that he had seen a vision,
  But seeing plaine when he a while had gaz'd,
  It was an act, and not an apparition:
  Good God (said he) are this Queenes eyes so daz'd,
  To love a Dwarfe, more worthy of derision?
  Whose husband is a Prince of worthy fame,
  So brave a man, such love? now fie for shame.

36

He now began to hold his wife excus'd,
  His anger now a little was relented:
  And though that she her body had abus'd,
  And to her servant had so soon consented;
  Not her for this, but he the sex accus'd,
  That never can with one man be contented:
  If all (quoth he) with one like staine are spotted,
  Yet on a monster, mine was not besotted.

37

The day ensuing he returned thither,
  And saw the dwarfe couragious still and jolly;
  Eke he another day repaired hither,
  And still he found the Queen committing folly:
  He oft returnes, he finds them oft together,
  They cease not work, on dayes prophane nor holy:
  Yea which was strange, the goodly Queen complain'd
  That of the dwarfe she found she was disdain'd.

38

One day when in the corner he had staid,
  He sees her come all sad and malecontent,
  Because the dwarfe her comming still delaid,
  For whom of purpose twice before she sent;
  Once more she sends, this answer brings the maid,
  Forsooth unto his play he is so bent,
  That for mistrust at chesse to leese a shilling,
  To come to you the apes face is not willing.

39

Iocundo who before had still been sad,
  Vpon this sight became of better cheare;
  The paines, the plaints, the cloudy stormes he had,
  Away were blown, the coast began to cleare:
  Most ruddie faire he chearfull grew and glad,
  That angell-like his beauty did appeare,
  So as the King and others thought it strange,
  In so short time to find so great a change.

40

Now as the King desired much to know,
  The mean whereby his hurt so soon was heal'd,
  No lesse *Iocundo* did desire to show,
  And would not have the thing from him conceal'd,
  So as his choler might no greater grow,
  Then his had been, when as it were reveal'd:
  But first he made him sweare on his salvation,
  Vpon the parties to use no castigation.

41

He made him sweare for ought he heard or saw,
  Wherewith his mind might fortune be diseas'd,
  Yet from his choler so much to withdraw,
  As that in shew he may not seem displeas'd,
  Nor punish it by might nor yet by law,
  Nor first nor last, but hold himselfe appeas'd,
  So as th'offenders might not have suspected,
  That their misdeeds were to his grace detected.

42

The King so sure, by oth so solemne bound,
  As one that little thought his Queene so stain'd,
  Iocundo first his own griefe doth expound,
  Why he so long so dolefull had remain'd,
  And in whose armes his own wife he had found,
  And how the griefe thereof so sore him pain'd,
  Had not that salve unlook'd for been applied,
  Of that conceit no doubt he should have died.

43

But lying in your highnesse house forlorn,
  I saw (quoth he) that minisht much my mone;
  For though it grieved me to weare a horn,
  It pleas'd me well, I ware it not alone:
  This said, he brought him where the wall was torn,
  And shew'd him that that made his heart to grone,
  For why the dwarfe did mannage with such skill,
  Though she curvets he keeps his styrup still.

44

Much did the King this foule prospect mislike,
  Believe my words I say, I need not sweare,
  Horn wood he was, he was about to strike
  All those he met, and his own flesh to teare;
  His promise to have broken he was like,
  If of his oath he had not had some feare;
  But unrevenged all must now be born,
  For on his *Agnus Dei* he had sworn.

45

Now to *Iocundo* gently he doth speak,
  Good brother mine, advise me what to do,
  Sith I am bound by oath, I may not wreak
  The fact, with such revenge as longs thereto;
  Forsooth let's trie if others be as weak,
  (*Iocundo* said) and make no more ado:
  This was the counsell he did give the King,
  Into their order other men to bring.

46

We both are yong, and of such pleasing hew,
  Not to be matcht with such another paire:
  What she will be so obstinately true,
  But will be won with youth, and being faire?
  If youth and beauty both do misse their due,
  The want herein our purses shall repaire:
  Let us not spare our beauty, youth, and treasure,
  Till of a thousand we have had our pleasure.

47

To see strange countries placed farre apart,
  Of other women eke to make some triall,
  Will ease the paine that whilom pierc'd our heart,
  And salve our sore, there can be no deniall:
  The King that long'd to ease his new-found smart,
  Consented straight, and to avoid espiall,
  Himselfe, the Knight, two pages, and no mo,
  Out of the Realme forthwith disguised go.

48

Away they past through *Italy* and *France*,
  And through the *Flemish* and the *English* land,
  And those whose beauties highest did advance,
  Those still they found most ready to their hand:
  They give, they take, so luckie is their chance,
  To see their stock at one stay still to stand:
  Some must be woo'd forsooth they were so chast,
  And some there were that wooed them as fast.

49

In countries some a moneth or two they taried,
  In some a week, in others but a day;
  In all of them they find the women maried,
  Like to their wives, too gentle to say nay:
  At last because they doubt to have miscaried,
  They mean to leave this sport, and go their way;
  They found it full of danger and debate,
  To keep their standings in anothers gate.

50

They do agree to take by common voice,
  Some one whose shape and face may please them both,
  In whom without suspect they might rejoyce;
  For wherefore (quoth the King) should I be loth,
  To have your selfe a partner in my choice?
  I must have one, and I believe for troth,
  Among all women kind there is not one
  That can content her selfe with one alone.

51

But of some one we two might take our pleasure,
  And not inforce our selves beyond our ease,
  But as they say, take meat, and drink, and leasure,
  And by our doings other not displease;
  Well might that woman think she had a treasure,
  That had us two her appetite to please:
  And though to one man faithfull none remaine,
  No doubt but faithfull they would be to twaine.

52

The *Roman* youth much prais'd the Princes mind,
  And to perform it, seemed very faine,
  Away they posted as they had assign'd,
  By town and city, over hill and plaine,
  Till at the last a prettie peece they find,
  The daughter of an Inkeeper in *Spaine*,
  A gyrle of person tall, and faire of favour,
  Of comely presence, and of good behaviour.

53

She was new entring in the flower and pride
  Of those well pleasing youthfull yeares and tender,
  Her father many children had beside,
  And poverty had made his portion slender,
  And for them all unable to provide,
  It made him soon consent, away to send her;
  The price agreed, away the strangers carie her,
  Because the father money wants to marie her.

54

In concord great she did with them remaine,
  Who took their pleasure one and one by turn,
  As bellowes do, where *Vulcans* wonted paine
  By mutuall blast doth make the metall burn:
  Their meaning is, now they had travel'd *Spaine*,
  By *Siphax* realme to make their home return;
  And having left *Valenza* out of sight,
  At faire *Zativa* they did lodge at night.

55

The masters go abroad to view the town,
  And first the Churches for devotions sake;
  And then the monuments of most renown,
  As travellers a common custome take:
  The gyrle within the chamber sate her down,
  The men are busied, some the beds do make,
  Some care to dresse their wearied horse, and some
  Make ready meat against their masters come.

56

In this same house the gyrle a *Greeke* had spi'd,
  That in her fathers house a boy had been,
  And slept full often sweetly by her side,
  And much good sport had passed them between;
  Yet fearing lest their love should be descri'd,
  In open talk they durst not to be seen,
  But when by hap the pages down were gone,
  Old love renew'd, and thus they talk thereon.

57

The Greek demands her whither she was going,
  And which of these two great estates her keeps?
  She told them all, she needs no further woing,
  And how a night between them both she sleeps:
  Ah (quoth the Greek) thou tellest my undoing,
  My deare *Fiametta*, and with that he weeps;
  With these two Lords wilt thou from *Spaine* be banish'd?
  Are all my hopes thus into nothing vanish'd?

58

My sweet designements turned are to sowre,
  My service long finds little recompence;
  I made a stock according to my power,
  By hoarding up my wages, and the pence
  That guests did give, that came in luckie houre;
  I meant ere long to have departed hence,
  And to have ask'd thy sires good will to marie thee,
  And that obtain'd, vnto a house to carie thee.

59

The wench of her hard fortune doth complaine,
  And saith that now she doubts he sucs too late:
  The *Greeke* doth sigh and sob, and part doth faine,
  And shall I die (quoth he) in this estate?
  Let me enjoy thy sweetnesse once againe,
  Before my dayes draw to their dolefull date;
  One small refreshing ere we quite depart,
  Will make me die with more contented heart.

60

The gyrle with pitie moved, thus replies,
  Think not (quoth she) but I desire the same;
  But hard it is among so many eyes,
  Without incurring punishment and shame.
  Ah (quoth the *Greeke*) some meanes thou wouldst devise,
  If thou but felt a quarter of my flame,
  To meet this night in some convenient place,
  And be together but a little space.

61

Tush (answer'd she) you sue now out of season,
  For ev'ry night I lie betwixt them two,
  And they will quickly feare, and find the treason,
  Sith still with one of them I have to do.
  Well (quoth the *Greeke*) I could refute that reason,
  If you would put your helping hand thereto,
  You must (said he) some pretie scuse devise,
  And find occasion from them both to rise.

62

She first bethinks her selfe, and after bad
  He should return when all were sound asleep,
  And learned him, who was thereof right glad,
  To go and come, what order he should keep.
  Now came the *Greeke*, as he his lesson had,
  When all was husht, as soft as he could creep,
  First to the doore, which open'd when he push'd,
  Then to the chamber, which was softly rush'd.

63

He takes a long and leisurable stride,
  And longest on the hinder foot he staid,
  So soft he treads, although his steps were wide,
  As though to tread on eggs he were afraid;
  And as he goes, he gropes on either side
  To find the bed, with hands abroad displaid,
  And having found the bottome of the bed,
  He creepeth in, and forward go'th his head.

64

Between *Fiamettas* tender thighes he came,
  That lay upright, as ready to receive,
  At last they fell unto their merry game,
  Embracing sweetly now to take their leave;
  He rode in post, ne can he bait for shame,
  The beast was good, and would not him deceive,
  He thinks her pace so easie and so sure,
  That all the night to ride he could endure.

65

Iocundo and the King do both perceive
  The bed to rock, as oft it comes to passe,
  And both of them one errour did deceive,
  For either thought it his companion was:
  Now hath the *Greeke* taken his latter leave,
  And as he came, he back againe doth passe,
  And *Phœbus* beames did now to shine begin,
  Fiametta rose and let the pages in.

66

Now with *Iocundo* gan the King to jest,
  Brother (quoth he) I doubt we do you wrong,
  It were more time for you to take your rest,
  That have this night a journey rode so long.
  Iocundo answers him againe in jest,
  Oh sir, you do mistake, you sing my song;
  Take you your ease, and much good do your grace,
  That all this night have rid a hunting pace.

67

I, quoth the King? I would in faith I sweare
  Have lent my dog a course among the rest,
  But that I found your selfe so busie were,
  And rode so hard, you could not spare the beast.
  Well (said the Knight) it seemeth me to beare,
  Although you brake your promise and behest,
  Yet privy quips and taunts here needed none,
  You might have bid me let the wench alone.

68

One urg'd so farre, the tother so repli'd,
  That unto bitter words their tongues were moov'd,
  Scarce one forbare to say the tother li'd:
  And plaine to trie whose truth should be reproov'd,
  They cal'd the gyrle the matter to decide,
  Who was afraid, as well it her behoov'd;
  And she must tell (they standing face to face)
  Which of them two deserved this disgrace.

69

Tell (quoth the King) with grim and angry sight,
  Nor feare not him nor me, but tell us true,
  Which of us two it was, that all this night
  So gallantly performed all his due.
  Thus either deeming he did hold the right,
  They looked both which should be found untrue:
  Fiametta lowly laid her selfe on ground,
  Doubting to die because her fault was found.

70

She humbly pardon craves for her offence,
  And that they pitie would her wofull case,
  That she with pitie mov'd to recompence
  His love, that lasted had no little space,
  And who it was, she told them, and of whence,
  Had this ill luck in this unluckie place,
  How she had hop'd that though they hapt to wake,
  Yet for his partner either would it take.

71

The King and his companion greatly mus'd,
  When they had heard the practice so detected,
And their conceits not little were confus'd,
  To heare a hap so strange and unexpected:
And though no two were ever so abus'd,
  Yet had they so all wrathfull mind rejected,
That down they lay, and fell in such a laughter,
They could not see nor speak an houre after.

72

And when at last their stomacks and their eyes
  Water'd and ak'd, they laughed had so much,
Such shifts (quoth they) these women will devise,
  Do what we can, their chastity is such:
If both our cares could not for one suffice,
  That lay betwixt us both, and did us touch,
If all our haires were eyes, yet sure they said,
We husbands of our wives should be betraid.

73

We had a thousand women prov'd before,
  And none of them denied our request,
Nor would and if we tri'd ten thousand more,
  But this one triall passeth all the rest:
Let us not then condemne our wives so sore,
  That are as chast and honest as the best,
Sith they be as all other women be,
Let us turn home, and well with them agree.

74

When on this point they both were thus resolv'd,
  They gave the Greeke *Fiametta* for his wife,
And ti'd the knot that cannot be dissolv'd,
  With portion large, to keep them all their life:
Themselves went home, and had their sins absolv'd,
  And take againe their wives, and end all strife:
And thus mine Host the prettie storie ended,
With which he prayth them not to be offended.

75

The *Pagan* Prince, of whom I erst made mention,
  Was pleased with this story passing well,
And heard the same with heed and great attention,
  And praised it, and said it did excell,
And sweares he thought no wit nor no invention,
  No pen could write, no tongue attaine to tell,
By force of eloquence, or help of art,
Of womens trecheries the hundredth part.

76

But at the table sate another guest,
  Of riper yeares, and judgement more discreet,
Who such untruths to heare could not digest,
  And see their praises so trod under feet;
Wherefore his speech he presently addrest
  Vnto his host, and said, we daily meet
With slanders and with lying fables told,
And this is one, to say I dare be bold.

77

Nor thee, nor him that told thee trust I will,
  No though in other things he gospell spake,
I dare affirm it well, that evill will,
  Not any triall that himselfe could make,
Mov'd him of all the kind to speak so ill,
  Belike for some one naughty womans sake:
But he that would enter in womens praise,
On higher steps aloft his stile might raise.

78

But tell me now, if any one of you
  That married are, have not awry yet stept?
No scarce a man, that hath not been untrue,
  And with some other woman hath not slept:
Nay that is more, they woo, they seek, they sew,
  They trie, they tempt those that be safest kept,
Yet women seek not after men I ween,
(I meane not such as common harlots been.)

79

Surely the man on whom your tale you father,
  Cannot himselfe nor other men excuse,
Who still to take an unknown piece had rather,
  Although their own were better far to chuse:
But if themselves were wood, I surely gather
  Such curtesies they never would refuse,
But rather straine themselves beyond their might,
Such kindnesse with more kindnesse to requite.

80

But bee't some woman breaks chast wedlocks lawes,
  And leaves her husband, and becomes unchast,
Yet commonly it is not without cause,
  She sees her man in sin his substance wast;
She feels that he his love from her withdrawes,
  And hath on some (perhap) lesse worthy plac'd,
Who strikes with sword, the scabberd him may strike,
And sure love craveth love, like asketh like.

81

Indeed in their behalfe agree would I
  That all wives that adultery do commit,
Should by a law condemned be to die,
  If so their husbands guiltlesse be of it.
But if that men unpunish'd walk awry,
  Doubtlesse in sense and reason 'tis not fit,
The weaker sexe should for this sin be vext,
Do as you would be done to, saith the text.

82

Yet when a man is bent to speak his worst,
  That in despite he can of women say,
He cals them but incontinent and curst,
  No greater fault he to their charge can lay:
To rob, to spoile, houses to break and burst,
  Whole cities, townes, and countries to betray.
Vsury, murder, all such sinnes appeare
Proper to men, women of them are cleare.

83

This said this grave wise man, and would have told
  Some story to the same, his speech to verifie,
  Of women that had liv'd till they were old,
  Chastly and vertuously, and with sincerity,
  But that the cruell *Turke* did him behold,
  With so grim look as did the poore man terrifie,
  And made him hold his peace with threats and terror,
  Yet hating inwardly the *Pagans* error.

84

These brables ended, night on them did creep,
  To rest they went, having their bodies fed:
  But *Rodomont* scant all the night could sleep,
  For cares that ran still in his troubled head,
  His unkind mistresse him doth waking keep,
  She troubles him, whether he lie on bed,
  Whether he go, or ride, or sit, or stand,
  Whether it be by water or by land.

85

But though himselfe could take but little rest,
  Yet of his horse he takes no little care,
  Both that he should be diligently drest,
  And have good provender, to mend his fare:
  To go by water now he thought it best,
  Himselfe to ease, and his good horse to spare,
  That horse he gat, as he might justly vant,
  Spite of *Rogero*, and of *Sacrapant*.

86

He takes a bark, and down the pleasant streame
  Of *Sonna* he doth passe, with wind and ore,
  Great hast he makes, to get to his own Reame,
  But changing place doth help him ne'r the more;
  In sleep, of her unkindnesse he doth dreame,
  Awake, he sighs and still renewes the sore:
  To talk was best, and yet not much the better,
  Say what he list, yet cannot he forget her.

87

Annoid by boat, againe he taking land,
  Vienna, *Lions*, and *Valenza* past,
  (All which then were in *Agramantes* hand,
  His late good hap had so them all agast:
  To *Aquamort* he turnes on his right hand,
  And thence he will to *Algier* turn in hast,
  And in his way, his journey to abridge,
  He past *Avignon* at the sumptuous bridge.

88

Not far from *Mompelier* a towne he saw,
  Of *Bacchus*, and of *Ceres* well belov'd,
  Though then so spoil'd by souldiers that for aw,
  The dwellers all themselves from thence remov'd:
  Also there was a Church for Christen law,
  But yet the Priests (in this to be reprov'd)
  To save themselves, their Church had quite forsaken,
  So as the same by *Rodomont* was taken.

89

This seat, this place, did so the *Pagan* please,
  That here he minds to make his firm abode;
  For of the tone side he might see the seas,
  On tother side the ground with corn well load:
  Here all provisions he might find with ease,
  Here he doth cause his men his stuffe unload,
  And makes that Church (oh horrible abuse)
  Serve him, to his profane ungodly use.

90

Now standing pensive in this pleasing place,
  As still he us'd, he saw a Lady faire,
  (Though mourning, yet most full of pleasing grace)
  Who with a Frier made thither her repaire:
  A goodly horse they led a soft slow pace,
  And as they went he taught her many a praier:
  That horse did beare a coffin on his back,
  All overspread in mourning sort, with black.

91

Me think by this description you may guesse,
  Who this same Frier, and who this damsell is,
  Yet for more plainnesse sake, I will expresse
  Her name, lest any may the matter misse.
  'Twas *Isabella*, who did late professe
  That state that leadeth straight to heav'nly blisse,
  He was the Frier, that to that mind converted her,
  When as despaire had almost quite subverted her.

92

Within the mourning coffin was inclos'd
  His corse, whom she so lov'd alive and dead,
  And though to griefe she seemed all dispos'd,
  Though all in black she went from foot to head,
  Yet in that wofull shew there was disclosed
  So worthy grace, as in the *Pagan* bred
  A fancy, moving such an alteration,
  As made him change his first determination.

93

For where before he did dispraise and scorn
  All women, now againe he doth commend
  That sex, that doth indeed the world adorn:
  His second love to place he doth intend
  On this, sith that his first hath him forlorn;
  Here now he hopeth all his wo to end;
  And with this passion to drive out the tother,
  As men do drive out one naile with another.

94

And straight in mildest manner that he can,
  Saluting her, he ask'd what caus'd her paine?
  And she the wofull tale to tell began,
  How her true love by *Mandricard* was slaine,
  For whose sake she would never marrie man,
  But serve God all her life that doth remaine:
  The *Pagan* laughs at that the damsell saith,
  As one that knowes no God, and hath no faith.

95

And greatly he her good intent controld,
  Affirming her to merit as great blame,
  As doth the miser that hoards up his gold,
  And neither doth himselfe imploy the same,
  And yet from those that would, doth it withhold:
  So shut not up your selfe (quoth he) for shame;
  Fierce Lions, Bears, and Serpents that have stings,
  Should be shut up, not faire and harmlesse things.

96

The godly Frier that took no little care,
  Lest this ill speech might turn her to small good,
  With new exhortings, bad her to beware,
  That such intisements strongly be withstood:
  And for that end forthwith he doth prepare
  A sumptuous messe of ghostly inward food:
  But this vile *Pagan* did no sooner tast it,
  But up againe his squemish stomack cast it.

97

And seeing that the speeches of this Frire,
  (Whom he could make by no means hold his peace)
  Seem'd greatly to contrary his desire;
  Wrath kindled, and at last did so increase,
  That this poore priest got but a sorie hire.
  But here a while my story now shall cease,
  Lest my mishap or punishment be such
  As was this Priests, for talking overmuch.

THE TWENTY-NINTH BOOKE OF
ORLANDO FVRIOSO

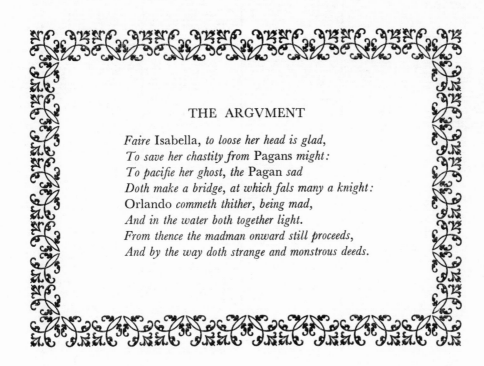

THE ARGVMENT

Faire Isabella, *to loose her head is glad,*
To save her chastity from Pagans *might:*
To pacifie her ghost, the Pagan *sad*
Doth make a bridge, at which fals many a knight:
Orlando *commeth thither, being mad,*
And in the water both together light.
From thence the madman onward still proceeds,
And by the way doth strange and monstrous deeds.

ORLANDO FVRIOSO
THE TWENTY-NINTH BOOKE

1

Oh thoughts of men, unconstant and unstable,
　As subject unto change, as Western wind,
　In all designments fond and variable,
　But chiefly those that love breeds in the mind:
　Lo he that late devis'd all he was able,
　To slander and deface all women kind,
　Yet now with them whom he so sore revil'd,
　Ev'n on the sudden he is reconcil'd.

2

Indeed (most noble Dames) I am so wroth
　With this vile *Turke*, for this his wicked sin,
　For speaking so great slander and untroth,
　Of that sweet sex, whose grace I faine would win,
　That till such time he shall confesse the troth,
　And what a damned errour he was in:
　I shall him make be so in conscience stung,
　As he shall teare his flesh, and bite his tongue.

3

But with what folly he was then possest,
　The sequell of the matter plaine doth show,
　For he that yesterday himselfe profest
　To all the kind a sworn and open foe:
　Now to this stranger one in state distrest,
　Whose birth, whose kin, whose name he doth not know,
　With one small glance, and sober cast of ey,
　Was so enthral'd, he woos her by and by.

4

And as new fancy doth his heart inflame,
　So to new speech it doth his tongue direct,
　A new discourse, new reasons he doth frame,
　With great perswasions, but to small effect:
　For still the godly Frire refutes the same,
　Exhorting her such speeches to neglect,
　And fast to hold her purpose good and holy
　Of serving God, and leaving worldly folly.

5

He saith the way of death is large and spacious,
　But that to life is straight and full of paine:
　But *Rodomont* that saw him so audacious,
　In spite of him this doctrine to maintaine;
　Steps to him, and with hand and tongue ungracious,
　First bids him get him to his cell againe;
　Then his long beard grown on his aged chin,
　All at one pull he pilleth from the skin.

6

And so farre forth his wrath and fury grew,
　He wrings his neck, as pincers wring a naile,
　And twice or thrice about his head him threw,
　As husbandmen that thresh do tosse a flaile:
　Reports most divers afterwards ensew,
　But which be true, and which of truth do faile,
　Is hard to say: some say he was so battered,
　That all his limbs about a rock were scattered.

7

Some say that to the sea he hurled him,
　Though diverse furlongs distant from the place,
　And that he di'd because he could not swim:
　Some others tell, some saint did him that grace,
　To save his life, and heale each broken lim,
　And to the shore did bring him in short space.
　The likelihood hereof who list may way,
　For now of him I have no more to say.

8

Thus cruell *Rodomont* that had removed
　The babling *Frire* that did him so much spight;
　The fearfull damsels love to win he proved,
　By all kind words and gestures that he might;
　He cals her his deare heart, his sole beloved,
　His joyfull comfort, and his sweet delight,
　His mistresse and his goddesse, and such names,
　As loving Knights apply to lovely dames.

9

Her reasons he doth curteously confute,
　(Love soone had made him such a learned clarke)
　In phrases mannerly he moves his sute,
　And still his sute was leueld at one marke,
　And though he might by force have pluckt the frute,
　Yet for that time he doth but kisse the barke:
　He thinkes it will more sweet and pleasing make it,
　If she do give him leave before he take it.

10

Wherefore a while he is content to pawse,
　In hope by time to win her love and grace:
　She deems her selfe like mouse in cats sharpe clawes,
　In strangers hands, and in as strange a place;
　She sees he feard not Gods nor humane lawes,
　Nor had no pittie of her wofull case,
　That onely for his lust would her perswade,
　To breake the vow that she to God had made.

11

Her heart and eyes oft times to heav'n she lifts,
  And prayes the blessed *Virgin* and her *Sonne*,
To save her from this *Pagans* filthy drifts,
  That unto her no villanie be donne:
She doth bethinke her of an hundred shifts,
  How she his beastly lust may safely shunne,
That like an open gulfe on her did gape,
So as it seemd unpossible to scape.

12

She finds out many scuses and delayes,
  That to prolong, which faine she would prevent,
Sometime in humble manner him she prayes,
  That to release her he would be content:
But being still repulst at all assayes,
  At last she doth a way and meanes invent,
Not onely how to shun that present shame,
But merit to her selfe eternall name.

13

Vnto the cruell *Turke* that now began
  From all good course of curtesie to swarve,
She commeth in the meekest sort she can,
  And saith, if he her honour will preserve;
(Which is the part of each true valiant man)
  She would of him that favour well deserve,
And give him such a gift as in due measure,
Should farre surpasse this momentarie pleasure.

14

But if you needs will me defloure, I wis
  (She said) when you have done you will repent,
To thinke how fondly you have done amisse,
  And lost that might have bred you true content:
As for your carnall love, you need not misse
  More faire then I, and fitter for your bent,
But in ten thousand, one you shall not know,
That such a gift upon you can bestow.

15

I know (quoth she) an herbe, and I have seene
  A little since the place where as it grew,
That boild upon a fire of cypresse cleene,
  And mixt with elder berries and with rew;
And after strained harmelesse hands betweene,
  Will yeeld a juyce, that who in order dew,
Annoint therewith, shall never domage feele,
By flame of fire, nor yet by dint of steele.

16

I say if one therewith annoint him thrise,
  These strange effects thereof will strait ensew,
Provided alwayes that in any wise
  He must each month the liquors strength renew:
I have the way to make it in a trice,
  And you shall see by proofe that it is true;
This thing I thinke should joy you more to gaine,
Then if you conquerd had all *France* or *Spaine*.

17

And now for my reward of you, I pray
  Let me obtaine this favourable meed,
To sweare that you henceforth will not assay
  My chastity, by either word or deed:
Fell *Rodomont* thinks this a blessed day,
  And hopes he now shall never armor need,
And sweares he will her honour safe defend,
Though to performe it he doth not intend.

18

Yet still she might this worke bring to effect,
  He doth himselfe against his mind inforce,
And that she might no violence expect,
  He doth not offer any signe of force;
But that once done, his oth he will neglect,
  For of an oth he never had remorce;
But specially he thought it least disgrace,
His oth to violate in such a case.

19

He makes to her a solemne protestation,
  And with most damned oaths the same doth bind,
That he will never do her molestation,
  If she procure a juyce of such a kind:
This sinks so deepe in his imagination,
  Of *Cygnus* and *Achilles* runs his mind,
For by this meanes he doth himselfe assure,
Such priviledge as they had to procure.

20

Poore *Isabella* glad of this delay,
  By which a while her chastitie she shields,
Receiving this his promise, go'th straightway
  To seeke these herbs amid the open fields,
In ev'ry bank and grove, and hedge and way,
  She gathers some, such as the country yeelds;
And all the while the *Pagan* walketh by,
And to the damsell casteth still an eye.

21

And least she should want cypresse wood to burne,
  He with his sword cuts downe whole cypresse trees,
And in all other things to serve her turne,
  That each thing may provided be he sees:
Now with her herbs she made her home returne,
  The caldrons are on fire (no time to leese)
She boyles and perboyles all those herbs and flowres,
In which he thought there were such hidden powres.

22

At all these ceremonies he stands by,
  And what she doth he many times doth looke,
The smoke and heate at last him made so dry,
  That want of drinke he could no longer brooke,
Greeke wines there were, and those he doth apply,
  Two firkins late from passengers he tooke,
He and his men by drinking both that night,
Their heads full heavie made, their hearts full light.

23

Though by their law they are forbidden wine,
　Yet now that here they did the liquor tast,
　They thought it was so sweet and so divine,
　That *Nectar* and that *Manna* farre it past:
At that restraint they greatly do repine,
　That did debar them of so sweet repast,
　And at their owne law and religion laffing,
　They spend that night carowsing and in quaffing.

24

Now had faire *Isbell* finisht that confection,
　Which this grosse *Pagan* doth beleeve to be,
　Against both steele and fire a safe protection:
　Now sir (she said) you shall the trial see,
And that you may be sure than no infection
　Is in these drugs, you first shall prove by me,
　I shall you shew thereof so perfect triall,
　As you shall see the proofe past all deniall.

25

My selfe (quoth she) mind first to take the say,
　That you may see I do not faine nor lie,
　Then after on your selfe you prove it may,
　When you have made a witnes of your eie:
Now therefore bid your men to go away,
　That none be present here but you and I,
　And thus, as with her selfe she had appointed,
　Her neck and brests, and shoulders she annointed.

26

Which done, in chearefull sort she open layd
　Her naked necke before the beastly *Turke*,
　And bad him strike, for she was not afraid,
　She had such skill and trust in this rare worke:
He unadvis'd, and haply overlayd
　With wine, that in his idle braine did worke,
　Was with her speech so undiscreetly led,
　That at one blow he quite cut off her head.

27

The head where love and all the graces dwelt,
　By heedlesse hand is from the bodie severed,
　Alas whose heart at such hap could not melt?
　Yea that is more, the head cut off endevered
To shew what pleasure of her death she felt,
　And how she still in her first love persevered:
　Thrise from the floore the head was seene rebound,
　Thrise it was heard *Zerbinos* name to sound.

28

His name to whom so great love she did beare,
　As she to follow him would leave her life,
　To whom tis hard to say if that she were
　A truer widow or a kinder wife;
O soule that didst not death nor danger feare,
　(A sample in these latter times not rife)
　To save thy chastitie and vowed truth,
　Ev'n in thy tender yeares and greenest youth.

29

Go soule, go sweetest soule for ever blest,
　So may my verse please those whom I desire,
　As my poore *Muse* shall ever do her best,
　As farre as pen can paint, and speech aspire,
That thy just praises may be plaine exprest
　To future times. Go soule to heaven or hyer;
　And if my verse can graunt to thee this chartir,
　Thou shalt be cald of chastitie the Martir.

30

At this her deed so strange and admirable,
　He that above all heav'ns doth ay remaine,
　Lookt downe, and said it was more commendable
　Then hers for whom *Tarquinio* lost his raigne.
And straight an ordinance inviolable,
　Ay to be kept on earth he doth ordaine,
　And thus he said, ev'n by my selfe I sweare,
　Whose powre, heav'n, earth, sprites, men and Angels
　　　　　　　　　　　　　　　　　　　　(feare,

31

That for her sake that dide of this name last,
　Who ever shall hereafter beare that name,
　Shall be both wise and continent and chast,
　Of faultlesse manners, and of spotlesse fame,
Let writers strive to make their glorie last,
　And oft in prose and verse record the same,
　Let *Hellicon, Pindus, Parnassus* hill,
　Sound *Isabella, Isabella* still.

32

Thus said the Hy'st, and then there did ensew
　A wondrous calme in waters and in aire,
　The chast soule up into the third heav'n flew,
　Where *Zerbin* was, to that she did repaire:
Now when the beastly *Turke* saw plaine in vew,
　How he had prov'd himselfe a womanslayre,
　When once his drunken surfet was digested,
　He blam'd himselfe and his owne deed detested.

33

In part to satisfie for this offence,
　And to appease her ghost as twere in part,
　Although he thought no pardon could dispence,
　Nor punishment suffice for such desart;
He vowes a monument of great expence,
　Of costly workmanship and cunning art,
　To raise for her, nor minds he to go furder,
　Then that selfe church where he had done the murder.

34

Of that selfe place he minds her tombe to make,
　And for that cause he gets of workmen store,
　For love, for mony, and for terrors sake,
　Six thousand men he set to worke and more;
From out the mountaines massie stones they take,
　With which wel wrought, & hewd, & squard therfore
　With hie and stately arch that Church he covers,
　And in the midst intombs the blessed lovers.

35

And over this was rais'd with curious sleight,
  A *Pyramid*, a huge and stately towre,
  Which towre an hundred cubits had in height,
  By measure from the top unto the flowre;
  It seemd a worke of as great charge and weight,
  As *Adrian* made, to bost his wealth and powre,
  Of goodly stones, all rais'd in seemly ranks,
  Vpon the edge of stately *Tybris* banks.

36

Now when this goodly worke was once begunne,
  He makes a bridge upon the water by,
  That of great depth and force did ever runne,
  In former time a ferrie there did lye,
  For such as would a further circuit shunne,
  And passe this way more easy and more nye;
  The *Pagan* takes away the ancient ferrie,
  And leaves for passengers, nor bote, nor wherrie.

37

But makes a bridge where men to row are wont,
  And though the same were strõg, & of great length,
  Yet might two horses hardly meet a front,
  Nor had the sides a raile or any strength,
  Who comes this way he meanes shall bide a bront,
  Except he have both courage good and strength,
  For with the armes of all that this way come,
  He means to bewtifie faire *Isbels* toome.

38

A thousand brave Atchievments he doth vow,
  Wherewith he will adorne his stately worke,
  From whom he taketh all these spoiles or how,
  He cares not whether *Christian* or *Turke*.
  Now was the bridge full finished, and now
  His watchmen on each side in corners lurke,
  To make him know when any one coms neare,
  For all that come, he means shall buy it deare.

39

And further his fantastike braine doth thinke,
  That sith by drinking wine he did that sin,
  In lieu thereof he now would water drinke,
  As oft as by mishap he should fall in:
  For when he should unto the bottome sinke,
  The top would be an ell above his chin,
  As who should say, for ev'rie evill action
  That wine procures, were water satisfaction.

40

Full many there arrived in few days,
  Some men, as in the way from *Spaine* to *France*,
  Some others fondly thirsting after prayse,
  In hope by this exploit their names t'advance,
  But *Rodomont* doth meet them both the ways,
  And such his vallew was so good his chance,
  That still as many men as there arrives,
  Lost all of them their arms, and some their lives.

41

Among the many prisners that he tooke,
  All those were *Christians* to *Algyre* he sent,
  And willd his men safely to them to looke,
  Because ere long himselfe to come he ment;
  The rest, save that their armors they forsooke,
  All harmelesse backe into their countries went:
  Now while such feats were by the *Pagan* wrought,
  Orlando thither came of wits bestraught.

42

At that same instant that *Orlando* came,
  Was *Rodomont* all armed save his hed,
  The naked *Earle* with wits quite out of frame,
  Leaps ov'r the bar, and went (as folly led)
  To passe the bridge, the *Pagan* him doth blame,
  For his presumption, and withall he sed,
  Stay sawcy villen, proud, and undiscreet,
  For such as thee this passage is not meet.

43

For Lords and Knights and Squyres of good estate,
  This bridge was built, and not for thee thou beast:
  He that no sence had in his idle pate,
  Not heeding what was said still onward prest:
  I must (the *Pagan* thinks) this fools pride bare,
  It seems belike he thinks I am in jest,
  And thereupon he makes the madman towards,
  And minds to drowne him, sith he was so frowards.

44

He little lookt to find a match so hard,
  Now while they two together gan to strive,
  Behold a gallant dame of great regard,
  At that same bridge by fortune did arrive,
  Faire *Fiordeliege*, that late before had hard,
  How love did of his witts this Earle deprive;
  She hither came to seeke out *Brandimart*,
  That now in *Paris* was with pensive hart.

45

And thus this Ladie (as before I told)
  Came at that season to this dangerous place,
  And knew this *Earle*, when she did him behold,
  And wonderd much to see him in such case:
  Now held *Orlando* with his foe hard hold,
  In vaine the *Pagan* strives him to displace,
  And grinning, to himselfe he said at length,
  Who could have thought, a foole had had such strength?

46

And fretting that he had his purpose mist,
  He doth by sleight the madmans force assay,
  Sometime he puts his hand below his twist,
  Sometime above, sometime another way:
  Orlando stands unmov'd, do what he list;
  The *Pagan* seemd to do by him that day,
  As doth the Beare, that would dig up the tree,
  From whence she fell, but sees it will not be.

47

Orlando full of force, though void of sence,
　About the middle tooke the *Pagan* fast,
And heaves him up from ground, and so from thence,
　Into the streame himselfe he backward cast:
Vnto the bottome both do sinke, from whence
　Each one was glad to get him in great hast,
Orlando nak't and light, swam like a fish,
　So that he soone gat out as he would wish.

48

And being out, away he straight doth runne,
　Nor tarries he to heare, or to expect,
If men do blame or praise that he had donne,
　But follows on his former course direct:
This while the *Pagan* dranke nye halfe a tunne
　Of water, ere he could himselfe erect,
And hardly he escaped being drownd,
　So heavie arm'd, and in place so profound.

49

Now, while the *Pagan* swimmeth for his life,
　Faire *Fiordeliege* with sad and pensive hart,
A lively patterne of a vertuous wife,
　Doth search the sepulcher for *Brandimart*,
Shee tooke her time while they fell first at strife,
　And up and downe she lookt in ev'rie part,
But here she finds nor arms nor yet his mantell,
　Nor meets with such as of him tydings can tell.

50

But leave we her awhile thus mourning sad,
　And seeking him each where save where he was,
And tell we now what hap *Orlando* had,
　And what strange feats his furie brought to passe,
You might perchance beleeve that I were mad,
　If none of his mad pranks I overpasse.
Which were so strange, and in so great a number,
　As you to heare, and me to tell would cumber.

51

I onely shall some few of those recite,
　As to my present purpose shall pertaine
The madman westward held his course forthright,
　Straight to the hils that sever *France* fro *Spaine*,
He seldome bayts, but travels day and night,
　So much he was distemper'd in his braine,
And by the mountaines side as he did passe,
　He met two young men driving of an asse.

52

This asse they loden had with clefts of wood,
　Fast bound upon his burden-bearing backe;
They seeing one runne nak't as he were wood,
　Amid their way, they cride, hoe sirra backe,
But he makes answer neither bad nor good,
　For sence and understanding he did lacke,
But with his foote the poore asse he so spurned,
　That both his lode and him he overturned.

53

He tost him like a football up on hy,
　Whence downe he fell and brake his necke with it;
Then at the men he doth with furie fly,
　Of which the tone had better hap then wit,
For downe the rocke the tone lept by and by,
　Deep threescore yards, and by the way did hit
Vpon a banke of furze, growne in the place,
　And scap't with onely scratching of his face.

54

The tother that of feare like passion feels,
　Did thinke to clammer up upon the rocke,
But straight *Orlando* takes him by the heels,
　And puls him downe and beats him like a stocke,
As fishers use to beat their sliding Eels,
　And ev'n as fawlkners teare some time a cocke,
To give unto their hawks their intrals warme,
　So he tears leg from leg, and arme from arme.

55

These same and other like stupendious deeds,
　He put in practise while those hils he past,
Ev'n such as speech and credit all exceeds,
　His fits so furious were, his strength so vast:
So far unto the westward he proceeds,
　That to the sea, he now was come at last,
Ev'n to the sandie shoars of *Tarracona*,
　That leadeth right the way to *Barcellona*.

56

Vpon those sands (such was his mad conceat)
　He purpos'd with himselfe a house to build,
And being noyed with the parching heat,
　He thinks with sand his skin therefro to shild:
Straight with his hands he digs him out a seat,
　And though the oes his bodie all defild,
Yet with that mould his members all he covered,
　That nothing but his head could be discovered.

57

Now as he lay halfe burid in the sand,
　(For save his head, the rest was all unseen,)
There thither came, as in their way by land,
　Medoro with *Angelica* his Queen,
She not aware what in her way did stand,
　(Of her lorne lovers bosting then I ween)
Came unto him so neare and on such soden,
　That upon him her horse had welny troden.

58

But seeing straight up start a naked man,
　The sight did her greatly amaze and fright,
She knows him not, nor guesse at him she can,
　She thinketh sure, he is some hellish spright:
Rough grisly beard, eyes staring, visage wan,
　All parcht, and sunne burnd, and deformd in sight,
In fine he lookt (to make a true description)
　In face like death, in cullor like a *Gyptian*.

59

But she at this strange sight (as erst I said)
  Did gallop thence as fast as she could ride,
  And screeching lowd, she crieth out for aid,
  Vnto *Medoro* her beloved guide:
  The mad *Orlando* was not ill apaid,
  When such a prettie damzell he had spide:
  Though he no knowledge nor remembrance had,
  How this was she, for whom he first fell mad.

60

Yet, as delighted with her pleasing hew,
  And liking well to see so faire a face,
  With great desire he straight doth her pursew,
  Ev'n as a hound the fearfull Doe doth chase,
  Medoro mov'd herewith, his rapier drew,
  And after this mad fellow rides apase,
  And with his horse he thinketh downe to tred him,
  And with his blade he thinketh to behed him.

61

But by effect, contrariwise he found,
  That he without his host his reckning made,
  The madman shrinketh not an inch of ground,
  And his bare skin was harder then the blade,
  Yet sodenly when as the madman found,
  That one behinde his backe did him invade,
  He turnd and with his fist so smote the horse,
  As made him ly on ground a senslesse corse.

62

And in a trise he backe againe doth goe,
  To catch *Angelica* who spurrs with speed,
  And thinketh still her palfreys pase too sloe
  For such a turne, and so it was indeed,
  For had it gone like arrow from a boe,
  It hardly could have holpe her at this need;
  At last her onely hope was in the ring,
  For now to helpe her was none other thing.

63

The ring that never faild her at her need,
  Did make her now to vanish out of sight,
  But whether that it were for want of heed,
  Or that the sodainenesse did her affright,
  Or that her beast did founder with the speed,
  Or that she did determine to alight,
  Of all these which it was I cannot tell,
  But topsie turvie from the beast she fell.

64

Had she falne shorter, or on tother side,
  In likelihood the madman had her caught,
  Which if he had, she doubtles should have dide,
  But great good fortune her deliverie wrought:
  But now another beast she must provide,
  For this another pase will soone be taught,
  Orlando still doth her pursue so fast,
  That needs he must ov'rget her at the last.

65

As for *Angelica* I take no care,
  I know that she a beast long will not lacke,
  But rather steale one, as she did that Mare,
  That now in madmans hands will suffer wracke.
  To follow her *Orlando* doth not spare,
  Till he her staid and lept upon her backe,
  Then gallopt he as long as she was able,
  And lets her rest in neither field nor stable.

66

Vntill at last in leaping ov'r a ditch,
  The poore Mare put her shoulder out of joynt,
  He with his fall, took neither ach nor stitch,
  Nor of the bruse he passeth not a poynt;
  Nor seeketh he for turpentine or pitch,
  The poore beasts brused members to annoynt,
  Though he might see with this fall he had mard her,
  Yet faine he would, she should have borne him farder.

67

At last on his owne shoulder her he laid,
  And bare her so about an arrow shoot,
  But feeling then that she too heavie waid,
  He leadeth her and lets her go on foot,
  She limping follows him, and still he said,
  Come on, come on, but little did it boot.
  At last to make her her slow pace to alter,
  About his right leg he doth tie her halter.

68

And tels her now with ease she follow may,
  And so to harry her he doth begin,
  The sharpe stones lying in the rugged way,
  Fret of her haire, and afterward the skin,
  The beast misused thus, lives scarse a day:
  Orlando hath her tyde unto his shinne;
  He sees not, nor he knows not she is ded,
  But on he draws her as his furie led.

69

And sure he would have serv'd her such a tuch,
  I meane his mistres if he could have caught her,
  Had not the vertue of the ring beene such,
  As how to walke invisible it taught her:
  Ah cursed be that ring, and curst as much
  Be he that so unluckily it brought her;
  Else sure *Orlando* had revenged then
  Her often wrongs, to him and other men.

70

Yet why wish I this curse on her alone?
  I would the like might hap to all the kinde,
  For in a thousand good there is not one,
  All be so proud, unthankfull and unkinde,
  With flinty hearts, carelesse of others mone,
  In their owne lusts carrid most headlong blinde,
  But more herein to speake I am forbidden,
  Sometime for saying truth one may be chidden.

THE THIRTIETH BOOKE OF
ORLANDO FVRIOSO

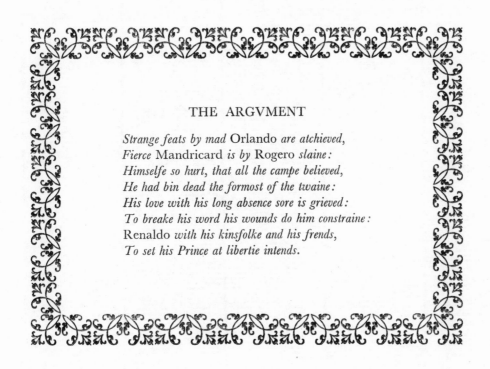

THE ARGVMENT

Strange feats by mad Orlando *are atchieved,*
Fierce Mandricard *is by* Rogero *slaine:*
Himselfe so hurt, that all the campe believed,
He had bin dead the formost of the twaine:
His love with his long absence sore is grieved:
To breake his word his wounds do him constraine:
Renaldo *with his kinsfolke and his frends,*
To set his Prince at libertie intends.

ORLANDO FVRIOSO

THE THIRTIETH BOOKE

1

When men with wrath and sodaine pangs of ire,
  Permit themselves to be orewhelm'd & drown'd,
And hot revenge that burns like flaming fire,
Moves hearts to hurt, or tongs or hands to wound,
Though after to amend it they desire,
Yet place of pardon seldome can be found:
  Ah (worthy Ladies) I do you beseech,
  To pardon that my former foolish speech.

2

For I am growne like a diseased man,
  That when he finds by phisicke no reliefe,
And now no more with patience suffer can
The burning torture of his lingring griefe,
Doth fall to rave and rage, and curse and ban,
Blaspheming God, renouncing his beliefe:
  But when that fit is past, then would he faine,
  But ah he cannot call it backe againe.

3

Yet Ladies of your clemencie I hope,
  I pittie shall, not onely pardon finde,
Although I somewhat swarve from reasons scope,
And rash words flow from unadvised minde:
She onely beares the blame that slayes my hope,
And for true service shews her selfe unkinde:
  That I did speake was partly of compassion,
  With sympathy mov'd of *Orlandos* passion.

4

Who (as I partly did before declare)
  In monstrous sort, survay'd *Marsilios* raigne,
And wrought great wo, great danger, and great care,
To all the then inhabitants of *Spaine*,
I told you how he drew the silly Mare,
Tide to his leg, till she was dead with paine:
  And how he had so small sense in his head,
  He drew her after him when she was dead.

5

But comming to a great deepe running water,
  He was constraind to let her there abide,
And (for he swimmes as perfect as an Atter)
He quickly passed to the tother side,
Where then a herdman came his beasts to water,
And on a curtall he himselfe did ride:
  And though he saw the madman and did view him,
  Yet being naked he would not eschew him.

6

The madman prayeth him that he would spare
  His horse; that they two might together cope:
I left (quoth he) on tother side my Mare,
And fast about her necke I left a rope:
I left her dead; but yet with heed and care,
Of her recoverie there is good hope:
  The herdman laugheth at his sencelesse words,
  And unto him no answer he affords.

7

Ho (saith *Orlando*) fellow, dost not heare?
  I must thy curtall have, thou needst not laffe:
And with that word approching somewhat neare,
The crabbed herdman with a crabtree staffe,
Gave him a bastinado on his eare,
Which put the mad Erle into such a chafe,
  That with his fist he made the herdman reele,
  Till paine it selfe made him no paine to feele.

8

This done he leapeth on the horses backe,
  And at adventure on he takes his way,
Where ere he comes he putteth all to wracke,
His horse tasts neither provender nor hay:
But though this tyrd, a horse he may not lacke,
The next he meets by force he takes away:
  To strive with him it was but little boote,
  He is resolved not to go a foote.

9

He passeth to the straits of Gibraltar,
  Or Zibelterra (call it which you will)
And as he went, with force of open war,
Townes he did burne, and all the dwellers kill:
Ten yeares will hardly make that he would mar
Within one houre, and thus he traveld still,
  Till on a day, riding upon the sand,
  He saw a ship new loosed from the land.

10

The aire was cleare and mild, and calme the wether,
  And certaine Gentlefolke had hyr'd the barke,
With mind to take their solace there together,
And to returne againe ere it were darke:
The madman cries, hoe sirs let me come thither:
His deeds, his words, they neither marke nor harke,
  Or if they did you may be sure they thought,
  They would not comberd be with such a fraught.

11

He hallows after them, and whoopes and hayles,
  To have them stay, & with faire words doth wo thē,
  Glad might they be they went with oars and sayls,
  For might he come, he surely would undoe them,
  The foole that sees how small his speech prevails,
  Beats on his horse, and meanes to ride unto them:
  In vaine his horse would shun this hard adventer,
  But he perforce makes him the sea to enter.

12

First he his feete doth wet, and then his knees,
  And next his belly, after that his backe,
  Now scant his nose one in the water sees,
  And still he layes him on; poore horse alacke,
  That either in these seas his life must leese,
  Or swim to Affricke ere he can turne backe:
  At last with swimming tyrd, with water cloyd,
  His belly fild, till limbs of life were void.

13

The horse unto the bottome quickly sunke,
  And had for company his burthen drownd,
  If fortune that helps frantike men and drunke,
  Had not him safe conveyd to Affricke ground:
  Orlando at the danger never shrunke,
  But to the shore he swam both safe and sound:
  It happie was the seas were then so still,
  Else had the Erle bin drownd for all his skill.

14

Now being safe arrived at the shore,
  Neare Setta strayt he ranged ov'r the cost,
  And did such deeds as he had done before,
  On tother side to many poore mens cost;
  At last he came where as he found great store,
  Of warlike weapons, and a mighty host:
  But how with them this madman disagreed,
  I may not in this booke to tell proceed.

15

And further how Angelica the faire,
  Did meete her love againe, and what a Lord
  He grew, by matching with so great an haire,
  And liv'd with her in love and sweet accord,
  (Although in birth an unfit matched paire)
  I leave for other Muses to record:
  For now I must addresse my selfe to tell,
  What haps in Agramantes campe befell.

16

I told you two bookes past, or thereabout,
  How Mandricard was Doralices choice:
  And how in face of all the Pagan rout,
  She gave that doome, that made him much rejoyce,
  For she was deemd for beauty (out of doubt)
  The best in Europe by the common voice:
  Now chiefe since faire Angelica was fled,
  And worthy Isabella lost her hed.

17

But yet this pleasure was not so entire,
  But that it sawced was with some annoy,
  For wrath and envie set his heart on fire,
  And much abated of his present joy:
  It spites him that Rogero dare aspire,
  To give his coat, being a berdlesse boy:
  And further that the King of Sericane,
  Should openly lay claime to Durindane.

18

And first Rogero will by no meanes yeeld,
  By no intreatie, nor by no request,
  That Mandricard should carrie that same sheeld,
  Which had the Argent Eagle on the crest,
  Except he first could win it in the feeld:
  On tother side Gradasso doth not rest,
  But he will be the first to trie by fight,
  Which of them two had to the sword most right.

19

With Agramant Marsilio tooke great paine,
  In all or part these quarrels to appease,
  But when they saw their labour was in vaine,
  To governe or perswade with one of these:
  The chance (quoth Agramant) shal make that plaine,
  For which you strive, and ev'n as fortune please,
  So let it be, and let some lots be cast,
  Which two or three, shall fight the first or last.

20

And yet this just request denie me not,
  Before the matter any further goth,
  (Though now you be so violent and hot,
  That speech of peace and all accord you loth)
  To grant that who shall combat first by lot,
  May leesing leese, and winning win for both:
  This motion, most indifferent must seeme,
  Sith both their vallews equall we esteeme.

21

This motion neither of them do mislike,
  And straight Gradassos and Rogeros name,
  Vpon two scroles were writ so passing like
  You would have judg'd them both to be the same:
  A boy of fourteene yeare of age they pike,
  To draw the lot, and he that first out came,
  Must fight with Mandricard, and make it knowne,
  He fights for tothers title and his owne.

22

When on this order all parts were agreed,
  The lot to fight upon Rogero fell,
  Which hap great griefe did in Gradasso breed,
  Although in shew he seemd to take it well:
  Contrariwise it did all joy exceed,
  The joy Rogero had, it so befell:
  So well of his owne vallew he believed,
  He joyd at that at which the tother grieved.

23

But yet *Gradasso* doth with great regard,
  Both favour and advance *Rogeros* side,
  And sheweth him how he must lie to ward
  A comming blow, how he might slip aside:
  How for a thrust he may be best prepard:
  Which blowes be firme, and which be falsifide,
  When best time is to follow thrust or blow:
  How one may best take vantage of his foe.

24

The rest of that same day that did remaine,
  Ensuing this same course of casting lots,
  They spent as pleased each mans pleasing vaine,
  In talke, or banquetting, or tossing pots:
  To see this fight the people glad and faine,
  Clammer the scaffolds, gazing still like sots,
  Some for desire do come by breake of day,
  And some all night within the place do stay.

25

Thus (as I say) these simple fooles do long,
  To see the combat these brave Knights betwixt,
  And blame the stay, and thinke the time too long,
  That for the same the *Heralds* had prefixt:
  But sober men that knew what did belong
  To such exploits, whose wiser heads were fixt
  On publike good, this quarrell much lament,
  And traveld all they can it to prevent.

26

And chiefe *Marsilio* and *Sobrino* sage,
  Advise King *Agramant* to stay the fight,
  And these same champions furie to asswage,
  And to take up the quarrell if they might:
  Forewarning him when he must battell wage,
  With *Charles* of *France*, the losse of one such Knight
  Will do him greater hurt and damage then,
  Then would the losse of thousands other men.

27

But *Agramant* knew all was true they spoke,
  And faine he would their counsell wise obay,
  But could not tell his grant how to revoke:
  Onely he doth in curteous sort them pray,
  That he may strike with them so great a stroke,
  Either to end or to defer the fray;
  And yeeld the rather unto his perswasion,
  Because it rose upon so light occasion.

28

Or if they did esteeme such toyes so far,
  As though they matters were of true renowne;
  That yet they would the fight so long defar,
  Vntill the sonne of *Pipen* were put downe:
  And till they conquerd had the *Realme* by war,
  And tane from him his mantle and his crowne,
  This motion had in likelihood taken place,
  Save each thought first consent would be disgrace.

29

Above them all and more then all the rest,
  That in this sort their speech in vaine had spent:
  Faire *Doralyce* doth *Mandricard* request,
  That to the Kings desire he would assent:
  She doth exhort, intreat, perswade, protest,
  She doth complaine, and languish, and lament:
  To thinke that by his over hastie choler,
  She still must live in anguish and in dolor.

30

How can I hope (said she) that ere I shall
  Live any houre in solace and in joy?
  When still I see you readie be to brall,
  With ev'rie man, for ev'rie trifling toy:
  The *Sarzans* foile doth me no good at all,
  My choyce of you hath bred me more annoy:
  To end that quarrell, ah what did it boot,
  Sith straight another quarrell is on foot?

31

I simple foole, in minde was proud and glad,
  That such a Prince, so brave a man as you,
  For love of me his whole state venterd had;
  But now I finde by this that doth ensew,
  That I had far more reason to be sad,
  Sith each like cause, like danger doth renew;
  And not my love, but your owne native furie,
  To bide such hard adventures did procure yee.

32

But if your love be such as in your speech,
  You do professe, and in your open show:
  Then by that love I humbly you beseech,
  And by that fancie which too well I know,
  Doth ev'n my heart and soule with love bewitch,
  Let not this quarrell any further grow:
  I see not why it should you so molest,
  To see your *Eagle* in anothers crest.

33

If needs you will attempt this hardie feat,
  And venter life upon a thing so vaine,
  The hazard that you make must needs be great,
  But none, or very small can be the gaine:
  But if that fortune change her fickle seat,
  Thinke then, ô thinke, what woe shall I sustaine?
  There never yet was Emperor or King,
  Could boast that he had Fortune in a string.

34

But if that life be unto you lesse deare,
  Then is a painted bird upon a sheeld;
  Yet for my sake, whom it doth touch more neare,
  Let me intreat you to this motion yeeld:
  If you were slaine, what joy could I have heare?
  Death sole from wo, both could and should me sheeld
  Nor feare I death; my onely griefe would bee,
  Before my death thy wofull end to see.

35

Thus earnestly faire *Doralycee* dealt,
  All that same night, as in his armes she lyes,
  And as she spake, the teares distill and melt,
  In watrie streames, downe from her crystall eyes:
  The *Tartar* that no little passion felt,
  To comfort her saith all he can devise:
  And wipes her cheekes, and her sweet lip doth kisse,
  And weeps for company, and answers this.

36

Ah do not grieve thy selfe so sore (my deare)
  Ah do not grieve thy selfe for such a toy,
  Plucke up thy sprights, and be of better cheare,
  There is no cause of feare mine onely joy:
  No though that all the Kings and captains heare,
  Had sworne my death, and vowed mine annoy:
  Yet all the Kings and captaines I would vanquish,
  Why then should you causles in sorrow languish?

37

What, did not I with trunchen of a speare,
  (You know your selfe whether I say the truth)
  Not having sword nor other weapon theare,
  Win you from all your gard? and shall a youth,
  A beardlesse boy, cause you my safetie feare,
  And breed in you so unadvised ruth?
  Well might you deeme I were a dastard lout,
  If of *Rogero* I should stand in doubt.

38

Gradasso, though unto his griefe and shame,
  Yet if one aske him can it not gainesay,
  That when he last unto *Sorya* came,
  I met and tooke him prisner by the way,
  Yet he is of another manner same,
  Then is *Rogero*, you your selfe will say:
  I had him there a prisner at my will,
  And if I listed might have kept him still.

39

And least I should of this good witnes want,
  Beside *Gradasso*, there be hundreds more,
  As namely *Isolyr*, and *Sacrapant*,
  Whom I set free and had great thanks therefore:
  Also the famous *Griffin* and *Aquilant*,
  That there were taken, but few dayes before:
  With divers more both *Turkish* and baptised,
  That by my force were taken and surprised.

40

Their wonder in those countries still doth last,
  Of that great vallew I that time did show,
  And should I now a doubt or perill cast?
  Am I in greater danger now you trow?
  Shall one young youth me hand to hand agast?
  Shall I now doubt his force, or feare his blow?
  Now having *Durindana* by my side,
  And *Hectors* armour on my backe beside?

41

Why did not I, as pointed was by lot,
  With *Rodomont* first bloudie battell wage?
  That by his ill successe you might forewot,
  The speedie end of this young sorrie page.
  Drie up these teares (my deare) and bring me not,
  Before the combat such an ill presage:
  Nor thinke an *Eagle* on a target painted
  Moves me hereto, but doubt of honor tainted.

42

Thus much said he, but she such answer made him,
  With words expressing such a loving mone,
  As were not onely able to perswade him,
  But might (I thinke) have mov'd a marble stone:
  The force was great wherewith she did invade him,
  In fine so farre she conquers him alone,
  He grants thus farre to be at her devotion,
  If peace be offerd, to accept the motion.

43

And so I thinke indeed he would have done,
  Had not *Rogero* early in the morne,
  Got up before the rising of the Sunne,
  And enterd in the lists, and blowne his horne,
  To shew that he the battell would not shunne,
  And that *Ioves* bird by him was justly borne:
  Which either he will carrie on his shield,
  Or else will leave his carkas in the field.

44

But when the *Tartar* fierce did heare that sound,
  And that his men thereof had brought him word:
  He thinks great shame should unto him redound,
  If any treatie he of peace afford:
  Arme arme he cries, & straight he armes him round,
  And by his side he hangs his trustie sword.
  And in his countenance he lookes so grim,
  Scarse *Doralyce* her selfe dares speake to him.

45

And armed at all pieces, up in hast
  He gets, and that same courser he bestrides,
  That was that *Christen* champions in time past,
  Who now doth runne his wit and sense besides:
  And thus he comes unto the lists at last,
  The place that all such quarrels still decides,
  The King and all his court soone after came,
  And now ere long begins the bloudie game.

46

Now on their heads their helmets are made fast,
  Now are the Lances put into their hands,
  Now was the token giv'n by trumpets blast,
  Which both the horse and horseman understands:
  Now in a full carryre they gallop fast,
  And either strongly to his takle stands:
  Now with such force the tone the tother strake,
  As though that heav'n did fall, and earth did shake.

47

The *Argent Eagle* comes on either side,
　With wings displaid on either captaines sheeld,
　The bird which *Iove* (men say) was seene to ride,
　(Though better wing'd) ov'r the *Thessalian* feeld:
　As for their mighty strength and courage tride,
　Their massie speares sufficient witnesse yeeld:
　Nor sturd they more with those tempestuous knocks,
　Then wind sturs towres, or waves do stur the rocks.

48

The splinters of the spears flew to the skie,
　(As *Turpin* writeth that was present there)
　And were on fire by having bin so nie,
　Vnto the scorching of the fierie Spheare:
　The champions out their swords draw by and by,
　As those that neither sword nor fire did feare,
　And either thrusteth at the tothers face,
　And seekes by force the tother to displace.

49

They never sought to hurt each others steed,
　Not that they made together such accord,
　But that they deemd it an unworthy deed,
　Not worthy of a worthy Knight or Lord:
　Of base revenge they count that act proceed,
　And meet of noble minds to be abhord,
　So that in those dayes none were knowne to kill
　A horse, except it were against his will.

50

Vpon their vizers both do strike at once,
　And though the same were firme and plated double,
　As being made of proofe and for the nonce,
　Yet did the force of such fell strokes them trouble;
　And still they lay on lode as thicke as stones
　Of haile, that often turne the corne to stubble:
　I thinke it needlesse further to alledge,
　If they have strength, or if their swords have edge.

51

Yet long they fought together in that field,
　Ere any signe of any blow was left,
　Such wary heed each tooke himselfe to shield;
　But *Durindan* at last fell with such heft,
　Full on the circle of *Rogeros* shield,
　That halfe way through the argent bird it cleft,
　And pierst the coate of male that was within,
　And found a passage to the very skin.

52

The cruell blow made many hearts full cold,
　Of such as wisht well to *Rogeros* part,
　For most of those that stood by to behold,
　Rogero favourd in their mind and hart,
　So that afore to say one might be bold,
　If fortune follow would the greater part,
　Fierce *Mandricard* were slaine, or else should yeeld,
　So that this blow offended halfe the field.

53

But surely some good Angell I beleeve,
　The force of this so fearfull stroke abated,
　Rogero though the wound him somewhat grieve,
　Yet was his mind therewith no whit amated,
　Great usury he mindeth him to give,
　And that the strife may quickly be debated,
　He frankly strikes with his whole force and might,
　Full on the helmet of the *Tartar* Knight.

54

With so great force and furie came the blow,
　As to the teeth no doubt had clov'n his head,
　Saving by what mishap I do not know,
　But want of heed that too much hast had bred,
　It lighted flatling on him, else I trow
　That stroke alone had him most surely sped,
　But as it was it made his head so idle,
　He opend both his hands and loos'd his bridle.

55

Good *Brigliadore* that felt the slacked raine,
　(I thinke still mourning for his masters change)
　Ran up and downe at randon on the plaine,
　His senslesse rider suffering him to range;
　Who when he came unto himselfe againe,
　And saw his horse to run a course so strange,
　A spurned Viper hath not so much wrath,
　Nor wounded Lion, as the *Tartar* hath.

56

He claps the spurs to *Brigliadoros* side,
　And on his stirrops he himselfe advances,
　And to his fo with furie he doth ride,
　And up on hie his right arme he inhances,
　To strike a blow; but when *Rogero* spide
　His arme lie ope, as oft in fight it chances,
　He chopt his swords point under tothers arme,
　And puld it out with blood both wet and warme.

57

By which he did not onely maime his fo,
　By letting blood upon so large a vaine,
　But bated much the furie of the blo,
　Which notwithstanding fell with force so maine,
　As made *Rogero* stagger to and fro,
　And mazd his head, and dazd his eyes with paine;
　And much it was that time for his behoofe,
　To have his helmet of so gocd a proofe.

58

But having now againe recoverd force,
　And as it were new wak'ned from his dreame,
　Vpon the *Tartar* Prince he turn'd his horse,
　And on his thigh he strikes with strength extreame,
　That through the steele he did the sword enforce:
　Out spins the blood in pure vermilion streame,
　Nought could availe inchanted *Hectors* armes,
　Against his sword with stronger temperd charmes.

AA

59

The *Tartar* feeling to his great disease,
  His body wounded as he litle thought,
  Did rage as terrible as do the seas,
  With highest winds and strongest tempests wrought,
  He curseth heav'ns, his smarting pangs to ease,
  The shield that had the bird for which he fought,
  Away he hurleth from him for the nonce,
  And to his sword he sets both hands at once.

60

Ah (quoth *Rogero*) too plaine triall this is,
  That to that *Eagle* thou no title hast,
  That first didst with thy sword cut mine in peeces,
  And now thine owne away from thee dost cast:
  Thus much said he, but whatsoever he sees,
  He must the force of *Durindana* tast,
  Which fell upon his forehead with such might,
  A mountaine might have seem'd to fall as light.

61

I say the blow upon his forehead fell,
  But yet his beaver sav'd it from his face,
  It happend at that time for him full well,
  That in the hollow there was so much space;
  Yet harmlesse quite to scape him not befell,
  For why the sword that ever cuts apace,
  Did pierce his plated sadle, and beside
  An inch did enter into *Rogeros* side.

62

Thus each with crimson had his armor dide,
  And bloud did streame from both a double way,
  Yet hitherto it could not be descride,
  On whether side would chances ballance sway:
  At last *Rogero* did that doubt decide,
  With that same sword that ever home doth pay,
  And where the tothers target wants, there just
  Rogero payes him with a speeding thrust.

63

The blade, gainst which prevailes no Magick art,
  His curats pierst, and ribs and flesh it tore,
  And found a passage to the naked hart:
  Now must the *Tartar* Prince for evermore
  In sword and painted shield forsake his part,
  Not onely so, but that which grieves him more,
  He must forsake his much beloved life,
  More loved honour, and most loved wife.

64

The wretch yet unrevenged did not die,
  But gave hard recompence ere he departed,
  At good *Rogeros* head he doth let flie,
  And had (no doubt) the same in sunder parted,
  Save that his arme was maymd, and so thereby
  Much of his force from thence had bin divarted,
  Much of his force diverted was from thence
  Before, when for his arme he wanted fence.

65

But as it was, yet too too hard it fell,
  And caus'd the noble Knight great paine to feele,
  His helmet it did cleave, though plated well,
  And made for proofe of tough well temperd steele,
  And in the very skull it clove a spell,
  Two fingers deepe, and made him backward reele,
  He backward fals, the paine was so exceeding,
  With grievous wound his hed most freshly bleeding.

66

Rogero was the first that tumbled downe,
  And *Mandricardo* fell a good while after,
  All thought *Rogero* dead, because his crowne
  Still bled, but chiefly *Stordilanos* daughter
  Ioyes, that her spouse had won this fights renowne,
  Now hopes she, she shal turne her teares to laughter,
  And as she thought, so was the common voice,
  So that the *Tartars* friends did all rejoyce.

67

But when there did appeare by certaine signes,
  The live man living, and the dead man slaine,
  Then *Doralycee* wrings her hands and whines,
  And griefe came there, and comfort here againe:
  The chiefest part, whose favour all inclines
  Vnto *Rogero*, are full glad and faine,
  And gratulate his good successe, and grace him,
  And runne to him, and in their armes embrace him.

68

Nor was this shew of love, dissimulation,
  But true unfained kindnesse, and good faith,
  But yet *Gradassos* faint congratulation
  Makes men surmise he thinks not as he saith:
  He secretly envies such reputation,
  Though outwardly the flatterer he playth,
  And curseth (were it destinie or chance)
  That to this enterprise did him advance.

69

But *Agramant* that ever did before,
  Do him great honor, and him well esteeme,
  Now he doth him admire, extoll, adore,
  So highly of his valew he doth deeme:
  In him alone he puts affiance more,
  Then all his campe together it should seeme,
  Now that the seed of *Agricane* was spent,
  And *Rodomont* gone thence a malcontent.

70

What should I tell the praise that many a Ladie
  Gave of this Knight, of *Affricke* and of *Spaine*?
  Who knew that *Mandricardo* was no babie,
  And saw him now by this mans valew slaine;
  Yea dolefull *Doralyce* her selfe (it may be)
  Save that for modestie she must refraine,
  Would have bene moved with a small request,
  To speake as well of him as did the rest.

71

I say it may be, but I cannot tell,
  For why? before unconstant she was proved;
  And sure *Rogeros* parts did so excell,
  As any Ladie doubtlesse might have moved.
  While tother liv'd, perhap she lik't him well,
  But now to seeke a new it her behoved,
  Such one as she her selfe might able warrant,
  To ride both day and nightly on her arrant.

72

Now brought the King *Rogero* with great care
  To his owne tent, that there he may be cured,
  The best Physitions thither sent for are,
  To search his wounds, they straight his life assured:
  The shield and armes that *Mandricardo* bare,
  The which this bloudie battell first procured,
  All save the sword that was *Gradassos* right,
  Were hanged up by his beds head that night.

73

Howbeit that brave courser *Brigliadore*,
  Rogero needs would give unto the King,
  Who tooke it thankfully, and set more store
  By that same steed then any such like thing:
  But hereof now a while I treate no more,
  First must you heare what news the maide did bring,
  (I meane *Hyppalca*) to her mistris deare,
  Whom love had made to be of heavie cheare.

74

She told her first what hap to her befell,
  How *Frontine* by a *Turke* was tane away;
  And after, how she found at *Merlins* well
  Richardo and *Rogero* that same day,
  To whom she did her hard adventure tell,
  And how *Rogero* went with her straightway,
  To win the horse out of the *Pagans* fist,
  But at that season he his purpose mist.

75

Also she told to *Bradamant* the cause,
  Why her deare love himselfe did now absent,
  Who promist her, to take a little pawse,
  And then her mind most thoroughly content:
  In fine *Hyppalca* from her bosome drawes
  That letter which was to her mistris sent,
  Who so much lesse did seeme to like the letter,
  Because she would have lik't his presence better.

76

For sith before she did himselfe expect,
  Now paper in his steed to have and inke,
  It caused her to feare and to suspect,
  And made some doubts into her thoughts to sinke,
  Yet lik't she well the meaning and effect,
  And kist the letter oft, and sure I thinke,
  Had burnd it with the heate of her desire,
  Save that the teares she shed did quench that fire.

77

She read the writing ov'r, five times or six,
  The words, the phrase, the sence her pleas'd so well,
  And then she made the maid, each time betwix,
  The message that *Rogero* sent to tell,
  And save he did so short a time prefix
  To come to her, and ay with her to dwell,
  I thinke she never would have ceased mourning,
  Till she had seene or heard of his returning.

78

Rogero to *Hippalca* promis'd had,
  Fifteen or twenty dayes at most to stay,
  And her, to tell her mistresse so he bad,
  But swearing to come sooner if he may:
  But ne'erthelesse good *Bradamant* is sad,
  Still doubting chances to prolong that day.
  All things (said she) to fortune are subjected,
  And chiefe in warres that are by chance directed.

79

Ay (my *Rogero*) who could once have thought,
  Sith I more then my selfe esteemed thee,
  That thou by any meanes couldst have been brought
  To beare thy very foes more love then me?
  Whom thou shouldst hurt, by thee their help is sought
  Whom thou shouldst save, by thee they spoiled be;
  Needs must I blame thy negligent regarding,
  As well in punishing as in rewarding.

80

Trajano slue thy sire, I think thou knowst,
  (For sure the stones it know) yet to his sonne,
  Thou thinkst in honour thou such dutie owest,
  That thou must see no hurt may him be done:
  Is this sufficient a revenge thou trowest,
  Thinkst thou true fame can by such facts be won?
  Lo unto what thy shew of honour tends,
  To serve thine enemies, and slay thy friends.

81

Thus *Bradamant* spake to her absent love,
  With passion great, and evermore her maid
  With reason seeks that fancy to remove,
  Assuring her she need not be affraid:
  And wishing her with patient mind to prove,
  If so he would not do as he had said,
  And that she would in all things hope the best,
  And then to God and fortune leave the rest.

82

With this good speech of hers, and strong perswasion,
  She doth his comming till the day expect,
  Which good *Rogero* brake, not by occasion
  That he his word and promise did neglect;
  But that which hapt against his expectation,
  His wounds had bred so dangerous effect,
  But chiefe the same he last took in his head,
  Which made him forty dayes to keep his bed.

83

Now *Bradamant* doth wait the twenty dayes,
  And staid at *Montalbano* with her mother,
  And making still enquiry many wayes,
  If she might heare some newes of one or other,
  But none she heard, save that which to his praise
  Was told her after by her younger brother,
  Which though she joy'd to heare, as was most meet,
  Yet mingled was some sowre with that same sweet.

84

For why the value of *Marfisa* stout
  Which did assist them greatly, as he told,
  To win their kinsmen from the moorish rout,
  That unto *Bertolage* should have been sold,
  This bred in *Bradamantes* mind some doubt,
  And strake into her heart a jealous cold;
  Because 'twas said they two together went
  To *Agramant*, that in his camp was pent.

85

For though she could not chuse but greatly praise her,
  That did her selfe so stout and valiant prove,
  Yet on the tother side, her beauty frayes her,
  Lest he perhap on her might set his love:
  But yet in fine, hope of his promise stayes her,
  So that in twenty dayes he did not move
  From *Montalbano*, and in that same space,
  There thither came the chiefe man of her race.

86

I mean not chiefe of birth, but chiefe of name,
  For two there were, in birth more old then he,
  Renaldo unto *Montalbano* came,
  His brothers, cosins, and his friends to see,
  Whom he had heard by speech of flying fame,
  Now safe arrived at that place to be,
  And how *Rogero* and *Marfisa* wrought
  Their liberty, when they were sold and bought.

87

Wherefore he came to see them face to face,
  And understand with them how each thing stood,
  It seem'd he was as welcome to the place,
  As is the swallow to her tender brood,
  That almost starved, and in sorie case
  Have long expected sustenance and food,
  And when they there had staid a day or twaine,
  Both they and he to *Paris* went againe.

88

Alardo and *Guicchiardo*, *Richardet*,
  And *Malagigy* and good *Viviane*,
  Close after this brave Lord themselves do get,
  And *Bradamant* with them they would have tane,
  But she alledg'd she could not come as yet;
  (But hopes ere long they should be overtane)
  She prayes them for that time content to hold them,
  For why she was not well at ease she told them.

89

And true it was, she was not well at ease,
  Not that she had a fit of any feaver,
  Or any other corporall disease,
  It was a fit of love, that burneth ever;
  Whose heat no herb nor physick can appease;
  This fit did her from that brave crew dissever:
  But in another book I shall repeat,
  What succour they did bring to *Charles* the great.

THE THIRTY-FIRST BOOKE OF
ORLANDO FVRIOSO

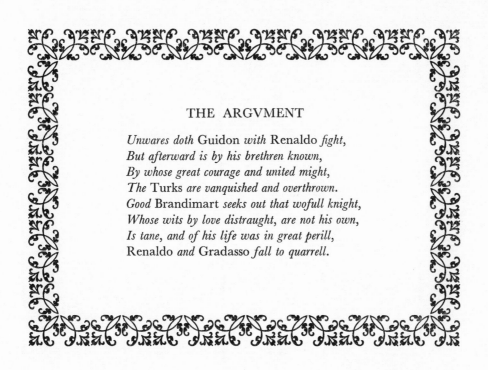

THE ARGVMENT

Unwares doth Guidon *with* Renaldo *fight,*
But afterward is by his brethren known,
By whose great courage and united might,
The Turks *are vanquished and overthrown.*
Good Brandimart *seeks out that wofull knight,*
Whose wits by love distraught, are not his own,
Is tane, and of his life was in great perill,
Renaldo *and* Gradasso *fall to quarrell.*

ORLANDO FVRIOSO
THE THIRTY-FIRST BOOKE

1

What state of life more pleasing may we find,
  Then theirs, that true and hearty love do beare?
  Whom that sweet yoke doth fast together bind,
  That man in Paradise first learn'd to weare:
  Were not some so tormented in their mind,
  With that same vile suspect, that filthy feare,
  That torture great, that foolish frenesie,
  That raging madnesse, called jealousie.

2

For ev'ry other sowre that gets a place,
  To seat it selfe amid this pleasant sweet,
  Doth help in th'end to give a greater grace,
  And makes loves joy more grateful when they meet,
  Who so abstaines from sustenance a space,
  Shall find both bread and water relish sweet:
  Men know not peace, nor rightly how to deem it,
  That have not first by war been taught t'esteem it.

3

Though eyes want sight of that they would see faine,
  The thought yet sees, & hearts with patience take it,
  Long absence grieves, yet when they meet againe,
  That absence doth more sweet and pleasant make it:
  To serve and sue long time for little gaine,
  (So that all hope do not ev'n quite forsake it)
  One may endure, for when the paine is past,
  Reward, though long it stay, yet comes at last.

4

The sharp repulses, and the deep disdaines,
  And all the torments that in love are found,
  At last with pleasure recompence the paines,
  And make far more contentment to abound:
  But if this hellish plague infect the braines,
  Though afterward it seem both whole and sound,
  The quality thereof is so mischievous,
  The very thought is to a lover grievous.

5

This is that cruell wound, against whose smart
  No liquors force prevailes, nor any plaster,
  No skill of starres, no depth of Magick art
  Devised by that great clark *Zoroaster*:
  A wound that so infects the soule and heart,
  As all our sense and reason it doth master;
  A wound whose pang and torment is so durable,
  As it may rightly called be incurable.

6

That is a plague that quickly doth infect
  All lovers hearts, and doth possesse their thought,
  As well with causelesse as with just suspect;
  By this a man to madnesse meere is brought:
  Oh plague, by whose most damnable effect
  In deep despaire to die have divers sought;
  Oh jealousie, that didst without desert
  Possesse the noble *Bradamantes* heart.

7

Not for the tale her maid or brother told,
  Which made within her mind a sharp impression,
  But other newes that made her heart full cold,
  How her love of new love did make profession;
  As I more plaine hereafter shall unfold,
  For now I needs a while must make digression
  To brave *Renaldo*, that to *Paris* ward
  Did march, with that same crew of great regard.

8

The day ensuing ere it yet was night,
  They met an armed knight upon the way,
  A Lady faire accompani'd the knight,
  His armour all was black, save that there lay
  Athwart the brest a wreath of Argent bright.
  And straight the formost man in their array,
  Which *Richardetto* was, as then did chance,
  He challenged with him to break a lance.

9

The gallant youth that never man refus'd,
  Straight turn'd his horse, a space for course to take,
  As one that (for his time) had often us'd
  Such feats as this to do, and undertake:
  Renaldo standeth still, and them perus'd,
  To see which knight the fairest course would make,
  Now *Richardet* thinks, if I hit him just,
  I shall this gallant tumble in the dust.

10

But otherwise it then to him befell,
  And of his reckning he was quite deceiv'd,
  The tother knew to hit, and sit so well,
  That *Richardet* was from the saddle heav'd:
  Alardo seeing how his brother fell,
  Did think t'avenge the foile that he receiv'd,
  But he likewise inferiour did remaine,
  His arm was bruis'd, his shield was rent in twaine.

11

Guicchiardo next the selfe same fortune tri'd,
    And was constrain'd unto the ground t'incline,
    Although to him *Renaldo* lowdly cri'd,
    Stay, hold your hands, for this course should be mine.
Vivian and *Malagige*, and more beside,
    That at their kinsmens foile did much repine,
    Would then have fought with this same stranger knight,
    Save that *Renaldo* claim'd it as his right.

12

And said, my friends, we must to *Paris* hast,
    But to himselfe he said, it were a jest,
    For me to stay till all they down were cast
    By one and one, Ile fight and they shall rest;
This said, he spurs his horse, and commeth fast,
    And as he runs he sets his speare in rest;
    The tother doth as much, and eithers speare
    The stroke doth in a thousand peeces teare.

13

The horsmen with the stroke stir not an inch,
    They both had learn'd so perfectly to sit,
    But on their horses it did shrewdly pinch,
    Yet *Bayard* scarce his course doth intermit,
The tothers horse had such a parlous wrinch,
    That mar'd him quite, and brake his back with it,
    His master that was greatly griev'd to see't,
    Forsakes his seat, and takes him to his feet.

14

And to *Renaldo*, that with naked hand
    Came toward him in shew of truce, he said,
    Sir knight I give you here to understand,
    I lik'd so well this horse that here is dead,
I think it would not with mine honour stand,
    To leave him unreveng'd, which hath me led
    To challenge you, ev'n as you are true knight,
    That you will answer me againe in fight.

15

Renaldo answer'd, if your horse you lost,
    The onely cause of this your quarrell be,
    Then comfort you, for of mine onely cost,
    Your want herein shall be suppli'd by me,
With such a horse, as I may boldly boast,
    To be as good a one as ere was he:
    Not so sir, said the tother, you mistake it,
    I will expound my mind, and plainer make it.

16

Though I lik'd well my serviceable horse,
    Yet sith he now is in this conflict slaine,
    Think not that of his death I so much force,
    As that alone moves me to fight againe;
But in plaine termes on foot to trie your force,
    As well as erst on horseback I would faine.
Renaldo, that of no mans force accounted,
    Without delay straight from his horse dismounted.

17

And sith (quoth he) I see your noble mind,
    Of this my company hath no suspition,
    They shall go on, and I will stay behind,
    And so will fight with you on ev'n condition.
This said, his band to part thence he assign'd,
    Who went their way upon their Lords commission,
    Which bred great admiration in the stranger,
    To find a man so little fearing danger.

18

Now when his standerd quite was out of sight,
    And all *Renaldos* company was gone,
    Then hand to hand they do apply the fight,
    With force and fury great they lay it on;
Each marvels at the tothers passing might,
    And yet of either side the gaine is none,
    They felt the blowes so heavy and so hard,
    That glad they were to lie well to their ward.

19

Thus these two knights, for honours only sake,
    Together combat in such eager sort,
    That ev'ry little errour they should make,
    Endanger'd life in this unpleasant sport:
An houre and halfe this travell they did take,
    Each labouring to cut the tother short,
    And in his mind *Renaldo* labours much,
    Who this should be, whose skill and force was such.

20

And, save that he could not with his reputation,
    He would have wisht the battell at an end,
    And offer'd of a truce communication,
    And of his unknown foe have made his friend:
Likewise the tother felt such inclination,
    Now finding scarce he could himselfe defend,
    That he repented his rash hardy part,
    And would have had a truce with all his heart.

21

It waxed dark, there fell an ev'ning mist,
    So that at last they neither of them know
    When he did hit aright, or when he mist,
    Nor how to give, nor how to ward a blow:
When first *Renaldo* wisht him to desist,
    Sith now the Sun descended was so low,
    And that the combat might be now rejourn'd,
    Till *Phœbus* were about the world return'd.

22

Offring (at which the stranger greatly mus'd,
    And his rare curtesie therein commended)
    To lodge him where he should both be well us'd,
    And like a man of honour well attended:
The tother his great curt'sie not refus'd,
    And so between them two the fray was ended:
    And straight *Renaldo* gave him as his gift,
    His pages horse, that was both strong and swift.

23

Thus on they rode unto *Renaldos* tent,
  And grew acquainted ere they thither came,
By meanes in certaine speeches as they went,
Renaldo happened to tell his name;
By which the stranger knew incontinent,
That this was that same *Palladine* of fame,
And that himselfe was to *Renaldo* brother,
By fathers side alone, and not by mother.

24

The savage *Guidon*, this brave warrier hight,
  That travel'd had full many a hundred mile,
With those two brothers, nam'd the black and white,
And *Sansonet*, untill by craft and guile
They were surprised, as you heard last night,
And made against their wils to wait a while,
For maintenance of lawes unjust and bad,
That wicked *Pinnabell* devised had.

25

Now when as noble *Guidon* certaine knew
  That this *Renaldo* was, whom he before
Desired long to see, he much did rew
That he had done, and did lament it sore:
A blind man would not be more glad to view
The light, he doubted he should ne'r see more,
Then *Guidon* in his mind was well appaid,
To see this knight, and thus to him he said.

26

What strange mishap, what sinister adventer,
  Hath bred this fault in me, my noble Lord,
That I with you into this strife should enter,
With whom I ought to have all kind accord?
I am your fathers sonne, not by one venter,
I ever have your name and stock ador'd,
Guidon I hight, *Constanza* was my mother:
Born beyond *Euxin* seas, and yet your brother.

27

Wherefore I pray, pardon my fond offence,
  That have instead of duty offer'd wrong,
And tell me wherein I may recompence
This oversight, and I will do ere long:
Renaldo that had heard of him long since,
And to have seen him did not little long,
Embrac'd him, and not onely did forgive him,
But commendation great and praise did give him.

28

He said his valew was a perfect signe,
  To shew himselfe in fight so fierce and stout,
That he was truly come of that same line,
Whose noble brute was blown the world about:
For if your manners did to peace incline,
Then had there been (said he) more cause of doubt,
The fearfull Hart comes not of Lions seed,
Nor doth a silly Dove a Faulcon breed.

29

Thus fell they two acquainted on the way,
  And talk'd together friendly as they went,
But neither did their talk the journey stay,
Nor did their riding make their speech relent,
Vntill they came where all their brothers lay,
When as a great part of the night was spent,
Who with great joy and pleasure did behold them,
And chiefe when who this was *Renaldo* told them.

30

For though he must to them (no doubt) have ever
  Been very welcome as a brother deare,
Yet could he be to them more welcome never,
Then now, what time as you before did heare,
They all did mind to do their best endeaver
To rescue *Charles* that was of heavy cheare:
Wherefore for this one cause above the rest,
He was unto them all a welcome guest.

31

Thus now the day ensuing on went *Guidon*,
  Ioyning himselfe unto *Renaldos* crew,
And as to *Paris* wals they forward ride on,
They met two valiant youths that well him knew:
Further with them conferring, they describe one,
A Lady richly clad, and faire of hew:
These warlike youths had *Gismond* to their mother,
White *Griffin* and black *Aquilant* his brother.

32

Now *Guidon* knew them, and to them was known,
  As having been together many dayes,
By whom they were unto *Renaldo* shown,
And prais'd for gallant men at all assayes:
As in your judgement, likewise in mine own,
(*Renaldo* said) these youths do merit praise,
For they have oft been prov'd two perfect warriers,
As well in spite as sport, at tilt and barriers.

33

Renaldo did by their apparell know them,
  Tone ever wearing white, the tother black,
And friendly countenance he now did show them,
Chiefly because the King did succour lack:
Wherefore into his band he doth bestow them,
That band that to the *Turks* did bring much wrack,
And they do joyne them to *Renaldos* banner,
Forgetting all old jars in loving manner.

34

Between the house of *Ammon* and these twins,
  About one *Truffaldin* a jarre there fell,
The matter at the first not worth two pins,
Wherefore the circumstance I will not tell,
But now *Renaldo* their affection wins,
By using them so curteously and well,
For curteous speech and usage mild and kind,
Wipes malice out of ev'ry noble mind.

35

Now after these another knight there came,
  Hight *Sansonet* a man of great account,
  Who welcom'd was, and took it for no shame,
  Of stout *Renaldos* band himselfe to count:
  While this thus past, behold the gallant dame,
  That knew this noble Lord of *Clarimount,*
  (For she was one that all the *French* Lords knew)
  Told him a tale that made him greatly rew.

36

My Lord (said she) I bring you sorie tiding,
  He whom the Church and Empire held so deare,
  Runs all about, in no one place abiding,
  Of sense and argument deprived cleare:
  He naked goes, not natures secrets hiding,
  Which me to tell, and you must grieve to heare,
  Orlando (that same light and lamp of *France*)
  Hath lost his wits, God knowes by what mischance.

37

His armes and sword that he away had throwne,
  As things by him left and forsaken clearly,
  I saw a courteous knight, to me unknowne,
  But one (it seem'd) that lov'd *Orlando* dearly,
  Them gather where they scatter'd were and sowne,
  And ev'n of charity, as seemed meerly,
  In triumph wise on tree he hang'd the same,
  And underneath he grav'd *Orlandos* name.

38

But straight the sword that hanged on the tree,
  With force and scornfull speech away was tane,
  (As I can witnesse well that did it see)
  By *Mandricard* the sonne of *Agricane:*
  Think you what hurt this will to *Europe* be,
  That once againe the *Turks* have *Durindane:*
  The gentle knight strave long with him to save it,
  But in the end was forc'd to let him have it.

39

I saw *Orlando* late in monstrous guise,
  To run about uncouth and all unclad,
  With strangest clamours and most hideous cries:
  In fine I do conclude that he is mad;
  And save I saw it so with these mine eyes,
  I would not trust if any told it had.
  She further told how she had seene him later,
  With *Rodomont* to tumble in the water.

40

And last of all she told him she had heard,
  How that about this sword there grew some strife,
  Between *Gradasso* stout and *Mandricard:*
  And how the *Tartar* having lost his life,
  The sword was giv'n *Gradasso* afterward,
  As over all the *Pagan* camp was rife:
  And having ended this so sad narration,
  Thereto she addeth this short exhortation.

41

That he and ev'ry one that were not foe
  To stout *Orlando,* would take so much paine,
  In *Paris* or elswhere him to bestow,
  Till he had purged his distemper'd braine:
  Mine husband *Brandimart* (said she) I know,
  To do him any good himselfe would straine:
  Thus *Fiordeliege* spake, the loving wife
  Of *Brandimart,* that lov'd her as his life.

42

At this strange tale and wofull accident,
  Such inward griefe the good *Renaldo* felt,
  That with the thought his heart incontinent
  Did seem like snow against the Sun to melt,
  And with all speed he might to go he meant,
  And by all meanes he might so to have dealt,
  To seek *Orlando,* whom if he can find,
  He hopes to bring him to a better mind.

43

But sith he now had hither brought his band,
  Or were't the will of God, or were it chance,
  He first doth mind to end the cause in hand,
  And rescue *Paris* and the king of *France:*
  Wherefore he makes his men all quiet stand
  Till night, what time himselfe will lead the dance,
  And then between the fourth and second watch,
  He meanes at once the matter to dispatch.

44

He makes his men lie close for all that day,
  By way of Ambuscado in a wood,
  And ease themselves and horses all they may,
  And take the sustenance of rest and food,
  The place within three leagues of *Paris* lay,
  And when the Sun was set, he thought it good,
  What time the world doth use his lesser lamp,
  To *Paris* ward to move his silent camp.

45

And as he purpos'd, he perform'd indeed,
  For straight himselfe with that same gallant crew,
  Set out by night, as first they had decreed,
  In silent sort suspition to eschew.
  Now came the time that they must do the deed,
  Now neare unto the *Turkish* camp they drew,
  When first the heedlesse Sentinels intrapping,
  They kil'd them all because they took them napping.

46

The watch once slaine, they are no longer dumbe,
  But after stout *Renaldo* soon they came,
  They sound the trumpet, and strike up the drum,
  And calling still upon that noble name,
  That often had the *Pagans* overcome,
  (I meane *Renaldos* house of *Montalbane*)
  Which crie he caus'd both his own men to quicken,
  And that the *Turks* might in more feare be stricken.

47

Himselfe well mounted on his famous horse,
  Doth presse amidst the *Pagan* Princes tents,
  And with his own, and with his horses force,
  He treads them down, and all in peeces rents,
  Vnarm'd, or arm'd he kils without remorse,
  Who ever commeth in his way, repents,
  The drowsie men halfe arm'd make poore resistance,
  Against so brave a man with such assistance.

48

For why, beside those men I nam'd before,
  Whose vertue and whose value oft were shown,
  Renaldo had six hundred men and more,
  All perfect train'd, of strength and courage known,
  Which about *Clarimont* he kept in store,
  For his own use and causes of his own,
  Though at this need his Princes turn to furnish,
  He soon agreed his own towns to unfurnish.

49

And though *Renaldo* had no great revenue,
  The which chiefe sinewes unto warre affords,
  Yet kept he still six hundred in retinue,
  What with good usage and with gentle words,
  That all of them did still with him continue,
  At his command with launces, horse and swords,
  Nor was there any that from him away went,
  Though diverse others offer'd greater payment.

50

Now think when this brave crew the *Turks* assail'd,
  At unawares, halfe wake or halfe asleep,
  How that same name & that same noise them quail'd
  How here they fled and there, with hold and keep:
  But smally flight, and lesse their fight prevail'd;
  But ev'n as Goats from Lions, or as sheep
  From Wolves make small defence, such in comparison
  These *Pagans* made against *Renaldos* garison.

51

On tother side king *Charles* (that by espiall)
  Had notice of *Renaldos* comming hither,
  With all that crue so noble and so loyall,
  That to his aid combined were together,
  With diverse Lords came forth in person royall,
  And all his men of armes likewise came thither:
  Eke *Brandimart*, rich *Monodontes* heire,
  Did with king *Charles* unto the field repaire.

52

Whom when his spouse that neare about did hover,
  Had found out by his standard and his armes,
  And plainly saw it was her dearest lover,
  She rusheth in among the men of armes,
  And unto him her selfe she doth discover,
  Who straight embraced her in open armes;
  And leaving then the battell, drew apart,
  That each to other might their minds impart.

53

And after sweet embracing oftentimes,
  They did conferre together of their state:
  O vertue of those unsuspicious times,
  When Ladies early wander might and late,
  And yet be faultlesse deem'd and free of crimes,
  Where now each small suspect turnes love to hate,
  Yea ev'n for all their watching and safe keeping,
  They doubt their wives do wake while they are sleeping.

54

Among the conference this couple had,
  The Lady did unto her spouse unfold,
  How his good friend *Orlando* was fal'n mad,
  How she her selfe his madnesse did behold,
  His running naked, carelesse and unclad,
  Not credible had any els it told,
  But credible it was now she had sed it,
  For in far greater things he gave her credit.

55

She further did to *Brandimart* recount,
  How she had seen the bridge the *Pagan* made,
  (I meane the cruell *Pagan Rodomount*)
  Vpon the streame so deep as none could wade,
  Where he the passengers of best account
  Did from each side with fury great invade,
  And with the spoiles of those he kil'd and took,
  Did beautifie a tombe made by the brook.

56

And last she told how with his strength extreme
  Orlando heav'd the *Turke* arm'd from the ground,
  And so with him fell backward in the streame,
  With perill great there to have both been drownd,
  From whence *Orlando* went about the Reame,
  Where his mad parts would make him soon be found.
  This tale in *Brandimart* did breed such sorrow,
  He staid not for the next ensuing morrow.

57

But taking for his guide faire *Fiordeliege*,
  And being ready arm'd, as then he was,
  He go'th to seek that foresaid parlous bridge,
  In mind (what ever hap) the same to passe,
  Where many men their lives line did abridge,
  As in such dangers soon it comes to passe:
  No sooner came he to the utmost ward,
  But *Rodomont* had notice by his guard.

58

He greatly did to heare such newes rejoyce,
  And straight he commeth forth with warlike gesture,
  And bids him with a loud and scornfull voice,
  Vnto the tombe to yeeld his armes and vesture:
  Or threatens him, if he refuse his choice,
  To make him drink beyond all good disgesture:
  But *Brandimart* his threats did nothing feare,
  And makes no answer but with couched speare.

59

Then straight to horses side he sets the spurs,
  The horse he rode upon *Batoldo* hight,
  The horse though good, yet snores, and starts, & stirs,
  Much scar'd with narrow bridge, and waters sight:
  Eke *Rodomont* his good *Frontino* spurs,
  Who ever starts, as used to this fight,
  Although the bridge did shake all under feet,
  When in the middle way these knights did meet.

60

Their speares that were of firm well season'd wood,
  With so great force upon their armour strake,
  That though their horses were both strong and good
  Yet both fell from the bridge into the lake,
  Quite overwhelm'd with water and with mud,
  Yet neither horseman did his horse forsake;
  Long taried they within the streame below,
  To search if any Nymph dwelt there, I trow.

61

This had not been the first time nor the fift,   (down,
  That from this bridge the *Turke* had been throwne
  Wherefore his horse and he could better shift,
  For neither horse nor he did doubt to drown;
  For where the streame was most profound and swift,
  He often had been plung'd above his crown,
  Which made his horse and him the more audacious
  Amid the streame, although profound and spacious.

62

He knew by proofe (for he had tri'd it oft)
  Where all the shelves, and where the channell lay,
  Which parts were gravelly, and which were soft:
  The tother ignorant, was born away,
  Tost here and there, now low, and then aloft,
  The while the *Pagan* greedy of his prey,
  At all advantages doth still assaile him,
  Whose horses footing more and more did faile him.

63

At last with plunging and with striving tir'd,
  He backward fell into the weeds and mud,
  Where he was like to have been drownd and mir'd,
  Save that his spouse that by the river stood,
  In humble wise the *Pagan* Prince desir'd,
  And in most earnest manner that she could,
  Ev'n for her sake, whose ghost he did adore,
  To help her worthy knight unto the shore.

64

Ah gentle sir, if ever you did tast
  Of love (she said) or of a lovers passion,
  Save that same knight, on whom my love is plac'd,
  And let him not be drown'd in so vile fashion:
  Suffice it you, your tombe will be more grac'd
  With one such prisner of such reputation,
  Then hundreds other that shall here arrive;
  Then take his spoiles, and save himselfe alive.

65

These words that might have mov'd a stone I think,
  Mov'd him to rescue noble *Brandimart*,
  Who without thirst had tane such store of drink,
  As from his limbs, his life did welnigh part:
  But ere he brought him to the rivers brink,
  He caus'd him with his sword and armes depart,
  And made him sweare now he was in his power,
  To yeeld himselfe true prisner to his tower.

66

The dame of comfort all was quite bereav'd,
  When as she saw how ill her spouse had sped,
  And yet lesse griefe of this chance she conceiv'd,
  Then if he had been in the water dead:
  She cals her selfe the cause that he receiv'd
  This harme, that fondly had him thither led,
  Into a place of danger such and jeopardie,
  As needs must hazard either life or libertie.

67

About the place in vaine she long did hover,
  Then parted she in mind to seek some knight,
  Of *Charles* his camp, that might her losse recover,
  And prove himselfe, though not more strong in fight,
  At least more fortunate then was her lover:
  Long did she travell all that day and night,
  And eke the day ensuing, ere she met one,
  Yet was it her good hap at last to get one.

68

A champion in a rich artire she met,
  All wrought with withered leaves of Cypresse tree,
  Hereafter I will tell you, but not yet,
  What wight this was, whether a he or she:
  Now turn I to the camp, lest I forget
  The noble knights that set their soveraigne free,
  I meane *Renaldo* and his new come brother,
  With cunning *Malagige* and many other.

69

Vnpossible it was account to keep
  Of those were kil'd that night, and those that fled,
  Fierce *Agramant* was wak'ned from his sleep,
  And with all speed that might be up he sped,
  He weighs the perill and the danger deep,
  His souldiers run away, ne'r making head:
  Marsilio, with *Sobrino*, and the rest,
  Wish him to flie, for feare he be distrest.

70

Advising him, sith fortune now gan frown,
  Vnto this tempest wisely to give place,
  And go to *Arly*, or some other town,
  So strong to dure assault no little space:
  So might he save his person and his crown,
  As first was to be car'd for in such case:
  And then with wisdome warily proceeding,
  To wait till time might serve of better speeding.

71

Thus *Agramant*, to so great danger brought,
  Well knew not what to do, nor what to say,
But did as by his counsell he was taught,
  And in great hast convey'd himselfe away:
The while much woe unto his men was wrought,
  The Christens them discomfite, kill and slay:
The darknesse caus'd the number be unknown,
That in this fight were kil'd and overthrown.

72

With hast full many were in water drown'd,
  That saw there was no safetie in the land,
More succour in their heeles then hands they found,
  Against such fierce assaylants few durst stand;
But greatest dammage did to them redound,
  By those six hundred of *Renaldos* band:
Who did distribute strokes in so great plenty,
As ev'ry one of them massacred twenty.

73

Some think that *Malagigi* plaid his part
  In this conflict, not wounding men nor slaying,
But making of their foes by Magick art
  To heare so huge a noise of horses naying,
Such sound of Drums, such shouts from ev'ry part,
  As all the world had vowed their decaying:
By which they all were stricken in such feare,
As not a man of them durst tarie there.

74

Yet though the *Turkish* Prince fled thence so fast,
  The brave *Rogero* he would not forget,
But caused him from danger to be plac'd,
  And on an easie paced horse him set:
Thus now the *Turks* were by the Christens chas'd,
  And glad they were a walled town to get:
But yet *Gradasso* and his valiant band
Did still unto their tackle stoutly stand.

75

Nay, which was more, when as he understood,
  How that *Renaldo* Palladine of *France*,
Was he that shed such store of *Turkish* blood
  He was so glad he ready was to dance;
He thanks his gods that were to him so good,
  To send him this so much desired chance,
By which he hopes and makes account most clearly,
To win that horse *Renaldo* held so dearly.

76

For why *Gradasso* king of *Serycane*,
  Long since to *France* came with an army Royall,
With onely hope to conquer *Durindan*,
  That famous blade of so good proofe and triall:
And eke *Renaldos* courser to have tane,
  That *Bayard* hight: and now when by espiall,
He knew *Renaldo* was on that beast mounted,
The conquest sure, the horse his own he counted.

77

So much the rather, for that once before,
  About this matter they had made a fray,
Fast by the sea upon the sandy shore;
  (To tell the circumstance I may not stay)
But *Malagigi* thence his cosin bore,
  And did into a barge him safe convay:
And thereupon *Renaldo* ever since
Was tane but for a coward by this Prince.

78

Wherefore in hope so rich a spoile to reape,
  Two houres before the rising of the sun,
All armed on *Alfana* he doth leape,
  And with his lance to death are diverse done:
On *French* the *Moores*, on *Moores* the *French* doth heape,
  And all he meeteth he doth over-run:
So did ambition set his heart on fire,
To meet *Renaldo*, such was his desire.

79

Soon after this, each met with speare in rest,
  (But neither then at first the tother knew)
Each brake his speare upon the tothers crest,
  Vnto the heav'nly car the splinters flew:
Then with their swords either was ready prest,
  (Their lances thrown away, their swords they drew)
Each laying on the tother so fell strokes,
As if not knights had fought, but clownes feld okes.

80

Gradasso though he knew him not by sight,
  (For yet the morning beames were not displaid)
Yet did he guesse both by the horses might,
  And those fierce strokes the tother on him laid;
Wherfore with words that savour'd scorn and spight,
  He straight begins *Renaldo* to upbraid:
And said he had his challenge disappointed,
And not appeared at the day appointed.

81

Belike you thought I should have met you never,
  But now (said he) you here are met right well,
Assure your selfe I will pursue you ever,
  Were you tane up to heav'n, or down to hell;
No height nor depth should hinder mine endever,
  I meane to find you out where ere you dwell,
To shun the fight with me it doth not boot,
Vntill you leave your horse and go on foot.

82

At this his speech were diverse standing by,
  As *Guidon*, *Richardet*, and others more,
Who would have slaine *Gradasso* by and by,
  Had not *Renaldo* stepped them before,
And said in wrath, what masters am not I
  Well able wreake my private wrongs therefore?
Then to the Pagan gently thus he spake,
And wisht him mark the answer he did make.

83

Who ever saith, that I did fight eschue,
　Or shew defect of value any way,
　I say and do avouch he saith untrue,
　And I will prove by combat what I say;
　I came unto the place to meet with you,
　No scuses I did seek, nor no delay,
　And frankly here to you I offer fight,
　But first I wish you were informed right.

84

Then took he him aside, and more at large
　He told what hapned him, and how by art
　His cosin *Malagige* into a barge
　Conveighed him, and forc'd him to depart:
　In fine himselfe of blame quite to discharge,
　He brought him out to witnesse ev'ry part,
　And then to prove that this was true indeed,
　He offer'd in the combat to proceed.

85

Gradasso that both curteous was, and stout,
　Gave eare unto the tale *Renaldo* told,
　And though it seem'd he stood thereof in doubt,
　Yet him in all his speech he not controld:
　But in conclusion, having heard it out,
　He doth his former purpose firmly hold:
　Which was by combat fierce to try and know,
　If so he could *Bayardo* win or no.

86

The *Palladine* that passed not a point
　Of no mans force, to meet him gave his word:
　The place in which to meet they did appoint,
　Was neare a wood, and by a pleasant foord,
　There onely added was a further point;
　Which was that *Durindan, Orlandos* sword
　Should to *Renaldo* as of right accrew,
　If he the *Pagan* ouercame or slew.

87

Thus for the present time departed they,
　Vntill the time approch'd of pointed fight,
　Although *Renaldo* friendly did him pray,
　To rest him in his tent that day and night:
　And offer'd frank safe conduct for his stay,
　So curteous was this same couragious knight:
　Gradasso greatly prais'd the noble offer,
　But yet refus'd the curtsie he doth profer.

88

The feare was great that secretly did lurk
　In all the minds of all *Renaldos* kin,
　Who knew, the strength and cunning of this *Turke*
　Was such, as doubt it was which side should win:
　Faine *Malagigi* by his art would work
　To end this stay, before it should begin:
　Save that he fear'd *Renaldos* utter enmity,
　In so base sort for working this indemnity.

89

But though his friends did feare more then was meet,
　Himselfe assur'd himselfe of good successe:
　Now at the pointed time and place they meet,
　Both at one very instant, as I guesse,
　And first they kindly do embrace and greet
　The tone the tother with all gentlenesse;
　But how sweet words did turn to bitter blowes,
　The next booke saving one the sequell showes.

THE THIRTY-SECOND BOOKE OF

ORLANDO FVRIOSO

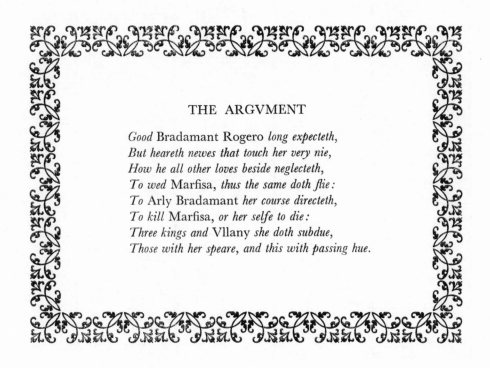

THE ARGVMENT

Good Bradamant Rogero *long expecteth,*
But heareth newes that touch her very nie,
How he all other loves beside neglecteth,
To wed Marfisa, *thus the same doth flie:*
To Arly Bradamant *her course directeth,*
To kill Marfisa, *or her selfe to die:*
Three kings and Vllany *she doth subdue,*
Those with her speare, and this with passing hue.

ORLANDO FVRIOSO
THE THIRTY-SECOND BOOKE

1

I now remember how by promise bound
  Before this time I should have made you know
  Vpon what cause faire *Bradamant* did ground,
  The jealous humours overcharg'd her so:
  She never took before so sore a wound,
  She never felt before such bitter wo,
  No not the tale which *Richardetto* told her,
  In such a fit and so great pangs did hold her.

2

To tell you first, when I should have begun,
  Renaldo call'd my tale another way;
  No sooner with *Renaldo* had I done,
  But straight with *Guidon* I was forc'd to stay:
  From this to that thus unawares I run,
  That I forgot of *Bradamant* to say:
  But now I mean to speak of her, before
  I speak of those two champions any more.

3

Yet needs I borrow must a word or twaine,
  How *Agramant* to *Arly* did retire,
  And gather'd there the few that did remaine,
  Escaped from the fury of the fire:
  Where not farre off from *Affrica* nor *Spaine*,
  He plants as fit as he could well desire,
  For lying on a flood so neare the seas
  Both men and vittell were suppli'd at ease.

4

To muster men *Marsilio* had commission,
  That may supply the place of them were lost,
  Of ships of warre there was no small provision,
  Soone had he gather'd up a mighty host:
  There was no want of armour and munition,
  There was no spare of labour nor of cost,
  That with such taxes *Affrica* was sessed,
  That all the Cities were full sore oppressed.

5

And further *Agramant*, that he might win
  Fierce *Rodomont* to aid him with his power,
  Did offer him a match of his neare kin,
  King *Almonts* daughter with a Realme in dower;
  But he his profer weighs not worth a pin,
  But keeps the bridge, and doth the passage scowre,
  That with his spoiles the place was welnigh fil'd,
  Of those he had dismounted, tane, and kil'd.

6

But faire *Marfisa* took another way:
  For when she heard how long the siege had lasted,
  How *Agramant* his camp at *Arly* lay,
  How both his men were slaine, and store was wasted,
  She sought no cause of any more delay,
  But thither straight without inviting hasted,
  Her purse and person offring in the fight,
  In just defending of his crown and right.

7

She brings *Brunello*, and the king she gave him,
  Who had giv'n cause of very just offence,
  Ten dayes and ten, she did of curtsie save him,
  To see who durst to stand in his defence;
  But when that no man made the means to have him,
  Though she to kill him had so good pretence,
  She thought it base, her noble hands to file,
  Vpon an abject dastard, and a vile.

8

She will deferre reveng of all his wrong;
  And unto *Arly* brought him to the King;
  Whose joy to tell, would aske a learned tongue,
  Both for the aid, and present she did bring:
  (For shew whereof, before it should be long,
  He offerd her to make *Brunello* wring:
  And at what time she pleased to appoint,
  To have him sent to crack his chiefest joynt).

9

Vnto some desart place he banisht was,
  To serve for meat for carrion crowes and pyes,
  Rogero that had helpt him oft (alas)
  Now cannot heare his piteous mones and cryes:
  He lyes sore wounded, as it comes to passe,
  And little knowes where poore *Brunello* lyes:
  And when he understands thereof at last,
  It is so late alreadie it is past.

10

This while what torments *Bradamant* indured,
  Those twenty days, how did she waile and mourne?
  Against which time she thought her selfe assured,
  Her loue to her, and to the faith should turne:
  She makes no doubt but he might have procured,
  Within that space to make his home returne,
  (Yea though he were in prison kept or banished)
  If troth and care of promise were not vanished.

11

In this long looking she would often blame,
　　The fierie coursers of the heavenly light,
　She thought that *Phœbus* wheeles were out of frame,
　Or that his charriot was not in good plight:
　Great *Iosuahs* day seemd shorter then these same,
　And shorter seemd the false *Amphitrions* night:
　Each day and night she thought was more then doubled
　So fancie blind her sence and reason troubled.

12

She now envyes the Dormouse of his rest,
　And wisht some heavy sleepe might overtake her,
　Wherewith she might most deadly be possest,
　Till her *Rogero* should returne to wake her:
　But waking cares ay lodged in her brest,
　That her desired sleepe did quite forsake her:
　To sleepe so long doth so much passe her power,
　She cannot frame her eyes to wincke one hower.

13

But turnes and tosses in her restlesse bed,
　(Alas no turning turnes her cares away)
　Oft at the window she puts forth her hed,
　To see how neare it waxeth unto day;
　When by the dawning, darkesome night is fled,
　She notwithstanding stands at that same stay:
　And during all the time the day doth last,
　She wishes for the night againe as fast.

14

When fifteene dayes were of the twenty spent,
　She growes in hope that his approch is ny,
　Then from a towre with eyes to *Paris* bent,
　She waytes and watches if she can descry
　At least some messenger that he hath sent,
　May bring the news where her sweet heart doth ly,
　And satisfie her mind by what hard chance,
　He is constraind to stay so long in *France*.

15

If farre aloofe the shine of armour bright,
　Or any thing resembling it she spies,
　She straight way hopes it is her only Knight,
　And wipes her face and clears her blubbred eyes:
　If any one unarm'd do come in sight,
　It may be one from him, she doth surmise:
　And though by proofe she finde each hope untrue,
　She ceaseth not for that, to hope anew.

16

Sometime all arm'd she mounteth on her steed,
　And so rides forth in hope to meet her deare,
　But soone some fancie her conceit doth feed,
　That he is past some other way more neare:
　Then homeward hasteth she with as much speed,
　Yet she at home no newes of him can heare:
　From day to day she passeth on this fashion,
　Hither and thither tossed with her passion.

17

Now when her twenty daies were full expired,
　And that beside were passed some dayes more,
　Yet not *Rogero* come, whom she desired,
　Her heart with care and sorrowes waxed sore;
　With cryes & plaints the woods and caves she tyred,
　Her brests she beat, her golden locks she tore,
　Nor while these gripes of griefe her heart embrace,
　Doth she forbeare her eyes or Angels face.

18

Why then (quoth she) beseemes it me in vaine,
　To seeke him still, who thus from me doth slide?
　Shall I esteeme of him that doth disdaine
　My sute, and scorne the torments I abide?
　Him, in whose heart a hate of me doth raine,
　Him, that accounts his vertues so well tride,
　As though some goddesse should from heav'n descēd,
　Before that he his heart to love would bend?

19

Though stout he is, he knows how well I love him,
　And how I honor him with soule and hart,
　Yet can my hot affection nothing move him,
　To let me of his love possesse some part:
　And lest he might perceive it would behove him
　To ease my griefe, if he did know my smart,
　To give me hearing of my plaint he feares,
　As to the charme the Adder stoppes his eares.

20

Love; stop his course that doth so loosely range,
　And flit so fast before my sorrie pace;
　Or with my former state else let me change,
　When I sought not to tracke thy tedious trace:
　I hope in vaine; remorce to thee is strange,
　Thou dost triumph upon my piteous case:
　For hearts thy meat, thy drinke is lovers teares,
　Their cries the Musicke doth delight thine eares.

21

But whom blame I? it was my fond desire,
　That first entist me to this killing call,
　And made me past my reach so far aspire,
　That now I feele the greater is my fall:
　For when aloft my wings be toucht with fire,
　Then farewell flight and I am left to fall:
　But still they spring, and still I upward tend,
　And still I see my fall, and finde no end.

22

Desire quoth I? my selfe I was too light,
　To give desire an entrance in my brest,
　Who when he had my reason put to flight,
　And of my heart himselfe was full possest,
　No roome for joy is left, or hearts delight,
　Since I do harbour this unruly guest,
　Who though he guide me to my certaine fall,
　The long expectance grieves me worst of all.

23

Then mine the fault be, if it be a fault,
  To love a Knight deserves to be beloved,
  With all good inward parts so richly fraught,
  Whose vertues be so knowne, and well approved;
  And more, whom would not his sweet face haue caught?
  My self, I must confesse, his beautie moved:
  What blind unhappie wretch were she would shun,
  The pleasing prospect of the precious Sun?

24

Beside my destinie which drew me on,
  By others sugred speech I was entrained,
  As though I should by this great match anon,
  Another *Paradice* on earth have gained:
  But now their words into the wind be gon,
  And I in *Purgatorie* am restrained:
  Well may I *Merlin* curse the false deceiver,
  Yet my *Rogero* I shall love for ever.

25

I hop't of *Merlins* and *Melissas* promises,
  Who did such stories of our race foretell:
  Is this the profit of beleeving prophesies,
  And giving credit to the sprites of hell?
  Alas they might have found them better offices,
  Then me to flout that trusted them so well:
  But all for envie have they wrought me this,
  So to bereave me of my former blis.

26

Thus sighs and lamentations are not fained,
  Small place was left for comfort in her brest:
  Yet spite of sorrows hope was entertained,
  And though with much a do, yet in it prest;
  To ease her mourning heart when she complained,
  And giving her sometimes, some little rest,
  By sweet remembrance of the words he spake,
  When he was forst of her his leave to take.

27

The minding of those words did so recure
  Her wounded heart that she was well content,
  For one months space his absence to endure,
  Yea when his dayes of promise quite were spent;
  Yet still she lookt for him you may be sure,
  And many a time that way she came and went,
  Till by the way at last such news she hard,
  That all the hope she had before, was mard.

28

For she by chance did meet a *Gascoigne* Knight,
  That in the warres of *Affrica* was caught,
  One that was taken captive in that fight,
  Then when fore *Paris* the great field was fought,
  What she requires to know, he could recite,
  But carelesse of the other news he brought,
  Of her *Rogero* chiefly she enquires,
  To heare of him is all that she desires.

29

Of whom the Knight could let her understand,
  (For in that Court he late his life had led)
  How *Mandricard* and he fought hand to hand,
  And how much blood on either part was shed:
  And though by wounds himselfe in perrill stand,
  That he subdew'd his foe, and left him ded.
  Now if with this, his story he had ended,
  Rogeros scuse had very well bin mended.

30

But he proceeds to tell, how one was theare,
  A Ladie hight *Marfisa* in the feeld,
  Whose fame for martiall acts did shine most cleare,
  Whose beauty rare to few or none did yeeld,
  Rogero her, she held *Rogero* deare,
  They never were asunder or but seeld,
  And that they two, as ev'rie one there saith,
  The tone the tother plighted have their faith.

31

And if *Rogero* once were whole and sound,
  Their wedding should be celebrate with speed:
  That such a paire as yet was never found,
  And happie they should come of such a seed:
  How much it joy'd the *Pagan* Princes round,
  To thinke upon the race they two should breed,
  Which likely were all others to excell
  In feats of arms that erst on earth did dwell.

32

The *Gascoigne* Knight of all that he had sed,
  Himselfe had reason to beleeve was sooth,
  So generall a fame thereof was spred,
  There were but few but had it in their mouth.
  Some little kindnesse she did use had fed
  Their foolish humors of this false untrowth;
  Still fame will grow if once abroade it flie,
  Although the ground be troth or be a lye.

33

They came indeed together to this fight,
  And many times together they were seene,
  For he was warlike, stout and worthy Knight,
  And she a gallant, faire, and daintie Queene,
  By which, suspition never judging right,
  Did gather straight they had assured beene:
  And specially because when she departed,
  To visite him she was so soone reverted.

34

Of just suspect their reason was but slender,
  If they had weighed well their vertues rare,
  Though of his wounds she seemd to be so tender,
  And of his danger had so great a care;
  Against bad tongues no goodnes can defend her,
  For those most free from faults; they least wil spare,
  But prate of them whom they have scantly knowne,
  And judge their humors to be like their owne.

35

Now when the Knight avowd the tale he told,
  (And yet in truth you know t'was but a tale)
  The damsels heart was toucht with shivering cold,
  The little hope she had away it stale,
  Almost in sound her seate she scarce could hold:
  With mourning cheare, and face both wan and pale,
  She said no more: but mad with griefe and ire,
  Her horse she turn'd, and homeward did retire.

36

And all in armour on her bed she lyes,
  She wisht a thousand times she now were ded,
  She bytes the sheets to dampe her sobs and cries,
  The *Gascoigns* news still bearing in her hed:
  Her heart is swolne, and blubberd be her eyes,
  With trickling teares bedewed is her bed,
  When griefe would be no longer holden in,
  Needs out it must, and thus it doth begin.

37

Ah wretched me, whom might a maiden finde,
  In whom she might be bold to put her trust?
  Since you *Rogero* mine, become unkinde,
  And dread your faith and promise in the dust;
  You only you, mine eye so farre did blinde,
  I still esteem'd you faithfull, true and just:
  Ah never wench that loved so sincerely,
  Was in requitall punisht so severely.

38

Why (my *Rogero*) why do you forget?
  (Sith you in beautie passe each other Knight,
  And do in feats of armes such honor get,
  As none can match your chivalrie in fight)
  This golden vertue with the rest to set,
  By which your glorious name will shine more bright
  If as in other graces you abound,
  So in your promise constancie were found?

39

This is the vertue breeds most estimation,
  By which all other vertues shew more cleare,
  As things most faire do loose their commendation,
  Which by the want of light can not appeare:
  What glory was it by false protestation,
  Her to deceive whose Saint and God you were?
  Whom your fair speeches might have made beleeve
  That water would be carrid in a seeve.

40

From any haynous act wouldst thou refraine,
  That murdrest her who beares thee so good will?
  How wouldst thou use thy foe, that thus in paine
  Dost let thy frend to be tormented still?
  Thou that with breach of faith thy heart dost staine,
  No doubt thou dost not care for doing ill;
  Well this I know, that God is ever just,
  He will ere long revenge my wrongs I trust.

41

For why, unthankfulnesse is that great sin,
  Which made the Divell and his angels fall,
  Lost him and them the joyes that they were in,
  And now in hell detaines them bound and thrall:
  Then marke the guerdon thou art like to win;
  For why like faults like punishment do call,
  In being thus unthankfull unto me,
  That always was so faithfull unto thee.

42

Besides of theft thy selfe thou canst not quit,
  If theft it be to take that is not thine;
  The keeping of my heart: no that's not it,
  That thou shouldst have it I do not repine,
  Thy selfe thou stalst, which I can not remit,
  Thy selfe thou knowst thou art, or shouldst be mine,
  Thou knowst damnation doth to them belong,
  That do keepe backe anothers right by wrong.

43

Though thou *Rogero* do forsake me so,
  I can not will nor chuse but love thee still;
  And since there is no measure of my wo,
  Death is the only way to end mine ill;
  But thus to cut of life, and thou my fo
  It makes me do it with a worser will;
  Yet had I dyde when best I did thee please,
  I should have counted death, no death but ease.

44

When with these words she was resolv'd to dy,
  She tooke her sword in hand for that intent,
  And forst her selfe upon the point to ly,
  Her armour then her purpose did prevent,
  A better spirit checkt her by and by:
  And in her heart this secret reason went,
  O noble Ladie borne to so great fame,
  Wilt thou thus end thy dayes with so great shame?

45

Nay rather if thou beest resolv'd to dy,
  Vnto the campe why dost thou not repaire,
  Where bodies of brave Knights in heaps do ly?
  Lo there to honour the directest staire,
  The losse of life with glory thou mayst buy,
  To die in thy *Rogeros* sight were faire,
  And happily by him thou mayst be slaine,
  So he that wrought thy wo may rid thy paine.

46

Thou mayst be sure *Marfisa* there to see,
  Who hath so falsly stolne away thy frend;
  If first on her thou couldst revenged be,
  With more contented mind thy dayes would end.
  Vnto this counsell she doth best agree,
  And onward on this journey straight doth tend,
  She takes a new device that might implie
  A desperation, and a will to die.

47

The collour of her bases was almost,
  Like to the falling whitish leaves and drie,
  Which when the moisture of the branch is lost,
  Forsakenly about the tree doth lye.
  With Cipresse trunks embroderd and embost,
  (For Cipresse once but cut will alwaies die)
  A fine conceipt, she thinks to represent
  In secret sort her inward discontent.

48

She tooke *Astolfos* horse and *Goldélance*,
  As fittest both for this her present feat,
  That speare could make the bravest Knight to dance,
  And caper with a tuch beside his seate.
  But where *Astolfo* had it, by what chance,
  Or why he gave it, need I not repeate,
  She tooke it, notwithstanding her election,
  Not knowing of that magicall confection.

49

Thus all alone without both Squire and Page,
  Thus furnished she set her selfe in way,
  To *Paris* ward she traveld in a rage,
  Whereas the campe of *Sarzins* lately lay,
  And (as she thought) kept up King *Charles* in cage,
  Not understanding how before that day,
  Renaldo aiding *Charles* with *Malageege*,
  Had forced them from thence to raise their seege.

50

Now had she left mount *Dordon* at her backe,
  When little way behind her she describe,
  A gallant Damsell following of her tracke,
  A shield of gold unto her saddle tide,
  Of Squires and other servants none did lacke,
  And three brave Knights were riding by her side,
  But of the Squires that overtooke her last,
  She askt one what those were that by her past.

51

And straight the worthie Ladie it was told,
  How from *Pole Artike* that same damsell came,
  Sent from a Queene, with that faire shield of gold,
  Vnto King *Charles* (that there was knowne by fame)
  But so, as he must this condition hold,
  That on a Knight he must bestow the same,
  Such one as he in his imagination,
  For prowesse deemd most worthy reputation.

52

For she of Island Ile that holds the raigne,
  And is (and knows it) that she is most faire,
  Doth thinke she should her worth not little staine,
  And her great fame and honour much impaire,
  If any Knight her Ile and her should gaine,
  Except he stood so high on honors staire,
  As that he were adjudg'd in feats of warre,
  The prymer man, and passing others farre.

53

Wherefore the cause she sends to *France* is this,
  She thinks if she shall finde one any where,
  That in the Court of *France* he surely is:
  And therefore she doth send to greet him there.
  As for those three, because you shall not misse,
  To know the truth, Ile tell you what they were:
  They were 3 Kings, of whom great fame there goth,
  of *Norway* one, one *Swethland*, one of *Goth*.

54

These three, though far they dwell from Island Ile,
  Yet love of that same Queene hath brought them hither,
  This Ile is call'd *Perduta* otherwhile,
  Because the seamen leese it in foule weather:
  These Kings liv'd from their country in exile,
  And to this Queene were suters all together:
  And she that knew not well how to forbid them,
  With this same pretie shift from thence she rid them.

55

She saith, she minds to wed for her behoofe,
  That wight that most excels in warlike action,
  And though (quoth she) you shew no little proofe,
  Of valew here (as twere in privat faction)
  Yet I must have you tride more far aloofe,
  Before my mind can have full satisfaction:
  Wherefore I meane my selfe and crowne to yeeld
  Alone to him that bringeth backe my sheeld.

56

This is the cause that these three Kings did move
  Each one to come from so remote a nation,
  With purpose firme their utmost force to prove,
  To win the golden shield with reputation,
  Or leese their lives, for that faire Ladies love,
  If that they failed of their expectation.
  When he had told her thus, he her forsooke,
  And soone his company he overtooke.

57

The Damsell rode a softer pace behind,
  And so as in a while she lost their sight,
  And often she revolved in her mind,
  The tale the fellow told, with small delight.
  She doubts this shield bestow'd in such a kind,
  Will be in *France* a cause of brall and fight,
  That this will be a meanes she greatly feares,
  To set her kin together all by th'eares.

58

This fancie mov'd her much, but more then this,
  That former jealous fancie did her move,
  That her *Rogeros* kindnesse alterd is,
  That on *Marfisa* he had plast his love:
  This so possest her sence that she did misse
  Her way, nor never thought as did behove,
  Till night was almost come, and Sunne nigh set,
  Where she a lodging for her selfe may get.

59

Ev'n as an emptie vessell that was tide,
  Vnto the wharfe, with some old rotten cable,
If that the knot do hap to breake or slide,
So that to hold it be no longer able,
Is borne away, as please the wind and tide:
So *Bradamant*, with mind and thoughts unstable,
Was in such muse, as she the right way mist,
And so was borne, where *Rabicano* list.

60

But when she saw the Sunne was almost set,
  She tooke more heede, and asking of a clowne,
(A shepherd that by hap there by she met)
Where she might lodging get er Sunne went downe
The shepherd made her answer, that as yet
She was almost a league from any towne,
Or other place where she might eate or lodge,
Save at a Castle cald sir *Tristrams* lodge.

61

But ev'rie one that list, is not assured,
  Though he do thither come, to stay therein,
To martiall feats they must be well inured,
With speare and shield they must their lodging win:
Such custome in the place hath long indured,
And many years ago it did begin,
Wherefore tis good that one be well advised,
Ere such an act by him be enterprised.

62

In briefe thus is their order, if a Knight
  Do finde the lodgings void, they him receave,
With promise, that if more arive that night,
Either he shall to them his lodging leave,
Or else with each of them shall prove in fight,
Which of them can of lodging tother reave:
If none do come that night he shall in quiet,
Have both his horsemeat, lodging, and his diet.

63

If foure or five do come together first,
  The Castle keeper them must entertaine,
Who commeth single after, hath the worst,
For if he hope a lodging there to gaine,
He must (according to that law accurst)
Fight with all those, that did therein remaine:
Likewise if one come first, and more come later,
He must go fight with them yet nere the later.

64

The like case is, if any maid or dame
  Do come alone, or else accompanied,
Both they that first, and they that latest came,
Must by a Iurie have their beauties tried:
Then shall the fairest of them hold the same,
But to the rest that come shall be denied:
Thus much the shepheard unto her did say,
And with his finger shewd to her the way.

65

About three miles was distant then the place,
  The damsell thither hasts with great desire;
And though that *Rabicano* trot apace,
Yet was the way so deepe and full of mire,
The snow and drift still beating in their face,
She later came then manners good require;
But though it were as then both darke and late,
She boldly bounced at the castle gate.

66

The porter told her that the lodgings all
  Were fild by Knights that late before them tooke,
Who now stood by the fire amid the hall,
And did ere long to have their supper looke:
Well (answers she) then have they cause but small
(If they be supperlesse) to thanke the cooke;
I know (quoth she) the custome, and will keepe it,
And meane to win their lodging ere I sleepe yet.

67

The Porter went and did her message bold,
  To those great states then standing by the fire,
Who tooke small pleasure when they heard it told,
For thence to part they had so small desire;
Now chiefly when twas rainie, darke and cold;
But so their oth and order did require,
That they must do it, were it cold or warme,
And therefore quickly they themselves did arme.

68

These were those three great kings, whom that same day
  Dame *Bradamant* had seene but few houres past,
Though they had sooner finished their way,
Because she rode so soft, and they so fast.
Now when they were all arm'd, they make no stay,
But all on horsebacke mount themselves at last:
No doubt but few in strength these three did passe,
Yet of those few, sure one this damsell was.

69

Who purpos'd (as it seemeth) nothing lesse,
  Then in so wet and in so cold a night,
To lack a lodging and sleepe supperlesse:
Now those within at windowes see the fight,
The men themselves on horsebacke do addresse,
To looke thereon, for why the Moone gave light:
And thus at last, though first twere somewhat late,
They did abase the bridge and ope the gate.

70

Ev'n as a secret and lascivious lover,
  Rejoyceth much, when after long delayes,
And many feares, in which his hope did hover,
He heares at last the noise of pretie kayes:
So *Bradamant* that hopes now to recover
A lodging, for the which so long she stayes,
Did in her mind in such like sort rejoyce,
When as she heard the watchfull porters voyce.

71

Now when those Knights and some few of their traine,
　Were past the bridge, the dame her horse doth turne
　To take the field, and then with speed againe,
　With full careere she doth on them returne,
　And coucht that speare, yet never coucht in vaine,
　For whom it hits it still doth overturne;
This speare her cosin, when he went from *France*,
　Gave unto her, the name was *Goldelance*.

72

The valiant King of *Swethland* was the first
　That met her, and the next the King of *Goth*,
　The staffe doth hit them full, and never burst,
　But from their saddles it did heave them both;
　But yet the King of *Norway* sped the worst,
　It seem'd to leave his saddle he was loth,
His girses brake, and he fell upside downe,
　In danger with the mire to choke and drowne.

73

Thus with three blows, three kings she down did beare,
　And hoist their heeles full hie, their heads full low,
　Then enterd she the castle voyd of feare,
　They stand without that night in raine and snow;
　Yet ere she could get in, one caus'd her sweare
　To keepe the custome, which they made her know;
And then the master doth to her great honor,
　And entertainment great bestowed on her.

74

Now when the Ladie did disarme her head,
　Off with her helmet came her little caul,
　And all her haire her shoulders overspred,
　And both her sex and name was knowne withall,
　And wonder great and admiration bred
　In them that saw her make three Princes fall;
For why she shewd to be in all their sight,
　As faire in face as she was fierce in fight.

75

Ev'n as a stage set forth with pompe and pride,
　Where rich men cost and cunning art bestow,
　When curtaines be remov'd that all did hide,
　Doth make by light of torch a glittering show;
　Or as the Sunne that in a cloud did bide,
　When that is gone, doth clearer seeme to grow:
So *Bradamant* when as her head was barest,
　Her colour and her beautie seemed rarest.

76

Now stood the guests all round about the fire,
　Expecting food, with talke their eares yet feeding,
　While ev'ry one doth wonder and admire,
　Her speech and grace, the others all exceeding,
　The while her host to tell she doth desire,
　From whence and whō this custome was proceeding,
That men were driv'n unto their disquiet,
　To combat for their lodging and their diet.

77

Faire dame (said he) sometime there rul'd in *France*,
　King *Feramont*, whose sonne a comely Knight,
　Clodian by name, by good or evill chance,
　Vpon a lovely Ladie did alight:
　But as we see it oftentimes doth chance,
　That jealousie in love marres mans delight;
Thus he of her in time so jealous grew,
　He durst not let her go out of his vew.

78

Nor ever *Argus* kept the milkwhite cow
　More straight, then *Clodian* here did keepe his wife,
　Ten Knights eke to this place he doth allow,
　Thereby for to prevent all casuall strife;
　Thus hope and feare betweene, I know not how,
　As he prolongs his selfe-tormenting life,
The good sir *Tristram* thither did repaire,
　And in his company a Ladie faire.

79

Whom he had rescue but a little since
　From Giants hand, with whom he did her find,
　Sir *Tristram* sought for lodging with the Prince,
　For then the Sunne was very low declin'd:
　But as a horse with galled backe will wince,
　Ev'n so our *Clodian* with as galled mind:
For casting doubts and dreading ev'ry danger,
　Would by no meanes be won to lodge a stranger.

80

When as sir *Tristram* long had prayd in vaine,
　And still denide the thing he did demaund,
　That which I cannot with your will obtaine,
　In spite of you (said he) I will commaund;
　I here will prove your villanie most plaine,
　With launce in rest, and with my sword in hand:
And straight he challenged the combat then,
　To fight with *Clodian* and the other ten.

81

Thus onely they agreed upon the case,
　If *Clodian* and his men were overthrowne,
　That all then presently should voyd the place,
　And that sir *Tristram* there should lie alone:
　Sir *Clodian* to avoid so great disgrace,
　The challenge tooke, for why excuse was none:
In fine, both *Clodian* and his men well knockt,
　And from the castle that same night were lockt.

82

Triumphant *Tristram* to the Castle came,
　And for that night, as on his owne he seased,
　And there he saw the Princes, lovely dame,
　And talkt with her, who him not little pleased:
　This while sir *Clodian* was in part with shame,
　And more with thought and jealous feare diseased,
Disdaining not in humble sort to woo him,
　By message mild to send his wife unto him.

83

But he, though her he do not much esteeme,
  For why, by meanes of an inchanted potion,
Isotta fairest unto him did seeme,
  To whom he vowed had his whole devotion:
Yet for he did the jealous *Clodian* deeme
  Some plague to merit, he denide his motion;
And sweares it were no manners nor no reason,
A Ladie to unlodge at such a season.

84

But if (saith he) it do his mind offend,
  To lie all night alone and eke abrode,
Tell him I will this other Ladie send
  To him, that shall with him make her abode:
Now tell him that to keepe this I intend,
  The which to win, I have such paine bestow'd;
Tis reason that the fairest should remaine
With him that is the strongest of us twaine.

85

Clodian in mind was wondrous malcontent,
  Vs'd so not like a Prince but like a patch,
That puffing, blowing up and downe he went
  All night, as one were set to keepe a watch:
But whether he do chase or else lament,
  He found the Knight for him too hard a match.
Next day sir *Tristram* let him have his wife,
And so for that time finisht was the strife.

86

For openly he on his honour swore,
  That he her honour had that night preserved,
Although discourtesies he had before
  Had at his hands a great revenge deserved;
Yet in that *Clodian* had lod'gd out of dore,
  He was content that penance should have served;
He nathelesse tooke it for no good excuse,
To say that love was cause of such abuse.

87

For love should gentle make rude hearts and base,
  And not in gentle mind breed humors vile:
Now when sir *Tristram* parted from the place,
  Sir *Clodian* meant to stay there but a while,
But to a Knight that stood much in his grace,
  He graunts the keeping of this stately pile:
Keeping one law for him and for his heires,
With ev'ry one that to the place repaires.

88

That namely ever he that was most strong,
  Should there be lodg'd, and she that was most faire,
And that the rest should take it for no wrong,
  To walke abrode into the open aire:
This is the law which hath endured long,
  And no man may the strength thereof impaire:
Now while the man this storie did repeate,
The steward on the boord did set the meate.

89

The boord was coverd in a stately hall,
  Whose match was scarce in all the country seene,
With goodly pictures drawne upon the wall,
  All round about, but chiefly on the screene;
These they did looke on, with delight not small,
  And would have quite forgot their meate I weene,
Save that their noble host did them advise,
To feed their bellies first, and then their eyes.

90

Now as they downe did at the table sit,
  The master of the house began to lowre,
And said they did an error great commit,
  To lodge two Ladies come in sundry howre;
Needs one must be put out, where ere it hit,
  And go abrode into the cold and showre:
The fairest (sith they came not both together)
Must bide, the foulest must go trie the wether.

91

Two aged men and women more beside
  He cald, and bad them quickly take a vew,
Which of the twaine should in the place abide,
  And namely which of twaine had fairest hew:
This Iurie do the matter soone decide,
  And gave their verdit, as it was most trew,
That *Bradamant* past her in hew as farre,
As she exceld the men in feates of warre.

92

Then spake the Knight unto the Island dame,
  Whose mind was full of timorous suspition,
I pray you thinke it not a scorne or shame,
  For hence you must, there can be no remission.
Poore *Vllany* (so was the damsels name)
  Doth thinke she now is driv'n to hard condition,
Yet in her conscience true she knew it was,
That *Bradamant* in beauty her did passe.

93

Ev'n as we see the Sunne obscur'd sometime,
  By sudden rising of a mistie cloud,
Engendred by the vapor-breeding slime,
  And in the middle region then embow'd:
So when the damsell plainly saw that time,
  Her presence in the place was not allow'd,
She was so chang'd in count'nance and in cheare,
That ev'n unlike her selfe she did appeare.

94

But much astonyd with the sudden passion,
  She readie was to sound in all their sight;
But *Bradamant* that would not for compassion
  Permit that she should go abrode that night,
Did say, this triall was of no good fashion,
  And that the judgement hardly could be right,
When men observe not this same chiefe regard,
As not to judge before both parts be hard.

95

I, that on me do take her to defend,
 Say thus, that be I faire, or lesse or more,
I came not as a woman, nor intend
 As woman now to be adjudg'd therefore;
Who knowes my sex, except I condescend
 To shew the same? and one should evermore
Shun to confirme things doubtfull, or deny it,
When chiefly others may be harmed by it.

96

Yet who can say precisely what I am?
 For many men do weare their haire as long,
And you do know that as a man I came,
 And all my gestures to a man belong;
Wherefore in giving me a womans name,
 To both of us perhaps you may do wrong;
Your law points women (if their right be donne)
By women, not by warriers to be wonne.

97

But yet admit it were as you do guesse,
 That I indeed were of the female gender,
Though that it is so, I do not confesse;
 Should I to her my lodging then surrender,
If that my beauty of the two were lesse?
 No sure, in that the reason were but slender:
The price that unto vertue longs of dewtie,
Should not be tane away for want of bewtie.

98

And if your law were such, that needs of force,
 Vnto the fairest lodging should be given,
Yet at this feast I tary would perforce,
 And from my lodging I would not be driven:
Wherefore mine argument I thus enforce,
 That this same match betweene us is not even,
For striving here with me, the case is plaine,
She much may leese, and little she may gaine.

99

And where the gaine and losse unequall is,
 The match is evill made in common sence;
Wherefore I thinke it were not much amisse,
 With this same law for this time to dispence;
And if that any dare mislike of this,
 Or seeme to take the matter in offence,
I will with sword be readie to maintaine,
That mine advice is good, and his is vaine.

100

Thus noble *Ammons* daughter mov'd with pittie
 In her behalfe, who to her great disgrace
Should have bin sent, where neither towne nor citie
 Was neare almost in three leagues of the place,
Fram'd her defence so stout and eke so wittie,
 That to her reason all the rest gave place;
But chiefe the perill great and hazard waying,
That might have grown to them by her gainsaying.

101

As when the Sunne in sommer hath most powre,
 And that the ground with heate thereof is rived,
For want of raine the drie and parched flowre
 Doth fade, and is as twere of life deprived,
But if in season come a fruitfull showre,
 It riseth up and is againe revived:
So when the damsell this defence did heare,
She waxed faire againe, of better cheare.

102

And thus at last they fell unto their feast
 In quiet sort, for none did come that night,
To challenge any of them, or molest,
 No traveller, nor any wandring Knight;
All merry were but *Bradamante* least,
 Fell jealousie bard her of all delight,
Her stomacke so distempring, and her tast,
She tooke no pleasure of that sweet repast.

103

When supper ended was, they all arise,
 Although perhaps they would have longer sate,
Saue for desire they had to feed their eyes;
 And now the night was spent and waxed late,
The master of the house in seemly wise,
 Doth call for torches to set out his state,
And straight with torch light filled was the hall,
But what they saw, hereafter shew I shall.

THE THIRTY-THIRD BOOKE OF

ORLANDO FVRIOSO

THE ARGVMENT

Faire Bradamant *sees grav'n by passing art,*
The future wars of France *upon a screene,*
Bayardos *flight the combat fierce doth part,*
Renaldo *and the* Sericane *betweene.*
Astolfo *having past the greater part*
Of all the world, and many countries seene,
Vnto Senapos *kingdome last arrives,*
And from his boord the foule Harpias drives.

ORLANDO FVRIOSO
THE THIRTY-THIRD BOOKE

1

Tymagoras, Parrhasius, Polignote,
  Timant, Protogenes, Apollodore,
With *Zeuxis*, one for skill of speciall note:
Apelles eke, past all the rest before:
Whose skill in drawing, all the world doth note,
And talke of still (to writers thanks therefore)
Whose works and bodies, time and death did wast,
Yet spite of time and death their fames do last.

2

With others that in these our later daies
  Have liv'd, as *Leonard* and *Iohn Bélline*,
And he that carves and drawes with equall praise,
Michell more then a man, Angell divine,
And *Flores*, whom the Flemmings greatly praise,
With *Raphael* and *Titian* passing fine,
With divers others that by due desart,
Do merit in this praise to have a part.

3

Yet all these cunning drawers with their skill,
  Could not attaine by picture to expresse,
What strange events should happen well or ill,
In future times, no not so much as guesse:
This art is proper unto Magike still:
Or to a Prophet, or a Prophetesse,
By this rare art, the Brittish *Merlin* painted
Strange things, with which our age hath bin acquainted.

4

He made by Magike art, that stately hall,
  And by the selfe same art he caus'd to be,
Strange histories ingraved on the wall,
Which (as I said) the guests desir'd to see.
Now when they were from supper risen all,
The pages lighted torches two or three,
Making the roome to shine as bright as day,
When to his guests the owner thus did say.

5

I would (quoth he) my guests, that you should know,
  That these same stories that here painted are,
Of future warres the sequels sad do show,
That shall to Italie bring wo and care:
Whereas the *French* full many a bloodie blow
Shall take, while others they to harme prepare,
As *Merlin* here hath layd downe, being sent
From *English Arthur*, chiefe for this intent.

6

King *Fieramont* that was the first that past
  The streame of *Rhine* with armie great of *France*,
And being in possession quiet plast
Or all those parts, sturd with so luckie chance,
Straight in ambitious thought began to cast,
His rule and scepter higher to advance.
Which that he might to passe the better bring,
He made a league with *Arthur English* King.

7

Informing him how that his meaning was,
  Of *Italie* the rule and crowne to get,
And askt his ayd to bring the same to passe,
Which never had atchieved bin as yet,
Now *Merlin* that did all men far surpasse
In Magike art, his purpose sought to let,
For *Merlin* had with *Arthur* so great credit,
He thought all Gospell was, if once he sed it.

8

This *Merlin* then did first to *Arthur* show,
  And then by *Arthur* was of purpose sent,
To *Fieramont* of *France*, to let him know
The cause why he misliked his intent,
As namely, many mischiefs that would grow,
To all that now, or that hereafter ment
The like attempt, advising him abstaine
From certaine trouble, for uncertaine gaine.

9

And that he might his courage more appall,
  And quite remove him from this enterprise,
He made by Magicke, this so stately hall,
Adorned as you see in sumptuous wise,
And drew these histories upon the wall,
That what he saw in mind, they might with eyes,
And thereby know, that in Italian ground
The Flour de luce can near take root profound.

10

And how as often as the *French* shall come,
  As frends to aid and free them from distresse,
So oft they shall their foes all overcome,
And fight with honor great, and good successe:
But be they sure to have that place their toome,
If so they come their freedome to oppresse;
Thus much the owner of the house them told,
And so went on, the storie to unfold.

11

Lo first how *Sigisbert* in hope of gaine,
  And promises of Emperour *Mauricius*,
Doth passe the mountaines with a mighty traine,
  With mind to *Lombardie* to be pernicious:
But *Ewtar* drives him backe by force againe,
  When he of such attempt is least suspicious,
So that his enterprise is quite reversed,
Himselfe doth flie, and leave his men dispersed.

12

Next after him the proud *Clodoveus* went,
  And had with him one hundred thousand men,
But him doth meet the Duke of *Benevent*,
  With scarse for ev'rie hundred souldiers, ten,
Who doth intrap him in an ambushment,
  So as the *French* might well be lik'ned then,
While *Lombard* wines too greedily they took,
To fish beguiled with a baited hooke.

13

Straight *Childibertus* with a mighty host,
  Doth come with mind to wipe away this blot:
But of his gamings he may make small bost,
  For of his purpose he prevailed not:
His enterprise by heav'nly sword is crost,
  The plague doth grow among his men so hot,
What with the burning feaver, and the flixe,
Of sixtie men, there scant returneth sixe.

14

Another picture lively doth expresse,
  How that King *Pepin* and King *Charles* his sonne,
Fought both in Italie with good successe;
  Not with intent that Realme to overrunne,
But to set free Pope *Stev'n* from sharpe distresse
  And wrongs, that by *Astolfo* were him done,
One tames *Astolfo* that was *Stev'ns* oppressor
Tother takes *Desiderius* his successor.

15

Behold another *Pepin* yet a youth,
  Not like his father, doth that Realme invade,
And thinking to procure his wofull truth,
  Of ships and boats a mighty bridge he made:
But marke what ill successe to him ensuth,
  Ear he through his great enterprise could wade,
A tempest did his massie worke confound,
His bridge was broken, and his souldiers drownd.

16

Lo *Lews* of *Burgundie*, descending theare
  Where, as it seemes he taken is and bound,
And he that takes him, maketh him to sweare,
  That he shall neare beare arms gainst *Latian* ground,
Low how he breakes his oth without all feare,
  Lo how againe his foes do him confound,
And like a moldwarpe, make him loose his eyes:
A just reward for such as oths despise.

17

See here how *Hugh* of *Arly* doth great feats,
  Driving the *Beringars* from native soile,
Forcing them twise or thrise to change their seats,
  And cause the *Hunnes* and *Baviers* backe recoile:
But greater force at last his acts defeats,
  First he compounds, and after all his toile,
He dies, nor after long his heire doth tarie,
But yeeldeth up his crowne to *Beringarie*.

18

Lo heare another *Charles* that by perswasion,
  Of evill shepherd, sets on fire the fold,
And kills two Kings in this his fierce invasion,
  Manfred and *Corradin*, which makes him bold:
But his owne faults of his fall gave occasion;
  His crueltie was such, so uncontrold,
That he and his were all kild (as they tell)
Ev'n at the ringing of an ev'nsong bell.

19

Now after these about one hundred yeares,
  For so the space betweene did seeme to say,
From *France*, one shall invade those famous peeres,
  The Vicount *Galeasses*, and shall lay
Siege unto *Alexandria* as appeares,
  By those that here do stand in battell ray.
Lo how the *Duke* preuenting ev'rie doubt,
Provideth strength within, deceipt without.

20

And with this warie policie proceeding,
  He doth the *Frenchmen* at advantage take,
Not finding his ambushment, and not heeding,
  Together with the Lord of *Arminake*,
Who dieth of his hurts with overbleeding:
  Lo how the streame of bloud there spilt doth make
A sanguin colour in the streame of *Poe*,
By meanes *Tanarus* into it doth goe.

21

After all these, one comes that *Marca* hight,
  And three that do of *Aniom* house proceed,
All these to those of *Naples* do much spite,
  Yet none of these can brag of their good speed:
For though to *French* they joyne some Latian might,
  Of greedie sort, that with their crownes they feed:
Yet still for all their paine and their expence,
Alfonse and *Ferdinando* drive them thence.

22

Lo *Charles* the eight descending like a thunder,
  Downe from the *Alps* with all the floure of *France*,
And conqu'ring all (to all mens passing wonder)
  Not drawing once a sword, nor breaking lance,
(Except that rocke that *Typheus* lyeth under
  While he too high himselfe strave to advance)
This Ile and castle both, that *Iskia* hight,
Defended was by *Vasto* gallant Knight.

23

Now as the master of the castle told,
  And pointed out each storie in his place,
It came into his fancy to unfold,
  The worthy praise of *Alvas* noble race;
Which (as for certaintie they all did hold)
  Wise *Merlin* propheside, who had the grace
To shew before hand, both with tongue and pen,
What accidents should hap, and where, and when.

24

And namely that this Knight whom here you see,
  Defending so the castle and the rocke,
As though he feard not those same fires that flee,
  As far as *Fare*, but them did scorne and mocke.
From this same Knight there shal descend (quoth he)
  Out of the root of this most worthy stocke,
A Knight shall win such fame and reputation,
As all the world shall hold in admiration.

25

Though *Nereus* were faire, *Achilles* strong,
  Though *Ladas* swift, though *Nestor* was most wise,
That knew so much, and lived had so long;
  Though bold *Vlysses* could both well devise,
And execute what doth to warre belong,
  Though *Cæsars* bountie prais'd be to the skies,
Yet place to give all these may thinke no scorne,
To one that shall in *Iskia* Ile be borne.

26

And if that ancient *Creta* may be prowd,
  Because that *Celus* nephew sprang therein:
If *Thebes* of *Bacchus* birth doth vant so lowd,
  And *Hercules;* if *Delus* of their twin:
Then may that Ile no lesse be well allowd,
  To vant it selfe, that hath so happie bin,
To have that Marquesse borne within that place,
On whom the heav'ns shall powre so great a grace.

27

Thus *Merlin* us'd to tell and oft repeat,
  How he should be for such a time reserved,
When *Roman* Empires high and stately seat,
  At lowest eb should be, and welnigh starved;
That his rare parts againe might make it great,
  And that by him it might be safe preserved,
Which that you may see plainly to his glory,
Marke in this table the ensuing story.

28

Lo here (said he) how *Lodwicke* doth repent,
  That he had thither brought King *Charles* the eight,
Which at the first he did but with intent
  To weaken, not to presse with so hard weight
His ancient foe; for now gainst *Charles* he went,
  Making new leagues according to his sleight,
He thinks to take him prisner by the way,
But *Charles* by force through thē doth make his way.

29

But yet the souldiers that behinde him staid,
  Had not the like good fortune nor successe,
For *Ferdinando* grew by *Mantuan* aid
  So strong, that soone he did the *French* distresse:
To whose great griefe, this Marquesse was betraid
  By *Gypson* vile, when he fear'd nothing lesse,
Which doth in *Ferdinand* so great griefe breed,
As doth his joy of victorie exceed.

30

Next after these, he shews them *Lews* the twelfth,
  That puls out *Lodwicke Sforse* with mighty hand,
And gets by force, what he had got by stelth,
  And plants the Flour de luce in *Millen* land;
Yet he no long time there in quiet dwelth,
  The great *Consalvo* with a *Spanish* band,
His Captaines and Lievtenants oft repulses,
And in the end from *Millen* quite expulses.

31

Lo here (which I forgat before to show)
  How *Lodwickes* frends, and his own men betray him,
One sells his castell never striking blow;
  The *Swizzers* eke that might away convay him,
And had his pay, and did him service ow,
  For filthy lucres sake they do bewray him;
Whereby without once breaking of a lance,
Two victories came to the King of *France*.

32

Lo how by favour of this mighty King,
  The bastard *Cæsar Borgia* grew full great,
And doth the necks of many nobles wring
  Of *Italie*, that had most ancient seat.
Lo how this King doth eke the akornes bring
  To Bulloign, lo how with another feat
He doth the *Genowais* in fight subdue,
And maketh them their late revolt to rue.

33

Lo here not far from thence, how all the feeld
  With dead mens bones is held at *Geriadad*,
How all the cities unto *Lews* do yeeld,
  How *Venice* to shut up her gates is glad;
And scarse her selfe from this great storme can sheeld:
  Lo how the Pope (his part that herein had)
Doth take away unto his great rebuke,
Modone, and more, from good *Ferraras* Duke.

34

At which King *Lews* (with rightfull choller moved)
  Gives *Bulloign* to the *Bentivols* againe,
And thence to *Breskie* all his force removed,
  And succours to *Felsina* doth ordaine,
What time the Churches souldiers felt and proved,
  The *French* mens force unto their mickle paine:
Lo after where both armies meet to fight,
Neare *Chassie* shore, to trie their utmost might.

35

On this side *France*, on that the powre of *Spaine*,
　Vnited is, and deadly blows ensew,
　The ditches all seemd fild with bodies slaine,
　A hap to make a stonie heart to rew;
　Long time in doubt doth victorie remaine,
　Which way the sway would carry no man knew,
　Till by the vertue of *Alfonse* alone,
　The *French* prevaile, the *Spanish* (forst) are gone.

36

Lo how the Pope his lip doth bite for griefe,
　Because the *Frenchmen* do *Ravenna* sack;
　Low how he sent to *Swizzers* for reliefe,
　Lo how they come and drive the *Frenchmen* back;
　And they that with their treason caused chiefe
　Of *Lodowike* the overthrow and wrack,
　To make some mends for that they erst had done,
　Vnto the fathers place restore the sonne.

37

But lo a Prince of *France* then new created,
　Meets with the *Swizzers* to their mickle cost,
　And so their courage quail'd, and force abated,
　As all the nation seemed welnigh lost;
　And of their title that them animated,
　Those villens vile hereafter need not bost,
　Defenders of the Church, tamers of Kings,
　They cleaped were, now clipped are their wings.

38

Lo how the *French* king *Francis* in despite
　Of all the league, faire *Millen* doth surprise,
　Bourbon defending it from *Genoas* might;
　Lo while this king doth practise and devise,
　Some great exploit, while by foule oversight,
　His lawlesse men the town did tyrannize;
　Their having too much pride and want of pitie,
　Doth cause them suddenly to lose the city.

39

Lo yet another *Francis Sforse*, a man
　Like to his grandsire both in acts and name,
　Who to drive out the *Frenchmen* well began,
　And *Millen* did recover with great fame;
　Lo *France* againe endeavour all they can,
　To win with praise that they had lost with shame,
　But *Mantuas* worthy Duke on *Tycian* streame,
　Cuts off his way, and kept him from that Realme.

40

Yong *Fredericke*, yet but a beardlesse boy,
　Scant having on his chin a little downe,
　Lo how he saves *Pavia* from annoy,
　When furiously the *French* besiege the towne;
　He makes their earnest plots turn to a toy,
　The Lion of the sea he beateth down:
　Lo here two Marquesses both of one blood,
　Both born to do their country endlesse good.

41

The first of these is that *Alfonsos* sonne,
　That by the *Negro* erst you saw betraid,
　Behold what feats of armes by him are done,
　How at their greatest need he them doth aid,
　How oft he hath on *Frenchmen* glory wonne,
　That of his very name they seem afraid:
　The tother that so mild doth look in sight,
　Is Lord of *Vasto*, and *Alfonso* hight.

42

This is that worthy knight, of whom I told,
　Then when I did the Ile of *Iskia* show,
　Of whom I said that *Merlin* had foretold
　To *Feramont* what he by skill did know,
　That when this world were worn and waxen old,
　And *Rome* and *Italy* were brought most low,
　Then he should spring, who to his endlesse praise
　Their foes should overthrow, and them should raise.

43

Lo how he with his cousin of *Pescare*,
　And with *Colonnas* prosprous aid no lesse,
　The *French* and *Dutch* that at *Bycocca* are,
　Do foile and slay, and drive to great distresse;
　Lo how againe the *Frenchmen* do prepare,
　With new attempts to mend their bad successe,
　One camp the king in *Lombardie* doth make,
　And with another *Naples* he would take.

44

But she that useth men as wind doth dust,
　First take it up and blow it very high,
　And from that highest place straight when she lust,
　She throwes it down whereas it first did lie:
　She makes this king devoid of all mistrust,
　Think he hath men an hundred thousand nie
　At *Pavie* siege, believing others muster,
　(But wo to kings whose servants are no juster.)

45

So while this noble Prince mistrusts no harme,
　His wicked Captaines greedy gaine to win,
　Caus'd that the soldiers in the night alarm,
　Came to their colours slow and very thin,
　Within their tents they feel their skirmish warme;
　The warie *Spaniards* soon had entred in
　With those two guides, with whom they durst assay
　In hell or els in heav'n to break a way.

46

Lo how the chiefe nobility of *France*
　Lie dead on ground, a cause of many teares,
　How many an hargabush, a sword and lance
　This stout king hath alone about his eares:
　His horse slaine under him by hard mischance,
　And yet he nothing yeelds, nor nothing feares,
　Though all the host assaulted him alone,
　And all the rescues and supplies were gone.

47

The valiant King defends him on his feet,
  Bathing his blade long time in enemies blood,
  But vertue that with too much force doth meet,
  Must yeeld at last, it cannot be withstood;
  Lo him here prisner, lo how in a fleet
  He passeth into *Spaine* the salt sea flood,
  Whence *Vasto* doth the chiefest honour bring
  Of the field won, and of the prisner king.

48

Thus both that hoast the king had thither brought,
  And that he meant to *Naples* to have sent,
  Were both dispersed quite, and came to nought,
  Much like a lamp when all the oyle is spent
  Lo how the King againe so well hath wrought,
  He leaves his sonnes for pledge, and homeward went,
  Lo how abroad he doth new quarrels pike,
  Lo how at home some do to him the like.

49

Lo here the wofull murders and the rapes
  That *Rome* doth suffer in the cruell sack,
  Where neither thing prophane nor holy scapes,
  But all alike do go to spoile and wrack:
  The league that should relieve, sits still and gapes,
  And where they should step forward, they shrinke back,
  Thus *Peters* successor by them forsaken,
  Is straight besieged, and at length is taken.

50

The King sends *Lautrek* new supplies to gather,
  Not that he should to *Lombardie* do ought,
  But that he might set free the holy father,
  That to so low an ebb so soon was brought:
  But *Lautrek* should have come a little rather,
  The Popes own coyn hath his own freedome bought,
  Lautrek attempts to conquer *Naples* town,
  And soon turnes all the country upside down.

51

Lo how a faire imperiall navy bends
  His course to succour the distressed town,
  But *Doria* back with heave and ho them sends,
  And some of them doth burn, and some doth drown:
  Lo, fickle fortune once againe intends
  To change her cheare and on the *French* to frown,
  With agues not with swords they all are slaine,
  Scarce of an hundred one turnes home againe.

52

These and such stories had the stately hall
  In marble rich ingraved on the skreen,
  As were too tedious to recite them all,
  Though then by them they were perus'd and seen;
  Their wonder great, their pleasure was not small,
  And oft they read the writings were between,
  That in faire *Roman* letters all of gold,
  The circumstance of ev'ry picture told.

53

Now when the Ladies faire and all the rest,
  Had seen and ask'd as much as they desir'd,
  Their host doth bring them to their rooms of rest,
  Where sleep renewes the strength of bodies tir'd,
  Onely Duke *Ammons* daughter could not rest,
  Though bed were soft, room warm, and well attir'd,
  Yet still she tost from left side to the right,
  And could not sleep one wink all that same night.

54

With much ado her eyes at last she clos'd,
  Not much afore the dawning of the day,
  And as she slept, she in her sleep suppos'd
  Rogero present was, and thus did say,
  My deare, what ailes thee to be thus dispos'd,
  That false beliefe in thee doth beare such sway?
  First shall the rivers to the mountaines clime,
  Ere I will guilty be of such a crime.

55

Beside she thought she heard him thus to say,
  Lo I am come to be baptiz'd my love,
  And that I seem'd my comming to delay,
  Another wound, and not a wound of love,
  Hath been the cause of my constrained stay,
  Suspitions vaine, and causlesse feare remove:
  With this the damsell wak'd, and up she started,
  But found her dreame and lover both departed.

56

Then freshly she doth her complaints renew,
  And in her mind thus to her selfe she spake,
  Lo what I like, are dreames vaine and untrue,
  And in a moment me do quite forsake;
  But ah, what me offends is too too true,
  I dream of good, but none I find awake,
  How are mine eyes alas in so ill taking,
  That clos'd see good, and nought but evill waking?

57

Sweet dream did promise me a quiet peace,
  But bitter waking turneth all to warre;
  Sweet dreame deluded me, and soon did cease,
  But bitter waking plagues, and doth not arre:
  If falshood ease, and truth my paine increase,
  I wish my selfe from truth I still might barre,
  If dreames breed joy, and waking cause my paine,
  Ay might I dream, and never wake againe.

58

Oh happy wights whom sleep doth so possesse,
  As in six moneths you never open eye,
  For sure such sleep is like to death I guesse,
  But waking thus, is not like life (think I)
  How strange are then the pangs that me oppresse,
  That sleeping seem to live, and waking die?
  But if such sleep resemblance be of death,
  Come death and close mine eyes, and stop my breath.

59

Now were those Eastern parts of heav'n made red,
　Where *Phœbus* beames do first begin appeare,
　And all the thick and rainie clouds were fled,
　And promised a morning faire and cleare;
　When *Bradamant* forsook her restlesse bed,
　And giving for her lodging and good cheare,
　Right courteous thanks unto her noble host,
　She leaves his house, and minds to part in post.

60

But first she found how that the damsell faire
　The messenger that sup'd with her last night,
　Was gone before, with purpose to repaire
　To those three knights that lately felt her might,
　When she did cause them caper in the aire,
　Driv'n without styrups from their steeds to light,
　She found they had all night to their great paine
　Abid the wind, the tempest and the raine.

61

And that which greatly did increase their griefe,
　Was that while those within had cheare great store,
　They and their horse lack'd lodging and reliefe:
　But that which did offend their stomacks more,
　And was indeed of all their sorrowes chiefe,
　Was lest the maid (of whom I spake before)
　Would tell their mistresse of their hard mischance,
　They had at their arrivall first in *France*.

62

And having full resolved and design'd,
　To die or venge the foile receiv'd last night,
　To th'end the messenger might change her mind,
　(The messenger that *Vllania* hight)
　Who thought their force and value far behind
　The vaunts that they had made of their great might,
　Therefore as soon as *Bradamant* they spi'd,
　Straight each of them to combat her defi'd.

63

Not thinking though she should a damsell be,
　For of a damsell gesture none she us'd;
　The Lady gently spake unto them three,
　And thought her hast the fight might have excus'd,
　But they did urge her still so farre, that she
　Without disgrace could not have it refus'd;
　Wherefore she coucht the golden-headed lance,
　And from their saddles made them all to dance.

64

And for that time thus ended was that fray,
　For she set spurs to horse, and rode so post,
　That ere they rose, she quite was gone away:
　They that their seats had twice together lost,
　Were so asham'd, they knew not what to say:
　For why they wonted were to make their bost,
　No knight of *France* should able be to stand
　Against the worst of them, with speare in hand.

65

But *Vllania* further them to taunt,
　That *Bradamant* a Lady was, them told,
　Now sirs (said she) you that were wont to vaunt,
　From *Palladins* to win the shield of gold,
　Lo how a womans forces can you daunt,
　Now is (I hope) your lofty courage cold:
　Sure for those knights you be too weak a match,
　When one poore damsell you can overmatch.

66

What need (said she) be **further** triall had,
　You have already that for which you came,
　Except that any of you be so mad,
　To joyne a future losse to present shame;
　Or if perhaps ye would be faine and glad,
　To end your lives by men of worthy fame:
　Trow you that vanquisht are by womans hand,
　Renaldo or *Orlando* to withstand?

67

Now when as *Vllanie* declared had,
　How that a damsell them had overthrown,
　With griefe and with disdaine they were so mad,
　That scarce their wits and senses were their own,
　Each one himselfe, or armour all unclad,　　(thrown,
　Their horse turn'd loose, their swords away were
　And vow'd for penance of so great disgrace,
　To touch no armour in a twelve-moneths space.

68

They further vow they ne'er will ride againe,
　No not when that same yeare should be expir'd,
　Although the way were mountanie or plaine,
　And though the way were gravelly or mir'd,
　Vntill they could by force of armes regaine
　Such horses, as for service are requir'd,
　And furniture for three such champions meet;
　Till then they vow'd to travell on their feet.

69

Thus wilfully they walk'd while others rode,
　But *Bradamant* went on, and that same night,
　She at a castle maketh her abode,
　Neare to the way that leads to *Paris* right:
　Here by her host, the Lady faire was show'd,
　How *Agramant* was vanquisht in the fight:
　Good meat, good lodging, and good newes she had,
　Yet eat she not, nor slept, nor was she glad.

70

But now of her so much I must not say,
　That I forget my story out to tell,
　Of those two knights that met this other day,
　And ti'd their horses at the running well:
　No lands nor townes were causes of their fray,
　Nor who in rule nor office should excell,
　But ev'n that he that strongest was of twaine,
　Should *Bayard* win, and *Durindana* gaine.

71

There needs no signe of war, nor trumpets sound,
To warn them when to strike or when to pawse,
No *Heralds* need to limit out the ground,
Nor read them lectures of their warlike lawes.
They met as they by promise firm were bound,
And each his weapon at one instant drawes,
And then they laid about them strong and nimble,
Blowes bred their smart; and smart their wrath did
(kindle.

72

Two blades more firm in triall, and more sure,
Could not in all the world have been prepar'd,
That having been (as these were) put in ure,
Would not have been in peeces burst and mar'd:
But both these blades were of such temper pure,
So keen so tough, and therewithall so hard,
They might a thousand times at hard-edge met,
And neither blade thereby a gap would get.

73

Renaldo quick hither and thither goes,
And oftentime was forc'd to change his place,
And traverse ground, for why the weight he knowes
Of *Durindana*, that would cut apace:
Gradasso ever gave the stronger blowes,
But tother still to scape them had the grace;
Or if they hit, they hit in some such part,
Where though they made great sound, they caus'd no
(smart.

74

Renaldo with lesse strength, but far more art,
Strake once or twice the *Pagan* on the arm,
And with a thrust had surely pierc'd his heart,
Save that his armour strengthened was by charm,
So that no maile out of his place would start:
But while each sought to do the other harm,
A sodaine noise did part their earnest quarrell,
They look'd and saw *Bayardo* in great parell.

75

I say they look'd about, and spi'd at length
Bayardo fighting with a monstrous fowle,
Bigger then he, her beak three yards of length,
In other shape and making like an owle,
Her talents huge and sharp, and of great strength,
The feathers of her wings all black and fowle,
Her eyes like fire, a long and hideous taile,
Her wings so huge, they seemed like a saile.

76

Perhaps it was a fowle, but I think not,
Nor ever heard I erst of such a bird;
Onely so *Turpin* calle it well I wot,
If any will credit to him affoord:
Rather I deem that *Malagigi* got
Some sprite infernall, that himselfe had stir'd,
To come in shape as I did shew before,
Because the champions fierce might fight no more.

77

Renaldo eke himselfe believ'd the same,
And with his cousin *Malagige* fell out,
And to his charge laid not a little blame,
And gave him evill language thereabout,
The tother sware by him that heav'ns did frame,
It was not he, to put him out of doubt.
But were it fowle, or were it a foule devill,
Certaine to *Bayard* it did work much evill.

78

The horse that was puissant, brake his raine,
When as the sharpnesse of her clawes he feels,
And what with terrour mov'd, and what with paine,
He yerketh at her fiercely with his heels:
She soar'd aloft, and downe she comes againe,
And strikes him so, that *Bayard* almost reels,
And sith of other fence no meane he had,
He runs away as if he had been mad.

79

Vnto the nearest wood he right doth run
And still the feather'd beast him held in chase,
Till the thick boughs holp him her gripes to shun,
So that she gave him over in short space,
And seeing that her sport with him was done,
She sored up on high, and left this place,
And to another coast her flight doth frame,
Where as she thought to find some other game.

80

Gradasso and *Renaldo* when they saw,
The horse was fled that caused all the fray,
Do by consent themselves from thence withdraw,
To find *Bayardo* out and if they may:
But first each promis'd to observe this law,
That he that found him first of both, should stay
At this same well, till tother should come thither,
And then againe to fight it out together.

81

Thus when each had his word to th'other past,
That they would meet there at their comming back,
They after go, but *Bayard* ran so fast,
As soone they lost the sight of any track:
Gradasso rode, and therefore made more hast,
The *Palladine* that his good horse did lack,
Remain'd behind, all sad and grieved more,
And malecontent then ere he was before.

82

And when he travel'd had about in vaine,
In body wearie, discontent in mind,
With losse of all his travell and his paine,
He turneth to the place they first assign'd,
In hope the tother would return againe,
And bring the horse, if so he could him find:
But when he saw his looking did not boot,
He travel'd back unto the camp on foot.

83

But yet *Gradassos* paine succeeded well,
  For why, a while before the lights decaying,
  He passed neare the place, as it befell,
  Where in a cave he found him by his naying,
  Still fearing that same monstrous imp of hell:
  He takes him thence, and then but little waying
  His promise made, he turnes another way,
  And to himselfe in secret thus doth say.

84

Let them that list hold things in strife and war,
  I mean to hold mine own with peace and ease;
  Onely to get this horse I came so far,
  And past so many lands, and many seas:
  My promise breach to me shall be no bar,
  To keep that I so quietly do sease:
  If he desire to win his horse againe,
  To come to *India* let him take the paine.

85

As safe as *France* hath been from me now twice,
  So safe from him shall be my *Serycane*,
  I thither wish him come if he be wise,
  Els of *Bayardo* now his leave is tane:
  If he will have him he shall know the prise,
  Now mine *Bayardo* is and *Durindane*:
  This said, he mounted on the steed so warly,
  And by another way went back to *Arly*.

86

Where finding ships new-rigg'd to sea-ward bent,
  Though then at anker in the harbour lying,
  With those rich spoiles, to passe the seas he meant,
  In all post hast into his country hying:
  Hereafter you shall heare which way he went,
  And of his last conflict and of his dying:
  Now him I leave, *Renaldo*, and all *France*,
  And tell you what did to *Astolfo* chance.

87

Who mounted on his stately winged steed,
  Well tamed late by *Logestillas* wit,
  Took perfect view of *France* with passing speed,
  And saw how ev'ry town of worth did fit,
  Which having well observ'd and mark'd with heed,
  From *Rhine* to *Pyren* mount he thought it fit,
  In manner like all over *Spaine* to ride,
  And many countries of the world beside.

88

To *Aragon* he passed through *Navar*,
  Each man that saw him wondring at the sight,
  Then *Taracon* he did descry not far
  Vpon his left hand, *Biskie* on his right,
  Where *Castill*, *Lisbon*, and *Galicia* are,
  And *Cordove* neare, and *Sivill* see he might,
  With diverse crownes now joyned in one raigne,
  Are govern'd by the mighty king of *Spaine*.

89

There saw he *Gades* where erst by *Hercles* hand,
  Two pillars, marks for Mariners were plac'd,
  Then over *Atlant* sea, to *Egypt* land,
  And over *Affrica* forthwith he past,
  And saw where *Balearick* Iles do stand,
  Then travel'd to *Eviza* with like hast,
  And to *Arzilla*-ward he thence departeth,
  Quite ore that sea that it from *Spagna* parteth.

90

Oran he saw, *Ippon*, *Marocco*, *Fesse*,
  Algier, *Buzea*, and those stately townes,
  Whose Princes with great pomp and pride possesse
  Of diverse Provinces the stately crownes,
  He saw *Byserta*, and *Tunigi* no lesse,
  And flying over many dales and downes,
  He saw *Capisse* and *Alzerbee* Ile,
  And all the cities to the flood of *Nyle*.

91

Tripolie, *Bernick*, *Tolomit*, and all
  Between the sea and *Atlas* woodie sides,
  Then on the *Cereneys* he right doth fall,
  And past *Carena* mounts, and more besides;
  Then crossing ov'r the barren fields and pall,
  Where sands with wind do ebb and flow like tides,
  The tombe of *Battus* he doth leave behind,
  And *Ammons* temple now worn out of mind.

92

Then came he by another *Tremisen*,
  That followes eke of *Mahomet* the law,
  Vnto another *Æthiopia* then
  He went, the which before he never saw,
  That differs both in language and in men:
  From thence he toward *Nubia* doth draw,
  Dobada and *Coallee* just between,
  Of which these Christen'd, and those Turkish been.

93

The bord'rers still are arm'd in heat and cold,
  Senapo yet of *Æthiop* is the chief,
  And hath great store of jewels and of gold,
  And much he varies not from our belief;
  For he those principles most firm doth hold,
  That can defend from everlasting grief.
  Here is it (if mine author be no lier)
  Where they do use to be baptiz'd with fier.

94

The Duke here lighted after travell long,
  And to *Senapos* stately Court was led;
  The castle was more sumptuous then strong,
  And admiration more then terrour bred;
  The locks, bars, chaines, and all that did belong
  Vnto the bridge and gates from foot to head,
  Which we make here of iron to endure,
  Was there faire wrought in massie gold most pure.

95

And though they have great store of metals fine,
  Yet were the chambers and the lodgings here
  Born up with crystall collumns, that did shine
  All ov'r the stately court most bright and cleare;
  A stately border, caus'd unto the eyne
  Red, white, green, blew, and yellow to appeare,
  Enriched with divisions for the nones,
  Of *Rubie, Smarag, Zaphyr, Topas* stones.

96

Most orient pearls and gems of passing price
  Were sprinkled on the pavements here and there,
  Hence balme doth come, hence other precious spice,
  Which from *Ierusalem* men wont to beare;
  Hence commeth musk, for odours sweet and nice,
  And amber pure, that some in bracelets weare;
  And finally all things grow there in plenty,
  That in this country are esteem'd most deintie.

97

Most true it is, els some have written lies,
  The *Sowdan* to this King doth tribute pay,
  For that in this Kings power alone it lies,
  Great *Cayre* and fertile *Egypt* to decay,
  Because that by those means he may devise,
  He may turn *Nyle* from them another way:
  This Prince *Senapo* there is cal'd of many,
  We call him *Prester Iohn* or *Preter Iany*.

98

Of all the Kings that ever there did raigne,
  This King exceld in riches and in treasure,
  But losse of sight made all his comforts vaine,
  And bard him ev'ry tast of worldly pleasure,
  And this did much increase his care and paine,
  And grieved him indeed beyond all measure,
  That all his wealth and treasure not prevented,
  But that with famine he was aye tormented.

99

For when this Prince (as hunger meet him drew)
  Did but prepare himself to drink or eat,
  Straight of *Harpias* came a cursed crew,
  With mighty wings, huge pawes, and bellies great,
  And all the dishes quite they overthrew,
  And greedily devoured all the meat;
  And that they left they did so file and flaver,
  As few could brook the sight, but none the saver.

100

The cause was this, why his great plague was such,
  Because in youth (when men most carelesse are)
  Finding himself to be extold so much,
  And passing other Kings in wealth so far,
  So foul a pride his lofty heart did touch,
  Against his maker, he would needs move war,
  To which intent a mighty power he led,
  Vnto that mount whence *Nylus* hath his head.

101

He had been told, and did it firm believe,
  That on that mount, whose top did touch the skie,
  Was that same place where *Adam* dwelt and *Eve*,
  Before their fall did cause them thence to flie.
  He hoping some rare conquest to atchieve,
  A mighty host prepared by and by,
  With mind (so high his heart with pride did swell)
  To make them tribute pay that there did dwell.

102

But high *Iehova* their foule pride represt,
  And down he sent his Angell that same night,
  Who slue an hundred thousand for the least,
  And him condemn'd for aye to lose his sight;
  Then sent he monsters vile him to molest,
  Those ugly monsters, that *Harpias* hight,
  Which so devoure and so spoile all his meat,
  Scarce they permit him once to drink or eat.

103

And that which drave him into meere despaire,
  Was that one told by way of prophecie,
  How those foule creatures ever should repaire
  Vnto that place, till time they might espie
  A gallant knight all armed in the aire,
  Vpon a winged beast aloft to flie:
  And for that this unpossible he deem'd,
  Past hope of help himselfe he then esteem'd.

104

Now when the people saw from ev'ry wall,
  And from each towre the strangely flying knight,
  He happy thought himselfe, that first of all
  Could tell the king of this unused sight;
  Who straight the prophecie to mind did call,
  And with the sudden joy, forgetting quite
  His trustie staffe, went groping with his hand,
  To welcome him that now came down to land.

105

Astolfo being lighted, nearer drew,
  And as he was the great court entring in,
  Behold the King stood ready in his vew,
  And kneeling down, to speak did thus begin,
  O heav'nly Angell, O *Messias* new,
  Though I deserve not pardon for my sin,
  Yet think to us is proper to offend,
  To you, to pardon those that will amend.

106

My guilt so heavy on my conscience lies,
  I dare not sue thou shouldst my sight restore,
  Though well I wot that thou couldst heal mine eyes,
  That art of those that aye stand God before,
  Let then this plague my want of sight suffice,
  And let me not be sterv'd thus evermore,
  At least from me these filthy monsters drive,
  And let me eat with quiet while I live.

107

And I do vow a temple unto thee,
  Of marble faire to build here in this place,
  Whose gates and cover all of gold shall be,
  Adorn'd with costly jewels in like case,
  Nam'd by thy name, and grav'd that men may see
  Thy miracle, which no time shall deface:
  Thus saith the prostrate King that nothing sees,
  And gropes to have embrac'd *Astolfos* knees.

108

The Duke to him thus friendly doth reply,
  Nor Angell I, nor new *Messias* am,
  Nor come from heav'n, but mortall man am I,
  And thrall to sinne, unworthy so high name;
  But for your sake my best skill I will trie,
  To kill or drive those fowle from whence they came,
  Which if I do, give God, not me the praise,
  That for your help did hither guide my waies.

109

For him your Churches and your altars make,
  That must of duty Church and altars have:
  This said, he up from ground the King doth take,
  And went with him and other Barons grave:
  Straightwaies of meat provision new they make,
  For so the hungry King in hast doth crave,
  In hope that now the monsters would be quiet,
  And not to interrupt him at his diet.

110

Forthwith a sumptuous dinner was prepar'd,
  In stately sort great store and of the best,
  Senapo hopes *Astolfo* can him guard
  From those foule fowles that did him so molest;
  But lo a sodain noise forthwith was heard,
  The sent of those same viands that were drest
  Had brought them thither, ere the men were able
  To set down all the dishes on the table.

111

Of them came sev'n together in a knot,
  With womans faces, wan with deadly cold,
  So hunger-starv'd, as death it selfe might not
  Be at first sight more hideous to behold,
  Their wings were great, but foule blacke wings God wot,
  Their talents sharp to gripe, but strong to hold,
  A large foule paunch, a filthy taile and long,
  From whence there came an odour mighty strong.

112

As sodaine heard, so sodaine were they seen,
  For on the table all at once they fell,
  And spoil'd the meat, and from their wombs uncleen
  Cast lothsome filth to see, irksome to smell:
  The Duke with blade of mettall sharp and keen,
  Strikes at the monsters, thinking them to quell;
  But all in vaine, his bootlesse blade turn'd back,
  As he had smitten on a woollen sack.

113

Some rav'nously devour'd the sweet repast,
  And did so eager fill their greedy gorge,
  That by and by they were compeld as fast,
  The same in beastly manner to disgorge:
  The wofull King thinks now all succour past,
  Till good *Astolfo* sware by sweet Saint *George*,
  Sith force was vaine, he would another way
  To drive these monsters from the King assay.

114

The horn which ever he about him beares,
  He means against these monsters to employ,
  He caus'd the King and his to stop their eares
  With molted waxe, that no noise them may noy,
  Els might his blast have bred in them such feares,
  To drive them thence, and all the land destroy;
  Then caus'd he them prepare another feast,
  And up he gets him on his winged beast.

115

The steward that did know his mind by signes,
  Straightwaies another dinner doth addresse,
  With store of dainty meats and costly wines;
  But in a trice more soon then one could guesse,
  The filthy flock (as famine them inclines)
  Came down, and seaz'd upon the costly messe,
  But straight *Astolfo* blew them such a blast,
  As on the sodaine made them all agast.

116

The noise into their open eares so enter'd,
  That had no means to stop them, nor defence,
  As so their stomacks and their tasts distemper'd,
  They fled, as feare expeld all other sence:
  The *English* Duke to follow them adventer'd,
  And winding still his horn, he chas'd them thence,
  To that hils foot, whence *Nylus* first doth fall,
  If so that *Nyle* have any head at all.

117

About the bottome of this mighty mount
  There is a cave descending like a well,
  By which (as dwellers by do oft recount)
  A speedy passage one may have to hell;
  To this the monsters fled, and made account
  Within this cave safe from the noise to dwell,
  Which seen, *Astolfo* from his beast allighted,
  And ceast the blowing that them so affrighted.

118

And for he did with heed the caves mouth mark,
  He nearer doth approch unto the same,
  And with a listning eare he then doth hark
  If any sound from thence unto him came;
  The entrance lookt all like a dungeon dark,
  With smoke that seem'd to come from smother'd flame:
  But more of this hereafter I will treat,
  For now this book begins to be too great.

THE THIRTY-FOVRTH BOOKE OF
ORLANDO FVRIOSO

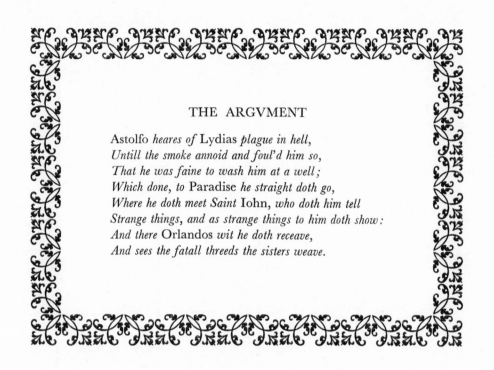

THE ARGVMENT

Astolfo *heares of* Lydias *plague in hell,*
Untill the smoke annoid and foul'd him so,
That he was faine to wash him at a well;
Which done, to Paradise *he straight doth go,*
Where he doth meet Saint Iohn, *who doth him tell*
Strange things, and as strange things to him doth show:
And there Orlandos *wit he doth receave,*
And sees the fatall threeds the sisters weave.

ORLANDO FVRIOSO
THE THIRTY-FOVRTH BOOKE

1

Oh foule *Harpias*, greedy, hunger starv'd,
  Whom wrath divine for just revenge hath sent
To blinded *Italy*, that hath deserv'd
  For sinnes both old and late so to be shent.
The sustenance that should for food have serv'd,
  For widowes poore and orphans innocent,
These filthy monsters do consume and wast it
Oft at one meale, before the owners tast it.

2

He doubtlesse guilty is of grievous sin,
  That first set open that long closed cave,
From which all filth and greedinesse came in
  To *Italy*, and it infected have,
Then ended good then did bad dayes begin,
  And discord foule so fane off all peace drave,
That now in warres, in poverty and paine,
It long hath tari'd, and shall long remaine.

3

Vntill she can her slothfull sonnes awake,
  From drowsie sleep, that now themselves forget,
And say to them, for shame example take,
  Let others valiant deeds your courage whet:
Why should not you the like acts undertake,
  As in time past did *Calai* and *Zet?*
That erst like aid to *Phineas* did bring,
As did *Astolfo* th'Ethiopian king.

4

Who having driv'n away these monsters fell,
  From blind *Senapos* boord, as erst I told,
And chased them so farre, untill they fell
  Into the cave most fearfull to behold;
That fearfull cave that was the mouth of hell,
  To hearken at the same he waxed bold,
And heard most wofull mourning, plaints and cries,
Such as from hell were likely to arise.

5

Astolfo minds into the place to enter,
  And visit those that have forgone this light,
And pierce the earth ev'n to the middle center,
  To see if ought may there be worth the sight;
For why he thought, what need I feare to venter,
  That have this horn, with which I can affright
Foule *Sathan*, *Cerberus* with triple chaps,
And safely keep my selfe from all mishaps?

6

He ties his flying beast fast by the reines,
  With mind to hell it selfe to bid defiance,
His horn fast ti'd about his neck remaines,
  In which much more then sword he puts affiance:
But at his very entrance he complaines
  Of that same smoke that bred him much annoyance,
That savour'd strong of brimstone and of pitch,
Yet still *Astolfo* goeth thorow stitch.

7

But still the further that he forward goes,
  He feels the smoke more noisome and more thick,
That in himselfe he gan now to suppose,
  If further he should wade he should be sick,
When lo a shadow seemed to disclose
  It selfe to him, of somwhat that was quick,
And to his thinking hither wav'd and thither,
Much like a carcasse hanged long in weather.

8

The *English* Duke that had desire to know,
  If so he saw a body or a vision,
Strake with his sword thereat so fierce a blow,
  As would indeed thereof have made division,
If it had been as it did seem in show:
  But when he saw his sword made no incision,
He guessed that it was (by that blowes giving)
A passed spirit, not a body living.

9

Then heard he how thus wofully it said,
  Oh you that to these lower parts descend,
Bring us no hurt, though you can bring no aid,
  And be not so to those whom none can friend.
The Duke amaz'd, both hands and footsteps staid,
  And said unto the ghost, so God thee send
Some speedy ease of this thy painfull smart,
As thou wilt deine to tell me who thou art.

10

And if to work your good lay in my lot,
  Above or here I should be glad to do it.
Ah (said the ghost) my plague with such a knot
  Is ti'd, as mortall strength cannot undo it,
Yet your request deny you will I not,
  Because you have so great a mind unto it,
I will declare to you my stock and name,
And eke the cause why to this place I came.

11

My name is *Lydia*, born of princely birth,
  And bred in pomp and solaces delightfull,
  Though now in place excluded from all mirth,
  I lie condemn'd by Gods high doom and rightfull,
  Because while I did live above on earth,
  Vnto my love I shew'd my selfe so spightfull;
  And many more be here for like offences,
  As he that all doth rule, their plague dispences.

12

Here lies that faire, but cruell *Anaxaritee*,
  Whose corps a stone divine revenge did make,
  Her ghost in smoke that no light ay shall clarifie,
  Doth most severe, but most just penance take,
  Because she could without all sense of charity,
  Behold her lover hanging for her sake:
  Here *Daphne* lies, that now repents her shunning
  Of *Phœbus*, whom she scap'd with over-running.

13

Too tedious it would be for me to tell
  The sev'rall names of ev'ry female spirit,
  That for reward of their hard hearts, in hell
  Appointed are such portions to inherit.
  Yet farre more are the men that there do dwell,
  For like offence, who for their evill merit   (them,
  Are placed much more low, though somwhat nigh,
  Where fume doth smother them, and flame doth fry
                                                    (them.

14

And reason good, for sith our sex is weak,
  The greater sinne it is us to deceive,
  As *Theseus* and *Iason* well can speak,
  And he that *Latin* did of rule bereave,
  With him, on whom faire *Absolon* did wreak
  The wrong that ravisht *Thamar* did receive,
  With diverse that of tone and tother gender,
  Refus'd or left their loves for causes slender.

15

But that I may particularly touch
  The cause that brought me to this endlesse paine,
  My beauty while I liv'd, and pride was such,
  As none or few did to the like attaine,
  And both of them in me excel'd so much,
  'Twas hard to say which greater was of twaine:
  But this I know full well, my proud mind grew
  Out of conceit of my well pleasing hew.

16

It hapned that a valiant knight of *Thrace*
  In state and living of the better sort,
  And hearing praise of my praise-worthy face,
  Confirmed oft by more then one report,
  He purpos'd, and perform'd it in short space,
  Vnto my fathers kingdome to resort,
  That he might sue to me, and only serve me,
  In hope by his great value to deserve me.

17

In gallant sort when he to *Lydia* came,
  And saw with eye what he had heard with eare,
  He calleth scant report, and niggard fame,
  That did to him so barren tidings beare:
  And ravisht with my look, he straight doth frame
  Himselfe to wait in court, and tarrie there,
  And shew'd such worth, and used such behaviour,
  As justly might deserve my fathers favour.

18

Exceeding was his service and desert,
  If to a gratefull Prince it had been done,
  So perfectly he had of warre the art,
  That for my sire, by his conduct he won
  All *Caria*, and of *Cilicia* part,
  And after these exploits, he then begun,
  For recompence of these his merits rife,
  To pray my father I might be his wife.

19

My father him repuls'd with answer sowre,
  Because to match me higher was his will,
  Not to a private knight, whose chiefest dowre
  Was vertue, of whose worth he could not skill,
  His greedy thoughts did nought but gaine devoure,
  And covetise the branch and root of ill,
  Made him no more regard his vertuous sute,
  Then doth an Asse the sound of sweetest Lute.

20

Alceste (so was nam'd the worthy Knight)
  Took this so foul repulse in great disdaine,
  Proceeding thence, from whence he ought of right
  Expect great recompence for his great paine;
  Wherefore he parted thence in great despight,
  And vow'd revenge, nor was his vow in vaine.
  Vnto th'*Armenian* king he thence doth go,
  My fathers emulous and ancient foe.

21

Him (ready to accept each light occasion)
  He soon perswades, without all intermission,
  To make upon my father fierce invasion,
  And make him chiefe Lievtenant by commission:
  And having won him thereto by perswasion,
  They thus agreed of spoiles to make partition,
  As namely all the towns he won should be
  The kings, and for himselfe he ask'd but me.

22

This league thus made, what woes my sire he wrought,
  I know not how in speeches to expresse,
  Foure royall armies quickly came to nought,
  Disperst or dead in half a yeare and lesse;
  In fine *Alcesté* by his value brought
  My father and his friends to such distresse,
  They took them to a fort with such small treasure,
  As in so Scarbrow warning they had leasure.

23

When here a while he us besieged had,
  To such despaire he then my father drave,
  To yeeld me up he would have been full glad,
  To be his wife, yea ev'n to be his slave;
  Nor would my sire have thought the bargaine bad,
  If halfe the Realme with me for dowre he gave,
  So sore he fear'd, ere long to leese it all,
  And die in wofull bands a captive thrall.

24

Wherefore in season to prevent the worst,
  Me that had been the cause of all this ill,
  He minds to offer to *Alcesté* first,
  To win thereby his favour and good will:
  I went (for why none other do I trust)
  With mind herein my sires mind to fulfill,
  And offer mine own self at his devotion,
  With halfe the Realme, if he accept the motion.

25

Alcesté hearing I came him to look,
  Against me forth he comes all pale and trembling,
  Not like a conqueror was then his look,
  But rather a captived man resembling;
  Which when I found, my first plot I forsook,
  For well I saw that this was not dissembling,
  With lowring look I held my peace a while,
  Then fit for his estate I fram'd my stile.

26

I waxed bold the more I see him faint,
  And first I cursed this unluckie love,
  And of his cruelty I made complaint,
  Which harm'd my friends, and chiefe that he would
  Against my will to have me by constraint,   (prove
  I further did most sharply him reprove,
  That he so parted with the first deniall,
  And never sought to make new friendly triall.

27

I told him that his manners were too fierce,
  That though my father his just suit deny'd,
  Because perhaps his nature is perverse,
  And would not at the first attempt be ply'd,
  He should not though, all his good deeds reverse,
  But rather ought with constancy have try'd,
  By patient suffring, and by painfull serving,
  To come unto reward of well deserving.

28

And if my father would not have been won,
  I would (I said) his favour have procur'd,
  And would have praid him, to make him his sonne,
  If I had found his love to me had dur'd;
  Or else in secret I would that have done,
  By which of me he should have been assur'd;
  But sith he needs would trie another mean,
  I told him plaine, my love was alter'd clean.

29

And though I now came in this humble sort,
  To yeeld my body, as the price of peace,
  Because my father, whom he held so short,
  Intreated me to sue for his release;
  Yet did I vow to marre his hoped sport,
  And if to offer force he would not cease,
  I sware that rather I my selfe would kill,
  Then grant such joyes constrain'd against my will.

30

These words and such as these to him I spake,
  Finding my power was over him so great,
  Wherewith I did him as repentant make,
  As ere was Saint in Hermits desart seat:
  He fell down at my feet, and praid me take
  His naked dagger, and did me intreat,
  To stab him with the same into his heart,
  To take just vengeance of his lewd desart.

31

Now when I saw him at this passe, I thought
  To follow this great conquest to his end,
  And straight a little hope to him I brought,
  Of favour, if his errour he would mend,
  And if my fathers freedome might be wrought,
  And state restor'd, and he continue friend,
  And not attempt hereafter to constraine me,
  But with his serviceable love to gaine me.

32

He promised hereof he would not misse,
  And back unto my sire me safe did send,
  Nor once presumed he my mouth to kisse;
  Think you, how he unto my yoke did bend;
  I think that love plaid well his part in this,
  And needed not for him more arrowes spend;
  Hence straight unto th'*Armenian* king he went,
  Whose all the winnings should be, by consent.

33

And in the mildest manner that he could,
  He prayeth him to grant his good assent,
  That my poore sire might *Lydia* quiet hold,
  And he would with *Armenia* be content.
  The king *Alcesté* sharply then controld,
  And in plaine terms he told he never meant
  To cease that bloudy warre at any hand,
  While that my father had a foot of land.

34

What if (said he) *Alcestés* wav'ring braine
  Is turn'd with womans words? his dammage be it:
  Shall I therefore lose all a whole yeares gaine
  At his request? I never will agree it:
  Againe *Alcesté* prayes him, and againe,
  But all in vaine, he sees it will not be yet:
  And last he waxed angry, and did sweare,
  That he should do it, or for love or feare.

35

Thus wrath ingendred many a bitter word,
  And bitter words did breed more bloudy blowes,
  Alcesté in that fury drew his sword,
  And straight the guard on each side him inclose,
  But he among them so himselfe bestir'd,
  He slue the king, and by the help of those
  Of *Thrace*, and of *Cilicia* in his pay,
  Th'*Armenians* all he put to flight that day.

36

And then his happy victory pursuing,
  First he my fathers friends did all inlarge,
  And next the Realme within one month ensuing,
  He gat again, without my fathers charge;
  And for the better shunning and eschuing
  Of all unkindnesse, with amends most large,
  For recompence of all harms he had done,
  He gave him all the spoiles that he had won.

37

Yea fully to content him to his asking,
  In all the countries that did neare confine,
  He rais'd such summes of coine, by cursed tasking,
  As made them grieve and greatly to repine.
  The while my hate in loves faire vizar masking,
  In outward show, I seem'd him to incline;
  Yet secretly I studi'd to annoy him,
  And many wayes devised to destroy him.

38

In stead of triumph by a privy train,
  At his return to kill him we intended,
  But from such fact feare forc'd us to refrain,
  Because we found he was so strongly friended;
  I seemed of his comming glad and fain,
  And promis'd when our troubles all were ended,
  That I his faithfull yokefellow would be,
  In wo or weale, to take such part as he.

39

Wherefore I praid him first, that for my sake,
  He would subdue some of our private foes,
  And he each hard exploit doth undertake,
  And now alone, and then with few he goes,
  And safe returns, yet oft I did him make,
  To fight with cruell Giants, and with those
  That past his strength, oft with some monstrous beast,
  Or Dragon fell, that did our Realme molest.

40

Don *Hercles* never by his cruell Aunt,
  Nor by the hard *Euristeus* was so wrought
  In *Lerna, Thrace,* in *Nemea Eremaunt,*
  Numid, Etolia, Tebrus where he fought,
  Nor *Spaine,* nor no where els, as I might vaunt,
  With mild perswasion, but with murdring thought,
  I made my lover still to put in ure,
  In hope hereby his ruine to procure.

41

But as the Palm the more the top is prest,
  The thicker do the under branches grow,
  Ev'n so, the more his vertue was opprest
  By hard attempts the brighter it did show:
  Which when I found, forthwith I thought it best,
  Another way to work his overthrow,
  A way by which indeed I wrought the feat,
  Which yet I shame and sorrow to repeat.

42

Against all such as bare him best affection,
  I secretly did still his mind incense,
  And ever one and one by my direction,
  I made him wrong, till all were driv'n from thence:
  So was his heart and soul in my subjection,
  So had my beauty blinded all his sence,
  Had I but wink'd, or up my finger hild,
  He had not car'd whom he had hurt or kild.

43

Now when I thus had foil'd my fathers foes,
  And by *Alcesté,* had *Alcesté* won,
  And made him for my sake forsake all those,
  That for his sake no high attempt would shun;
  I then began my self plain to disclose;
  And let him know what wise thred he had spun,
  With bitter spitefull words I all to rated him,
  And told him plain that in my heart I hated him.

44

And that I wish'd his life and dayes were ended,
  And would have kild him, if I could for shame,
  Save then I should of all men be condemned,
  Because his high deserts were of such fame;
  Yet him and them I utterly contemned,
  And loath'd to see his face, or heare his name,
  And sware I would wish him thenceforth no better,
  Nor heare his message, nor receive his letter.

45

At this my cruell usage and ungrate
  He took such grief, that in a while he di'd:
  Now for this sin, he that all sin did hate,
  Condemnes me here in this smoke to be ti'd,
  Where I in vain repent my self too late,
  That I his suit so causlesly deni'd,
  For which, in smoke eternall I must dwell,
  Sith no redemption can be had from hell.

46

Here *Lidia* this her wofull tale doth end,
  And faded thence; now when her speech did cease,
  The Duke a farther passage did intend,
  But this tormenting smoke did so increase,
  That backward he was forc'd his steps to bend,
  For vitall sprites already did decrease,
  Wherefore the smoke to shun, and life to save,
  He clammerd to the top of that same cave.

47

And lest those woman-faced monsters fell
  Might after come from out that lothsome ledge,
  He dig'd up stones, and great trees down did fell,
  (His sword sufficing both for axe and sledge)
  He hew'd and brake, and labour'd it so well,
  That gainst the cave he made a thick strong hedge,
  So stop'd with stones, and many a ragged rafter,
  As kept th'*Harpias* in a great while after.

48

But now the Duke, both with his present toile,
  That did with dirt and dust him all to dash,
  And with the smoke that erst did him so soile,
  As black as soot, was driv'n to seek some plash,
  Where he himself might of his clothes dispoile,
  And both his raiment and his armour wash,
  For why the smoke without and eke within,
  Did taint his clothes, his armour, and his skin.

49

Soon after he a chrystall stream espying,
  From foot to head he wash'd himself therein,
  Then up he gets him on his courser flying,
  And of the aire he more and more doth win,
  Affecting heav'n, all earthly thoughts defying:
  As fishes cut the liquid streame with fin,
  So cutteth he the aire and doth not stop,
  Till he was come unto that mountaines top.

50

This hill nigh touch'd the circle of the Moone,
  The top was all a fruitfull pleasant field,
  And light at night, as ours is here at noone,
  The sweetest place that ever man beheld;
  (There would I dwell if God gave me my boone)
  The soyle thereof most fragrant flowres did yeeld,
  Like *Rubies, Gold, Pearles, Saphyrs, Topas* stones,
  Chrysolites, Diamonds, Iacints for the nones.

51

The trees that there did grow were ever green,
  The fruits that thereon grew were never fading,
  The sundry colour'd birds did sit between,
  And sing most sweet, the fruitfull boughs them shading:
  The rivers cleare as crystall to be seen,
  The fragrant smell the sense and soule invading,
  With aire so temperate and so delightsome,
  As all the place beside was cleare and lightsome.

52

Amid the plaine a pallace passing faire
  There stood, above conceit of mortall men,
  Built of great height, unto the clearest aire,
  And was in circuit twenty mile and ten;
  To this faire place the Duke did straight repaire,
  And viewing all that goodly country then,
  He thought this world, compared with that pallace,
  A dunghill vile, or prison void of solace.

53

But when as nearer to the place he came,
  He was amazed at the wondrous sight;
  The wall was all one precious stone, the same,
  And then the carbuncle more sanguine bright;
  O workman rare, O most stupendious frame,
  What *Dedalus* of this had oversight?
  Peace ye that wont to praise the wonders seav'n.
  Those earthly kings made, this the King of heav'n.

54

Now while the Duke his eyes with wonder fed,
  Behold a faire old man in th'entrie stood,
  Whose gown was white, but yet his jacket red,
  The tone as snow, the tother look'd as blood,
  His beard was long and white, so was his head,
  His countnance was so grave, his grace so good,
  A man thereby might at first sight suspect,
  He was a Saint, and one of Gods elect.

55

He comming to the Duke with chearfull face,
  Who now alighted was for rev'rence sake,
  Bold Baron (said the Saint) by speciall grace,
  That suffer'd wast this voyage strange to make,
  And to arrive at this most blessed place,
  Not knowing why thou didst this journey take,
  Yet know that not without the will celestiall,
  Thou commest here to *Paradise* terrestriall.

56

The cause you came a journey of such length,
  Is here of me to learn what must be done,
  That *Charles* and holy Church may now at length
  Be freed, that erst were welnigh overrun,
  Wherefore impute it not to thine own strength,
  Nor to thy courage, nor thy wit, my son,
  For neither could thy horn nor winged steed
  Without Gods help stand thee in any steed.

57

But at more leisure hereof we will reason,
  And more at large I mind with you to speak,
  Now with some meat refresh you, as is reason,
  Lest fasting long may make your stomack weak;
  Our fruits (said he) be never out of season:
  The Duke rejoyced much, and marvel'd eke;
  Then chiefe when by his speeches and his coat
  He knew 'twas he that the fourth Gospell wrote.

58

That holy *Iohn* whom *Christ* did hold so deare,
  That others thought he death should never see,
  Though in the Gospell it appeares not cleare,
  But thus he said, What if it pleased me,
  O *Peter*, that thy fellow tarry here
  Vntill my comming, what is that to thee?
  So though our Saviour not directly spake it,
  Yet sure it was, so ev'ry one did take it.

59

He here assumed was in happy houre,
　Whereas before *Enoch* the Patriark was,
　And where the Prophet bides of mighty power,
　That in the fierie coach did thither passe:
　These three in that so happy sacred bowre
　In high felicity their dayes did passe:
　Where in such sort to stand they are allow'd,
　Till *Christ* return upon the burning cloud.

60

These Saints him welcome to that sacred seat,
　And to a stately lodging him they brought;
　And for his horse likewise ordained meat,
　And then the Duke himselfe by them was taught;
　The dainty fruits of *Paradise* to eat,
　So delicate in tast, as sure he thought
　Our first two parents were to be excus'd,
　That for such fruit obedience they refus'd.

61

Now when the Duke had nature satisfi'd,
　With meat and drink, and with his due repose,
　(For there were lodgings faire, and all beside
　That needfull for mans use man can suppose)
　He gets up early in the morning tide,
　What time with us alow, the Sun arose,
　But ere that he from out his lodging mov'd,
　Came that Disciple whom our Saviour lov'd.

62

And by the hand the Duke abroad he led,
　And said some things to him, I may not name,
　But in the end (I think) my son he sed,
　Although that you from *France* so lately came,
　You little know how those in *France* have sped,
　There your *Orlando* quite is out of frame,
　For God his sinne most sharply now rewardeth,
　Who most doth punish whom he most regardeth.

63

Know that the champion your *Orlando*, whom
　God so great strength and so great courage gave,
　And so rare grace, that from his mothers wombe,
　By force of steel his skin no hurt might have,
　To th'end that he might fight for his own home,
　And those that hold the Christian faith to save;
　As *Sampson* erst enabled was to stand,
　Against *Philistins* for the *Hebrew* land.

64

This your *Orlando* hath bin so ungrate
　(For so great grace receiv'd) unto his maker,
　That when his country was in weakest state,
　And needed succour most, he did forsake her,
　For love (O wofull love that breeds Gods hate)
　To woo a *Pagan* wench, with mind to take her,
　And to such sin this love did him intice,
　He would have kild his kinsman once or twice.

65

For this same cause doth mighty God permit
　Him mad to run, with belly bare and breast,
　And so to daze his reason and his wit,
　He knowes not others, and himselfe knowes least:
　So in times past our Lord did deem it fit,
　To turn the king of *Babel* to a beast,
　In which estate he sev'n whole yeares did passe,
　And like an oxe did feed on hay and grasse.

66

But for the *Palladins* offence is not
　So great as was the King of *Babels* crime,
　The mighty Lord of mercy doth allot
　Vnto his punishment a shorter time,
　Twelve weeks in all he must remaine a sot,
　And for this cause you suffer'd were to clime
　To this high place, that here you may be taught
　How to his wits *Orlando* may be brought.

67

Here you shall learn to work the feat I warrant,
　But yet before you can be fully sped
　Of this your great, but not forethought on arrant,
　You must with me a more strange way be led,
　Vp to the *Planet* that of all starres errant
　Is nearest us, when she comes over head,
　Then will I bring you where the medicine lies,
　That you must have to make *Orlando* wise.

68

Thus all that day they spent in divers talk,
　With solace great, as never wanteth there,
　But when the Sun began this earth to balk,
　And passe into the tother hemispheare,
　Then they prepar'd to fetch a further walk,
　And straight the firie charet that did beare
　Elias, when he up to heav'n was cari'd,
　Was ready in a trice, and for them tari'd.

69

Foure horses fierce, as red as flaming fire,
　Th'*Apostle* doth into the charet set,
　Which when he framed had to his desire,
　Astolfo in the carre by him he set,
　Then up they went, and still ascending higher,
　Above the firie region they did get,
　Whose nature so th'*Apostle* then did turn,
　That though they went through fire, they did not burn.

70

I say although the fire were wondrous hot,
　Yet in their passage they no heat did feel,
　So that it burn'd them, nor offends them not;
　Thence to the *Moone* he guides the running wheel,
　The *Moone* was like a glasse all void of spot,
　Or like a peece of purely burnisht steel,
　And look'd, although to us it seem'd so small,
　Welnigh as big as earth and sea and all.

71

Here had *Astolfo* cause of double wonder,
    One, that that region seemeth there so wide,
    That unto us that are so farre asunder,
    Seems but a little circle, and beside,
    That to behold the ground that him lay under,
    A man had need to have been sharply ey'd,
    And bend his browes, and mark ev'n all they might,
    It seem'd so small, now chiefly wanting light.

72

'Twere infinite to tell what wondrous things
    He saw, that passed ours not few degrees,
    What towns, what hils, what rivers, and what springs,
    What dales, what pallaces, what goodly trees;
    But to be short, at last his guide him brings
    Vnto a goodly valley, where he sees
    A mighty masse of things strangely confus'd,
    Things that on earth were lost, or were abus'd.

73

A store-house strange, that what on earth is lost,
    By fault, by time, by fortune, there is found,
    And like a merchandize is there ingrost,
    In stranger sort then I can well expound;
    Nor speak I sole of wealth, or things of cost,
    In which blind fortunes power doth most abound,
    But ev'n of things quite out of fortunes power,
    Which wilfully we wast each day and houre.

74

The precious time that fooles mis-spend in play,
    The vaine attempts that never take effect,
    The vowes that sinners make, and never pay,
    The counsels wise that carelesse men neglect,
    The fond desires that lead us oft astray,
    The praises that with pride the heart infect,
    And all we lose with folly and mis-spending,
    May there be found unto this place ascending.

75

Now as *Astolfo* by those regions past,
    He asked many questions of his guide,
    And as he on tone side his eye did cast,
    A wondrous hill of bladders he espi'd;
    And he was told they had been in time past,
    The pompous crowns and scepters full of pride,
    Of monarchs of *Assyria* and of *Greece*,
    Of which now scantly there is left a peece.

76

He saw great store of baited hooks with gold,
    And those were gifts that foolish men preferd
    To give to Princes covetous and old,
    With fondest hope of future vaine reward;
    Then were there ropes all in sweet garlands rold,
    And those were all false flatteries he hard.
    Then heard he crickets songs, like to the verses
    The servant in his masters praise reherses.

77

There did he see fond loves, that men pursue,
    To look like golden gives with stones all set,
    Then things like Eagles Talents he did view,
    Those offices that favourites do get:
    Then saw he bellowes large that much wind blew,
    Large promises that Lords make, and forget,
    Vnto their *Ganimeds* in flowre of youth,
    But after nought but beggery ensu'th.

78

He saw great Cities seated in faire places,
    That overthrowne quite topsie turvie stood,
    He ask'd and learn'd, the cause of their defaces
    Was treason, that doth never turne to good:
    He saw foule serpents with faire womens faces,
    Of coyners and of theeves the cursed brood,
    He saw fine glasses all in peeces broken,
    Of service lost in Court, a wofull token.

79

Of mingled broth he saw a mighty masse
    That to no use all spilt on ground did lie,
    He ask'd his teacher, and he heard it was
    The fruitlesse almes that men give when they die:
    Then by a faire green mountaine he did passe,
    That once smelt sweet, but now it stinks perdye,
    This was that gift (be't said without offence)
    That *Constantine* gave *Silvester* long since.

80

Of birdlime-rods he saw no little store,
    And these (O Ladies faire) your beauties be,
    I do omit ten thousand things and more
    Like vnto these, that there the Duke did see:
    For all that here is lost, there evermore
    Is kept, and thither in a trice doth flee,
    Howbeit more nor lesse there was no folly,
    For still that here with us remaineth wholly.

81

He saw some of his own lost time and deeds,
    But yet he knew them not to be his own,
    They seem'd to him disguis'd in so strange weeds,
    Till his instructer made them better known:
    But last, the thing which no man thinks he needs,
    Yet each man needeth most, to him was shown,
    By name mans wit, which here we leese so fast,
    As that one substance all the other past.

82

It seem'd to be a body moist and soft,
    And apt to mount by ev'ry exhalation,
    And when it hither mounted was aloft,
    It there was kept in pots of such a fashion,
    As we call jarrs, where oyle is kept in oft:
    The Duke beheld (with no small admiration)
    The jarrs of wit, amongst which one had writ
    Vpon the side thereof, *Orlandos* wit.

83

This vessell bigger was than all the rest,
 And ev'ry vessell had ingrav'n with art
 His name that erst the wit therein possest:
 There of his own the Duke did find a part,
 And much he mus'd, and much himselfe he blest,
 To see some names of men of great desert,
 That think they have great store of wit, and boast it,
 When here it plaine appear'd they quite had lost it.

84

Some lose their wit with love, some with ambition,
 Some running to the sea, great wealth to get,
 Some following Lords, and men of high condition,
 And some in faire jewels rich and costly set:
 One hath desire to prove a rare Magician,
 And some with Poetrie their wit forget,
 Another thinks to be an Alcumist,
 Till all be spent, and he his number mist.

85

Astolfo takes his own before he goes,
 For so th'*Evangelist* doth him permit;
 He set the vessels mouth but to his nose,
 And to his place he snuft vp all his wit:
 Long after wise he liv'd, as *Turpin* showes,
 Vntill one fault he after did commit:
 By name the love of one faire Northerne lasse,
 Sent up his wit into the place it was.

86

The vessell where *Orlandos* wit was clos'd,
 Astolfo took, and thence with him did beare;
 It was far heavier then he had suppos'd,
 So great a quantity of wit was there;
 But yet ere back their journey they dispos'd,
 The holy Prophet brought *Astolfo*, where
 A pallace (seldome seen by mortall man)
 Was plac'd, by which a thick dark river ran.

87

Each room therein was full of diverse fleeces,
 Of wooll, of lint, of silk, or els of cotten,
 An aged woman spun the diverse peeces,
 Whose look and hew did shew her old and rotten:
 Not much unlike unto that labour, this is,
 By which in Sommer new made silk is gotten,
 Where from the silk worme his fine garment taking,
 They reave him of the clothes of his own making.

88

For first in one large roome a woman span
 Threds infinite, of diverse stuffe and hew;
 Another doth with all the speed she can,
 With other stuffe the distaves still renew;
 The third in feature like, and pale and wan,
 Doth sever faire from foule, and old from new:
 Now who be these? the Duke demands his guide,
 These be the fatall sisters, he repli'd;

89

The *Parcees* that the thred of life do spin
 To mortall men, hence death and nature know
 When life must end, and when it must begin:
 Now, she that doth divide them, and bestow
 The course from finer, and the thick from thin,
 To that end works, that those that finest grow,
 For ornaments in *Paradise* may dwell,
 The course are curst to be consum'd in hell.

90

The Duke did further in the place behold,
 That when the threds were spent that had been spun,
 Their names in brasse, in silver, or in gold
 Were wrote, and so into great heapes were done;
 From which a man that seemed wondrous old,
 With whole loads of those names away did run,
 And turn'd againe as fast the way he went,
 Nor ever wearie was, nor ever spent.

91

This aged man did hold his pace so swift,
 As though to run he onely had been born,
 Or had it giv'n him as a speciall gift:
 And in the lappet of his cloke were born,
 The names of men, with which he made such shift:
 But now a while I crave to be forborn,
 For in the book ensuing shalbe show'd,
 How this old sire his cariage ill bestow'd.

THE THIRTY-FIFT BOOKE OF
ORLANDO FVRIOSO

THE ARGVMENT

Saint Iohn *the praise of writers doth recount:*
Bradamant *doth with good successe recover*
The prisners that were tane by Rodomount:
This done, she sends a challenge to her lover,
And sends withall an horse of good account,
Which makes Rogero *long in doubt to hover;*
The while before his face the fall he saw,
Of Serpentine, Grandonio, *and* Ferraw.

ORLANDO FVRIOSO
THE THIRTY-FIFT BOOKE

1

Faire mistresse who for me to heav'n shall flie,
　To bring againe from thence my wandring wit,
　Which I still lose, since from that piercing eye
　The dart came forth that first my heart did hit?
　Nor of my losse at all complaine would I,
　Might I but keep that which remaineth yet:
　But if it still decrease, within short space
　I doubt I shall be in *Orlandos* case.

2

Yet well I wot where to recover mine,
　Though not in Paradise nor *Cynthias* sphere,
　Yet doubtlesse in a place no lesse divine,
　In that sweet face of yours, in that faire heare,
　That rubie lip, in those two starlike eyne,
　There is my wit, I know it wanders there;
　And with my lips (if you would give me leave)
　I there would search, I thence it would receave.

3

But to returne unto that *English* Prince,
　Whom (if you do remember) with S. *Iohn*,
　By ugly streame I left a little since,
　The fatall sister spinners looking on,
　Who somtime do prolong, and somtime mince
　Our thred of life, I say he saw anon,
　Among a million more, one passing fleece,
　More fine than that that *Iason* brought to *Greece*.

4

So shone the thred that from that fleece out came,
　No gold, nor orient pearle could look so bright,
　Astolfo much desir'd to know his name,
　And time of birth, that to that thred had right.
　Straightwayes this answer unto him doth frame,
　He that the darke *Apocalyps* did write;
　The number of his name shall noted be,
　When twenty shall be tane from M and D.

5

And as the fleece which here so faire doth show,
　In finest substance passeth all the rest;
　So shall the person that the same doth owe,
　Make that same age in which he liveth, blest,
　For all the gifts that nature can bestow,
　Or with which study can a man invest,
　Shall powred be on him with large proportion,
　Assigned from above to be his portion.

6

There stands (said he) neare to the banks of *Poe*
　A village, now of small or none account,
　Whose moorish seat the streame doth overflow,
　But in that time that I to you recount,
　Vnto a City of such state shall grow,
　As all the neighbour townes it shall surmount;
　Nor sole in walls, and buildings fine and stately,
　But in good arts of old found out, or lately.

7

Nor think you this preferment to proceed
　By peradventure, or as 'twere by chance,
　But ev'n as a thing by God himselfe decreed,
　For one mans sake his native soile t'advance;
　As still we see those that good fruit will breed,
　Do grasse the stock, and prune and pick the branch,
　Or as the goldsmith pollisheth the mettell,
　In which he means a gemme of price to settell.

8

For nere shall soule that shall to earth descend,
　With mortall garment be more comly clad,
　Never did God a soule from hence down send,
　That more choice gifts, nor more rare vertues had
　Then this, which unto him he doth intend,
　That shall his country and his friends make glad,
　Hippolito of *Est* his name shall be,
　To whom the heav'ns such favours do decree.

9

For all those vertues great that wonted are,
　To set forth diverse, diversly divided,
　Shall joyned be in this same man most rare,
　Vnto such place, by heav'ns appointment guided;
　Maintain'd shall studies be by his great care,
　All quarrels cease, and broiles shall be decided,
　Whose vertues all, if I to tell prolong,
　Orlando should expect his wit too long.

10

Thus much the follower of *Iesus* spake,
　The while *Astolfo* those same webs doth view,
　From whence our lives end and beginning take:
　One spun, one cut, the third doth stuffe renew,
　Then came they to the foul and lothsome lake,
　Dark, deep, and miry, of a deadly hew,
　Where was the aged man that never stinted
　To carie bundels of the names imprinted.

11

This was the man, whom (as I told before)
  Both use and nature so swift pac'd had made,
He never rested, but ran evermore,
  And with his running he did use this trade;
A heap of names within his cloke he bore,
  And in the river did them all unlade;
Or (plaine to speak) away he cast them all
Into this stream, which *Lethe* we do call.

12

This prodigall old wretch no sooner came
  Vnto this cursed rivers barren bank,
But desp'rately, without all feare of blame,
  Or caring to deserve reward or thank,
He hurld therein full many a precious name,
  Where millions soon into the bottome sank,
And scant in ev'ry thousand one was found,
That was not in the gulf quite lost and drownd.

13

Yet all about great store of birds there flew,
  As vultures, carren crowes, and chattring pies,
And many more of sundry kinds and hew,
  That made lewd harmony with their lowd cries:
These when the carelesse wretch the tresor threw
  Into that stream, did all they could devise,
What with their talents some, and some with beak,
To save those names, but find themselves too weak.

14

For ever as they sought themselves to raise,
  To beare away those names of great renown,
The weight of them so heavy downward waies,
  They in the stream were driv'n to cast them down,
Only two swans sustain'd so great a praise,
  In spite of him that sought them all to drown,
These two do still take up whose names they list,
And bare them safe away, and never mist.

15

Somtime all under that foule lake they div'd,
  And took up some that were with water cover'd,
And those that seem'd condemned they repriv'd,
  And often, as about the bank they hover'd,
They caught them ere they to the stream arriv'd:
  Then went they with the names they had recover'd
Vp to a hill that stood the water nigh,
On which a stately Church was built on high.

16

This place is sacred to immortall fame,
  And evermore a *Nymph* stands at the gate,
And took the names wherwith the two swans came,
  (Whether they early come, or whether late)
Then all about the Church she hang'd the same,
  Before the sacred image in such rate,
As they might then well be assur'd for ever,
Spite of that wretch in safety to persever.

17

Astolfo had a great desire to know
  The mysteries most high, and hidden sence
Of that old man, that still ran to and fro,
  And precious things so lewdly did dispence,
And of the birds, and of the nymph also,
  That from the swans took names, and bare them thence,
And therefore asked what they signifi'd,
To whom the man of God thus wise repli'd:

18

Know first (said he) there cannot wag a straw
  Below on earth, but that the signe is here:
And each small act doth correspondence draw,
  Although in other shew it doth appeare:
That aged man, that running erst you saw,
  And never baits, nor resteth all the yeare,
To work the like effects above is bound,
As time doth work below upon the ground.

19

When here the fatall threed of life is spun,
  Then doth below the life of man decline,
There fame, and here their names in metall done,
  Would make them both immortall and divine,
Save here this aged sire that so doth run,
  And there below, time doth thereat repine,
He here flings all their names into a puddle,
Time there doth all in dark oblivion huddle.

20

And ev'n as here Rav'ns, Vultures, Pies, and crowes,
  And such like birds, endeavour all they may
To save those names that worthiest they suppose,
  But wanting strength, the names stil downward sway;
So there promooters, ruffins, bawds, and those
  That can the parasites and jesters play,
That by great Lords are oft more made of, then
The true, and plaine, and vertuous minded men.

21

And these (forsooth) good fellowes call you must,
  Because they learn like Asse and Pork to be,
But when their Lords be laid full low in dust,
  Their line of life cut off by sisters three,
Yea oft by their own surfetting and lust,
  Then these same goodly squires of base degree,
In their vile mouthes their names beare up and down
A while, and after in oblivion drown.

22

But as the swans that here still flying are,
  With written names unto the sacred port,
So there *Historians* learn'd and *Poets* rare
  Preserve them in cleare fame and good report;
O happy Princes, whose foresight and care
  Can win the love of writers in such sort,
As *Cæsar* did, so as you need not dread
The lake of *Lethe* after ye be dead.

23

But surely God their reason so doth blind,
  And takes from them all sence of wit and skill,
  That when their rooms on earth they have resign'd,
  Death both their bodies and their fames might kill;
  Where at the least some fame would stay behind,
  (Admit in part their manners were but ill)
  Had they but wit to get some grace with *Cirra*,
  Their fame should sweeter smel then nard or mirrha.

24

Perhaps *Æneas* was not so devout,
  Nor *Hector* nor *Achilles* were so brave,
  But thousands have as honest been and stout,
  And worthy by desert more praise to have;
  But those faire lands and castles out of doubt,
  That their successors unto writers gave,
  Made them so famous over forraigne lands,
  Canoniz'd by the *Poets* sacred hands.

25

Augustus Cæsar was not such a Saint,
  As *Virgil* maketh him by his description,
  His love of learning scuseth that complaint,
  That men might justly make of his proscription;
  Nor had the shame that *Neros* name doth taint,
  Confirm'd now by a thousand yeares prescription,
  Been as it is, if he had had the wit,
  To have been frank to such as Poems writ.

26

Blind *Homer* writ how *Agamemnon* fought,
  And wan at last great Troy that long resisted;
  And how *Penelope*, though greatly sought
  By many suters, yet in faith persisted.
  Yet sure (for ought you know) he might have taught
  The contrary to this, if he had listed,
  That *Troy* prevail'd, that *Greeks* were conquer'd clean,
  And that *Penelope* was but a quean.

27

On tother side, we see Queen *Didos* name
  That worthy was indeed to be commended,
  Is subject now to slander and to shame,
  Because that she by *Virgil* is not friended.
  But on this point I now more tedious am
  Then I was ware, or then I had intended,
  For I love writers well, and would not wrong them,
  And I my self do count my self among them.

28

I wrate a volume of my masters praise,
  For which to me he hath not been ungrate,
  But to this height of honour me doth raise,
  Where (as you see) I live in happy state;
  I pitie those that in these later dayes
  Do write, when bounty hath shut up her gate,
  Where day and night in vaine good writers knock,
  And for their labours oft have but a mock.

29

So as indeed this reason is the chief,
  That wits decay, because they want their hire,
  For where no succour is, nor no relief,
  The very beasts will from such place retire.
  Thus said the Saint, and (as it were with grief
  Of such offence) his eyes did flame like fire,
  But turning to the Duke with sober lafter,
  He pacifi'd himself a little after.

30

But here I leave *Astolfo* safe and sound
  With holy *Iohn*, for forthwith leap must I,
  As far as from the Moon unto the ground;
  My wings would faile, if I still soar'd so hie:
  Now come I unto her that had the wound,
  That ever smarting wound of jealousie,
  I told she had, when last of her I spoke,
  Vnhorst three kings with goldelaunces stroke.

31

And how she lay all at a castle sad,
  Although in vaine she sought her grief to smother,
  How at that place she perfect knowledge had,
  That *Agramant* was foiled by her brother,
  And that to flie to Arlie he was glad,
  With good *Rogero* and with many other;
  This made her unto *Provence* then to hast,
  Because she heard that *Charles* pursu'd him fast.

32

Now unto *Provence* onward as she went,
  A comely damsell in her way she view'd,
  Who though she lookt like one that did lament,
  Yet could not griefe her comly grace exclude;
  This dame had travel'd long, with this intent,
  To find some knight that from the Pagan rude,
  (Fierce *Rodomont*, that prisner held her lover)
  By force of arms againe might him recover.

33

Now when the comfortlesse dame *Bradamant*
  Had met a dame as comfortlesse as she,
  Such sympathy she felt of griefe, that scant
  She kept in teares, so sad a sight to see,
  She ask'd her what misfortune or what want,
  Of her sad plight, unworthy cause might be:
  Faire *Fiordeliege* that for a knight did hold her,
  The circumstance of all the matter told her.

34

And in most rufull sort she did recount,
  Both of the tombe and bridge the wofull storie,
  And how the cruell Pagan *Rodomount*
  Had taken him, for whom she was so sorie,
  Not that he could in value him surmount,
  That for his value had obtain'd much glory,
  But that the Pagan not to strength did trust,
  But to a bridge, and vantages unjust.

35

Wherefore most noble minded knight (said she)
  If such you be, as by your speech I guesse,
  Help my deare spouse from bondage vile to free,
  And plague the Pagan that doth him oppresse;
  Or if you cannot so, yet counsell me,
  Where I may find some aid for my distresse,
  Some knight so stout of heart, and strong of hand,
  As may this cruell Sarazen withstand.

36

So shall you do a brave and noble deed,
  That wandring knights do think they ought of due,
  So might you aid a worthy man indeed,
  And one in love most faithfull and most true:
  As for his other praise, it is no need
  For me to tell mine own griefes to renew,
  Sith well I know they plainly are appearing,
  To all that have their sense of sight and hearing.

37

The worthy Dame that thirsted still for praise,
  Agrees to take this hard exploit in hand,
  As one that ready was at all assaies,
  On horse, on foot, by water, or by land:
  For either thus she shall her glory raise,
  If so she shall the Pagans force withstand,
  Or die she shall, which danger lesse doth move her,
  Because she thinks *Rogero* doth not love her.

38

And thus she said, most lovely loving Dame,
  Gladly I shall my utmost forces prove,
  To succour one that merits so great fame,
  Yet of his praises chiefly me doth move,
  Because you give him such a noble name,
  That he is true and faithfull in his love:
  Which sith you speak by triall, I must ween so,
  Els I durst sweare no man alive had been so.

39

These last words ending with a scalding sigh,
  A sigh that came indeed from grievous thought,
  Then on they went, till they approched nigh
  The parlous bridge, that *Rodomont* had wrought:
  And straight the watch descri'd them from on high,
  And blew a horn, by which the Pagan thought,
  That travellers were come the bridge to passe,
  Came out all armed, as his manner was.

40

But when that he one all in armour saw,
  He greets them lowd with this lewd salutation:
  Ho stay, and ere you passe observe this law,
  Vnto this tombe, humbly to make oblation,
  Of horse and armes, with feare and rev'rent aw:
  Els with this speare expect sharp castigation.
  She that before had heard of *Isbels* death,
  And of this tombe thus stoutly to him seth.

41

Ah damned wretch, why should the innocent
  Indure the penance of thy grievous guilt?
  Thy self shouldst die, or suffer punishment,
  That killedst her, if please her ghost thou wilt:
  Her soule (upon my soule) would be content,
  If by my hand thy guilty blood were spilt,
  More then with all the armors, men, and horses,
  That thou dost win by thy unlawfull forces.

42

And so much more it will accepted be
  To her, if thou by my right hand maist die,
  Because I am a woman as was she,
  And onely come on thee my force to trie:
  But let us first upon these points agree;
  That if you hap to vanquish me, then I
  Shall suffer at your hands, so and no more,
  Then other prisoners have done before.

43

But if I vanquish you (as sure I trust)
  Then I will have the spoile of all the rest,
  And make your horse, and armes, a gift more just,
  Vpon the tombe of her for ever blest:
  And then withall, to me you promise must,
  That all your prisners straight shall be releast,
  When thus the Dame her mind had signifi'd,
  Thus the fierce Turk mildly to her repli'd.

44

Faire Dame, you seem to me to speak but reason,
  And thereto I my frank assent affoord:
  But true it is, that I for feare of treason,
  My prisners all, have sent from hence aboord,
  So as I cannot free them at this season,
  But firmly here to you I passe my word,
  If you foile me, of which there is small jeoberty,
  I will send word to set them all at liberty.

45

But if I conquer you, as sure I shall,
  (For so it is most likely, and most meet)
  I will not hang your armour on the wall,
  Nor send you hence a prisner in my fleet,
  I will remit to you my conquest all,
  For that faire faces sake, and look so sweet;
  Suffice it that this curtesie may move thee,
  Where now thou seem'st to hate me, then to love me.

46

Be not (faire Dame) in your own strength beguil'd,
  I offer not such grace to ev'ry stranger,
  For I am strong; at this the damsell smil'd,
  But such a smile, as shew'd not mirth, but anger;
  And whether courage had all feare exil'd,
  Or that despaire made her to doubt no danger;
  She spur'd her horse, nor other answer made him,
  But with her speare in rest she doth invade him.

47

This so did move the cruell *Rodomount*,
  Vpon his horse he doth himself advance,
  Not making doubt, but that he would dismount
  Out of her seat, the noble Dame of *France*;
  But he was quite deceiv'd of his account,
  No sooner was he toucht with *Goldelance*,
  But ev'n as if of strength he had bin reav'd,
  Quite from the saddle backward he was heav'd.

48

But yet the Dame her self in danger was,
  To fall into the streame so swift and fleet,
  By meanes the bridge so narrow was to passe,
  That hardly two at once thereon could meet;
  But *Rabican*, whose swiftnesse did surpasse
  All foure foot beasts, did firmly keep his feet:
  Although so straight and narrow was the bridge,
  He was constrain'd to run upon the ridge.

49

Now when the Pagan lay thus overthrown,
  She turn'd to him, and sporting, thus she spake,
  Now sir (said she) I hope it may be known,
  Of us two which the worser cause did take.
  But he, like one whose wits were not his own,
  He either could or would no answer make;
  But still he stood, looking on ground and musing,
  Neither his foile denying nor excusing.

50

And having walk'd some half a dozen paces,
  He suddenly cast all his armour off,
  And hurles it gainst the stones, and it defaces,
  That scant he left unbroke one peece thereof:
  Determining after such foule disgraces,
  To hide himselfe, and go a great way off:
  But ere he went, he granted full commission,
  To free his prisners without intermission.

51

So thence he went, and what of him became,
  Or what he did, no notice cleare I have,
  But onely this, that ev'n for very shame,
  He long liv'd close within a secret cave:
  The while his armes by that victorious Dame,
  Were hang'd up at the tombe for triumph brave,
  The tother armes and furnitures among,
  That erst to Pagan Princes did belong.

52

But for all those that were from Christens won,
  She laid them up, and did in safety set,
  Among the which was *Monodantes* son,
  And *Olivero* and stout *Sansonet*,
  Who late before with ill successe did run,
  So that the Pagan did their armour get,
  And them themselves as prisners did convay
  Vnto *Algirie*, farre from thence away.

53

Among the rest that had their armour lost,
  Was *Sacrapant* the fierce *Circassen* Prince,
  Who sought for *Frantlet*, to his paine and cost,
  And with the Pagan fought but little since;
  But being foil'd, he quite forsook that coast,
  Where men, of such disgrace might him convince,
  And with great shame, but what could shame him boot?
  He came on horsback, & went thence on foot.

54

Wherefore asham'd in such sort to return,
  He minds to follow that his former quest
  Of her, whose love long since his heart did burn,
  Although her love he never yet possest:
  For still her froward mind did ever spurn,
  Against his earnest, and most just request.
  Of her return he late had heard the newes,
  (I know not how) but now he her pursues.

55

And let him her pursue, for I proceed,
  Of noble *Bradamantes* acts to tell,
  Who having done this brave and worthy deed,
  To free the passage where so many fell,
  She wrate it, so as ev'ry one might read,
  How all the circumstance thereof befell;
  Which having done, then she demands to know,
  Which way Dame *Fiordeliege* did mind to go.

56

Who straight her purpose unto her unfolding,
  Told her, to passe the sea by ship she meant,
  At *Arly*, least the *Turke* his word not holding,
  Might keep her spouse too long in prison pent:
  Then shall you (saith the Dame) be more beholding
  To me, for sure (said she) tis mine intent,
  Vnto that town to guard you in your passage,
  So you will do for me but one embassage.

57

And that withall, you me this grace affoord,
  To give *Rogero* this same horse for me,
  And say an unknown champion sends him word,
  To challenge him, that all the world may see
  He hath been false of promise and of word;
  Of which our combat shall the triall be:
  And tell him plainly there is no deniall,
  But that by challenge I will make this triall.

58

This say, and say no more; and if he ask
  My name, then tell him plaine you may not tell;
  The while mine armes shall serve me for a mask,
  This I desire, do this, and so farewell;
  This is (said *Fiordeliege*) an easie task
  From you, that have of me deserv'd so well,
  As binds me both to this that you demand me,
  And to what ever els you would command me.

EE

59

This said, she takes the bridle in her hand,
  And with her leads *Frontino* on the way,
Vntill they both came to the salt sea sand,
  That next vnto the town of *Arly* lay;
But *Fiordeliege* goes to the town by land,
  And *Bradamant* doth in the suburbs stay,
To th'end she may convenient respit give her,
To him the horse and message to deliver.

60

Who when the bridge and gate she quite had past,
  She prayeth one of those that kept the ward,
To bring her to *Rogero* in great hast,
  And through the town of curtsie her to guard;
This done, she to *Rogero* came at last,
  And did her message with most due regard,
And gave *Frontino*, and then went her way,
Nor would she once to heare his answer stay.

61

Rogero standeth still all in a muse,
  The messenger and message so beguile him,
He wonders who it is, that both doth use
  Such curtesie, and yet withall revile him.
He thinks the partie doth him much abuse,
  With fowlest blot of breach of word to file him:
And of all others, least of all he thought,
That *Bradamant* of him the combat sought.

62

To think it *Rodomont* he was inclin'd,
  But yet it could not sink into his reach,
Why of a sudden he should be so kind,
  And wherein he could blame his promise breach;
And save with him, he cannot call to mind,
  With whom he had of friendship any breach:
The while the Lady with a stately scorn,
In token of defiance blew her horn.

63

Straightwayes the newes to *Agramant* doth fly,
  That one without did challenge some within,
And *Serpentine*, that then by chance was by,
  Ask'd leave to fight, with sured hope to win,
And swears the knight should yeeld or els should dy,
  And then the people flockt both thick and thin,
And stood upon the wals with young and old,
Between these two the combat to behold.

64

Out *Serpentino* came in brave array,
  And bravely with his speare in rest he ran,
But at the first encounter downe he lay,
  The horse runnes leere away without the man,
But noble *Bradamant*, the horse doth stay,
  And backe restore: then finely as she can,
She prayes him to King *Agramant* to speake,
To send a stronger Knight, sith he was weake.

65

The mightie Kings of *Affricke* and of *Spaine*,
  That from the wall the courteous act did vew,
From praising of the same could not refraine,
  Though none of them, thereof the author knew;
Now *Serpentino* backe returnd againe,
  And to his Prince he told his message trew,
How that same champion did desire to fight,
With some more stout and more renowned Knight.

66

And then *Grandonio* fierce of *Volaterne*,
  The proudest Knight that *Spaine* long time had bred
Obtain'd next place, and with a visage sterne,
  And threatning voice thus to the damsell sed:
Your curtsie small reward for you shall earne;
  For either here in fight you must be ded,
Or at the least, I will you prisner bring,
Vnto *Marsilio*, of great *Spaine* the King.

67

Well (answer'd she) keepe these your threats in store,
  Your villany my curtsie shall not let,
But that ile frendly monish you before,
  That backe againe unto your King you get,
Ere that your fall, may make your body sore;
  And say that I desired to have met
A man indeed of courage, and of worth,
And not your selfe, nor him that last came forth.

68

This her replie so mild, and yet so bitter,
  The Pagan with more furie did enflame;
With speare then speech, he thought an answer fitter
  And toward her in full carreer he came,
Intending sure, some deadly blow to hit her;
  But she that was accustom'd to this game,
Bare well his blow, and with her *Goldelance*,
She taught him how the somersaut to dance.

69

But yet his horse, that loose about did runne,
  She brought him backe, and thus to him she said,
Loe sir, you had bin better to have donne
  My message, when I curteouslie you prayd;
Yet here I will release my prisner wonne,
  So you will tell your King that I have stayd,
To combat with a man in fight well seene,
And not with novices, of skill so greene.

70

The lookers on that sure thought nothing lesse,
  Then that a virgin so could guide a speare,
With murmurings their wonder great expresse;
  Still ayming with surmises who it were;
Some *Brandimart*, and some *Renaldo* guesse,
  Or others whom the *Turks* had cause to feare,
But most they would *Orlando* have suspected,
Save they had heard his sences were distracted.

71

Next stout *Ferraw* desir'd to have the place,
  Not that he hop't the conquest to have wonne,
  But that these Knights may have the lesse disgrace,
  If I (quoth he) shall do as they have donne:
  A strong swift horse he takes, and sure of pace,
  Well made to beare the shocke, and free to runne,
  The choisest of an hundred that he kept,
  And thus all arm'd upon the beast he lept.

72

Against the femall champion forth he goes,
  And first they interchangeably salute,
  Please it you (said the Ladie) to disclose
  Your name to me? that shall be all my sute:
  He (that what longs to civill manners knowes,)
  To satisfie her therein was not mute,
  And I refuse you not, then said the tother,
  Although I rather would have had another.

73

Whom? (quoth *Ferraw*) *Rogero* (she replyed)
  And scarse she fully could bring forth his name,
  But that a blush with rosie colour dyed
  Her lovely cheekes, with secret honest shame:
  (Further she addeth) him whose vallew tryed,
  And so much prays'd, was cause I hither came,
  None else I seeke, nor for none else care I,
  Onely his manhood I desire to try.

74

She spake the word in plaine and simple sence,
  Which some perhaps will subtlie wrest awry,
  Well (said *Ferraw*) yet now ere I go hence,
  Let me with you have leave on course to try;
  To see if I can make no more defence,
  Then those whom last you made on earth to ly,
  If I fall as did they, then I will send
  That gentle Knight, that may our errour mend.

75

Her beaver open was while they confard,
  At which, when her the *Spaniard* well had vewed,
  And markt her bewtie worthy of regard,
  He was alreadie more then halfe subdewed:
  He thought an Angell of the heav'nly guard,
  Could not with greater bewtie be endewed;
  Against her speare, what fence can he devise,
  That is already conquerd with her eyes?

76

Now tooke they field, and ran with all their force,
  And now *Ferraw* is from his saddle borne,
  The damsell doth of curtsie stay his horse,
  The *Spaniard* lyeth like a man forlorne;
  But backe he must unto the King perforce,
  Nor true to do his message doth he scorne;
  He tels *Rogero* plaine before them all,
  How this same Knight onely for him doth call.

77

Rogero who it is yet little knowing,
  In hast to make him readie doth begin,
  A setled hope of conquest plainly showing,
  Willing to fight, with mind assur'd to win:
  As for their foyles, and their fowle overthrowing,
  That went before, he weigh'd them not a pin;
  But how they met, how kindly him she served,
  Vnto the booke ensuing is reserved.

THE THIRTY-SIXT BOOKE OF
ORLANDO FVRIOSO

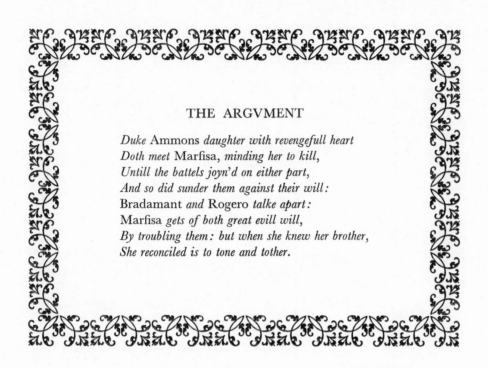

THE ARGVMENT

Duke Ammons *daughter with revengefull heart*
Doth meet Marfisa, *minding her to kill,*
Untill the battels joyn'd on either part,
And so did sunder them against their will:
Bradamant *and* Rogero *talke apart:*
Marfisa *gets of both great evill will,*
By troubling them: but when she knew her brother,
She reconciled is to tone and tother.

ORLANDO FVRIOSO
THE THIRTY-SIXT BOOKE

1

Tis meet a gentle heart should ever show
 By curtesie the fruits of true gentilitie,
Which will by practice to an habit grow,
And make men do the same with great facilitie:
Likewise the dunghill blood a man shall know
By churlish parts and acts of incivility,
Whose nature apt to take each lewd infection,
Custome confirmes, and makes ill in perfection.

2

Of curteous acts, old stories he that reads,
 In ancient times shall find there hath been store;
But in our dayes of bloudy cruell deeds
Is greater plenty then hath been before;
For charity brings forth but barren seeds,
And hatred still is sow'd in so great store,
That when the fruits of both come to be reap'd,
The tone is scarce, the tother over-heap'd.

3

What fierce *Barbarian*, *Tartar*, *Moore*, or *Turke*,
 Could use more cruelty then now of late
In *Latian* land *Venetian* force did work?
Not by consent of the wise men of state,
But by the filthy nature that did lurk
In wicked hirelings, and a hidden hate;
I speak not of the dammage and defaces,
They did by fire in all our pleasant places.

4

Though that revenge was foule and too too cruell,
 And chiefe against *Hippolito*, who late,
When *Cæsar* sieged *Padoa*, as they knew well,
And brought it to low ebbe and wofull state,
He both withdrew the matter all and fewell,
And quencht the fires kindled by deadly hate,
Preserving many a Church and many a village
By his rare clemency from fire and pillage.

5

Not those I meane, nor many actions more,
 That cannot be excused or defended,
But such an act as stones might weep therefore,
As oft as it is talk'd of or remembred:
Then when my Lord his houshold sent before,
There where his foes were secretly assembled,
And left their vessels on the saltish sand,
While in ambushment close they lay on land.

6

As *Hector* and *Æneas* did by fire
 Assault the Greekish fleet with hardy fight,
So saw I two, whose hearts to fame aspire,
(One *Alexander*, tother *Hercles* hight)
Assault their foes, and drive them to retire
Vnto their trenches, nay within them quite;
But one of them returned thence full hard,
The tother of returning clean was bar'd.

7

For *Feruffino* scap'd, *Cantelmo* staid,
 O Duke of *Sore*, what great sore didst thou find,
To see thy noble sonne so foule betraid,
Among a thousand blades left there behind?
His naked neck on side of gally laid,
And chopped off: now surely in my mind,
When that same bloudy stroke his neck smit off,
You felt like stroke, ev'n with the sight thereof.

8

Slavonian vile, where didst thou learne to know
 Such lawes of warre? within that *Scithian* land,
Vse men to kill a prisner taken so,
That yeelds, and hath no weapon in his hand?
Or was it such a grievous sinne you trow,
The foes of his deare country to withstand?
Why hast thou Sunne, so long on this age shinde,
That breeds of *Atrews* and *Thiestes* kinde?

9

Barbarian vile, that kild so sweet a youth,
 To satisfie thy rancor and thy rage,
So rare a youth, as to confesse the truth,
His match could not be found in this our age,
Whose beautie might have bred sufficient ruth,
Fierce *Poliphemus* anger to asswage,
But not fierce thee, more cruell and more fell,
Then any monsters that in deserts dwell.

10

The valiant men did studie in time past,
 With clemencie their honors to increase,
And hate no longer then the fight did last,
With victorie revenge did ever cease:
So *Bradamant*, of whom I told you last,
The prisners she had tane, did still release,
And staid their horses when themselves were downe,
And sent them backe againe into the towne.

11

And praid them but her challenge to deliver,
　Vnto *Rogero*, and to call him out,
　Who meant with speare in rest her answer give her,
　Vnto her challenge that she sent so stout.
　Now when the other Knights were all togither,
　In presence of the Kings, they cast a doubt,
　Who this should be, and then they aske *Ferraw*,
　That talkt with her, and her bare visage saw.

12

Sure (said *Ferraw*) it is not tone nor tother,
　Of those on whom before your thoughts were set;
　I tooke it first it was *Renaldos* brother,
　Who is in yeares a very youth as yet:
　But now I rather judge it is another,
　For so much force is not in *Richardet*,
　I thinke it is his sister by her usage,
　Who I have heard is like him much in visage.

13

She hath ere this of value had great fame,
　Renaldo and the *Palladins* among,
　I must confesse I found it to my shame,
　Her, then her brothers to be farre more strong:
　Rogero, when he heard them her to name,
　Was guiltie straight that he had done her wrong,
　And blusht in countenance with bashfull grace,
　And oft his heart shot blood into his face.

14

Yea feare invaded him, not feare of danger,
　For force he feared not of any wight,
　Of *Turke* nor *Christen*, countryman or stranger;
　The very cause of this his dolefull plight
　Was love, for love feares nothing more then anger,
　He doubts least she conceiv'd not of him right:
　Thus waving thoughts his mind do both waies cary,
　If so he better were to go or tary.

15

The while *Marfisa* that was present there,
　And ever had a forward will to just,
　Could now no longer from the same forbeare,
　Though seeing some before her lie on dust.
　For all their fals did breed in her no feare,
　So much in her great value she did trust,
　Wherefore least good *Rogero* might prevent her,
　First she rides forth, and in the lists doth enter.

16

And mounted on her horse came swiftly running,
　Vnto the place where *Bradamant* did stay,
　With panting heart to wait *Rogeros* comming,
　With mind to take him prisner if she may,
　She thinks how she might guide her staffe with cunning,
　As with her stroke do him least hurt she may:
　Thus commeth out *Marfisa*, nothing fearing,
　Vpon her loftie crest the *Phenix* bearing.

17

Or that thereby to bost her strength she ment,
　Of her rare strength, of which she tooke some pride,
　Or else thereby to note her chast intent
　She had, a warlike virgin still to bide;
　But *Bradamant*, who first to meet her went,
　And not to be *Rogero* now espide,
　Did aske her name, and by her name she knew
　That this was she that made her love untrew.

18

Or to say better, whom she did surmise,
　To be the sole withholder of her deare,
　Her whom she hates, gainst whom her blood doth rise,
　And minding now to make her buy it deare,
　With furie great and rage at her she flies;
　And that she may make all suspitions cleare,
　With couched speare she fiercely runneth on her,
　And meanes to kill her, or to die upon her.

19

Marfisa was constrained with the stroke,
　To kisse the ground as those before her had,
　Which to such rage her courage did provoke,
　That with disdaine she seemd as one halfe mad;
　Not knowing how so great a foile to cloke,
　She drawes her sword with an intention bad,
　But *Bradamant* cry'th out with loftie hart,
　What dost thou traitor? thou my prisner art.

20

And though I used curtsie to the rest,
　To use it unto thee I am not tide,
　Whose mind (as I have heard) is ev'n a nest,
　Wherin is bred all villanie and pride:
　Looke how great waters rage and do not rest,
　When as the winds do strive against the tide,
　So rag'd *Marfisa* rather more then lesse,
　And for meere spite could not a word expresse.

21

But hurles about her blade with all her force,
　Not caring what she strikes, nor where, nor how,
　Vpon the horseman or upon the horse,
　Her rage in her no reason did allow:
　And *Bradamant* as void of all remorse,
　With mind to breake that, that refus'd to bow,
　Ranne at her with the speare that would not misse,
　And made her once againe the ground to kisse.

22

But once againe upon her feet she getteth,
　And with her sword revengement she intends,
　Each fall she hath, her furie sharper whetteth,
　Yet still she fals, and can have no amends,
　Nor golde lance his wonted force forgetteth,
　For all it touches, to the ground it sends;
　Had not the speare bene (as it was) inchaunted,
　It could not so *Marfisas* force have daunted.

23

Some of our men were hither come the while,
  I meane some of the Christen host, that lay
Encamped neare the towne within a mile,
  So as the wals of *Arlie* see they may,
And thinking (for her sex did them beguile)
  Some Knight of theirs maintain'd so great a fray,
They thither came with will and with delight,
To see so fierce and well maintaind a fight.

24

Whom when as *Agramant* from far espide,
  And thinks they came to bring their knight assistance
He thought it best in wisedome to provide,
  If they should offer force to make resistance;
Wherefore he pointed some that of their side,
  May stand from that same place a little distance,
Of this last crew *Rogero* was the first,
With whom the damsell so to fight did thirst.

25

And seeing now how fierce the combat gro'th,
  Betwixt these two, to whom he wisht none ill,
Although in sundry kinds he favour'd both,
  For tone was love, the tother bare good will;
To suffer them to fight he was full loth,
  Although for honors sake he must be still,
Else sure he could have found it in his hart,
To step betweene them, and the fray to part.

26

But they that with him from the citie came,
  And saw the Christen champion was so strong,
Stept in betwixt her and the tother dame,
  And so withdrew *Marfisa* them among,
Which act the other Christens did inflame,
  So that with mind to venge so foule a wrong,
They stept in too: thus both sides cride alarme,
And soone the skirmish waxed fresh and warme.

27

Such as before were armed, out do runne,
  They that unarmed were, their armor take,
And some runne out on foot, on horsebacke some,
  Each to his standerd doth himselfe betake;
The divers sound of trumpet and of drum,
  That doth the horsemen, this the footmen wake,
But *Bradamant* is malcontent and wrath,
To thinke *Marfisa* thus escaped hath.

28

Then lookt she wishly all about the place,
  To finde out him that caused all her care,
At last she knew him, though not by his face,
  Yet by the *argent Eagle* that he bare,
And viewing well his person and good grace,
  His goodly stature and his feature rare,
She rag'd to thinke another should possesse it,
And in these secret words she doth expresse it.

29

Shall any other then that sweet lip kisse?
  And I in love thereof still mourne and pine?
Shall any other then possesse my blisse:
  Shalt thou anothers be, if none of mine?
No certes, rather then to suffer this,
  Thou by my hand shalt die, or I by thine,
If in this life we shall be joyned never,
Death onely be the meane to joyne us ever.

30

Although that thou shouldst fortune me to kill,
  Thy death by right should pacifie my spirit,
For lawes appoint, who guiltlesse blood do spill,
  Shall for reward the doome of death inherit;
Yet still I shall sustaine the greater ill,
  For I should guiltlesse die, but thou by merit,
I killing thee, kill one that hates me meerely,
Thou killing me, kilst one that loves thee deerly.

31

Why shouldst not thou (my hand) be strong and bold,
  That by thy stroke his hard heart may be riven?
Who unto me sharp wounds and manifold,
  In time of loves sweet peace and truce hath given,
And doth ev'n now with stonie heart behold
  The wofull state to which poore I am driven,
Heart now be stout to take thy just revenge,
Let this one death thy thousand deaths avenge.

32

With that at him she runs, but first aloud,
  Defend thy selfe (*Rogero* false) she said,
And think not thou shalt scape with spoiles so proud
  Of heart subdued of a silly maid.
Rogero, who to her himselfe had vow'd,
  And to offend her greatly was afraid,
Held up his gantlet unto her in token,
That he with her desired to have spoken.

33

He would her wrath with kind words have appeased,
  And shew'd her how the cause he brake his day,
Was that with grievous wounds he lay diseased,
  Which forced him against his will to stay;
But at this time she was so sore displeased,
  She would not hearken what he had to say,
But with her speare in rest, on him she runneth,
Who such unkind encounter greatly shunneth.

34

But when he saw she was so rash and headie,
  And that her choler now so great did grow,
That she was in her full careere alreadie,
  He puts his speare in rest, at least for show,
And forward sets, but when she was ev'n readie,
  Him to have giv'n a sharpe disgracefull blow,
(Or that it were that she ev'n then recanted,
Or that her heart to harme him courage wanted)

35

She bare her launce aloft quite ore his crest,
  And so of purpose that same course she mist,
  Yet so, as by the manner might be guest,
  She could have hit him surer, had she list,
  And wrath and rage still boiling in her brest,
  To bend her force gainst him she did desist,
  But in that mood no little harme she workes,
  Vnto the other souldiers of the *Turkes*.

36

In little time, she with her gilded lance
  Had caus'd three hundred men on ground to lie,
  So that the conquest to the part of *France*,
  Was thought to have bene gained sole thereby:
  Rogero seekes her out, and last by chance,
  He speakes to her, and saith, my deare I die,
  But I may talke with you, what have I done
  Alas, that you my conference should shunne.

37

As when the Southerne wind with luke-warme blast,
  Doth breath on hils where winter long had dwelt,
  Resolves the rocks of ice that hung so fast,
  And all the new made mounts of snow doth melt:
  So with this gentle prayre, though spoke in hast,
  The damsell such an inward motion felt,
  That sodainly her hardned heart did soften,
  As unto women kind it chanceth often.

38

Yet answer made she none, but held her peace,
  She onely turned *Rabican* aside,
  And hasting to get out of that same prease,
  She beckned him that after her he ride:
  Thus went she thence, with mind inclind to peace,
  Vnto a valley, where on either side,
  A grove of Cypres so ev'n set was seene,
  As if they all of one selfe stampe had beene.

39

Amid this grove a goodly sepulture
  Was built, which these faire Cypres trees did shade,
  Of Porphyrie and marble white and pure,
  And faire engrav'n, to shew why it was made;
  But of the tombe she tooke no care nor cure,
  But there expected in the open glade,
  Vntill *Rogero* having made good hast,
  Approcht the wood and damsell at the last.

40

But of *Marfisa* now I must you tell,
  Who having got by this her horse againe,
  Her loftie heart with rancor great did swell,
  To be reveng'd of this foule sufferd staine,
  And seeing where she went, as it befell,
  And how *Rogero* followd her amaine,
  She little thinketh that it is for love,
  But rather that they may the combat prove.

41

Wherefore to follow them she thinks it best,
  So as she came almost as soone as they,
  But what a tedious and unwelcome guest
  She seem'd to both, one soone conjecture may:
  Much sure it did the *Dordon* dame molest,
  Who sole to her *Rogeros* faults did lay,
  She deemd that to come thither nothing mov'd her,
  But that *Rogero* in ill sort had lov'd her.

42

And false, *Rogero* she againe doth name,
  And was it not enough false man, said she,
  That of thy falshood I should heare by fame,
  But that I with these eyes the same should see?
  But sith I find thou dost thy actions frame,
  To drive me with unkindnesses from thee,
  I am content to die, but ere I die yet,
  She that did cause it, dearly shall abuy it.

43

Thus as a Viper angrie and malicious,
  With mind indeed to do her best to kill
  Her, that was come in manner so suspitious;
  (Though she came more for wrath, thē for good wil)
  With gilded launce she gives a blow pernicious,
  That quite unhorsed her for all her skill,
  Backward *Marfisa* fell, and in the durt,
  Her beaver stucke, but had no further hurt.

44

Duke *Ammons* daughter that resolves to die,
  Or kill her fo, so much her selfe forgetteth,
  That thinking to dispatch her by and by,
  Before her head out of the mire she getteth,
  The golden launce she will no farther trie,
  But throwes it downe, as wrath her courage whetteth,
  And to performe the feate, her sword she drawes,
  Therewith of feare to cut away the cause.

45

But ere she came so neare, *Marfisa* met her,
  Like one with rage, with spite and scorne halfe mad,
  To thinke that now againe she sped no better,
  And that a while before she sped so bad;
  So that *Rogero* could by no meanes let her
  From fighting, which to stop great will he had,
  But both of them with choler were so blinded,
  They fought like bedlem folk, and desprat minded.

46

They came unto the halfe sword at the first,
  And with their rage forgetting rules of skill,
  Their overmuch desire to do their worst,
  Was only cause that they could do none ill;
  Their hearts were ready for despite to burst,
  And either purposing to die or kill,
  Did leave her sword aside, in mind supposing,
  With stab to kill each other at the closing.

47

Rogero sunders them, and both intreateth,
  To pacifie themselves, but all in vaine,
  Then of their daggers he them both defeateth,
  And by perswasions mov'd them both againe;
  Sometime he speaketh faire, somtime he threateth,
  Except they wil at his request abstaine;
  But these viragoes will not thoe desist,
  Though weapons want, they fight with feet and fist.

48

He steps betweene againe, and back he drawes,
  Now one, and then the tother by the sleeves,
  And makes them both against their wils to pause,
  At which *Marfisa* not a little greeves;
  Her selfe too greatly wronged in the cause,
  And him to be too partiall she beleeves,
  Wherefore his friendship she doth quite disclaime,
  And open warres with him she doth proclaime.

49

And taking up her sword, in termes most vile,
  She saith he plaies the churlish villens part,
  And that he greatly doth himselfe beguile,
  To thinke her fight against her will to part,
  She sweares she will, within a little while,
  Of his owne folly make him feele the smart;
  And that she will henceforth so short him curbe,
  He shall not dare her combat to disturbe.

50

Rogero still bare all her words as words,
  And sought by speech her to have pacified;
  But seeing that it needs must come to swords,
  And that with blowes, not speeches she replied,
  No longer time to walking he affords,
  But to his weapon he himselfe applied,
  And being moved now with rightfull anger,
  To save himselfe, he oft put her in danger.

51

But nere did spectacle breed more delight,
  In stately Rome or Athens so well learned,
  Then *Bradamant* did take to see this fight,
  In which she now apparently discerned,
  That of their love she had not judged right;
  Now jealousie, and all that it concerned,
  Suspition, feare, mistrust, and wrath, and franzie,
  Are of the sodaine quite put from her fancie.

52

And taking up her sword, she stands not farre,
  With mind not yet awhile the fray to part,
  She thinkes in him she sees the God of warre,
  Such grace *Rogero* us'd, such skill, such art:
  And tother seem'd in that unpleasant jarre,
  Some hellish furie, (so she playd her part)
  Yet true it is that he a while forbare her,
  Nor did his worst, but did of purpose spare her.

53

He knew the secret vertue of this blade,
  Which he had tride in many battels well,
  That evermore a way and entrance made,
  Whose charme all charmed armes did far excell;
  Wherefore he doth not fiercely her invade,
  With bloudy blowes nor fearfull thrusts and full,
  But flatling still he caus'd his blowes to light,
  Till once he was of patience put out quite.

54

For once *Marfisa*, with intention shrowd,
  Strake with such furie at *Rogeros* beaver,
  That with that blow she very plainly showd,
  That to have kild him she did her endever,
  Rogero with his *argent Eagle* trowd,
  From danger of the stroke himselfe to sever,
  But though the shield brake not, gramercy charme,
  Yet underneath the shield it stound his arme.

55

It happie was Don *Hectors* shield was there,
  Else had she put him unto further paine,
  Scarce could he now the massie target beare,
  Scarce now the silver bird he could sustaine:
  Now he intends no longer to forbeare,
  But hurleth out a foyne with force so maine,
  In rage with that late blow so fierce and bitter,
  Wo unto poore *Marfisa*, had it hit her.

56

I know not what good Angell did her keepe,
  The thrust mist her, and in a tree it strake,
  And enterd in the same a shaftman deepe,
  And on the sodaine all the hill did quake:
  A secret horror on them all did creepe,
  They see the hill, the trees and tombe to shake,
  Till from that sepulcher a voice proceeding,
  Spake unto them all humane voice exceeding.

57

The voice to them with no small terror cride,
  File not your hands and hearts with so great sin,
  It is a kinde of cruell parricide,
  To seeke to kill, and be so neare of kin:
  Wherefore I charge you lay all hate aside,
  And marke my speech, and all containd therein,
  I say you both were gotten of one seed,
  One wombe you bare, one brest you both did feed.

58

My deare *Rogero*, my *Marfisa* deare,
  Let not the sister seeke to kill the brother,
  But learne of me some things that touch you neere,
  Which former times in ignorance did smother;
  Your sire, *Rogero* hight, who that same yeare
  He gat you of dame *Gallacell* your mother,
  Was by your uncles of his life deprived,
  Who also your destruction thus contrived.

59

They put your mother in a steerlesse bote,
  Who was as then of you twaine great with child,
And in the Ocean wide they let her flote,
  There to be starv'd or drown'd in waters wilde:
But lo how fortune holpe the lucklesse lot,
  And ere you yet were borne, upon you smild,
For why against all hope or expectation,
  Your mother made a happie navigation.

60

And being safe arriv'd at *Syrtee* shore,
  There at one burden she brought forth both you,
And then (as if she ought this world no more)
  Her blessed soule to Paradise up flew;
But there by hap (to God be thanks therefore)
  Was I at hand, and when the cause I knew,
I did as much, ere I the place did leave,
  As such a barren soile would give me leave.

61

Your mother then in dust of earth I lapt,
  (Our auncient mother) whereto all must go,
And in my cloke your little selves I wrapt,
  To seeke some meanes to nourish you, when lo,
A Lionesse that late had whelpt there hapt,
  To come in sight while I went to and fro,
Her did I make to leave her proper whelpes,
  And give you sucke, then wanting other helpes.

62

Ten months and ten in forrests wilde and moorish,
  The Lions tets you used were to sucke,
I after learnd with wilde flesh you to nourish,
  Such as I could, of Beares, or Stag and Bucke;
But when you now began in strength to flourish,
  One day while I was lacke, by evill lucke,
A band of fierce *Arabians* comming thither,
  Would have convaid you both from thence togither.

63

But thou *Rogero* when thou sawst them comming,
  Didst save thy selfe from that mishap by flight,
But thou *Marfisa*, not so swiftly running,
  Wert tane, and quickly carrid out of sight,
To fetch thee backe againe I wanted cunning,
  For which I soride many day and night,
But as the losse of tone did make me sad,
  So of the tother greater care I had.

64

Ah my *Rogero*, thou thy selfe canst tell
  If thine *Atlanta* lov'd thee while he liv'd,
I saw the starres some evill haps foretell,
  That thou shouldst have, which me no little griev'd:
Yet I endeavour'd still, as thou know'st well,
  That by my means thou mightst have been reliev'd:
But finding thee still contrary inclin'd,
  For very griefe at last I di'd and pin'd.

65

But here I built this tombe afore I di'd,
  Where I foresaw you two should make this fray;
And being dead, to *Charon* lowd I cri'd,
  To suffer in this wood my ghost to stray,
Vntill this fight, to me foresignifi'd,
  Should happen, which was done this present day,
Now shall my soule from hence depart in peace,
  Now *Bradamant* thy jealousie may cease.

66

Thus said the voice, and left them all amaz'd,
  With wonder great, and strangenesse of the case,
And when a while each had on other gaz'd,
  They met in kindest manner, and embrace;
Nor *Bradamant* her selfe, who erst was craz'd
  With jealousie, now took it in disgrace,
To see her spouse, when he most kindly kist her,
  Now well assured that she was his sister.

67

Thus they agreed at last, and either twin
  Do call to mind some acts of childish yeares,
What they had said and done, where they had bin,
  Which ev'n with tender heart did move their teares;
At last the worthy brother doth begin
  To tell *Marfisa* what great love he beares
To *Bradamant*, whom he to wed intends,
  And so at length he made them faithfull friends.

68

Then all parts pacifi'd so well at length,
  Marfisa doth intreat her noble brother,
To tell to her the story more at length,
  Of that so strange exiling of her mother,
And if their sire were slaine by fraud or strength,
  And who it was that wrought the tone or tother,
For sure (said she) I think I never heard it,
  Or childishnesse did make me not regard it.

69

Rogero tels her, how of *Trojan* race,
  From *Hector* they be lineally descended,
By meanes *Astianax* (of speciall grace,
  That scap'd *Vlysses* and the snares intended)
Did leave a child of like yeares in his place,
  And from that country to the sea descended,
And came to *Sicill* after travell long,
  And took *Mesina* and grew very strong.

70

His of-spring still increasing in renown,
  Calabria rul'd in part, and thence to *Phare*,
And came at last to dwell in *Mars* his town,
  And many a noble Emperour and rare
In stately *Rome* have worn th'Imperiall crown,
  Of such as from this stock descended are,
From *Constance* and from *Constantine* accounting,
  To *Pepin* and his sonne, them all surmounting.

71

Rogero first, and *Iambaron* of these,
  Rovus, *Rambaldus*, and *Rogero* againe,
Of whom (as *Atlant* told) sav'd from the seas,
Our mother by the shore brought forth us twaine,
Their acts in ancient stories they that please
To look, may find them there recorded plaine;
Then tels he how there came king *Agolant*,
With *Almont*, and the sire of *Agramant*.

72

How that Kings daughter, a most noble maid,
  In feats of armes so valorous did prove,
That diverse *Palladines* she overlaid;
And then with that *Rogero* fell in love,
And of her fathers anger not afraid,
Did match in Christen state, as did behove,
How after this one *Beltram* sought by treason,
Incestuous love of her without all reason.

73

And for that cause his brothers and his sire,
  And his own native soile he did betray,
And open *Risa* at his foes desire;
Which being tane, and seiz'd on as a pray,
Fierce *Agolant* and his inflam'd with ire,
Took *Gallacell* our mother where she lay
Six months with child, and put her in a boat,
And in the *Ocean* wide they let her float.

74

Marfisa all this while with gladsome cheare,
  Vnto her new known brothers tale attended,
And in her mind rejoyced much to heare,
That of so noble house she was descended,
From which *Mongrana* came, as doth appeare,
And that of *Clarimount* so much commended,
Which houses both long in great fame had flourished,
For divers noble persons they had nourished.

75

But when of *Agramant* she heard him say,
  How both his grandsire, uncle, and some other,
Consented had their father to betray,
And in so cruell sort to use their mother,
She could not suffer any longer stay,
But breaking of his tale, said, noble brother,
(With your good favour) you have too much wrong
To leave your father unreveng'd so long.

76

If not in *Almont* nor *Trajanos* blood,
  You can avenge this ill sith they be gone,
Yet ought you to avenge it on their brood;
Live you, and let you *Agramant* alone?

This blot except it quickly be withstood,
Will shame you ever, if it once be known,
That he that did this wrong not onely liveth,
But that to you he entertainment giveth.

77

But for my part (said she) by *Christ* I vow,
  (Whom as my father did, so serve I will)
That I will not leave armes, till I know how
To venge my fathers and my mothers ill;
And much I shall lament, and do ev'n now,
If in that Pagan camp you tarry still,
Or ever should be seene therein hereafter,
Except it were to work their harm and slaughter.

78

Oh how did *Bradamant* at this rejoyce,
  Advising him to follow that direction,
And to give eare unto his sisters voice,
To leave so vile a place and base subjection,
And cleave to *Charles* as to the better choice,
Who gladly would receive him in protection,
Of which (she said) one sure signe she did gather,
She heard him often so extoll his father.

79

Rogero answers thus with great regard,
  (My deare) to have done this at first I ought,
But then indeed the troth I had not heard,
Whereby I might my duty have been taught:
Now sith that *Agramant* hath me prefer'd,
If his destruction should by me be sought,
That am his servant and a daily waiter,
The world might justly deem I were a traiter.

80

But this my meaning was, and so it is,
  To find some means I may (with honour) part,
Which when I have, then sure I will not misse,
To come and to requite your great desert;
And that (quoth he) I had perform'd ere this,
Save that a cause (of which I felt the smart)
Enforc'd my stay, the wounds the *Tartar* gave me,
So as my friends had much to do to save me.

81

As she knowes well that holp me at my need,
  And ev'ry day did sit by my beds side:
Thus much he said, but they that took good heed
To all he said, in earnest sort repli'd,
Howbeit at the last it was agreed,
That he so long with *Agramant* should bide,
Till he some honourable cause might find
To leave his master and to change his mind.

82

Well (quoth *Marfisa*) if he needs will go,
  Then let him go, but I will you assure,
  That shortly I will use the matter so,
  He shall not long with *Agramant* endure:
  This said she unto *Bradamant*, but tho
  She told not how she would the same procure:
  Thus for that time *Rogero* brake this parlie,
  And turn'd his horse to turn againe to *Arlie*.

83

When lo they chanc'd a sudden crie to heare,
  Proceeding from the next adjoyning vale,
  The voice did seem (when they approached neare)
  To be some damsels that for help did call:
  But who it was hereafter you shall heare,
  For now of force I must cut off my tale,
  And pray you my abruptnesse to excuse,
  For in the next you shall heare further newes.

THE THIRTY-SEVENTH BOOKE OF
ORLANDO FVRIOSO

THE ARGVMENT

Rogero *with his sister and his spouse,*
Find Vllanie *halfe stript and strangely used,*
Straight each of them, but chiefe Marfisa *vowes*
To be aveng'd on him that her misused:
She heares the law that women none allowes;
She finds the man that hath the sex refused:
She plagues the tyrant, for his proud behaviour,
And makes another law in womens favour.

ORLANDO FVRIOSO
THE THIRTY-SEVENTH BOOKE

1

If worthie Ladies would but take such paine,
  In studies that immortall glorie raise,
As they do often take in matters vaine,
  Deserving none at all, or little praise,
Which notwithstanding that they might obtain,
  They have employed many nights and dayes;
To have thereby some trifling want supplied,
That niggard nature had to them denied.

2

And further, if they could with their owne pen,
  Set forth the worthie praise of their owne kind,
And not to be beholding unto men,
  Whom hate and envie often so doth blind,
To make us heare the good but now and then,
  But ev'rie place full of their ill we find;
Then sure I judge, their praises would be such,
As hardly men should have attaind so much.

3

For many writers do not onely strive,
  Too highly to extoll our sexes fame,
But that they thinke they must withall contriue,
  To publish womens blemish and their blame;
As fearing haply, lest they might arrive,
  By their most due desart, to greater name;
And so they might thereby obscure our praise,
As doth a cloud the Sunnes bright shining rayes.

4

But yet, for all such sparing pens do write,
  Or lavish tongues can speake in their disgrace,
Enforcing ev'rie il report for spite,
  That may their credit slander and deface,
We still shall find their glorie shining bright,
  We still shall see, it keepes a worthie place,
Though wanting of that height the greater part,
To which it should attaine to by desart.

5

Harpalice and *Thomeris* beside,
  With those that *Turnus* did and *Hector* ayd,
Besides that dame that in an *Oxes* hide,
  The first foundation of faire *Carthage* layd,
Zenobia eke, and she that quayld the pride
  Of *Assur*, and both *Inde* and *Persia* frayd:
I say there have bin many more then these,
That have bin famous both by land and seas.

6

Nor only *Rome* and *Greece* have bred such store,
  Of faithfull matrons, chast, and stout, and wise,
But all the world beside, some lesse, some more,
  From whence it sets, to where the Sun doth rise:
Though now their names obscured are so sore,
  That few or none are laid before our eys:
And all because that they in those dayes wrate,
Were envious, and false, and full of hate.

7

Yet cease not Ladies, ye that vertue love,
  To follow that your course, and so good way,
And let not feare your minds from it remove,
  That your great fame hereafter may decay;
For true it is, as we do daylie prove,
  No good nor ill can still stand at a stay;
Though writers in time past were not your frends,
The present time shall make you large amends.

8

The worthie writers of this present time,
  Have set your worthy praises so to vew,
Some in grave prose, and some in learned rime,
  As none shall need this want hereafter rew:
And though they were infected with this crime,
  Yet in this age, so learn'd are some of you,
So well acquainted with the noble muses,
You could your selves remedie such abuses.

9

And if I should recite the names of those,
  That by the writers of our times are prais'd,
Or that themselves have wrote in verse or prose,
  And have their owne and others glory rais'd,
As I might please some few, so I suppose,
  I might be blam'd of others and dispraisd,
Or in omitting some, to do them wrong,
Or reckning all, too tedious wax and long.

10

Shall I then all omit? that were not well,
  Sith that to please them all I do desire:
Then will I chuse some one, that doth excell
  The rest so fane, as none may dare envie her;
Whose name doth in such height of honor dwell,
  As hard it is, for any to come nye her,
Whose learned pen such priviledge can give,
As it can make ev'n those are dead to live.

11

For ev'n as *Phebus* shines on ev'rie star,
  Yet on his sister casts his fairest light,
So eloquence and grace ay shining are,
  Much more on her, then any other wight,
And maketh her to passe the rest as farre,
  As *Phebe* doth the other starrs in night,
Her light so splendent is, and so divine,
As makes another Sunne on earth to shine.

12

Vittoria is her name, a most fit name,
  For one in triumphs borne, in triumphs bred,
That passeth *Artimesia* in the fame
  Of doing honor to her husband ded;
For though she did erect a wondrous frame,
  For her *Mausolio,* with a Pyramed,
Yet which is more, to lay the dead in grave,
Or else from death, with learned pen to save.

13

If *Laodamie,* and if *Brutus* wife,
  Argia, Arria, and *Evadne* chast,
Be to be praised, as they are so rife,
  Because when as their husbands dayes were past,
They willingly forsooke this mortall life:
  Then in what height must she of right be plast?
That such a gift unto her spouse doth give,
That being dead she still doth make him live.

14

And if the great *Macedon* envie bare
  Vnto *Achilles,* for *Meonian* Lyre,
Much more to noble *Francis* of *Pescare,*
  He would have borne, whose praise is sounded hyre;
By such a wife, so vertuous, chast, and rare
  As ev'n thy soule it selfe could not desire
A louder trumpe thy praises out to sound,
Sith hardly can a match to this be found.

15

But to conclude both these and others prayse,
  That I may follow on my present storie,
I say that both in these and former dayes,
  Faire dames have merited great fame and glorie;
Which though by writers envie much decayes,
  Yet need you not therefore now to be sorie,
Because amongst us all it is intended,
That this foule fault hereafter shall be mended.

16

Now of *Marfisa* and of *Bradamant,*
  I meane to tell, that still were so victorious,
As both my voice too faint, and skill too scant
  Would be, to count their famous deeds and glorious;
Yet shall good will so farre supply my want,
  As I will reckon those were most notorious,
And were my might agreeing to my mind,
I would deserve as well of all their kind.

17

If you remember, I declared erst,
  How good *Rogero* purpos'd to returne,
And how he heard the sound I then reherst,
  Of some that seemed wofully to mourne;
Which wayling so his mind with pittie pierst,
  As he a while his journey did adjourne,
Both that to know the parties he desired,
And ment to succour them, if cause required.

18

With him those dames the noble cosins went,
  And when they nearer came unto the place,
They saw three damsels wofully lament,
  Appareld strangely and in sorie case,
Their clothing all had bene clipt off and rent,
  Vp to their navels, to their foule disgrace,
They sitting on the grand and durst not rise,
To hide their secret parts from strangers eyes.

19

As *Vulcans* sonne (by *Pallas* pointment nurst)
  Whom (without mother) got of earth he had,
(For whom *Aglaur* was plagu'd, because she durst
  Looke on him when the Goddesse had forbad)
Sat in a coach (by him devised furst)
  To hide his leggs, that were deform'd and bad:
So sat the wofull maids their secrets hiding,
Scarse from the ground to lift their looks abiding.

20

The foule prospect, did with great wrath inflame
  The worthie dames when they did plaine it vew,
And in the maids behalfs, they blusht for shame,
  As do in *Pestus* gardens roses new:
But *Bradamant,* when as more neare she came,
  Was grieved more, for one of them she knew,
Whose name was *Vllanie,* that since a while,
Was unto *France* sent from the *Island* Ile.

21

She also knew both tother in effect,
  For she had met them trav'ling on that cost,
But yet her speech she chiefly did direct,
  To *Vllany,* whom she regarded most;
And askt her what vile wight did so neglect
  All law, and had all humane nature lost,
As that without remorse he could abide,
To leave that bare that nature seekes to hide?

22

Poore *Vllanie,* that both by speech and sight,
  The worthie damsell *Bradamant* did know,
To be a Ladie, whom she saw last night,
  To give three Princes such an ouerthrow;
When first a while she sobbed had and sight,
  The manner and the matter plaine doth show,
How people neare that place, did ill intreat them,
And clippe their cloths, and also whip and beat them.

23

Fast by (said she) the Castle you may see,
  Where they do keepe, that us so ill did use,
  As for the shield of gold and Princes three,
  That came to win it, she could tell no newes:
  We only ment to trudge on foote (said she)
  To make complaint of those did us abuse,
  Vnto the noble *Christen* Emp'rour *Charles*,
  Who punish will I trust such lawlesse carles.

24

Brave *Bradamant* and stout *Marfisa* longs,
  To go immediatly unto this place,
  And be aveng'd on such enormous wrongs,
  Done as they deeme, to all the sexe disgrace:
  Rogero eke, that knows well what belongs,
  Vnto the law of Knight-hood, in such case,
  (To succour all that are by wrong opprest,
  But chieflie women) goes without request.

25

With one consent, they all put off their bases,
  Which serv'd the maidens very fit to hide
  The secret parts, of those same privie places,
  That modestie to show cannot abide.
  Then *Bradamant* straightway behind her places
  Faire *Vllany*, and makes her so to ride,
  Marfisa and *Rogero* take the paine,
  Behind themselves, to place the other twaine.

26

The dame of *Dordan* led them all the way,
  The tother two do follow with great hast,
  But *Vllany* show'd where the Castle lay,
  To which they many a hill and valley past.
  But now so much was spent of that same day,
  That they were quite benighted at the last,
  At night to take a village they were glad,
  Where they good meat, good drinke, good lodging had.

27

But when to looke about them they began,
  They none could see but women in the place,
  The women drest, brought all, and not a man,
  In all the village that did show his face:
  Among themselves, they on the matter scan,
  And much they mused at so strange a case,
  Among so many, fayre, foule, young, and old,
  As there they saw, not one man to behold.

28

I thinke that *Iason* never marveld more,
  Nor those his *Argonauts*, that with him came,
  Then when they first arriv'd at *Lemnos* shore,
  Where they found none but women void of shame,
  That had their sires, and brethren slaine before,
  And did a common wealth of women frame:
  Then did *Rogero* with the Ladies wonder,
  To see no men, but women such a nomber.

29

Wherefore (when first they had in seemly sort,
  Provided raiment for the damsels three,
  If not so sumptuous, certes not so short,
  But to conceale that which men should not see)
  Then they desir'd some dweller there, report
  To them, what might the cause and reason be,
  Why in this towne there were allow'd no men,
  And in this sort the woman answerd then.

30

This order at the which you seeme to wonder,
  Was by a tyrant pointed for our paine,
  A tyrant, whose subjection we are under,
  Who by his proclamation doth ordaine,
  From mothers sons, from husbands wives to sunder,
  And in such hard exile we must remaine,
  And suffer not by merit, but by force,
  From our deare spouses, such a long divorce.

31

Thrise have the trees with winter bene deleaved,
  Since we have bene into this place confind,
  Of husbands, fathers, and of sonnes bereaved,
  So sore the tyrant hateth all our kinde:
  And if that any chance to be perceaved,
  (As some perhaps there be, that are so kinde)
  To come but once to looke upon his wife,
  The man and woman both, shall loose their life.

32

The lawlesse wretch, that makes this cruell law,
  Dwels two leagues hence, and is of such behaviour,
  As from his purpose no man can him draw,
  How much so ever he be in his favour;
  He doth all women from his land withdraw,
  As if he were infected with their favour,
  He is so fierce, so sturdie, and so strong,
  That none dare once protect, whom he will wrong.

33

And which is strange, he useth strangers worst,
  If any happen to his house arrive,
  (It seems he hath of womens bloud some thurst)
  For though he let them part from thence alive,
  Yet first with whipping, and with usage curst,
  He doth their torment, and reproch contrive:
  Wherefore if you your safeties do regard,
  I wish you not to travell thither-ward.

34

At this *Marfisa* and the *Dordon* dame,
  Were much incenst, and did desire to know,
  How he was cald, and whence his furie came,
  That made him first to such a madnes grow:
  The woman maketh answer thus, his name
  Is *Marganor*, and if you please Ile show
  The whole discourse: to this they all agreed,
  And she then on her tale did thus proceed.

35

This *Marganor*, that makes full many weepe,
  Was bloodie from his birth by disposition,
  But yet a while he did dissemble deepe,
  That of the same there was but some suspistion;
  His sonnes did make him it the closer keepe,
  Because they were of contrary condition,
  Both bounteous, frank, & curteous, of good qualitie,
  Of strangers lovers and of hospitalitie.

36

Faire dames and Knights that hapt to passe this way,
  Were still by them so frendly entertained,
  That by such kind of curteous usage, thay
  The love and praise of ev'rie one had gained;
  Their honors also farther to display,
  The sacred right of Knighthood they obtained;
  Both stout, both strong, comly and of good stature,
  Not wanting ornaments of art or nature.

37

Cylandro and *Tanacro* nam'd they are,
  And long they liv'd with no dishonor stained,
  And longer had, if they had bene so ware,
  As not in *Cupids* snares to have bene trained;
  This foolish passion foyld all their welfare,
  The passion men call love, this them constrained,
  To change the worthie course they had begonne,
  And do that by the which they were undonne.

38

It happend that there thither came a Knight,
  Belonging to this Emperour of *Greece*,
  Who brought with him a Ladie faire and bright,
  Of good behaviour, and a lovely peece,
  With whom *Cylandro* fell in love that night,
  And fully bent of her to have a fleece,
  He thought her beautie so possest his hart,
  That he should surely dye, if she depart.

39

And, for he deemd it labour lost to pray,
  To open force he doth himselfe dispose,
  And secretly all arm'd, unto the way
  Where tother needs must passe, afore he goes,
  And seeing him he would no longer stay,
  But trusting to his manhood, comes to bloes,
  Not seeking vantage, but with lance to lance,
  He minds to trie of fight the doubtfull chance.

40

Not thinking though but with his suer running,
  To beat him downe, and beare away his wife,
  But this same Knight, that in this art was cunning,
  Did pierce his shield, and rest him of his life:
  The newes hereof unto his father comming,
  Fild all the court with plaints and sorrows rife;
  At last, when long the time had bene deferred,
  By his great ancestors they him interred.

41

Nor did this foule mishap and ill successe,
  Make *Marganor* to minish ought his port,
  Tanacro still did courtesie professe,
  To strangers all, and us'd them in good sort:
  But loe, it chanc't within a yeare and lesse,
  A noble Baron thither did resort,
  A comely man of personage to see,
  With him a Ladie faire as faire might be.

42

And to her beautie her behaviour fitted,
  Her looks are modest, manners sober are,
  Her words are ware, and shew her sharply witted;
  Likewise her Lord, himselfe most comely bare,
  As fit to whom the charge should be committed,
  Of one in shape and qualities so rare:
  He hight *Olindro*, Lord of *Longavilla*,
  The lovely Lady named was *Drusilla*.

43

No lesse *Tanacro* doted on this Dame,
  Then had his brother done on that before,
  But that foule end to which his brother came,
  Made him more warie, though not honest more;
  By former good report that bred him fame,
  And all his passed praise, he sets no store:
  Be fame, be vertue troden in the dust,
  So he may but fulfill his present lust.

44

Thus caring onely to avoid the danger,
  In which he saw before his brother dyde,
  He secretly that night way-laid the stranger,
  There as he knew next day he needs must ride,
  Not meaning his owne person to endanger;
  In fine, the Baron that to save his bride,
  Did stoutly give and take full many a wound,
  At last they left foule murderd on the ground.

45

Drusilla se'ing her deare *Olindro* ded,
  In deadly sound unto the ground she sanke,
  But thence in curteous sort the men her led,
  Whom to have kild her, she would give more thanke:
  But griefe in her such will to die had bred,
  That wilfully she leapt downe from a banke,
  To kill her selfe, but poore soule could not dy,
  But all her head and face was brus'd thereby.

46

Tanacro gets some surgeons and Phisicions,
  To looke unto her health, and hurts to cure,
  He causeth her to heare most rare musicions,
  To cheare her heart, and solace to procure:
  He makes great brags of her so chast conditions,
  With mind by marriage to make her sure,
  He thinks a woman of so vertuous life,
  Must not be term'd a lemman, but a wife.

47

To marrie her he inwardly intends,
　This outwardly in shew he doth make knowne,
　And evermore he highly her commends;
　And though her griefe was by his doings growne,
　He saith he will for this make large amends,
　And that he will her love, and be her owne:
　But still the more that on that point he grateth,
　The more in heart she him detests and hateth.

48

But yet her hate did not so blind her wit,
　But that to keepe it close she tooke good heed;
　She knew full well she must dissemble it,
　If she will be reveng'd of him indeed;
　Wherefore untill the time may serve her fit,
　She seemes unto his meaning halfe agreed,
　And did in shew the same so smoothly carrie,
　That lastly she consented him to marrie.

49

Sweet peace and love were written in her eyes,
　Revenge and hate were in her heart engraved,
　To kill him, in her thought she doth devise,
　When with most kindnesse she her selfe behaved:
　He needs must die, needs die in any wise,
　But ev'n thus long to live of God she craved:
　How can I better end my life (she seth)
　Then in revenging my deare husbands deth?

50

Thus seeming to forget all former wrong,
　She chearfully expects the wedding day,
　As though that she did for this marriage long,
　And so she did, although another way,
　She shortens all that might the time prolong,
　And paints her selfe, and tricks her trim and gay:
　She onely crav'd thus much for *Christ* his Passion,
　She might be marry'd of her country fashion.

51

Not that her speech herein indeed was trew,
　That such the custome was as she pretended;
　But she doth mind to forge a custome new,
　With trust assuredly to be revenged
　On him, that her beloved husband slew;
　Revenge, revenge was all that she intended:
　She pray'th, she might observe her countrie guise,
　Which in this sort, she doth to them devise.

52

The widdow that to marrie new intends,
　According as our countrie law allows,
　Must first appease the ghost whom she offends,
　I meane (saith she) that of her former spouse,
　And make unto his spirit some amends,
　By Dirges, trentals, masses, pray'rs and vows,
　In that same Church, whereas his bones be resting,
　Then may she marrie new, without molesting.

53

But when of her new spouse she takes the ring,
　The Priest in sight of all that stand about,
　Of hallowd wine, a bottle then must bring,
　And in the Challice he must powre it out;
　Then over it he must both say and sing,
　Effectual prayrs, and Psalmes, and hymnes devout,
　Then must the woman take it of the Vicker,
　And drinke unto her spouse the blessed licker.

54

Tanacro liketh well of this her motion,
　Respecting little how much it imported,
　To let her marrie with so strange devotion,
　He onely wisht to have the season shorted;
　And not mistrusting that same hallow'd potion,
　To cut of all delays he her exhorted,
　Each makes like hast, though sundry in construction,
　He to her wedding, she to his destruction.

55

Among her women servants that were theare,
　Drusilla had one old ilfavord trot,
　She calleth her, and bad her in her eare,
　That some strong sodaine poyson may be got,
　You know (said she) to get it, how and wheare,
　Convay it safe into some pretie pot,
　For I (quoth she) have found the way and skill,
　The wicked sonne of *Marganor* to kill.

56

And doubt not, I know how to save us both,
　As I will let thee know at better leasure,
　The woman doth the feat though seeming loth,
　Save onely, that it was her mistres pleasure:
　Then for a cup of *Candie* wine she goth,
　And mingles this and that in so due measure,
　As made it with but little alteration,
　Not sowre in tast, yet sure in operation.

57

Now came *Drusilla* on the wedding day,
　With gorgeous gowns and costly jewels dect,
　There where *Olindros* corps intombed lay,
　Rais'd high on collumns as she did direct;
　The Priest began the solemne Masse to say,
　To which came great resort, without suspect,
　And *Marganor* himselfe now most contenting,
　Came with his son and frends the place frequenting.

58

When all the solemne rites to end were brought,
　Then in a cup of massie gold and fine,
　The Priest powrd out, as she before had taught,
　The cursed poyson, with the blessed wine;
　She soberly drinks a convenient draught,
　Inough to do the feat she did designe,
　Then to *Tanacro* with a lovely cheare,
　She gave it, who supt up the challice cleare.

59

And rendring then the challice to the Frire,
  He thought in open arms her to embrace,
  But then she sodainly began retire,
  Then her sweet looks, and words so full of grace,
  Were gone, her eyes did seeme to flame like fire,
  Then wrath and spite were written in her face,
  She cries with grisly looke, and voice unpleasant,
  Avaunt, and touch not me thou traitor peasant.

60

Thoughtst thou of me solace to have and sport,
  And bring me cause of torment, teares, and woe,
  No, now I trow that I have cut thee short,
  That drinke was poyson, if you do not know:
  But ah this death is of too gentle sort,
  And I too noble hangman am I trow,
  A hangman ought with halter stop thy breath,
  This was for thee, too honorable death.

61

My onely sorrow is that ere I dyde,
  My sacrifice was not in full perfection,
  And that thy wicked sire and more beside,
  Did not with thee, tast of that strong confection:
  But pardon me (my deare dead spouse) she cride,
  If I have fayld for fault of good direction,
  If I perhaps have not done all I should do,
  Yet sure I have performed all I could do.

62

And looke what I do want in all or part,
  In working him torture condigne, and shame,
  I hope the world to come, with greater smart,
  Will pay it him, and I shall see the same.
  Thus much she said, and then with chearfull hart,
  Still calling on her former spouses name,
  Take here in worth (said she) this sacrifice,
  That thy poore wife did for thy sake devise.

63

And of our Lord for me a place obtaine,
  In Paradise, with thy most blessed spirit,
  And if he say that none must there remaine,
  But they that by good works the same inherit;
  Tell him I have a cruell tyrant slaine,
  Of tyrants death I bring with me the merit;
  To kill a tyrant, what can be more glorious,
  Or in the sight of God more meritorious?

64

Thus much she said, and fell dead therewithall,
  And being dead, she kept a chearfull looke,
  And sure to her the comfort was not small,
  That for her spouse so sharpe revenge she tooke.
  I know not if *Tanacro* in his fall,
  Did follow her, or else her overtooke,
  He overtooke her sure, as may be thought,
  That dranke the bottome, and the greater draught.

65

Fell *Marganor* that heard his sonnes last grone,
  And seeing him lie dead past all reliefe,
  Made at the first so great and grievous mone,
  As though he would have dide of very griefe:
  Two sons he had of late, now hath he none,
  Two women had hereof bin causes chiefe,
  One mov'd the first to hazard life, the tother
  With her owne hands gave poison to his brother.

66

Love, pitie, griefe, disdaine, and hate, and wrath,
  Desire of death and of revenge together,
  The dolefull parent so inraged hath,
  Like to the roaring seas in fowlest wether:
  Faine to *Drusilla* he would do some scath,
  But she was dead before, yet goes he thether,
  As blinded hate did him still forward pricke,
  He seeks to harme the corse that was not quicke.

67

Ev'n as a snake whom speare to ground doth naile,
  Doth bite the steele and wood that sense hath none,
  Or as a dog that doth a man assaile,
  If one do fling at him a sticke or stone,
  Doth runne and bite the same without availe,
  Till he that hurled it is past and gone:
  So *Marganor* more fierce then dog or snake,
  Seeks on the senslesse corse revenge to take.

68

And when that harrying it, and all to tearing,
  Could not in any part his wrath asswage,
  Ev'n in the Church on us, no such thing fearing,
  He drawes his sword, and in his senslesse rage
  Doth hew and mangle women, none forbearing,
  For dignity, for beautie, nor for age;
  While we cride out, and at his furie wondred,
  He thirtie kild, and hurt and maimd an hundred.

69

So sorely of his people he is dreaded,
  That no man dare against his acts oppose him,
  Vnto his will he is so firmely wedded,
  That for the time starke mad ye would suppose him;
  Who would reforme him, hang'd shall be & headed,
  For guerdon of his paine, when once he knows him:
  His servants do, as doth the proverbe say,
  When furie runs, let furie have her sway.

70

But when at last himselfe was almost tired
  With killing us, though voyd of all remorce,
  Then by his friends request he was desired,
  And as it were constrain'd by honest force;
  And to his castle he himselfe retired,
  Appointing there this law of our divorce,
  And clemencie forsooth he doth it call,
  In that he did forbeare to kill us all.

71

Thus whether they obeyd or else repined,
  Men are from wives, babes frō their dames devided,
And hither all the women be confined;
  This towne of purpose is for us provided,
Where if that any man to love inclined,
  And by a good and kind affection guided,
Come but to see his wife, and thereby show it,
Wo be to him if *Marganor* may know it.

72

And worse then this, he hath ordaind an order,
  Such one I thinke was never heard before,
All women that are tane within his border,
  Must first be whipt with rods till they be sore,
And then he doth their vestiments disorder,
  By clipping them behind and eke before;
And so away he sendeth them halfe stripped,
When first they have bin beaten well and whipped.

73

And if that any hope to have assistance,
  Or bring some Knights them to defend and save,
Forthwith he killeth them and their assistants,
  As sacrifices on his childrens grave:
So as no hope there is to make resistance,
  For evermore he if he list can have
At his commaund, of men a mighty powre,
By name one thousand ev'n within an houre.

74

And further all men in his realme he takes,
  By either faire perswasions or by feare,
Vpon the Sacrament to sweare he makes,
  That ay they shall to women hatred beare.
Now for your owne and these faire Ladies sakes,
  Iudge you if you have reason to forbeare,
Vnto his castle nearer to approch,
Except you will be sham'd with foule reproch.

75

This tale so much did move the warriers three,
  With pitie first, and then with high disdaine,
That save it was so darke they could not see,
  They would have gone ev'n then him to have slain:
Now for that night they rest, but they decree,
  So soone as *Phebus* should returne againe,
To arme themselves, and boldly to adventer,
Vpon the tyrants hold by force to enter.

76

Now as they were about their horse to take,
  They saw before them at the mountaines root,
Some twentie men, that no great hast did make,
  But some on horseback were, and some on foote,
All arm'd, these three them soone did overtake,
  Before they full had rode an arrow shoot,
And then they saw how they did beare by force,
An aged beldam on a sumpter horse.

77

This was forsooth *Drusillas* chamber mayd,
  That to her mistris that same poison gave,
And being then mistrustfull and afrayd,
  What strange effect it fortune might to have,
Vpon the wedding day from Church she staid,
  And so by secret flight her selfe did save,
And kept her selfe three yeares from law and triall,
Till *Marganor* had found her by espiall.

78

What cannot gaine and hope of money worke?
  First by his coyne he learned where she lay,
Then with his coyne he set these men a worke,
  Who in this sort did fetch her thence away,
And of a Lord (in whose land she did lurke,
  With promise that she safely there should stay)
With coyne of that same Baron her he bought;
Ah noble men, can nobles make you nought?

79

Looke how the great and stately streame of *Poe*,
  The nearer he unto the sea descends,
When *Lambra*, *Tycin*, *Adda*, with some mo,
  Fall into him, and their due tribute sends,
The broader and the deeper still doth grow:
  Ev'n so the more that *Marganor* offends,
The greater will in these three champions breeds,
To be avenged on so vile misdeeds.

80

Yet first to free this woman they intend,
  Who else (at least) should have bin hang'd in chaines,
Straight on those lowts all three their forces bend,
  They couch their speares and slacke their horses rains:
An host of men could scarce such force defend;
  Much lesse a sort of dastard hireling swaines:
Wherefore they cast away their warlike tooles,
Their cariage left, and went away like fooles.

81

Ev'n as a greedie wolfe that runneth loden
  With his desired pray unto his den,
That finds unwares the way to him forboden,
  By hunting dogs, or by the hunting men,
Hurles downe his pray, and by the paths untroden
  Doth flie for life; so did these cullions then,
Not onely that their prisoner enlarge,
But leave their horses and their other charge.

82

Some, others force, some, their owne feare unhorses,
  By meanes whereof they did at ease provide,
For those three damsels good convenient horses,
  That yesterday behind them three did ride:
Also *Rogero* that old trot inforces,
  (Though she in vaine refused and denide)
To go with them, lamenting sore and wailing,
But all her lamentation nought availing.

83

Now were they come unto the towne at length,
  About the which there was no ditch nor wall,
  Yet were the houses built in bredth and length
  Both orderly and very strong withall:
  A castle in the midst of mightie strength,
  Stood on a rocke that overlookt them all:
  To this they march with great desire and longing,
  Because it was to *Marganor* belonging.

84

Within this towne no sooner set they feet,
  But that the guard that kept the watch, began
  Behind them step, and chained fast the street:
  Some others, with the greatest hast they can,
  Cald *Marganor*, that straight came them to meet,
  With guard of many a tall and sturdie man,
  Who with a speech but short yet full of pride,
  The leud law of his Citie signifide.

85

Marfisa who before hand had agreed,
  Vpon the matter with the other two,
  Sets spurs to horse, and galloping in steed
  Of making answer, makes no more ado,
  But being of her person strong indeed,
  Employing neither launce nor sword thereto,
  With bended fist she gives him such a boxe,
  As stonid him, and would have feld an oxe.

86

Nor doth *Rogero*, nor the dame of *France*,
  Grant to the others any time of ease,
  But chiefe the damsell that with *Goldelance*,
  Doth throw to ground as many as she please;
  No man there was that durst himselfe advance,
  To stand unto the shocke with one of these;
  Rogero seven, she threw downe seven times seaven,
  Ev'n as if thunder had falne downe from heaven.

87

The hurtlesse people to their houses fled,
  The hartlesse souldiers followd them as fast,
  None stayd behind but those were maimd or dead,
  And *Marganor* alone was left at last,
  And by *Marfisa* now is captive led,
  Who (with his armes behind him piniond fast)
  Gave him *Drusillas* maid to be tormented,
  And would have burnd the town, had they consented.

88

But all consent the law to abrogate,
  The people easily were wonne thereto,
  And to accept one of another rate,
  Which there was ratifide, with small ado
  His law and him they did detest and hate,
  Yet as him list they were content to do,
  As still we see the foolish common use,
  Obey him best that doth them most abuse.

89

And why, they dare not one another trust,
  Nor tell to one another their complaints,
  They let him kill and banish whom he lust;
  Ones goods he takes, anothers house he taints,
  The silent soule yet cries for vengeance just
  Vnto the mighty God and to his Saints,
  Who though they seeme in punishing but slow,
  Yet pay they home at last, with heave and how.

90

So now these silly soules inflam'd with ire,
  With speech and deeds do make their stomacks knowne,
  And (as the proverbe saith) each man beares fire,
  To burne the tree the wind hath overthrowne.
  Ye Princes that to tyrannize desire,
  Marke this mans end, and make his case your owne,
  Beleeve it well, that God doth ever send
  Vnto a wicked life a wretched end.

91

Out came the yong and old, the great and small,
  In words and workes to do him great disgrace:
  He that so terrible was erst to all,
  Is now despisde of all (a wondrous case)
  Yea those three warriers had ado not small,
  To keepe him now from killing in the place,
  Not that they car'd to have his life preserved,
  But unto greater paines they him reserved.

92

They gave him bound unto that woman aged,
  That erst upon *Drusilla* did attend,
  And to those three, whose minds were yet inraged,
  Whom whipt and stript he lately thence did send;
  These with sharp goads and knives his body gaged,
  And to torment him, all their wits did bend,   (him;
  Now some cast stones, and some with needles pricke
  Some scratch, some bite, with feet some spurn & kick
                                        (him.

93

Ev'n as a brooke new swolne with rage of raine,
  Or with a sodaine thaw of melting snow,
  Oft bears down rocks and trees with force so maine,
  As heards doth drowne and houses overthrow,
  A drouth doth come, and then that brooke againe
  Abates his pride, and is at last so low,
  A woman, yea a child with small adoe,
  May passe the same, and never wet their shoe.

94

So *Marganor* that erst in pompe and pride,
  Made hearts of men to quake when he was named,
  To lowest ebb now turned sees his tyde,
  His combe now cut, his furie now is tamed;
  Now kennel-rakers scorne him, and deride,
  To looke men in the face he is ashamed,
  Small children, yea the babes, be not affeard,
  To pull away his haire from head and beard.

95

The while *Rogero* with those champions twaine,
  The castle summon'd that did gladly yeeld,
  Here *Vllanie* recovered againe,
  Which lately she had lost, her golden shield:
  Here met they those three kings, which to their pain,
  Dame *Bradamant* had twise ov'rthrowne in field,
  At the same castle, where before I told
  She wan their lodging, and made them lie cold.

96

Since which, on foote unarm'd they vow'd to go,
  Which want faire *Vllanie* from death did save,
  For all that went with arm'd men garded so,
  Were sacrificed on *Tanacros* grave;
  Yet better of the twaine it was to show,
  The parts that modestie conceald would have,
  For why both this and ev'ry other shame,
  Is halfe excus'd, if force procure the same.

97

Marfisa straight a Parliament did call
  Of all the towne, and made them take an oth,
  Of high and low, rich, poore, and great and small,
  Although they were content, or else were loth,
  That to their wives they should be subject all;
  That in their houses and the Citie both,
  The women should have rule, such powre, such graces,
  As men are wont to have in other places.

98

She further made this notable decree,
  That lodging, meate and drinke should be forbode
  To travellers, of whatsoere degree,
  Admit they go on foote, or that they rode,
  (Within that towne) except they first agree
  To sweare by some great Saint, or else by God,
  That they should evermore be womens friends,
  And foe unto their foes to their lives ends.

99

And whatsoever stranger there arrives,
  Must further sweare, before they go their way,
  If, or they have, or meane to marry wives,
  That evermore they shall their wils obay:
  This must they keepe on perill of their lives,
  For why she vowes to come ere twelve months day,
  And if she find her law broke in that Citie,
  To sacke and burne the same without all pitie.

100

This done, the warriers three did hasten hence,
  But yet their going they so long deferred,
  Vntill *Drusillas* corse was tane from thence,
  Where (as it seem'd)it was but homely berred,
  And order tane, with cost and good expence,
  Her spouse and she might nobly be interred,
  With Epitaphs, by which was signified,
  In how great honour they both liv'd and died.

101

Marfisa made her law in marble faire,
  Vpon a pillar to be written downe,
  And then *Rogero* with the warlike paire
  Of damsels, took their leaves of all the towne:
  But *Vllanie* her garments doth repaire,
  And stayes to make some new and costly gowne,
  She thinks to come to Court were great dishoner,
  Except she had some sumptuous clothing on her.

102

Therefore she staid behind, and in her powre
  Was *Marganor*, by those same warriers given,
  Who had new torments taught him ev'ry howre,
  And was at last by his sharpe judges driven,
  To leape downe headlong from a mighty towre,
  Where all his bones and flesh were broke and riven:
  Of him nor these I have no more to say,
  But of those three that went the tother way.

103

The rest of that same day together riding,
  And halfe the next in company they spent,
  Vntill they found a way in twaine dividing,
  One to the campe, tother to *Arlie* went;
  Here oft they take their leaves, yet still abiding,
  For ever parting makes friends ill content:
  In fine the Knight the way to *Arlie* tooke,
  They to the campe, and thus I end this booke.

THE THIRTY-EIGHT BOOKE OF
ORLANDO FVRIOSO

THE ARGVMENT

Marfisa *doth present her selfe before*
King Charles, *and in his presence is baptized:*
Astolfo *doth* Senapos *sight restore,*
By whom such hardie feats are enterprised,
That Agramant *therewith molested sore,*
Is by Sobrino *finally advised,*
To make a challenge on Rogeros *hed,*
To end the troubles that the warre had bred.

ORLANDO FVRIOSO
THE THIRTY-EIGHT BOOKE

1

Faire Ladies, you with gracious eare that heare
  My present storie, now me seemes I see,
  By this unwonted changing of your cheare,
  That with *Rogero* you offended be,
  For thus againe departing from his deare,
  And that you take the same as ill as she,
  As though you thought, and durst affirme it boldly,
  That fire of love in him did burne but coldly.

2

And sure had he bin moved hereunto,
  By any other cause, then that I told,
  No though thereby he had attained to
  Rich *Crassus* wealth, or richer *Gresus* gold,
  Yet would I thinke (as now it seemes ye do)
  Loves darts in him had tane but shallow hold:
  For so sweet joy, as this was to be thought,
  With gold nor silver never could be bought.

3

But when ones honour shall thereon depend,
  Then should it merit not excuse but praise,
  And chiefe when one so truly may pretend,
  He cannot save his honor otherwayes:
  And that same woman that her selfe should bend,
  To stop the same by prayre, or by delayes,
  Should give just cause to ev'rie one to guesse,
  Her love were little, or her wit were lesse.

4

For if a woman should of him she loves,
  Esteeme the life and safetie as her owne,
  (I speake of such, whose choice no change removes,
  And whose affections are not rashly growne)
  Then sure much more in reason it behoves,
  That of his honour should more care be showne;
  By how much more, it should in due account,
  Both pleasures all, and life it selfe surmount.

5

In following of his Lord so faithfully,
  Rogero did but ev'n as he was bound,
  And if he should have left him then, thinke I,
  He should have done it but on slender ground:
  What though *Almonte* made his father die?
  On *Agramant* that fault could not redound,
  Who had for all his ancestors offences,
  Giv'n to *Rogero* many recompences,

6

He did but well in going to his Lord,
  And she as well (it cannot be denied)
  In that she thereto granted her accord,
  Which she might hap have stopt, had she replied,
  That from the same her liking had abhord;
  What now she wants, henceforth may be supplied,
  But if that honor have one minutes staine,
  An hundred yeares scant can it cleanse againe.

7

Now while *Rogero* unto *Arly* went,
  As duty bound him to *Trajanos* haire,
  Vnto the Christen campe incontinent,
  Rogeros spouse and sister (noble paire)
  As loving friends and cosins now they went,
  And unto *Charles* his tent they did repaire;
  Who minds by siege, or battels doubtfull chance,
  To drive these tedious troubles out of *France*.

8

When in the campe it was made knowne and bruted,
  That *Bradamant* was come, her noblest brothers
  Came forth to her, and kindly her saluted,
  With *Guidon*, though they came of sundry mothers;
  And she, as for her sexe and calling suted,
  Did resalute both them, and divers others,
  By kissing some, and speaking to the best,
  And making frendly gestures to the rest.

9

But when *Marfisas* name was heard and knowne,
  Whose noble acts ev'n from *Catay* to *Spaine*,
  And over all the world beside were blowne,
  To looke on her all were so glad and faine,
  With presse and thrust not few were overthrowne;
  And scarse a man could in the tents remaine,
  But heaving, shoving, hither-ward and thither,
  To see so brave a paire as these togither.

10

Now when to *Charles* his presence come they be,
  Vpon her knee *Marfisa* did decline,
  And (as *Turpinon* writes) no man did see
  Her knee to touch the ground before that time,
  To none of any calling, or degree,
  Not unto *Christen* Prince or *Sarazine*:
  She onely doth esteeme King *Pepins* sonne,
  As worthie whom such honor should be donne.

11

But *Charles* arose, and met her halfe the way,
  And in kinde stately sort did her embrace,
  And set her by his side that present day,
  Above the Princes all, and gave her place.
  Then voided was the roome that none might stay,
  But Lords and Knights well worthie so great grace,
  Excluding all the sawcie baser sort,
  And then *Marfisa* spake in such like sort.

12

Most mighty *Cæsar*, high renownd and glorious,
  That from our *Indies*, to *Tyrinthian* shore,
  From *Scythia*, frosen still with breath of *Boreas*,
  To *Æthiopia* scorching evermore,
  Mak'st thy white crosse, so famous and victorious,
  By value much, but by thy justice more;
  Thy praise (O Prince) and thy renowned name,
  Were cause from countries farre I hither came.

13

And to say troth, flat envie mov'd me chiefe,
  Because thy powre to reach so farre I saw,
  I must confesse I tooke disdaine and griefe,
  That any Prince that favord not our law,
  And was to us of contrarie beliefe,
  Should grow so great, to keepe us all in aw;
  Wherefore I came with mind to have destroid thee,
  Or by all meanes I could, to have annoyd thee.

14

For this I came, for this I stayd in *France*,
  To seeke your ruine and your overthrow,
  When lo a chance (if such a thing can chance)
  Made me a frend and subject of a fo,
  I will not stay to tell each circumstance,
  But this in substance, it did make me know,
  That I, your bloodie enemie *Marfisa*,
  Was daughter to *Rogero* late of *Rysa*.

15

He by my wicked uncles was betraid,
  And left my wofull mother big with child,
  Who neare to *Syrté* downe her bellie laid,
  As strangely sav'd, as wrongfully exild;
  She brought a twin, a man child and a maid,
  We fosterd were, seven yeares in forrest wild,
  By one that had in Magicke art great skill,
  But I was stolne from him against his will.

16

For some *Arabians* sold me for a slave,
  Vnto a *Persian* King, whom (growne in yeares)
  Because he my virginity would have,
  I killed him and all his Lords and Peeres
  And then such hap, God and good fortune gave,
  I gat his crowne and armes, as yet appeares;
  And ere I fully was twise ten yeare old,
  Seven crownes I gat beside, which yet I hold.

17

And being envious of your endlesse fame,
  (As erst I told) I came with firme intent,
  By all the meanes I could, to quaile the same,
  And haply might have done the hurt I ment;
  But now a better minde, that minde doth tame,
  Now of my malice I do much repent,
  Since by good hap, I lately understood,
  That I was neare allide to you in blood.

18

And sith I know my father was your man,
  I meane no lesse then he did, you to serve,
  As for the hate and envie I began,
  To beare you I now do the same reserve,
  For *Agramant*, and all the harme I can,
  To all his kin, that do the same deserve,
  Because I now do know, and am assured,
  His ancestors my parents death procured.

19

This said *Marfisa*, and withall did adde,
  That she would be baptized out of hand,
  And when that *Agramant* she vanquisht had,
  Returne (if *Charles* so pleas'd) to her owne land,
  And Christen them, and farther would be glad,
  Against all those that would *Christs* law withstand,
  Ay to beare armes, with vow that all her gaine
  To *Charles* and holy Church should ay remaine.

20

The noble *Charles* of tongue as eloquent,
  As wise in head, as valorous in heart,
  Did much extoll the Ladie excellent,
  And all her kin and sire by just desart:
  And of her former speech incontinent,
  Most graciouslie he answerd ev'rie part,
  Concluding that he would for ever after,
  Accept her as his cousin, and his daughter.

21

And her againe he did embrace of new:
  And kist her forhead as his child indeed:
  It long would be to tell how brave a crew,
  From *Clairmount*, and *Mongrane* did proceed,
  To welcome her, or when *Renaldo* knew
  Marfisas name, what joy in him did breed,
  He calls to mind what force in her he found,
  Then when *Albracca* he besieged round.

22

It long would be to tell of *Guidons* joy,
  With *Griffin*, *Aquilant* and *Sansonet*,
  That scapt with her their land, that do destroy,
  Those men that in their Realme they hap to get:
  No lesse did *Malagige* and *Vivian* joy,
  Remembring how she joynd with *Richardet*,
  To rescue them, as long before I told,
  When unto *Bertolage* they had bene sold.

23

Now was prepard against th'ensuing day,
 A place, as was by *Charles* himselfe devised,
 Set stately forth, and hang'd with rich aray,
 Where this most worthy dame should be baptised,
 Then Bishops were employd by whom she may
 Be taught the *Christen* faith and Catechised,
 And all that day a learned Clarke and Preacher,
 The principles of *Christen* faith did teach her.

24

Then *Turpin* Archbishop of chiefe account,
 In his robes pontificiall doth baptise her,
 Charles with great rev'rence standeth by the fount,
 And what to answer, he did still advise her.
 But now tis time that to the Moone I mount,
 For that receit must make *Orlando* wiser,
 From whence the Duke, descending by strange byas,
 Came with *S. Iohn* in charret of *Elyas*.

25

And by his guide he backe againe was led,
 And keeps still in his hand that pot or Iarre,
 That should againe make wise the mased hed,
 Of that same *Palladin* well seene in warre.
 Likewise the Saint unto *Astolfo* sed,
 Assoone as they allighted from the carre,
 That with an herbe (of which there grew great store)
 He should againe *Senapos* sight restore.

26

For which, and for his former great desart,
 He should have men t'assault *Biserta* land,
 He teacheth him those people unexpart,
 He should so traine, to make them to his hand:
 He further learned him the way and art,
 How he might safely passe th'unstable sand;
 And plainly thus *S. Iohn*, from point to point,
 What th'English Duke should do, did him appoint.

27

Then did *Astolfo* take his winged steed,
 And of the Saint devoutly tooke his leave,
 And soaring downe, he makes no little speed,
 To do that which in charge he did receave;
 So farre by *Nylus* bankes he doth proceed,
 Vntill that *Nubia* he did plaine perceave;
 And following the course of that same streame,
 Came to *Senapo*, head of that same Reame.

28

Great was the pleasure, triumph, and the joy,
 Senapo tooke when he thereof had woord,
 Remembring well the trouble and annoy,
 The foule *Harpias* brought him at his boord:
 But when he made him eke his sight enjoy,
 And did so rare a grace to him affoord,
 That by his meanes his eye sight was restord him,
 He worship him and like a God ador'd him.

29

Nor onely did he give him souldiers then,
 Wherewith he might *Biserta* towne invade,
 But for each one he askt he gave him ten,
 That soone two hundred thousand men he made:
 Scarse had the fields roome for so many men,
 But footmen all: so is that countryes trade,
 For horses in that Region are but dentie,
 But *Elephants* and *Camells* they have plentie.

30

Now that same day that went before the day,
 In which the men of *Nubia* made account,
 To march on forward, some part of their way,
 Astolfo on his Griffith horse doth mount;
 And Southward he doth passe, and doth not stay,
 Vntill he came neare to a mighty mount:
 At foote whereof a vast cave he doth finde,
 Which was the lodging of the Sotherne winde.

31

The mighty cave had but a narrow mouth,
 At which the Duke (as *Christs* Apostle taught)
 Did watch so long, untill the wind of South,
 Came home to ease his spirits overwrought,
 To enter in *Astolfo* him allowth,
 But when anone, to have come out he thought,
 Within a leather sacke the Duke had plast
 At that caves mouth, he caught and tyde him fast.

32

The *Palladin*, full proud of such a pray,
 Returnes to *Nubia* ward, before twas night,
 And to the *Negros* then he show'd the way,
 Appointing them how they should travell right;
 He victualls doth and cariages convay,
 All safe unto that hill, that *Atlas* hight;
 Quite ore those fields where many have bene found,
 With wind for want of water, more then drownd.

33

And being come unto the mountaines side,
 There, where he might discover all the plaine,
 He doth his bands and companies devide,
 And chuseth those that are most apt to traine,
 And those he parts and putteth them aside,
 And orders for the rest he doth ordaine,
 Then he in sight of all the hill ascendeth,
 And lookt like one that some great feat intendeth.

34

And kneeling downe (as one that did beleeve,
 His prayre should granted be, as well as hard)
 He prayd his master their great want releeve:
 Then casting stones that were before prepard,
 (What cannot firme beleefe in *Christ* atcheeve?)
 The very stones (a thing to credit hard)
 Did grow, and live, and move by hidden cause,
 And had both bellyes, legges, and necke, and jawes.

35

And naying lowd, fild all the place with sound,
  Of horse, some bay, some roane, some daple gray,
  And of all them were readie horses found,
  The spurre, the wand, the leg and voyce t'obay;
  To stop, to start, to passe carier, to bound,
  To gallop straight, or round, or any way:
  Thus were the men well horst, with little paines,
  For ev'rie horse had saddle, bit and raines.

36

Thus by this vertuous Duke, within one houre,
  Were fourescore thousand footmen, horsemen made,
  With which so great and unexpected powre,
  Full fiercely he all *Affrike* did invade,
  And burnt and spoild full many a towne and towre,
  All giving way to his victorious blade,
  Vntill three Princes, *Agramants* vicegerents,
  Made head against the Duke, with their adherents.

37

The King of *Aldyzer*, and he of *Ferse*,
  With stout *Bransardo*, all three mighty Kings,
  That find their enemies to grow so fierce,
  Do send their Lord by sea, word of these things.
  A little fricket straight the waves doth pierce,
  And of these evill newes quicke notice brings
  To *Agramant* that lay that time in *Arlie*,
  Besieged by an army strong and warlie.

38

Who hearing of his countries wofull case,
  And by his absence what did them betide,
  He cald his Lords and Princes to the place,
  Consulting how for this harme to provide;
  And looking once or twise with stately grace,
  Now on the tone, then on the tother side,
  But on *Marsilio* and *Sobrino* chiefe,
  In such like words he told to them his griefe.

39

Although I wot it worst beseemes of all,
  A Generall to say, I had not thought,
  Yet so say I, for when a harme doth fall,
  Beyond the reach of humane sence or thought,
  Then sure the blame is either none or small,
  And in this compasse may my fault be brought:
  My fault it was, *Affricke* to leave unarmed,
  If of the *Nubians* now they could be harmed.

40

But who could thinke (but God that understands
  The things to come as well as those are past)
  So great an host could passe so many lands,
  That were from us so great a distance plast,
  Twixt whom and us lies those unstable sands,
  That dangerously are mov'd with Southerne blast;
  Yet are they come, and have so farre prevailed,
  Biserta selfe is now by them assailed.

41

Now on this point your counsels here I crave,
  If so I shall all fruitlesse hence retire,
  Or trie before I go, if I can have
  The crowne of *France*, to which I do aspire,
  Or how I may at home my country save,
  And this destroy, which is my most desire;
  If any know the meane, then speake he to it,
  To th'end that we may know the best, and do it.

42

Thus much the sonne of great *Trajano* spake,
  And on *Marsilio* fixt his eyes, that he
  As chiefe in place, thereby might notice take,
  That first by him he would advised be:
  Who when he had stood up for rev'rence sake,
  And bow'd his body, and withall his knee,
  Downe sate him in his honorable seate,
  And spake such words as I shall here repeate:

43

What ever fame doth bring, of good or ill,
  To make it greater it doth ever use,
  Wherefore (my soveraigne Lord) I never will
  Be bold or basht with hearing flying newes,
  But move such doubt and such assurance still,
  As though I would not all reports refuse,
  Yet would I thinke the truth of other sort,
  Then as so many mouthes shall make report.

44

And I beleeve each tale so much the lesse,
  By how much more from likelihood it doth arre:
  Now in this present cause let any guesse,
  If like it be, a King that dwels so farre,
  Could come with such an host, as they expresse,
  To *Affrica*, so often us'd to warre,
  And passe those parlous sands, where to his cost,
  Cambises erst did leese his mighty host.

45

But they be *Nubians*, let it be allowd,
  By miracle come in a showre of raine,
  Or closely carrid thither in some clowd,
  Sith by the way none saw so large a traine:
  Hath *Affrike* ever to such people bow'd,
  Must they have aide to drive them home againe?
  I sure may think you kept a sorie garison,
  If them and yours betweene there be comparison.

46

I rather thinke th'*Arabians* are come downe,
  From those their hils, and done some spoile or wast,
  And tane some men, and burnt some baggage towne,
  But small resistance finding as they past,
  And that *Bransardo* for his owne renowne,
  Whom as your deputie you there had plast,
  For one sets downe one hundred in his letter,
  To th'end that his excuse may seeme the better.

47

But if you will but send some ship or twaine,
That but your standard may therein appeare,
No doubt but they will hie them home againe,
By that time these but weigh their ankers here,
If they *Arabians*, that can bide no paine,
Or if they *Nubians* be, the case is cleare,
Who onely taken have this heart of grace,
To know your person absent from the place.

48

This therefore is the sum of my perswasion,
Make sure the conquest here ere you go hence,
Charles can no more endure your sharpe evasion,
Now that his nephew is distraught of sence:
Now by the forehead let us take *Occasion*,
Least after all our travell and expence,
He hide away his haire, and turne his bald,
And we unprovident be thought and cald.

49

With these so warie words, and such as these,
The subtle *Spaniard* labour'd to perswade,
The King of *Affrike* not to passe the seas,
Till of the warres in *France* an end were made:
But sage *Sobrino*, that espide with ease,
How deepe he seemd in shallow streames to wade,
Respecting privat more then publike cause,
Did answer thus after a little pause.

50

My Liege, when first to peace I counseld you,
I would I had not bin so true a Prophet,
Or if my sayings needs must prove so true,
I would you had beleev'd them for your profit;
Not *Rodomont*, with that rash youthfull crue
Of *Alcyrd, Marbalust*, that then did scoffe it,
Whom now I wish here present, face to face,
But chiefly *Rodomont* I wish in place.

51

He that then undertooke to make all *France*,
But like the dust that flies before the wind,
He that did vow, in heav'n or hell, your lance
To follow, nay to leave it farre behind,
Now when he should the matter most advance,
Vnprofitably lurkes in corners blind,
And I that then (because I told you true)
Was cald a coward, still abide with you.

52

And still I will abide, what ere ensuth,
During this life, which though made weake with age,
I will not feare, against the strongest youth
That lives in *France*, in your defence to gage;
Nor yet can any charge me with untruth,
Nor from the proudest Prince to poorest page,
And well I wot, I have done more then some,
That promist much ere they were hither come.

53

Thus much I say, thereby more plaine to prove,
That what I then did say, or now impart,
Came from true service, and of loyall love,
And not of faint, much lesse of hollow hart:
Now I advise you hence with speed remove,
And that you homeward in all hast depart,
For well you wot, that wisedome it is none,
In winning other mens, to leese ones owne.

54

Yet know not I why we should call it winning,
If of our losses just account we yeeld,
Thirtie two Kings we were at the beginning,
A third part now scarce tarries in the field;
And we our selves here up in corners pinning,
Scant safe within these rampiers can us shield,
We so decay, except in time we cease,
At last we shall be driv'n to sue for peace.

55

Orlando is not there, tis true, what tho?
Had he bin there, we had all dide ere this,
His want doth but prolong our ouerthrow,
By other men, our state in danger is:
They have *Renaldo* there, that plaine doth show
His force and courage not much lesse then his,
There are his cousins, all the *Palladins*,
Eternall terror to our *Sarazins*.

56

They further have a man in strength and hart,
(I needs must praise my foe against my will)
A second *Mars*, I meane King *Brandimart*,
Whose great puissance joynd to active skill,
My selfe in single fight have found in part,
And further proofe have seene by others ill:
Besides, *Orlando* wanted long ago,
Since which we more have lost then won you know.

57

Now if we sped no better in time past,
We shall speed worse hereafter I do dread,
We see *Gradasso* over sea is past,
And that the valiant *Mandricard* is dead;
Marfisa hath forsaken us at last,
And *Rodomont*, of whom it may be sed,
Were but his faith with force to be compared,
The rest might in a manner have bin spared.

58

Now when as so great helpes and succors faile us,
So many thousands of our souldiers slaine,
And all supplies that should at all availe us,
Already come from *Affrike* and from *Spaine*;
They have of late got foure new Knights to quaile us,
Compard with any of the Christen traine,
Foure Knights, that if you search from hence to *Inde*,
Foure Knights to match these foure you shal not find.

59

I known not if you ever heard before,
  Of *Oliveros* sons, and *Sansonet*,
With *Guidon* savage, whom I value more
  Then all their other succors that they get,
From *Almanie* the higher or the lower,
  Although such aids at nought we cannot set,
And we do plainly see before our eyes,
That ev'ry day they may have fresh supplies.

60

We may assure our selves if any more
  We take the field, our side goes to the pot,
For if when we were two for one before,
  Yet we must needs confesse we gained not,
Now they so much increased have their store,
  With forraine powre, both *English*, *Dutch* and *Scot*,
What can we hope but after all our toyle,
To have bad recompence of shame and foyle.

61

Yet all is well, if you will part betime,
  And hie you home before it prove too late;
But if you tarry any longer time,
  You here will leese your men, at home your state:
Now if to leave *Marsilio* seeme a crime,
  For feare the world condemne you for ungrate,
To save him harmlesse you for peace must sue,
Which they will so accept, if so will you.

62

But if you thinke such motion may not stand,
  With honour of your state and high degree,
And hope by fight to make a surer hand,
  Which yet how it succeeded hath you see;
Yet seeke at least to have the upper hand
  By this device, and herein follow me:
Put all the quarrels triall, if you can,
To one, and let *Rogero* be the man.

63

I know, and you do know, and so we all
  Do know, that our *Rogero* hath such might,
No *Christen* can so sturdie be or tall,
  As hand to hand to conquer him in fight:
But if you meane to make warre generall,
  Though he in strength far passe each other Knight,
Yet in the fight he but for one can stand,
And what is one against a mightie band?

64

I thinke it best, if so you thinke it good,
  To offer this to *Charles*, that if he will,
If with his worthy courage so it stood,
  For saving those, whom you on both sides kill,
And shunning of the shedding guiltlesse blood,
  Which both of you, on each side dayly spill,
Each side to chuse one champion at whose parrell,
To make a full conclusion of the quarrell.

65

Provided first, that which so ere of these
  Shall dye, his Prince shall pay the tother tribute:
I know this motion will not *Charles* displease,
  For all his Lords, will there-unto contribute;
And this would worke our safetie, and our ease,
  For to *Rogero*, so much I attribute,
That such his vallew is, this cause so just,
Were *Mars Antagonist*, yet yeeld he must.

66

These words *Sobrino* spake with such effect,
  As *Agramant* thereto gave his consent,
And then Interpreters he did direct,
  Who straight to *Charles* with such a challenge went:
Charles meanes not such occasion to neglect,
  He thinks the combat wonne incontinent,
He had such store of champions, nere the latter,
Vnto *Renaldo* he commits the matter.

67

Glad were both armies of this new accord,
  Henceforth to live in quiet they intend,
And either part doth praise his soveraigne Lord,
  That of these broyles would make so speedie end.
Each one in mind these foolish bralls abhord,
  That made them thus in warres their dayes to spend,
Each man could say, and no man then denyd it,
That warre is sweet to those that have not tryd it.

68

Renaldo, he in mind doth much rejoyse,
  To thinke his Prince had done him such a grace,
To make of him above so many choyse,
  For triall of so great importing case:
And though *Rogero* were by common voyce,
  The chiefe man deemd of all the *Turkish* race,
And hand to hand had killed *Mandricard*,
Renaldo this but little did regard.

69

But good *Rogero* he was nothing glad,
  Though of so many gallant men and stout,
His King to his great praise, him chosen had,
  Above all other Knights, and pikt him out;
His heart was heavie, and his looke was sad,
  Not that in mind he ought did dread or doubt,
Renaldos forces, or *Orlandos* either,
No scarse and if they had beene both togither.

70

But this procur'd his griefe, because he knew,
  Renaldo brother was unto his deare,
Who did her plaints with letters oft renew,
  And charged him so deepe, as toucht him neare:
Now if he should to old wrongs, add this new,
  To kill *Renaldo*, then the case is cleare,
She should have so great reason to reprove him,
He doubts she never will hereafter love him.

71

Now if *Rogero* do in silent sort,
    Lament this combat tane against his will,
No doubt his spouse which heard this sad report,
    Was worse appaid then he, at least as ill;
She beats her brest, and breakes her tresses short,
    And many teares with sorrow she did spill,
And calls *Rogero* oftentimes ungrate,
And curseth evermore her cruell fate.

72

It needs must turne unto her griefe and paine,
    Who ere is overcome, who ever win,
She dare not thinke *Rogero* can be slaine,
    Her heart such anguish doth conceive therein;
And if it pleased *Christ* so to ordaine,
    For chastising his wretched peoples sin,
That man should dye, that of her house was chiefe,
Besides his death, that brought a further griefe.

73

A griefe that was indeed beyond all measure,
    To thinke she never might henceforth for shame,
Go to her spouse, without the flat displeasure,
    Of all her kin and house of whence she came:
And when she weigh'd the case at better leasure,
    Each thing to her seemd worse and worse to frame,
For why she knew, her tongue that knot had tyde,
That while she liv'd, might never loose, nor slide.

74

But that deare frend of hers, that never faild,
    To helpe at chiefest needs, the noble maid,
I meane the sage *Melissa*, so prevaild,
    That *Bradamantes* guese was part alaid,
For when she knew the cause, and what she aild,
    Against the time, she promised her aid;
And undertooke, that of that bloudy quarrell,
To her nor hers, there should arise no parrell.

75

This while the gallant Knights against the fight,
    Themselves, and eke their weapons do provide,
The choise whereof did appertaine in right,
    Vnto the champion of the Christen side,
Who, as a man that tooke but small delight,
    (Since he had lost his famous horse) to ride,
Did chuse to fight on foot, and in this sort,
All arm'd, with axes long, and daggers short.

76

Or were it chance, or were it in regard,
    That *Malagige* advised him thereto,
Because he knew the force of *Balysard*,
    Of powre all charms of armour to undoe,
(Of whose sharpe edge you have ere this time hard)
    But this they did appoint betweene them two,
About the place likewise they do agree,
A plaine neare *Arlie* walls, the same to be.

77

Now when *Aurora* left the lothed bed,
    Of *Tytan* (unto whom she hath no list)
To th'end that no disorder may be bred,
    On either side the marshalls part the list,
At end whereof, were rich pavillions spred,
    Where nothing that belongs to state was mist,
And distant from each tent a little space,
On either side, they did an alter place.

78

Not long time after this, in battell ray,
    The *Turkish* armie with their King came out,
Glistring in gold, and stately rich aray,
    In show, with all *Barbarian* pompe set out,
A swift *Arabian* horse, of colour bay
    He rode, and by his side *Rogero* stout,
Rode cheeke by cheeke, and to his greater fame,
On him to wait, *Marsilio* thought no shame.

79

His helmet (for the which the *Tartar* dyde,
    Slaine by *Rogero* as I did rehearse)
(Which since a thousand yeares, and more beside,
    Was celebrated in more stately verse)
Marsilio carrid, by *Rogeros* side,
    Well mounted on a *Spanish* genet fearce,
His arms, and all that did thereto belong,
Some other states divided them among.

80

On tother side came worthie *Charlemayne*,
    From out his tents, strongly intrencht, anone,
And all his bands of men he did ordaine,
    So as if to battell he should then have gone:
About him was of Peers a noble trayne,
    Renaldo in the mids, with armour on,
That onely helmet erst from *Mambryn* tane,
Was by *Vggero* borne, the noble *Dane*.

81

Two axes, both alike in each respect,
    Salemon and Duke *Namus* beare before,
The Chieftaines on each side their men direct,
    To keepe within their limits evermore;
And in the midst was left a large prospect,
    Betweene each company, and roome good store,
For present death it was, if any venter,
Save those two champions, in the list to enter.

82

When second choise of weapon (as was fit)
    Was giv'n *Rogero* to avoid suspect,
Two Priests before the rest came forth, to wit,
    Of each side one, and one of either sect,
Each had a booke, ours had *Christs* holy writ,
    Theirs *Alcoran*, with errours foule infect,
With ours came forth the *Christen* Prince devout,
With that of theirs, the King of *Turks* came out.

83

Now first King *Charles* neare to his altar stands,
  And this great protestation there did make,
  And lifts to heaven both heart, and eyes and hands,
  O God, O *Christ*, that sufferdst for our sake,
  O blessed Ladie, that in swathing bands,
  Heldst him that mortall flesh of thee did take,
  And didst nine months inclose that high divinitie,
  In sacred wombe, still keeping true virginitie.

84

Be witnesses, that here I make it knowne,
  And promise faithfully for me and mine,
  To *Agramant*, and who so ere shall owne
  The crowne of *Affrike* in ensuing time,
  That if my champion shall be overthrowne,
  To pay to them, each yeare of gold most fine,
  Ten horslode, and forthwith the warres to cease,
  And evermore hereafter to have peace.

85

And if I fayle, then let the fearfull wrath
  Of both, on me at once this folly wreake,
  And worke unto my sect all wo and scath,
  That all insuing ages plaine may speake,
  Loe what a plague, and just reward he hath,
  That durst his oth to you, and promise breake:
  This said, his hand he laid upon the booke,
  And up on heaven he fixt his stedfast looke.

86

When this was done, then all departed thence,
  There where the *Turks* had with much superstition
  Adorn'd their altar with no small expence,
  And their King *Agramant*, with like condition,
  Vow'd never after this, to do offence
  To *Charles*, but passe the seas with expendition,
  And ay keepe peace, and equall tribute pay,
  If that *Rogero* vanquisht were that day.

87

And in like sort he did protest alowd,
  And cald on *Mahomet*, his Idol great,
  And by that booke, that his Priest held, he vow'd
  To keepe most duly all he did repeat:
  This done, to part from thence were all allow'd,
  And either Prince retired to his seat;
  Then in like sort they sweare the champions both,
  And thus much in effect contain'd their oth.

88

Rogero promiseth, that if the fight,
  By *Agramant* shall be disturb'd or parted,
  That never after he will be his Knight,
  But serve King *Charles*, and be to him true harted.
  Renaldo in like sort his faith doth plight,
  That if to him, *Charles* any aid imparted,
  Before that one of them were overcome,
  That then himselfe to *Agramant* would come.

89

Now when these ceremonies all were ended,
  That ev'rie man departed to his side,
  And then the warriours onely now attended,
  The trumpets sound, that battell signifide;
  Which when both heard, then each of them intended,
  To show the utmost of his vallew tride:
  Now sounds the steele with blows, not few nor soft,
  Now they themselves, strike low and now aloft.

90

Sometime they would beguile the tone the tother,
  With mind unto their strength, to ad their art,
  They profer at one place, and strike another,
  Invading still the least defended part:
  But good *Rogero*, that against the brother,
  Of her did fight, that did possesse his hart,
  Did oft bestow his blows, with such regard,
  Most thought *Renaldo* was for him too hard.

91

He seemed readier to ward then strike,
  For he himselfe well knew not what he ment,
  To kill *Renaldo*, that he did not like,
  To dy himselfe that was not his intent:
  But now I hope that none will it mislike,
  Sith in this booke so much time hath bene spent,
  And least my tediousnesse may some molest,
  In this ensuing booke to heare the rest.

THE THIRTY-NINTH BOOKE OF
ORLANDO FVRIOSO

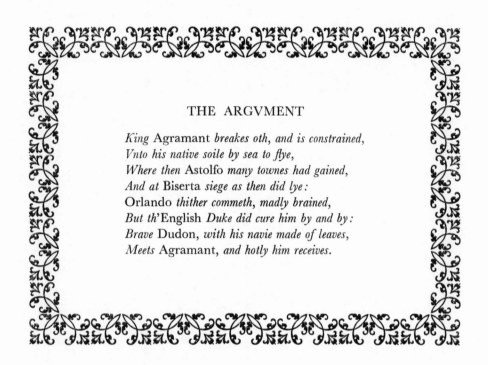

THE ARGVMENT

King Agramant *breakes oth, and is constrained,*
Vnto his native soile by sea to flye,
Where then Astolfo *many townes had gained,*
And at Biserta *siege as then did lye :*
Orlando *thither commeth, madly brained,*
*But th'*English *Duke did cure him by and by :*
Brave Dudon, *with his navie made of leaves,*
Meets Agramant, *and hotly him receives.*

ORLANDO FVRIOSO
THE THIRTY-NINTH BOOKE

1

What tongue can tell, or learned pen expresse
  The woes, to which *Rogero* now did runne?
In mind, and body, driv'n to such distresse,
That of two deaths, the tone he cannot shun:
If he be slaine, and if he kill no lesse,
Both wayes he sees he shall be quite undonne:
  By shame in death, and if he win and live,
  By that offence he shall his true love give.

2

The tother Knight whom no such thought encombred
  Lets frankly fly his blows without regard,
In so great store as was not to be numbred,
No time, no place, nor no advantage spard:
Rogero seem'd to him, as if he slumbred,
Small list he had to strike, but all to ward,
  And if he did, in such a place he strake,
  His blow great sound, but little signe did make.

3

The *Pagan* Lords now doubt it will go wrong,
  They see the combat so unequall grow,
Renaldo seem'd too lustie and too strong,
Rogero seem'd too lasie and too slow.
But *Agramant* that sate the rest among,
Doth fret, and fume, and chafe, and sweat, and blow,
  Doth blame *Sobrino* chiefly, whose perswasion,
  Was of this combat chiefe and sole occasion.

4

This while *Melissa* sage, whose skill was great
  In Magicke art, repaired to the place,
And with some secret words she did repeat,
She chang'd her voice, her stature, and her face,
In mind hereby to worke a wondrous feat;
She seem'd all armed in a Dragons case,
  In sword, in shield, in shew, in ev'rie thing,
  She seemed *Rodomont* the *Sarzan* King.

5

To wofull *Agramant* she straight doth ride,
  (In likenesse of an horse, she rode a sprite)
And comming to his presence, lowd she cride,
(My Liege) this was too fowle an oversight,
To match a beardlesse boy so meanly tride,
With such a famous and renowned Knight,
  And chiefe in matter that imports so much,
  As doth the whole estate of *Affricke* tuch.

6

Wherefore that you in time this losse may save,
  Permit the combat to proceed no more,
Let *Rodomont* the blame and blemish have,
Of breaking that, which you so rashly swore;
Now each man shew how well his sword can shave,
Now I am here, each man is worth a score.
  These words in *Agramant* had so much force,
  That without more advice, he straight tooke horse.

7

And thinking sure fierce *Rodomont* was theare,
  Forthwith the *Christens* host he doth invade,
Of oth nor promise he hath now no feare,
This one mans presence him so bold had made:
Each man doth in a moment couch his speare,
Or charge his pike, or draw his glittering blade:
  Melissa having set them thus togither,
  With this illusion vanisht (God knows whither).

8

The two stout champions when they plainly saw,
  Their combat, that all quarrell should descide,
Disturb'd against all promise, and all law,
They cease all force, and lay all wrath aside,
And by consent, themselves they do withdraw,
Vntill it might more plainly be descride,
  In whether Prince of faith were found such want:
  In aged *Charles*, or youthfull *Agramant*.

9

And each of them of new doth vow and sweare,
  That unto him that first did cov'nant breake,
They will for ever endlesse hatred beare,
And joyne together such offence to wreake:
The while the hosts of neither side forbeare
To make quicke triall who be strong or weake,
  For lightly at the first conflict they shoe,
  Their hearts if they be resolute or no.

10

Even as a grewnd which hunters hold in slip,
  Doth strive to breake the string, or slide the coller,
(That sees the tearfull Deare, before him skip,
Pursewd belike with some *Actæons* scholler)
And when he sees he can by no meanes slip,
Doth howle, and whine, and bites the string for choler
  In such like case within the tents did stay,
  Marfisa with dame *Bradamant* that day.

11

All that same day unto that present howre,
  They had beheld with great despite and paine,
  Such tempting baites, yet had they not the powre,
  To set their foote in that forbidden plaine:
But now they do the field on each side scowre,
  Though erst for duties sake they did abstaine,
  Now finding such a true and just excuse,
  That *Agramant* had lewdly broke the truse.

12

Marfisa ran the first quite through the brest,
  And made the speare come forth a yard behind;
  Then with her sword she flies among the rest,
  There chiefe where most resistance she doth finde:
And *Bradamant* puts *Goldélance* in rest,
  With like effects, but of another kind,
  For all she toucht therewith she overthrew,
  And yet not one among them all she slew.

13

Thus these two warriours ever as they went,
  Subdewd their enemies, and kept them under,
  Who ever met them surely should be shent,
  And each of them at tothers force did wonder:
But being both to sharpe revengement bent,
  At last they part themselves, and went asunder,
  Each by her selfe, such high exploits performing,
  As gave the *Turks* long after cause of mourning.

14

As when the Southerne winds do melt the snow,
  Congeald on tops of mountaines many dayes,
  It often happens that two streames do flow,
  And taking in their course, two sundrie wayes,
At last so violent and furious grow,
  That bearing downe, and breaking usuall bayes,
  They wast the fields, and seeme on vye to runne,
  By which of them most damage may be donne.

15

Ev'n so these twaine, incenst with rage and wrath,
  And each in sev'rall acts their forces trying,
  Do worke the *Turks*, no little woe and scath,
  And leave them overthrowne, or maymd, or dying:
Scarse *Agramant* the powre by this time hath,
  (Say what he list) to keepe his men from flying,
  Himselfe not shrinking though, nor once retiring,
  But evermore for *Rodomont* enquiring.

16

By onely his advise and exhortation,
  (For so the unadvised Prince doth thinke)
  He broken had his solemne protestation,
  He marvels now, to find him so to shrinke:
Likewise *Sobrino* with great lamentation,
  (Religion in his mind so deepe did sinke)
  Retyrd to *Arly*, evermore protesting
  His faultlesse mind, that perjurie detesting.

17

Marsilio eke unto his countrie fled,
  The shamefull promise breach of *Agramant*
  Strake in his mind such superstitious dred,
  He leaveth him to beare the brunt, who scant
Against the Christen souldiers could make hed:
  That no supplies of forren powres did want,
  With *Palladines* among them fierce and bold,
  Mixt like rich gemmes in faire embroderd gold.

18

But now a while I linquish this conflict,
  And passe beyond the seas without a barke,
  For to this tale I am not tyde so strict,
  But that I will repeat (if you will harke)
Astolfos acts, who forward dayly prickt,
  With new made horsemen, as (if you did marke)
  I told you erst, and did all *Affrike* wast,
  Vntill three Kings resisted him at last.

19

The King of *Algazer*, and stout *Bransard*,
  Did levy powres, such as in hast they could,
  And put them all in armes without regard,
  That some too young were found and some too old;
Yea from the musters, women scant were spar'd,
  For *Agramant* (as hath before bene told)
  With hope of vaine revenge, without advise,
  Of able men, unpeopled *Affrike* twise.

20

Thus few were there, and of those few were theare,
  (So quite his countrie weale he did neglect)
  The greater part unskilfull, armes to beare,
  As was more plainly proved in effect,
For at first brunt they fled from thence for feare,
  In hope *Biserta* walls should them protect:
  Brave *Bucifer* was taken in the fight,
  Bransardo scapt, and sav'd himselfe by flight.

21

But *Bucifer* alone, he tooke more griefe,
  Then all the rest (he did him so esteeme)
  Because *Biserta* asked great reliefe,
  For which this *Bucifer* most fit did seeme,
Who was in all those parts of credit chiefe;
  Wherefore *Bransardo* faine would him redeeme,
  He many wayes doth cast, but none conclude on,
  Till at the last he did remember *Dudon*.

22

This *Dudon* was by blood and birth a *Dane*,
  But yet esteemd the *Palladins* among,
  He lately at the Bridge was prisner tane,
  Where *Rodomont* the sturdie Turke and strong,
Brought many worthy men unto their bane:
  To Affrike *Dudon* then he sent ere long,
  Now *Bransard* thinkes (nor was his thought amisse)
  Stout *Bucifer* by change to get for this.

23

He perfect notice had, by true espiall,
  The *Nubians* leader was an *English* Lord,
Who love a *Dane* (there can be no deniall)
And once were *Danes*, as writers do record:
Wherefore he sends a messenger for triall
Vnto *Astolfo*, who doth soone accord,
  To free his kinsman, whom he lov'd so dearly,
  And joyned was in blood to him so nearly.

24

Thus *Dudon* by the *English* Duke was freed,
  Who afterward his service did employ,
Now (as Saint *Iohn* had wild him to proceed)
He sought to worke the *Turks* some more annoy;
And that he might set *Provence* free with speed,
Which *Agramant* and his did then enjoy,
  He maketh of his men a new election,
  Whom he may send to free them from subjection.

25

And having chosen forth some men of these,
  As best from his huge armie might be mist,
Whose number was so great, as he at ease
With halfe of them three *Affricks* might resist:
He caus'd them to be trained for the seas,
And praying God his purpose to assist,
  That night was shew'd *Astolfo* in a vision,
  How he of ships might make a large provision.

26

Next day the weather being faire and calme,
  Astolfo walketh to the salt sea shore,
And holding in his hands in either palme,
Great store of leaves that he had tane before,
Of Bayes, of Cedar trees, of Oke, of Palme,
Into the sea he flang them in great store;
  O metamorphosis beyond all credit,
  O admirable powre divine that bred it!

27

No sooner had the water wet the leaves,
  But presently they chang'd their former hue,
The veines that were in them, each man perceaves
To grow to ribs and posts in order due,
And still at each end sharp each leafe receaves,
Ev'n of a sailing ship proportion true:
  And of the ships as many sorts there weare,
  As there were trees that those same leaves did beare.

28

A miracle it was to see them growne
  To ships and barks, with gallies, bulks and crayes,
Each vessell having tackling of their owne,
With sailes and oares to helpe at all assayes.
The Duke provided, when it once was knowne,
Both marriners and masters in few dayes,
  For with his present pay he soone allured
  From *Sard* and *Corsie* men to seas inured.

29

Those that take shipping then, were counted more
  Then six and twentie thousand strong of hand,
Great Admirall was *Dudon*, who before
Had learnd the service both of sea and land:
Now while they lay at anker nigh the shore,
To wait when wind would for their purpose stand,
  It fortuned a man of warre came by them,
  Full lode with prisners, and cast anker nie them.

30

These were those prisners whom fierce *Rodomount*,
  (As oft I have declar'd) did daily get,
When at the bridge he did them so dismount,
And sometime backward in the river set:
Here were (among some more of good account)
Brave *Brandimart* and worthy *Sansonet*,
  With *Oliver*, and some I now not tutch,
  Both *French*, *Italian*, *Gascoigne* Knights and *Dutch*.

31

The master of the barke had first assign'd,
  His prisoners at *Algier* to unlode,
But being driv'n by overblowing wind,
Farre past the place, he thought to make abode
Neare great *Biserta*, where he thinks to find
None but his countrimen within the rode;
  To which he thinks himselfe as welcome guest,
  As *Progne* is unto her chirping nest.

32

But after, when th'Imperiall bird he saw,
  Conjoyned to the *Pard* and flowre of *France*,
He was abasht, and looked pale for aw,
Much like to him that waking new, doth chance
On poisond serpent tred, and faine would draw
Himselfe from thence, for feare of more mischance;
  He quakes, and from the serpent doth retire,
  Whose poison swels, and eyes do flame like fire.

33

But now the wretched Pilot could not flie,
  And lesse could keepe the prisners he had caught,
For both himselfe, and all they by and by,
Vnto the place against his will were brought,
Whereas the Duke and *Dudon* then did lie,
Who welcom'd well the *Christens* as they ought,
  And he that brought them thither, for his paines,
  Was made a gally slave, and bound in chaines.

34

Thus were the Knights most frendly entertained,
  And greatly welcomed by *Otons* sonne,
Who horse and furniture for them ordained,
And caus'd to them great honor to be donne:
Eke *Dudon* with these Knights some days remained,
And thinks the time so spent, not lost but wonne:
  His journey purposely three dayes deferring,
  To spend the same with these brave knights conferring.

35

By their relation he doth understand,
  In what estate King *Charles* and th'empire stood,
  What are the hav'ns, where he may safely land,
  And where they thought the same would be withstood.
  Thus while discreetly on each point they scand;
  And each man told what he thought ill or good,
  There suddenly rose in the campe alarme,
  The cause unknown, but ech man cride, arme, arme.

36

The Duke *Astolfo* with his noble crew,
  That at that time conferring were together,
  Straight arm'd themselves, and out their swords they
  And went enquiring hither still and thither,   (drew
  To learne of whence this sudden tumult grew,
  But yet no cause they could suspect or gether,
  At last they saw a madman stare and stampe,
  That nak't alone did trouble all the campe.

37

Those that had seene him first belike did flout him,
  But when some few unto their cost had found,
  That with a bat he so did play about him,
  His blowes made many fall in deadly sound:
  They now began so much to dread and doubt him,
  That they had giv'n to him no little ground,
  And none of them to meet him had the harts,
  They onely shot at him, or cast some darts.

38

The noble Duke, and those with him did see,
  The wondrous force and most stupendious wracke,
  The madman wrought, and marveld much that he
  Alone could drive so many souldiers backe:
  When lo, a Ladie of no meane degree,
  Rode towards them attyred all in blacke,
  And unto *Brandimart* she came in hast,
  And claspt her arms about his necke full fast.

39

I know you know, without my further showing,
  This was the spouse of noble *Brandimart*,
  Who ever since his wofull overthrowing,
  By *Rodomont*, did with a pensive hart,
  Seeke his release, till at the last she knowing,
  (As I before did more at large impart)
  How he beyond the seas was prisner sent,
  Her selfe at *Arly* to take shipping ment.

40

But while that loving purpose she pursewth,
  Bardino met with her, an Easterne Knight,
  Who brought up *Brandimart* in tender youth,
  And kept him at a Castell (*Silvan* hight)
  He hearing at her mouth at large the truth,
  And how in *Affrica* they find him might,
  They soone agreed, no long time overslipping,
  To seeke him out and so forthwith tooke shipping.

41

No sooner they on *Affrike* shore did land,
  (*Bardino* sage, and faithfull *Fiordeliege*)
  But first the people let them understand,
  Astolfo great *Biserta* did besiege,
  With many a Captaine brave, and gallant band;
  Likewise a brute of *Brandimart* their liege
  Was spred, that he was there arived newly,
  But none was able to confirme it truly.

42

Vntill so long they traveld on the cost,
  At last she found and saw him with her eyes,
  Among those Lords, amid the *Nubian* host,
  With which such joy did in her thoughts arise,
  As vitall sprites did faile in her almost,
  Nor any word to speake could she devise,
  But hang'd about his necke a burden sweet,
  And he as lovingly his spouse did greet.

43

Full glad was he to see her, and as glad
  To see his ancient tutor and his friend,
  And further talke with them he would have had,
  But he was forst to make a speedie end,
  By meanes the man that naked ran and mad,
  Did keepe such rule as did them all offend.
  Faire *Fiordeliege* that lookt with eye more curious,
  Cride, ah my deare, this is *Orlando* furious.

44

Astolfo eke when as he did behold him,
  And saw how madly he about did range,
  And no man durst him meet, nor none could hold him,
  He wonderd greatly at the sight so strange,
  And by the marks that erst S. *Iohn* had told him,
  He knew it was the man; but such a change
  There was in all his shape, from top to toe,
  He rather seemd a beast, more then a man in show.

45

Astolfo straight did call unto the rest,
  And said my Lords, this man that you had vewd,
  Orlando is: at this themselves they blest,
  And ev'rie one his wofull pickle rewd:
  Well (said the Duke) to helpe our friend is best,
  And not to wayle; and therefore to conclude,
  Come joyne your force to mine, and let us take him
  And I do hope ere long Ile sober make him.

46

To this they soone assent, and *Brandimart*,
  With *Sansonet* and *Olivero* jolly,
  And *Dudon* clos'd him round, on ev'rie part,
  But he as full of strength, as foole of folly,
  At *Dudon* strake, and save the blow in part
  Was broke by *Oliver*, and fell not wholy
  On *Dudon*, sure I thinke that staffe accurst,
  His shield, his headpeece, head and all had burst.

47

His shield it brake, and thunderd on his scull,
 That noble *Dudon* therewithall fell backe,
But *Sansonet* strake with his sword so full,
 That of the staffe three yards he made him lacke:
Now *Brandimart* thinks backward him to pull,
 And leaps behind, a pick pack, on his backe,
And holds his armes: the Duke doth then devise,
To hold his legs, and *Oliver* his thyes.

48

Orlando shakes himselfe, and with a spring,
 Ten paces off, the *English* Duke he cast,
But *Brandimart* from him he could not fling,
 That was behind him, and did hold him fast,
But yet with *Oliver* he was to bring,
 For with his fist he smote him as he past,
That downe he fell, and hardly scaped killing,
From mouth, nose, eyes, the bloud apace distilling.

49

Of headpeece strong he never had more need,
 For sure he could not have escaped death,
Except it had a good one bene indeed.
 This while *Astolfo* now had taken breath,
And *Dudon* both who late for want of heed,
 Were by *Orlando* tumbled on the heath,
With *Sansonet*, that par'd his staffe so well,
All these at once upon *Orlando* fell.

50

Good *Dudon* that endevors him to cast,
 With *Brandimart*, about his shoulders hangs;
Astolfo and the rest his arms hold fast,
 He seeks to loose himselfe with sudden pangs:
Who so hath seene a Bull with mastives chast,
 That in his eares have fixt their cruell fangs,
How he doth runne, and rore, and with him beares
The eager doggs, that still hold fast his eares.

51

Let him imagine that *Orlando* now,
 In such sort drew the warriours on the plaine;
But *Oliver*, that had the broken brow,
 Againe on foote recoverd up againe,
Did cast within his mind a reason how,
 To do with ease, that they did seeke with paine:
He doth bethinke a way, that will not misse,
To do the feat: and his device was this.

52

Full many a halser, and full many a cord,
 With sliding knots all knit he doth provide,
And to the leggs and armes of this mad Lord,
 He made them on the sudden to be tyde,
And then their ends on each side by accord,
 They all of them amongst themselves devide,
Thus were those Princes faine to do unto him,
As Smiths do to an oxe, when they do shoe him,

53

Then fell they on him when he lay on ground,
 And then they bind him sure, both hand and foote:
Orlando when he felt himselfe thus bound,
 Doth strive in vaine, for striving will not boote.
Astolfo that doth meane to make him sound,
 And saw his skin looke blacke as any soote,
Requested them unto the shore to beare him,
Which soone was done, for now they need not feare him.

54

Then seav'n times was he washed in the place,
 And seav'n times dipped over eares and hed,
To get the scurfe from of his skin and face,
 Which with his naked going had bene bred:
Then with some herbs, the Duke gat in this space,
 He made them stop his mouth, for why he sed,
For certaine secret reasons that he knowes,
He must not fetch his breath but at his nose.

55

Then kneeling downe as if he askt some boone
 Of God, or some great Saint, that pot he brought,
Which he had carride from beyond the Moone,
 The *Iarre*, in which *Orlandos* wit was caught,
And clos'd it to his nostrills, and eftsoone,
 He drawing breath, this miracle was wrought,
The *Iarre* was void, and empty'd ev'rie whit,
And he restord unto his perfect wit.

56

As one that in some dreame or fearfull vision,
 Hath dreamt of monstrous beasts, and ugly fends
Is troubled when he wakes with superstition,
 And feareth what such ugly sight intends,
And lying wake, thinks of that apparition,
 And long time after in that fancie spends:
So now *Orlando* lay, not little musing,
At this his present state, and uncouth using.

57

He holds his peace, but lifting up his eyes,
 He sees his ancient frends King *Brandimart*,
And *Oliver*, and him that made him wise,
 All whom he knew, and loved from his hart;
He thinks, but cannot with himselfe devise,
 How he should come to play so mad a part,
He wonders he is nak't, and that he feeles
Such store of cords about his hands and heeles.

58

At last he said, as erst *Sileno* said,
 To those that tooke him napping in the cave,
Solvite me: with countenance so stayd,
 And with a cheare so sober and so grave,
That they unloosed him, as he them prayde,
 And sufferd him his liberty to have,
And clothed him, and comforted his sadnesse,
That he conceived of his former madnesse,

59

Thus being to his former wits restord,
  He was likewise delivered cleane from love;
  The Ladie whom he erst so much adord,
  And did esteeme all earthly joyes above,
  Now he despisde, yea rather quite abhord:
  Now onely he applies his wits to prove,
  That fame and former glory to recover,
  Which he had lost, the while he was a lover.

60

This while *Bardino* told to *Brandimart*,
  How that his father *Monodant* was dead,
  And how his brother *Gylyant* on the part
  Of all that those East Iles inhabited,
  Him sent of purpose these news to impart,
  And pray him (as he ought) to be their head:
  Sith all the world had not a Realme more wealthy,
  Nor any Prince could wish a seate more healthy.

61

Wherefore (saith he) deare sir, it is most meet,
  That you should now repaire to your owne home,
  For home though homely twere, yet is it sweet,
  And native soile is best: you would not rome
  About the world, did you once tast and see't,
  Thus much he said, but *Brandimart* in whome
  True love and great renown were bands more strong
  Then privat profit, answerd this ere long.

62

My brothers message, and your frendly paine
  I kindly take, but lo, my word is past,
  With *Charles* and with *Orlando* to remaine,
  And them to serve while these garboyles do last:
  Now in my steed, I will my brother raigne,
  Let him be my vice-roy, and I will hast,
  When once these warres are at a finall end,
  To come, and there my life with them to spend.

63

Thus these did part, and next ensuing day,
  Went *Dudon* with his fleet to *Provence* ward,
  Orlando with the British Prince doth stay;
  And when the state of those same warres he hard,
  Vnto *Biserta* straight a siege they lay,
  But evermore *Orlando* had regard,
  That (as *Astolfo* follow'd his advise)
  To give him th'honor of each enterprise.

64

But how they did the great *Biserta* win,
  When they assaulted it, and on which side,
  How at the first assault, the men within
  Did yeeld, and durst no longer try all byde,
  I cannot farther now proceed herein,
  But must deferre it to another tyde:
  Now I do purpose unto you to show,
  How *Agramant* receiv'd an overthrow.

65

Who was welnye abandond of his men,
  Ev'n in the very furie of the fight,
  For why *Marsilio* and *Sobrino* then
  Were gone, in minde to save themselves by flight;
  In walled townes they feard themselves to pen,
  But went to sea with all the hast they might,
  And many Princes of the *Turkish* trayne,
  The sample follow giv'n them by these twayne.

66

Yet *Agramant* did beare it out a space,
  But when he saw there was no other shift,
  Then from his enemies he turnd his face,
  To get into the towne was all his drift:
  Him *Bradamant* pursew'd a wondrous pace,
  Still spurring *Rabican*, that ran full swift,
  She wisht upon his corps to venge the wrong,
  In keeping of her deare from her so long.

67

On tother side *Marfisa* rode as fast,
  To venge though late, her fathers wofull end,
  She makes her horse to feele she is in hast,
  But each of them doth misse that they intend:
  He got within the gates and made them fast,
  And then to sea he doth himselfe commend,
  He sees he was not able to withstand,
  The forces of his enemies by land.

68

As two couragious Pards, that held in chase
  An Hart, or bearded Goat upon a plaine,
  That scaped then by swiftnesse of his pace,
  With no small wrath, and chase turne backe againe,
  As though they thought they had a great disgrace,
  In that they follow'd had the prey in vaine,
  So did the damsels chase, and sigh, and fret,
  That they to *Agramant* no neare could get.

69

But though he scap't their hands, yet sure the rest
  Escaped not, full dearely then abuying,
  Some wounded in the side, in backe, and brest,
  Some slaine outright, some worse then dead a dying,
  How sorily (poore soules) had they bene drest,
  Whose safetie was not wrought, no not by flying,
  For *Agramant*, himselfe more sure to save,
  To shut the Citie gates commandment gave.

70

He made the bridges eke to be cut downe,
  On *Rodon* streame, that was both large and deepe,
  Ah wofull subjects unto tyrants crowne,
  Who that they may their persons safely keepe,
  Regard not if their people swim or drowne,
  But deeme of them like beasts, or silly sheepe,
  That so themselves they pamper may and cherish,
  They care not if their men in millions perish.

71

Twas infinite the number that was slaine,
   In this same last conflict, nor fewer drownd,
   While they attempted despratly in vaine,
   To passe the streame, so brode and so profound;
   Of which great slaughter yet the signes remaine,
   For dayly neare to *Arlie* walls are found,
   Huge heapes of dead mens bones, and of their sculls,
   Whose flesh was then devourd by crows and gulls.

72

Now *Agramant* made speedie preparation,
   And caus'd his ships forth in the deepe to lanch,
   Providing all that longs to navigation,
   In mind for ay to bid farwell to *France*:
   Two dayes the winde stopt his determination,
   The third it serv'd, and then he did advance
   His sayles, and ev'rie one did ship his ore,
   And so away they parted from the shore.

73

Marsilio doubting least his Realme of *Spaine*,
   Should now be driv'n to pay this costly shot,
   And fearing to be forced to sustaine
   That storme alone, which fell in *France* so hot,
   Doth land at *Valence*, where he did ordaine
   All furniture, that might for warre be got,
   Repairing all his townes against that warre,
   That after him, and all his frends did marre.

74

But *Agramant*, his ships to *Affrike* bent,
   Ill arm'd, halfe void of men, but full of griefe,
   For most of them were sad and malcontent,
   Three parts of foure were lost past all reliefe:
   And though for feare perhaps, of being shent,
   None dare in publike speake to his repriefe,
   Yet secretly, their burning hate to coole,
   Some cald him proud, some cruell, some a foole.

75

But (as I say) they speake this in their sleeves,
   For feare of blame, except some two or three,
   That each to other open dare their greeves,
   Yet wretched *Agramant*, he doth not see,
   How he is scorned; but he still beleeves,
   That he is lov'd, and why, because that he,
   Saw never lookes but fawningly disguised,
   Heard never words, but fainingly devised.

76

Now he was fully purpos'd in his landing,
   To leaue *Biserta* and seeke harbour nyer,
   Because he late had perfect understanding,
   The *Nubians* spoyld those parts with sword and fier
   Wherefore for doubt of dangerous withstanding,
   He meant to shun that port, and land farre hyer,
   And thence withall unto his parts addicted,
   To bring reliefe unto the towne afflicted.

77

But loe his cruell fate doth overthrow
   His counsell sage; and quite his hope deceaves,
   For while scant winde did make him sayle but slow,
   Stout *Dudon* with that navie made of leaves,
   Met him full butt, that no such thing did know,
   And with a fierce assault him there receaves,
   Enforcing him to unexpected fight,
   In that darke, cloudie, and tempestuous night.

78

For *Agramant* no spyall had till now,
   Of these same ships, and would have deemd a fable,
   If one had told him of a little bow,
   To make a hundred ships, a man was able:
   Wherefore he sayled on he car'd not how,
   And doubts no foe but wave, and wind unstable,
   And not expecting such strange sodaine stops,
   He never set his watchmen in his tops.

79

On tother side, our men that had espyde
   Their enemies at sea, an houre ere night,
   Came with great speed, although all undeseride,
   For ev'ry ship kept close their fire and light:
   At last when as they saw their time, they tryde
   Their utmost force, and with full sayles they light
   On their foes shipping, that at first did shrinke,
   And many did unto the bottome sinke.

80

Now *Dudons* men began to play their parts,
   Some using fire, some heavie stones, some steele,
   Vpon the *Turks* fell such a storme of darts,
   As they before, the like did never feele:
   On our side God with courage fill'd their harts,
   On their side, each mans hart was in his heele,
   They stood amazd with feare, and quite astonished,
   The time now come their old sins should be punished.

81

Thus *Agramant* was clos'd on ev'rie side,
   With many a pike, and sword, and hooke, and axe,
   The stones that fell from high, made breaches wide,
   And much sea enterd at the new made cracks,
   But most the fire, which they could least abide,
   That takes in pitched boords, and wreathed flax,
   To kindle very quicke, but slow to quench,
   Annoyd them sore with heat, and smoke, and stench.

82

Some over boord do fall in water cold,
   And there are drownd: some take them to their swim-
   But on another bark while they take hold,   (ming,
   They now full fraught, and fearing overtrimming,
   With cruell sword (a foule sight to behold)
   Cut of their hands, with which they now were climing
   The bleeding stumps all mingled their remained,
   And with fresh blood, the water salt was stained.

83

Some few to save their lives that had desier,
  Or at the least, to leese them with least paine,
  Do leape in water to escape the fier,
  Till with new feare of drowning, they againe,
  Vnto the flaming shipwracks do retier,
  And there, with much ado are glad and faine,
  To catch some burning boord: and being loth
  To dye of either death, they dye of both.

84

Some one for feare of sword, or axe, or pike,
  Doth all in vaine, unto the sea betake him,
  For why some stone, or arrow, or such like,
  Ere he be farre from thence, doth overtake him:
  But least the reader haply may mislike,
  My too long tale, this motion I would make him,
  That to another season he defarre,
  To heare the sequell of this bloudy warre.

THE FORTIETH BOOKE OF
ORLANDO FVRIOSO

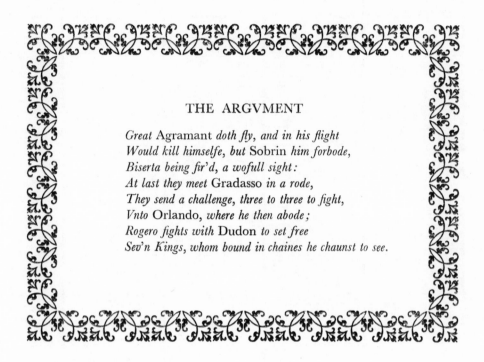

THE ARGVMENT

Great Agramant *doth fly, and in his flight*
Would kill himselfe, but Sobrin *him forbode,*
Biserta being fir'd, a wofull sight:
At last they meet Gradasso *in a rode,*
They send a challenge, three to three to fight,
Vnto Orlando, *where he then abode;*
Rogero fights with Dudon *to set free*
Sev'n Kings, whom bound in chaines he chaunst to see.

ORLANDO FVRIOSO

THE FORTIETH BOOKE

1

Twere long (my Lord) to tell of all that fought,
  In that sea fight, and certes all the while,
  That I should tell it you, I should be thought,
  To beare pots (as they say) to *Samos* Ile,
  Where earthen vessels in great store are wrought,
  Or Owles to *Athens*, Crocodils to *Nyle*,
  For more then can of this by me be told,
  Your selfe have caused many to behold.

2

Your faithfull people had a long prospect,
  When all a day upon the streame of *Poe*,
  Your men, as your great vallew did direct,
  The shipping of your foes assaulted so,
  That with their blood the streame they did infect,
  And brought upon them all, a world of woe;
  Then both your selfe, and others plaine did see,
  How sundry deaths, in fights of sea there be.

3

It was not then indeed, my hap to see't,
  (Sent then to *Rome* six dayes before in post,
  To crave then, at the holy fathers feet,
  Reliefe and aid against so great an host)
  And in that time your grace with them did meet,
  In such a sort, so sorely to their cost,
  And so you par'd the Lyons teeth and pawes,
  That since that time to feare we had no cause.

4

But *Alfonsin*, and *Moore* that saw the same,
  Affranio, *Anniball*, and *Zerbinet*,
  Albert, and *Baygn*, and three that beare my name,
  Declar'd to me the conquest you did get:
  Also their banners, monuments of fame,
  Which offerd in the Churches you did set,
  With fifteene Gallies tane a thousand botes,
  Of that rich conquest, give us open notes.

5

He that had seene the fire and wondrous wreake,
  That at that time was wrought upon your foes,
  When for your few, their many were too weake,
  He might describe the deaths and divers woes,
  Of *Agramantes* host, of which I speake,
  And of their great and grievous overthrowes,
  Then when amids the surging waves and salt,
  Stout *Dudon* in the night did them assault.

6

When first the fight began, the night was darke,
  But when the flame upon the pitch tooke hold,
  The fire gave light, and did so clearly sparke,
  That *Agramant* might plainly now behold
  His enemies, and their great number marke,
  Incredible, if any had it told:
  Wherefore in season to prevent the worst,
  He chang'd the course he had intended furst.

7

And chusing out a vessell swift of sayle,
  And placing there his things of greatest price,
  With *Brigliadore* (sith all hope now doth fayle)
  To steale from thence he closlie doth devise:
  And while that *Dudon* doth his men assayle,
  In all the hast he can, away he flyes,
  His men the sword, the sea, the fire destroyes,
  And he is fled that caused their annoyes.

8

And in that Barke, with him *Sobrino* fled,
  Who much complain'd and was not little greeved,
  That that which he before so truly sed,
  Yet then by *Agramant* was not beleeved:
  But tell we now how good *Astolfo* sped,
  And what exploits *Orlando* had atcheeved,
  Who counseld so to raze *Biserta* towne,
  That it might never noy th'Imperiall crowne.

9

And so it was in publicke sort proclaym'd,
  That the third day th'assault they should expect,
  Astolfo had some ships before ordayn'd,
  (For *Dudon* had not all) for this effect,
  And these same ships with *Sansonet* remayn'd,
  A man that could by sea and land direct,
  Who rode at anker neere *Biserta* shore,
  But distant from the hav'n a myle and more.

10

The *Brittish* Duke, and valiant *Palladine*,
  That like good Christens used evermore,
  To pray to God for grace and aide divine,
  Proclaimed in the campe, three dayes before,
  That to assault the towne they did assigne,
  By fast and publike prayre, *Christ* to adore,
  And crave his aid against that wicked towne,
  That they might raze it quite and beat it downe.

11

And having ended that their solemne fast,
  And made their vowes, accustom'd in such case,
  Then frendly they together take repast,
  And each his frend, and parent doth embrace,
  And spake as if those words should be their last,
  The kindly tears, oft trickling downe their face,
  And ev'rie one resolved by and by,
  Either to win the towne, or in the place to dy.

12

Also the wretched Priests within the towne,
  With fayned show of foolish superstition,
  Pray unto *Macon*, that he do not frowne
  On them: and vow to him on that condition,
  Great Holocausts, with cost of many a crowne,
  Of him they seeke to have their sinnes remission,
  And as if he the fates could mend or alter,
  They offer sacrifices on his alter.

13

Then when they were by their great Cady blest,
  They went (but faintly) to their Citie wall,
  Yet did the fayre *Aurora* take her rest,
  And scarce the Esterne coast yet looked pale,
  When *Sansonet, Astolfo*, and the rest,
  That had the needfull things provided all,
  The noble enterprise did take in hand,
  And did assault the towne by sea and land.

14

Biserta hath this manner situation,
  Two parts thereof with water are enclosed,
  Two parts with goodly wall of ancient fashion,
  But not so strong, as one would have supposed:
  And though to make new strength and reparation,
  The King *Bransardo* all the towne disposed,
  His time and warning were so short and small,
  He could do little good, or none at all.

15

Astolfo did appoint the *Nubian* King
  Such wise to noy the keepers of the wall,
  With darts, and Turkish bowes, and many a sling,
  That from the battlements he drave them all,
  That now he might both horse and footmen bring,
  Vpon the ditch in perill none or small;
  And each according to his powre and skill,
  Brought matter wherewithall the ditch to fill.

16

Some fagots brought, and some brought store of helme,
  Some heavy stones, and some light planks and boords,
  And lest the streame their worke might overwhelme,
  They turned it away by other foords;
  Great store of wood there grew in that same Realme
  The which to them great store of stuffe affoords,
  And now that Proverbe see performd you might,
  That many hands make heavie works but light.

17

The *Nubians* fierce impatient of all stay,
  And by desire of gaine all headlong led,
  The perill great and danger do not way,
  But each man clapps his target on his hed:
  And then their battrie to the walls they lay,
  With rammes, and engines strongly furnished,
  With which to shake the walls they do begin,
  Nor were they all unfurnished within.

18

Darts, stones, and planks, yea ev'n their houses tyle,
  They flang down on thē, whē they drew more neare
  By which they brake and pierced otherwhile,
  Their engines huge, so as it might appeare,
  Dame Fortune seem'd at first on *Turks* to smile,
  But after soone againe she chang'd her cheare,
  No sooner night was gone, and Sun once up,
  But that they tasted of another cup.

19

Then on each side they had so hot a charge,
  As hardly they were able to sustaine:
  Sansonet of the shipping had the charge,
  And he by sea assaults them to their paine;
  And, for their powre was great, and place was large,
  Each Captaine tooke with him a severall traine,
  Thereby the more to trouble all their foes,
  And of their vertue, to make larger shoes.

20

And for that speciall cause, they do divide,
  Their mightie host into foure sev'rall parts,
  To th'end that by that meanes it might be spide,
  Which men had stout, and which had fainting harts,
  Great towres on mighty wheeles did seeme to ride,
  Drawne with great force like ordinary carts,
  And Elephants did carrie towres so tall,
  As did in height surpasse the Citie wall.

21

A scaling ladder *Brandimart* doth beare,
  And clymes himselfe and causeth others clyme:
  For what man having such a guide, could feare?
  Each man to stay doth thinke it haynous crime:
  The ladders strength was weigh'd by no man there,
  Each roung a man, and some beares two sometime:
  Now *Brandimart* to conquest wholy bent,
  Gets to the top, and winnes a battlement.

22

With hand and foote he clammerd in such sort,
  He wan a batlement and did it keepe,
  Then with his sword he made them all such sport,
  As caus'd the lookers on, not laugh, but weepe:
  The ladder now charg'd with too great resort,
  Standing aslope, and not upright and steepe,
  Brake in the midst, so that save *Brandimart*,
  All of them fell, unto their paine and smart.

23

Their Captaine though, with this no whit dismayd,
  Keepes still his place though he the hap did marke,
Although he saw his men him could not ayd,
  Though he alone were all their shooting marke;
His men below cryde out to him, and prayd
  Him to retire, but he no whit could harke;
But boldly from the wall into the towne,
Which was thrise ten foote deepe, he leaped downe.

24

As if the pav'ment had bene straw, not stone,
  So lept he downe, so nimble and so light,
And being there, layd so about alone,
  He made them all give place unto his might:
Of those that fought he killed many a one,
  The rest thought best to save themselves by flight,
But they that saw him leape downe from without,
Within their minds were full of dread and doubt.

25

Straightwayes about the campe a rumor spred,
  From mouth to mouth, and man to man doth come,
And same doth fly, and flying gathers hed,
  Of that hard feat, that *Brandimart* had done;
And comes at last whereas *Orlando* led
  His band, and after to King *Otons* sonne,
And then to *Olivero*, never ceasing,
But in her going still her tale increasing.

26

All these but chiefe *Orlando* all among,
  That *Brandimart* in minde did dearely love,
And hearing it from thence they tarrid long,
  It would be hard his danger to remove;
Vnto the walls set scaling ladders strong,
  Resolved now their utmost force to prove;
And up they mount, with looks so grim and bold,
As scant their enemies durst them behold.

27

As when the seas are wrought with sturdie wind,
  The ventrous vessell tost with many a wave,
Is sometime smote before, sometime behind,
  And each surge strives a passage free to haue;
The fearfull Pilot with astonisht minde,
  Knowes not which way himselfe he should behave,
Till at the last one surge the whole possesseth,
And so both Pilot, ship, and all oppresseth.

28

So when those three, of whom before I spake,
  Had got the wall, they did the souldiers teach,
To follow them, and so large path did make,
  As thousands of them now the wall did reach:
This while the monstrous rammes the walls did shake
  In other places, and made such a breach,
That now in many parts without resistance,
They might to *Brandimart* bring good assistance.

29

Looke how that streame surnam'd of streams the king,
  With damage great above his bankes doth grow,
When some strong wind or tyde of highest spring,
  Makes him beyond accustom'd bounds to flow,
And thereby hurt unto the fields doth bring,
  And drowneth flockes, and houses overthrow,
Then trees do harbour fish, as new come guests,
Where flying birds were wont to build their nests.

30

So now *Biserta* walls were farre too weake,
  To save the Citie from both sword and fire;
The valiant Captaines first the Ice do breake,
  To follow whom, the souldiers do aspire;
And what with will their ancient wrongs to wreake,
  And what with hope of booties, and desire,
They ruind soone that Citie, that had beene
Of *Affrica*, the sole triumphant Queene.

31

Now multitudes lay slaine in ev'ry street,
  And with the bloud that of their wounds did runne,
The channels flow'd vermillion under feet;
  But when the fire to take had once begunne,
No doubt it was a wofull sight to seet,
  What spoile upon the towne by fire was done:
Such cryes, such plaints were over all the Citie,
As might have moved any hearts to pitie.

32

Their helples Gods now under foot were troden,
  Their sacred jewels taken all for pray,
The conquerers come forth of houses, loden,
  With gold, with plate, with faire and rich aray;
And though the souldiers flatly were forboden
  Foule beastly lust, this was to them no stay,
Young children and old matrones could not scape,
Deflouring forced, not ungodly rape.

33

Stout *Olivero* with a sound blow slew,
  King *Bucifer*, and brought him to his end,
Bransardo kild himselfe, when as he knew,
  The Citie could not now it selfe defend;
Astolfo did in single fight subdew
  Fulvo, and tooke him prisner in the end:
These three were those, whom (as before you hard)
King *Agramant* those countryes left to guard.

34

But *Agramant*, who as before I told,
  Stole from his men, and so away did sayle,
When as he did these flames from farre behold,
  Much did the state of that same towne bewaile;
But when a messenger did plaine unfold,
  How farre his foes in *Affricke* did prevaile,
He would have slaine himselfe, of woes to rid him,
Save that the sage *Sobrino* did forbid him.

35

Ah sir said he (in frendly sort him chiding)
 Drive from your worthy minde such wretched thought,
What could be to your foes more welcome tiding,
 Then that your selfe, your owne destruction sought?
They doubt, while you in safetie are abiding,
 But hard to keepe, that they have easlie caught;
Not one of them but dreads, and greatly feares,
That *Affricke* while you live, cannot be theirs.

36

Your death would all your frends of hope deprive,
 (The onely helpe that in our case is left)
All they have got, while you remaine alive,
 They can but count it robberie and theft:
But if you die, who shall against them strive?
 Both *Affricke* lost, and we of hope are reft:
Wherefore though for your selfe you life abhord,
Live for our sake (at least) my soveraigne Lord.

37

The Souldan sure will helpe your cause t'advance,
 To him you may for men and money send,
Be sure he will be loth the King of *France*
 Should nest in *Affricke*, being not his frend:
If *Norandino* knew of your mischance,
 He would both men, and horse, and monie send,
The states of *Media*, *Persia*, and *Armenie*,
With *Arabia*, will helpe you with their menie.

38

These words then spake the grave wise man and old,
 To move his Prince a better minde to carrie,
And bad him cheare himselfe, and still he told,
 What hopes there were (tho sure he thought cõtrary)
He saw and knew their comfort was but cold,
 That long they use to pray, and sue, and tarie,
Who having lost their crownes, to sue are faine
To other Kings, to helpe them home againe.

39

Both *Hanniball* and *Iugurth* samples be,
 To Princes all, that trust in forren ayd,
With *Lodwicke Sforce* whom this last age did see,
 Vnto a stronger *Lodwicke* foule betraid:
Wherefore vnto that sentence I agree,
 The Duke *Alfonso* of *Ferrara* said,
A greater signe of folly is not showne,
Then trusting others force, distrust ones owne.

40

Wherefore in that conflict and bitter warre,
 In which he found Christs Vicar not his frend,
And that the Venice state with him did jarre,
 And he that promised him to defend,
From *Italie* was driv'n and absent farre,
 Yet never would *Alfonso* condiscend,
To put himselfe in other mens subjection,
And leave his state to forren powres protection.

41

But *Agramant* of comfort all bereft,
 Forsooke the shore, and lanched to the deepe,
To thinke in what estate his Realme was left,
 Does make him bitterly to wayle and weepe,
From right hand now they sayld vnto the left,
 And Eastward all the night their course did keepe,
Vntill a storme that rose within a while,
Did cause them harbour in a little Ile.

42

A little Ile voyde of inhabitants,
 But full of Hares, and Conies, and of Deare,
With coverts great, of trees and slender plants,
 That had not bene cut downe in many a yeare:
Else there was nothing to supply their wants,
 Onely some tokens plainly did appeare,
That fishers used there their nets to drye,
The while the fish in sea do quiet lye.

43

Here onely in the harbour they did find,
 A ship that had bene weatherbeaten sore,
Gradasso forced by contrary wind,
 Came in that ship from *Arly* late before,
With princely gesture, and behaviour kind,
 Each King salutes the tother on the shore;
For well they lov'd together, and were late,
Fellows in arms neare *Paris* walles and gate.

44

The King of *Sericane* with no small griefe,
 Did heare the storie of their late distresse,
And which did comfort *Agramante* chiefe,
 His person offerd these harms to redresse,
But that he shall in *Ægypt* finde reliefe,
 He greatly doubts, and thinketh nothing lesse,
Pompeys example teacheth you (he said)
That banisht men finde there but sorie aid.

45

But sith the case so stands, and that you say,
 English *Astolfo* with a *Nubian* host,
And mad *Orlando*, who this other day,
 As I did heare, for love his wit had lost,
Have done such hurt, I have bethought a way,
 That at this time I thinke will profite most:
I will *Orlando* challenge hand to hand,
Who (sure I am) in my hands cannot stand.

46

Were he once dead, the rest I count as straw,
 And for the *Nubians*, though I cannot dreame
How they should come, yet know I how to draw
 Them backe againe from yours, to their own Reame
Those other *Nubians*, whom a divers law
 Sunders from these, as well as *Nylus* streame,
Shall with *Arabian* and *Macrobian* forces
Assaile them, (these have gold, & those good horses).

47

The King of *Affricke* prais'd this offer kind,
  And called it a good and blessed storme,
  That caus'd him such a frend as this to find,
  And thanks him for his offer: but the forme
  Of it (he said) doth no whit please my mind,
  No though thereby I might all harmes reforme,
  And that I might *Biserta* towne regaine,
  I would not do mine honor such a staine.

48

If any man must challenge him, then I
  It is, that am in honor tide unto it,
  And whether I shall kill or else shall die,
  I am resolved, surely I will do it
  Nay then sir (said *Gradasso*) I will trie
  Another way, if you assent but to it,
  We two will make one challenge thus: to fight
  Against *Orlando* and some other Knight.

49

So I be one (then *Agramant* replide)
  I care not, though I second be or furst,
  For in the world is not a man beside,
  To trust whose courage more then yours, I durst.
  Sobrino that stood all the while aside,
  Into such speech, upon the sudden burst,
  Hath age (quoth he) brought me in such contempt,
  To be excluded from so brave attempt?

50

Disgrace me not so much, to leave out me,
  Age hath not tane away my vigor cleene,
  Skill and experience good companions be,
  Age knoweth whatsoever youth hath beene;
  Wherefore let me be one, and you shall see,
  That I am stronger, then perhaps you weene:
  To this request of his they soone agree,
  And so they send their challenge three to three.

51

They send a Herald, as it is the use,
  The challeng to *Orlando* stout to beare,
  With number like to meet at *Lippaduse*,
  And so by combat, end all matters theare:
  The while each side should grant the other truse,
  And all acts of hostilitie forbeare;
  This *Lippadusa* is a little Ile,
  Distant from *Affricke* shore some twentie mile.

52

The Herald made good hast, and went apace,
  And us'd all helpe of oares and sailes he could,
  And comming to *Orlando* with good grace,
  His message and the challenge plaine he told:
  Amids *Biserta* in the market place,
  He found him parting summes of coyne and gold,
  (Of that same sacked towne the many spoiles)
  Vnto his men for guerdon of their toiles.

53

Now when *Orlando* this brave challenge hard,
  He did accept it, and did much rejoyce,
  And gave unto the Herald in reward,
  Of many sumptuous gifts great store and choise;
  He knew before the death of *Mandricard*,
  And heard of *Durindan* by common voice,
  How that *Gradasso* had it, whom to find,
  A voiage unto th'*Indies* he assign'd.

54

But knowing that he need not go so farre,
  And that his great good fortune so had wrought,
  That he should send to offer single warre,
  Whom he farre of had purpos'd to have sought;
  He now doth hope that long they should not barre
  Him of his sword, that he so deare had bought,
  Eke *Brigliadore* he hopes now to regaine,
  That did in *Agramantes* hands remaine.

55

He chuseth for his frends to take his part,
  In this so great and dangerous a fray,
  His cousin, and that faithfull *Brandimart*,
  Both whom he oft saw tride before that day;
  Armours and horse, and swords on ev'ry part,
  He seekes to get for them the best he may,
  For none of them had armour of his owne;
  As I before this time have made it knowne.

56

Orlando when he first of all fell mad,
  Lost both his sword and armour that same howre,
  The tothers twaine, the *Sarzan* taken had,
  And now they were safe lockt up in a towre:
  In *Affrica* their armour was but bad,
  The warres in *France* did dayly theirs devowre:
  They seldome had in those parts any store,
  And *Agramant* what was, had had before.

57

Such as he could, though it were old and rustie,
  He caused to be scowrd and furbusht new,
  And ev'rie day with his companions trustie,
  He talked of the fight that should ensew.
  One day, as in a morning fresh and lustie,
  They walkt upon the shore, they saw in vew
  A great ship under saile with treble top,
  Saile to the shore, without all stay or stop.

58

No saylers, passengers, nor anie guide,
  Within the ship to be discoverd were,
  But as the tempest drave her and the tide,
  She came, and safely so arived there:
  But here a while the emptie ship shall bide,
  And these three Knights, because the love I beare
  Vnto *Rogero* and *Renaldo* both,
  To overpasse them longer makes me loth.

59

You heard how they themselves aside did draw,
  And of their owne accords their combat cease,
  When as they saw, against all right and law,
  On either side the battell to increase:
  They were so earnest, neither of them saw
  Which side was first, that brake their vowed peace:
  Wherefore they aske of those that neare them came,
  Which King of this foule breach should have the blame.

60

Rogero had a valiant trustie man,
  That served him with faithfulnesse and care,
  Who never since the combat first began,
  Had lost the sight of him, and being ware
  Of this new breach, with all the speed he can,
  He did his masters sword and horse prepare,
  And brought it him, and wished him to use it,
  But for that day *Rogero* did refuse it.

61

Howbe't from thence he did his course direct,
  And promise with *Renaldo* doth renew,
  That if his King were first did oath neglect,
  And shew'd himselfe in promise so untrue,
  That he would leave him and his wicked sect;
  This said, he bad *Renaldo* then adew,
  Demanding all he met, who was in fault,
  Of this ungodly and unjust assault.

62

Of all the world he heares it plainly spoken,
  How that of youthfull *Agramantes* part,
  The law of armes, and late sworne truce was broken
  Which now was turnd unto his losse and smart:
  Yet thinks he, men would deeme it were a token
  In him of faint or of unfaithfull hart,
  To leave his Master in so great distresse,
  Although his falshood had deserv'd no lesse.

63

The thought thereof drave him to no small muse,
  If better twere for him to goe or tarrie,
  If he do go, he much shall her abuse
  Whom he so oft had promised to marrie;
  Againe he thinketh that he cannot chuse;
  In his returne to *Affricke* but miscarie,
  He knowes how perjurie offendeth God,
  How over it ay hangs a heavie rod.

64

On tother side, he feares the great disgrace,
  Men would impute to him his Lord to leave,
  And thinke it comes of fearfull heart and base:
  What if some men perhaps his scuse receave,
  When they do know, and understand the case?
  Yet most will say, he doth his Lord deceave:
  And that a man such promise may forsake,
  As at the first, unlawfull was to make.

65

All that same day, and all that night ensuing,
  He did the matter with himselfe debate,
  His love, his Lord, on either side renewing
  The doubtfull question, each in divers rate:
  But noble minde, the greater shame eschewing,
  Chose lastly to releeve his masters state,
  Much lov'd he *Bradamant*, much thought he on her,
  But more he lov'd his duty and his honer.

66

Wherefore resolved to depart the Reame,
  He sought at *Arly*, ships him to transport,
  But neither at the sea, nor in the streame,
  Could he there find a ship of any sort,
  For *Agramant* in hast and feare extreame,
  Had all from thence, or burnd them in the port,
  Which when *Rogero* once did understand,
  He went unto *Marsilia*-ward by land.

67

In *Arly*, nor from *Arly* all the way,
  He saw no living *Turke*, but many a corse,
  He mindeth at *Marsilia*, if he may,
  To get a ship, by faire meanes or by force,
  That into *Affrica* shall straight convay
  Him and *Frontino*, his well tried horse:
  But while such thoughts he in his mind contrived,
  Great *Dudon* with his navie there arrived.

68

That *Dudon*, whom King *Agramant* on seas
  Met to his cost, when erst his men were slaine:
  He fled, his frends tane prisners, and in thease
  Seaven Kings that erst in *Affrica* did raigne;
  A man as then, might hardly cast a pease
  Into that streame, or any little graine,
  The Navie, and the prises, in such number,
  Did so the river pester up, and cumber.

69

But *Dudon* selfe was newly come on land,
  And his chiefe prisners he had set on shore,
  And as in way of triumph made them stand,
  The chiefe behind, the meaner set before,
  With souldiers garded of his choisest band,
  Who with their warlike voices evermore,
  Made that same towne, and all the places round,
  Of *Dudons* praise, and *Dudons* name to sound.

70

Rogero when he saw these bands appeare,
  First thought it was the fleet of *Agramant*,
  But when as he approched now more neare,
  He saw how much his guesse of truth did want;
  He sees his captive frends, with heavie cheare,
  Bambyrage, Agricalt, and *Ferurant,*
  Balastro, Rimedont, and *Manilard,*
  And *Nasamon,* that wayle their hap so hard,

71

Rogero could by no meanes it endure,
To see in misery his noble frends,
He doubts his prayre no succour can procure,
And therefore he to trie his force intends:
His lance he presently doth put in ure,
With which not few unto the ground he sends;
His sword he drawes, and therewith in short space,
He doth an hundred hurt, kill, maime, displace.

72

Now *Dudon* heares the noise, the harme doth see,
Done by *Rogero*, yet to him unknowne,
He sees his men displac't and foyled be,
And by one onely man their hurt is growne:
He takes his horse, and to that end that he
May venge these harms, or joyne thereto his owne,
He setteth in his rest, a mightie lance,
To prove himselfe a *Palladine* of *France*.

73

He bids his men in order to retire,
That of the field they two may have good scope:
Rogero, that to rescue did desire
His frends, and now had put them in some hope:
And seeing vertuous *Dudon* did aspire,
In combat hand to hand with him to cope,
Did deeme he was the Captaine chiefe and guide,
And with great courage toward him did ride.

74

First *Dudon* came, but when he nearer came,
And saw *Rogero* had no speare in sight,
He cast away his owne, as counting shame
To use advantages in any fight.
Then saith *Rogero* to himselfe, this same
Is token of a most brave minded Knight;
And sure, except mine aime be much amisse,
One of the *Palladines* of *France* he is.

75

Wherefore he minds, ere any more ensew,
Or any force of either part were donne,
To learne his name: and asking him, he knew
How that he was the Dane *Vggeros* sonne;
Now (saith good *Dudon*) let me know of you
Your name, before our combat be begonne:
Rogero in like sort him satisfied,
And so they both each other then defied.

76

Now *Dudon* had that Axe or iron Mace,
Wherewith he wonne such fame in many fights,
As proved him to be of that same race
Of *Palladines*, so brave and worthie Knights:
Rogero hath the sword that cuts apace,
And frustrateth all charms, where ere it lights,
So that he had the vantage, had he us'd it,
But for that time, it seemed he refus'd it.

77

The cause was this, he was afeard perchance,
It would offend his loving *Bradamant*,
For being skilfull in the lines of *France*,
He knew that *Dudons* mother was her Ant:
So though his conquest might his name advance,
He doubts her love it may not little daunt:
For *Turpin* thinks, this was the onely reason,
That *Dudon* scaped killing at that season.

78

Rogero never foynd, and seldome strake,
But flatling, and his sword was so good steele,
The backe so thicke, as it no hurt did take,
Yet oft therewith he made good *Dudon* feele
Such thundring knocks, as caus'd his head to ake,
And made him readie many times to reele,
But least much reading may annoy your eyes,
To lay this booke aside I you advise.

THE FORTY-FIRST BOOKE OF
ORLANDO FVRIOSO

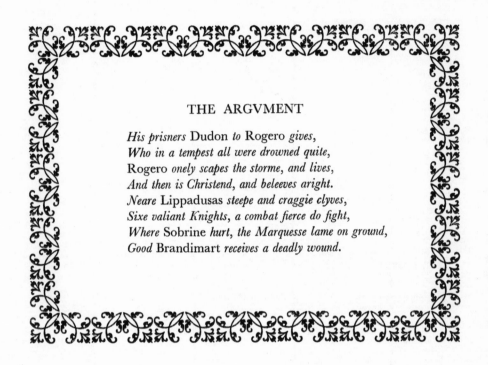

THE ARGVMENT

His prisners Dudon *to* Rogero *gives,*
Who in a tempest all were drowned quite,
Rogero *onely scapes the storme, and lives,*
And then is Christend, and beleeves aright.
Neare Lippadusas *steepe and craggie clyves,*
Six valiant Knights, a combat fierce do fight,
Where Sobrine *hurt, the Marquesse lame on ground,*
Good Brandimart *receives a deadly wound.*

ORLANDO FVRIOSO
THE FORTY-FIRST BOOKE

1

That odor sweet wherewith an amorous youth
 Of either sexe, their garments do perfume,
 Or head or beard, when (full of loving ruth)
 In flames of *Cupids* fire they co consume:
 We say that odor perfect was in truth.
 And of his goodnesse we do much presume,
 If so a good while after it be felt,
 And that the sweetnesse be long after smelt.

2

That pleasant juyce that *Icarus* unwise,
 Did cause his men (to his great harme) to tast,
 And did the *Gauls* to *Italie* entise,
 Where they committed so great spoile and wast,
 Was doubtlesse perfect good, and of great price,
 If so at twelvemonths end it pleasant last.
 The tree that doth his leaves in winter nourish,
 Without all question did in sommer florish.

3

The bountie that so many hundred yeare,
 In your most Princely stocke did ever shine,
 Is to the world an open proofe and cleare,
 That he, from whom was first deriv'd your line,
 Was sure a great, and worthie minded Peare,
 And had that noble vertue and divine,
 Which chiefly makes a man so rare and od,
 As in that one, they most resemble God.

4

I shew'd you in the booke that went before,
 How good *Rogero* tooke great care and heed,
 That as in other acts he shew'd great store
 Of vertues rare, that other men exceed,
 So in this fight he shewd as much or more,
 Then he had done in any other deed:
 With noble mind ambitious to all good,
 For glory thirsting still, but not for blood.

5

Good *Dudon* found (for well discerne he might)
 How that *Rogero* him to hurt forbare,
 How though he had great vantage in the fight,
 Yet that to use the same he still did spare;
 Wherefore though he were overmatcht in might,
 Yet therewithall he shew'd his speciall care,
 That though *Rogero* were in force superiour,
 Himselfe in courtsie would not be inferiour.

6

Perdie sir let (saith he) our combat cease,
 Your courtsie hath alreadie conquerd me,
 I cannot winne, and therefore seeke I peace;
 And I (saith tother) will to peace agree:
 I onely crave this grace, that you release
 Those seav'n, whom standing there in bonds I see,
 Those were the Kings, whom late near *Affrike* shore
 Had taken bene a day or two before.

7

At his request thus *Dudon* gave remission,
 But ere they went, he made them first to sweare,
 That neither they, nor none by their permission,
 Gainst any Christen state, should armour beare;
 He gave them also leave on like condition,
 To take the choisest vessell that was theare,
 Who no convenient season overslipping,
 For *Affrica* immediately tooke shipping.

8

Thus had those kings their ransomes all remitted,
 And with *Rogero* shipt themselves that day,
 And then to faithlesse winds themselves committed,
 They weigh their ankers, and their sailes display:
 A friendly gale at first their journey fitted,
 And bare them from the shore full far away:
 But afterward within a little season,
 The wind discoverd his deceit and treason.

9

First from the poop, it changed to the side,
 Then to the prore, at last it turned round,
 In one place long it never would abide,
 Which doth the Pilots wit and skill confound:
 The surging waves swell still in higher pride,
 While *Proteus* flock did more and more abound,
 And seem to him as many deaths to threaten,
 As that ships sides with divers waves are beaten.

10

Now in their face the wind, straight in their back,
 And forward this, and backward that it blowes,
 Then on the side it makes the ship to crack,
 Among the Mariners confusion growes;
 The Master ruine doubts, and present wrack,
 For none his will, nor none his meaning knowes,
 To whistle, becken, crie it nought availes,
 Somtime to strike, somtime to turn their sailes.

11

But none there was could heare, nor see, nor mark,
  Their eares so stopt, so dazeld were their eyes,
  With weather so tempestuous and so dark,
  And black thick clouds that with the storme did rise,
  From whence somtime great gastly flames did spark,
  And thunderclaps that seem'd to rend the skies:
  Which made them in a manner deaf and blind,
  That no man understood the Masters mind.

12

Nor lesse, nor much lesse fearfull is the sound
  The cruell tempest in the tackle makes,
  Yet each one for himselfe some businesse found,
  And to some speciall office him betakes:
  One this unti'd, another that hath bound,
  He the Main bowling, now restraines, now slakes:
  Some take an oare, some at the pump take paine,
  And powre the sea into the sea againe.

13

Behold a horrible and hideous blast,
  That *Boreas* from his frozen lips doth send,
  Doth backward force the saile against the mast,
  And makes the waves unto the skies ascend:
  Then brake their oares and rudder eke at last,
  Now nothing left from tempest to defend,
  So that the ship was swaid now quite aside,
  And to the waves laid ope her naked side.

14

Then all aside the staggring ship did reel,
  For one side quite beneath the water lay,
  And on the tother side the very keel,
  Above the water cleare discern you may.
  Then thought they all hope past, & down they kneel,
  And unto God to take their soules they pray,
  Worse danger grew then this, when this was past,
  By means the ship gan after leak so fast.

15

The wind, the waves to them no respite gave,
  But ready ev'ry houre to overthrow them,
  Oft they were hoist so high upon the wave,
  They thought the middle region was below them,
  Oft times so low the same their vessell drave,
  As though that *Caron* there his boat would show thē
  Scant had they time and power to fetch their breath,
  All things did threaten them so present death.

16

Thus all that night they could have no release,
  But when the morning somwhat nearer drew,
  And that by course the furious wind should cease,
  (A strange mishap) the wind then fiercer grew,
  And while their troubles more and more increase,
  Behold a rock stood plainly in their view,
  And right upon the same the spitefull blast
  Bare them perforce, which made them all agast.

17

Yet did the master by all means assay
  To steare out roomer, or to keep aloof,
  Or at the least to strike sailes if they may,
  As in such danger was for their behoof.
  But now the wind did beare so great a sway,
  His enterprizes had but little proof:
  At last with striving yard and all was torn,
  And part thereof into the sea was born.

18

Then each man saw all hope of safety past,
  No means there was the vessell to direct,
  No help there was, but all away are cast,
  Wherefore their common safety they neglect,
  But out they get the ship-boat, and in hast
  Each man therein his life strives to protect,
  Of King, nor Prince no man takes heed nor note,
  But well was he could get him in the boat.

19

Among the rest, *Rogero* doth suppose
  The safest way to be, to leave the ship,
  And being in his dublet and his hose,
  He nimbly down into the boat did skip,
  But after him so great a number goes,
  Before they could the rope unwind or slip,
  The boat at length did sink with over-lading,
  And to the bottome cari'd all her lading.

20

'Twas lamentable then to heare the cries,
  Of companies of ev'ry sort confus'd,
  In vaine to heav'n they lift their hands and eyes,
  And make late vowes, as in such case is us'd,
  For over them the wrathfull sea doth rise,
  As though to give them eare it had refus'd,
  And made them hold their peace by hard constraint,
  And stopt the passage whence came out the plaint.

21

Some swam a while, some to the bottome sank,
  Some flote upon the wave, though being dead,
  Rogero for the matter neuer shranke,
  But stil aboue the water keeps his head,
  And not farre off he sees that rockie banke,
  From which in vaine he and his fellowes fled:
  He thither laboureth to get with swimming,
  In hope to get vpon the same by climing.

22

With legs and armes he doth him so behave,
  That still he kept upon the floods aloft,
  He blowes out from his face the boistrous wave
  That ready was to overwhelm him oft.
  This while the wind aloof the vessell drave,
  Which huld away with pace but slow and soft,
  Frō those, that while they thought their deth to shun
  Now di'd perhaps before their glasse was run.

23

O hopes of men uncertaine, vaine and fraile,
  The ship that all forsook, as quite forlorn,
  When all her wonted guides and helps did faile,
  Her sailers drownd, and all her tackle torn,
  A safe course held with broken mast and saile,
  And by an Eddie from the rock was born,
  And ev'n as if the storm had chang'd his mind,
  It went with merry gale afore the wind.

24

And where with mariners it went awry,
  Now wanting them it went to *Affricke* right,
  And came on land unto *Biserta* ny,
  And gently on the sands it did alight,
  What time *Orlando* then was walking by,
  Conferring with his fellowes of their fight,
  The which was undertaken by them three,
  Against three Princes of no mean degree.

25

And for they saw the ship was fast on ground,
  They took a boat, and went on her aboord,
  With mind to question whither she was bound,
  Or what good merchandise she can affoord;
  But under hatches lading none they found,
  Save good *Rogeros* armour, horse, and sword,
  Which he behind him left, when in bad taking,
  He took the boat, the ship itself forsaking.

26

Orlando view'd them well with good regard,
  And having chiefly mark'd the noble blade,
  He knew it was that famous *Ballisard*,
  With which he did some yeares before invade
  Fallarius garden, spite of all her guard,
  Who by strong charms, the sword and garden made,
  It may be you ere this have heard the tale,
  And how this sword from him *Brunello* stale.

27

And after to the good *Rogero* gave it,
  Who late had left it in this wofull wrack,
  Glad was *Orlando* now againe to have it,
  That oft had triall both of edge and back;
  He deem'd that God did ev'n of purpose save it,
  Now to supply therewith his present lack:
  And after oft he said, and thought indeed,
  That God did send it him at so great need.

28

At so great need, when as he was to fight,
  Against *Gradasso* king of *Sericane*,
  Who had, beside his great and passing might,
  Renaldos horse, and fearfull *Durindane*.
  Rogeros armour though it looked bright,
  Yet was it not as thing so precious tane,
  As being priz'd more for the sumptuous show,
  Then for the goodnesse, which they did not know.

29

And sith himselfe for armour did not care,
  And never did the dint of weapon feare,
  He doth that armour to his cosin spare,
  But not the sword, for that himself doth weare:
  The horse that was of shape and goodnesse rare,
  Had *Brandimart*, and thus divided were,
  Among these three, in guerdon of their paines,
  An equall share and portion in the gaines.

30

Now each prepar'd against the day of fight
  Brave furniture, with cost of many a crown:
  Orlando on his quarter, bare in sight,
  High Babels tower with lightning stricken down,
  His cosin had a Lyme hound argent bright,
  His Lyme laid on his back, he couching down,
  The word or mot was this, *untill he commeth*,
  The rest was rich, and such as him becommeth.

31

But *Brandimart*, who as I erst made mention,
  Had heard his fathers death, went all in black:
  Of braveries he now had no intention,
  Lest men might think he did discretion lack,
  He car'd for no device, nor new invention,
  Nor ware he sumptuous clothing on his back,
  He only had one border richly set
  With stones, but darkned over with a net.

32

A net that *Fiordeliege* his dearest Queene
  With her own hands against that day did make,
  But neither then, nor all the time between
  That first she undertook it for his sake,
  Till she had done it, was she ever seen
  To laugh or smile, or any joy to take:
  Her heart still heavy was, her look still sad,
  And yet her self did know no cause she had.

33

But still in feare, and still in doubt she is,
  Her spouse by death shall now from her be sunderd:
  Oft times her self hath seen him be, ere this
  In greater fights an hunderd and an hunderd,
  Yet never did her heart so give amisse,
  Wherefore at her own feare she greatly wonder'd:
  And ev'n that reason made her feare the more,
  Because she was not us'd to feare before.

34

Now when each thing in order fit was set,
  The champions three were shipped with their horses:
  Vnto *Astolfo* and to *Sansonet*,
  The charge was left of all those Christen forces,
  But dolefull *Fiordeliege*, although as yet
  To hide her sorrow, she her self inforces,
  Yet when the wind away the vessell beares,
  She bursteth out to open cries and teares.

35

With *Sansonet Astolfo* took much paine,
  To bring her to her chamber from the shore,
Who lying on her bed, she still doth plaine,
  That she hath lost her spouse for evermore:
To seek to comfort her it was in vaine,
  For talking made her feare increase the more,
But now the worthy champions in this while
Were safe arriv'd at *Lippadusa* Ile.

36

No sooner set they foot upon the land,
  But (on the Eastern side) they pitcht a tent,
Because perhap that part was nearest hand,
  Or els upon some politick intent:
On tother side, with such an equall band,
  Came *Agramant:* but sith this day was spent,
They all agreed all fight to be forborn,
Vntill the very next ensuing morn.

37

A watch was charged then on either part,
  That neither side the tother may deceive,
But ere it yet was dark, king *Brandimart*,
  (Though not without *Orlandos* speciall leave)
Doth mean a wondrous favour to impart
  To *Agramant*, if he the same receive:
For why the tone the tother oft had seen
As friends, and had in *France* together been.

38

Now after joyning hands and salutation,
  The noble minded *Brandimart* begun
To use unto the *Turke* an exhortation;
  That with *Orlando* he the combat shun:
Affirming unto him with protestation,
  Would he believe but in the *Virgins* Son,
That he both present peace would then assure him,
And all his Realmes in *Affricke* safe procure him.

39

Because you are, and have been deare to me,
  Therefore (he saith) this counsell I you give,
And sith I follow it my self you see,
  Thereby you may be sure I it believe;
Christ is a God, a God indeed is he;
  An Idol *Mammet* is, that doth not live:
Wherefore deare sir, I do desire to move
From errours foule, your self and all I love.

40

This is indeed the way of truth and life,
  All other wayes but this do lead astray;
Why should you live in error and in strife,
  When in true peace and knowledge live you may?
Tempestuous cares this world hath ever rife,
  And if your present state you would but way,
You plainly may perceive your venter such,
As you to win but little hazard much.

41

What if you could the sonne of *Milo* kill?
  Or us that come with him to win, or die?
Think you that then you shall have all you will?
  Think you your state you can restore thereby?
No sure, the state of *Charles* is not so ill,
  But that he quickly can our lack supply:
Wherefore deare Sir unto my counsell listen,
All would be well, if you would be a Christen.

42

Thus much said *Brandimart*, and more beside
  He would have said, to peace him to exhort,
Save that with scornfull speech and full of pride,
  Fierce *Agramant* this wise did cut him short;
A madnesse meet it is (thus he repli'd)
  In you, or any man that in such sort
Will counsell and advise men what to do,
Not being cal'd of counsell thereunto.

43

And where you say, to this love mov'd you chief,
  That you have born, and still do beare to me,
Herein you pardon must my hard belief,
  While in *Orlandos* company you be;
I rather think despaire, and spite, and grief
  Hath mov'd you hereunto, because you see
Your soule is damned to eternall fire,
To draw us thither with you, you desire.

44

What victories, or els what overthrowes
  I shall hereafter have, God onely knoweth,
Nor you nor I, nor yet *Orlando* knowes,
  God onely where he list the same bestoweth:
But as for me, no feare nor foolish showes
  Shall daunt my courage, howsoere it goeth,
Die first I will with torment and with paine,
Much rather then to yeeld, my stock to staine.

45

Now when you list, depart from hence you may,
  As little thankt, and slenderly rewarded,
And if to morrow you the Champion play
  No better, nor no more to be regarded,
Then you have plaid the Orator to day,
  Orlando sure will be but weakly guarded;
And these last words in manner such he said,
As that thereby much choler he bewraid.

46

Thus parted they, and rested all that night,
  But ready they were all by break of day,
All arm'd, and ready for the future fight,
  Small speech was us'd, no lingring nor no stay,
They couch their spears, & run with all their might:
  But while I tell you of this bloudy fray,
I doubt I do unto *Rogero* wrong,
To leave him swimming in the sea so long.

47

The gallant youth had labour'd many an houre
  To swim, and save himself from being drownd,
  The surging wave still threats him to devoure,
  But guilty conscience more doth him confound;
  He thinks that God will of his mighty power
  Sith he foresloed when he was on ground
  To he baptiz'd in waters fresh, and fitter,
  To sowse him now in waves both salt and bitter.

48

He now remembers he had plighted troth
  To *Bradamant*, nor done as he had spoken,
  How to *Renaldo* he had made an oath,
  And that the same by him was foully broken;
  Most earnestly he now repents them both,
  And cals to God for mercy, and in token
  Of true contrition voweth out of hand,
  To be baptiz'd, if ere he come to land.

49

And that he would renounce all Turkish lawes,
  Nor gainst a Christen Prince once weapon carrie,
  But serve king *Charles*, and aid the Churches cause,
  And from the same hereafter not to varie,
  And never seek delay or farther pause,
  His vertuous spouse Dame *Bradamant* to marrie.
  ('Twas strange) no sooner he this vow had ended,
  But that his strength increast, & swimming mended.

50

And where before he greatly was affraid,
  That those same surging waters him would drown,
  He thinketh now they do his swimming aid:
  And somtime rising, somtime going down,
  He passeth on with courage undismaid,
  And scarce he seemed once to wet his crown:
  That so with cunning part, and part with strength,
  He reached to the little Ile at length.

51

The rest of all his company was drownd,
  Nor ever was a man of them seen more,
  But by Gods onely grace *Rogero* found
  This little Ile, and clammerd up the shore:
  And finding it a small and barren ground,
  A new feare rose no lesse then that before,
  Lest in a place of needfull things too scant,
  He should be starv'd with penury and want.

52

But yet with constant mind and unappal'd,
  Resolv'd to suffer all that God would send,
  Vpon the rock with much ado he cral'd,
  And gat upon the levell ground in th'end;
  When lo an aged man whose head was bald,
  And beard below his girdle did descend,
  That was an Hermit that did there inhabit,
  Came forth to him in godly rev'rent habit.

53

And comming neare he cri'd, O *Saul*, O *Saul*,
  Why persecutest thou my people so?
  As erst our Saviour spake unto Saint *Paul*,
  Then when he gave to him that blessed blow,
  Behold how God when pleaseth him can call,
  From sea, from land, from places high and low,
  When you did ween him farthest he was nighest,
  So strong an arm, so long reach hath the highest.

54

Thus spake this Hermit so devout and old,
  Who by an Angell in his sleep that night
  Of good *Rogeros* comming was foretold,
  And of all chances should on him allight,
  With all his valiant actions manifold,
  That he had done, and should perform in fight,
  And of his death, and of his noble race,
  That should succeed him after in his place.

55

Now (as I said) this wise this Hermit spoke,
  And part doth comfort him, and part doth check,
  He blameth him, that in that pleasant yoke
  He had so long deferd to put his neck,
  But did to wrath his maker still provoke,
  And did not come at his first call and beck,
  But still did hide himself away from God,
  Vntill he saw him comming with his rod.

56

Then did he comfort him, and make him know,
  That grace is nere deni'd to such as ask:
  (As do the workmen of the Gospell show,
  Receiving pay alike for divers task)
  Provided that our prayr of zeal do grow,
  And serve not as a viser or a mask:
  This did the man of God *Rogero* tell,
  And so from thence he led him to his cell.

57

The cell a chappell had on th'Eastern side,
  Vpon the Western side a grove or berie,
  Forth of the which he did his food provide,
  Small chear God wot, wherwith to make folk merie,
  Yet forty yeare he had that living tri'd,
  And yet thereof it seem'd he was not wearie:
  But eating berries, drinking water cleare,
  He had in strength and health liv'd fourscore yeare.

58

Now kindled had the man of God some wood,
  And on his boord he set a little fruit,
  The youth to drie his clothes not far off stood,
  For why, to change he hath no other sute;
  Then he by th'old mans teaching understood
  The faith, and how to *Christ* he must impute
  The pardon of his sins, yet nere the later,
  He told him he must be baptiz'd in water.

59

And so he was the next ensuing day,
　And afterward he rested in that place
A while, and with the man of God did stay,
　Resolving him of ev'ry doubtfull case:
Somtime of heav'n, and of the later day,
　Somtime of earth, and of his noble race,
That should in time to come hold mighty Reames,
As was reveal'd to him in former dreames.

60

And further unto him he doth repeat,
　How his chief house should be sirnamed *Esté*,
Because in time to come king *Charles* the great
　Should say to them in Latin words, *Hic este*,
Which is as much to say, be here the seat,
　In which you shall hereafter ever rest ye,
And many future things to him he told,
Which were too long for me now to unfold.

61

This while *Orlando* and king *Brandimart*
　With Marquesse *Olivero*, (as I told)
Met with those three of the contrary part,
　Yong *Agramante* and *Gradasso* bold,
With good *Sobrino*, who for valiant heart,
　Gives place to few of them, though being old;
Each spurs his horse, that ran a wondrous pace,
And of their blowes resounded all the place.

62

In this same course each plaid his part so well,
　That up to heav'n flew shiver'd ev'ry lance,
The hideous noise did cause the seas to swell,
　And some report, 'twas heard as far as France;
Gradasso and *Orlando* (as befell)
　Did meet together, were it choice or chance;
The match was ev'n, save that their horses differ,
And made *Gradasso* seem to run the stiffer.

63

The weaker horse on which *Orlando* rode,
　Was bruised so with this so fearfull shock,
As now he could no longer beare his lode,
　But sinking down, lay senslesse with the knock;
Orlando then did make but small abode,
　His courser lying senslesse like a stock,
Sith that with neither raines nor spurs he sturd,
He left his saddle, and drew forth his sword.

64

With *Agramant* the Marquesse hand to hand
　Did most, betweene them equall went the game,
Sobrino was by *Brandimartés* hand,
　Cast from his horse, I know not how it came,
But at that time it could not well be scand,
　If so the horse or horseman were to blame:
But whether beast or rider wanted force,
Sobrino certaine downe was from his horse.

65

King *Brandimart* nere offerd once to touch
　Sobrino, when he saw him downe in vew,
But to *Gradasso* that had done as much
　Vnto *Orlando*, in great hast he flew
The Marquesse fight with *Agramant* was such,
　As which side had the vantage no man knew,
For when their staues were shiuered all and rent,
Their axes then they vsd incontinent.

66

Orlando who by hap a horse did lacke,
　And saw *Gradasso* bent another way,
Whome *Brandimart* did hold so hardly tacke,
　That he enforced him thereby to stay;
I say the *Palladine* then looking backe,
　Saw old *Sobrino* standing in his way,
And toward him he go'th with looke so fierce,
As though his eye, as well as sword could pierce.

67

Sobrino gainst the force of such a man,
　Sought with his surest ward himselfe to saue,
And as a Pilot doth the best he can,
　To shunne the furie of the surging waue,
Eu'n so this well experienc't *Turke* began,
　Himselfe in this great danger to behaue,
With sword and shield his best defence he made,
Against the fearfull edge of that same blade.

68

Which blade, of such an edge, in such an arme,
　No maruell if to pierce it seldom faile,
Against the which in vaine was any charme,
　For though his shield was steeld, his cote of male,
Yet quite through shield and armore it did harme,
　To saue his shoulder all could not auaile.
But he to wound *Orlando* was not able,
For God hath made his skinne impenetrable.

69

The valiant Earle redoubled still his blow,
　And thinks from shoulders off to cut his head,
He, that the force of *Clarimont* did know,
　Gaue backward, or his ground still trauersed,
But in his trauersing he was so slow,
　That with one blow he laid him downe for dead,
The blow fell flatling, but with force so maine,
As crusht his helmet, and amaz'd his braine.

70

Downe fell *Sobrino* backward on the ground,
　From whence long time it was ere he arose,
Orlando thinks that he was safe and sound,
　And that he was starke dead he doth suppose:
Wherefore since single foe he no where found,
　Vnto *Gradasso* presently he goes,
To whom king *Brandimart* in armes, and horse,
In sword, inferiour was, perhaps in force.

71

But yet the noble minded *Brandimart*,
Vpon *Rogeros* horse *Frontino* mounted,
With that same *Sarasin* so plaid his part,
As if his forces he but little counted:
And sure *Gradasso* not in skill nor heart,
But in his sword and armour him surmounted:
Enforcing him oft times to stand aloofe,
Because his armour was of no good proofe.

72

But good *Frontino* bare away the bell,
For being ready to the riders hand,
It seem'd where euer *Durindana* fell,
Frontino had such wit to vnderstand,
That evermore he did escape it well:
But all this while it hardly could be scand,
In tother twaine on which side fortune works,
In *Olivero*, or the king of *Turks*.

73

Orlando had (as late before I told)
Left good *Sobrino* on the ground for dead,
Wherefore on foot he goes with courage bold,
To succour *Brandimart* if ill he sped;
But in the way by hap he did behold
Sobrinos horse that without rider fled,
Orlando straight into the saddle valted,
Not looking if he went upright or halted.

74

One hand his sword, the tother holds his raine,
And so he rideth to *Gradasso* ward,
Who when he saw him come, did not refraine,
But to encounter with him straight prepar'd:
To fight with one of them, or els with twaine,
It seem'd he little reckoned nor car'd;
He minds and hopeth to effect it soon,
To make them both to think it night ere noone.

75

Yet for a while king *Brandimart* he leaves,
And turnes him to the Earle, and with a thrust
Whereas his armour weakest he perceives,
There doth the fierce *Gradasso* hit him just,
And enter'd, but his cunning him deceives,
Orlandos skin be pierced never must.
But when with *Ballisard Orlando* strake,
His helmet, coat of maile, and shield he brake.

76

So that both in his face, his breast, and side,
He wounded sore the king of *Sericane*,
Who marvels much what strange chance did betide,
For never erst such sore hurt he had tane:
He thought there could not be a blade beside
To pierce his coat, he having *Durindane*;
And sure that blow had him dispatched clearly,
If it had had more strength, or come more nearely.

77

He sees that now he must take better heed,
And not trust armour, but a surer ward,
To seek to save himselfe he now hath need,
And looke unto his limbs with more regard:
Now while twixt them the fight did thus proceed,
Good *Brandimart* did see he might be spar'd,
Wherefore to breath himselfe he then retir'd,
Still ready t'aid each part, if cause requir'd.

78

Now had *Sobrino* long laine in a trance,
With that same bruse, and with that bloody wound,
Giu'n him by that great *Palladine* of *France*,
That at two blowes had laid him on the ground,
With much ado he doth himselfe aduance,
And standing on his feete, and looking round,
He thought his Master was in weakest case,
And to his aid he moues his silent pace.

79

At *Oliueros* backe he comes vnspide,
Who sole on *Agramant* did fixe his eyes,
And that same horse that *Oliuer* did ride,
He hought behind in such despitefull wise,
That wanting strength, he fell downe on his side,
And was not able any more to rise:
And which was worse then his vnlookt for fall,
His foot hung in the stirop therewithall.

80

Sobrino doubled then his blowes againe,
Thinking from shoulders off his head to pare,
But yet the steele made that attempt but vaine,
That *Vulcan* tempred erst, and *Hector* ware:
King *Brandimart* at *Sobrin* runnes amaine,
When of his doings he was well aware,
And ouerthrew him quite, and stoutly smote him,
But th'old fierce man, soone on his feet vp got him.

81

And once againe at *Oliuer* he flies,
And once again he thinketh him to kill,
Or at the least cause him he shall not rise;
But he that had his better arme at will,
Layd with his sword about him in such wise,
As that he kept himselfe from further ill:
And made his foe, that was of no great strength
Stand distant from him, almost twise his length.

82

The Marquesse hopes ere long to ease his paine,
If he can cause *Sobrino* stand aloofe,
Who bled so fast, as now from fight t'abstaine
He thought it would be best for his behoofe:
Now *Oliuero* all his force doth straine,
And to get loose he maketh manie a proofe,
But still his foot was fast to his great hurt,
And still the horse lay tumbling in the durt.

83

This while king *Brandimart* doth go to find
  Traianos sonn, and now he hath him found,
Frontino now before, and straight behind:
  That good *Frontino* that can turne so round:
The horse was sure and of a passing kind,
  The Sotherne kings was readie, strong, and sound:
He had that famous courser *Brigliadore*,
The which *Rogero* gaue him late before.

84

But sure the Turke great ods in armour had,
  For he had one of proofe, well tride, and sure,
And *Brandimartés* was indeed but bad,
  Such as he could in warning short procure,
Wherefore to change it now he would be glad,
  And that he shall, his heart doth him assure:
So that he waxed stouter still and bolder,
Though *Agramant* had hurt him in the shoulder.

85

Gradasso further had about his thye,
  Him giu'n a blow, not to be tane in sport,
But yet the king did so the fight apply,
  And laid on lode in so couragious sort,
As that he wounded his left arme therby,
  And pricked his right hand (thus they report)
But all this was but May-game and delight,
Vnto *Gradassos* and *Orlandos* fight.

86

Gradasso hath *Orlando* halfe disarmd,
  And made him with one blowe his shield forsake,
He could not wound him, for his skin was charmd,
  But yet his headpeece on both sides he brake;
But him *Orlando* hath in worse sort harmd,
  Beside that hurt of which before I spake,
He hath drawn blood of him in many a place,
As namely in brest, in throate, and in his face.

87

Gradasso sees himselfe with blood besmeard,
  And smarting paine in many places found,
And sees that Earle like one that nothing feard,
  Stand whole and quite vnwounded safe and sound;
Wherefore with both his hands his sword he reard,
  With mind to cleaue him, rather then to wound,
And eu'n as he desir'd, with all his strength,
He strake him on his head, at halfe sword length.

88

And sure had clou'd him to the saddle bow,
  Had it another then *Orlando* bene,
But now as if it had falne flatling thoe,
  The blade rebounded from him bright and cleene,
But yet that Earle was daz'd so with the bloe,
  I think some starres on ground by him were seene;
He lost his bridle, and his sword had mist,
Saue that a chaine did bind it to his wrist.

89

The horse on which the good *Orlando* rode,
  Was eke so scared with the fearfull sound,
As there he durst no longer make abode,
  But on the sands at randon runneth round,
And beares *Orlando* as a senslesse lode,
  That with the paine still stood as in a sound,
And had *Gradasso* little harder spurred,
He might haue tane the Earle ere he had sturred.

90

But as he rode, he saw king *Agramant*,
  Vnto extremest point of danger brought,
For why the valiant sonne of *Monodant*,
  Had loosd his beuer, and such hold had caught
Vpon his gorget, that but small did want,
  Eu'n with one stab his last end to haue wrought:
For why the noble minded Christen Prince,
Had wonne his sword from him a good while since.

91

Gradasso doth no more that Earle pursew,
  But maketh hast king *Agramant* to ayd,
And vnto *Brandimart* that nothing knew,
  Nor of no such misfortune was affrayd,
He comes behind his back quite out of vew,
  And both his hands at once on sword he laid,
And in that sort, he strake with all his might,
Full on the helmet of the noble knight.

92

Oh heau'nly Father grant a resting place
  In Paradice, for this thy Martyrs spirit,
That hauing run all his tempestuous race,
  He may with thee an harbour safe inherit.
Ah *Durindan*, hadst thou so little grace,
  So ill to quite thy noblest Masters merit,
That in his sight thou could of life depriue,
His best and kindest friend he had aliue?

93

The sword did pierce a double plate of steele,
  That little lesse was then two fingers thick,
Good *Brandimart* gan with the blow to reele,
  It pierced had so deepe vnto the quicke.
His braines all cut therewith he plain did feele,
  And downe he fell like one most deadly sicke;
A streame of blood out of the grieuous wound,
Ran forth, and dyde with crimson all the ground.

94

By this *Orlando* waked, and behild
  His *Brandimart* that lay now a la mort:
He sees the *Sericane* that him had kild,
  This angerd him, and grieu'd him in such sort,
Twas hard to say which more his stomacke fild,
  His wrath or griefe, but time to mourne was short,
That griefe gaue place, and wrath bare chiefest sway,
But now I thinke it best awhile to stay.

THE FORTY-SECOND BOOKE OF
ORLANDO FVRIOSO

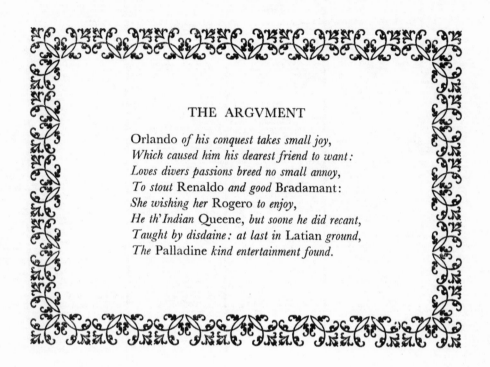

THE ARGVMENT

Orlando *of his conquest takes small joy,*
Which caused him his dearest friend to want:
Loves divers passions breed no small annoy,
To stout Renaldo *and good* Bradamant:
She wishing her Rogero *to enjoy,*
He th'Indian Queene, *but soone he did recant,*
Taught by disdaine: at last in Latian *ground,*
The Palladine *kind entertainment found.*

ORLANDO FVRIOSO
THE FORTY-SECOND BOOKE

1

What iron band, or what sharp hard mouth'd bit,
  What chaine of diamond (if such might be)
Can bridle wrathfulnesse and conquer it,
  And keep it in his bounds and due degree?
When one to us in bonds of friendship knit,
  And dearly lov'd, before our face we see,
By violence or fraud to suffer wrong,
By one for him too crafty, or too strong.

2

And if before we can such pang digest,
  We swerve somtime from law, and run astray,
It may be well excus'd, sith in ones brest
  Pure reason at such time beares little sway;
Achilles when with counterfeited crest,
  He saw *Patroclus* bleeding all the way,
To kill his killer was not satisfi'd,
Except he hal'd and tare him all beside.

3

So now a little since when in his brow,
  Alfonso wounded was with cursed stone,
And all his men and souldiers thought that now
  His soule from earth to heav'n had been up flowne,
They kild and spoil'd, they car'd not whom nor how,
  Strong rampiers, wals, to them defence were none,
But in that fury they put all to wrack,
Both old and yong, and all the town to sack.

4

Our men were so enraged with this fall,
  To think they had their Captaine lost for aye,
That to the sword they put both great and small,
  That happen'd then to come within their way:
And so their fortune did prevaile withall,
  That they the Castle did regaine that day,
In fewer houres to their great fame and praise,
Then had the *Spaniards* got it erst in dayes.

5

It may be, God ordained (as I guesse)
  That he that time should wounded be so sore,
To punish that same sin and foule excesse,
  His foes committed had a while before,
When *Vestidell* forlorn and in distresse
  Did yeeld, and should have had his life therefore:
Yet was he kild when they had him surpris'd,
By men whose greater part were circumcis'd.

6

Wherefore I justly may conclude thus much,
  That nothing can more hotly kindle wrath,
Then if one shall the life and honour touch,
  Of our deare friend, or do him wrong or scath.
Now (as I said) *Orlandos* grief is such,
  And such occasion of just griefe he hath,
He sees his friend, for lack of better heeding,
Lie flat on ground, and almost dead with bleeding.

7

As the *Nomadian* Shepheard, that a Snake
  Along the grasse and herbes hath sliding seen,
Which late before with tooth most poyson'd strake
  His little son, that plaid upon the green,
Doth bruise and beat, and kill him with a stake:
  So goes this Earle with blade most sharp and keen,
And yet far more with wrath and choler whet;
And *Agramant* was then the first he met.

8

Vnhappy he that in his passage stood,
  His sword was gone, as I declar'd before,
Himselfe besmeared all with his own blood,
  Brave *Brandimart* had wounded him so sore,
Orlando comes, and in his wrathfull mood,
  With *Ballisard*, that payes home evermore,
He strikes (by fortune were it or by art)
Iust where the shoulders from the head do part.

9

Loos'd was his helmet, as I erst did tell,
  That like a Poppie quite fell off his head,
The carkas of the *Lybian* Monarch fell
  Down to the ground and lay along stark dead,
His soule by *Charon*, ferrie-man of hell,
  To *Plutos* house or *Stygian* lake was led,
Orlando staid no whit, but straight prepar'd
To find *Gradasso* eke with *Ballisard*.

10

But when *Gradasso* plain beheld and saw
  Of *Agramant* the wofull end and fall,
He felt an unaccustom'd dread and aw,
  Who never wonted was to feare at all;
And ev'n as if his own fate he foresaw,
  He made the *Palladine* resistance small:
Feare had so maz'd his head and daz'd his sence,
That for the blow he quite forgat his sence.

11

Orlando thrust *Gradasso* in the side,
  About the ribs, as he before him stood,
  The sword came forth a span on tother side,
  And to the hilt was varnisht all with blood,
  By that same thrust alone it might be tri'd,
  That he that gave it was a warriour good,
  That with one thrust did vanquish and subdue
  The stoutest champion of the *Turkish* crew.

12

Orlando of this conquest nothing glad,
  Doth from his saddle in great hast alight,
  And with a heavy heart and count'nance sad,
  He runs unto his deare beloved knight,
  He sees his helmet cut, as if it had
  Been cloven quite with axe (a wofull sight)
  And ev'n as if it had been made of glasse,
  And not of steel, and plated well with brasse.

13

The *Palladine* his helmet then unties,
  And finds the scull clov'n down unto the chin,
  And sees the braine all cut before his eyes;
  Yet so much breath and life remain'd within,
  That he is able yet before he dies,
  To call to God for mercy for his sin,
  And pray *Orlando* joyne with him in praying,
  And use to him this comfortable saying.

14

My deare *Orlando*, see that to our Lord,
  Thou in thy good devotions me commend:
  Likewise to thee commend I my deare *Fiorde-*
  And *liege* he would have said, but there did end;
  Straight Angels voices with most sweet accord,
  Were heard the while his spirit did ascend,
  The which dissolved from this fleshly masse,
  In sweetest melody to heav'n did passe.

15

Orlando though he should rejoyce in heart,
  Of this his end so holy and devout,
  Because he knew his loving *Brandimart*
  Was taken up to heav'n without all doubt,
  Yet flesh and bloud in him so plaid their part,
  That without teares he cannot beare it out,
  But that he needs must shew some change in cheare,
  To leese one more then any brother deare.

16

This while *Sobrino* bruised in his head,
  And wounded sorely in his side and thye,
  Vpon the ground so great a streame had bled,
  It seem'd his life in perill was thereby;
  And *Olivero* little better sped,
  On whom his horse still overthrown doth lie,
  He striving, but his striving did not boot,
  To get at liberty his bruised foot.

17

And sure it seems he had been worse apaid,
  Had not his dolefull cosin quickly come,
  And brought to him both quick and needfull aid,
  Before the paine had him quite overcome:
  His foot that long had in the stirop staid,
  Was therewithall so void of sence and numme,
  That when he stood upright he was not able
  To touch the ground, much lesse tred firm and stable.

18

So that indeed *Orlando* in his heart,
  But little joy of so great conquest had,
  He wailes the death of his deare *Brandimart*,
  And that his kinsman was in state so bad:
  Now lay *Sobrino*, though alive in part,
  Yet with a look so chearlesse and so sad,
  And so much blood his aged veines had bled,
  That doubtlesse in few howres he had been dead.

19

Saue that *Orlando* with compassion mov'd,
  To see him lie so lorn, and so distressed,
  Gate him such needfull things as best behov'd,
  And charitably made his wounds be dressed:
  So kindly, that some kinsman deare belov'd,
  And not his foe, a man might him have guessed:
  Such was this Earles good nature, fierce in fight,
  But fight once done, from malice free or spight.

20

The horse, and bodies of the other twaine
  He took away, and left their men the rest,
  To be dispos'd to their own private gaine,
  Or to interre their Lords, as they thought best.
  But here, that in my story I do faine,
  Fredericke Fulgoso (as I heare) hath guest,
  Sith at this Ile he late arriving found
  In all the same no levell foot of ground.

21

Nor doth he probable it deem or take,
  That six such knights as had in armes no peere,
  On horseback should a combat undertake,
  Where no one foot of plaine ground doth appeare,
  To which objection I this answer make,
  That then, in times now past sev'n hundred yeare,
  Plaine ground there was, but now some inundation,
  Or earthquake might procure this alteration.

22

Wherefore *Fulgoso*, honour of thy name,
  Bright *Fulgor*, causing all thy stock to shine,
  If in this point thou hadst imputed blame
  To me, perhaps before that Prince divine,
  From whom thy countries good and quiet came,
  And did it first to love and peace incline,
  Inform him now, that ev'n perhaps in this
  My tale of truth or likelihood doth not misse.

23

This while *Orlando* looking from the shore,
  A little Frigot did far off descrie,
  That both with saile and with the help of ore,
  Vnto that Ile seem'd in great hast to flie;
  But ere of this I tell you any more,
  I must to *France* as fast as I can hie,
  To see if they be merry there or sad,
  Now they from thence the *Turks* expulsed had.

24

First let us see how faithfull *Bradamant*
  Doth take his absence whom she loveth most,
  Who in his oath due care of faith did want,
  Which he had tane in sight of either host:
  Now sure she thinks his love and faith too scant,
  To heare he quite had left the Chistren cost:
  If in his publike oath he be unjust,
  Whereto alas, then whereto can she trust?

25

And still returning to her former plaints,
  And still bemoning her unluckie fate,
  With which her selfe she too too well acquaints,
  She cals her selfe accurst, and him ungrate,
  Yea blaming God himself, and all his Saints,
  For not redressing this her wofull state,
  She scarce abstaines high blasphemie to speak,
  That God unjust, and that Saints powers are weak.

26

Then she *Melissa* (absent) doth reprove,
  And curst that Oracles perswasion blind,
  That lapt her in this Labyrinth of love,
  Whence she her self by no means can unwinde,
  But to *Marfisa* all the rest above,
  She open layes her stomack and her mind,
  With her she chides and utters all her choler,
  And yet she prayes her comfort this her doler.

27

Marfisa comforts her in all she may,
  And tels her what a vertue patience is,
  And partly doth excuse *Rogeros* stay:
  And further giveth her her faith in this,
  That if she find he wilfully delay,
  She will constraine him mend all is amisse,
  Or if she find that he refuse to do it,
  To fight with him, and so compell him to it.

28

With this she did in part her paine asswage,
  For why it is in sorrow great relief,
  To those of either sex or any age,
  To have some friend to whom to tell their grief,
  But now if *Bradamant* be in such rage,
  No lesse is he that of her house was chief,
  I meane *Renaldo*, that cannot expulse
  Loves fire, from ev'ry sinew, veine and pulse.

29

I think I need not now to you repeat
  A thing by me so often told before,
  By name that love and that affection great,
  That to *Angelica Renaldo* bore:
  Nor did her beauty cause so much his heat,
  As did that spring of which he drank such store,
  Now all the other *Palladines* were free
  From all their foes, now *Cupids* thrall is he.

30

An hundred messengers he sends about,
  Himselfe the while an hundred wayes more riding,
  To ask of her, or els to find her out,
  Who hath her now, or where is her abiding.
  At last, because he thinketh out of doubt,
  That *Malagige* of her can learn some tiding,
  He asketh him (but blushing sore with shame)
  If he knew what of th'*Indian* Queene became.

31

His cosin wonders at so strange a case,
  And in his mind thereon long time he mused,
  That when *Renaldo* had both time and place,
  Her offers large and kind he still refused,
  When both her self did sue to have his grace,
  And many of his friends perswasions used:
  And *Malagige* himself among the rest,
  Had prov'd him oft with prayer and with request.

32

The rather eke, because *Renaldo* then
  By taking her, had set his cosin free,
  Who then was kept close prisner in a den,
  And for that cause in perill slaine to be;
  He marvels that he now would seek her, when
  No hope nor cause there was, and further he
  With angry look did bid him call to mind,
  How in this point he had been too unkind.

33

But good *Renaldo* now quite out of tune,
  Pray'th him old quarrels from his mind to move,
  And doth most earnestly him importune
  Vnto his help, his skill and books to prove:
  Which made his cosin so much more presume
  Vpon his reconcilement and true love,
  And promist to assist him if he may,
  And for his answer he prefixt a day.

34

And straight from thence he go'th unto the place,
  Where he was wont the spirits to conjure,
  A strong vast cave, in which there was great space,
  The precepts of his art to put in ure:
  One sprite he cals, that of each doubtfull case
  Of *Cupids* court, could give him notice sure:
  Of him he askt what bred *Renaldos* change,
  By him he heard of those two fountaines strange.

35

And how *Renaldo* by misfortune led,
  First happen'd of that hatefull spring to drink,
Which his dislike of that faire Lady bred,
And made her love and proferd service stink:
And how againe by some ill star misled,
He drank of th'other spring, which caus'd him think
Her only to be loved and admir'd,
Whom erst he hated more then cause requir'd.

36

Moreover he to *Malagigis* show'd,
  How that same famous *Indian* Queen (nay quean)
Had on a *Pagan* youth her self bestow'd,
Of parentage, of state, of living mean:
And how from *Spaine* they in a galley row'd,
All *Christendome* and *Spaine* forsaking clean,
And passing both with safety and with ease,
(In ventrous bark of *Catalyn*) the seas.

37

Now when *Renaldo* for his answer came,
  His learned cosin seeks him to perswade,
Vnto some better thought his mind to frame,
Nor further in this gulf of love to wade;
Alledging what a slander and a shame,
It was to fancy one her self had made,
Not like a Queen, but like a vile maid Marian,
A wife (nay slave) unto a base *Barbarian*.

38

In fine he said, she was to th'*Indies* gone,
  With her *Medoro*, and was welnigh there:
Renaldo not a little mus'd thereon,
Yet all the rest he could with patience beare,
And for the paine, he counts it small or none,
So he at last might find her any where;
Wherefore of it he had no care nor keep,
Nor could that make him once to break his sleep.

39

But when he heard that one of birth so base
  Had with his mistris laid his knife aboord,
It seem'd this strake him speechlesse in the place,
He was not able to pronounce a word:
His heart did quake within, his lips like case
So trembled, answer he could none afford;
But overcome with anguish of the passion,
He flang away from thence in carelesse fashion.

40

And much lamenting this her foule abuse,
  He vowes to follow her what ere ensue,
But yet to *Charles* he faineth this excuse,
That sith *Gradasso*, of his word untrue,
Had tane his horse contrary to the use
Of valiant knights, he means him to pursue;
Alledging that it were his great dishoner,
To let *Bayardo* have a forren owner.

41

And that a Turke should boast another day,
  That he by fight did him thereof bereave:
King *Charles* (though loth) yet could not say him nay
To such an honest suit, but gave him leave;
Which tane, alone from thence he goes his way,
And all his friends in *Paris* he doth leave:
With *Guidon*, *Dudon* stout to him do profer
Their company, but he refus'd their offer.

42

Away he goes alone, yet not alone,
  Griefs, teares, and plaints still his companions are:
And oft in heart he bitterly doth grone,
To think that erst he should so little care
For her great love, which wilfully forgone,
He now esteemes at rate so high and rare,
He could have wish'd (thus was his mind perplext)
But one day to enjoy, and die the next.

43

Then he bethinks with no lesse grief, nay rage,
  How she could find in that her lofty heart,
To set her love on such a sorrie page,
The merits all, and service put apart,
Done unto her ev'n from her tender age,
By men of high renown, and great desert:
Thus with a fired heart and watred eyne
He rode untill he toucht the banks of *Rhyne*.

44

Ere long into *Ardenna* woods he enters,
  Soone after he *Basylea* quite had past:
Ardenna woods, whence many come repenters,
And in that forrest have been sore agast,
To travell through the same *Renaldo* venters,
When suddenly the skie did overcast,
And there arose a black and hideous storm,
And then appear'd a monster of strange form.

45

She seem'd of womans shape, but in her head
  A thousand eyes she had, that watch did keep,
As many eares, with which she harkened,
Her eyes want lids, and therefore never sleep,
In stead of haire her crown snakes overspred,
Thus marched she forth of the darknesse deep,
Her taile one Serpent bigger then the rest,
Which she with knots had ti'd about her brest.

46

This sight *Renaldos* mind appald so sore,
  He feels his heart already gan to faile him,
And sith it never had done so before,
He marvels very much what now should aile him:
Yet still his mind misgave him more and more,
To see the monster comming to assaile him,
He nathlesse counterfeits his wonted boldnesse,
Though quaking hands bewraid his inward coldnes.

47

The monster straight assaulted him, much like
  To one that perfect was and skild in fence,
  And when againe he with his sword did strike,
  He missed, and could do her none offence.
  Much doth *Renaldo* this ill match mislike,
  And little wants to quite distract his sense,
  Right blowes and reardemaine he striketh many,
  But yet he cannot hit her right with any.

48

The monster sticks a Serpent in his brest,
  That strake his heart into a freezing cold,
  Another fixed is below his crest,
  And on his neck and shoulders taketh hold;
  Renaldo thinks to get him gone is best,
  And spurs away with all the speed he could,
  But that vile monster was not lame to find him,
  But overtook him; and leapt up behind him.

49

And whether he go straight, or go he wide,
  The monster sitteth sure and holds him fast,
  He knowes not how to be from her unti'd,
  Nor any mean within his mind can cast,
  His heart ev'n quakes within him, and beside
  That he was with this hideous plague agast,
  He sorrow'd so not knowing how to mend it,
  He loth'd his life, and did desire to end it.

50

He spurs amaine, and purposely he takes
  The rugged wayes, the worst that he could find,
  By craggie rocks, and hils, through bryers and brakes,
  Through copsies thick, by narrow paths and blind,
  But sure the knight the matter much mistakes,
  He cannot from the monster him unwind:
  And like it was, great harme had him betided,
  Had not for him been help in time provided.

51

For lo a knight unto his succour went,
  All arm'd in shining steel, and on his shield
  He bare a yoke in sundry peeces rent,
  And flames of fire all in a yellow field,
  So weaponed he was, as if he meant
  To make all that encountred him to yeeld.
  A sword and speare he had, and to the same,
  A Mace from whence he threw continuall flame.

52

His Mace was stor'd with everlasting fire,
  That ever burned, and did never wast,
  No other weapon needed one desire,
  To make good way with, wheresoev'r he past,
  And sure *Renaldos* danger did require
  Quick remedy, wherefore the knight doth hast:
  And when he saw this monster, and did view her,
  With his stiffe speare forthwith he overthrew her.

53

But this same fall did her no whit annoy,
  Wherefore to use his speare he now misliketh,
  He onely wils his fiery Mace imploy,
  And with that same the monster foule he striketh:
  Then she no longer could her force enjoy;
  Renaldo while she fled, occasion piketh
  To scape away, as him that knight perswaded,
  While he this monster more and more invaded.

54

Now when the knight had with his fiery Mace
  Driv'n back this monster to her darksome den,
  Where she for spite doth beat her head and face,
  Repining at the good of other men,
  Then to *Renaldo* he doth ride apace,
  And when he had soon overtane him, then
  He offerd in kind sort with him to ride,
  From out the darksome places him to guide.

55

But when *Renaldo* was from danger free,
  And that same knight by whom his safety came,
  So courteously to come to him did see,
  His speech to him in kind words he did frame,
  And gave him many thanks in high degree.
  And then besought him he might know his name,
  That th'Emperour and all his court might know,
  What knight did so great grace on him bestow.

56

The knight in courteous manner thus repli'd,
  I would not you should take it in displeasure,
  That I my name from you a while shall hide,
  But ere the shadow grow a yard by measure,
  I shall you tell: thus onward still they ride,
  Renaldo being pleas'd to stay his leasure,
  So long they went together till they found
  A chrystall spring that ran along the ground.

57

At which full oft the herdmen that did dwell
  Neare those same woods, have in their loving fits
  Drunk love away, with tasting of that well,
  And of those passions purged clean their wits:
  Now (for the knight that rode with him could tell
  That for *Renaldos* ill, this Physick fits)
  He doth advise him there to stay a space,
  And make that well their bait and resting place.

58

Renaldo of the motion well allowth,
  And lighteth straight, and to the well doth go,
  Both for that heat and travell bred his drowth,
  And that the monster had disturb'd him so;
  Vnto the Chrystall well he puts his mouth,
  And greedily drinks down five gulps or mo,
  And from his brest doth with one draught remove
  His burning thirst and his more burning love.

59

Now when that other knight that with him went,
  Saw him lift up himself from that same brook,
  And found he did his foolish love repent,
  And that he now that humour quite forsook,
  Then to declare his name he was content,
  And looking with a grave and lofty look,
  He said, *Renaldo*, know I hight *Disdaine*,
  That came to loose thee from loves foolish chaine.

60

This said, he vanish'd from *Renaldo* quite,
  His horse nor him he could not after see,
  Renaldo marvels at this wondrous sight,
  And looks about, and saith, what where is he?
  At last he thinks 'tis some familiar spright,
  That by good *Malagigis* sent might be:
  To rid him of that tedious care and wo,
  That many months had him afflicted so.

61

Or els that God to him this help did lend,
  Of his especiall grace and loving kindnesse,
  As erst he did unto *Tobias* send
  His Angell to deliver him from blindnesse:
  But let it Angell be, or be it fiend,
  Renaldo takes against him no unkindnesse:
  He thanks and praises it, and doth acknowledge
  To have receiv'd of him grace, wit, and knowledge.

62

Now that same great mislike and hate returned
  Of faire *Angelica*, whom late he lov'd,
  Now he despised her, and greatly scorned
  To think that he for her one foot had mov'd:
  Yet onward into *India* ward he journed,
  As for *Bayardos* sake it him behov'd:
  Because both honour did compell him to it,
  And to his Prince he undertook to do it.

63

He rides to *Basile* next ensuing night,
  Where very late before some newes were heard,
  How that *Orlando* challeng'd was to fight,
  And for that fight how he himself prepar'd,
  Not, that *Orlando* newes hereof did write,
  But one that came from *Sicill* thitherward,
  Affirmed he had heard the same reported,
  By many that to *Sicily* resorted.

64

These newes do set on edge *Renaldos* heart,
  He faine would present be at this conflict,
  He faine would take therein *Orlandos* part,
  To whom he bounden was in bonds most strict,
  Of friendship, of alliance, and desert:
  Wherefore he takes post horse, and spur'd and prickt,
  And chang'd both beasts & guides each tē miles end
  And toward *Italy* he still doth bend.

65

At *Constance* he did passe the stream of *Rhine*,
  And then beyond the *Alpes* he soon doth go,
  To *Mantoa*, and ere the Sun decline,
  He passed ore the stately stream of *Poe*,
  Here he did doubt, and did not soon designe,
  If he should travell all the night or no:
  Till at the last a well behaviour'd knight
  And full of curtesie, came in his sight.

66

This knight forthwith unto *Renaldo* went,
  And ask'd him if he were a marri'd man,
  Renaldo marvels what the question meant,
  But answerd yea, then tother straight began,
  And praid him, that he would be then content
  To be his guest, at such cheare as he can:
  Offring to show him, while with him he tarri'd,
  A sight well pleasing unto all were marri'd.

67

Renaldo glad so good a bait to make,
  And no lesse willing, haps most rare to heare,
  Would not the offer of this knight forsake,
  Of entertainment good and friendly cheare,
  But onward with him doth his journey take,
  Vntill he saw a goodly place appeare,
  So well set forth both for the shew and sence,
  As seem'd not for a private mans expence.

68

The porch was all of Porpherie and Tuch,
  Of which the sumptuous building raised was,
  With images that seem'd to move, see, tuch,
  Some hew'd in stone, some carv'd and cut in brasse,
  Likewise within the beauty was as much:
  Beneath a stately arch they straight did passe
  Vnto a court that good proportion bare,
  And was each way one hundred cubites square.

69

And either side a Porch had passing faire,
  That with an arch is on two collumns plac'd,
  Of equall size they seemed ev'ry paire,
  Yet sundry works; which them the better grac'd,
  At each of these a wide, large, easie staire,
  Without the which all buildings are defac'd,
  And those same staires, so stately mounting, led
  Each to a chamber richly furnished.

70

The collumns high, the chapters built with gold,
  The cornishes enrich'd with things of cost,
  The Marbles set from far, and dearly sold,
  By cunning workmen carved and imbost,
  With Images, and antikes new and old,
  (Though now the night thereof concealed most)
  Shew that that work so rich beyond all measure,
  Could scant be builded with a Princes treasure.

71

But nothing did so much the sight enrich,
  As did the plenteous fountaine, that did stand
  Iust placed in the middle, under which
  The Pages spred a table out of hand,
  And brought forth napty rich, and plate more rich,
  And meats the choicest of the sea or land:
  For though the house had stately roomes full many,
  In summer season this was best of any.

72

This fountaine was by curious workmen brought
  To answer to the rest with double square,
  Eight femall statues of white marble wrought,
  With their left hands an azure skie up bare,
  Which raining still, expelled heat and drought,
  From all that under it, or neare it are,
  In their right hands was *Amaltheas* horn
  By ev'ry one of those eight statues born.

73

Each of these statues rested both their feet
  Vpon two images of men below,
  That seem'd delighted with the noise so sweet
  That from the water came, that there did flow,
  They also seem'd the Ladies low to greet,
  As though they did their names and vertues know:
  And in their hands they hold long scroles of writings
  Of their own pennings and their own enditings.

74

And in faire golden letters were the names
  Both of the women wrote, and of the men,
  The women were eight chast and sober dames,
  That now do live, but were unborn as then:
  The men were Poets, that their worthy fames
  In time to come should praise with learned pen:
  These Images bare up a brazen tressell,
  On which there stood a large white Marble vessell.

75

This took the water from the azure skie,
  From whence, with turning of some cock or vice,
  Great store of water would mount up on high,
  And wet all that same court ev'n in a trice;
  With sight of these *Renaldo* fed his eye,
  So that his host could scarcely him intice,
  To feed his stomack, yet he oft him told,
  His meat would marre, and sallets would be cold.

76

Then down at last they sate them at the boord,
  And pleasant talk did help digest their meat,
  His host that was no niggard, did affoord
  Great store of delicates to drink and eat,

And all this while *Renaldo* spake no word,
  Although he did it oft in mind repeat,
  And though his tongue did itch, to pray him tell,
  What 'twas that would please marri'd men so well.

77

At last he put him mannerly in mind
  Of that he first did promise him to show,
  Ev'n then he plainly saw his host inclin'd
  To inward grief, and did more pensive grow,
  With secret sighs, and leaving half behind;
  At last a Page came in with curtsie low,
  And beares a standing cup of gold most fine,
  Without of gemmes, and full within of wine.

78

With this, the Master of the feast did smile,
  And on *Renaldo* look'd with pleasant cheare,
  But one that well had marked him that while,
  Might see more griefe then mirth in him appeare:
  Now noble guest (quoth he) within a while
  You shall see prov'd a strange conclusion here,
  That needs must be full welcome to be tri'd,
  By all that are in bonds of wedlock ti'd.

79

For sure I think (he said) each husband ought,
  Make search if so his wife esteem him dearly,
  If fame or shame by her to him be brought,
  If man or beast he be reputed meerly:
  The burthen of the horne though it be thought
  To weigh so heavie, and to touch so nearly,
  No doubt but many get them in their mariage,
  Yet feel them not, they be so light in cariage.

80

But if a man by certaine signes may know,
  How that his wife to him is true and just,
  He hath more cause more kindnesse her to show,
  Then he that lives in right or wrong mistrust:
  For some without a cause do jealous grow,
  Whose wives are chast, and free from lawlesse lust:
  And some that for their wives truth durst have sworn,
  Have for their labours in their head a horn.

81

Now sir, if you believe your wife is true,
  As sure till one do find contrary proofe,
  I think both you and all men ought of due,
  For that no doubt is best for their behoofe,
  Here you shall see it tri'd within your view,
  For which I praid you harbour in my roofe:
  This cup (said he) if you desire to know it,
  By drinking in the same, will clearly show it.

82

Now drink hereof, and prove this passing skill,
  For if *Acteons* armes be on your crest,
  Do what you can, you shall the liquor spill
  Beside your mouth, upon your lap and brest:
  But if your wife be chast, then drink your fill,
  No such mischance your draught will then molest,
  Thus much he said, and fixt on him his eyne,
  And thinks *Renaldo* sure would spill the wine.

83

Renaldo halfe allured to assay
  To find a thing, which found he might repent,
  Did take in hand the golden cup straight way,
  As if to quaffe it off, were his intent:
  Yet first he doth the certaine danger way,
  To which by tasting such a cup he went.
  But give me leave a while some breath to take,
  Before you heare what answer he did make.

THE FORTY-THIRD BOOKE OF
ORLANDO FVRIOSO

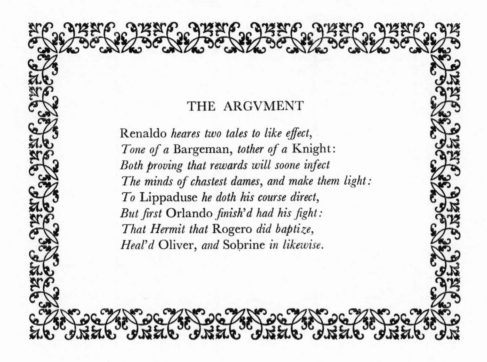

THE ARGVMENT

Renaldo *heares two tales to like effect,*
Tone of a Bargeman, *tother of a* Knight:
Both proving that rewards will soone infect
The minds of chastest dames, and make them light:
To Lippaduse *he doth his course direct,*
But first Orlando *finish'd had his fight:*
That Hermit that Rogero *did baptize,*
Heal'd Oliver, *and* Sobrine *in likewise.*

ORLANDO FVRIOSO
THE FORTY-THIRD BOOKE

1

O curst, ô greedy, ô unsatiable
  Desire of gaine, I do not marvell sure,
If thou the base and filthy minds art able
  To cause to stoope unto thy carren lure,
Sith oft we see some persons honorable,
  Can scarce thy weak and base assaults endure,
Who if they could thy foule inticements shun,
No doubt but they great glory should have won.

2

Some men can measure earth, and sea, and skie,
  And tell the change and cause of ev'ry season,
And wade so far with wit, and mount so hie,
  They search both heav'n & hel with depth of reason,
But when thou com'st in place, then by and by
  Thou putst their dainty tasts so out of season,
They place their whole delight, their hope, their health
In onely scraping and in heaping wealth.

3

Another man in wars hath great renown,
  And gets the conquest in each bloudy strife,
And wins this fortresse and that walled town,
  Opposing his stout brest to perils rife,
Thou only conquerst him, and thrusts him down,
  And keepest him thy prisner all his life:
Some men excelling in each art and studie,
Thou dost obscure, with base desires and muddie.

4

What should I speak of dames of worth not small,
  That having lovers, men of great deserts,
Oppose their honours as a brazen wall,
  Against their suits with unrelenting hearts?
But come some miser, base deformed squall,
  That save his riches hath no worthy parts,
They break the wall, and make therein a gap,
To take the showre that fell in *Danaes* lap.

5

Nor without cause hereof complaine do I,
  Take me that can, for I do rightly take it,
Nor from my matter do I swerve awry,
  Or by **a** vaine digression do forsake it:
Yet to my former speech I not apply,
  But tending to a future tale I spake it:
Now let me tell you of *Renaldo* first,
That with one draught would swage his double thirst.

6

But whether that his courage did him faile,
  Or that on more advice he changed mind,
He thought and said, what should it one availe,
  To seek a thing he would be loth to find?
My wife a woman is, their sex is fraile,
  I yet am to believe the best inclin'd;
I know I cannot better my belief,
And if I change it, it will be my grief.

7

What good may come by such a straight espiall,
  Into my sences surely cannot sink,
Much hurt may come, there can be no deniall,
  Let nothing sever those whom God doth link:
Wherefore to make so unaccustom'd triall,
  Were sin, and tempting God, as I do think:
Then drink this cup (quoth he) that list, not I,
I am not, nor I mind not to be drie.

8

God would such skill from mortall men be hid,
  And ev'n as *Adam* wrought his overthrow,
By tasting fruit that God did him forbid,
  So he that curiously will search to know
All that his wife hath said, or what she did,
  May fortune at the last himself beshrow,
And shall confound himself (this think I verily)
And live in sorrow, that did erst live merrily.

9

Thus much said good *Renaldo*, and withall
  He thrust away that hatefull cup of wine,
And then he saw of teares a stream not small,
  Flow from the master of that house his eyne:
Which past, he said, now foule may them befall,
  That first procur'd this misery of mine:
To prove (which I shall sorrow all my life)
That, which bereft me of my dearest wife.

10

Why was not I (said he) with you acquainted,
  Ten yeares ere this, to take advice so sound,
Before my heart was thus with sorrow tainted,
  Of which no ease can now, nor end be found:
But that you may (as in a table painted)
  Behold my griefs, I will to you expound,
What caus'd this my incomparable woe,
And then you sure will pitie me I know.

11

Not far from hence you left a little town,
  About the which there runs a pretie lake,
That fals into this stream of great renown,
  But from *Banaco* first his head doth take,
Erected when those wals were beaten down,
  That erst *Agenors* dragon there did make;
There was I born of house and stock not base,
Though of mean wealth inferiour to my race.

12

But though to me dame Fortune was but spare,
  That by my birth small wealth to me there grew,
Yet nature did with bounty great and care
  Supply that want, by faire and comly hew,
My seemly personage, my beauty rare,
  To me the liking of full many drew:
My qualities thereto were quaint and jolly,
Although I know to praise ones self is folly.

13

Within this town a great rich man did tarie,
  Well learn'd and wise, and old beyond all credit,
For ere he di'd, he on his back did carie
  Full six score yeares and eight at least, he sed it:
An hundred yeares he lived solitarie,
  But after that (you know what humor bred it)
He lov'd a dame, & with his wealth so wrought her,
That at the last he gat of her a daughter.

14

And lest the daughter should prove like the mother,
  To sell her chastity for filthy pelf,
Which whosoever sels, it quite undoth her,
  Although she thinks she doth enrich her self,
Therefore he bred her far from sight of other,
  And by the help of many a hellish elf,
Which by his skill in Magick he could master,
He built this house of Tutch and Alablaster.

15

He caused chast old women her to nourish
  In this same house, in which she grew so faire,
And in those years when youth doth chiefly flourish,
  He let not any thither to repaire,
That were in looks, or speech, or manners whorish,
  But contrary, he caus'd in marble faire,
Or els on tables to be drawn and carv'd,
All such whose chastities had praise deserv'd.

16

Nor only such as have in ancient times,
  Been patterns true of manners chast and pure,
And have oppos'd against all fleshly crimes,
  Most chast and vertuous thoughts (a buckler sure)
By which their name to such high honour climes,
  As their great praise shall evermore endure:
But such as shall excell in times to come,
Of which those eight that erst you saw be some.

17

Now when this aged sire had with his skill
  Procur'd his daughter be thus choicely bred,
It was my hap, (shall I say good or ill?)
  That I was deem'd most worthy her to wed;
And that old man bare her so great good will,
  He gave to me this house thus furnished
With needfull things within it and without it,
And all the lands in twenty mile about it.

18

But her own shape so pleas'd my heart and eyne,
  That for the rest I did but little care,
For needle works and for embroidries fine,
  I think her skill with *Pallas* may compare;
To heare her play or sing, a thing divine
  It was, her stroke so sweet, her voice so rare:
In other sciences her skill was such
As was her fathers, or almost as much.

19

Great was her wit, no lesse then wit, her favour,
  As might in senslesse stones affection move,
To this she had a sweet and kind behaviour,
  As more then all the rest ingendred love,
It seem'd her sole delight was in my favour,
  Out of my sight she was most loth to move:
So lived I, and still had lived so,
But that my self did work my self this wo.

20

For when her father finish'd had his life,
  Full five years after I had got his daughter,
Then grew the causes of this wofull strife,
  That unto sorrow turneth all my laughter;
For when I doted most upon my wife,
  And of the world the chiefest jewell thought her,
A dame of noble birth, of person seemly,
Did hap to fall in love with me extremely.

21

This dame, for passing skill in Magick art,
  Was comparable to the best Magicion,
But yet for all her skill, my constant heart,
  She could not move nor turn on no condition,
To cure her malady, or ease her smart,
  I still refused to be her Physition,
Because the med'cine that of me she sought,
As injurie unto my wife I thought.

22

Yet was her beauty much, I must confesse,
  And greater offers she to me did make,
Beside the love she did to me professe,
  Would moue a man some care of her to take,
But my wives love did me so firm possesse,
  I all rejected, only for her sake,
And that which most to her my liking drew,
Was that I found her still so kind and true.

23

The good opinion, and the strong surmise,
  I had of my wives chastity and truth,
  Would without doubt have made me to despise
  The Dame, whose beauty bred to *Troy* such ruth.
  And all the wealth (though laid before mine eyes)
  That *Iuno* offer'd to the *Trojan* youth,
  Yet my refusall, and her oft repulses,
  No part of her great love from her expulses.

24

Melissa, so was this inchantresse name,
  Perceiving still in vaine to me she sewed,
  Once finding me at leisure, to me came,
  And in most cunning sort her suit renewed,
  And secretly she kindled jealous flame
  Within my brest, which oft I since have rued.
  She saith, I do but well so true to be
  Vnto my wife, if she were so to me.

25

But how know you (saith she) your wife is true,
  That of her faith as yet no proof have made,
  You never let her go scant from your view,
  When none can come to vice her to perswade,
  When none can see her, none to her can sue,
  'Tis easie to resist where none invade,
  To praise her truth untri'd, is too much hast,
  Your care, and not her vertue keeps her chast.

26

But get you but from home some little while,
  That men to sue to her might take occasion,
  And thinking you are absent many a mile,
  With letters and with gifts to make invasion,
  And then if you shall find in her no guile,
  Except she yeeld to gifts and to perswasion,
  So she have hope to do it unespi'd,
  Then think your wife is chast when that is tri'd.

27

With these and such like words th'Inchantresse sly
  Did make me do that that hath me undone,
  By name, to give consent my wife to try,
  If so she could by such assaults be won:
  But how shall I be well assur'd (said I)
  To know at my return, what she hath done,
  And whether she, with these so great assayes,
  Have at my hands deserved blame or praise?

28

Forsooth (saith she) I will on you bestow
  A drinking bowle, not much unlike that cup
  With which *Morgana* made her brother know
  Genewras fraud, when he thereon did sup.
  Who drinks hereof, his wives truth plain shall know,
  If she be chast, he drinks the liquor up,
  But if a cuckold to carrowse doth think,
  He sheddeth in his bosome all the drink.

29

Now ere you go the cup I wish you tast,
  And you shall drink, perhaps and shall not spill,
  Because as yet I think your wife is chast,
  As never being tempted unto ill:
  But try againe when as a month is past,
  And you shall see (I trow) a prettie skill,
  For then I grant, that if you drink it cleanly,
  Aboue all men you blessed are not meanly.

30

I took her offer, and I took the say
  Of that same cursed cup, with sweet successe,
  I find my wife unspotted to that day,
  As I my self was sure, and she did guesse:
  Now straight (quoth she) to part from hence away,
  For one or two months space, your self addresse,
  Then try at your return how you have sped,
  If you drink clean, or if the drink you shed.

31

But now this parting such a penance seem'd,
  As I indeed could by no means indure,
  Not that of my deare wife I ought misdeem'd,
  For her of all the rest, I thought cocksure;
  But that her company I so esteem'd:
  Well then (*Melissa* saith) I will procure,
  If you will do but what I shall you teach,
  That you shall change your clothes, your shape, and
                                                (speech.

32

And so you shall your self to her present,
  And make your self a plaine and perfect proof,
  I foolishly to this device assent,
  And so it hapt that hence not far aloof,
  A knight of large revenue and of rent
  Dwelt at *Giabana*, fit for this behoof,
  His personage was brave, his purse well lin'd,
  His yeares but young, to *Venus* all inclin'd.

33

That gallant youth had one day been a halking,
  His hawke by hap into my garden flew,
  He comming thither, found my wife a walking,
  And much he lik'd her at the very view;
  But when he had a while with her been talking,
  To burning love his warm affection grew,
  That after that full many waies he prov'd her,
  If his request to grant he could have mov'd her.

34

But having still such short and sharp repulses,
  He means no more in that fond suit to wade,
  But from his thought her shape he not expulses,
  That first to give the bold attempt him made;
  So well *Melissa* knew to touch my pulses,
  To take his form she doth me soon perswade,
  I straight was chang'd I know not how nor where,
  In face, in clothes, in speech, in eyes, in heare.

35

Now having to my wife a tale devis'd,
  As though to th'East I then my journey took,
And being like this youth, so strange disguis'd,
  In gate, in voice, apparell, and in look,
I came as slie *Melissa* me advis'd,
  And she did like my Page or Lackie look,
Vpon her arm she beares a little flasket,
In which of jewels rich she had a casket.

36

I that well knew each room, came in securely
  Into the house, my Page and I together;
There where my Lady sate alone demurely,
  For neither groome as then, nor maid was with her,
Then I expound my suit, and that more surely
  She might believe my words, I needs would give her
Pearles, Rubies, Diamonds of passing price,
The wicked baits to draw good minds to vice.

37

I bad she should esteem this gift but small,
  To that she might of me in time expect:
I said her husbands absence fit did fall,
  And wisdome bids occasions not neglect:
I praid her weigh my constant love withall,
  Which long had lasted, though without effect,
And last, I sware I had some grace deserv'd,
That had so long, that had so truly serv'd.

38

At first she blush'd, and look'd with lowring cheare,
  And would not hearken, but did still retire,
But th'Orient Pearls and stones that shone so cleare,
  Did mollifie her heart, to my desire:
She softly saith, but so as I might heare,
  That for the thing which I so oft require,
She grant it would, and would on me bestow it,
So she were sure that none beside might know it.

39

This answer was to me a poyson'd dart,
  To strike my soule in desperate disease,
And straight my heart, my head, and ev'ry part
  I felt a frozen jealousie to seize:
And presently *Melissa* by her art
  Restor'd my shape (as she could do with ease.)
How look'd my wife (think you) whē by my trapping
She found her self thus foully taken napping.

40

We both do look like ashes, pale and wan,
  We both stand dumb, we both cast down our eye,
Scarce able was my voice (do what I can)
  To serve my turn, while I did think to cry:
Then wouldst thou wife unto another man
  Mine honour sell, if he the same could buy?
She held her peace, and answer made me none,
But onely wept, and made a piteous mone.

41

The shame was much, but much more the disdaine,
  That of my foolish usage tane she hath,
Within due bonds she could not it containe,
  But that it brake to spite, to hate, to wrath,
Resolv'd with me no longer to remaine,
  When *Phœbus* charret trod his Western path,
That ev'ning in a small barge of her own,
Down stream she swimmeth as if she had flown.

42

Betimes next day she doth unto that knight
  Her self present, that her before had lov'd,
In whose disguised shape, I her last night
  Both gainst mine own, and gainst her honour prov'd,
You well may judge it was a welcome sight
  To him, that long before such suit had mov'd,
From thence she sends to me this message plaine,
That she would never come at me againe.

43

Ah wo was me, for from that houre to this,
  She bides with him, where me they lout and scorn,
And I that could not see my sugred blisse,
  Now by forgoing it am quite forlorn;
Nor can I say but just my penance is,
  Which still growes more, and will till I be worn,
And sure one yeare of life had quite bereft me,
Save for one only comfort that was left me.

44

This only comfort brought me some relief,
  That for the space of ten years all my guests,
(Though many of their wives had great belief)
  Yet still they shed the drink upon their brests;
To find so many partners in my grief,
  Asswageth much the paine that me molests,
Your only self hath been the onely stranger,
That hath refus'd a draught of so great danger.

45

My overmuch desire to sift my wife
  In so precise and in so straight a sort,
Doth cause that now I shall not all my life
  Live one good houre, endure it long or short:
Glad was *Melissa* that procur'd this strife,
  But soon I turn'd and marred all her sport,
For finding she was of my harm procurer,
I hated her and could no more endure her.

46

But she that finds her selfe disdained mearly,
  Where she had hoped to have found reward,
And me, whom she profest to love so dearly,
  Her love and kindnesse nothing to regard,
The grief hereof did touch her mind so nearly,
  To leave this country she forthwith prepar'd,
And ever since farre hence she is abiding,
Whereas of her we heare no newes nor tiding.

47

Thus told the wofull knight in dolefull wise,
  This rufull tale unto his noble guest,
  Who with compassion moved, thus replies,
  Melissas counsell certes was not best,
  That did without discretion you advise,
  To anger wasps, or so to stir their nest,
  And you your self did greatly over-shoot you,
  To seek a thing, whose finding would not boot you.

48

What marvell is it, if your wife were won
  With gifts, and were to lightnesse soon allur'd?
  Is she the first (think you) that hath so done?
  No, nor the fiftieth be you well assur'd,
  Yea, minds full sound have wanted power to shun
  Such baits, and have not such assaults endur'd:
  Have you not heard of men that have for gold
  Their masters and their friends most dearest sold?

49

You should not with a dart so fierce assaile,
  If to see her defend her self you sought,
  What, know you not stone wals cannot availe,
  Nor steel, if gold be to the batt'rie brought?
  Now sure your self of duty more did faile,
  In tempting her, then she in being caught,
  Perhaps if she had tempted you so sore,
  Your folly would have been as much, or more.

50

Thus spake *Renaldo*, and withall he rose,
  And prayd he might betake him to his rest,
  He minds a while himselfe there to repose,
  And after to depart he doth request;
  Small time he hath, and that he would dispose
  With great regard, for so he thinks it best:
  The gentle knight doth tel him when it please him
  He may within his chamber rest and ease him.

51

But if you will vnto my counsell harke,
  And that you haue (as you pretend) such hast,
  I will appoint for you a little barke,
  That shall with oares conuey you safe and fast,
  There may you sleepe the while you finde it darke,
  And when your stomake serues you, take repast:
  Thus may you, downe the streame in safty sliding,
  Win one whole night, & saue a whole daies riding.

52

Renaldo this good offer doth accept,
  And gaue him hartie thanks, then tooke his barge:
  He found his host with him had promise kept,
  And makes of needfull things prouision large;
  No sooner was he setled, but he slept,
  But yet before he gaue the stearman charge,
  If that to sleepe too long it did befall him,
  When he came neare *Ferrara*, then to call him.

53

Now did the knight of *France* in quiet sleepe,
  And past by diuers townes of count the whiles,
  And still the barge a pace most swift doth keepe,
  Vpon that hand, where *Poe* makes diuers Iles:
  And now the Rosie colour gan to creepe
  To th'Esterne skie, when hauing past some miles,
  Bandano then the stearsman wakt *Renaldo*,
  When they discouered both rocks of *Tealdo*.

54

Whereon when as the knight his eye had fixt,
  He saith, O happie place that I behold,
  Of which, by vew of wandring starres and fixt,
  My cosin *Malagigis* oft foretold,
  How that by heau'nly doome it was prefixt,
  On thee to lay such blessings manifold,
  As that thy glorie to such height should rise,
  Of *Italie* to hold the chiefest prise.

55

Thus good *Renaldo* spake, the while his bote
  Down that same streame did swim, or rather fly,
  And when the knight came nearer he did note
  The place, that seemed then all wast to ly,
  And with a moorish water all on flote:
  Yet did he much reioice thereof, for why,
  He knew that that same towne in future time,
  Ordained was to great renowne to clime.

56

His cosin *Malagige* and he while eare
  Had past that way, what time his cosin told,
  That when the Ram had tane the golden spheare,
  That fourth is plac'd in height, sev'n hundred fold,
  Then should there be the bravest Iland there,
  That ever sea, or streame, or lake did hold,
  So well replenished, that none should dare
  With this *Nausicas* Iland to compare.

57

And that it should for building faire, disgrace
  Tiberius Ile, that *Capry* they do call,
  And that th'*Hesperides* should give it place,
  For passing fruits, and sundry sorts withall:
  Beside, more store of beasts, for use or chase,
  Then *Circes* erst did keep in field or stall,
  That *Venus* with her sonne, and all the Graces,
  Should chuse this seat, and leave all other places.

58

And that a certaine Prince should this fulfill,
  So provident, so stout, so wise, so staid,
  As having power united to his will,
  Should with strong Rampires fence the town, he said,
  That foes should have no force to work her ill,
  Nor she should never feed of forraine aid:
  And that the man by whom this must be done,
  Should be both *Hercles* Sire, and *Hercles* sonne.

59

Thus while the knight of *France* with great delight
  Did call to mind what should another day
  Vpon that happy City there alight,
  His water-men did give so lusty way,
  That of the place he soon had left the sight,
  And keeping on the right hand all the way,
  They went beyond Saint *Georges* in an houre,
  And passed by *Grabanas* ditch and Tower.

60

And now *Renaldo*, as doth oft befall,
  That one conceipt another out doth drive,
  Began the knight to memorie to call,
  That last did him kind entertainment giue,
  That had iust cause this City more then all
  To hate, and should haue still while he did liue:
  The cursed cup he further cald to mind,
  In which men may their spouses falshood find.

61

And last of his hosts later speech he thought,
  Concerning that same cup, and how they sped,
  I meane his guests, that that same triall sought,
  Into their bosoms still the liquor shed:
  Now he doth half repent he mist the draught,
  Yet was he glad thereof, for why (he said)
  Had it faln well, what had I got thereby?
  If not, in what a case had then been I?

62

I now believe so well, as having tri'd
  With good success believe I better should not;
  So that I might have well been damnifi'd,
  But by my triall mend my state I could not:
  But what grief had it been if I had spi'd,
  By my most deare *Clarice*, that I would not?
  Much may they leese, but gains get small or none,
  That will in play a thousand lay to one.

63

These later words so lowd and plaine he spake,
  (Though to himselfe) that he that steard the boat,
  Who to his speech and gestures heed did take,
  The words and meaning of his words did note:
  Wherefore a further cause of speech to make,
  As one that though he ware a liv'ry coat,
  Yet was well spoken, and of good bold sprite,
  He straight doth fall to reason with the knight.

64

In fine, the summe of all their argument,
  Was that his wit was much to be controld,
  That sought to make too great experiment,
  Of womens truths, more then their force can hold:
  For she that can with chast and firm intent,
  Maintaine her truth, against assault of gold,
  Might ev'n as easily defend the same,
  Against a thousand swords in midst of flame.

65

To this the Bargeman said, you sure may sweare it,
  They must not be assail'd with darts so fierce,
  For their soft breasts too tender are to beare it,
  Sith coats of sounder proofe such shot will pierce:
  I could (saith he) to this effect rehearse,
  And sure a pietie tale (if you would heare it)
  Of one who though his wife had sore offended,
  By her, in greater sinne was apprehended.

66

I meane the tale of that *Adonio*, which
  The great gift gave unto the Iudges wife,
  A little dogge that made his owner rich,
  A thing that in these parts is known so rife,
  The knight repli'd, mine eares to heare it itch,
  For never yet I heard it in my life:
  Then if it please you, heare it now you shall,
  The Stears-man said, and thus began his tale.

67

There was a learned Lawyer, cal'd by name
  Anselmus, borne here in our neighbour towne,
  That so long studied *Vlpian*, till he came
  To be a Iudge, and weare a scarlet gowne,
  And having won great wealth, he woo'd a dame
  For beauty and for state of great renowne;
  They wedded were, for better and for worse,
  So he her person lik'd, so she his purse.

68

Her qualities and haviour past the rest,
  She seemed all of lovelinesse compos'd,
  Not fit indeed for him, that was to rest,
  And to his bookes, more then to sports dispos'd:
  Wherefore foule jealous thoughts his mind possest,
  And that his wife plaid false, he still suppos'd,
  Yet cause was none, of her so to misdeem,
  Save that too faire, and wittie she did seem.

69

Now in the selfe same City dwelt a knight,
  (Too neare a neighbour to this man of law)
  That was of that same stock descended right,
  That had their off-spring from the serpents jaw,
  From whence the *Fairy* eke, that *Manto* hight,
  And built our City, doth her linage draw,
  This knight that was *Adonio* cal'd by name,
  Was much enamor'd on the lovely dame.

70

And that he might attaine this Ladies love,
  He doth begin to spend beyond all measure,
  In clothes, in feasts, his calling farre above,
  In showes, in playes, to do his mistris pleasure:
  To beare the charge thereof it would behove
  To have that Emperour *Tiberius* treasure,
  So as I ween ere winters twaine were past,
  His lands were quite consum'd, he spent so fast.

71

Wherefore compeld to strike his lofty sailes,
  He suddenly surceast his stately port,
  The house (now that the Lords revenue failes)
  Stood solitary, quite without resort:
  There was no Feasants, Partridges, nor Quailes,
  His pittance now was grown but bare and short,
  And he that erst was king of all this feasting,
  Plaid least in sight, now doubting of arresting.

72

And therefore lothing to be known or seen,
  He purpos'd in his place not long to tarie,
  But with a mind to leave his country clean,
  He stale away from thence all solitarie:
  Her only love, that of his heart was Queen,
  In all his woes he still with him doth carie,
  But lo, when as his Ebb did seem most low,
  Good fortune made his tide most high to flow.

73

For as he wander'd here and there abroad,
  He saw how that a sturdy clown and stout,
  With sturdy staffe, laid on no little load
  Vpon a bush, still beating thereabout:
  Adonio in the place makes some aboad,
  And ask'd the cause of that same country lout,
  Who told him that a monstrous snake and huge
  Had taken that same bush for a refuge.

74

And told him further he that stir did make,
  With mind to find and kill it ere he part.
  Adonio for his crest did give the Snake,
  And therefore lov'd and favour'd Snakes in hart,
  As from whose kind he did his gentry take;
  Wherefore unto the clown he doth impart
  His mind so farre, at last he him perswaded,
  To let alone the Snake he so invaded.

75

This done, he went as he was bent before,
  Farre from his country, where he was unknown,
  And so indur'd till sev'n whole yeares and more
  Of woe and want quite ore his head were blown:
  But that great love he to his mistris bore,
  Him forc'd, though now all out of fashion grown,
  With bushie beard, lean cheeks, and ragged clothes,
  To turne unto the place that most he lothes.

76

In this mean time, our town had cause to send
  Some sage Ambassadour unto the *Pope*,
  That must upon his Holinesse attend,
  And for his suit to take a whole yeares scope:
  The Iudge by lot was chosen to that end,
  (O cursed lot that killed all his hope)
  To shun this office he tries many shifts,
  By scuses, promises, by prai'rs and gifts.

77

But finding that he strave against the streame,
  At last against his will he takes the place,
  Though to depart into another Reame,
  It seemed unto him a grievous case:
  His jealousie therewith grew most extreame,
  Misdoubting his wives truth, so long a space,
  Yet nath'lesse her, in grave and friendlesse speech,
  To have great care thereof he doth beseech.

78

He saith, a woman cannot take upon her,
  With beauty, riches, nor with high Nobility,
  To claime the true deserved praise of honour,
  If chastity do faile by her fragility,
  This is the vertue that defends her owner,
  And now she may (he saith) with great facility
  Attaine great praise, and shew thereof great proof,
  While he is forc'd to stay so far aloof.

79

These words he spake, and many such as these,
  Thereby to move her to continue true,
  And she (poore soule) yet free from such disease,
  His parting thence did much lament and rue;
  She swears that sooner men should draine the seas,
  Then draw her mind so to forget her due;
  Yea first she will ev'n die the death she saith,
  Much rather then to falsifie her faith.

80

The Iudge appeas'd with this her protestation,
  Began to have of her the lesse mistrust,
  But yet his fond and jealous inclination
  So moves him, that search further needs he must:
  He had a friend that could by conjuration
  Foretell of future matters true and just:
  That were it skill in Magick, or in starres,
  His guesse was such, as that it seldome erres.

81

He speaketh to that friend to this effect,
  That he his wives nativity would cast,
  To learn if he did right or wrong suspect,
  That she would in his absence live unchast:
  The man thus praid, the figure doth erect,
  And in their place the Planets all he plac'd,
  Anselmus leaves him busie, and next day
  Doth come to heare him what he hath to say.

82

'Twas long before th'Astronomer would speak,
  As loth to speak, that would the Iudge offend,
  With many scuses frivolous and weak,
  He shifts him off, but urged by his friend,
  He told him flatly she would wedlock break,
  And that she would to him prove false in th'end,
  Not mov'd by beauty, nor by suit desir'd,
  But ev'n for lucres sake directly hir'd.

83

Now when *Anselmus* former bad belief
  Was newly reconfirm'd by Spheares supernall,
  It doubtlesse did so much augment his grief,
  I think his torture past the paines infernall:
  And more then all the rest, this griev'd him chief,
  And to his heart a corsive was eternall,
  To think that Avarice should her entice,
  Vpon her chastity to set a price.

84

Yet to prevent all that such mind might breed,
  Most earnestly he bendeth all his power,
  For (as they say) man is compeld by need
  To rob the Church, and hallow'd things devoure:
  His jewels, plate, and stock that did exceed,
  He put all in her hands that present houre,
  And made it all her own by deed of gift,
  And told her plaine what was herein his drift.

85

He saith he gives it her on this condition,
  Not that she should strive to increase or mend it,
  For why (he said) she should have free commission,
  To sell, to give, cast it away and spend it,
  But only that she should avoid suspition
  Of wedlock breach, and by no means offend it,
  On this condition, all he then bequeaths her,
  That he may find her such as now he leaves her.

86

He further doth her earnestly exhort,
  That presently when he is gone away,
  She should (for more eschuing of resort)
  Not any longer in the City stay,
  But at his countrey house, where in good sort
  Till his return the season passe she may:
  Belike, he thought in tillers of the ground,
  And country swaines, inticements none are found.

87

His loving wife *Argia* all this space
  Still hanging on his neck while he did speak,
  With kindly teares bedeawed all his face,
  And much it griev'd her to be judg'd so weak,
  And to be deemed so devoid of grace,
  That in his absence she would wedlock break,
  Her manners have not been so light and vicious,
  (She saith) to move him to be thus suspicious.

88

I should too long in this one matter dwell,
  If all that past between them two at large,
  When he departed, I to you should tell,
  Still iterating that his former charge:
  Now on his way he goes, God speed him well,
  The grief was great that did his heart surcharge,
  But thus they part, her eyes all full of teares,
  His mind of jealousies and thousand feares.

89

This while *Adonio* looking pale and wan,
  As erst I told, and overgrown with haire,
  To travell to his country-ward began,
  In hope that no man now would know him there,
  He travels in the secret'st sort he can,
  Vnseen, unknown, till he arrived where
  He rescu'd had the snake sev'n yeares before,
  That by the clown pursued was so sore.

90

Arriving at this place by break of day,
  He saw a Lady walking neare the lake,
  Who though she seem'd attir'd in strange array,
  Yet for some great estate one would her take,
  Her count'nance did such majesty bewray:
  She toward him with stately gate did make,
  And looking on him with a gracious cheare,
  She spake these words so loud as he might heare.

91

Gentleman, though you do not know my face,
  Yet am I bound to you, and am your friend,
  I am your cosin, and of *Cadmus* race
  Our royall stock doth lineally descend,
  I am that *Manto*, that in yond same place
  To build that town did first begin and end,
  And *Mantua*, according to my name,
  'Tis cald, as you perhaps have heard by fame.

92

I am a *Fayrie*, and to make you know,
  To be a *Fayrie* what it doth import,
  We cannot die how old so ere we grow:
  Of paine and harmes of ev'ry other sort
  We tast, but yet no death we nature ow;
  But which is worse then if our lives were short,
  Each sev'nth day we constrained are to take
  Vpon our selves the person of a snake.

93

To be transform'd to Serpents ugly hew,
  That creepeth still, and on his belly go'th,
  Is such a grief to us, to tell you true,
  Not one of us but then to live doth loth.
  Now that I further may declare to you,
  From whence this kindnesse that I speak of, groth,
  Know this, what day we have this cursed shape,
  We hardly dangers infinite escape.

94

No living thing is lothed more then they,
  So that no sooner one of us is spi'd,
  But we are chas'd and hunted out straightway;
  And if we find no place our selves to hide,
  They lay on load, and beat us so that day,
  That we the paine thereof long after bide,
  And who would not rather one death have chus'd,
  Then beaten evermore to be and brus'd?

95

Now Sir, the benefit that I confesse
  I have receiv'd, in which your merit stands,
  Was this, some sev'n yeares since, or not much lesse,
  As you did wander ov'r these woods and lands,
  You saved me from danger and distresse,
  I should have sufferd at a villens hands:
  Who though he could not slay me, neare the latter,
  Did seek with cudgill me to bruise and batter.

96

For why those dayes that we be snakes (she saith)
  And creeping groveling, bellies on the ground,
  The heav'ns, that other times our hest obay'th,
  Denies their aid, in us no force is found:
  Somtimes the Sun at our commandment stay'th,
  The steadie earth doth move and turneth round,
  As we can by our power cause in a trice,
  Ice turn to flame, and fire congeal to ice.

97

Now here I come your curtsie to requite,
  Which sev'n years since I to me done did note,
  Now to reward you I have power and might,
  While I am free from serpents cursed coat,
  Three times your fathers wealth you shall ere night
  Possesse, and I will set you so aflote,
  You never shall be poore, to your lives end,
  But ever have the more, the more you spend.

98

And (for I know that in your former knot
  In which love bound you first; you still are ti'd)
  I will direct you so, by wayes I wot,
  Your sute shall not be unto you deni'd.
  Now that the jealous Iudge at home is not,
  Go thither straight, and I will be your guide,
  She now is at her husbands country village,
  Attending there good huswifrie and tillage.

99

She further doth at large to him devise,
  How he shall go, in what apparell clad,
  How he shall tempt her, in what manner wise,
  And how to grant his suit she should be glad;
  Then told she how she would her self disguise,
  For why, for ever in her power she had,
  Except the dayes in which she was a snake,
  What shape she list upon her self to take.

100

Thus she disguis'd him like a Pilgrim poore,
  That on his shoulders doth a wallet beare,
  And doth for Gods sake beg from doore to doore,
  A gown of Fryers gray she made him weare,
  A strange apparell for a gallant woer:
  Into an Island dog, with shagged haire,
  As white as Ermin, and the prettiest elf,
  That ever nature made, she chang'd her self.

101

And thus unto *Argias* they resort,
  First to some utter rooms, in which were biding
  The Hinds and Labourers of meaner sort,
  Here he with certaine pipes of his providing,
  His dog made dance, and make such prettie sport,
  That glad was he could bring his mistres tiding,
  Who needs would see as much as they had seen,
  Such was the Doctors destinie I ween.

102

Adonio to her presence thus admitted,
  Commands the dog, which in all points obayd,
  His turns, his dances, and his gestures fitted,
  So due and just, to all the Pilgrim said.
  They mus'd to see a dog so rarely witted,
  And marking still the qualities he plaid,
  In seeing them they take great mirth and pleasure,
  And prais'd the little dog beyond all measure.

103

Much wonder first, but after much desire
  Bred in the Iudges wife, the dog to get,
  She bids the nurse the dog to buy or hire,
  And try what price the man thereof would set:
  Dame (said the Pilgrim) had your mistres by her
  In coyned gold, as much as ever yet
  A womans thought did wish, it would not boot,
  Of this same dog of mine to buy one foot.

104

And plaine to shew that that was true he said,
  And that it rather better was then worse,
  He took her straight aside with him, and praid
  The dog to give two duckats to the nurse,
  The dog but shook his eares, and out he laid
  The gold; there take and put it in thy purse,
  Adonio saith, and think what price is able
  To buy a dog that is so profitable.

105

What ere I ask this dog to me will bring,
  Embroider'd gowns and kirtles, cloth of gold,
  A chaine of pearle, a jewell, or a ring,
  In shorter time then it can well be told;
  Yet tell my Lady this, she hath a thing,
  For which alone my Spaniell can be sold,
  To pay me gold or coyne I count it dodging,
  But I will sell it her for one nights lodging.

106

This said, he sent by her as for a token,
  A gem of passing price, then newly made;
  The nurse rewarded thus, and fairely spoken,
  And vs'd (perhaps) to trafficke in such trade,
  Went backe therewith, and hauing fitly broken
  The matter first, her mistres doth perswade,
  To buy the dog, and said she might atchieue it,
  With such a price, as is no losse to giue it.

107

At first, the fayre *Argia* backward drew,
  As partly, being loth to breake her faith,
And partly doubting all could not be trew,
  The which the tatling nurse before her laith;
But she with oathes doth her first tale renew,
  And that such offers seldome come she saith,
In fine she wan her mistres to agree,
Next day more priuatly the dog to see.

108

Adonios next apparance in the place,
  Became the Doctors ruine and confusion,
Suck duckets, such spur Ryals in like case,
  Such gems he shew'd indeed, or by illusion,
He mollifi'd thereby my Ladies grace,
  And mov'd her marke the bargaine in conclusion,
And this did (then perhaps) the rather moue her,
When as she knew he was her ancient louer.

109

Thus her true louers presence, and his prayer,
  The comforts of her nurse, that whorish drudge,
The great rewards he presently did pay her,
  The absence long of that same iealous Iudge;
And lastly hope that sure none would bewray her,
  Wip't from her conscience scruple all and grudge,
So that she tooke his dog, and for his laber,
Gaue him free leaue to play vpon her taber.

110

Thus now *Adonio* frankly reapt the fruit,
  Of that faire Ladies loue that he had wonne,
The which he followd still with sweet pursuit,
  Vnto their likings both: this while the Sun,
Before the iudg full ended had his suit,
  Through twice six signes his yearly course had run,
And home he came at last, suspecting sore,
That which th'Astronomer had told before.

111

But ere vnto his owne house he would go,
  First of th'Astronomer to aske he ment,
If so his wife had taryed chast or no,
  Since he from home on his Ambassage went:
The cunning man, that meant the troth to show,
  Doth calculate, to see how starres were bent,
And when that he the planets well had vewd,
That she had plaid the quean, he doth conclude.

112

And that it was befalne as he forshowed,
  How she, with mightie gifts and bribes allured,
Her selfe vpon another had bestowed.
  The wretched Iudge, with no small griefe indured,
To heare these news, & though too true he trowed
  The same, yet seeking to be more assured,
He cals the nurse aside, at his home comming,
And seekes to sift her with no little cunning.

113

With diuers circumquaques and deuises
  He seeketh of the nurse to finde the trace,
But she in speech so warie and so nice is,
  As one belike well studied in the case,
That all his cunning speech her not intices,
  But that she still denide with shamelesse face,
That which she knew, and whereof her perswasion
Had bene in part, though not the chiefe occasion.

114

When as the iealous Iudge long time in vaine,
  Had tempted her with promises and gifts,
And that he saw for all his search and paine,
  He found lesse certentie, the more he sifts,
He doth expect to try a further traine,
  As one not vnacquainted with such drifts,
He watcht a time, when they should fall to bralling,
As still where women are, is oft befalling.

115

And as he thought indeed so fell it out,
  The testie nurse one day not pleased well,
Came vnto him at their next falling out,
  And of her owne accord the truth doth tell:
Thinke you, when as the Iudge had heard her out,
  How he did chase, and fret and fume, and swell,
So neare vnto his heart and braine it sits,
It little wanted to haue reau'd his wits.

116

And in this agonie resolu'd to dye,
  And finish both his owne dayes and his wives,
And so his griefe, and her great shame thereby
  To wipe away, with ending both their lives,
He turneth to the Citie by and by,
  As that same desperat desire him driues,
And thence a trustie seruant with instruction,
He sends of purpose for his wiues destruction.

117

He bids him tell *Argia* in his name,
  That on the sodaine he was falne so sicke,
That but to him without delay she came,
  The doubt was great she could not find him quick,
Wherefore her iourney with more speed to frame,
  To ryde behind this man, who in a thicke,
That was right in the way vnto the Citie,
Had charge to kill her there without all pitie.

118

And straight accordingly the servant went,
  To say and do, as much as he was bidden,
But she foretold of that their fell intent,
  (For nothing from her little dogge was hidden)
And taught withall, the same for to preuent,
  Away with this same servant she is ridden,
And in few houres arived at the wood,
Where he was purpos'd to have shed her blood.

119

Then did he tell to her his masters will,
  And drew his sword a speedie death to giue her,
  He onely offered, ere he would her kill,
  To grant her time, to pray God to forgive her,
  I cannot tell you by what manner skill,
  She did her selfe forth of his hands deliuer,
  But gon she was, he seeking all about,
  And for his life he could not find her out.

120

Backe went the fellow, with astonied face,
  With trembling heart, and courage all dismayd,
  And made his master, at the wondrous case,
  No lesse then he had bene afore afrayd,
  He knew not how; by Faery *Mantos* grace,
  His wife could when she list, haue helpe and ayd,
  For why the nurse that did the rest vnfold,
  I knew not why, but this she neuer told.

121

The Doctor now was plagu'd with griefe extreame,
  Far more then euer he had felt before,
  What erst was but a mote, is now a beame,
  Nor he one iot reuenged is the more;
  His shame will now be blazd ov'r all the Reame,
  And all men now, will laugh at him therefore,
  The former errour, might haue bene concealed,
  But this to all the world will be revealed.

122

He thinks that sure, vpon this plaine detection,
  Of his fellonious mind, of which I spake,
  She will, to keepe her out of his subiection,
  To some great Lord, forthwith her selfe betake,
  And liue in spite of him, with such protection,
  And so a mocking stocke of him to make,
  But most he doubts, least to some man she go'th,
  As is a leacher, and a ruffin both.

123

Wherefore so foule a mischiefe to preuent,
  He spares no paine, no trauell nor no cost,
  To ev'rie towne, in *Lombardie* he sent,
  With letters and with messages in post;
  And further he himselfe in person went
  To seeke his wife that was so strangely lost,
  But all in vaine, for why of her abiding,
  No inckling he could heare nor any tyding.

124

And to conclude, at last he cald his man,
  That man that made to him the strange report,
  And bids him show the place, and if he can,
  Where his lewd mistres vanisht in such sort:
  The seruant straight to lead the way began,
  And to the place, together they resort,
  But (which was strange) where erst he left a wood,
  A wondrous stately Palace now there stood.

125

The fayre *Argia* caused had this space,
  Her *Faery* to erect there for her pleasure,
  An house of Allablaster in the place,
  Adornd and guilt, with cost beyond all measure:
  Twere hard to thinke, much lesse to tell with grace,
  What beautie was without, within what treasure;
  My masters house, frō whence last night you came,
  Was but a paltrie Alehouse to this same.

126

Of costly Arras, there was so great plentie,
  Of beds of silke, imbroidred, fresh and new,
  As furnisht chambers, more then ten times twentie,
  And halls, and what soeuer was in view,
  Cups, candlesticks, and bowls of stones most dentie,
  Of precious substance, and of sundrie hew,
  To be imploid for eating, and for drinking,
  And store of gold, and silke beyond all thinking.

127

Now sir, the wretched Iudge, as I said earst,
  That out to seeke his wife had here assignd,
  And findes this house, in state as I rehearst,
  Where he had nothing thought, but woods to find,
  With wonder great his mazed head was pearst,
  And doubted not a little in his mind,
  If so himselfe were sleeping then or waking,
  Or if his troubled brayne, were in due taking.

128

He sees a *Gibsen* standing at the doore,
  All blab-lipt, beetle browd, and bottle nozed,
  Most greasie, nastie, his apparell poore,
  His other parts, as Painters are disposed,
  To giue to *Esop*, such a Blackamore
  Could not be seene elsewhere, as he supposed,
  So vile a visage, and so bad a grace,
  To make ev'n Paradise a loathsome place.

129

Anselmus seeing none but this same drudge,
  Went vnto him, and praith him make it knowne,
  Whose house is this: the *Gipsen* tels the Iudge,
  That he himselfe, the stately house doth owne:
  The Iudge, that he doth mocke him sure doth iudge,
  And prayes the certaine truth to him be showne:
  The *Negro* doth affirme with many an oth,
  That that which he had said before, was troth.

130

And that he plainly might the truth perceaue,
  He prayes him vew the house at better leasure,
  And offreth him free libertie and leaue,
  Of any thing was there, at his owne pleasure,
  For him or for his friends, to take and leaue,
  And eu'n as of his owne, to make free seasure,
  The Doctor maruels that such liberalitie
  Could be in one, of so base show and qualitie.

131

But yet the Iudge, so fayre and kind intreated,
  In frendly sort, doth from his horse alight,
  And sees the house as I before repeated,
  With wonder great, and with as great delight,
  So richly furnished, so Princely seated,
  So brauely built for vse, as well as sight,
  And eu'rie part with other so agreeing,
  He could not satisfie his eyes with seeing.

132

Now when the Iudge came backe againe, he told
  He nere saw house, so pleasing to his eye,
  And sweares he thought that ten times *Crœsus* gold,
  Were scant a price, so rare a house to buy:
  Yet may (the *Negro* saith) this house be sold,
  Though not for coyne (for not for coyne care I)
  Yet for some other ware, which sure I guesse,
  You will esteeme at price a great deale lesse.

133

In fine, he made to him the like request,
  As Sodomits did make for guests of *Lot*:
  The Iudge his motion doth and him detest,
  Who though fiue times repulst, yet ceaseth not,
  But him with so large offers still he prest,
  That in conclusion, like a beastly sot,
  So as it might be done, in hugger mugger,
  The Iudge agreed, the Negro him should (   ).

134

Argia that there by unseene had stayd,
  And seene him falne into the sinne forenamed,
  Disclos'd her selfe, and sharply did upbrayd
  His filthy fact, that justly might be blamed;
  A Iudge (said she) reputed wise, and stayd,
  Sinne thus? wherewith the Doctor was so shamed,
  He wisht the earth would cleave unto the center,
  That he to hide himselfe, therein might enter.

135

But she exclaimeth on him still anew,
  For his more shame, and for her more excuse,
  And said, what punishment were fit for you,
  For this foule sinne, against all natures use?
  That did no lesse then death to me thinke dew,
  For such a small and naturall abuse,
  With one that lov'd me, and whose gift was such,
  As ten such houses are not worth so much.

136

If one death did unto my fault belong,
  One hundred deaths were fit to thine to give,
  And though my selfe am in this place so strong,
  That if I list, thou shouldst no longer live,
  Yet will I do to thee no further wrong,
  But pardon thee, and thou shalt me forgive,
  And quite each other, all old debts and driblets,
  And set the hares head against the goose gyblets.

137

And let henceforth peace follow in effect,
  As ought to be betweene the man and wife,
  Nor ever tone to tother once object,
  Our former fault in all our future life:
  The Iudge was glad, and did it not neglect,
  To take this frendly end of cursed strife;
  Thus as good frends, they lived many a yeare,
  And while they liv'd, they lov'd each other deare.

138

And there the steers-man did his story end,
  With which he mov'd the worthy knight to lafter,
  Who blam'd the Doctor, that did so offend,
  And talked of the same a good while after:
  But much he did *Argias* wit commend,
  Or at the least, the wit of her that taught her,
  To make the Iudge into that net fall in,
  In which her selfe was falne with far lesse sin.

139

Now when the Sunne gan mount unto the South,
  A little Table in the Barge was spred,
  And then the knight began to feed his mouth,
  When sleepe his eyes, and talke his eares had fed:
  The *Mantuan* at his charges, him allowth,
  All fine Acates that that same country bred,
  The while his swimming vessell doth forsake
  The pleasant country, and unpleasant lake.

140

From thence, he held his course still forward right,
  The river running straight as any lyne,
  Which when they passed had with speedie flight,
  Vpon the tother hand they did decline:
  And by a ditch, and standing poole in sight,
  Ere of that day, were spent full howers nine,
  Vnto *Ravenna* as they were commanded,
  They went, and there the brave *Renaldo* landed:

141

Although *Renaldo* could but seldome bost
  Of store of coyne, yet now such store he had,
  As to the Bargemen of his frendly host,
  He gave a largesse such, as made them glad:
  From thence to *Rimini*, he went in post,
  And changing horses still, now good, now bad,
  That night at *Mountefior*, he did but sup,
  And so t'*Vrbyno*, ere next Sunne was up.

142

Then *Caglie*, and from thence the *Alpes* he past,
  Then th'*Vmbrys* and *Etruscians*, thence to *Rome*,
  And so by Barke, to *Ostia* in great hast
  He went, and to that Citie he doth come,
  Which good *Æneas* many ages past,
  Ennobled with his sire *Anchyses* toome:
  Then straight by sea he went unto this Ile,
  Where I did leave *Orlando*, since a while.

143

I meane that Ile, that *Lippadusa* hight,
  Wherein the famous warriors, three to three,
  The combat that I spake of erst did fight,
  The which *Renaldo* longing sore to see,
  With ores and sayles, made all the hast he might,
  But yet for all his hast, it would not be,
  The wind did for his purpose serve so slacke,
  More then an houre too late it kept him backe.

144

So that ev'n much about that time he came,
  When as *Orlando* had that conquest wonne,
  In which unto his everlasting fame,
  Two Turkish Princes, unto death were donne;
  Yet was some sorrow mingled with the same,
  Both for the death of *Monodantés* sonne,
  And *Oliveros* hurt, of which he found
  Such griefe, he could not set his foote to ground.

145

Now as the Earle *Renaldo* did imbrace,
  He could not chuse, but shed a streame of teares,
  When as he show'd him, in the present place,
  Good *Brandimart*, to whom such love he beares,
  Lye newly slaine, with pale and livelesse face:
  Likewise to weepe, *Renaldo* not forbeares,
  To see his death, and eke his cosins bruse,
  So grievous, that his foote he could not use.

146

Renaldo comforts them in all he may,
  Although himselfe of comfort tasted least,
  And chiefe to thinke by his unluckie stay,
  He was come tardie, to so great a feast:
  This while the wofull servants did convay,
  Their masters coarses, to the towne distrest,
  I meane *Biserta*, where they made it knowne,
  Which side prevaild, and which was overthrowne.

147

Of this same conquest that *Orlando* wonne,
  Astolfo and stout *Sansonet* were glad;
  Yet joy'd they not, so as they would have donne,
  If *Brandimart* his death then had not had:
  The fall of noble *Monodantes* sonne,
  Strake them into a dumpe and made them sad,
  But who shall now impart to *Fiordeliege*,
  The wofull losse of her deare Lord and liege?

148

Her self had dream'd a strange dream overnight,
  Which did her mind in fearfull sort dismay,
  She dream'd the bases of her loved knight,
  Which she embroidred black this other day,
  With spots of red were powdred all in sight,
  And on the same like storm of hailstones lay:
  That she had done it so she sure believ'd,
  And with the thought thereof was greatly griev'd.

149

She further thought, that to her self she sed,
  Did not my Lord command me black to make it,
  What meant I then to mix it so with red,
  And in so strange a manner to mistake it?
  An ill presage in her this fancy bred,
  And for an evill token she did take it,
  Then came these newes which none imparted with her,
  Till th'*English* Duke and *Sansonet* came thither.

150

When they came in, and that she well had heeded
  Their count'nances, in such a conquest sad,
  No further newes, no further notice needed,
  To make her know, they brought her tidings bad:
  Forthwith her grief and sorrow so exceeded,
  Scarce any power her vitall spirits had,
  But presently in pale and deadly sound
  She fell in wofull trance upon the ground.

151

But when that life came to his course againe;
  Her tender cheeks and her faire haire she tare,
  Oft calling on his loved name in vaine,
  Whose losse had bred in her such wofull care,
  She screeches and cries out with grief and paine,
  Like those with Devils that possessed are,
  Or as the *Menades* with sound of horn
  In furious manner all about were born.

152

This man and that to lend she doth intreat
  A knife, wherewith her self she murder may,
  Straight to the hav'n she runs with fury great,
  There where the bodies of the dead kings lay,
  With mind to mangle them, and bruise, and beat:
  Then to the sea she will, there is no nay,
  And passe to *Lippaduse*, and there abide,
  And end her life by *Brandimarts* deare side.

153

Ah *Brandimart* my loved Lord (she said)
  What meant I without me, to let thee part?
  Ay me unluckie wretch, in that I staid,
  And was not present there to take thy part;
  Mine eye might unto thee have been an aid,
  My voice might have assisted thee in part,
  And if *Gradasso* thee behind had stricken,
  One cry of mine might thee both warn and quicken.

154

Or els perhaps, so well I might have sped me,
  As to have stept the blow and thee between,
  If thou hadst scap'd, although it did behead me,
  I would have said that it had happy been:
  Now die I will, though death no whit can sted me,
  And though I know my death is fruitlesse cleane;
  Whereas if I had di'd in thy defence,
  My death had profit bred, and not offence.

155

And if the heav'ns had been so hard in this,
  That I could not have holp thee in the place,
  At least my last farewell and solemne kisse,
  I should have giv'n thee, and thy lovely face,
  Bedew'd with teares, and ere to heav'nly blisse
  Thy soule had flown, I should have had the space
  To say, depart from hence in peace my deare,
  And know, I have not long to tarie here.

156

Is this (deare *Brandimart* is this thy raigne,
  Of *Damagyre*, whose scepter I should take?
  Is this the dowre thou dost to me ordaine?
  Is this the royal seat, of which you spake?
  Ah fortune hard, how frivolous and vaine
  Dost thou my hopes and my designements make?
  Ah why cease I, sith so great good is reft me,
  To cast away what ever els is left me?

157

With this, againe so great her fury grew,
  She made upon her self a fresh assault,
  And her faire haire she rent, and tare anew,
  As if her haire had been in all the fault,
  Ev'n from her tender cheeks the bloud she drew,
  Still dewing them with watry teares and salt:
  But let her here a while lament and mourn,
  For to *Orlando* I must now return.

158

Who with his kinsman that did now require
  Some cunning leach his grievous wound to cure,
  And (for to *Brandimart* he did desire
  To give an honourable sepulture)
  To that hill went that doth the night with fire
  Make cleare, and doth the day with smoke obscure,
  And so the wind did favour his intent,
  In twenty houres he came to *Agringent*.

159

Here when they were down from their ships alighted,
  The Sun ev'n then preparing to go down,
  They sent abroad and in great hast invited
  The chief Nobility of all the town:
  Straight at the shore of torches store was lighted,
  And many men of honour and renown,
  When as *Orlando* to the shore return'd,
  Went with him to the corps, and with him mourn'd.

160

There *Bardyn* stood, a man well strick in yeares
  And in such sort to waile he did persever,
  That with abundant shedding of his teares,
  Men thought he would have lost his eyes for ever;
  To blame the heav'ns and stars he not forbeares,
  But roaring like a Lion in a fever,
  Tare his gray haire, and all about it sprinkled,
  And spared not his aged skin and wrinkled.

161

When as the *Palladine* approched neare,
  Straight doubled was the mourning noise and cry,
  Each striv'd who should most sorrowfull appeare,
  And ev'ry one lift up his voice on high;
  Orlando with more heavy heart then cheare,
  Still keeping fixed on the beare his eye,
  When silence first by signes procur'd he had,
  Pronounc'd these words with mourning voice & sad.

162

O stout, ô deare champion mine, and friend,
  That here art dead, but liv'st in heav'nly seat,
  Where thy great joyes shall never have an end,
  Nor ever be empair'd with cold or heat:
  Yet pardon me in that I do offend,
  To waile my woe, and misery so great,
  My sorrow is not for thy parting hence,
  But that my selfe am so long absent thence.

163

To think that he is sever'd now so far,
  In whom I joy'd, this doth my paine increase,
  I was with thee in tempests and in war;
  Why am not I with thee in calm and peace?
  O mirie flesh, that me from blisse doth bar,
  Why cannot I obtaine a like release,
  Sith still I was copartner of thy paine,
  Why am I kept from part of so great gaine?

164

To you the happy guerdon and the gaine,
  To us the losse and dammage all is left,
  France, *Germany*, and *Italy* complaine,
  Their chiefe defence, and their chiefe buckler rest:
  How shall my Prince and uncle now sustaine,
  (Depriv'd of so good help) so great a heft,
  Thy losse of succour hath bereaved wholy
  Both holy Church, and eke the empire holy.

165

The *Pagans* whom thou dantedst in thy life,
  How will they gather heart now with thy death?
  How will they stir new storms of fearfull strife,
  Now having so good meanes to gather breath?
  But how great sorrow will thy dearest wife
  Sustaine? me thinks I heare ev'n now she seth
  I am to blame, and that she hates me most,
  And saith by me she hath her worlds joy lost.

166

Yet *Fiordeliege*, this comfort may revive
  Both thee, and all that for his death are sorie,
  That all the valiant knights that him survive,
  Have cause to envy, and admire his glory:
  The *Decij*, nor the knight that leapt alive
  In *Curtian* lake, so prais'd in *Latin* story,
  Nor *Codrus* by the *Greeks* so magnifi'd,
  With greater praise, nor honour never di'd.

167

These words, and such as these *Orlando* spake,
  The while the Fryres, both white, and black, and gray
A solemne and a long procession make,
  In goodly rank, and in devout array:
That God to heav'n the dead mans spirit take,
  Requiem æternam for his soule they pray,
And tapers in the midst, before, behind,
Did cause that knight, like to the noone day shin'd.

168

Then diverse Earles and knights the hearse uphold,
  All over which a mantle rich was spread,
Of purple silk, embroider'd brave with gold,
  And with faire pearle, and stone well garnished,
Of equall cost and beauty to behold,
  The coffin was that held the body dead,
Provided by the *Palladine* to be,
Fit for his calling and his high degree.

169

Three hundred people of the poorer sort
  Of dwellers that inhabited the town,
Vnto the funerals did then resort,
  And unto each was giv'n a mourning gown;
An hundred Pages, mounted in good sort,
  On warlike steeds, cloth'd to the ground adown,
And both the Pages, and the gallant steeds
From top to toe were clad in mourning weeds.

170

Then bare they divers banners faire displaid,
  And painted divers armes, that he obtain'd
From armed bands alone, without all aid,
  And had to *Cæsar* and to *Peter* gain'd:
With hundreds more, all in black gowns arraid,
  To whom were divers offices ordain'd,
And last *Renaldo* and *Orlando* came,
But *Olivero* staid (for he was lame.)

171

It long would be ere I could it rehearse,
  And tell what ceremonies used were,
Nor can I comprehend them well in verse,
  How orderly they were accomplish'd there:
Vnto the chiefest Church they bare a hearse,
  The while nor old nor young to weep forbeare,
His noblenesse, his value, and his youth
Did breed in all their hearts so wondrous ruth.

172

Now when the women finish'd had and done
  Their bootlesse weeping, and their fruitlesse paine,
The Priest had said their *Kyrieleisonne*,
  And all the rites that thereunto pertaine:
The carkasse of great *Monodantes* sonne,
  So chested, on two collumns to remaine
Orlando caus'd, till time he might procure
A costly and more stately sepulture.

173

From *Sicilie Orlando* not departs,
  Till he for Tutch and Porpherie had sent,
And all that were most skilfull of those arts,
  Had talk'd withall, and told them his intent:
Then *Fiordeliege* comming to those parts,
  Her time, her travell, and her treasure spent,
To make the tombe most stately for her spouse,
At which to spend her future time she vowes.

174

And sith her plaints and teares were never tir'd,
  In that self place she means her dayes to passe,
And for her husbands soule she still desir'd
  Continuall Dirges, and perpetuall Masse;
From company her selfe she quite retir'd,
  And to the place (such her devotion was)
That by the tombe she built a little cell,
In which till death she purposed to dwell.

175

Orlando divers messages did send
  To her, and after that in person went
To fetch her into *France*, and did pretend
  That her to place with *Galeran* he meant,
Or if the time in prayer she still would spend,
  He would a Nunry build for that intent,
Or that he would, if so she so had rather,
Attend her to her country, and her father.

176

But at the tombe she tari'd obstinate,
  And would from thence by no mean be remov'd,
Still doing, saying, both betime and late,
  Penance and prayrs, for him that she so lov'd,
Till death in th'end cut off her dolefull date,
  And sent her soon, to find her deare belov'd:
But now the knights of *France* from *Sicill* parted,
For losse of their companion heavy hearted.

177

And *Oliver* still of his foot complain'd,
  For why, no salve nor surgery prevail'd,
But that he was with griefe so greatly pain'd,
  They doubted that his life would then have fail'd:
Thus while they all in doubtfull dump remain'd,
  The man that stear'd the bark in which they sail'd,
Did make to them this motion sage and wise,
And they agreed to follow his advise.

178

He told them that not far from thence there dwelled
  An Hermit in a solitary place,
That so in sanctity of life excelled,
  That he could remedy each doubtfull case,
Diseases divers were by him expelled,
  Dumbe, blind, and lame were heal'd (such was his grace)
And that he could with one signe of the crosse
Allay the waves when they do highest tosse.

179

In fine, he told them sure there was no doubt,
  To find relief, ev'n present at the hands
  Of that same man, so holy and devout,
  As scarce his match was found in many lands.
Orlando having heard the Pylot out,
  Inquired of the place, which way it stands,
  And presently the place to him was show'd,
  And toward it in hast they sail'd and row'd.

180

Next morning they discover'd all the Ile,
  But kept aloof, so as their ship might float,
  And there they cast their anchor, and the while
  Convaid the wounded Marquesse in a boat,
  Vpon the shallow waves, scant half a mile,
  Vnto the blessed Hermits simple coat,
  That very Hermit that before but late
  Had brought *Rogero* unto Christian state.

181

The man of God that had his dwelling here,
  Came forth, and met *Orlando* at the gate,
  And welcom'd him with kind and friendly cheare,
  Inquiring of his arrant, and their state,
  (Although to him it was apparant cleare:
  For God that night had sent his Angell late
  To tell the Saint thereof) *Orlando* said,
  His arrant was to get his kinsman aid.

182

Who had a great and grievous maime receav'd,
  In fighting for the Empire and the faith,
  And was of hope and comfort quite bereav'd,
  Be of good cheare (the godly Hermit saith)
  Who trust in God shall never be deceav'd,
  Yet ointment none unto his hurt he layth,
  But first to Church he go'th, and makes his prayre,
  Then with great boldnesse doth to them repayre.

183

And calling on that treble sov'raigne name,
  Of God the Father, Sonne, and Holy Ghost,
  He blest the knight that maimed was and lame,
  (Oh wōdrous grace, of which Gods Saints may bost)
  Straight to his use each veine and sinew came,
  No part of all his former strength was lost,
  And as it pleased God of his great grace,
  Sobrino present was then in the place.

184

And being now so weak with bleeding brought,
  That ev'n his vitall sprites were almost spent,
  And seeing plainly such a wonder wrought,
  So great, so gracious, and so evident,
  To leave his *Macon* he thereby was taught,
  And to confesse our Christ omnipotent,
  He praid in most contrite and humble manner,
  To be a souldier under Christian banner.

185

The just old man did grant him his request,
  And christen'd him, and did his health restore,
  At which *Orlando* stout and all the rest
  Rejoyced much, and praised God therefore.
Rogero eke as joyfull as the best
  Increased in devotion more and more,
  To see those mysteries divine and Oracles,
  Confirmed so by plaine apparant miracles.

186

Thus all this company in sweet consort
  In this same blessed Hermits house do stay,
  Who doth them all most fatherly exhort,
  To bend their whole endeavours all they may,
  That in this Inne where mans abode is short,
  They seek to wash away the dirt and clay,
  That some call life, and greatly do commend,
  And sole to heav'n their eyes and hearts to bend.

187

Then sent *Orlando* to his ship in hast
  For bread and wine, and other dainty dishes,
  And this old man whom abstinence and fast
  Had made forget the tast of beasts and fishes,
  Of charity they praid some flesh to tast,
  And he therein consented to their wishes,
  And when they had all eat to their contents,
  They found discourse of sundry arguments.

188

And as in speech it often doth befall,
  That one thing doth another bring to light,
Rogero was at last known to them all,
  For that *Rogero* that exceld in fight,
  The first that him to memory did call,
  Was *Sobrin*, who did know him well by sight:
  The next that knew his lovely look and stately,
  Was good *Renaldo* that fought with him lately.

189

They all do come to him with friendly face,
  When of his christendome they understand,
  And some do kisse him, others him embrace
  In kindest sort, some take him by the hand,
  And chiefe *Renaldo* strives to do him grace:
  Yet if that you desire to understand,
  Why more then all the rest *Renaldo* sought it,
  Turn ore the leaf, and there you shall be taught it.

THE FORTY-FOVRTH BOOKE OF
ORLANDO FVRIOSO

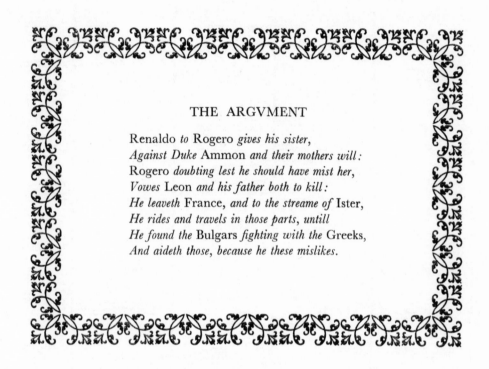

THE ARGVMENT

Renaldo *to* Rogero *gives his sister,*
Against Duke Ammon *and their mothers will :*
Rogero *doubting lest he should have mist her,*
Vowes Leon *and his father both to kill :*
He leaveth France, *and to the streame of* Ister,
He rides and travels in those parts, untill
He found the Bulgars *fighting with the* Greeks,
And aideth those, because he these mislikes.

ORLANDO FVRIOSO

THE FORTY-FOVRTH BOOKE

1

Oft times we see in house of mean estate,
  In fortune bad, and chances overthwart,
  That men do sooner lay aside debate,
  And joyne in sound accord with hand and heart,
  Then Princes Courts, where riches gender hate,
  And vile suspect that loving mind doth part,
  Where charity is clean consum'd and vanish'd,
  And friendship firm is quite cast out and banish'd.

2

Hence comes it that 'twixt Princes and great Lords,
  Agreements all and cov'nants are so fraile,
  To day Kings, Popes, and Emp'rors make accords,
  To morrow deadly wars with tooth and naile:
  And why? their thoughts still varie from their words,
  They keep not oaths but for their own availe:
  Nor weigh they wrong or right, or reckon of it,
  But as the same may turn to their own profit.

3

Now though such men as yet were never taught,
  What friendship is, nor ever knew the same,
  (For friendship never growes where there is nought
  But shewes disguis'd, in earnest or in game)
  Yet if ill fortune them so low have brought,
  To meet in meaner place, they straight do frame
  Their proud high minds to friendship true and plaine,
  Which erst they knew not, or they did disdaine.

4

The saintlike man had in his Cell more power,
  His guests in firm and sound accord do bind,
  Then others should have had in Princely bowre:
  And more, this friendship was of such a kind,
  That ever after from that present houre
  Ev'n to their ends they all agreed in mind:
  Appearing to this old man and devout,
  As white within, as swans are white without.

5

He found them all both gentle, kind, and meek,
  And not in sort of which I erst complain'd,
  Of those that never think and speak alike,
  But ever go with speech and visage fain'd.
  They cleare forgat all grudge and old mislike;
  No signe nor memory thereof remain'd:
  But love together, as if they had come
  All of one seed, and laine all in one wombe.

6

But good *Renaldo* could by no means rest,
  To shew *Rogero* kindnesse great and love,
  Both for his prowesse great, and valiant brest,
  Which hand to hand in fight he late did prove:
  And for his courtsie, that did passe the rest,
  And was praise-worthy all the rest above:
  But chiefe the cause was this, because he found
  His friends to him had sundry wayes been bound.

7

He knew, for often he had heard it told,
  How first *Rogero* saved *Richardet*,
  Whom then *Marsilio* kept in cruell hold,
  Because with child he did his daughter get:
  And further, *Bovos* sons should have been sold,
  But them *Rogero* did at freedome set:
  These things in honour true and reputation,
  He knew were matters of great obligation.

8

And though before he could no kindnesse show
  To him, while he profest himself a *Turke*,
  Yet now that him a *Christian* he did know,
  He would now let his love no longer lurk:
  Which when the Hermit saw, he was not slow,
  A farther kindnes them between to work:
  He moves them (sith he so good friends had seene them)
  That he might make affinity between them.

9

He said it was foreshow'd him from on hie,
  That by the joyning their two lines in one,
  Such ofspring should arise, as under skie
  To passe or match the same, there should be none;
  Wherefore he wisheth them that by and by
  By his advice they would agree thereon:
  Renaldo at his motion straight allowes
  That *Bradamant* should be *Rogeros* spouse.

10

Orlando, Olivero soon to that
  Gave their good will, and favour, and assent,
  Affirming that all *France* may joy thereat;
  They little knew how good Duke *Ammon* meant
  To match his daughter higher far, and that
  King *Charles* thereto did willingly consent:
  To *Leon* namely *Constantinos* heire,
  Emp'rour of *Greece*, who sought the Lady faire.

11

Duke *Ammon* meant not such a match to shun,
　But yet his answer he a while defer'd
　Vntill such time as with his absent son
　He had on such a weighty cause confer'd:
　Not doubting but he thereto would be won,
　And glad to have his sister so prefer'd;
　But yet, though herein he did nothing doubt him,
　Yet would he not resolve thereon without him.

12

But now *Renaldo* absent from his father,
　And ignorant of that imperiall plot,
　Vnto *Rogero* promist her the rather,
　Because his present friends mislik'd it not;
　But chief that he by th'Hermits speech did gather,
　That God ordain'd it by eternall lot;
　And of his father firmly he believ'd,
　At such alliance he could not be griev'd.

13

All that same day and night, and half the next,
　They made abode with that same saintlike sire,
　Still preaching, teaching them the blessed text,
　Expounding ev'ry place at their desire:
　The mariners with their long tarrying vext,
　Oft sent to pray them to the ship retire,
　Because the wind blew well to serve their turn,
　Compelling them in fine to make return.

14

Rogero that had liv'd in long exile,
　(Now glad to do as that old man had told him)
　Doth bid farewell, and left that happy Ile,
　When he had learnd that faith that sole must save him
　Orlando unto him his sword this while,
　And *Hectors* armes, and good *Frontino* gave him,
　Both to declare his love so much the more,
　And that he knew they had been his before.

15

And though the *Palladine* in common sence
　Had juster claime unto the blade inchaunted,
　As having won it in his own defence,
　Forth of the garden with foule spirits haunted,
　Whereas *Rogeros* title and pretence
　Came from *Brunello*, that of theft was taunted,
　Yet gave he it of his good nature meerly,
　Although his right thereto appeared clearly.

16

Then by the holy man they were all blessed,
　And to their ship they made their back repaire,
　Their oares for waves, their sails for winds addressed,
　Which then blew very temperate and faire:
　No feare of wrack, no doubt to be distressed;
　No need there was of vowes, or yet of praier:
　But here I leave them sailing in faire weather,
　Till th'*English* Duke and them I bring together.

17

Who when the victory he understood
　Orlando got, of which he was lesse glad,
　Because the same was won with so much blood,
　And sith now *France* no feare of *Affricke* had;
　To send *Senapo* home he thought it good,
　And therefore with a countnance grave and sad,
　Yet kind and friendly he did give him thank,
　For lending him his aid so free and frank.

18

And *Dudon* sent a little while before,
　All that his great triumphant navy back,
　Wherewith he plagued had the *Turks* so sore,
　And brought them all to ruine great and wrack:
　Which ships no sooner touch'd that *Affricke* shore,
　And quite disburden'd of the people black,
　But ev'ry ship his shape forsakes and leaves,
　And all of them were turn'd againe to leaves.

19

And now on parting were the *Nubian* bands:
　Some mounted, some on foot pell mell together,
　The winds that wont to move the troublous sands,
　Astolfo gave their king in bags of leather,
　So firmly ti'd, and in so sured bands,
　As feare they need not any change of weather:
　And will'd him, when they were past all jeoperty,
　That they should grant unto the wind his liberty.

20

Turpino writes that they no sooner came
　Vnto the mountaine *Atlas* stony root,
　But that their horses stones againe became,
　And so they all went home againe on foot:
　But after how each thing with them did frame,
　In this discourse to tell it shall not boot:
　Now tell we of your *English* Dukes proceeding,
　Of his return to *France*, and of his speeding.

21

Who having rulers for those parts ordain'd,
　That might as pleas'd them ruine or repaire,
　No longer then in *Affrica* remain'd,
　But unto *France* he quickly did repaire,
　By land or sea to travell he disdain'd,
　But with his winged beast he cuts the aire,
　And quickly came to *Province*, where he did
　As much as erst th'Evangelist did bid.

22

Which was that entred into *Province*, he
　Should take away his saddle and his raines,
　And grant him liberty and set him free,
　And put him now vnto no further paines:
　For *Cinthias* spheare, in which our lost wits be,
　That maketh of our losses greatest gaines
　Had made his horne long since to loose his sound,
　That now no vertue in the same was found.

23

Now th'English Duke vnto *Marsilio* came,
  And iust at that same time arriued there,
  When those three *Palladines*, of worthy fame,
  With *Sobrin* and *Rogero* landed were:
Much was their joy, yet lesson'd was the same,
  And outward showes thereof they do forbeare:
So great a sadnes in them all it bred,
To thinke their friend king *Brandimart* was ded.

24

But *Charles* that from *Sicilia* notice had,
  How those two kings were slaine, and *Sobrine* taken,
  And *Brandimart* deceast (which made him sad)
  And that *Rogero* had the *Turkes* forsaken;
Was in his minde now well apaid and glad,
  That such a peise, he from his neck had shaken,
Which for a long time had so grieuous wayed,
As he therewith was welny ouerlayed.

25

Wherefore to do them honour, as was meete,
  That with their courage did his crowne sustaine,
  He sent his Peeres and nobles them to greete,
  Vnto the verie confines of his raigne:
Himselfe in person, after did them meete,
  With Lords and Princes of his chiefest traine:
And neare the town, the Queene with many a Ladie
Came forth, to do them honor all that may be.

26

King *Charles* himselfe with chearfull friendly face,
  The *Palladines*, their kinsfolke and their friends,
  The noble men, and people meane and base,
  To make them for their merits some amends,
With friendly shouts did fill vp all the place,
  Each man and euery child his voice extends,
And cride on those two houses of account,
That of *Mongrana*, and of *Clarimount*.

27

Now to the Prince *Rogero* they did bring,
  And told him how he was apparent haire
  To *Risa*, and of that great house did spring:
  And while they spake these words, *Marfisa* faire
Saluted him in presence of the King,
  But *Bradamant* (who thither did repaire)
Yet kept her selfe aloofe with more respect,
Least openly she should her loue detect.

28

Then *Charls* doth welcom him with words most sweet,
  And vsd him like a man of rare account,
  And for he was allighted on his feet,
  For reu'rence sake, againe he made him mount;
And cheeke by cheeke, to ride through ev'ry street:
  He knew and ioy'd, that at the sacred fount,
Rogero by the hermit was baptised,
As he by former letters was aduised.

29

In triumph and in feasts they spent the day,
  And riding through the towne at sundry houres,
  Some straw greene leaues, or rushes in the way,
  Some cast downe garlands made of sundry flowres.
The streets were hanged all with rich array,
  And damsels from the windowes high and towers,
To gratulate their prosperous deeds and haps,
Cast showres of Roses from their tender laps.

30

At eu'ry corner, market-crosse or gate,
  High arches triumph-like were new erected,
  Some of *Bisertas* fall and wofull state,
  Which they had ouerthrowne and quite deiected:
Some of the combate that was fought so late,
  With playes and new deuises vnexpected:
Thus dedicate and thus entitled wholly,
To those Redeemers of the Empire holy.

31

With gratefull sound, of instruments and voice,
  With sundrie sweet and musicall consorts,
  The people shew how greatly they reioyce,
  With *Iubiles*, and shouts, and playes and sports.
Then *Charles* and all his knights, and Barons choise
  To his owne house, and his owne court resorts:
And there with tilting, turneis, and with playes,
They spent a few of then ensuing dayes.

32

Renaldo taking time, vpon a day,
  The mariage matter to his father brake,
  And told him he had promist by the way,
  His sister should for spouse, *Rogero* take:
By which, allyance such procure they may,
  As men may count great folly to forsake:
In which himselfe the further did proceed,
Because *Orlando* was thereto agreed.

33

With much disdaine this speech Duke *Ammon* hard,
  Affirming he presumptuously had donne,
  To promise so, sith he had now prepar'd,
  To match her to the *Greekish* Emp'rors sonne,
And not this priuate knight, who he had hard,
  Had not one foote of land scant vnder Sunne;
Alas (quoth he) poore gentrie small auailes,
And vertue lesse, if land and riches failes.

34

But chiefly *Ammons* wife, dame *Beatrice*,
  Doth call her sonne vngrate and arrogant,
  And thinks to worke so by her wise advise,
  To make an Empresse of her *Bradamant*:
Renaldo much condemneth that deuice,
  Nor will not of his word one title want:
But said, his sister (vnder their correction)
Would therein ruled be by his direction.

35

The mother (in her daughter much beguild)
  Perswades with her, and comforts her to say,
That she will rather dye and be exild,
Then match so meane, when higher match she may.
She saith, she will not take her for her child,
If she will let her brother beare such sway:
Wherefore (saith she) be bold, and do denie it,
And with your brother giue me leaue to try it.

36

Poore *Bradamant* doth silent stand and still,
  She dares not scarse in thought, for reu'rence sake,
Gainsay her mother, or withstand her will,
On tother side, she dare not promise make,
Of that, which to performe did passe her skill,
And was aboue her power to vndertake:
Now power she had in this nor great nor small,
For long ere this, loue seased on it all.

37

She dares not giue consent, nor yet deny,
  She onely sighes, and answer maketh none,
But when she is alone that none are by,
Vnto her selfe she makes a piteous mone;
She makes her brests and her faire haire to trie
In part her griefe, for why she beates the tone,
In spitefull wise, the tother short she teares.
And thus she speakes amid her plaints and feares.

38

Wo me, shall then my will and fancie varie
  From hers, whose will should rule and gouerne mine?
Shall my will to my mothers be contrarie,
Or that disdaine, my mother doth designe?
Shall I presume with such a man to marrie,
At whom my parents both do so repine?
What fowler blot can staine a damsels praise,
Then when her parents will she disobayes?

39

Shall then my mothers rev'rence and my sires,
  Make me my deare *Rogero* to forget?
And to new loues, new hopes, and new desires
Betake my selfe, and him at nought to set?
Or shall the rev'rence which their age requires,
And which my selfe hath borne them euer yet,
Be now forgot, and I be wholly bent,
To mine owne ioy, and solace, and content?

40

I know (alas I know) my dutie well,
  But powre I have not to performe the same,
My fancie reasons rule doth quite expell,
And my well ordred thoughts, put out of frame:
And tyrant Love, gainst whom who dare rebell,
Makes me cast off all feare of others blame:
My speech, my deeds, my thoughts he doth dispose,
And ruleth them, against my will God knowes.

41

To *Ammon* daughter, and to *Beatrice*
  I am, but vnto Loue I am a slaue,
Though I do now refuse their wise advice,
Of them I may hereafter pardon haue.
But if I Love resist, who knowes the price,
Or who can me from his great furie saue?
He will not stay to harken to my scuses,
But slay me presently, for such his vse is.

42

With much adoe, and with long time I drew
  My deare *Rogero*, to the *Christian* faith,
What profit doth thereof to me ensew,
If still ill hap my purpose good gainsaith?
So doth the Bee, not for himselfe renew,
The hony that in combes he safely laith:
But sooner of my life they shall me reaue,
Then force me my *Rogero* deare to leaue.

43

But though herein I disobey my mother,
  And father too, which I to do am loth:
What though? yet I therein obey my brother,
That is reputed wiser then they both:
Orlando eke, for me speakes tone and tother,
And favour will this match, how ere it goth;
And sure I am, the world doth of them twaine,
Make more esteeme then all our house againe.

44

Sith then the world esteemes and calleth those,
  The glorie and the flower of *Clarimount*,
Lesse shame it is for me, as I suppose,
If that I suffer men of such account,
Of me in marriage matters to dispose,
That all my kin in credit do surmount:
Beside they haue the word directly spoken,
But to the *Greeke* the matter is but broken.

45

But now if *Bradamant* her selfe torment,
  And doth her euill hap bewaile and blame,
No doubt *Rogero* is as malcontent,
Who had some priuie inckling of the same:
He secretly doth his ill state lament,
And curseth fortune that vnconstant dame,
That had for wealth, so sparing left his lot,
Which diuers base vnworthy men had got.

46

In each thing else that nature man can graunt,
  Or that is got by industrie or art,
He knowth, and each man saith that none can vaunt
To haue a greater no nor such a part: (daunt,
His strength was such, no strength the same could
His person past his strength; his noble hart,
His Princely manners, and his braue behauiour,
Wan each mans love, each mans applause & savour.

47

But this same vulgar sort vntaught and rude,
  That as them list distribute praise and shame,
  And (saue the wise and learned) I include
  All men that liue on earth, within that name;
  For Myters, states, nor crownes, may not exclude,
  Popes, mightie kings, nor Keysars from the same:
  But onely wisdome graue, and learning cleare,
  Gifts given from heav'n, that are not common here.

48

This vulgar sort (to tell my meaning out)
  That sauing wealth and riches, nought admyre,
  And nothing thinke praise worthy them without,
  And in their base conceits can looke no hyre:
  That be one nev'r so learned, so wise, so stout,
  Well shap't as eye can see, or heart desire,
  Well borne, well qualited of sober cariage,
  They nought esteeme all these in case of mariage.

49

Well (saith Rogero) if that Ammon needs
  Will make an Empresse of his daughter deare,
  At least this hast he makes, is more then needs,
  Let him yet giue me respite but one yeare:
  And if in that same yeare I do such deeds,
  That both the sonne and sire, I vanquish cleare:
  When both their crowns I conquer'd haue & wonne
  Then I may worthy be, to be his sonne.

50

But if he straight the mariage do effect,
  With Constantinos heire in so great hast,
  And will Renaldos promise quite neglect,
  And eke his Cosens, which so few dayes past,
  Before that blessed man of Gods elect,
  And that good Marques, they did bind so fast:
  If they shall wrong me so, what then shall I,
  What can I do in such a case but die?

51

What should I do? shall I then be auenged
  Of him that me contraries in this wise?
  Let me be blamed herein, or commended,
  Let me therein be deemd a foole or wise:
  But would my state alas, be then amended
  By th'old mans death? no, no, far otherwise:
  I doubt this would not worke my more content,
  But rather contrarie my first intent.

52

My first intention was, and yet is still,
  That Bradamant should beare me loue, not hate,
  Now then if I her father here should kill,
  Or ought attempt against her brothers state:
  Had she not cause of me to thinke then ill,
  And to refuse me for her spouse and mate?
  What shall I do? alas then shall I beare it?
  Ah no perdy, first I will dye I sweare it.

53

And yet I will not die, but Ile destroy
  That Leon that procur'd my harme and wo,
  And is disturber of my chiefest ioy,
  Him and his father I will kill also:
  Faire Helen to the louer lewd of Troy,
  Nor cost so deare, nor longer far ago,
  Proserpine cost Perythous price so hye,
  As I will cause them this my griefe to buy.

54

But were it possible (my deare) that thou,
  Canst leaue thine owne Rogero for this Greeke?
  Yea though that all thy brothers did allow
  This match, which Ammon doth so fondly seeke?
  Yes yes, I feare that thine owne minde doth bow
  To his desire, and could far better leeke,
  When with thy selfe, thou dost these offers scan,
  To haue a Cæsar then a priuate man.

55

Can then the dignitie and glorious name
  Of pompous shewes, and of imperiall seat,
  The noble heart of Bradamant so frame,
  Her vallew rare, and vertue to defeat,
  And go from her first promise, to her shame,
  Which me she made with many vowes and great?
  No sure I know she will them all forsake,
  Much rather then vnsay, that once she spake.

56

These words Rogero spake, and many such,
  And oftentimes he spake them in such sort,
  That diuers ouerheard him, in so much
  That they were told, by more then one report
  To Bradamant, whom they did chiefly tuch,
  Who tooke them not (you may be sure) in sport:
  But as her priuate griefe was great before,
  So this report of him did grieue her more.

57

But most it griv'd her and aboue the rest,
  That he mistrusted she would him forsake,
  At any mans commandment or request,
  And specially for this same Grecians sake:
  Wherefore to moue this scruple from his brest,
  And this foule error from his minde to take,
  She gat her pen and inke one night full late,
  And to Rogero such like words she wrate.

58

My deare, as erst I was I still will bide,
  While life shall dure, yea ev'n when life is past,
  Though toward me, loue shew his grace, or pride,
  Or fortune raise me vp, or downward cast:
  My stable faith shall neuer faile nor slide,
  For calme, nor storme, but as a Rocke stand fast,
  Against the surging waues still vnremoueable,
  So shall my faith stand firme and vnreproueable.

59

First shall a file, or knife of drossie lead,
  The Dyamond to sundrie figures carue,
Ere any chance by Fortunes frailtie bred,
Or power of loue shall cause my course to swarue:
First shall the streames runne backe vnto their hed,
Ere I will iustly such a blame deserue:
Or ere I shall, for chances good or ill,
Giue my consent to change my setled will.

60

To thee *Rogero* mine, a good while since,
  Of me, and of my heart I gaue dominion,
I should my selfe of lightnes great convince,
If I so sodainly could change opinion:
As for my true allegeance, sure no Prince,
Is faithfuller belov'd of dearest minion.
For me you need no fortresse nor no towre,
To be defences against forren powre.

61

You need no bands of men to entertaine,
  To keepe this fortres, strength enough haue I,
For riches make on me assault but vaine,
So base a price no gentle heart can buy:
Nor noble birth, nor name of crowne or raigne,
Which oft doth dase the common peoples eye,
Nor beautie, to the which light minds incline,
Though greater see I neuer shall then thine.

62

No, feare not, no man powre shall euer haue,
  My heart to other figure to transforme,
Loue did your shape therein so deepe ingraue,
As now it can receiue none other forme:
My heart is not of wax, for why Loue gaue,
(When to his worke he did it first conforme)
An hundred strokes with cheessell and with male,
Ere he could fetch therefrom one little scale.

63

Pure Iuorie, gemmes, and ev'rie hardest stone,
  That most withstandeth steel, a man may burst,
But other figure yet receiue they none,
Then that to which they formed were at furst:
My heart is not vnlike a precious stone,
Or Adamant, or what so cutteth worst:
Loue sooner shall it breake in thousand splints
Ere other beauties bring it to new prints.

64

These words she wrote, and many more to these,
  That him with faith, with loue, with hope so fed,
Of force to cure each desperate disease,
Or rather to reuiue him being ded:
But when they thought them safest from the seas,
And in the hav'n securely harbored,
A new and sodaine tempest rose so sore,
As draue them backe to sea from sight of shore.

65

For worthy *Bradamant* that had assign'd,
  To shew her meaning plaine was, and direct,
And calling wonted courage to her minde,
And quite reiecting womanly respect,
Came vnto *Charles*, and spake in such a kind;
My Liege, if ere my seruice did effect,
Ought worth your highnes thanks, at your cōmand
Let not your grace deny me one demand.

66

But promise me, vpon your Princely faith
  And royall word, which I may surely trust,
To grant one suit, what ere your handmaid praith
And I will promise that it shall be iust.
(Beloued worthy mayd, the Emp'ror saith)
Your many seruices confesse I must,
Deserue no lesse, and frankly here I vow it,
If of my Realme you aske part, Ile allow it.

67

My suit is that your highness will not yeeld,
  That I (said she) may any husband haue,
That shall not first of all, with speare and sheeld,
Or else with sword in hand him so behaue,
As that he can withstand me in the field,
Behold the only fauour that I craue;
I would be his that proues himselfe so stout,
The rest may be content to stand without.

68

Most noble maid (the Emp'ror straight replide)
  Thy stout demand, well to thy minde doth sute,
Wherefore by me it may not be denyde,
It is so noble and so iust a suite:
Now (for she sought not this her suit to hide)
All they that heard thereof, sure were not mute,
But eu'n ere night it publisht was so rife.
As it was knowne to *Ammon* and his wife.

69

And thereupon they presently conceau'd
  Against their daughter, great disdaine and wrath,
For by such motion plainly they perceiued,
She to *Rogero* most devotion hath:
Wherefore to th'end she might be quite bereaued
All hope, to follow that forbidden path,
From out the court they traind her by a flight,
And sent her to their castle that same night.

70

This was a fortresse that but few dayes past,
  The Prince had giu'n to them vpon request,
Betweene *Perpignan* and *Cirtasso* plast,
And neare the sea, not of importance least:
Here as a prisner they did keepe her fast,
With minde to send her one day vnto th'East,
They purpose, will she, nil she, she must take
Don *Leon*, and *Rogero* quite forsake.

71

The Damsell, though not kept with watch or guard,
  Yet bridled with the Parents awfull raine,
  Did keepe her close, with good and due regard,
  And of their rigor did no whit complaine:
  But yet to this her thoughts were full prepar'd,
  To bide imprisonment or any paine,
  Or death it selfe, by torture or by racke,
  More rather then from promise to go backe.

72

Renaldo finding that his suttle sire,
  Had tane his sister thus from out his fist,
  Nor able as his promise did require,
  Rogeros suit to further and assist,
  Forgets he is his sonne, and in his ire,
  Rebukes his Parents, but say what he list,
  They are content to giue the words to loosers,
  But in their daughters match they will be choosers.

73

Rogero hearing this, and greatly fearing,
  Least *Leon* should by loue, or by constraint,
  Possesse his ladie by his long forbearing,
  He minds (but none he doth therewith acquaint,)
  To giue a speedie death to *Leon*, swearing
  That he of *Cæsar*, will make him a saint,
  And that he will, except his hope deceiue him,
  Of scepter, life, and loue, and all bereaue him.

74

And in his minde resolued full thereon,
  Don *Hectors* armor that from *Mandricard*
  He late had wonne, forthwith he putteth on,
  Frontino eke he secretly prepar'd:
  But Eagle on his shield he would haue none,
  I cannot tell you well in what regard;
  In steed thereof an argent Vnicorne,
  In field of Gewls by him as then was borne.

75

One onely trustie seruant and no mo,
  He takes with him his purpose to conceale,
  He giueth him in charge where ere he go,
  That he his name to no man do reueale:
  Thus *Mosa, Rhyne*, he past with pace not slow,
  And *Austria* to th'*Vngarian* common weale:
  And vpon Isters banke, such speed he made,
  That in a while he came vnto *Belgrade*.

76

Where *Saua* doth into *Danubia* fall,
  And all along that streame he might discouer
  Ensignes and banners all Imperiall,
  That nye the streame in numbers great did houer:
  Great was the multitude, and *Grecians* all,
  Who with a hope that citie to recouer,
  Which late before from them the *Bulgars* wonne,
  Were thither brought by th'Emperor and his sonne.

77

Twixt *Belgrade*, and the streame in warlike rankes,
  The *Bulgars* stood eu'n to the mountaines ridge,
  Both armies watred at the riuers bankes,
  The *Greeks* endeuord there to cast a bridge;
  And for that end prepared boats and plankes,
  The *Bulgars* sought their purpose to abridge:
  Scarse had *Rogero* vewd them well, and seene them,
  But that there fell a skirmish hot betweene them.

78

The *Greeks* were foure to one, beside they haue
  Good store of boats with many a planke and boord,
  And to the place a sharp assault they gaue,
  And meane to passe although there were no foord:
  But this was but a policie, and braue,
  For *Leon* so this while himselfe besturd,
  That with a compasse that about he set
  Both he and his the streame past without let.

79

With little lesse then twentie thousand men,
  Along the banks he secretly doth ride,
  And gaue to them a fresh alarum then,
  Vnlooked for, vnwares, and vnespi'd:
  No lesse the Emp'ror *Constantino*, when
  He saw his sonne, on land on tother side,
  By ioyning planke to planke, and boat to boat,
  With all his power, an easie passage got.

80

The *Bulgar* Captaine that *Vatrano* hight,
  And was a valiant warrior and a wise,
  Endeuoured both by policie and fight
  To beare the bront, but nothing could suffice:
  For *Leon* both by multitude and might,
  Vnhorsed him, and ere he could arise;
  Sith he to yeeld him prisner did disdaine,
  Among a thousand swords he there was slaine.

81

Till then, the *Bulgars* valiantly made hed,
  But when they saw their king and Captaine slaine,
  So great a terror in their minds was bred,
  In their faint hearts no courage did remaine.
  Rogero seeing how the *Bulgars* fled,
  And none to stay or bring them backe againe:
  To helpe the weaker part resolueth briefly,
  For hate of *Constantine*, but *Leon* chiefly.

82

He spurres his horse that like the winde doth runne,
  And makes them stand, that fled with fainting brest,
  And hauing spide one brauer then the Sunne,
  A gallant youth, more forward then the rest:
  (This same was *Constantinos* sisters sonne)
  At him *Rogero* runnes with speare in rest:
  He brake his shield and coat like brittle glasse,
  And through his bodie made the speare to passe.

83

He leaues him dead, and *Ballisard* he drawes
 And with that blade he shewd himselfe so stout,
 Who meeteth with him, to repent haue cause,
 He presseth in among the thickest rout;
 Ones skull he cleaueth to the verie iawes,
 Heads, leggs, and armes flew all the field about:
 The streame that erst did run as Christall cleare,
 Vermillion now doth to the sight appeare.

84

No man that saw, much lesse that felt his blowes,
 Dare once make head against them, or resist them,
 Rogero in the field triumphant goes,
 The *Bulgars* now march freely where it list them:
 Nor was there one amongst them all that knowes,
 What wight it was that did so well assist them.
 This change they saw procur'd in little space,
 Who lately fled, now held their foes in chase.

85

The yong *Augustus* standing on a hill,
 A place aboue the rest much eminent,
 Seeing one man his men to slay and kill,
 And that their losse and flight was euident:
 He wonders at his courage and his skill,
 And thinkes that God had sure some Angel sent,
 To plague the *Grecians* for their old offences;
 And for the *Bulgars* succours and defences.

86

He sees both by his armes and Vnicorne,
 That sure he was a knight of forraine Nation,
 And whereas some, more hate would him haue born,
 He rather held him in more admiration:
 His heart, whom vertuous thoughts did still adorne
 And euer was of noble inclination,
 Made him extoll him for his deeds of armes,
 Although his men by him receiu'd such harmes.

87

Eu'n as a babe, whom somtime mou'd with ire,
 The mother beats with rod; or with it chaseth,
 Runnes not vnto the sister, nor the sire
 But to the Mam, and sweetly her imbraceth:
 So now though *Leons* men are made retire,
 And though *Rogero* killeth them and chaseth,
 Yet his great valew maketh *Leon* loue him,
 Much more then hate him, for the harme he doth him.

88

But if that *Leon* loue him and admire,
 Me thinks he hath but sorrie recompence,
 For why *Rogeros* hope and sole desire,
 Is to do *Leon* damage and offence:
 He lookes for him, and oft he doth enquire,
 Which way he was, but still the diligence,
 And long experience of the warie *Greeke*,
 Do cause *Rogero* him in vaine did seek.

89

Don *Leon* saw his soldiers flee so fast,
 He sounds retreit and to his father sent
 A messenger forthwith, in all post hast,
 And of his message this was chiefe content;
 To let him vnderstand how things had past,
 And wish him flie for feare of being shent:
 Likewise himselfe and his hast all they may,
 Back ore the streame themselues then to conuay.

90

But yet for all his hast, his men were slaine,
 And some with hast were drowned in the streame;
 The *Bulgars* now did conquerors remaine,
 That erst in perill were to loose their Reame:
 The knight of th'Vnicorne, they all see plaine,
 Caus'd all their good, wherefore with ioy extreame,
 To him they go acknowledging indeed,
 That all their glorie did from him proceed.

91

Some kisse his hands, and some do kisse his feete,
 And in most humble manner him salute,
 They thinke for him a praise diuine were meete,
 And power diuine they do to him impute:
 They send their chiefest Captaines him to meete,
 And all of them to him do make this sute:
 And vp to heau'n their ioyfull voices ring,
 That he would be their Captaine, guide, and king.

92

Rogero vnto them this answer made,
 That he will be their guide as they thinke best,
 But that he will not come into *Belgrade*,
 Nor staffe nor scepter touch at no request,
 Vntill that *Leon* that did them invade,
 He haue once slaine, or tane him at the least:
 For why a thousand miles for this alone,
 He ridden had, and other cause had none.

93

This said, forthwith he biddeth them adew,
 And would no longer stay at their desiring,
 But that way *Leon* fled, did him pursew,
 (For flight it was indeed, and not retyring)
 Howbeit *Leon* and his men that knew,
 What in such case for safetie was requiring, (past
 Brake downe the bridge, when they the streame had
 And so as then they made the passage fast.

94

Rogero failing of his first intent,
 Did seeke some place to passe to tother side,
 Along that streame till all that day was spent,
 And all that night vncessantly doth ride:
 Betime next morne vnto a towne he went,
 To ease his wearied bodie, and beside,
 To make his horse amends for so great wrong,
 In keeping him without a bait so long.

95

Vngardo, one of reckning good and state,
  Held this same towne to *Constantino* deare,
  And footmen had, and horsemen got of late,
  Since of these warres he did first tidings heare:
Rogero finding none to watch the gate,
  More boldly entred finding passage cleare,
  The towne it selfe within he likewise found,
  With meat and drinke, and lodging to abound.

96

Now where *Rogero* lodged that same night,
  One of *Romania*, happened there to oste,
  That present was at that precedent fight,
  When as *Rogero* holpe the *Bulgars* host:
  And at that time did him so sore affright,
  That though of his escaping he might bost;
  Yet still he feared him, and still did doubt him,
  And still he thought that Vnicorne about him.

97

Wherefore when as he saw that shield, he knew
  This was the man that ev'n before so late,
  So many of the *Grecian* armie slew,
  Straightway he hasted to the castle gate:
  And that he may haue audience he doth sew,
  For matter that concernes the Realme and state:
  But when he was admitted, what he told,
  Within the booke insuing ile vnfold.

THE FORTY-FIFT BOOKE OF
ORLANDO FVRIOSO

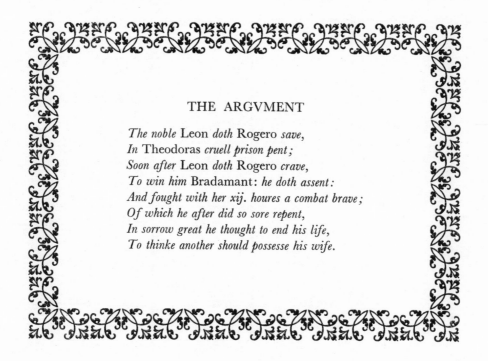

THE ARGVMENT

The noble Leon *doth* Rogero *save,*
In Theodoras *cruell prison pent;*
Soon after Leon *doth* Rogero *crave,*
To win him Bradamant: *he doth assent:*
And fought with her xij. houres a combat brave;
Of which he after did so sore repent,
In sorrow great he thought to end his life,
To thinke another should possesse his wife.

ORLANDO FVRIOSO
THE FORTY-FIFT BOOKE

1

Looke how much higher Fortune doth erect
  The climing wight, on her unstable wheel,
  So much the nigher may a man expect,
  To see his head, where late he saw his heele:
  Polycrates hath prov'd it in effect,
  And *Dionysius* that too true did feel:
  Who long were lul'd on high in Fortunes lap,
  And fell down sodainly to great mishap.

2

On tother side the more a man is pressed,
  And utterly ov'rthrown by Fortunes lowre,
  The sooner comes his state to be redressed,
  When wheel shall turn, and bring the happy houre:
  Some from the block have grown to be so blessed,
  Whole realmes have been subjected to their power,
  As *Marius* and *Ventidius* sample is
  In former age, and *Lews* of France in this.

3

That *Lews* of France (the story well is known)
  That to *Alfonsos* sonne did give his daughter,
  Who was at Saint *Albinos* overthrown,
  And ev'n with much ado escaped slaughter;
  A like misfortune by like danger grown,
  Corvino scaped but a little after:
  And having past that moment by good chance;
  One ruled *Hungary*, the tother *France*.

4

'Tis manifest in stories new and old,
  That good and ill each other do succeed,
  And worldly blisse hath but a slender hold;
  Wherefore a man of wisdome will take heed;
  And on his fortune never be too bold,
  Although his state and riches farre exceed:
  Nor yet in fortune ill, despaire or doubt,
  For evermore her wheel doth turn about.

5

Rogero (as I lately did repeat)
  Now having both repulst the sonne and sire,
  Grew to such pride therewith, and such conceit,
  (Ambition evermore aspiring hier,)
  He thinks by fortune and his force so great,
  To kill Don *Leon*, which was his chief desire,
  And for that purpose aid he asketh none,
  But thinketh sure to do the feat alone.

6

But she that cannot suffer nor abide,
  That any long should of her favour bost,
  Now in the midst of all his praise and pride,
  When in her favour he affied most,
  Did cause him of this knight to be descri'd;
  Who went unto *Vngardo* straight in post,
  And told him how that man that put to flight
  The *Greekish* host, would lie in town that night.

7

He said, 'twas happen'd ev'n as one could wish,
  If so they mar'd not all by ill contriving,
  That he was taken now as is a fish,
  That to the net approcheth without driving:
  Or rather layes itself into the dish,
  And makes resistance none nor any striving,
  Much did the Captaine at these newes rejoyce,
  And shew'd the same by gesture and by voice.

8

And presently provision such he made,
  That good *Rogero* taken was that night,
  And kept as prisner now in *Novengrade*,
  (For so the town where he was taken hight)
  What should he do? when arm'd men did invade
  Him naked and asleep, with so great might:
  Vnguardo straight doth send this joyfull tiding
  To *Constantine*, at *Beltrich* now abiding.

9

For since his forces late were beaten down,
  He thought it safest, quickly to withdraw
  Vnto some strength, or to some walled town,
  (For of the *Bulgars* now he had such aw)
  He doubted they would hazard ev'n his crown,
  Now having such a guide as erst he saw,
  And this same town was strong, and did pertaine
  To him, whose sonne was by *Rogero* slaine.

10

But when this message of their Captains taking,
  By letters and by post was brought to him,
  He was therewith in such a joyfull taking,
  He thought he now in seas of milk did swim;
  His face that pale, his heart that erst was quaking,
  Vpon this newes it chearfull was and trim;
  The Bulgars now he counts as overthrown,
  The victory he judgeth sure his own.

NN

11

As doth the father joy, so doth the son,
  Of this good hap, though for a further end,
  He hopeth this brave knight may now be won
  By curtesie, to be his faithfull friend,
  He needeth not envie (if that were done)
  King *Charles* the great (he thinks) but ev'n contend
  Both with his *Palladines* and all his garison,
  For flowre of Chivalry, to make comparison.

12

But *Theodora* was of other mind,
  Don *Leons* Ant, whose sonne *Rogero* slew,
  For she with choler carri'd headlong blind,
  And for his losse, whose death she most did rew,
  To *Constantine* her Lord, and brother kind
  She went, and at his feet her selfe she threw,
  And when she first had made a piteous plaint,
  She with her suit this wise did him acquaint.

13

I will not rise from these your feet (she seth)
  My liege, untill you grant me power to wreak
  My selfe on him, that brought my sonne to death,
  And did with cruell speare his bowels break:
  Besides he was your nephew, while his breath
  Did dure, you saw his love, and service eke,
  Your highnesse knowes it were too great a wrong,
  To let his death be unrevenged long.

14

You further see, that God of goodnesse meare
  Had caus'd that wretch the camp thus to forsake,
  And come like bird to bait (the case is cleare)
  Whereas *Vngardo* did him prisner take,
  Because my only sonne I lov'd so deare,
  Might not go unreveng'd to *Stygian* lake:
  Then give me him (my Lord) and be content,
  I swage my grief, with his sharp punishment.

15

Her plaints and mone so well she doth devise,
  So forcibly and heartily she praid,
  Nor would not stirre from thence in any wise,
  (Although the noble Emp'ror did and said
  Ev'n all he could, to make her thence arise)
  That sith she would by no means be denaid,
  But still renew'd her suit, with piteous weeping,
  He granteth her the prisner in her keeping.

16

And thus at last, to make the matter short,
  He sendeth for the knight of th'Vnicorn,
  And gave him her, whose chiefe delight and sport
  Was to devise to work him woe and scorn;
  All common deaths were of too mild a sort,
  To have him hang'd, and all in peeces torn,
  And on each gate to set a quarter'd lim,
  She thought it was not plague enough for him.

17

Chain'd hands and feet, and neck, she lockt him up
  In dungeon void of light, but full of stink,
  With mouldie bread she made him dine and sup,
  And gave him puddle water for his drink:
  She shortly means, that he a sorrie cup
  Shall tast, but till she may her selfe bethink
  The kind of death, she giveth him a keeper,
  Whose rancor was as deep as hers, or deeper.

18

Oh had Duke *Ammons* noble daughter known
  Of her *Rogeros* now distressed state,
  Or if it had been to *Marfisa* shown,
  Who lov'd him deare, though in another rate,
  But tone and tother thither would have flown,
  And would not cease to ride betimes and late,
  To rescue good *Rogero* and assist,
  Let *Ammon* and his wife say what they list.

19

Now *Charles* the great began to call to mind
  His promise, by the which himself was bound,
  That husband none should ever be assign'd
  To *Bradamant*, but he in fight were found
  Her match, and (as kings use in such a kind)
  He published the same by trumpets sound,
  Ov'r all his Empire sending proclamations,
  That soon the fame did flie to forrain nations.

20

Thus much the writing made men understand,
  That no man *Bradamant* to wife should get,
  But one that would attempt with sword in hand
  From rising of the Sun, untill it set,
  Her force in single combat to withstand;
  Which if that any could, there was no let,
  But she agrees, and *Charles* himselfe allowes,
  That such a one should have her for his spouse.

21

This Article was likewise there set down,
  That they should name the weapon if they list,
  For why her valew was of great renown,
  To fight on horse, on foot, in field, in list.
  Duke *Ammon* now that to withstand the crown,
  Wants force and will, no longer doth resist,
  But after long discourses with his daughter,
  Compeld in fine, back to the Court he brought her.

22

Her mother eke, though wroth and malecontent,
  Yet both for nature and for honours sake,
  Good store of costly clothes incontinent,
  Both gownes and kirtles she for her doth make;
  Thus *Bradamant* with both her parents went
  Vnto the Court, where she small joy did take,
  She scarce esteemed it a Court to be,
  When that her lover there she could not see.

23

As one that saw in Aprill or in May
  A pleasant garden full of fragrant flowres,
  Then when fresh earth new clad in garments gay,
  Decks ev'ry wood and grove with pleasant bowres,
  And comes againe on some Decembers day,
  And sees it mar'd, with winters storms and showres,
  So did this Court to *Bradamant* appeare,
  When as she saw *Rogero* was not here.

24

She dares not ask of any man for feare,
  Lest such a question might her love accuse,
  Howbeit secretly she lendeth eare,
  To others talk, as in such case men use:
  Each man saith gone he is, but none knowes where,
  For to the Court of him there came no newes,
  And he himselfe, when as he thence departed,
  His purpose unto no man there imparted.

25

Oh in what feare and rage these newes do set her,
  To heare *Rogero* was in manner fled,
  She thinks that sure, because he could not get her,
  And that her father nay to him had sed,
  That now he sought of purpose to forget her,
  And shun her sight, that all his sorrow bred;
  She thinks that he from thence himselfe withdrawes,
  For this alone, and for none other cause.

26

But more then all, this doubt her heart assailes,
  That he was gone to seek some forrain love,
  And sith that of his purpose here he failes,
  To speed some otherwhere he straight would prove,
  As from a boord men drive out nailes with nailes,
  So with new love he would her love remove;
  But straight another thought that thought gainsaith,
  She thinketh her *Rogero* full of faith.

27

And thereupon her selfe she reprehends,
  That she her lover should so much abuse,
  Thus in her mind one fancy him defends,
  And then another doth him sore accuse,
  And she her thought to either fancy lends,
  And in great doubt she is which part to chuse;
  But when a while she had her self bethought,
  She leaneth most unto best pleasing thought.

28

Then chief, when in her mind she doth repeat
  Rogeros promise, which he bad her trust,
  She thinks to him the injury is great,
  That causlesly she now should him mistrust,
  And ev'n as he were present, she doth beat
  Her breast that still doth harbour thoughts unjust,
  My self hath sin'd (she saith) which now I curse,
  But he that caused it is cause of worse.

29

Love was the cause (quoth she) that in my heart
  Your face and grace ingraved hath so seemly,
  And therewith hath set forth each vertuous part,
  Beseeming thee so sweetly and so trimly,
  That sure no dame, that knowes well what thou art,
  Can chuse but fall in love with thee extremely,
  And therewithall with all her power indever
  To win thy love, and make thee hers for ever.

30

Oh if that love had grav'd thy thoughts so well,
  As it hath grav'd thy visage in my mind,
  In how great joy and blisse should I then dwell,
  For well I know that they be true and kind;
  Then jealousie the onely plague of hell,
  (To which alas I am too much inclin'd)
  Should quickly cease, and I should free me from it,
  Nor would I in my heart once think upon it.

31

But as a miser hoording up his treasure,
  Doth doubt in absence still that theeves be there,
  So I when thou that art mine onely pleasure,
  Art absent farre from me (I know not where)
  I straight suspect, and straight I doubt false measure,
  And straight my hope grows lesse, and more my fear,
  Which though I think both bootlesse and unjust,
  Yet still I doubt, and still I do mistrust.

32

But yet no sooner shall the pleasing light
  Of thy sweet countnance come unto mine eyes,
  O thou my joy, O thou my lives delight,
  (Though where thou art I cannot now devise)
  But that true hope false feare shall put to flight,
  And knowledge plaine all doubts shall satisfie,
  Come then my deare, and hasten thy returning,
  Ere hope and fear shal wast me quite with mourning.

33

As when the night hath spread her mantle black,
  Faint hearted folk are wont to be affraid,
  But when again the day-light doth come back,
  They seem of better cheare and well appaid:
  So I do faint, when as my deare I lack,
  But in his presence I am undismaid:
  Come then my deare *Rogero*, come unto me,
  Before that hope and doubt do quite undo me.

34

As in the night each little fierie spark
  May plainly be discerned with our eyne,
  But when the day doth come we then shall mark,
  That all are damp'd, and do no longer shine,
  So kindles feare in mind with doubt made dark,
  Vntill my Sun in my Horizon shine:
  Turn then my deare, and with thy light illume me,
  And drive away this care that doth consume me.

35

As when the Sun declines to South most low,
  The land doth leese the beauty that she had,
And winter stormes breed raine, and ice, and snow,
  The pleasant birds all silent sit and sad:
So when as thou from me far off dost go,
  O shining Sun, whose beams do make me glad,
  A thousand feares but all unjust and vaine,
  Make winter in my heart, to my great paine.

36

Shine then on me, O my cleare Sun, and bring
  Thy beames more nye, this snow and ise to thaw,
Refresh these branches withred in their spring,
  And do no more thy self so farr withdraw:
As *Philomena* dolefully doth sing,
  When as her young ones all destroy'd she saw
  Or as the Turtle early mournes and late,
  When she hath lost her deare beloued mate.

37

So noble *Bradamant* still mournes and plaines,
  With feare *Rogero* had her loue reiected,
And with salt teares her louely cheeks distaines,
  Yet secretly, for feare to be detected:
O had she knowne that he was bound in chaines,
  And eu'rie houre a cruell death expected,
  What griefe of minde thinke you, should she then take,
  That was so grieu'd alreadie for his sake!

38

But loe, the heau'nly goodnes so ordaines,
  That *Theodoras* rage, and cruell spight,
Against her prisner, whom she keeps in chaines,
  And means to kill with torture all she might,
Reseruing him aliue for greater paines,
  Came to the eare of *Cæsars* sonne one night,
  And put into his heart to saue and cherish,
  And not to suffer so great vallew perish.

39

The noble *Leon* that *Rogero* loues,
  (Not knowing tho that this *Rogero* was)
Whom his rare vertue, and great vallew moues,
  Which he did thinke all humane farre to passe,
Deuising sundry wayes, this one he proues,
  And by the same, he brought the feat to passe,
  So that his cruell Aunt could not espy him,
  Nor once complaine that she was wronged by him.

40

He speaketh in the secretst sort he can,
  Vnto the bloudy wretch that kept the kayes,
And pray'th him show him the condemned man,
  For why he must examin him he sayes:
A knight a valiant man that was his man,
  He takes with him fit for all bold assayes,
  The cruell Jayler, that no fraud suspected,
  In all points did as *Leon* him directed.

41

He leads him secretly vnto the den,
  Where good *Rogero* was in prison pent,
Nor tooke he with him any of his men,
  But as their guide, the formost of them went:
Who when they saw the time best serued then
  No longer to defer th'occasion ment,
  But vnawares they at aduantage catch him,
  And with a sodaine stab they do dispatch him.

42

Then open they the trap doore out of hand,
  And downe they let the ladder that was by,
And *Leon* with a lanterne in his hand,
  Of light conceald, went where the knight did ly,
Fast bound vpon a grate with bitter band,
  Not in the water, but thereto so ny,
  The very dampe was such, that one might guesse,
  That sole would kill him, in a month or lesse.

43

With great compassion *Leon* him imbraced,
  And sayd, sir knight, the vertue you haue showne,
With sured knots my loue hath knit and laced
  To you, since first the same to me was knowne,
So as my heart and thoughts are wholly placed,
  To seeke your safetie, rather then mine owne,
  Ventring, your welfare and your loue to win,
  To leese my sires good will, and all my kin.

44

To tell you true, the Emp'rours sonne I am,
  Leon by name, as yet to you a stranger,
To set you free, of purpose now I came,
  And put my person, and my state in danger,
That both my father greatly me may blame,
  And looke vpon me euermore with anger;
  The losse at *Belgrade* which you wrought him late
  Makes him to beare to you so sharp an hate.

45

These sugred words, and many more beside,
  Which were for me too tedious to repeat,
He spake, and then his hands he all vntyde,
  And secretly he caus'd him moue his seat:
Rogero in this wise to him replyde,
  Your courtesie is such, your gift so great,
  To giue me life, that you shall ay command it,
  When euer it shall please you to demand it.

46

Thus *Leon* in this secret sort vnknowne,
  Rogero from the prison doth convay,
And send him to a castle of his owne,
  Whereas he might secure in silence stay,
Vntil this tumult all were ouerblowne,
  And till againe for him regaine he may
  His armes and gallant horse, and famous blade,
  Kept by *Vngardo*, Lord of *Nouengrade*.

47

The keeper slaine the next ensuing morne,
  The prison gates, from off the hinges heaued,
  The hinges, and the manicles in pieces torne
Each man might see, but none by whom perceaued:
All thought that *Leon* had him hatred borne,
  Wherefore of him they no mistrust conceaued,
  The cause he had of hate, each man doth know,
By name his late receaued ouerthrow.

48

At this great curtesie that *Leon* vsed,
  Rogero wonders much, and thinks it strange,
  And sore he was in mind and thought confused,
And sodainly he feels a wondrous change,
His heart relented, and all hate refused,
  And turnde it all to loue, by sweet exchange,
  What erst malicious, cruell was, and hatefull,
Is turned now to kinde, and milde, and gratefull.

49

So deepe into his head and heart it sinks,
  That it possessed all his soule and sense,
  On this he studies when he wakes or winkes,
How he may do to him some recompence:
To spend eu'n al his future dayes (he thinkes,)
  Sole in his seruice, and in his defence,
  Could not requite, no scarce the twentith part
Of so great curtsie, and so great desart.

50

In this meane while, the newes was come from *France*,
  Which *Charles* had notifi'd to many a nation,
  Of her that would be woo'd by sword and lance,
In single fight (so said the proclamation:)
Don *Leon* was quite out of countenance,
  To heare of this her strange determination,
  And as a man that wel his owne strength knowes,
Himselfe too weake for her he doth suppose.

51

And long debating how he might supply,
  His want of force and courage, by his wit,
  In fine he purpos'd with himselfe to try,
This new made frēd, whose name he knowes not yet,
Although he well could witnesse with his eye,
  That for no braue exploit he was vnfit,
  He hopeth by his manhood and his aid,
To conquer and to haue that hardie maid.

52

But two things he must do before he goes,
  One is the minde of this same vnknowne knight,
  Vnto this hardie enterprise dispose,
The tother is, to bring him to the fight
So secretly, as none might it disclose,
  And all that while to keepe himselfe from sight;
  First then, in earnest sort he doth intreat
Rogero take on him this hardie feat.

53

Much might the *Greeke* preuaile by eloquence,
  The which he vs'd to lead him thereunto,
  But more prevail'd the bond of recompence,
So firme as no time euer could vndo,
That though the motion bred him great offence,
  And seemd a thing vnpossible to do,
  With gladder looke then heart he doth reply,
Deare sir, I nothing may to you deny.

54

Though he no sooner had this word pronounced,
  But that he felt such griefe did gripe his hart,
  As if damnation were to him denounced,
Such pangs he had, such torture and such smart:
But yet his promise giu'n he not renounced,
  Nor from the same once purpos'd to depart,
  For first a thousand deaths he ment to chuse,
Then one request of *Leons* to refuse.

55

Dye sure he shall (he thinks) for if he leaue
  His loue, he knowes he cannot byde aliue,
  For either sorrow will of life him reaue,
Or if that nature shall with sorrow striue,
Of his owne hands he will his death receaue,
  And so his soule from hated harbor driue,
  Each other thing on earth to him seems possible,
But missing her, to liue he thinks impossible.

56

Then die he must, onely he doubts what kinde
  Of death, were for his state and fancie best,
  Once this conceit did come into his minde,
To lay in fight his naked open brest:
Might she him slay, he deemeth in his minde,
  That such a death, in death might make him blest,
  But then he sees what follow would of this,
That noble *Leon* should his purpose misse.

57

And then himselfe of promise eke should fayle
  Which was not to dissemble, but indever
  That *Leon* in his wooing might preuaile,
And make dame *Bradamant* his owne for euer:
Thus though that diuers thoughts his minde assayle,
  Yet wholly in that thought he doth perseuer,
  That moueth him most plaine to deale and trew,
And to all other thoughts he bids adew.

58

This while Don *Leon* with his fathers leaue,
  With such retinue as his state required,
  Of knights and squires, his natiue soyle did leaue,
And went to see the dame he so desired:
Rogero did of him before receaue,
  His armes and horse, and in strange clothes attired,
  Day after day they so their iourney frame,
That at the last to *Paris* wals they came.

59

Don *Leon* to the Citie would not go,
  But neare vnto the same he pitcht a tent:
And by Ambassage made the king to know,
  How he was come, and vnto what intent:
King *Charles* was glad and did his gladnes show
  With gifts, and vnto him in person went:
Don *Leon* tels what did his comming breed,
And prayes he may dispatched be with speed.

60

And that King *Charles* that noble maid would cause,
  To come the day ensuing to the field,
That would (against all common wedlocks lawes)
  Be wood and woone, with onely sword and shield:
King *Charles* her cals, and she that askt no pause,
  Vnto the motion willingly did yeeld,
And so accordingly next day she came,
Vnto the lists prepared for the same.

61

That day that went before the day of fight,
  Rogero passed with as great content,
As doth a man condemned spend the night,
  The which before his execution went,
He chus'd to fight all clad in armour bright,
  Because as then to be vnknowne he ment,
And (for to hurt her, was not his pretence)
Saue sword, he vs'd no weapon of offence.

62

Lance he would none, not that he feard the lance
  Which first *Argalia*, then *Astolfo* bare,
Which forced men beside their seat to dance,
  And vnto many men procurde great care,
For neither he that v'sd it first in *France*,
  Nor any of those other, was aware,
How all those feats were by inchantment donne,
Saue that same king, that gaue it to his sonne.

63

Likewise *Astolfo* and the *Dordon* dame,
  That with that speare full many did vnhorse,
Thought not that it from Negromancy came,
  But from their sleight, and their owne proper force,
They thought with any speare to do the same:
  But now *Rogero*, did both speare and horse
Refuse, because if he had vsde his owne,
He thought it would by *Bradamant* be knowne.

64

Needs must the damsell call to minde the steed,
  For why she kept him long at *Clarimount*,
And vsed him with her owne hands to feed,
  And made of him a speciall deare account:
Wherefore *Rogero* that took speciall heed
  To go vnknowne refus'd on horse to mount,
Or any other thing by which he may,
Vnto his dearest loue himselfe bewray.

65

He further needs another sword would take,
  For well he knew against his *Ballisard*,
No steele, nor armour none, defence could make,
  Whose edge so keene, whose mettall was so hard,
Of that new sword likewise he (for her sake)
  Rebates the edge, so great was his regard,
And thus himselfe both weakning and disguising,
He came into the field at *Phebus* rising.

66

And that each one for *Leon* might him note,
  Vntill the controuersie were decided,
He weares vpon his backe Don *Leons* cote,
  The golden Eagle with the head diuided,
(Their making both was like, from foote to throte)
  Thus when all things were readily prouided,
The tone presents him in the open greene,
The tother kept him close, and was not seene.

67

But *Bradamant* now farre in other rate,
  Herselfe in readines for fight doth set,
And if the knight do his swords edge rebate,
  As fast the damsel her swords edge doth whet:
She wisheth with a heart most full of hate,
  Her sword a passage to the quicke would get,
Yea comfort her it would and doe her good,
If she with eu'rie blow could draw the blood.

68

Ev'n as a Barbrye horse that runnes a race,
  And for the signe thereof hath long expected,
Against his will, doth stay his running pace,
  With swelling nostrils and with eares erected:
Eu'n so the noble damsell in like case,
  That of *Rogeros* presence naught suspected,
Did swell with wrath, and burnes like flaming fire:
Vnto the combat, such was her desire.

69

And as oftimes vpon some fearefull clap
  Of thunder, straight a hurlewinde doth arise,
And lifts the waues aloft, from *Thetys* lap,
  Ev'n in a moment vp vnto the skyes,
The Heardman doubting of some great mishap,
  About some tree, or caue, close hidden lyes,
So *Bradamant* with rage of anger driuen,
Assayld *Rogero* when the signe was giuen.

70

But neuer did a stiffe and aged oake,
  Against the Northern blast more firmely stand,
Nor better doth a rocke, indure the stroke,
  Of surging waues, still wallowing to the land,
Then good *Rogero*, guarded in the cloke
  Of *Hectors* armes, her forces did withstand,
Though she still layd on loade with spite and hate
Vpon his armes, his sides, his brest, and pate.

71

Sometimes she giues a blow, sometime a thrust,
  According as her vantage most she spide,
  And still she watcht, if she could hit him iust
  Betweene the plates or where the same were tide,
  Twas well the coate was such as one might trust,
  For she doth search it still on ev'ry side,
  And inwardly she fretteth in her minde,
  That nought fell out of that she had assignd.

72

So shall you see some men besiege a towne,
  Wel walld, and strongly flankt with rampiers mayne,
  Assault it oft, and striue to batter downe
  Some towers or gates, with perill great and payne,
  And wast their time, and spending many a crowne,
  To lose their men about the same in vayne,
  No more the damsels force did now preuaile,
  To pierce a plate, or to vnriuet nayle.

73

Sometime forth of his helmet and his sheeld,
  She made the sparkes of fire fly out in sight,
  Still smiting him with blowes not soft, nor feeld,
  Somtime at reardemaine, and oft downe right,
  As thicke as haylestones that vpon the feeld,
  Or on the tyled houses do alight:
  But still Rogero close lyes to his ward,
  And not to hurt her, still he hath regard.

74

Oft standing still, now turning, then retiring,
  He makes his foote accompanie his fist,
  With sword, with shield, with slip (cause so requiring)
  He wards the blowes, or shunnes them as him list,
  And euer not to damage her desiring,
  When he might hit, of purpose still he mist,
  Yet in such wise, that she her selfe was ware,
  And all the rest, that he the same forbare.

75

But Bradamant when she her selfe bethought,
  What was contain'd in th'Emperors Edict,
  That whosoeu'r with her a whole day fought,
  Should haue her at the end of such conflict,
  With all her force endeuord still and sought,
  To gall her aduersarie and afflict;
  And now the more she troubled was in minde,
  To see the Sun to West so low declinde.

76

And as her hope still lesse and lesser grew,
  So her desire increast still more and more,
  Her louing aduersarie to subdew,
  That she had fought withall the day before:
  As labourers whose worke by taske was dew,
  That loytred haue and now are sad therefore,
  When night drawes on bestur their lasie bones,
  Vntill their strength, and light fayle both at once.

77

Alas good Bradamant, if thou didst know,
  The man to whom thou wishest so much ill,
  That in this fight hath beene thy friendly foe,
  And winneth thee (perhaps against his will)
  Thou wouldest first haue kild thy selfe I trow,
  Then of his blood one little drop to spill,
  Thou that didst now so curse him and beshrow him
  Wouldst neither of them do, if thou didst know him.

78

But Charles and all his Lords, with full perswasion
  That this so valiant champion, Leon was,
  To praise him highly now they take occasion;
  And sith his strength did hers so greatly passe,
  They think for her there now was no euasion,
  The matter brought to such a narrow passe.
  Each man esteems this match for her most fit,
  Each man allowes, each man commendeth it.

79

Now gan Don Phebus dip his golden rays,
  (To swage their burning) in the Westerne seas,
  When Charles himselfe comes to them both & prays
  The damsell now her furie to appease,
  And giueth sentence, that without delayes,
  Don Leon may her marrie when he please:
  Rogero doth himselfe no whit disclose,
  But armed still backe to the tent he goes.

80

Don Leon, brotherly doth him imbrace,
  And then he holpe him to vntie his beauer,
  And with great kindnes kissed all his face,
  And said that he was bound to him for euer,
  And that no time such merit could deface,
  Which to reward he would for ay indeuer,
  Affirming frankly of his owne meere motion,
  That all he had, should be at his deuotion.

81

I neuer can such curtesie requite,
  Scant in this life (he saith) or in the next,
  No though I should surrender all my right
  Vnto my crowne, and all thereto annext.
  Rogero, that in speech tooke small delight,
  And was with inward passion so perplext,
  Restor'd to him his armes, that he had worne,
  And tooke againe his shield of th'Vnicorne.

82

Pretending (as he truly might pretend)
  He wearie was, and would himselfe repose,
  And therefore to his tent vnto that end,
  All priuat vnaccompany'd he goes;
  At midnight horse to take he doth intend,
  At midnight priuily from bed he rose.
  And armd, and mounted thence away departed,
  But why nor whither, he to none imparted.

83

And thus away he secretly doth ride,
　And giues *Frontino* leaue to chuse the way,
　Now neere a wood, then by the riuer side,
　(He neuer looking to what coast it lay)
　He faine would die, and still come death he cride,
　He thought death onely could his paine allay,
　He onely wisheth death to end his griefe,
　That while he liues, is sure past all reliefe.

84

Ah wretch (said he) of whom can I complaine,
　For sodain reauing me of all my blisse?
　Shall I so great an iniurie sustaine?
　Of whom else shall I be aueng'd for this?
　I did the fault, and now I feele the paine,
　Nor can I say, but iust the torment is,
　For punishment doth properly belong
　To him that is the author of the wrong.

85

But had I done my self the wrong alone,
　I might perhap forgiue my selfe the same,
　Though surely cause, nor reason there is none,
　To pardon such a fact, so worthie blame:
　But now I haue to her bene cause of mone,
　To suffer that, it were perpetuall shame;
　So though I should no iust reuengment take
　For mine owne cause, yet must I for her sake.

86

This wrong revenge I may, I will, I must,
　By onely death, sith this offence was such;
　To dye, I soone shall finde the way I trust,
　The care thereof my minde no whit doth tuch:
　Oh that I had long since bene layd in dust,
　Ere that I iniured my deare so much,
　I would I had bene put to death before,
　When I was prisner vnto *Theodore*.

87

If I had then bene martyr'd and tormented,
　With all the plagues her malice could deuise,
　At least my deare my death would haue lamented,
　With teares, from out her christall streaming eyes:
　Now when she knows, that I haue thus consented
　To *Leon*, to betray her in this wise,
　My part of her, vnto a stranger giuing,
　She will haue cause to hate me dead and liuing.

88

Now while the knight did thus lament and plaine,
　The Eastern parts of heau'n with light were cleared,
　And *Phebus* from his golden house againe,
　Lift vp his head, wherewith all creatures cheared,
　Betake them to their ordinarie paine:
　And then vnto *Rogero* it appeared,
　That he was in a wood, a most fit place,
　For one of such a mind, in such a case.

89

He lights, and off he takes *Frontinos* sadle,
　And giues him libertie, and thus he sayes,
　My gallant beast so good, so seruiceable,
　As I haue found thee still at all assayes,
　Go, here I set thee free, and were I able,
　As I am willing, to set forth thy prayse,
　Thou doubtlesse shouldst not need that horse enuie
　That was tane vp from earth vnto the skye.

90

Nor should *Arions* prayses make thee sory,
　Nor *Cillarus* that *Castor* did bestryde,
　Nor any praisd in *Greeke*, or Latin story,
　For why (thy shape and readines beside)
　Of all these famous steeds not one can glorie,
　As thou maist do, it cannot be denide,
　Of them none passeth thee in commendation,
　Nor iustly challenge can such reputation.

91

Thou hast bene cherished and loued deere,
　By such a Nymph, so faire and so diuine
　As all the world can hardly show her peere,
　She hath thee fed with that fayre hand and fine,
　I meane my loue, but ah why liue I here,
　Sith now I may no longer call her mine?
　No longer mine she is, ah cruell word,
　Why end not I my dayes by mine owne sword?

92

Now if *Rogero* thus himselfe tormented,
　And caus'd the birds and beasts, to mone his plaint,
　For none but birds and beasts the place frequented,
　Whom he with his great sorrow might acquaint;
　No doubt the damsell was as ill contented,
　And made a greater, or as great complaint,
　Sith for her selfe she nothing hath to say,
　Why she to *Leon* longer should say nay.

93

Yet all meanes possible she meanes to trye,
　Before that she will her *Rogero* leaue,
　And make king *Charles* and all his Lords to lye,
　And *Leon* of his promise to deceaue:
　Or if the worst shall hap, she meanes to dye,
　And with her hands of life her self bereaue,
　For present death she rather ment to chuse,
　Then her belou'd *Rogero* to refuse.

94

How commeth it to passe (said she) my deare
　That at this time thou art so farre from hence?
　How can a thing which all the world did heare,
　So strangely be concealed from thy sence?
　If thou hadst heard it, sure thou wouldst appeare;
　For that my drift, that was my sole pretence,
　Ah my ill fortune euermore accurst,
　What can I deeme, but eu'n the very worst.

95

Why then *Rogero* mine, can you alone,
  Not know that all the world doth know beside,
  For had you known it straight you would haue flown
  Of purpose hither combate to haue tride;
  Thou sure art taine, or slaine, for third is none:
  It may be *Leon* that thy praise enuide,
  Hath like a traytor, set for thee a trap,
  And thou art tane therein by some mishap.

96

I gat this grace of *Charles* to mary none,
  But one that were in fight for me too hard,
  Assured thou shouldst be that onely one,
  For no mans force but thine I did regard;
  I thought none else could vanquish me alone,
  But lo how God doth this my pride reward,
  That he that never erst in all his life
  Did manly deed, hath wonne me for his wife.

97

If I be won and vanquished, because
  He matched still my force at all assayes,
  But *Charles* doth not iudge rightly of the cause,
  And therefore I must seeke some new delayes;
  Ah if I now put in some baffling clause,
  I shall be cald vnconstant all my dayes,
  But ficklenes in maids is seldome wondred,
  Nor am I first that vsde it, by an hundred.

98

Sufficeth me that in the being trew
  Vnto my loue, I others all excell,
  And passe the paterns either old or new,
  Or neare or far, eu'n wheresoeu'r they dwell:
  Then will I bid that constancie adew,
  That may be hindrance to my doing well,
  So I and *Leon* may not match together,
  Let me be deemd as wau'ring as the wether.

99

This *Bradamant* vnto her selfe doth say,
  And oft she breaks her speech with sighs and teares,
  And that night that ensu'd that lucklesse day,
  To sleepe or close her eye lids she forbeares,
  But when *Apollos* beames had driu'n away
  Nocturnus shades, then lo supernall spheares,
  By which all humane actions are directed,
  Brought helpe to her, when least it was expected.

100

For why *Marfisa*, that braue minded dame,
  The next day came and sowd new seeds of strife,
  Alledging that it was great wrong and shame,
  A forrener should haue her brothers wife;
  And sweares her selfe could not endure the same;
  And that she would by combate gage her life,
  According as the law of armes allows,
  To proue *Rogero* was her lawfull spouse.

101

And if dame *Bradamant* would it deny,
  She said, she will it to her face auer,
  As hauing witnes bene with eare, and eye,
  That good *Rogero* was assur'd to her
  With words, as folkes in mariages apply,
  And adding shee would vnto law refer,
  If so the damsell to her noble brother
  Affianced, might iustly take another.

102

Now whether this she spake were false or true,
  I know not, but she spake it with intent,
  To stop the mariage likely to ensew
  With *Leon*, which she studi'd to preuent:
  Some thought perhaps that *Bradamant* it knew,
  And that twas done in part by her consent,
  As hauing no more safe nor honest way,
  Vnto her left, to say Don *Leon* nay.

103

In euill part these newes the Emp'ror tooke,
  And called for the damsell by and by,
  And told her what *Marfisa* vndertooke,
  (And loe by hap, Duke *Ammon* then stood by)
  She fixed on the ground her silent looke,
  And to the question, said nor no nor I,
  That by her gesture, eu'rie one did take,
  That that was true, that erst *Marfisa* spake.

104

This made *Orlando* and *Renaldo* glad,
  In hope that this might proue a lawfull meane,
  To make the match which they forepromist had,
  And hinder this new match, and dash it cleane:
  For sith Duke *Ammon* those first banes forbad,
  And vnto *Leons* side did wholy leane,
  To vse pretence of law, they both had rather,
  Then take by force, the damsell from her father.

105

For if that this pretence may stand for good,
  The neck of *Leons* match it then would breake,
  And moue no cause of warre, or shedding blood:
  But *Ammon* in great wrath, thus wise doth speake;
  This is a tale indeed of *Robinhood*,
  Which to beleeue, might show my wits but weake,
  But thinke not that I will be so besotted,
  Though this were true, that you haue vainly plotted.

106

For presuppose, which yet I not confesse,
  My daughter was by folly so allured,
  And that they are, which none of wit could guesse,
  Each vnto other, man and wife assured:
  I pray you yet, the time more plaine expresse,
  When this was done, how long it hath indured,
  This (sure I am) tis but a tale deuised,
  Except it were before he was baptised.

107

And if twere done before his *Christen* state,
To stand vnto the same I am not tyde,
Wherefore this caueat is put in too late,
His owne desire she hath not had denyde:
Now tis not fit, a Prince of such estate,
As for her sake, aduentur'd to haue dyde,
Should by our Empr'ours promise be deluded,
And by such craft, be from his right excluded.

108

You should haue spoken then of this contract,
Before our king had sent his proclamation,
I meane not thus to haue my credit crakt,
For more then so I weigh my reputation:
Thus pleaded he against that precontract,
The which to breake was his determination,
To either part his eare the Emperor lends,
Yet partially, to neither side he bends.

109

Looke what a murmure winds do make in woods,
When *Zephyrus* mild blasts among them are,
Or when one hears from farr the saltish floods,
When *Eolus* and *Neptune* are at square:
So did the common people in their moods,
Talke of these matters, and the same compare,
And as the manner is (for nine dayes space)
This was the newes and talke in eu'rie place.

110

This man *Rogero*, *Leon* that defends,
According to the fancies of the men,
But yet it seemd *Rogero* had most friends,
Scarse had the stranger one, for tothers ten,
But as I said, the king to no side bends,
And hauing duly weigh'd the matter then,
He points the mariage day to be deferred,
The case vnto his Parliament referred.

111

Next day *Marfisa* made another offer,
Sith that none could, during her brothers life,
Wed *Bradamant*, and be assured of her,
Her brother should (for ending of the strife)
To *Leon* hand to hand, the combate proffer,
So she might be the last suruiuers wife;
And he that tother could in battell kill,
Enioy her might alone at his owne will.

112

Charles vnto *Leon*, doth impart these newes,
As he before the other did impart,
That offer *Leon* ment not to refuse,
But saith he take it would, with all his hart,
He minds again the matter so to vse,
The knight of th'Vnicorne should play his part,
He little knew that in great care and anguish,
The noble knight did now consume and languish.

113

But missing him, he quickly did repent,
That he accepted had that stout defiance,
And therefore straight to seeke the knight he sent,
In whose tryde force, he put his whole affiance;
Him to *Rogero* to oppose he ment,
And all his friends and all his strong alliance:
Wherefore to shun both danger great and scorne,
He sent to seeke the Knight of th'Vnicorne.

114

To al the Cities, and the towns he sends,
And all the villages were there about,
And mounting on his horse himselfe intends
To go in person and to seeke him out,
But neither he nor all *Rogeros* friends,
In *France* had euer light on him I doubt,
Had not *Melissa* holpe him at his need,
As in the booke insuing you may reed.

THE FORTY-SIXT BOOKE OF

ORLANDO FVRIOSO

THE ARGVMENT

Leon *by search doth good* Rogero *find,*
And having learn'd the cause of his annoy,
He grants to him his love in manner kind,
Whom now Rogero *sweetly doth enjoy:*
Onely the Sarzan *king with hatefull mind*
Comes to disturbe Rogeros *ease and joy,*
Nathelesse he is deceiv'd of his account,
In fine, Rogero *kils fierce* Rodomount.

ORLANDO FVRIOSO
THE FORTY-SIXT BOOKE

1

Now if my compasse and my card be true,
  I am not far from that desired cost,
Where I shall pay my vow and promise due
Vnto my Saint, of whose great grace I bost:
I looked erst with pale and chearlesse hue,
  For feare in this wide *Ocean* to be lost,
But now me think I see, I now see surely
The hav'n, in which I harbor shall securely.

2

Hark, hark, what peals of Ord'nance great and Guns,
  Are shot in token of congratulation,
Hark how they sound the Trumpets and the Drums,
To gratulate my happy navigation:
See how on either shore the people runs,
  To see me after my long per'grination,
Behold a crew of peerlesse knights and dames,
Now I discern them, now I know their names.

3

But least my ship should perish in the port,
  As oft it doth befall for want of heed,
I will go forward in my first report,
And tell to you how well the Prince did speed
That sought *Rogero*, who in wofull sort
  Did pine and languished, and wish'd indeed,
Sith that dame *Bradamant* he might not marie,
To die all comfortlesse and solitarie.

4

But sage *Melyssa* that had ever sought,
  To make that match (as often hath been sed)
And evermore did take great care and thought,
That good *Rogero Bradamant* might wed,
By her great skill in Magick art so wrought,
  She had continuall notice how they sped;
Two sprites she did imploy for that intent.
And still as one came home, another went.

5

By them she quickly had intelligence,
  How he had tane so inward grief and great,
He tari'd in a wood with firm pretence,
To pine himself away with want of meat:
Melyssa parteth presently from thence,
  And with some secret words she did repeat,
In likenesse of a horse a sprite she took,
And so met *Leon*, that for him did look.

6

And thus she said to him, sir, if you be
  So gracious, as your semblance makes me ween,
If your good mind with your good looks agree,
If so you have not lost all pitie cleen;
Come then, ô come and help, and joyne with me,
  To aid the bravest knight that ere was seen,
Who for one curteous part that he hath done,
(Except you help) is like to be undone.

7

The noblest, stoutest, and the prowest knight,
  That ever cari'd shield, or blade forth drew,
The seemliest and most worthy minded wight,
That ever was in age, or old, or new,
Is like to perish in most wofull plight,
  Except he may relieved be by you;
Come quickly then unto his aid perdye,
And suffer not so brave a man to die.

8

Don *Leon* straight supposed in his minde,
  That this same knight, of whom the stranger spake,
Was he whom long he sought and could not finde,
And he for whom such care himselfe did take:
Melissa leads the way, he close behind
  Doth follow her, and so good shift they make,
That in some twaine, at most in three hours ryding
They came there where *Rogero* was abyding.

9

Now being at the place to which they hasted,
  They both alighted there, with minde to stay:
There saw they how he pinde away and wasted,
For in two dayes before, nor all that day,
No liquor he had drunke, nor meat had tasted,
  But in his armor on the ground he lay,
And made a pillow of that noble sheeld,
With th'Vnicorne upon vermillion feeld.

10

Here as I said, he lay along and mused
  On his owne miserie, and on that wrong,
With which he had his love so much abused,
And bites for griefe, his hands, and lips, and tong;
And his conceits, and wits were so confused,
  To set his thoughts upon one thing so long,
And having on his griefe so firmely fixt them,
He saw not them, although he were betwixt them.

11

Don *Leon* harkned to his lamentation,
  And heard him often call himselfe unkind,
  And saw him vexe himselfe in such a fashion,
  As unto pittie great his heart inclind:
  He finds that love bred all this molestation,
  But yet whose love it was he did not find,
  He heard how sundry times himselfe he blamed,
  But all that while his love he never named.

12

And therefore pitying much his wofull case,
  Although awhile he silent stood and mute,
  Yet after stood before him face to face,
  And with great lovingnesse doth him salute,
  And with affection great doth him imbrace,
  Intreating him, and making speciall sute,
  That he would tell him plaine, and make him know,
  What cause had bred him so great griefe and woe.

13

Rogero loth to live, resolv'd to dye,
  Prayes *Leon* now to trouble him no more,
  But he most sweetly doth to him reply,
  That God hath made a salve for ev'ry sore,
  If men would learne the same how to apply,
  And that no one thing may avayle man more,
  To cure a griefe, and perfectly to heale it,
  Then if he do unto some frend reveale it.

14

And sure (said he) I take it in ill part,
  Because you trust not me, that am your frend,
  Not onely, since with your late frendly part,
  You bound me unto you, to my lives end,
  But was ev'n then, when you with hatefull hart,
  At *Belgrade* siege did me and mine offend,
  Thinke not but I will still procure your good,
  Both with my lands, my frends, and with my blood.

15

Why should it grieve you to declare your griefe,
  To one that may perhaps your losse repayre:
  Bad haps are holpe with hope, and good beliefe,
  Wherefore a wise man never will dispayre:
  I hope my selfe shall bring you some reliefe,
  By force, by policie, or else by prayre,
  When all meanes have bene tryde, and all hope past
  Then dye, at least keepe that unto the last.

16

These words so earnestly Don *Leon* spake,
  And with such efficacie him he praid,
  Beseeching him, his frendly counsell take,
  That tother now, with kindnesse overlaid,
  Was forst an answer unto him to make;
  But in his answer, sodainly he staid,
  And stammerd twise, ere he could bring it out,
  Despaire still moving him to causlesse doubt.

17

Good sir (he said) when I my name shall show,
  As I do meane, and that ev'n by and by,
  You will be then full well content I trow,
  To grant me leave and liberty to dye:
  I am *Rogero* (if you needs will know)
  That went from *France* (and if I shall not lye)
  Mine arrant was, your sire and you to kill.
  And would have done it, had I had my will.

18

And all because indeed I then supposed,
  Your only life, did let me of my love,
  Man purposes, but all things are disposed,
  By that great God, that sits and rules above:
  Behold it hapt I was in prison closed,
  And there I did your noble courtsie prove,
  For there you did me such a great good turne,
  As all my hatred into love did turne.

19

And having bound me with so great desart,
  And ignorant, that I *Rogero* was,
  You did your secrets unto me impart,
  And praid me win for you, that warlike lasse,
  Which was all one, as to have askt my hart;
  Yet loe for you, I brought the same to passe,
  Now take her to your selfe, and much good do you,
  More good then to my selfe, I wish unto you.

20

But yet withall forbid me not to dye,
  As now I trust I shall, ere many houres,
  For live as well without a soule can I,
  As without her, that holds my vitall powres:
  And sure tis best for your behoofe, for why
  While I do live, she is not lawfull yours,
  For we two are betrotht, and law allowes,
  One woman, but of one to be the spouse.

21

Don *Leon* with these newes was so accrazed,
  He seemed in a traunce, he knew not how,
  And on *Rogero* stedfastly he gazed,
  Nor ever moving lip, nor hand, nor brow,
  But like an Image long he stood amazed,
  That some hath hallowd to performe his vow,
  This act of his, so curteous he doth weene,
  He thinks the like before had never beene.

22

So that he did not (when he knew his name)
  Repent him of the good he had him done,
  But rather greatly did increase the same,
  Proceeding in the course he had begun:
  Wherefore to shew from how great stock he came,
  And that he was indeed an Emperors sonne:
  Although in other things he was inferiour,
  In curtesie he means to be superiour.

23

And thus (he said) my deare *Rogero* know,
  As if I well had known your person, when
  As by your means I had an overthrow,
  And that you foiled me and all my men:
  Yet that great vertue that you there did show,
  Should ev'n in manner like have mov'd me then,
  And so I would all malice have remov'd,
  And so I would your vertue great have lov'd.

24

That once I did dislike *Rogeros* name,
  Before I knew you I must needs confesse,
  But that I now continue should the same,
  Assure your self I purpose nothing lesse:
  And if when first I to the prison came
  To set you free from danger and distresse,
  I known had all the truth, yet then I vow,
  I would have done the same I will do now.

25

And surely, if I would have done it then,
  When I had reason to have born you hate,
  Much rather now I ought to do it, when
  Not doing it I should be most ungrate,
  And most unthankfull of all other men;
  Sith you your love, your life, and whole estate
  Have freely giv'n for me, but as you gave it,
  Of me againe so freely you shall have it.

26

More due to you then me the Damsell is,
  Whom though I much esteem of due desert,
  Yet not so much, that if I her do misse,
  Straightwayes the grief thereof should kill my heart:
  Nor shall your death avantage me in this,
  Sith you in her already claime such part,
  That lawfully while you abide in life,
  She can by no means be anothers wife.

27

As for my part, first I will quite forsake
  Both her, and all my worldly joyes beside,
  Then it shall once be said, that for my sake
  A noble knight of so great worth had di'd:
  This only thing I could unkindly take,
  That you that had before my kindnesse tri'd,
  Would rather chuse to end your dayes with grief,
  Then at my hands have comfort and relief.

28

These words Don *Leon* spake, and many more,
  Which now would be too tedious to recite,
  Refuting good *Rogero* evermore,
  That in conclusion being vanquish'd quite:
  He said, I yeeld, and Ile resist no more,
  I will not die; but when I shall requite
  Your curtesie, that twice to me hath given
  My life, when I to greatest wo was driven.

29

Now had *Melissa* caused to be brought
  Both cordiall meats, and wines of her purvaying,
  And made him take the same, who now with thought
  And fasting long was ev'n almost decaying:
  His horse likewise (as nature hath them taught)
  Came where he heard the other horses naying:
  Don *Leon* caus'd his lackies him to get,
  And then his saddle on his back to set.

30

And so *Rogero* with Don *Leons* aid,
  With much ado did clammer to his seat,
  So greatly was his former strength decaid,
  With which he overthrew an army great:
  And lately did withstand that warlike maid,
  So weakly weapon'd, as I did repeat:
  And thus with all convenient speed they might,
  They brought him to an Abbey that same night.

31

Where all the night, and three dayes that ensew'd,
  They staid, and had of needfull things good store,
  Vntill *Rogero* had his strength renew'd,
  Which had with fasting long been weakned sore:
  Then privily among them they conclude,
  To turn to *Paris*, where the night before
  A few *Bulgarians* came with an embassage,
  And this was all the substance of their message.

32

They said how that the people of their Nation,
  To whom *Rogero* late such aid did bring,
  Beyond all hope, beyond all expectation,
  Had therefore chosen him to be their king:
  Rejecting all their own kings generation,
  And all his royall race (no usuall thing)
  So much they loved him, so well they like him,
  And therefore sent to *Charles* his Court to seek him.

33

Rogeros lackey that had been their guide,
  Told eke his masters friends how he had sped,
  As namely how the *Greeks* he damnifi'd,
  And how the *Bulgars* having lost their head,
  Chose him for king, how he alone did ride,
  To *Novengrade*, where he was tane in bed,
  And unto *Theodora* was presented,
  Who purposed to have him sore tormented.

34

And how he heard it commonly was spoken,
  That he his cruell keeper closely slew,
  And that the Prison gates were rent and broken,
  And he was gone, but whither no man knew:
  Now while *Rogeros* man such things did open,
  Rogero closely out of all mens view,
  Did come to town, and there that night did stay,
  And he and *Leon* came to *Charles* next day.

35

Don *Leon* arm in arm *Rogero* led,
(Thus it was then devised them between)
With that self cote and arms apparelled,
That were of late by all the people seen,
Then when dame *Bradamant* had combated
With *Leon* (as they falsly then did ween)
That batter'd sword, that coat, that plume all torn,
That headpeece now was by *Rogero* worn.

36

By which each man ev'n at first sight surmis'd,
This was that knight that had the Lady won,
Don *Leon* self bare faced, undisguis'd,
Came richly clothed, like an Emp'rors son,
And with retinue not to be despised:
And when he had to *Charles* due rev'rence done,
Rogero by the hand he then did take,
On whom all eyes were fixt, and thus he spake.

37

This is that stout and well approved knight,
That did with *Bradamant* fight hand to hand,
Whom sith she never took nor put to flight,
But that he did twelve houres her force withstand,
(Most worthy sir) to have her ought of right,
If your edict we rightly understand.
And therefore now accordingly he commeth,
To lay his claime to her, as best becommeth.

38

Besides his right by proclamation known,
That justly doth all others claime debar,
I think the value that he now hath shown,
Proves his sufficiency in feats of war:
If love may win her, she is sure his own,
His love to her doth passe all others far;
And here he stands prepared to aver
By law or force, that he hath right to her.

39

King *Charles* and all his court did greatly muse
At this, for why till then he little thought,
That he before did them so much abuse,
But that himself had that same combat fought:
This while *Marfisa*, that with flying newes
Of this same strange report was thither brought,
Scant him to end his speech she would permit,
But presently this wise she answerd it.

40

Sith now *Rogero* absent is from hence,
That might his right against this knight defend,
And prove that this is but a vaine pretence,
Because the strife shall not so easely end:
I that his sister am, in his defence,
And in defence of this same cause intend,
To fight with whomsoever in this place,
As shall deny his title, or disgrace.

41

And these last words she spake with such disdaine,
That some that knew her nature (hasty ever)
Did feare she scantly would ev'n then refraine,
But without leave to kill him straight endever:
Now *Leon* thinks it best no longer faine;
And forthwith pulling off *Rogeros* beaver,
Lo here himself now ready prest (he said)
To answer all shall to his charge be laid.

42

As old *Ægeus* at his cursed boord
Amazed sate, to find his spouses wile,
When to his sonne she poyson did affoord,
And if he lingred had a little while,
And had not known the handle of his sword
Had kild his sonne he gat by *Pitheus* guile:
So stood *Marfisa* mazed in the place,
When as she saw and knew *Rogeros* face.

43

And straight she runs, and on his neck doth fall,
And long it were ere from him she could part,
Renald', *Orlando*, *Charles*, afore them all
Embraced him, and welcom'd from their heart:
Good *Dudon*, *Oliver*, with joy not small,
And old *Sobrino*, health to him impart,
Eke all the other Lords, and Knights, and Squires
To bid him welcome shew most prompt desires.

44

Don *Leon* that in speech was eloquent,
When ev'ry one had done his gratulation,
Begins to tell to *Charles* incontinent,
And all the rest, *Rogeros* commendation:
And how he to the *Bulgars* succour lent,
(To no small dammage of the *Greekish* nation)
And shew'd such noble courage and such force,
As him to love *Rogero* did enforce.

45

So as when he was after tane and brought
To her that vow'd with torments him to slay,
Himself in spite of her, and all that sought
To hurt *Rogero*, brought him safe away:
For which kind part of his *Rogero* thought
Himself so bound to him, that he last day
Did him that curtesie that sure doth passe
The greatest curtesie that ever was.

46

He further doth from point to point declare
What for his sake *Rogero* hath atchiev'd,
But after this, with anguish great and care,
The losse of his belov'd so sore him griev'd,
As he to pine away did straight prepare,
Had not his sorrow been in time reliev'd:
All which so rufully Don *Leon* sed,
Scarce was an eye but teares with blindnesse shed.

47

Then spake he to that obstinate old man,
    I meane Duke *Ammon* that faire Ladies sire,
    And with all skill and Rhetorick he can,
    He wooes his love, and pacifies his ire.
    That by entreaty at the last he wan
    Himself to go in person, and desire
    Rogeros pardon: praying him in th'end
    To take him for his father-in-law and friend.

48

This while to *Bradamant* the joyfull tiding
    Was quickly brought, by more then one report,
    Who in her chamber all her sorrow hiding,
    Eschew'd all solace, shunning all resort:
    Whereby the blood about the heart abiding
    Was drawn now thence in such a sodaine sort,
    And this unlook'd for joy so overfild her,
    That ev'n the suddennesse had almost kild her.

49

Quite speechlesse, livelesse, sinking to the ground,
    (So strong a qualme her tender heart did feel)
    And she in whom such force was lately found,
    For want of strength did here and thither reel;
    But nev'r did thief with hands together bound,
    Condemned to the rope, the axe, or wheel,
    And blindfold, looking ev'ry houre to die,
    Ioy more to heare some man a pardon crie.

50

The houses of *Mongrane* and *Montalbane*,
    Rejoyce at these their branches newly knit,
    But by *Maganza* comfort small is tane,
    For in their hearts they sorrie were for it:
    Anselmus, *Falcon*, *Gynamus*, and *Gane*,
    Dissembling yet their thoughts with crafty wit:
    But for a time of vengeance they do watch,
    As doth the Fox the hurtlesse Hare to catch.

51

Beside old quarrels and their ancient hate,
    New matters done of late did them displease,
    Although the king and wise men of the state,
    For common quiet did the same appease:
    The death of *Pynabello* slaine but late,
    And *Bertolage* did much their minds disease:
    Yet now in shew they do dissemble deep,
    And close in mind they do their malice keep.

52

In this meane time th'Ambassadours that came
    To *Charles* his court by those *Bulgarians* sent,
    Rejoycing now that things so well did frame,
    In humble manner to *Rogero* went:
    And did salute him king, as in the name
    Of all their countrimen incontinent,
    And so accordingly did lowly greet,
    Their new made Prince, and kneeled at his feet.

53

They told him how their Scepter and their Crown
    Was safely kept, alone for his behoof,
    In *Adrianopolis* their chiefest town:
    And for they knew by many a former proof,
    That *Constantino* strave to keep them down,
    They pray him not to stay so far aloof;
    Affirming boldly that if he were there,
    The forces of all *Greece* they would not feare.

54

Rogero granteth them their just request,
    And promis'd to defend them from the *Greeks*,
    And vowes (if God permit) to do his best,
    To be with them within some thirteen weeks:
    But *Leon* bids them set their hearts at rest,
    He tels them that their choice so well he likes,
    He on his Princely word will undertake,
    'Twixt *Constantine* and them firm peace to make.

55

Thus each thing framed now in so good sort,
    As could be wisht by thought or by device,
    But neither did *Rogeros* good report,
    Get favour with ambitious *Beatrice*,
    Nor personage that past the common sort,
    Nor feats of armes, in which he wan the prize;
    And of the which all *Europe* now doth ring,
    But onely this to see him made a king.

56

In royall sort this mariage they prepare,
    (Whose charge it was, the state will make it known)
    Charles bare the charge, and took thereof such care,
    As if she were a daughter of his own:
    Of her and hers so great the merits are,
    And had to her so many wayes been shown;
    He thought the cost had not exceeded measure,
    If he had spent upon them half his treasure.

57

He kept an open court by proclamation,
    Where nine dayes space, who list may freely haunt,
    Men of their own, and men of forren nation,
    To all of them he did safe conduct grant:
    And all that stood upon their reputation,
    That sought their foes in single fight to daunt,
    Had licence frank to challenge whom they lists,
    For evermore prepared were the lists.

58

In open fields they pitched tents great store,
    Beside with Oken boughs they made such bowres,
    Strawing the pavements of them evermore,
    With fragrant Roses and sweet smelling flowres;
    That never had the like been seen before;
    Nor never since, from that same age to ours;
    Besides the furnitures of silk and gold,
    Was more then can conveniently be told.

59

Th'innumerable people of each sort,
  From *Greece*, from *England*, *Italy*, and *Spaine*,
Th'Ambassadours that thither did resort,
  Beside each severall Prince a severall traine,
Did cause the city walls to seem too short,
  To lodge them all, so they in fine were faine
In hovels, booths, in tents, and in pavillions,
  To lodge some thousands, if I say not millions.

60

Onely *Melissas* care was to foresee,
  The marriage chamber should be well attyr'd,
Which by her skill she meant should furnisht be,
  For long to make the match she had aspir'd:
Which now that she accomplished did see,
  She thought she had the thing she most desir'd:
For by her skill in magick she did know
  What passing fruit forth of that branch should grow.

61

Wherefore she plac'd the fruitfull wedding bed
  Amid a faire and large pavillion, which
Was ev'n the sumptuosest that ere was spred,
  Of silk and beaten gold wrought ev'ry stitch:
And more, from over *Constantinos* head,
  At *Thracyan* shore, where he his tents did pitch
Fast by the sea, for his more recreation,
  She took the same to his great admiration.

62

Were it that *Leon* gave consent thereto,
  Or that she did the same her skill to vaunt,
To shew what one by Magick art can do,
  That have the skill the fiends of hell to daunt:
(For what cannot their power atchieve unto,
  When for our plague God leave to them will grant!)
From *Thrace* to *Paris* in twelve houres it came,
  I trow she sent one in the divels name.

63

She caus'd it to be cari'd at noone day
  From *Constantino* Emp'ror then of *Greece*,
The beam, the staves, the cords they brought away,
  The pins, the hoops, and ev'ry little peece:
She placed it whereas she meant to lay
  Atlantas Nephew, with his new made Neece:
In this pavillion she did place their bedding,
  And sent it back when finisht was the wedding.

64

Two thousand yeare before, or not much lesse,
  This rich pavillion had in *Troy* been wrought,
By faire *Cassandra* that same Prophetesse,
  That had (but all in vaine) in youth been taught,
Of future things to give most certaine guesse,
  For her true speech was ever set at naught:
She wrought this same, with help of many other,
  And gave it *Hector*, her beloved brother.

65

The worthiest wight that ev'r man did behold,
  That should proceed forth of his noble line,
She here portrayd in work of silk and gold,
  Of precious substance, and of colour fine:
Also the time and season was foretold,
  Both of his birth, and of his praise divine:
Don *Hector* of this gift great count did make,
  Both for the work and for the workers sake.

66

But when himselfe by treason foule was slaine,
  And *Troy* was by the *Greeks* defaced quite,
Who enterd it by *Synons* subtill traine,
  And worse ensew'd thereof then Poets write:
Then *Menelaus* did this great relick gaine,
  And after on king *Proteus* hapt to light,
Who gave to him dame *Helen* ere he went,
  And for reward receiv'd of him this tent.

67

And thus to *Ægypt* at that time it came,
  Where with the *Ptolomeys* it long remain'd,
Till *Cleopatra* that lascivious dame
  As by inheritance the same obtain'd:
Agrippas men by sea then took the same,
  What time in *Rome Augustus Cæsar* raign'd:
And then in *Rome*, while *Rome* was th'Empires seat,
  It staid till time of *Constantine* the great.

68

That Emp'ror *Constantine* I mean, of whom
  Faire *Italy* for ever shall lament,
Who when he lothed *Tibris* banks and *Rome*,
  Vnto the city of *Byzantium* went,
A place of more receipt and larger roome,
  And thither this pavillion then he sent:
Of which the cords were golden wyre and silk,
  The staves and pins were Iv'rie white as milk.

69

In this *Cassandra* wrought such divers faces,
  More then *Apelles* erst with pensill drew,
A queen in child-bed lay, to whom the graces
  With pleasant grace perform'd *Lucynas* dew:
Iove, *Mercurie*, and *Mars* in other places,
  And *Venus* do receive the babe born new:
The sweetest babe that to the world came forth,
  From mans first age, ev'n down unto the fourth.

70

Hippolito they name him, as appeares
  Wrote in small letters on his swathing bands,
And when he is a little grown in yeares;
  On one side fortune, tother vertue stands:
Then in another picture divers Peeres,
  Clad in long raiments, sent from forren lands,
Vnto the father and the mother came,
  To beg the babe in great *Corvinos* name.

71

They part from *Hercles* with great rev'rence then,
  And from that infants mother *Elinore*,
Vnto *Danubia* ward, and there the men
  Still run to see that infant and adore:
Also the king *Corvino*, wonders when
  He saw in him both wit and judgement more,
In those his tender childish yeares and green,
Then many times in older men had been.

72

One doth endeavour in his childish hand,
  Of the *Strigonian* Realme to put the mace,
But evermore the tender youth doth stand
  So high in that same noble Princes grace,
That if he war in manly *Almans* land,
  Or in the *Turks* or any other place;
Hippolito is ever by his side,
And learneth vertue under such a guide.

73

Another place shewes how he doth dispence,
  His youthfull time in discipline and art,
Fusco instructs him in the hidden sence
  Of ancient writs, and precepts doth impart,
What actions praise, what actions breed offence,
  What be reward of good and ill desert:
All which the picture did so well expresse,
That at the meaning ev'ry one might guesse.

74

Lo where as yet a boy in *Vatican*
  Among the gravest Card'nals he doth sit,
And speaks so wisely that they all began
  To wonder at his towardnesse and wit;
What manner man (if once he were a man)
  Would this man prove? for *Peters* chaire how fit?
They seem to say; oh if he thither clime,
What holy age were that? what happy time?

75

Within another part described were
  His youthfull sports, when he more strong did grow
Oft in the mountaines he doth meet a Beare,
  Oft times a Bore, in marish grounds and low:
He rides his Genet fierce, and void of feare,
  He chaseth oft the Buck, the Hart and Roe,
And by his horse swift pace doth over-ride them,
And then doth with his sword in twaine divide them.

76

Of Poets then, and of Philosophers,
  About him you shall see a worthy band,
To make him know the course of wandring stars,
  How heav'n doth move, & why the earth doth stand,
Or reading of Elegies, or verse of wars,
  Fine Epigrams, Odes hard to understand:
Or somtime instruments of Musick hearing,
In all his acts a speciall grace appearing.

77

Then on another part was to be view'd
  His vertues, each one by it self distinct,
First Prudence, Temperance, and Fortitude,
  And justice, and a fift unto them linkt
So nigh, that who with it is not indew'd,
  The rest may seem or blotted, or extinct:
Good bounty, shew'd in giving and in spending,
A speciall grace to all the other lending.

78

This one place shewes he aids vnluckie *Sforse*,
  Him euermore most faithfully assisting,
Sometime with policie, sometime with force,
  Him helping, and his enemies resisting:
Of Fortunes change he doth but little force,
  In woe and weale, in one faith still persisting:
He comforts him when euill haps do grieue him,
In dangers he doth saue, in want relieue him.

79

Then stands he studying at another season,
  And for his countries safetie taking care,
He searcheth, and he finds by depth of reason,
  And finding, to his brother doth declare
Their most vnnaturall and filthy treason,
  That some of his owne blood for him prepaire,
By which he doth deserue such name to haue,
As *Rome* yet free, to famous *Tully* gaue.

80

Fast by he stands all clad in armour bright,
  And to relieue the Church he runs in post,
With sodaine souldiers, raw and armed light,
  Against a setled and wel ordred host:
Yet did his onely presence so affright
  The adverse part, that one may rightly bost,
It quencht the fire, ere it to burne began,
So he may say, *I came, I saw, I wan.*

81

Here stands he by his natiue riuers side,
  And straight encounters with the strongest fleete,
That euer yet *Venetians* did prouide,
  Gainst *Greeke*, or *Turke*, but he doth boldly meet,
And vanquisht them; and took them at one tide,
  And though the bootie and the gaine was sweet,
All (saue the praise) he left vnto his brother,
For only that cannot be giu'n another.

82

Thus this Pauillion, as before I told,
  The which *Melissa* brought so far from thence,
Did please the knights, and dames that did behold
  The goodly imag'rie, and rich expence:
Although they had not any to vnfold
  The meaning of the same and hidden sence;
But yet by good *Melissas* wise instruction
Dame *Bradamant* did know their whole cõstruction.

83

Rogero markt likewise with great attention,
  Those goodly figures calling to his minde,
  That oft his vnckle of that Prince made mention,
  Hippolito the flowre of all his kinde:
  But now king *Charles*, whose care is and intention,
  To giue to all men entertainment kinde,
  Made playes and feasts with sundry sports and great,
  And euermore the tables fild with meat.

84

There, men might plainly see and vnderstand,
  The courage and the strength of eu'rie knight,
  Sometimes in single wise, now band to band,
  In iusts, and turnaments resembling fight,
  But still *Rogero*, had the vpper hand,
  In all his exercise of day and night:
  In leaping, running, wrastling, and in dancing,
  All men him far aboue the rest aduancing.

85

But on the last of these dayes festiuall,
  Then when to take away they did prouide,
  What time king *Charles* was set amid them all,
  Eu'n iust between the Bridegroome and the Bride,
  Behold they saw a goodly man and tall,
  That seemd directly toward them to ride.
  Most proudly mounted on a coursers backe,
  But yet his horse and he, all clad in blacke.

86

This was fierce *Rodomont*, king of *Algyre*,
  Who at his late receiued foile, and scorne
  Of *Bradamant*, inflam'd with spite and ire,
  All vse of horse and armor had forsworne,
  Till one whole yeare, one month, one day expire,
  But liue that while an Hermit all forlorne:
  For so the knights were wont in ancient times,
  Of their owne selues, to punish their owne crimes.

87

And though this while he oft had notice how
  King *Agramant*, and how king *Charles* had sped,
  Yet nathelesse for not breaking of his vow,
  Forth of the doores he neuer put his hed:
  But when the yeare and month were ended now,
  And day beside, himselfe he furnished,
  With armour new, new horse, new sword, new lance,
  And came therewith vnto the court of France.

88

Not once allighting nor so much as rising,
  For reu'rence sake, to bow his head or knee,
  He bare the count'nance of a man despising
  Both *Charles*, and all those Peeres of great degree:
  At this each man amazed stands deuising,
  What proud and sawcy fellow this might be,
  From talking and from eating each man stayes,
  To hearken what this loftie warrier sayes.

89

Now when he was to th'Emp'ror come so nye,
  That he *Rogero* fully did confront,
  With stately voice, and with disdainfull crie,
  (He saith) I am the king of *Sarza Rodomont*,
  That thee *Rogero* flatly here defie,
  And ere the Sunne go downe make full account,
  To proue thou hast bene false vnto thy Prince,
  And openly of treason thee conuince.

90

For though thy trechery be knowne so cleare,
  In being *Christned*, thou canst not deny it,
  Yet that to all the world it may appeare,
  I offer here in single fight to trie it:
  Or if thy courage faile, if any here
  Will take on them thy quarrell, to supply it,
  I will accept of any one or more,
  Yea not to faile, of six or halfe a score.

91

Rogero, when he first had licence craued
  Of *Charles*, this wise to *Rodomont* replide,
  (And said) he euer had his honour saued,
  And who so said contrarie lowdly lide:
  For he had to his Prince himselfe behaued,
  Most loyally eu'n to the day he dide:
  And said he there was readie to maintaine,
  That yet his faith had neuer sufferd stain.

92

And that himselfe was bold enough and strong,
  With him to buckle hand to hand alone,
  And that he hop't to make him feele ere long,
  He had enough perhap too much of one:
  Straightwayes *Renaldo* to aueng this wrong,
  Orlando, and the Marquis would haue gone,
  Marfisa with the brothers white and blacke,
  And *Dudon* would be on the *Pagans* iacke.

93

Alledging, that sith he was newly mari'd,
  For him to fight, it was against all vse,
  But from their speeches his opinion vari'd,
  And swears that that for him was no excuse:
  Those armes that erst the famous *Tartar* carri'd,
  He takes, nor will he make one houre of truse:
  To arme him, all those states their aids afford,
  King *Charles* himselfe, holpe to put on his sword.

94

His wife takes care his Curats well may fit,
  Orlando tyes his spurres, *Marfisa* bold
  Doth fast vpon his head his beaver knit,
  Astolfo is content his horse to hold:
  His stirrop, *Dudon;* others thinke it fit,
  To rid the lysts, and driue out yong and old:
  Renaldo, *Namus*, *Oliuer*, take charge
  To martiall it, and make it cleare and large.

95

Faire dames and damzels stand with lookes dismaid,
　With feare and trembling, like to fearfull Doues.
Whō some blacke tēpest-bringing cloud hath fraid,
And driu'n from fields, to shrowd in houses rooues:
(Downe fals the haile with which the corne is laid,
And profitlesse vnto his owner proues)
So do they this fierce *Pagans* forces feare,
Which sure they iudge, *Rogero* cannot beare.

96

Nor onely do faint people so surmise,
But many knights of worth, the same did weene,
That cald to mind what erst before their eyes,
To their griefe they had in *Paris* seene:
When he with fire and sword in fearfull wise,
Did welny spoile the towne, and wast it cleane:
Of which the wofull signes did still appeare,
And would remaine yet many a month and yeare.

97

But *Bradamant* more feard then all the rest,
Not that she thought in strength or skill well tride,
The *Pagan* past her spouse, nor valiant brest,
Or that he had more reason of his side,
(Which vnto victorie availes not least,
When men by combat quarrels do discide)
Yet still her minde is sad, her lookes vnchearfull,
Nor blame her though, for loue is euer fearfull.

98

Great suit she makes, great labour to procure,
That vpon her she may the quarrell take,
Yea if to haue bene slaine she had bene sure,
To saue her spouse, but all in vaine she spake:
The champions now their lances put in vre,
And each with couched speare the tother strake:
The staues like Ise in shivers small did flie,
The splints like buds did mount vnto the skie.

99

The *Pagan* that his lance did full direct,
Against the middle of *Rogeros* sheeld,
Did smite on it to small or none effect,
For *Vulcan* had the same most firmly steeld:
The tothers Target had no knowne defect,
Yet to the stroke it did a passage yeeld:
Yet was it thicke a quarter of a foote
Of bone, and linde with plated steele to boot.

100

And saue the lance sustained not the blow,
But at the first did break and was dispersed,
So that the pieces of it seem'd in show,
To haue beene feathered foules (as I rehearsed,)
That stroke had finished that strife I trow,
And had his Curats and his bodie pearced:
But now it brake, and both gaue strokes so sound,
As made both horses cruppers kisse the ground.

101

The riders neare the lesse sate firme and stedie,
And laboured so well with spurre and raine,
Their horses were got vp on foote alreadie,
The men to fight addresse themselues againe
With swords; their horses both were stronge & redie
And each with skill some vantage sought to gaine,
And where they thought their armors were most thin,
With force they straue to pierce & enter in.

102

Fierce *Rodomont* had not that Serpents hide
He vsd to weare, nor yet that shauing blade,
That he was wont to carrie by his side,
For *Nimrod* his great ancestor first made;
He lost those armes, and many more beside,
Then when as *Bradamant* did him invade,
At that same church, where he a twelvemonth since,
Entombed *Isbell*, with that peerlesse Prince.

103

He had another armor good and sure,
But not like that so passing tough and hard,
But neither this, nor any else could dure,
Against the piercing edge of *Ballisard:*
No mixture such, no metall was so pure,
No charme so strong, but that this blade thē mard:
Rogero so besturd him with this blade,
More then one hole, in tothers coate he made.

104

Now though a little while the *Pagan* clokes
His hurts receiu'd, with vnappaled minde,
Yet when he saw his blood, and felt the strokes
So smart, that still they seem'd the quick to finde:
To so great wrath and rage it him prouokes,
Eu'n like the sea turmoyld with blustring winde,
He hurles away his shield, and doth endeuer,
With both his hands to cleaue *Rogeros* beauer.

105

With force as great he strikes, and as extreame,
As doth that engin in the Riuer *Poe,*
Borne twixt two shippes vpon the stately streame,
Enforcing downe with many a heauie bloe,
Some piece of timber or some sharpned beame:
I say the *Pagan* smote *Rogero* so,
Had not the charmed helmet bene of force,
He doubtlesse would haue clou'n him & his horse.

106

Rogero sitteth staggering in his seat,
His hand the bridle left, his thighes their hold,
Rodomont giues another blow as great,
To maze him more by all the meanes he could:
And last a third, but now he so did beate
His blade of mettal free, it would not hold,
But burst in twaine, with his continuall hammering,
And left the *Pagan* in no little mammering.

107

But yet for this the *Turke* doth not refraine,
But still inuades the knight that wants defence,
So had the blow amaz'd his head and braine,
So dazed had the blow his witt and sense:
The *Pagan* minds to waken him againe,
First he doth close with him, and so from thence,
Wringing him by the necke with all his force,
To leaue the saddle he doth him inforce.

108

He fell, but yet the ground he touched scant,
But he that rose, inflam'd with wrath and shame;
For looking vp, he saw faire *Bradamant*,
Whose blush did shew how ill shee tooke the same:
Yea eu'n of sounding she did little want,
And still her fainting colour went and came;
Which seene, *Rogero* with his sword intends,
For this so great disgrace to make amends.

109

The *Pagan* with his horse would ouer-runne him,
And iustles him, but he with little paine,
Doth step aside, and warily doth shunne him,
And with his left hand takes the horses raine:
(So as the *Turke* thereby no hurt hath done him)
The while he puts in ure his sword againe,
And with two thrusts, he did the *Pagan* harme,
One in his thigh, another in his arme.

110

The *Turke* with whom a peece did yet remaine,
Of that same blade that was in pieces flowne,
Smote on *Rogeros* headpiece so againe,
As had well-ny againe him ouerthrowne:
But good *Rogero* now perceiuing plaine,
His vantage that was erst to him vnknowne,
Takes him by his left arme with all his force
And (will he nill he) puls him from his horse.

111

Were it his strength or flight, I cannot tell,
But so he fell, no ods was them betweene,
My meaning is that on his feete he fell,
For in the swords, *Rogeros* odds was seene:
Rogero that did know his vantage well,
To keepe him now at bay his best doth weene;
It is not best for him he doth suppose,
With such a strong, and big bon'd man to close.

112

He further saw what store of blood he spilt,
So now he hopes by warily proceeding,
To force his foe to yeeld, and leaue the tilt,
Whose strength decaid, still more & more with bleeding:
The *Turke* then takes the pomell and the hilt
Of his owne sword, and with force so exceeding
Did hurle the same, he smote the knight so sore,
He stund him more then eu'r he was before.

113

It strake him twixt the shoulders and the head,
And gaue to him a blow so firme and sound,
That good *Rogero* therewith staggered,
And scant could keepe his feet vpon the ground.
The *Turke* to close with him then hastened,
But loe his foote did faile with former wound,
So that his too much hast (as oft we see)
Did hurt, and made him fall vpon his knee.

114

Rogero lost no time in manfull wise,
To strike fierce *Rodomont* in brest or face,
And holds him short, and so his force applies,
He laid him on the ground, but in short space:
In spyte of him, the *Pagan* doth arise,
And with small kindnesse he doth him embrace:
And then they striue, heaue, shoue, thrust to and fro,
And either seekes the tothers ouerthrow.

115

Each striues with all his skill, and his abilitie,
By force to lay the tother on the ground,
Now *Rodomont* was growne to some debilitie,
By meanes of more then one receiued wound,
Rogero had great practise and agilitie,
And vs'd to wrastle, and he quickly found
His vantage, which he did not ouerslip,
But on his weakest side his foe doth trip.

116

The *Turke* most full of wrath and of despite,
Vpon *Rogeros* necke tooke stedfast hold,
Now drawing toward him with all his might,
Now thrusting him backe from him all he could,
And by and by he heau'd him quite vpright,
As strong *Antheus* was in time of old:
Rogero notwithstanding sure doth stand,
And labord still to haue the vpper hand.

117

Full oft the valiant knight his hold doth shift,
And with much prettie sleight, the same did slippe:
In fine he doth applie one speciall drift,
Which was to get the *Pagan* on the hippe:
And hauing caught him right, he doth him lift,
By nimble sleight, and in such wise doth trippe:
That downe he threw him, and his fall was such,
His head-peice was the first that ground did tuch.

118

The *Turke* with such an hard and heauie fall,
Was sore perplext, and bruised in such wise,
His wounds fell fresh on bleeding therewithall,
And make the place Vermillion where he lyes.
Rogero giues him respite very small,
But keepes him downe and will not let him rise:
And presently presents his dagger point
Vnto his throat, and to his chiefest ioynt.

119

As those that digge and search for golden ore,
  Within *Pannonian* or *Iberian* hils,
  Not vnderpropping sure the ground before,
  Oft for a plague of their too greedie wills,
  With sodaine ruine, are surpris'd so sore,
  As to get forth againe, doth passe their skills:
  So was the *Turke* held downe, and pressed so,
  By braue *Rogero* his triumphant foe.

120

Who now his naked dagger did present,
  Vnto the others vizer at his eye,
  And with sharpe words he told him that he ment,
  Except he yeeld, to kill him by and by:
  But *Rodomont*, that rather then relent,
  Or shew base minde a thousand deaths would dy,
  No word doth speake, but straue himselfe to sunder
  From him, or if he could to get him vnder.

121

Eu'n as a Mastiue fell, whom Grewnd more fell,
  Hath tyrde, and in his throat now fastned hath
  His cruell fangs, yet doth in vaine rebell,
  Though vnder him, and seekes to doe some skath:
  For still the Grewnd preuailes, and doth excell
  In force of breath, though not in rage and wrath:
  So doth the cruell Pagan striue and straine,
  To get from vnder him, but all in vaine.

122

But with long striuing and with wondrous paines,
  He freed his better arme, and void of aw,
  His dagger that in his right hand remaines,
  Which in this later bick'ring he did draw,
  He seekes to stabbe into *Rogeros* raines;
  But now the valiant youth the perill saw,
  Then for his safeties sake he was constrained,
  To kill the cruell *Turke* that grace disdained.

123

And lifting his victorious hand on hie,
  In that *Turks* face he stabd his dagger twise
  Vp to the hilts, and quickly made him die,
  And rid himselfe of trouble in a trice:
  Downe to the lake, where damned ghosts do lie,
  Sunke his disdainfull soule, now cold as Ise,
  Blaspheming as it went, and cursing lowd,
  That was on earth so loftie and so proud.

NOTE

Harington appended a considerable quantity of editorial matter to his translation, including a life of Ariosto, a critical preface, an allegory of the poem, and a long index of characters and mythological allusions. These are omitted here; a synopsis of the whole poem and a list of the principal characters are supplied instead.

SYNOPSIS OF THE POEM

I. Introduction and dedication, 1-4. Angelica escapes from the Duke of Bavaria; meets Renaldo, then Ferraw; duel between Renaldo and Ferraw, 5-23. The ghost of Argalia, 23-31. Angelica meets Sacrapant, 32-59. Duel between Sacrapant and Bradamante, 60-71. Bayardo taken by Sacrapant, 71-81.

II. Duel between Sacrapant and Renaldo. Angelica flees; falls in with a hermit. Renaldo returns to Paris, 1-24. Renaldo sent to England for aid by Charlemain. A storm, 24-30. Bradamante meets Pinabello who relates his misadventures; she sets off for the castle of the magician Atlante, but is betrayed by Pinabello and falls into a cave, 31-76.

III. Bradamante in the cave meets Melissa, who leads her to the tomb of Merlin. She hears a prophecy of all the lineage that is to descend from her and Rogero, 1-52. Goes with Melissa towards Atlante's castle; meets Brunello, 52-63.

IV. Bradamante takes the magic ring from Brunello, overcomes Atlante and frees Rogero, 1-32. Rogero carried away on the Griffith horse (the Hippogriff), 32-38. Renaldo arrives at the Scottish court; undertakes the defence of Genevra; meets Dalinda, Genevra's maid, 35-59.

V. Dalinda tells Genevra's sad story and proves her innocence, 1-75. Renaldo reveals to the King, Genevra's father, that Polinesso has slandered his daughter; fights with Polinesso and kills him, 76-92.

VI. Genevra married to her lover Ariodante, 1-16. Rogero carried by the Hippogriff to Alcina's island, 16-25. Is warned by Astolfo who has been changed into a myrtle by Alcina's wiles, 25-53. Fights with monsters, 54-81.

VII. Rogero in Alcina's palace, 1-29. Melissa reproves him and rescues him, and he sets off for the island of Logistilla, 30-69.

VIII. Rogero escapes from Alcina's land; the other prisoners are freed, 1-17. Renaldo obtains the help desired from Scotland, 18-24. Angelica falls into the power of the hermit; is captured by pirates of Ebuda to be exposed to the Orc, 25-58. Orlando goes in search of her, Brandimarte follows, 59-81.

IX. Orlando hears of the evil customs of Ebuda; wishes to go there, but is brought by a tempest to Holland, 1-15. Story of Olimpia and Bireno, 16-51. Orlando kills Cymosco, frees Bireno, and goes on his way to Ebuda, 51-86. Marriage of Olimpia and Bireno, 87.

X. Bireno abandons Olimpia, 1-33. Rogero flees to Logistilla's domain, 34-57. Goes off on the Hippogriff, arrives in London, and sees the army assembled to help Charlemain, 57-77. Arrives at Ebuda and rescues Angelica from the Orc, 78-97.

XI. Angelica flees from Rogero, 1-14. Rogero in a delusive vision sees Bradamante carried off by a giant, 15-18. Orlando kills the Orc and frees Olimpia, 19-44. Olimpia continues the tale of her woes, and marries the King of Ireland. Orlando leaves, 45-66.

XII. Orlando and Rogero with other knights fall into the power of Atlante, 1-17. Angelica frees Orlando and others, then disappears, 17-26. Duel between Orlando and Ferraw, 26-47. Angelica meets a wounded youth, 47-50. Orlando makes great slaughter among enemy troops; finds Isabella and Gabrina in a cave, 51-70.

XIII. Story of Isabella, 1-38. Bradamante goes to Atlante's palace to rescue Rogero, but herself falls into the magician's power, 39-65. Agramante reviews his troops, 66-67.

XIV. A victory of the Duke Alfonso, 1-9. Agramante and Marsilio review their troops, 10-25. Mandricardo sets out in pursuit of Orlando, but meets Doralice on the way and takes possession of her, 26-55. Charlemain's preparations against the assault on Paris. Discord makes trouble in the pagan camp. Assault on Paris. Exploits of Rodomonte, 56-111.

XV. Assault on Paris continued, 1-5. Adventures of Astolfo; he leaves Logistilla, taking a magic book and horn; captures Caligorant and kills Orillo, 6-70. Goes to Jerusalem. Griffin sets out for Antioch to seek his love Orrigile, 71-83.

XVI. Griffin finds Orrigile with Martano and goes with them to Damascus, 1-15. Assault on Paris continued; Rodomonte again, 16-23. Renaldo and his forces, guided by Silence, arrive to help Charlemain. The battle continues, 24-63.

XVII. Tyrants sent by God as punishment for our sins, 1-5. Charlemain and his forces attack Rodomonte, 6-11. Story of Griffin and Orrigile continued; Griffin disgraced by a trick of the cowardly Martano ,11-89.

XVIII. Griffin vindicates his honour, 1-5. Rodomonte leaves Paris and goes in search of Doralice. The battle before Paris continues, 6-24. Griffin honoured, Martano and Orrigile punished, 25-42. Another tournament at Damascus, at which Astolfo and Marfisa arrive. They decide to embark for France. A storm, 43-67. The battle before Paris continues. Episode of Cloridano and Medoro; they go in search of the body of their dead lord Dardinello, and are surprised by a troop under Zerbino, 67-95.

XIX. Cloridano killed, Medoro wounded, 1-11. Angelica finds the wounded Medoro, heals him and falls in love with him; marries him and returns to the East, 12-33. Marfisa and her company arrive in the country of the Amazons. Meet with Guidon Savage, 33-71.

XX. Guidon Savage tells his story and is recognised as Renaldo's brother, 1-50. They plan to escape the Amazons, but Astolfo stays behind, 50-66. Marfisa arrives in Marseille; her further adventures; meets Gabrina; meets Zerbino; she makes him take Gabrina, who gives him news of Isabella, 67-98.

XXI. Zerbino defends Gabrina against Hermonida; Hermonida tells the story of Gabrina's infamies, 1-65. Zerbino goes on his way with Gabrina, 66-70.

XXII. Zerbino finds a dead knight, 1-4. Astolfo destroys Atlante's palace and frees the prisoners, 5-24. Rogero and Bradamante recognise each other and declare their mutual love, 25-28. Rogero overcomes several knights; Bradamante kills Pinabello, and then loses her way, 29-77.

XXIII. Bradamante's horse stolen by Rodomonte, 1-27. Zerbino is accused of the death of Pinabello. Orlando saves him; restores Isabella to him, 28-54. Duel between Orlando and Mandricardo, 55-67. Mandricardo meets Gabrina, 67-73. Orlando finds proof of the loves of Angelica and Medoro. His madness begins, 74-108.

XXIV. Orlando's madness, 1-12. Zerbino hears Isabella's story; gives Gabrina to Odorico, 13-39. Fights with Mandricardo and is killed. Isabella goes with a hermit to Provence, 39-96. Duel between Mandricardo and Rodomonte, 76-96.

XXV. Rogero saves Ricciardetto. Story of Ricciardetto and Fiordispina, 1-62. Captivity of Viviane and Malagigi. Rogero writes a letter to Bradamante; goes off to rescue Viviane and Malagigi; meets Marfisa, 62-77.

XXVI. Rescue of Viviane and Malagigi, 1-25. Story of Merlin's cave, 26-38. Rogero goes in search of Rodomonte; various single combats, 38-92. Malagigi has Doralice carried off by a demon; first Mandricardo, then Marfisa and Rogero go off in pursuit, 93-99.

XXVII. Rogero and other pagan knights make havoc in the Christian camp, 1-23. The archangel Michael stirs up new discord among the pagans, 24-83. It is agreed that Doralice should choose between Mandricardo and Rodomonte. She chooses Mandricardo. Anger of Rodomonte, 83-101. Rodomonte sets off for Africa, but stops at an inn, where the host begins to entertain him with a merry tale, 102-113.

XXVIII. The host's tale of Jocundo, 1-84. Rodomonte meets Isabella with the hermit, and falls in love with her, 84-96.

XXIX. Isabella by a subterfuge causes Rodomonte to kill her, to save her honour, 1-33. Rodomonte in remorse erects a splendid tomb and a bridge which he defends against all comers, 35-41. Orlando arrives, fights with Rodomonte and overthrows him. Renewed madness of Orlando, 41-70.

XXX. Orlando swims across the straits of Gibraltar, 1-14. Mandricardo fights with Rogero and is killed, 15-72. Grief of Bradamante at Rogero's absence, 72-84. Renaldo goes to join Charlemain, but Bradamante stays behind, 85-87.

XXXI. Renaldo fights with Guidon Savage unawares, 1-21. They meet Fiordiligi and others; learn from Fiordiligi that Orlando is mad, 21-41. Renaldo and Charlemain attack the Moors, 41-50. Brandimarte meets Fiordiligi, learns of Orlando's madness and sets out in search of him. Falls prisoner to Rodomonte at the bridge, 51-67. Agramante retreats to Arles. Gradasso and Renaldo agree to fight for possession of the horse Bayard, 68-89.

XXXII. Bradamante laments the absence of Rogero, 1-27. Hears that he is with Marfisa, becomes jealous, and sets out in search of him, 28-50. Meets Ullania, 50-60. Arrives at Tristram's lodge, 60-103.

XXXIII. Bradamante is shown the pictures on the walls of Tristram's lodge, 1-52. Sets out for Paris, 53-69. Duel between Renaldo and Gradasso interrupted by Malagigi; Gradasso takes Bayard, 69-86. Astolfo's voyage on the Hippogriff. Arrives in Nubia and drives the Harpies away into Hell, 86-118.

XXXIV. Astolfo hears the tale of Lydia in Hell, 1-46. Visits the Earthly Paradise, 46-69. And the moon, where he finds Orlando's lost wits, 69-87. The Parcae and Time, 88-91.

XXXV. Allegory of Time and the poets, 1-29. Bradamante goes to the bridge of Rodomonte and rescues his prisoners, 30-54. Goes on to Arles and sends a challenge to Rogero. Overthrows several warriors, 54-77.

XXXVI. Rogero perturbed about his forthcoming duel with Bradamante. Duel between Bradamante and Marfisa, 1-22. Skirmish between Christians and Saracens. Duel between Bradamante and Rogero; they make peace and converse together, 22-29. Another duel between Bradamante and Marfisa, then between Rogero and Marfisa, 39-55. The voice of Atlante is heard revealing that Rogero and Marfisa are brother and sister. It is determined that Rogero shall leave Agramante and join the Christian side, 56-83.

XXXVII. Praise of accomplished women, 1-15. Rogero, Bradamante and Marfisa meet Ullania, 15-25. They hear the tale of the tyrant Marganor, 25-75. They go to his castle, capture the tyrant and establish new laws, 76-103.

XXXVIII. Marfisa goes to Charlemain's camp and receives Christian baptism, 1-24. Further marvellous adventures of Astolfo, 25-35. Agramante proposes to decide the war by single combat. Duel between Rogero and Renaldo, in which Rogero refrains from injuring his adversary, 26-91.

XXXIX. Agramante breaks off the duel; general melée in which the pagans are routed, 1-17. Astolfo victorious at Biserta; miraculously creates a fleet, 17-29. Frees Rodomonte's prisoners; finds Orlando mad and cures him, 30-62. More fighting near Biserta; a sea-battle in which Agramante is defeated, 63-84.

XL. Biserta captured. Agramante and Sobrino flee to an island where they meet Gradasso. They send a challenge to Orlando, 1-58. Rogero comes to Marseille; fights Dudone to liberate the pagan kings, his prisoners, 59-78.

XLI. Rogero goes by ship to Africa, is wrecked in a storm, 1-22. Preparations for a duel in Lipadusa 23-46. Rogero swims to an island, repents and is christened by a hermit, 46-60. Fighting in Lipadusa, 61-91.

XLII. Agramante, Gradasso and Brandimarte killed, Oliver and Sobrino wounded, 1-23. Bradamante laments the absence of Rogero, 24-28. Renaldo in search of Angelica cures himself of his love by drinking of the magic fountain, 29-58. Goes to a castle and is shown a magic cup, 59-82.

XLIII. Renaldo hears two tales against women; arrives at Lipadusa, 1-144. Despair of Fiordiligi at Brandimarte's death; funeral of Brandimarte; death of Fiordiligi, 145-176. Orlando and his companions meet Rogero; the hermit heals Oliver and baptises Sobrino, 177-189.

XLIV. Renaldo promises Bradamante to Rogero, not knowing that her father Ammon has promised her to Leone; they set off for France, 1-16. Further adventures of Astolfo; he arrives at Marseille, 16-23. They are received by Charlemain; disputes about Bradamante's marriage; she receives a promise from Charlemain that she shall marry only the man who can defeat her in battle, 24-72. Rogero goes off to fight alongside the Bulgarians against Leone, but falls into the hands of the enemy, 73-97.

XLV. Imprisonment of Rogero, 1-17. Sorrow of Bradamante, 10-37. Leone rescues Rogero, and Rogero agrees to fight Bradamante on his behalf, 38-57. Rogero fights Bradamante and flees secretly, 58-83. Laments of Rogero and Bradamante, 84-99. Marfisa opposes the marriage of Bradamante to Leone, 100-114.

XLVI. Rogero helped by Melissa; Leone renounces Bradamante, 1-51. Rogero is made king of the Bulgarians. His marriage to Bradamante. The storied pavilion, 52-84. Rodomonte comes to trouble the feast. Duel between him and Rogero; Rodomonte is killed.

PRINCIPAL CHARACTERS

Where Harington's version of a name is notably idiosyncratic, the original or a more familiar form is added in brackets. Where a character appears in only one episode, reference is given to the relevant cantos.

AGRAMANTE, Emperor of Africa and leader of the pagan host.
ALCINA, a wicked enchantress who entraps Astolfo and Rogero. (V, VI, X).
AMMON (Amone, Aymon), father of Renaldo, Bradamante and Ricciardette (XLIV, XLVI).
ANGELICA, a princess of Cathay, beloved of Orlando, Renaldo and other champions, both Christian and pagan.
ARIODANTE, a knight at the court of Scotland, helped by Renaldo.
ASTOLPHO, an English prince, possessed of magical powers and hero of many miraculous adventures.
ATLANTE, an enchanter, formerly Rogero's guardian.

BIRENO, a Duke of Zealand, faithless lover of Olimpia. (IX, X).
BRADAMANTE, a warrior-maiden, daughter of Ammon and beloved of Rogero.
BRANDIMARTE, a loyal and brave knight, lover of Fiordiligi.

CHARLEMAIN (Carlo Magno, Charlemagne), Emperor of Rome, leader of Christendom against the pagans.
CLORIDANO, faithful follower of Dardinello and friend of Medoro. (XVIII, XIX).

DARDINELLO, a Moorish leader.
DORALICE, a princess loved by Rodomonte, but marries Mandricardo.
DUDONE, a Danish knight.

FERRAW (Ferrau), a pagan knight.
FIORDILIGI, the faithful lady-love of Brandimarte.
FIORDISPINA, paramour of Ricciardetto. (XXV).

GABRINA, a hag.
GENEVRA (Ginevra), a Scottish princess, loved by Ariodante.
GRADASSO, a pagan king.
GRIFFIN (Grifone), lover of Orrigile. (XV, XVII, XVIII).
GRIFFITH HORSE (the Hippogriff), a magical winged steed, ridden by both Rogero and Astolpho.
GUIDON SAVAGE (Guidon Selvaggio), a natural son of Ammon, half-brother of Renaldo and Bradamante.

ISABELLA, a princess of Galicia, married to Zerbino.

LOGISTILLA, a virtuous enchantress, sister of Alcina. (X, XV).

MALAGIGI, an enchanter.
MANDRICARDO, Emperor of Tartary, one of the great pagan leaders.
MARFISA, an Indian warrior-queen, sister of Rogero.
MARTANO, a coward, loved by Orrigile. (XVII, XVIII).
MEDORO, follower of Dardinello, friend of Cloridano, and ultimately Angelica's husband. (XVIII, XIX).
MELISSA, a benign enchantress.
MERLIN, the famous enchanter.

OLIMPIA, a princess of Holland, loved and betrayed by Bireno. (IX, X).
OLIVER, one of the most famous of Charlemain's peers, friend of Orlando.
ORLANDO, the greatest of all Charlemain's peers; celebrated in innumerable legends, but somewhat under a cloud in this poem as he is mad for love of Angelica.
ORRIGILE, the faithless mistress of Griffin. (XV, XVII, XVIII).

RENALDO (Rinaldo), brother of Bradamante, one of the greatest of the Christian warriors; in love with Angelica.
RICCIARDETTO, scapegrace brother of Renaldo and Bradamante. (XXV).
RODOMONTE, a fierce and boastful pagan warrior.
ROGERO (Ruggiero), a great pagan knight later converted to Christianity. Lover of Bradamante, marries her in the last canto.

SACRAPANT, a Saracen king.
ZERBINO, a Scottish prince.